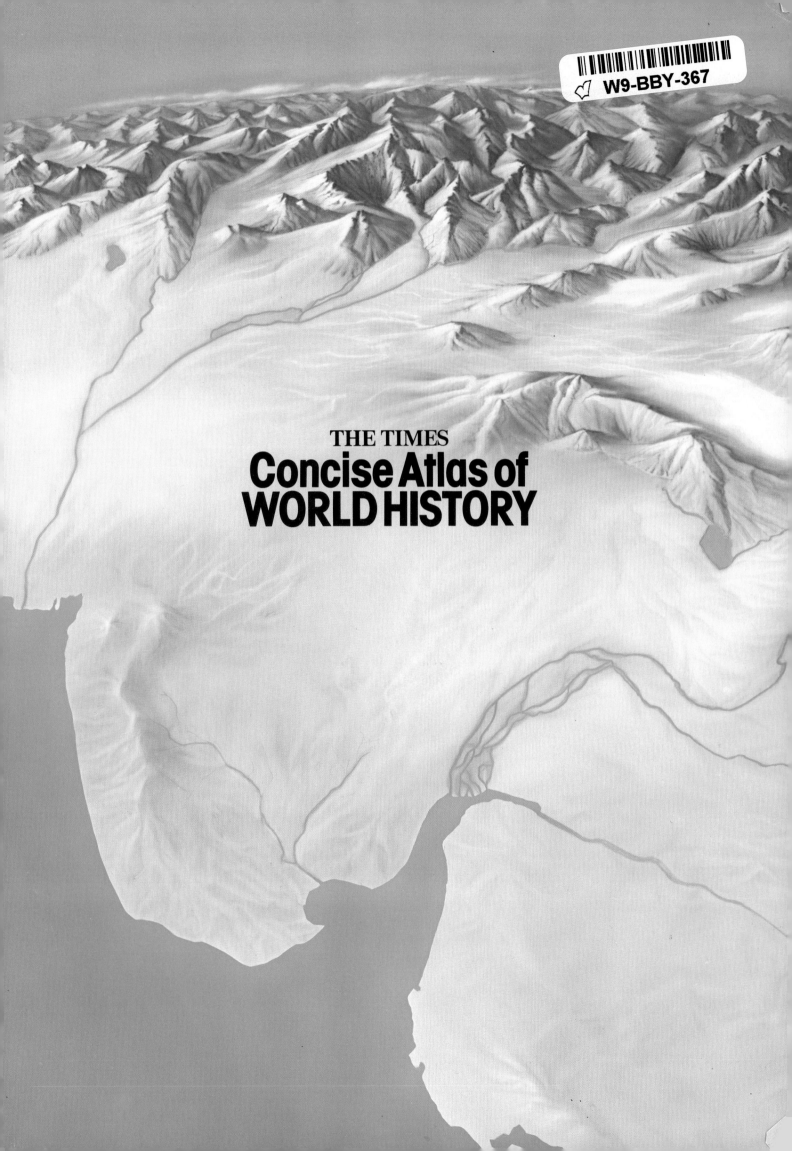

THE TIMES
Concise Atlas of
WORLD HISTORY

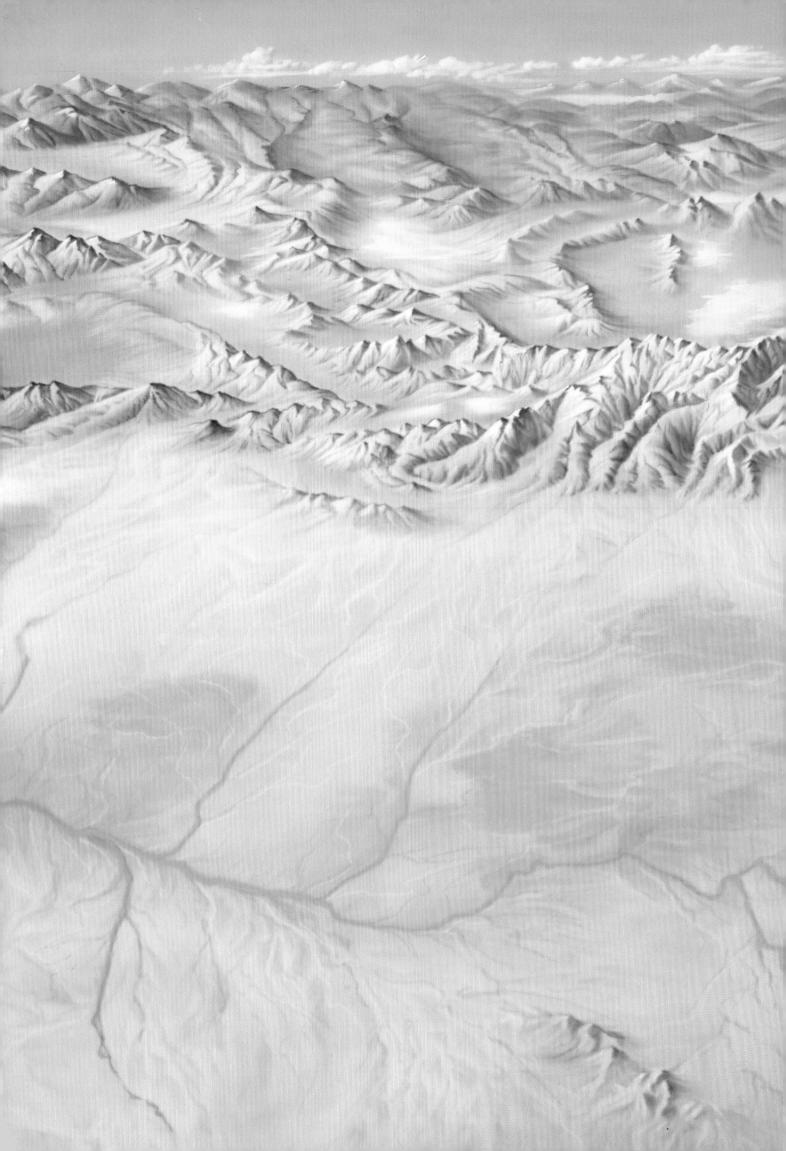

THE TIMES
Concise Atlas of
WORLD HISTORY

Edited by
GEOFFREY BARRACLOUGH

HAMMOND ®
INCORPORATED
MAPLEWOOD, NEW JERSEY 07040

Third edition first published in 1988 by
Times Books Limited,
16 Golden Square,
London, W1R 4BN

First published in 1982
Revised editions 1986, 1988
© Times Books Limited
1982, 1986, 1988

Library of Congress Cataloging in Publication Data
Main entry under title:

The Times concise atlas of world history.

Based on: The Times atlas of world history. c1978.
Bibliography: p.
Includes index.
1. Geography, Historical—Maps. I. Barraclough,
Geoffrey, 1908–   . II. Times (London, England)
III. Times atlas of world history. IV. Title: Concise
atlas of world history.
G1030.T56 1982   911   82-50111
                                      AACR2

ISBN 0-7230-0274-6 softcover Order No. 1131-0

HAMMOND®
INCORPORATED
MAPLEWOOD, NEW JERSEY 07040

EDITORIAL DIRECTION	Barry Winkleman Ailsa Hudson Andrew Heritage
DESIGN & ART DIRECTION	Ivan and Robin Dodd
MAP DESIGN AND ARTWORK	Swanston Graphics Ltd., Derby P.S.G. Ltd., Derby Peter Sullivan Ivan and Robin Dodd
PLACE NAMES AND INDEX	P.J.M. Geelan
COLOUR SEPARATION	Ensign Graphics, Hull D.S. Colour International Ltd., London
TYPESETTING	Oliver Burridge & Co. Ltd.
PRINTED AND BOUND IN ITALY BY	Mondadori, Verona

ACKNOWLEDGEMENTS

This atlas contains the work of many of the contributors to THE TIMES ATLAS OF WORLD HISTORY (1978) who are listed in that volume. We also wish to thank the following:
F.W. Boal, *Reader in Geography, Queens University, Belfast*
Professor Michael Crowder, *University of Botswana*
Dr Elizabeth Dunstan, *International African Institute*
Professor Norman Hammond, *Rutgers University, USA*
Sinclair Hood, *formerly Director, British School of Archaeology, Athens*
Raymond Hutchings, *Senior Editor, Abstract, Soviet and Eastern European Series*
Morton Keller, *Spector Professor of History, Brandeis University, Massachusetts*
John Lynch, *Professor of Latin American History and Director, Institute of Latin American Studies, University of London*
W.H. McNeill, *Robert A. Millitin Distinguished Services Professor of History, University of Chicago*
W.H. Parker, *formerly Lecturer of the Geography of the USSR, University of Oxford*
H.W.F. Saggs, *Professor of Semitic languages, University College, Cardiff*
Chris Scarre, *Faculty of Archaeology, University of Cambridge*
H.H. Scullard, *Emeritus Professor of Ancient History, King's College, University of London*
Peter Sluglett, *Lecturer in Modern Middle Eastern History, Durham University*
R.L. Sims, *Lecturer in the History of the Far East, School of Oriental and African Studies, University of London*

EDITORIAL CONSULTANT
(Third Edition)

Norman Stone, *Professor of Modern History, University of Oxford*

CONTENTS

INTRODUCTION

The welcome given to THE TIMES ATLAS OF WORLD HISTORY, first published in English in September 1978, and now available in nine languages, shows how widespread an interest there is today in the human story. It also led us to think that there might be a place for a shorter, less elaborate atlas on a reduced scale.

The present volume is the result. Nevertheless THE TIMES CONCISE ATLAS OF WORLD HISTORY is not merely a condensed and abbreviated version of the earlier work. No fewer than 70 of the 320 maps here presented are entirely new or radically changed, and many others have been revised and redesigned. THE TIMES CONCISE ATLAS is intended to stand on its own feet as a compact, easily available reference book covering the whole story of mankind from the earliest beginnings, when man's ancestors first emerged from the tropical forests of Africa, to the complex, highly articulated world in which we live.

Although the present volume incorporates new material and differs in a number of other ways from the larger work on which it is based, the principles which have guided us are the same. As in THE TIMES ATLAS OF WORLD HISTORY, we have endeavoured to make the coverage as universal as is possible in the present state of knowledge, and in particular to provide full and clear accounts of the civilisations of Asia, Africa and the Americas, both before and after the coming of the Europeans. We have paid close attention to the relations and interactions between these different regions in all their manifestations – cultural and economic, peaceful and warlike, including invasions and migrations, the spread of agriculture and the diffusion of technologies – because we believe these to be some of the main threads of world history. Although we have given more space in this volume to the intricate web of politics (wars, treaties, frontier changes) and to the internal development of particular countries (e.g. England, Russia, Japan, and the U.S.A.), it is our view that world history is more than a combination of national histories, and we have planned this work accordingly.

A long view and a wide historical perspective are vitally important in the world as it is constituted today. If THE TIMES CONCISE ATLAS OF WORLD HISTORY has succeeded in providing such a view, it will have fulfilled one of its objectives. Nevertheless it is important to emphasise that this is not an atlas of current affairs. We have sought, in the concluding plates, to pick out and illustrate some of the more significant trends and movements in the contemporary world, but no attempt has been made to cover the years between 1945 and 1980 in detail. That was not our purpose; but we believe that informed knowledge of the past is a key to the understanding of the present and – as the great Victorian historian, Lord Acton, said it should be – 'a power that goes to the making of the future.'

GEOFFREY BARRACLOUGH
Oxford, March 1982

This third edition brings many changes and updates to Professor Barraclough's first edition. The changes were planned and implemented after his death in December 1984, but the academic authorities to whom we have referred for revisions and updates are among the great team he assembled for this series of Times Historical Atlases and follow principles he laid down.

TIMES BOOKS
March 1988

Human origins

In the longer perspective of world history Man is comparatively a newcomer to the historical scene. Life on earth, as the geological time-chart (diagram 1) indicates, reaches back more than 3,000 million years. Birds and mammals appeared at least 130 million years ago. Modern Man (*Homo sapiens*) is at most 250,000 years old, probably considerably less. He and the great apes are believed to have descended from various ape-like species, the *Dryopithecinae*, whose fossil remains, dating from 15–20 million years ago, have been found in east Africa, northern India and Europe. But much in the subsequent process of human evolution and differentiation still remains obscure. Moreover, it must be borne in mind that evidence for the history of early Man and his ancestors (map 3) is largely accidental and haphazard, the result of chance survival or of the concentration of archaeologists on particular sites or areas. New discoveries could substantially modify the picture.

The original home of the early hominids was equatorial Africa. Why, unlike the tree-living apes, these creatures took to the ground, can only be surmised; presumably it was in search of foods. In any event it marked a decisive step in human evolution. Travelling upright on two feet, early Man developed unique physical characteristics. He was also free to use his hands for new purposes, e.g. to make tools and weapons from pebbles and later from flints and other sharp-edged materials. Along with increased manual dexterity went other characteristic developments, notably an increasingly large brain. At the same time the jaw and snout, no longer needed to seek out and masticate raw food, became less prominent. Indeed, the evolution of Man is most easily traced (diagram 2) in terms of jaw formation and cranial capacity, until about 40,000 years ago the latter attained today's average of 1500 cc.

The course of this evolutionary development is certainly not unilinear. The earliest hominids, dating from about 10 million years ago, belong to the genus *Ramapithecus*, but there is no certainty that these creatures were bipeds. The earliest definite evidence of terrestrial bipedal hominids was discovered at Taungs in southern Africa in 1924. They belong to the genus *Australopithecus*, of which there are at least two distinct species, *A. robustus* and *A. africanus*, the former larger and with prominent jaws, the latter smaller and probably a hunter and meat-eater. Whereas the fate of the former is obscure, *A. africanus* is almost certainly the ancestor of the first recognisably human creature, *Homo erectus*, who is found over a wide geographical range, extending to Java and Peking, indicating that by this time Man had fully developed the skills and organisation enabling him to spread far and wide from his African homeland across Asia and Europe. Except for the skull, with a brain capacity of 1000 cc, the bone structure of *Homo erectus* is indistinguishable from that of modern Man. His tools were far more sophisticated than those of *Australopithecus*, and at Peking (c.350,000 years ago) he was using fire, thus enabling him to live north of the frost line in the caves of Choukoutien.

Homo erectus survived for 1.5 million years or more and it is not clear when he gave way to *Homo sapiens*. The earliest remains which can properly be classified as human were found at Steinheim and Swanscombe and date from c.250,000 BC. But even here the cranial capacity is smaller than that of modern Man. The intermediate stage is commonly known as that of 'Neanderthal Man', named after a skull discovered in Germany in 1856. But 'classic' Neanderthal Man appears to have been an aberration and disappeared with the retreat of the glaciers. A more generalised 'progressive' Neanderthal type occurs widely in separate parts of the Old World, and it was from this type, somewhere between the eastern Mediterranean and the mountains of inner Asia, that modern Man first emerged. Once established he spread quickly over the whole world.

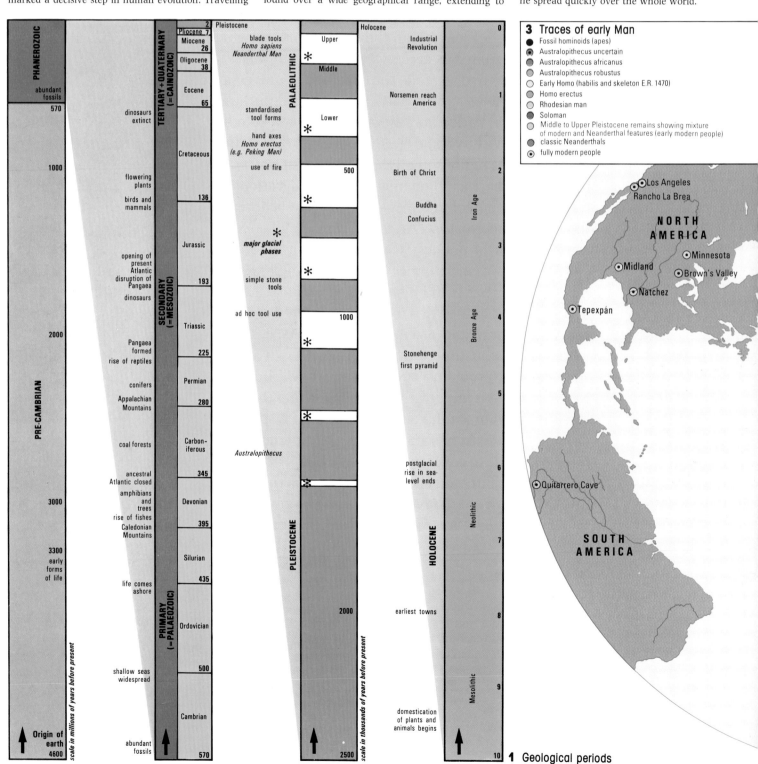

3 Traces of early Man
- Fossil hominoids (apes)
- Australopithecus uncertain
- Australopithecus africanus
- Australopithecus robustus
- Early Homo (habilis and skeleton E.R. 1470)
- Homo erectus
- Rhodesian man
- Soloman
- Middle to Upper Pleistocene remains showing mixture of modern and Neanderthal features (early modern people)
- classic Neanderthals
- fully modern people

1 Geological periods

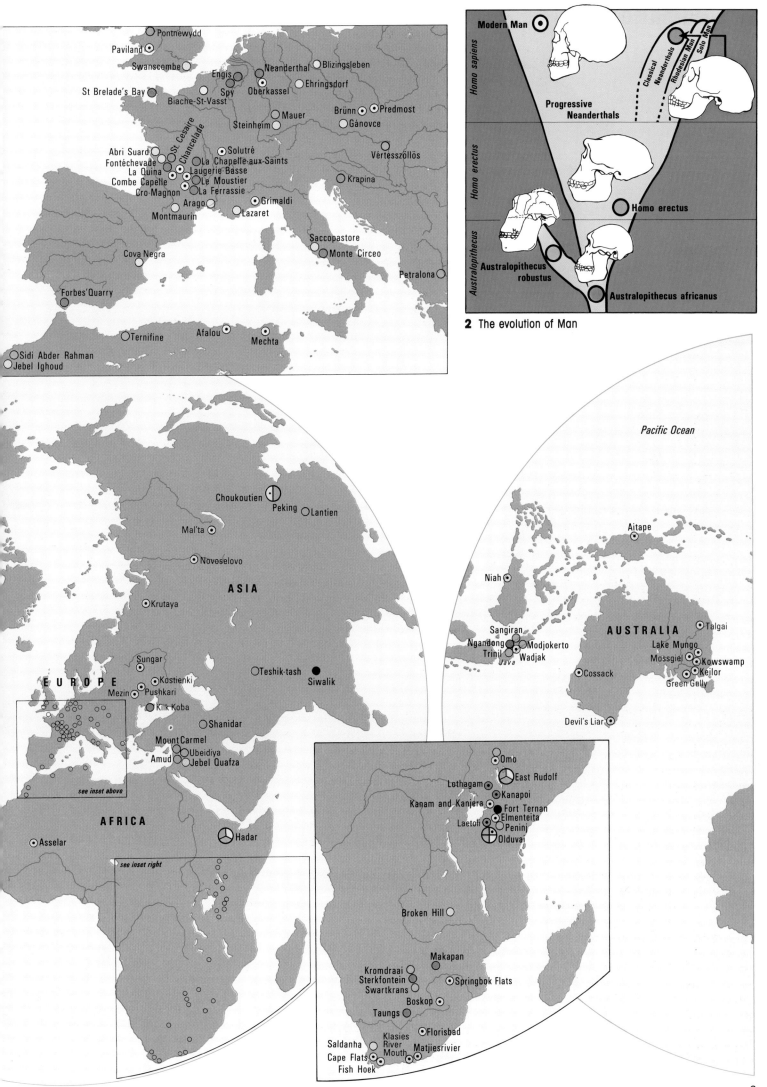

Modern Man ⊙

Homo sapiens

Progressive
Neanderthals

Classical Neanderthals

Rhodesian Man

Solo Man

Homo erectus

Homo erectus ⊙

Australopithecus

Australopithecus robustus

Australopithecus africanus

2 The evolution of Man

Pontnewydd
Paviland
Swanscombe
St Brelade's Bay
Engis
Neanderthal
Blizingsleben
Oberkassel
Ehringsdorf
Spy
Biache-St-Vasst
Mauer
Brünn
Predmost
Steinheim
Gánovce
St. Cesaire
Chancelade
Abri Suard
Fontéchevade
La Chapelle-aux-Saints
Vértesszöllös
La Quina
Laugerie-Basse
Combe Capelle
Le Moustier
Cro-Magnon
La Ferrassie
Krapina
Arago
Grimaldi
Montmaurin
Lazaret
Saccopastore
Cova Negra
Monte Circeo
Petralona
Forbes'Quarry
Ternifine
Afalou
Mechta
Sidi Abder Rahman
Jebel Ighoud

Pacific Ocean

Choukoutien
Peking
Lantien
Mal'ta
Novoselovo
ASIA
Krutaya
Aitape
Niah
Talgai
Sangiran
Ngandong
Trinil
Modjokerto
Wadjak
Java
AUSTRALIA
Lake Mungo
Mossgiel
Kowswamp
Keilor
Green Gully
Cossack
Sungar
Teshik-tash
Siwalik
EUROPE
Kostienki
Mezin
Pushkari
Kilk Koba
Shanidar
Devil's Liar
Mount Carmel
Amud
Ubeidiya
Jebel Quafza
see inset above
Omo
East Rudolf
Lothagam
Kanapoi
Kanam and Kanjera
Fort Ternan
Elmenteita
Penini
Laetoli
Olduvai
AFRICA
Asselar
Hadar
see inset right
Broken Hill
Makapan
Kromdraai
Sterkfontein
Springbok Flats
Swartkrans
Boskop
Taungs
Florisbad
Klasies
River
Mouth
Saldanha
Matjiesrivier
Cape Flats
Fish Hoek

3

Man and the Ice Age

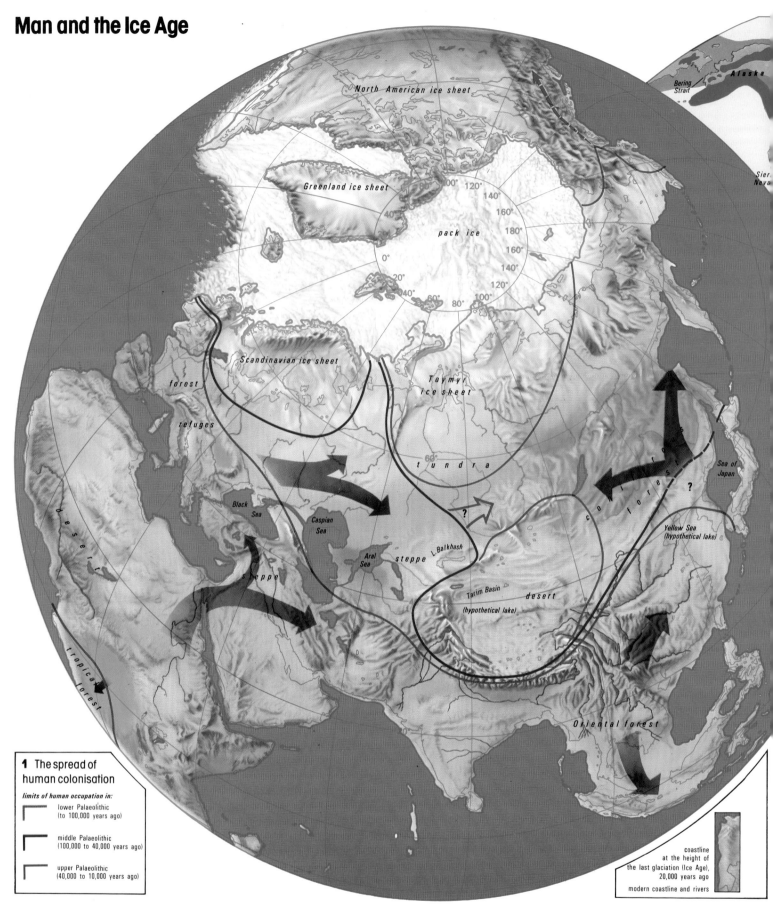

Labels on map:

North American ice sheet

Greenland ice sheet

pack ice

Scandinavian ice sheet

Taymyr ice sheet

forest

refuges

tundra

desert

Black Sea

Caspian Sea

Aral Sea

steppe L. Balkhash

Tarim Basin (hypothetical lake)

desert

steppe

tropical forest

Oriental forest

cool forest

Yellow Sea (hypothetical lake)

Sea of Japan

Bering Strait

Alaska

Sier. Neva

1 The spread of human colonisation

limits of human occupation in:

lower Palaeolithic
(to 100,000 years ago)

middle Palaeolithic
(100,000 to 40,000 years ago)

upper Palaeolithic
(40,000 to 10,000 years ago)

coastline
at the height of
the last glaciation (Ice Age),
20,000 years ago

modern coastline and rivers

The different ice ages of the Pleistocene era (page 2, diagram 1) marked a decisive phase in the history of Man. His ability to adapt himself to the environmental changes in this period of extreme climatic variation was a crucial factor both in his survival and in his ability to dominate other species. In northern latitudes the main determinant of animal existence throughout the Pleistocene era was the advance and retreat of the glaciers. Only when they shrank back, allowing the northward spread of the vegetation on which mammoths and reindeer browsed, was it possible for human beings to live outside the warmer equatorial regions. In these regions the pluvial age (i.e. the period of favourable rain and vegetation) fostered the emergence of more ad-

vanced tool- and weapon-making cultures, which emerged c.20,000 years ago.

The decisive phase came with the advance of the Würm glaciers in central Europe – the last European ice age – and the associated Weichsel and Wisconsin glacier fields in northern Europe and north America, some 75,000 years ago. By tying up water on a grand scale these reduced sea levels, and land bridges appeared, linking most major areas and many isolated islands (including the British Isles) into one single continental mainland. The result (map 2) was that Man was able to reach Australia and Tasmania (page 10). No less significant was the land bridge between eastern Asia and Alaska, which became a highway for human beings and

animals. When around 12,000 years ago an ice-free corridor opened through Canada, the hunters from Siberia advanced into the rich gamelands of the American plains (as schematically indicated on map 3), and then, as the abundant herds became depleted, moved through the Panama isthmus into South America.

The earliest tool-makers had been restricted by climatic conditions to the south of the Old World. During the last glacial phase (75,000–10,000 BC), when sea levels were low and ice expansion had restricted the forests, groups of hunters expanded northwards, where they could exploit the rich animal life of the steppe and tundra zones. The main lines of expansion are indicated on map 1, which also shows the limits of human habi-

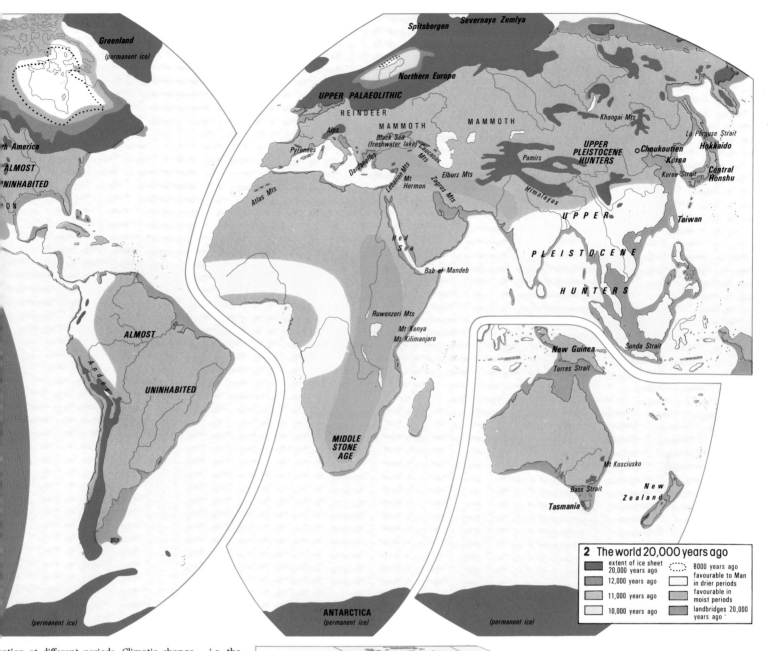

Greenland
(permanent ice)

ALMOST
UNINHABITED

Spitsbergen   Severnaya Zemlya

Northern Europe

UPPER PALAEOLITHIC

REINDEER

MAMMOTH   MAMMOTH

Khangai Mts

Alps
Black Sea
(freshwater lake)   Caucasus Mts

UPPER
PLEISTOCENE
HUNTERS

La Pérouse Strait
Hokkaido

Pyrenees

Dardanelles   Pamirs   Choukoutien

Korea

Lebanon Mts
Mt
Hermon   Elburz Mts   Korea Strait

Central
Honshu

Atlas Mts   Zagros Mts

Himalayas

U P P E R

Taiwan

Red
Sea

P L E I S T O C E N E

Bab el Mandeb

H U N T E R S

New Guinea

Ruwenzori Mts

Torres Strait   Sunda Strait

Mt Kenya
Mt Kilimanjaro

ALMOST

Andes

UNINHABITED

New
Zealand

Mt Kosciusko

MIDDLE
STONE
AGE

Bass Strait

Tasmania

(permanent ice)   ANTARCTICA
(permanent ice)   (permanent ice)

2 The world 20,000 years ago

extent of ice sheet 20,000 years ago	8000 years ago
12,000 years ago	favourable to Man in drier periods
11,000 years ago	favourable in moist periods
10,000 years ago	landbridges 20,000 years ago

ation at different periods. Climatic change – i.e. the
onset of warmer conditions – some 10,000 years ago,
profoundly affected the human situation. Rising sea
levels cut off Australia and the Americas, which henceforward pursued their own independent lines of development (pages 10 and 12). Elsewhere Man advanced, with
the help of fire and warm clothing (initially animal
skins), into areas hitherto precluded from human habi-
tation. At the same time the depletion of hunting resources, which thus far had been the main source of
foodstuffs, compelled men to turn to new sources of
subsistence. Hunters and gatherers persisted in the re-
moter areas down to modern times, but as the world
started slowly to warm up, more and more people were
driven by necessity to domesticate animals and plants
and to embark on what was subsequently called the
Neolithic or agricultural revolution (page 6). This, again,
was a major turning point in human history.

The ice age presented a great challenge to Man,
which he successfully overcame, largely by developing
his mental capacities and his aptitude for cooperation.
Cave paintings in the Dordogne and elsewhere show,
apart from their remarkable artistic merits, that by 6000
BC, probably considerably earlier, men had learnt to
work together in hunting food-producing animals, e.g.
herds of red deer. Much earlier, c.40,000 BC, the masto-
dons and mammoths had started to disappear from
Africa and South-East Asia, presumably as a result of
concerted attacks by groups of humans. The same was
true in the Americas where by 10,000 BC most of the
teeming animal life (including horses) had disappeared.
It is impossible to say how far primitive Man, with his
limited numbers, was responsible for this destruction;
but there is little doubt that late Palaeolithic Man, with
his greatly expanded population, played a major part in
the process.

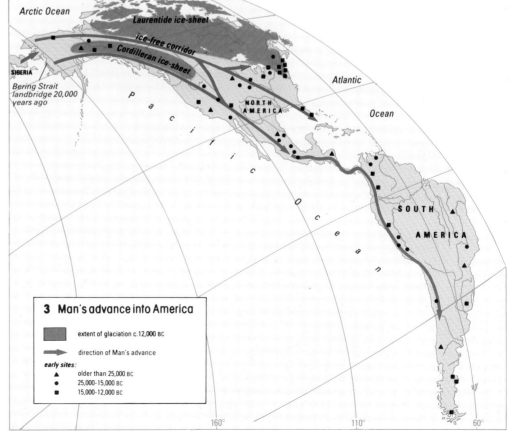

Arctic Ocean

Laurentide ice-sheet

ice-free corridor

Cordilleran ice-sheet

SIBERIA

Pacific

Atlantic

Bering Strait
landbridge 20,000
years ago

NORTH
AMERICA

Ocean

SOUTH

AMERICA

3 Man's advance into America

extent of glaciation c.12,000 BC

direction of Man's advance

early sites:
▲ older than 25,000 BC
● 25,000-15,000 BC
■ 15,000-12,000 BC

160°   110°   60°

From hunting to farming

Somewhere around 8000 BC Man began to select, breed, domesticate and cultivate various species of plant and animal. This was the beginning of agriculture and is sometimes called the Neolithic or agricultural revolution. In fact, it was a slow and partial process which occurred at different times and speeds in different parts of the world and was never complete, if only because climatic and soil variations precluded agriculture in many areas. The arid zones were the home of mobile pastoralists, who domesticated sheep and horses and colonised the grazing grounds of the steppes (map 3), while the densely afforested areas, in northern Europe and elsewhere, were inhabited, as earlier, by hunters. The result, following the spread of agriculture, was a differentiated world economy, with well defined zones, cereal and root-crop cultivation being characteristic of the temperate and tropical regions respectively (map 1).

Nevertheless, the transformation of Man from a hunter and fisher to an agriculturalist, and from a migratory to a sedentary life, was a decisive event in world history. The increase in food resources which followed made possible a spectacular growth of human population which is calculated to have multiplied sixteen times between 8000 and 4000 BC. It also required co-operative effort, particularly after the introduction of irrigation c.5000 BC, leading to the establishment of settled, organised societies, at first villages, then towns and cities. Urban civilisation dates from c.3500 BC, but already before 6000 BC there were 'proto-cities' covering extensive sites (up to 30 acres) at Jericho in the Jordan valley and Çatal Hüyük in Anatolia. Here also there is evidence of long-distance trade, stone for tools at Jericho, for example, coming from as far away as Anatolia.

There is no doubt that agriculture developed independently in different parts of the world (maize in Mexico, for example, millet and rice in China), presumably in response to similar stimuli. But the beginnings of cereal cultivation, which later spread to India and Europe (and in modern times was carried to the New World), are clearly associated with the Near East — that is, with the region bounded in the north by the Caucasus Mountains, in the west by the Mediterranean and Black Seas, and in the east by the Caspian Sea and the Persian Gulf. Here, on the remote mountain uplands, were found the wild ancestors of wheat and barley, and the villages where they were first cultivated (c.8000 BC) grew up on the edge of this zone, within the critical rainfall limit of 300 mm (12 ins) a year (map 2). Only with the introduction of irrigation was it possible to extend cultivation into the adjacent dry plains. This occurred during the fifth and fourth millennia BC.

Many other parts of the globe contributed their quota at different times to Man's supply of domesticated plants and animals (map 4). Their diffusion from their original habitat not only supplemented native food resources, but also affected human diet. Rice, which originated in South-East Asia and southern China, passed into the Near East and Mediterranean Europe, where it became a staple foodstuff. The yam and banana, later to be major African food crops, were introduced from Asia during the first millennium BC. The story of domestic animals is similar. The camel, first domesticated in central Asia, was introduced into Africa c.100 BC and made possible a rapid expansion of trans-Saharan trade. A new chapter opened after AD 1500, following the discovery of the New World (map 5). Without the potato, which originated in America, it would scarcely have been possible to feed the teeming population of Europe during the Industrial Revolution.

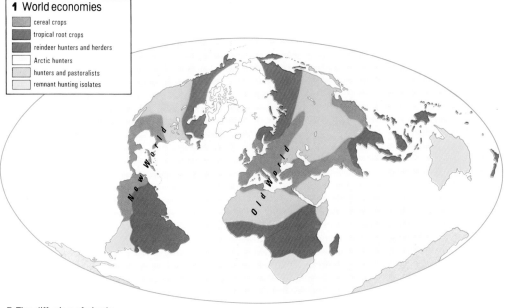

1 World economies
- cereal crops
- tropical root crops
- reindeer hunters and herders
- Arctic hunters
- hunters and pastoralists
- remnant hunting isolates

5 The diffusion of plants

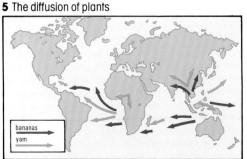

bananas
yam

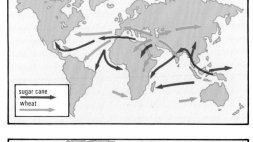

sugar cane
wheat

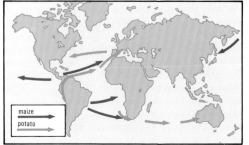

maize
potato

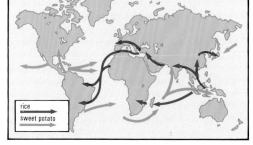

rice
sweet potato

NORTH AMERICA
Turkey

MESOAMERICA

ANDES

Llama   Guinea Pig   Alpaca

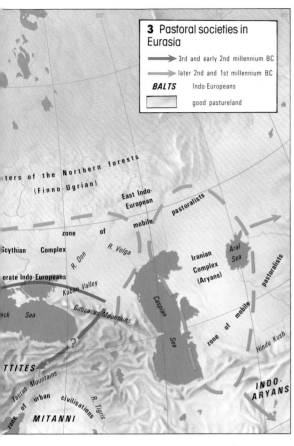

3 Pastoral societies in Eurasia

→ 3rd and early 2nd millennium BC

→ later 2nd and 1st millennium BC

BALTS Indo-Europeans

good pastureland

ters of the Northern forests
(Finno-Ugrian)

zone of

East Indo-
European

mobile pastoralists

Scythian Complex

erate Indo-Europeans

R. Don

R. Volga

Kuban Valley

Caucasus Mountains

Iranian
Complex
(Aryans)

Aral
Sea

Caspian Sea

zone of mobile pastoralists

Hindu Kush

ck Sea

TTITES

Taurus Mountains

?

zone of urban civilisations

MITANNI

R. Tigris

INDO-
ARYANS

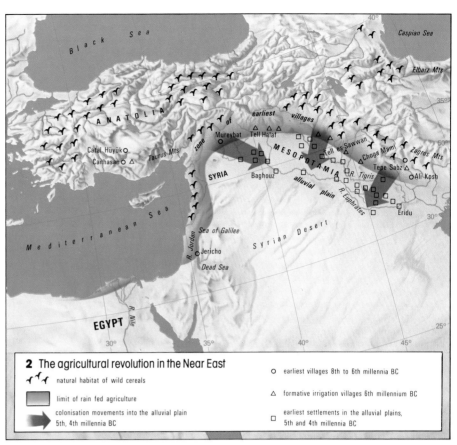

Black Sea

Caspian Sea

Elburz Mts

ANATOLIA

earliest villages

Mureybat Tell Halaf

zone of

Çatal Hüyük○

Canhasan○△ *Taurus Mts*

MESOPOTAMIA

Tell es Sawwan

Choga Mami

Zagros Mts

Baghouz

R. Tigris

Tepe Sabz△ Ali Kosh○

SYRIA

alluvial plain

R. Euphrates

Eridu

Mediterranean Sea

Sea of Galilee

R. Jordan

○Jericho

Dead Sea

Syrian Desert

R. Nile

EGYPT

2 The agricultural revolution in the Near East

⤙⤚ natural habitat of wild cereals

limit of rain fed agriculture

➤ colonisation movements into the alluvial plain
5th, 4th millennia BC

○ earliest villages 8th to 6th millennia BC

△ formative irrigation villages 6th millennium BC

□ earliest settlements in the alluvial plains,
5th and 4th millennia BC

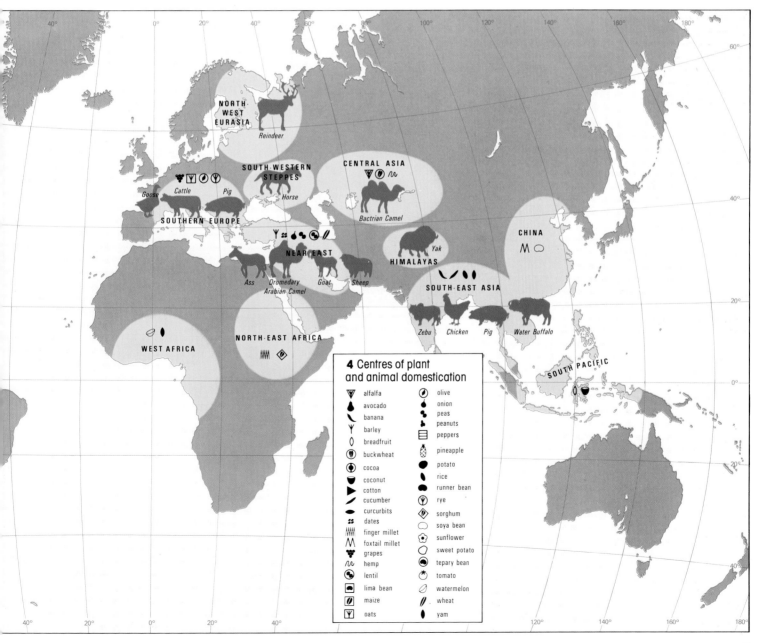

NORTH-WEST EURASIA

Reindeer

SOUTH-WESTERN STEPPES

Horse

CENTRAL ASIA

Bactrian Camel

Goose Cattle Pig

SOUTHERN EUROPE

NEAR EAST

Ass Dromedary
Arabian Camel

Goat Sheep

HIMALAYAS Yak

CHINA

SOUTH-EAST ASIA

Zebu Chicken Pig Water Buffalo

SOUTH PACIFIC

WEST AFRICA

NORTH-EAST AFRICA

4 Centres of plant
and animal domestication

- alfalfa
- avocado
- banana
- barley
- breadfruit
- buckwheat
- cocoa
- coconut
- cotton
- cucumber
- curcurbits
- dates
- finger millet
- foxtail millet
- grapes
- hemp
- lentil
- lima bean
- maize
- oats

- olive
- onion
- peas
- peanuts
- peppers
- pineapple
- potato
- rice
- runner bean
- rye
- sorghum
- soya bean
- sunflower
- sweet potato
- tepary bean
- tomato
- watermelon
- wheat
- yam

Early cultures of Asia

Early Man, or his immediate ancestors, is found widely spread throughout Asia during the Second Interglacial Period (400,000–200,000 BC). His appearance here seems to date from the Middle Pleistocene (page 2, diagram 1), but it is not possible to establish the stages of his advance. It is reasonable to assume that he first reached India, where hand-axes, chopping tools and flakes of the early Stone Age are found not only in the foothills of the Punjab but as far east as southern Bihar and northern Orissa and as far south as Madras (map 1), and that he later moved on to China and South-East Asia. But the discovery of Java Man in the Solo Valley of central Java (map 3) and of Peking Man in the limestone fissures at Choukoutien (map 2), both apparently of approximately the same age, suggests fairly uniform diffusion by c.350,000 BC. What, in any case, is note-worthy is the profusion of early sites, particularly in India, by com-parison with Europe, where, except for the Mediterranean littoral, Man's advance was held up by the extensive ice-fields.

These early hominids were hunters, and it was not until long after the appearance of *homo sapiens* (in Java c.40,000 BC, in China c.30,000 BC) that we find the beginnings of agriculture. Evidence from Spirit Cave in northern Siam suggests that rice cultivation had begun in South-East Asia by 6000 BC. In China the first agricultural communities arose c.4000 BC in the loess-covered highlands of the north and north-west, where the well-drained soil of the river terraces was ideal for primitive agriculture. Nevertheless, the first Neolithic culture, the Yangshao, still subsisted largely by hunting and fishing. Its successor, the Lungshan, covered a wider area and had more permanent villages and a higher level of organisation (map 2). In India there was a similar evolution. By the end of the fourth millen-nium more advanced settlements were widely scattered throughout Sind, Baluchistan and Rajasthan, and urban life was beginning to develop, with the appearance of copper and bronze.

The advent of copper and bronze (in South-East Asia perhaps as early as 3000, in China c.1600 BC) marked a new and decisive stage in the history of Asian civilisation. In China it is associated with the first historical dynasty, the Shang, dating approximately from 1700–1100 BC (map 4). In South-East Asia its impact is seen in the famous Dong Son bronze drums, distributed widely throughout the region but with a marked concentration c.1000 BC in northern Vietnam (map 3). In India craftsmanship was a feature of the great Indus civilisation, spreading from the highly developed cities of Harappa and Mohenjo-Daro – the largest of all the early civilisations of the Old World, covering nearly 1,295,000 sq. km (500,000 sq. miles) (map 5) – which survived for around 1000 years (c.2550–1550 BC) until it was destroyed by primitive tribal invaders from the north: the Aryans. In China, also, the Shang were defeated and dis-placed by a more primitive warrior people from the western border-lands of their domains, the Chou, who gradually extended control over a much larger area (map 6). Both the Shang and the Chou regimes were loose collections of feudal overlordships, rather than centralised monarchies, and both were forced to move their capitals frequently under political pressure. It was only later (page 28), with the introduction of iron technology (c.800–500 BC) that empires arose with adequate economic and administrative foundations.

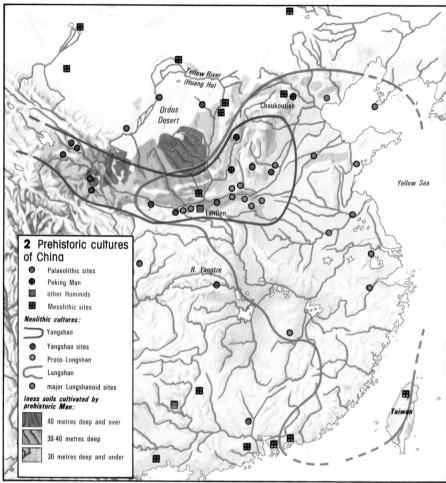

2 Prehistoric cultures of China

Palaeolithic sites
Peking Man
other Hominids
Mesolithic sites

Neolithic cultures:

Yangshao
Yangshao sites
Proto-Lungshan
Lungshan
major Lungshanoid sites

loess soils cultivated by prehistoric Man:

40 metres deep and over
30–40 metres deep
30 metres deep and under

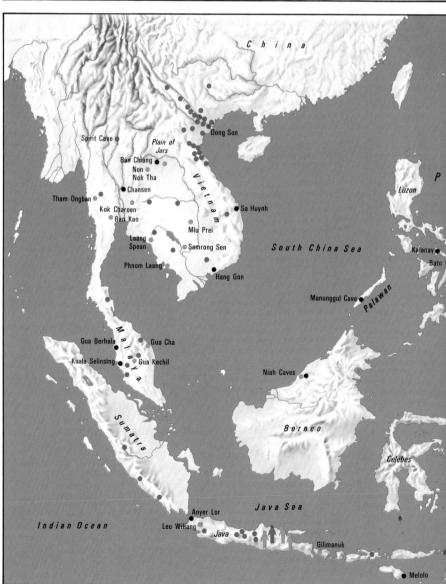

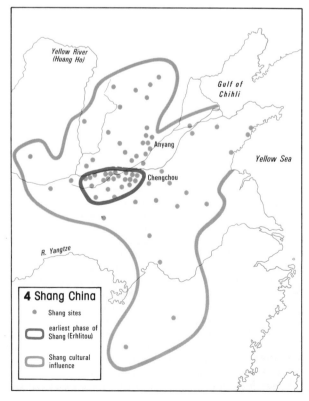

4 Shang China

Shang sites
earliest phase of Shang (Erhlitou)
Shang cultural influence

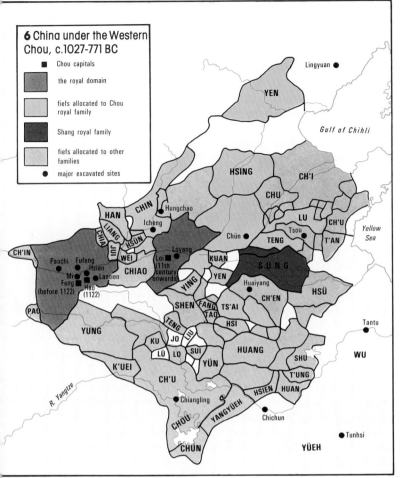

6 China under the Western Chou, c.1027-771 BC

- ■ Chou capitals
- the royal domain
- fiefs allocated to Chou royal family
- Shang royal family
- fiefs allocated to other families
- ● major excavated sites

YEN

Gulf of Chihli

HSING
CH'I
CHU
LU
CH'U
Yellow Sea

HAN
CHIN
CHIA
HSÜN
WEI
JUI
LIANG
Hungchao
Icheng
Chün
TENG
TSOU
T'AN

CH'IN
Paochi
Fufeng
Hsian
Loyang
Loi (11th century onwards)
KUAN
YEN
HSÜ

Mi Feng (before 1122)
Hao (1122)
Lantien
CHIAO
YING
SUNG

Huaiyang
CH'EN

SHEN
FANG
TAO
TS'AI
HSI

YUNG
TENG
JO
LIU
Tantu
WU

PAO
KU
LÜ
LO
SUI
YÜN
HUANG
SHÜ

K'UEI
YÜN
CH'U
T'UNG
HSIEN
HUAN

CHOU
Chiangling
YANGYÜEH
Chichun
Tunhsi

CHÜN
YÜEH

R. Yangtze

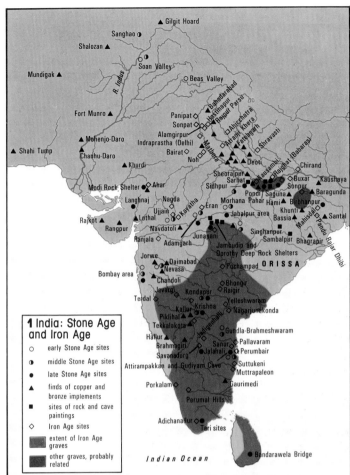

1 India: Stone Age and Iron Age

- ○ early Stone Age sites
- ◐ middle Stone Age sites
- ● late Stone Age sites
- ▲ finds of copper and bronze implements
- ■ sites of rock and cave paintings
- ◇ Iron Age sites
- extent of Iron Age graves
- other graves, probably related

Gilgit Hoard
Sanghao
Shalozan
Shalozan
Mundigak
Soan Valley
Beas Valley
Fort Munro
Panipat
Bahadarabad
Hastinapur
Atranji Khera
Alamgirpur
Sonpat
Ahichchatra
Rajpur Parsu
Fatehgarh
Shravasti
Chirand
Mohenjo-Daro
Indraprastha (Delhi)
Bairat
Noh
Shahi Tump
Chanhu-Daro
Khurdi
Sheorajpur
Kaushambi
Rajghat (Babargsi)
Buxar
Kaushaya
Sarbat
Sonpur
Baragunda
Modi Rock Shelter
Ahar
Sidhpur
Pondi
Saguna
Khunti
Santal
Mahisdi
Pandu Rajar Dhibi
Langhnaj
Nagda
Morhana Pahar
Hami
Birbhanpur
Ujjain
Karatha
Eran
Jabalpur area
Bassia
Bhagrapir
Rajkot
Lothal
Navdatoli
Singhanpur
Sambalpur
Rangpur
Ranjala
Adamgarh
Junapani
Jambudip and Dorothy Deep Rock Shelters
ORISSA
Jorwe
Daimabad
Pochampad
Bombay area
Nevasa
Bhongir
Chandoli
Kondapur
Raigir
Teral
Jevato
Kallur
Krishna
Yelleshwaram
Piklihal
Nagarjunakonda
Hallur
Sanur
Pallavaram
Brahmagiri
Jadigenhalli
Perumbair
Savanadurg
Jalahali
Suttukeni
Attirampakkan and Gudiyam Cave
Muttrapaleon
Porkalam
Gaurimedi
Perumal Hills
Tari sites
Adichanallur
Indian Ocean
Bandarawela Bridge

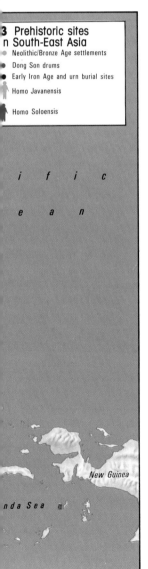

3 Prehistoric sites in South-East Asia

- Neolithic/Bronze Age settlements
- Dong Son drums
- Early Iron Age and urn burial sites
- Homo Javanensis
- Homo Soloensis

ific
ean

New Guinea
nda Sea

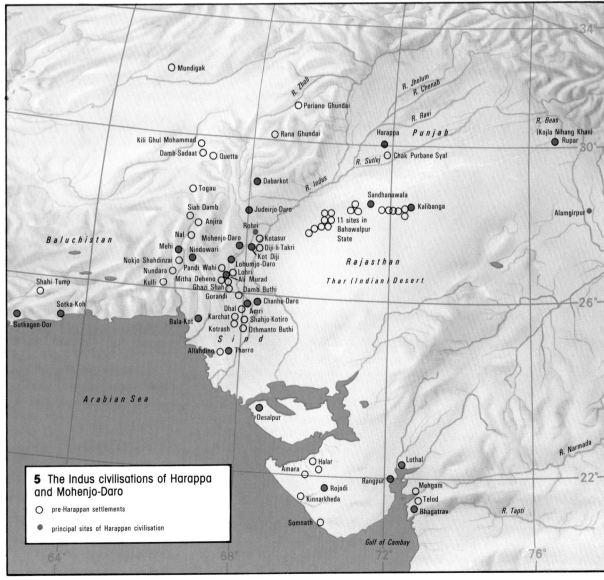

Mundigak
R. Zhob
R. Jhelum
R. Chenab
Periano Ghundai
R. Ravi
R. Beas
Rana Ghundai
Harappa
Punjab
(Kojla Nihang Khan)
Kili Ghul Mohammad
Rupar
Damb-Sadaat
Quetta
R. Sutlej
Chak Purbane Syal
Togau
Dabarkot
R. Indus
Siah Damb
Sandhanawala
Anjira
Judeirjo-Daro
Kalibanga
Nal
Rohri
Alamgirpur
Mehi
Mohenjo-Daro
Kotasur
11 sites in Bahawalpur State
Nindowari
Diji-li-Takri
Nokjo Shahdinzai
Kot Diji
Pandi Wahi
Lohumjo-Daro
Rajasthan
Nundara
Lohri
Kulli
Mitha Deheno
Ali Murad
Thar (Indian) Desert
Shahi Tump
Ghazi Shah
Damb Buthi
Gorandi
Sotka-Koh
Dhal
Chanhu-Daro
Sutkagen-Dor
Karchat
Amri
Bala-Kot
Kotrash
Shahjo-Kotiro
Othmanto Buthi
Sind
Allahdino
Tharro
Arabian Sea
Desalpur

5 The Indus civilisations of Harappa and Mohenjo-Daro

- ○ pre-Harappan settlements
- ● principal sites of Harappan civilisation

Halar
Lothal
Amara
R. Narmada
Rojadi
Mehgam
Rangpur
Kinnarkheda
Telod
Bhagatrav
R. Tapti
Somnath
Gulf of Cambay

Prehistoric Africa and Australasia

Climatic change, setting in 5–6000 years ago, profoundly influenced the early history of Africa and Australasia. North Africa, belonging to the temperate Mediterranean belt, developed in close association with western Asia, and by 3000 BC an advanced civilisation was established in Egypt (page 16). But Africa south of the equator, almost certainly the original home of Man (page 2), was cut off from the mainstream for centuries by the desiccation of the Sahara. Similar changes occurred in Australia which had been populated during the late Pleistocene ice age via the land bridge from New Guinea (page 4). Here the rise of the sea level, due to temperature change, severed the links with South-East Asia, and the Australasian continent developed thenceforth in geographical isolation. The colonisation of the islands of Melanesia occurred considerably later, when settlers from New Guinea, associated with the distinctive Lapita pottery, reached Fiji (c.1300 BC) and then made their way into Polynesia via Tonga and Samoa, reaching the Marquesas Islands c.AD 300 (map 2). From here they spread north to Hawaii (c.AD 800) and south-west via the Cook Islands to New Zealand between 850 and 1100 (map 3).

Geographical isolation was an important factor in shaping the cultures of southern Africa and of Oceania. In Australia the aborigines remained hunters and gatherers. They did not herd or cultivate, and there was no use of iron. Elsewhere in Oceania, notably in New Zealand, a mixed hunting-farming society developed after the depletion of animal food resources, and settlement, originally coastal, spread inland. But population remained small, about 300,000 in Australia and 100,000 in New Zealand when the Europeans arrived. The isolation of southern Africa was never so complete. In East Africa settlers spread down the Rift Valley from Ethiopia during the first millennium BC, and trans-Saharan trade increased in importance after the introduction of the camel from Asia c.100 BC (map 1). This facilitated the spread of iron tools and weapons, introduced in the north from Asia in 663 BC, which reached the Jos Plateau in Nigeria by c.450 BC and became widespread in the south after c.AD 100. The coming of iron had revolutionary effects, leading to the displacement of the Stone Age hunters and gatherers by settled Bantu-speaking agricultural and cattle-raising societies. These established themselves in Katanga during the late Stone Age and expanded into the rest of southern Africa during the early Iron Age.

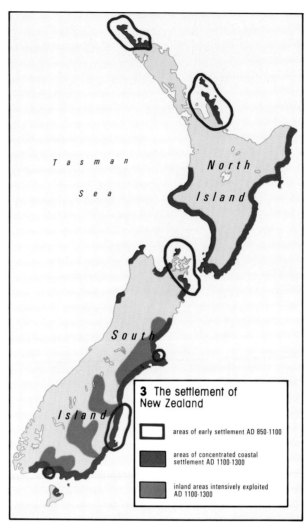

3 The settlement of New Zealand

☐ areas of early settlement AD 850-1100

■ areas of concentrated coastal settlement AD 1100-1300

▨ inland areas intensively exploited AD 1100-1300

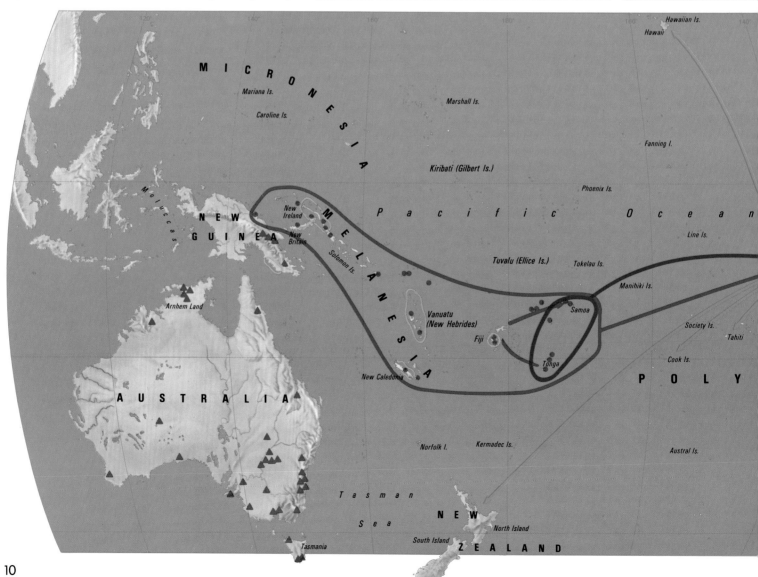

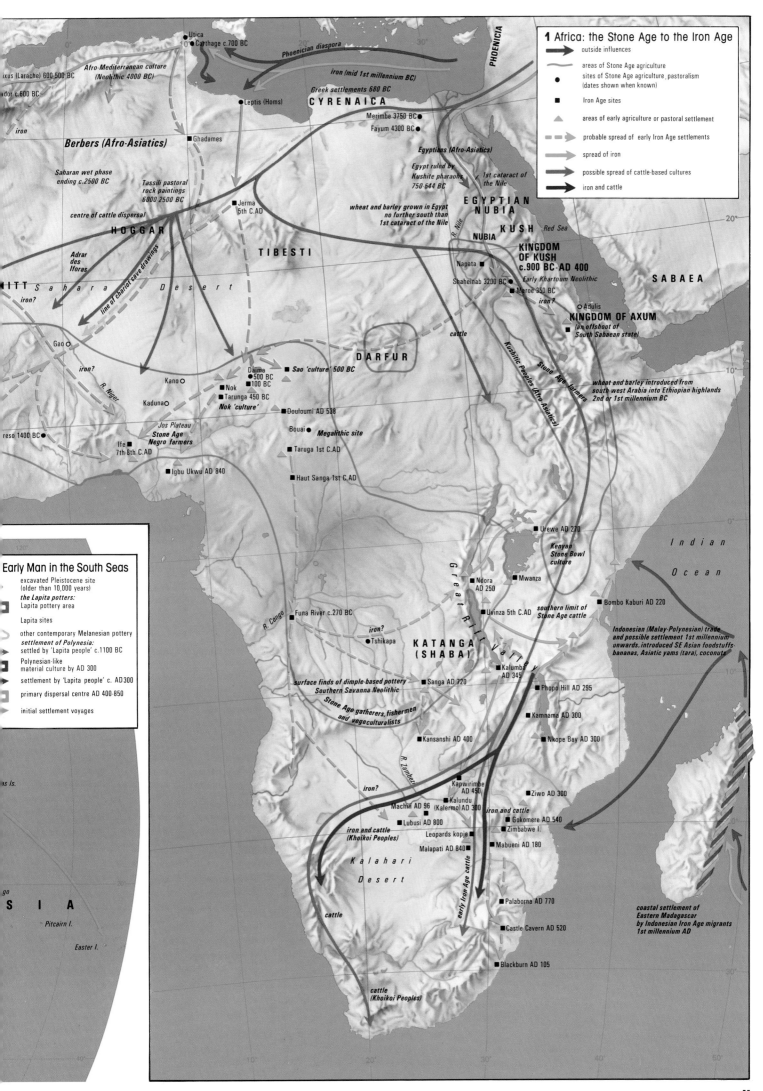

1 Africa: the Stone Age to the Iron Age

→ outside influences
∿ areas of Stone Age agriculture
• sites of Stone Age agriculture, pastoralism (dates shown when known)
■ Iron Age sites
▲ areas of early agriculture or pastoral settlement
⇢ probable spread of early Iron Age settlements
→ spread of iron
→ possible spread of cattle-based cultures
→ iron and cattle

○ Utica
● Carthage c.700 BC

Phoenician diaspora

Afro-Mediterranean culture (Neolithic 4000 BC)

ixus (Larache) 600-500 BC

dor c.600 BC

iron

○ Leptis (Homs)
■ Ghadames

iron (mid 1st millennium BC)

Greek settlements 680 BC

CYRENAICA

● Merimbe 3750 BC
● Fayum 4300 BC

PHOENICIA

Berbers (Afro-Asiatics)

Saharan wet phase ending c.2500 BC

Tassili pastoral rock paintings 6000-2500 BC

centre of cattle dispersal

■ Jerma 5th C.AD

HOGGAR

Egyptians (Afro-Asiatics)

Egypt ruled by Kushite pharaohs 750-644 BC

1st cataract of the Nile

EGYPTIAN NUBIA

KUSH

NUBIA

○ Adulis

Adrar des Iforas

line of chariot cave drawings

TIBESTI

wheat and barley grown in Egypt no further south than 1st cataract of the Nile

● Napata

KINGDOM OF KUSH c.900 BC-AD 400

Red Sea

SABAEA

ITT *Sahara Desert*

iron?

● Shaheinab 3200 BC

Early Khartoum Neolithic

■ Meroe 350 BC

iron?

KINGDOM OF AXUM (an offshoot of South Sabaean state)

○ Gao

iron?

R. Niger

DARFUR

cattle

Kushitic Peoples (Afro-Asiatics)

Stone Age farmers

wheat and barley introduced from south-west Arabia into Ethiopian highlands 2nd or 1st millennium BC

○ Kano
■ Nok
● Daima 500 BC
● 100 BC
■ Sao 'culture' 500 BC

○ Kaduna

■ Tarunga 450 BC

Nok 'culture'

■ Douloumi AD 538

Bouai ●

● Megalithic site

reso 1400 BC ●

Jos Plateau
Stone Age Negro farmers

▲ Ife 7th-8th C.AD

▲ Taruga 1st C.AD

■ Igbu Ukwu AD 840

■ Haut Sanga 1st C.AD

Early Man in the South Seas

▢ excavated Pleistocene site (older than 10,000 years)

the Lapita potters:
Lapita pottery area

Lapita sites

other contemporary Melanesian pottery

settlement of Polynesia:
settled by 'Lapita people' c.1100 BC

Polynesian-like material culture by AD 300

settlement by 'Lapita people' c. AD 300

primary dispersal centre AD 400-850

initial settlement voyages

R. Congo

Funa River c.270 BC

iron?

● Tshikapa

KATANGA (SHABA)

■ Urewe AD 270

Kenyan Stone Bowl culture

■ Ndora AD 250
■ Mwanza

■ Uvinza 5th C.AD

southern limit of Stone Age cattle

■ Bombo Kaburi AD 220

Indonesian (Malay-Polynesian) trade and possible settlement 1st millennium onwards, introduced SE Asian foodstuffs-bananas, Asiatic yams (tara), coconuts

Indian Ocean

Great Rift Valley

■ Kalumba AD 345

■ Sanga AD 720

■ Phopo Hill AD 295

surface finds of dimple-based pottery Southern Savanna Neolithic

Stone Age gatherers, fishermen and vegeculturalists

■ Kamnama AD 300

■ Nkope Bay AD 300

■ Kansanshi AD 400

R. Zambezi

iron?

Kapwirimbe AD 450
● Kalundu (Kalermo) AD 300
▲ Machili AD 96
■ Lubusi AD 800

● Kalundu (Kalermo) AD 300

iron and cattle

■ Gokomere AD 540

■ Ziwo AD 300

iron and cattle (Khoikoi Peoples)

Leopards kopje ■
■ Zimbabwe I.

Malapati AD 840 ■
■ Mabueni AD 180

Kalahari Desert

■ Palaborna AD 770

cattle

■ Castle Cavern AD 520

coastal settlement of Eastern Madagascar by Indonesian Iron Age migrants 1st millennium AD

early Iron Age cattle

cattle (Khoikoi Peoples)

■ Blackburn AD 105

SIA

Pitcairn I.

Easter I.

as Is.

go

Peoples and cultures of the Americas

America, like Australia (page 10), was colonised from Asia during the last cold age 30,000 or more years ago, and like Australia was later cut off from the Old World by the melting of the ice and the rise of the sea level which submerged the land bridge across the Bering Strait (page 4). Unlike the Australian aborigines, however, who never progressed beyond a Stone Age hunting and gathering culture, geographic isolation did not prevent the American Indians from developing independently a high level of civilisation, based on agriculture (particularly the cultivation of maize), mining (particularly obsidian for tools and weapons), pottery manufacture and gold, silver and copper working. It was a civilisation distinguished not only by magnificent art and remarkable mathematical and astronomical skills, but also by monumental building on a grand scale. In its prime, around AD 600, the city of Teotihuacán in the basin of Mexico covered 20 sq. km (8 sq. miles) and had a population of 125,000.

The first civilisations arose in the climatically favourable regions of Mesoamerica and the central Andes, where maize farming, permitting a rapid increase in population, became widespread from c.1500 BC. By 1000 BC the Olmecs on the Gulf of Mexico, the Zapotecs at Monte Albán, and the inhabitants of Chavín in Peru had established states with populations numbering tens of thousands, a priesthood, a civil service, and a hierarchy of social classes including craftsmen and traders (map 2). Mesoamerica and the central Andes remained the main centres of civilisation, but the diffusion of agriculture and growing commercial exchanges soon affected other regions. In North America the introduction of maize, beans and squashes from Mexico initiated a period of rapid development between 300 BC and AD 550. Its centre was the Hopewell territory in Illinois and Ohio, but trading contacts (mainly for precious metals) extended its influence as far as Florida and the Rockies (map 3). In South America a number of separate centres, each with its own distinctive artistic style, developed in the Andes (map 4), and were fused after AD 600 into the empires of Tiahuanaco and Huari (map 5). But this precarious unity broke down after AD 800 and it was not until the fifteenth century under the Incas that Peru was once again united (page 62).

In Mesoamerica the early Olmec and Zapotec civilisations were submerged by invaders coming from the north, first the Maya who reached Yucatán by the fifth century AD, then the Toltecs in the eleventh century and finally the Aztecs in the thirteenth century. The classic period of Maya civilisation falls between AD 300 and AD 900; but influences radiating from Teotihuacán were strong (map 2), and Maya civilisation, like all the other civilisations of the classical period, was essentially a variant of a common Mesoamerican culture pattern. Internecine warfare appears to have weakened these civilisations and left them prey to invaders from the north. Teotihuacán was destroyed c.750, Monte Albán allowed to go to ruin during the tenth century, and Maya civilisation collapsed between AD 800 and 900.

For all their brilliant architectural and artistic achievements, the civilisations of Mesoamerica and the Andes account for only a small area of the Americas taken as a whole (map 1). Climatic variation alone dictated disparate ways of life. Particularly in the far north and far south, where conditions were too harsh for farming, the small nomadic populations depended on hunting and fishing. Climate was also a determining factor for the desert gatherers in the interior. The continent the Europeans encountered when they arrived in the sixteenth century was at widely different levels of development; but even the simpler societies, far removed from the centres of civilisation, had adapted themselves to the environment and its requirements.

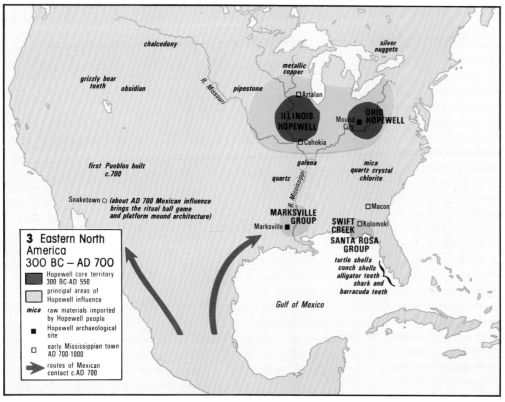

3 Eastern North America 300 BC – AD 700

- Hopewell core territory 300 BC-AD 550
- principal areas of Hopewell influence
- *mica* raw materials imported by Hopewell people
- ■ Hopewell archaeological site
- □ early Mississippian town AD 700-1000
- → routes of Mexican contact c.AD 700

Snaketown ○ (about AD 700 Mexican influence brings the ritual ball game and platform mound architecture)

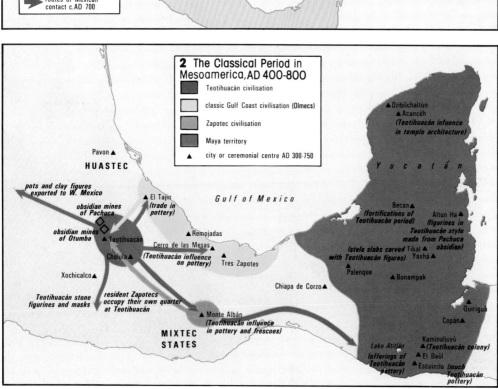

2 The Classical Period in Mesoamerica, AD 400-800

- Teotihuacán civilisation
- classic Gulf Coast civilisation (Olmecs)
- Zapotec civilisation
- Maya territory
- ▲ city or ceremonial centre AD 300-750

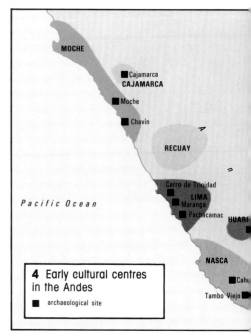

4 Early cultural centres in the Andes

- ■ archaeological site

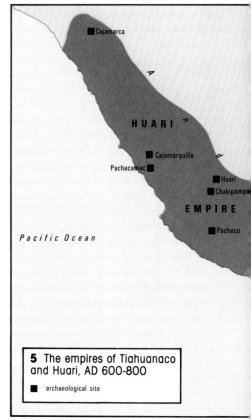

5 The empires of Tiahuanaco and Huari, AD 600-800

- ■ archaeological site

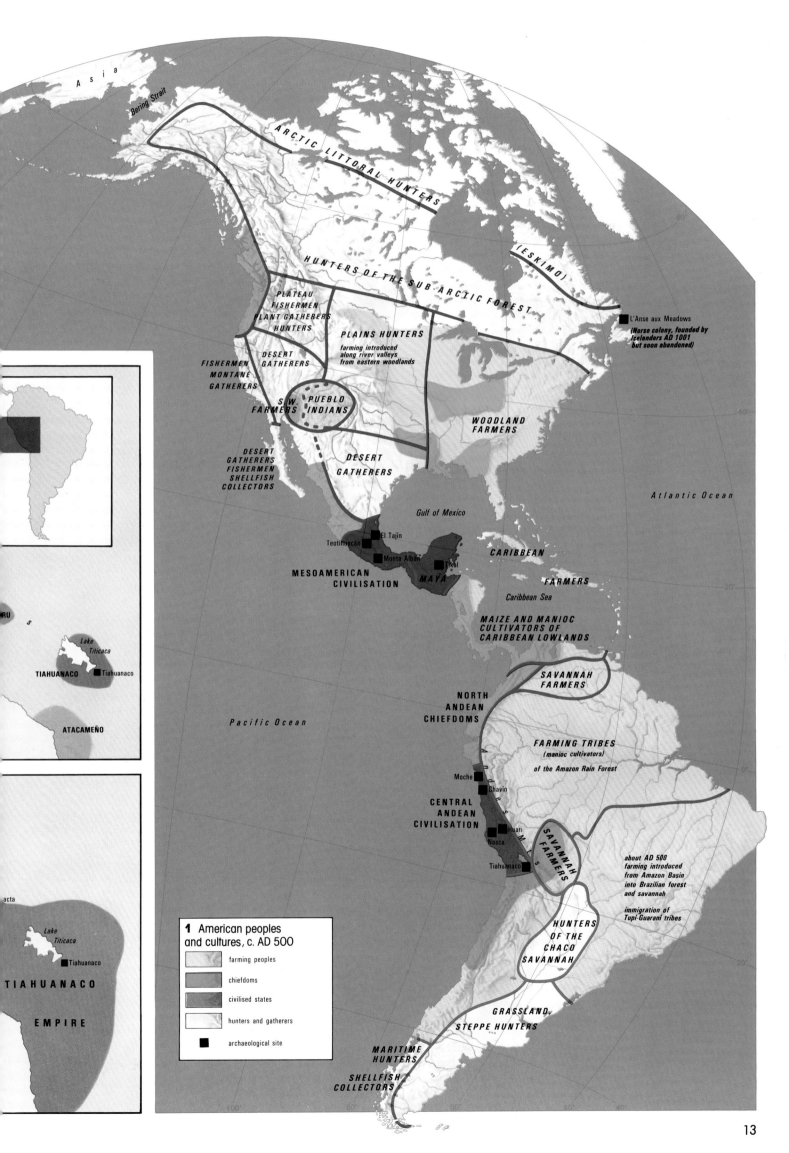

Asia

Bering Strait

ARCTIC LITTORAL HUNTERS

(ESKIMO)

HUNTERS OF THE SUB-ARCTIC FOREST

L'Anse aux Meadows
*(Norse colony, founded by
Icelanders AD 1001
but soon abandoned)*

PLATEAU
FISHERMEN
PLANT GATHERERS
HUNTERS

PLAINS HUNTERS
*farming introduced
along river valleys
from eastern woodlands*

DESERT
GATHERERS

FISHERMEN
MONTANE
GATHERERS

S.W.
FARMERS

PUEBLO
INDIANS

WOODLAND
FARMERS

DESERT
GATHERERS
FISHERMEN
SHELLFISH
COLLECTORS

DESERT
GATHERERS

Atlantic Ocean

Gulf of Mexico

El Tajín

Teotihuacán

Monte Albán

Tikal

MESOAMERICAN
CIVILISATION

MAYA

CARIBBEAN

FARMERS

Caribbean Sea

MAIZE AND MANIOC
CULTIVATORS OF
CARIBBEAN LOWLANDS

SAVANNAH
FARMERS

NORTH
ANDEAN
CHIEFDOMS

FARMING TRIBES
(manioc cultivators)
of the Amazon Rain Forest

Pacific Ocean

Moche

Chavin

CENTRAL
ANDEAN
CIVILISATION

Huari

Nasca

SAVANNAH
FARMERS

Tiahuanaco

*about AD 500
farming introduced
from Amazon Basin
into Brazilian forest
and savannah*

*immigration of
Tupi-Guarani tribes*

HUNTERS
OF THE
CHACO
SAVANNAH

GRASSLAND
STEEP HUNTERS

MARITIME
HUNTERS

SHELLFISH
COLLECTORS

1 American peoples
and cultures, c. AD 500

- farming peoples
- chiefdoms
- civilised states
- hunters and gatherers
- ■ archaeological site

Lake
Titicaca

TIAHUANACO

Tiahuanaco

ATACAMEÑO

PERU

Lake
Titicaca

Tiahuanaco

TIAHUANACO

EMPIRE

The colonisation of Europe, 6000-300 BC

Settlers from Anatolia, one of the original homes of agriculture (page 6), crossed the Aegean to Thessaly and Crete c.6000 BC. From there different groups, identifiable by their pottery, moved north and west reaching the British Isles c.4000 BC (map 1). About this time metallurgy, which originated in the copper belt of the Near East (map 2), was introduced into the Balkans and spread to Iberia and central Europe, where rich mineral deposits were available (map 3). Two main routes of colonisation were followed: the Mediterranean littoral and the Vardar-Danube-Rhine corridor to the north European plain and to the south Russian steppes. In the Mediterranean zone fishing, maritime trade, and the cultivation of vines and olives laid the economic foundations of Mycenaean civilisation (page 18). In the northern belt the economy was based on grazing (sheep and cattle) and cereals (predominantly wheat). Clearing the land as they went, the settlers slashed and burnt the inland forests, while on the Atlantic coast and the boulder-strewn moraines of north-west Europe they removed rock and stone, using the boulders to build impressive megalithic mortuary shrines, many of which still survive (map 4).

The opening-up of northern and western Europe in the fourth and early third millennia changed the cultural configuration of Europe. Wheeled vehicles and the plough, introduced probably by Indo-European speaking immigrants (page 6), made possible the cultivation of heavier soils. The result was a great increase in the population of Europe north of the Alps, and also the beginning of a more closely articulated political organisation, centred upon hill-forts where the aristocracy resided. The main focus of these developments, greatly stimulated by the introduction (1000–800 BC) of ironworking, was the territory of the so-called 'Urnfield culture' – a complex of related peoples in central Europe which dominated the Rhine-Danube axis. About 1000 BC these tribes expanded into adjacent areas. Their four main branches each gave rise to an important group of peoples: Celts in the west, Slavs in the north-east, Italic speakers in the south and Illyrians in the south-east (map 5).

During the first millennium BC the Celtic areas expanded at the expense of their neighbours, particularly in the direction of modern France. Ironworking on an industrial scale and superior arms and equipment probably accounted for this advance, which occurred in two phases, named respectively after Hallstatt in Austria and La Tène in Switzerland. The later, La Tène, phase (450 BC onwards) saw the Celtic occupation of much of Britain, but its main feature was raiding and settlement in the south and east (map 6). Contact with the Mediterranean world stimulated Celtic civilisation, but it also prepared the way for Caesar's campaigns, which brought the western Celtic world under Roman control by 49 BC.

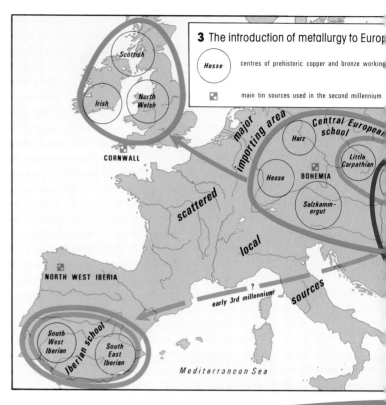

3 The introduction of metallurgy to Europe

Hesse — centres of prehistoric copper and bronze working

— main tin sources used in the second millennium

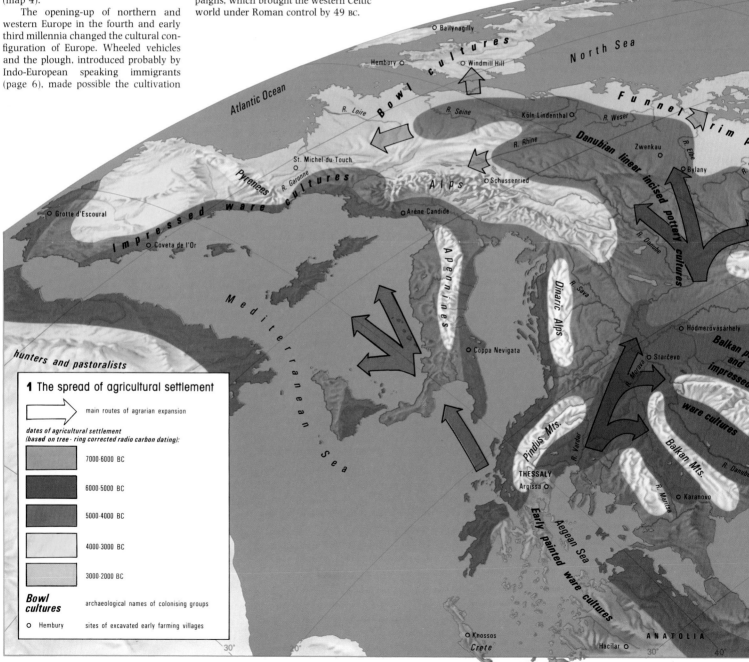

1 The spread of agricultural settlement

⟹ main routes of agrarian expansion

dates of agricultural settlement (based on tree-ring corrected radio carbon dating):

- 7000-6000 BC
- 6000-5000 BC
- 5000-4000 BC
- 4000-3000 BC
- 3000-2000 BC

Bowl cultures — archaeological names of colonising groups

○ Hembury — sites of excavated early farming villages

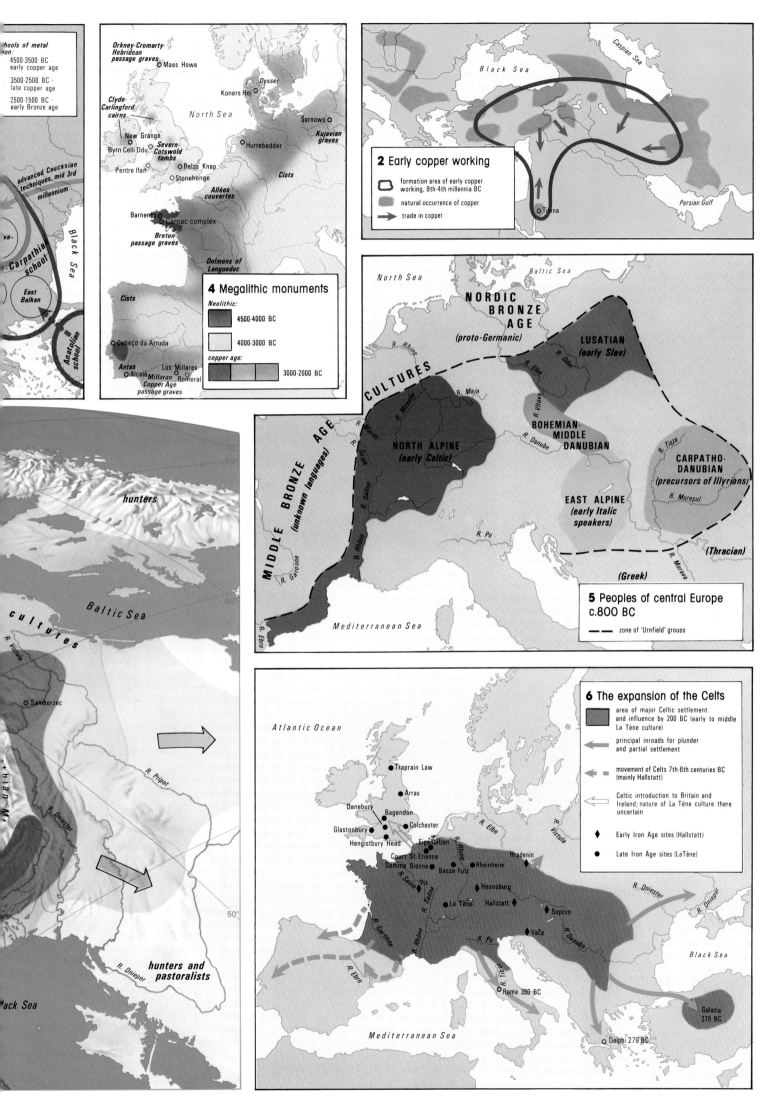

Schools of metal [production]:
4500-3500 BC - early copper age
3500-2500 BC - late copper age
2500-1500 BC - early Bronze age

advanced Caucasian techniques, mid 3rd millennium

...va-

Carpathian school

East Balkan

Anatolian school

Black Sea

4 Megalithic monuments

Neolithic:
4500-4000 BC
4000-3000 BC

copper age:
3000-2000 BC

Orkney-Cromarty-Hebridean passage graves
Maes Howe
Dysser
Koners Hoj
Clyde-Carlingford cairns
North Sea
Sarnowo
Kujavian graves
New Grange
Byrn Celli Ddu
Severn-Cotswold tombs
Hurrebedder
Pentre Ifan
Belas Knap
Stonehenge
Cists
Allées couvertes
Barnenez
Carnac complex
Breton passage graves
Dolmens of Languedoc
Cists
Cabeço da Arruda
Antas
Alcalá
Millares
Millaran
Romeral
Los Millares
Copper Age passage graves

2 Early copper working

Black Sea
Caspian Sea
Persian Gulf
Timna

formation area of early copper working, 8th-4th millennia BC
natural occurrence of copper
trade in copper

5 Peoples of central Europe c.800 BC

zone of 'Urnfield' groups

North Sea
Baltic Sea
NORDIC BRONZE AGE (proto-Germanic)
LUSATIAN (early Slav)
BOHEMIAN-MIDDLE DANUBIAN
CARPATHO-DANUBIAN (precursors of Illyrians)
NORTH ALPINE (early Celtic)
EAST ALPINE (early Italic speakers)
MIDDLE BRONZE AGE (unknown languages)
CULTURES
R. Rhine
R. Moselle
R. Marne
R. Seine
R. Saône
R. Rhône
R. Garonne
R. Ebro
R. Main
R. Elbe
R. Oder
R. Vltava
R. Danube
R. Tisza
R. Mureşul
R. Morava
R. Po
(Thracian)
(Greek)
Mediterranean Sea

hunters
Baltic Sea
cultures
R. Vistula
Samborzec
R. Pripet
R. Dniester
R. Dnieper
...thian Mts
hunters and pastoralists
Black Sea

6 The expansion of the Celts

area of major Celtic settlement and influence by 200 BC (early to middle La Tène culture)
principal inroads for plunder and partial settlement
movement of Celts 7th-6th centuries BC (mainly Hallstatt)
Celtic introduction to Britain and Ireland; nature of La Tène culture there uncertain
Early Iron Age sites (Hallstatt)
Late Iron Age sites (La Tène)

Atlantic Ocean
Traprain Law
Arras
Danebury
Bagendon
Glastonbury
Colchester
Hengistbury Head
Eigenbilzen
Court St. Étienne
Somme Bionne
Basse-Yutz
Vix
Rheinheim
Hradenin
Heuneburg
La Tène
Hallstatt
Sopron
Vače
R. Elbe
R. Vistula
R. Rhine
R. Seine
R. Saône
R. Rhône
R. Garonne
R. Ebro
R. Po
R. Tibr
R. Danube
R. Dniester
R. Dnieper
Rome 390 BC
Delphi 279 BC
Galatia 276 BC
Black Sea
Mediterranean Sea

15

Mesopotamia and the Near East, 3500-1600 BC

The rise of the great riverine civilisations in the fertile valleys of the Nile in Egypt, the Euphrates and Tigris in Mesopotamia, and also (page 8) in the Indus valley in north-west India, was a decisive stage in the development of human society. Previously cereal cultivation in the foothills of the Taurus and Zagros mountains permitted agriculture and flourishing villages, even urban settlements on the scale of Catal Hüyük and Jericho to develop (page 6). But the alluvial valleys of Egypt and Mesopotamia offered far greater potential, provided that a social organisation was available to carry out the necessary irrigation operations. This led after 3500 BC to the growth of cities and city-states, distinguished by size, planning, architecture and fortifications (map 1). It also led, because of the need for accounting procedures related to the collection and distribution of agricultural surpluses among a large and increasingly urban population, to the invention of writing, originally pictographic, but developing into cuneiform on clay tablets in Mesopotamia and hieroglyphic in Egypt.

Because of geographical factors political unification came earlier in Egypt than in Mesopotamia. The Egyptian settlements coalesced early into two kingdoms, Upper (south) Egypt and Lower Egypt (the Delta), which were united by King Menes c.3100 BC with the capital at Memphis. In Mesopotamia the basic organisation until the second half of the third millennium BC remained one of Sumerian city states, with a shifting hegemony between them but no centralised control. Ethnic movements also affected the course of development (map 2). In Egypt, though different ethnic groups can be traced in prehistoric times, in the historical period there was no immigration of significance until the Hyksos early in the 2nd millennium BC (page 20). The Sumerians of southern Mesopotamia are thought by some historians to be indigenous, by others to be immigrants via Iran from central Asia; in either case, they were responsible for the earliest development of cities (map 3), as well as for the invention of writing. Another factor affecting developments across the ancient Near East in this period was the need to acquire scarce resources. South Mesopotamia lacked stone, metals and timber, which led the Sumerians to exploit the Zagros mountains and to develop trading relations with Iran and Asia Minor, as well as by sea to Dilmun on the Persian Gulf. Egypt was more self-sufficient, but here also the need for timber stimulated trade with Syria, and Syria served as a link between Egypt and Mesopotamia.

The first significant attempt at empire in Mesopotamia came when Sargon (2371–16 BC), of Akkadian immigrant descent, founded the city of Agade (site uncertain) and made it his task to bring the old Sumerian city states under centralised control (map 4). From this base he and his successors, notably his grandson, Naram-Sin (2291–55 BC), undertook conquests from Elam in south-west Iran to Syria, including the recently excavated city of Ebla, and possibly also into central Asia Minor. Motivated by trade, this expansion extended sea-links which probably reached as far east as the Indus valley.

The subsequent course of events was complicated by the repeated incursions of mainly Semites, Hurrians and the Indo-European Hittites. Each of these peoples played political roles of considerable importance. Sargon's empire collapsed as a result of internal stresses and the invasion of hillmen from the central Zagros, and was followed by a revival of the Sumerian city-state system, in which Ur emerged as the dominant element.

This was a highly bureaucratic empire, more stable than that of Agade; but it collapsed in turn (c.2000 BC) under the pressure of a new wave of Semitic invaders, the Amorites from the Syrian desert, who established control over the whole region from Syria to southern Mesopotamia, where they set up a number of small kingdoms among which Assyria and Babylon eventually won pre-eminence. The former emerged under the Amorite Shamshi-Adad I (1813–1781 BC), who annexed the kingdom of Mari on the middle Euphrates and formed a powerful state extending from the Zagros mountains to the border of the Anatolian plateau. But the pre-eminence of Assyria was short-lived, and after Shamshi-Adad's death its place was taken by Babylon under Hammurabi (1792–50 BC). By the seventeenth century BC a new power centre was developing further north in Anatolia, where the Hittites set up a kingdom with its capital at Hattushash. After 1650 BC they began to spread southwards and in 1595 they sacked Babylon. In the dislocation which ensued the first Babylonian dynasty collapsed; but the ideal of a single south Mesopotamian kingdom with Babylon as its capital, survived as Hammurabi's enduring legacy.

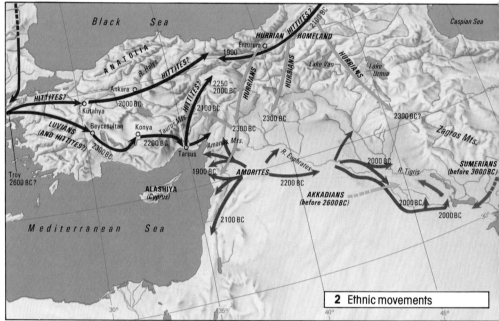

2 Ethnic movements

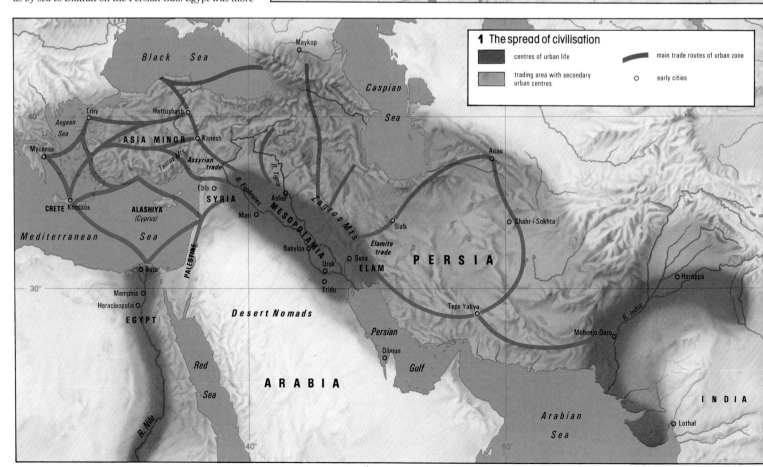

1 The spread of civilisation

- centres of urban life
- main trade routes of urban zone
- trading area with secondary urban centres
- early cities

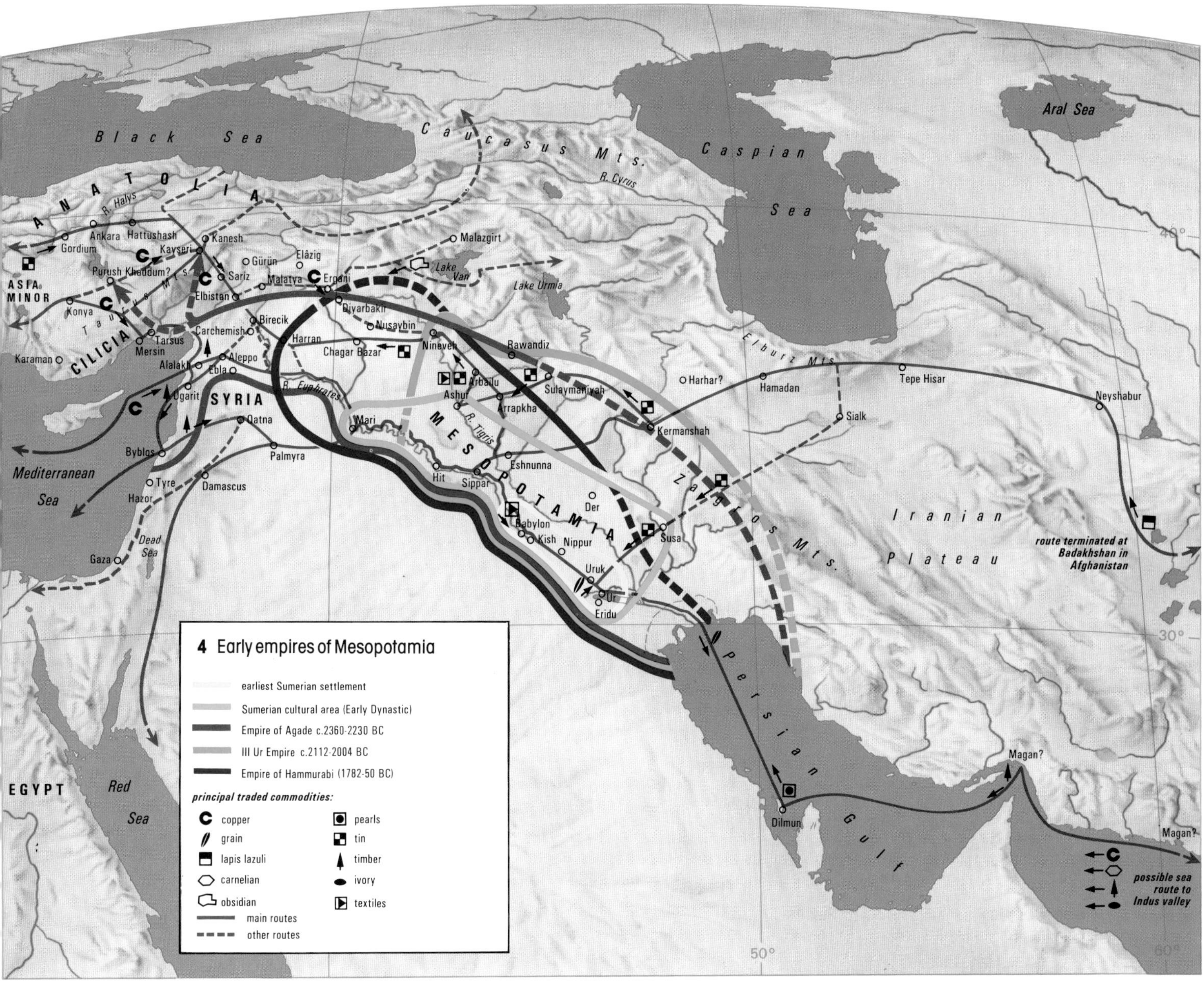
4 Early empires of Mesopotamia
earliest Sumerian settlement
Sumerian cultural area (Early Dynastic)
Empire of Agade c.2360-2230 BC
III Ur Empire c.2112-2004 BC
Empire of Hammurabi (1782-50 BC)
principal traded commodities:
copper
grain
lapis lazuli
carnelian
obsidian
pearls
tin
timber
ivory
textiles
main routes
other routes
Black Sea
Caucasus Mts.
R. Cyrus
Caspian Sea
Aral Sea
ANATOLIA
R. Halys
Ankara
Gordium
Hattushash
Kayseri
Kanesh
Purush Khaddum?
ASIA MINOR
Konya
Taurus Mts
CILICIA
Tarsus
Mersin
Karaman
Gürün
Elâzig
Sariz
Malatya
Ergani
Elbistan
Malazgirt
Lake Van
Lake Urmia
Diyarbakir
Nusaybin
Birecik
Carchemish
Harran
Chagar Bazar
Nineveh
Rawandiz
Arbailu
Ashur
Arrapkha
Sulaymaniyah
Alalakh
Aleppo
Ebla
Ugarit
SYRIA
R. Euphrates
Qatna
Byblos
Palmyra
Mediterranean Sea
Tyre
Hazor
Damascus
Dead Sea
Gaza
MESOPOTAMIA
Mari
R. Tigris
Eshnunna
Hit
Sippar
Der
Babylon
Kish
Nippur
Susa
Uruk
Ur
Eridu
Harhar?
Hamadan
Kermanshah
Sialk
Tepe Hisar
Neyshabur
Elburz Mts
Zagros Mts.
Iranian Plateau
route terminated at Badakhshan in Afghanistan
Persian Gulf
Dilmun
Magan?
possible sea route to Indus valley
EGYPT
Red Sea
40°
30°
50°
60°

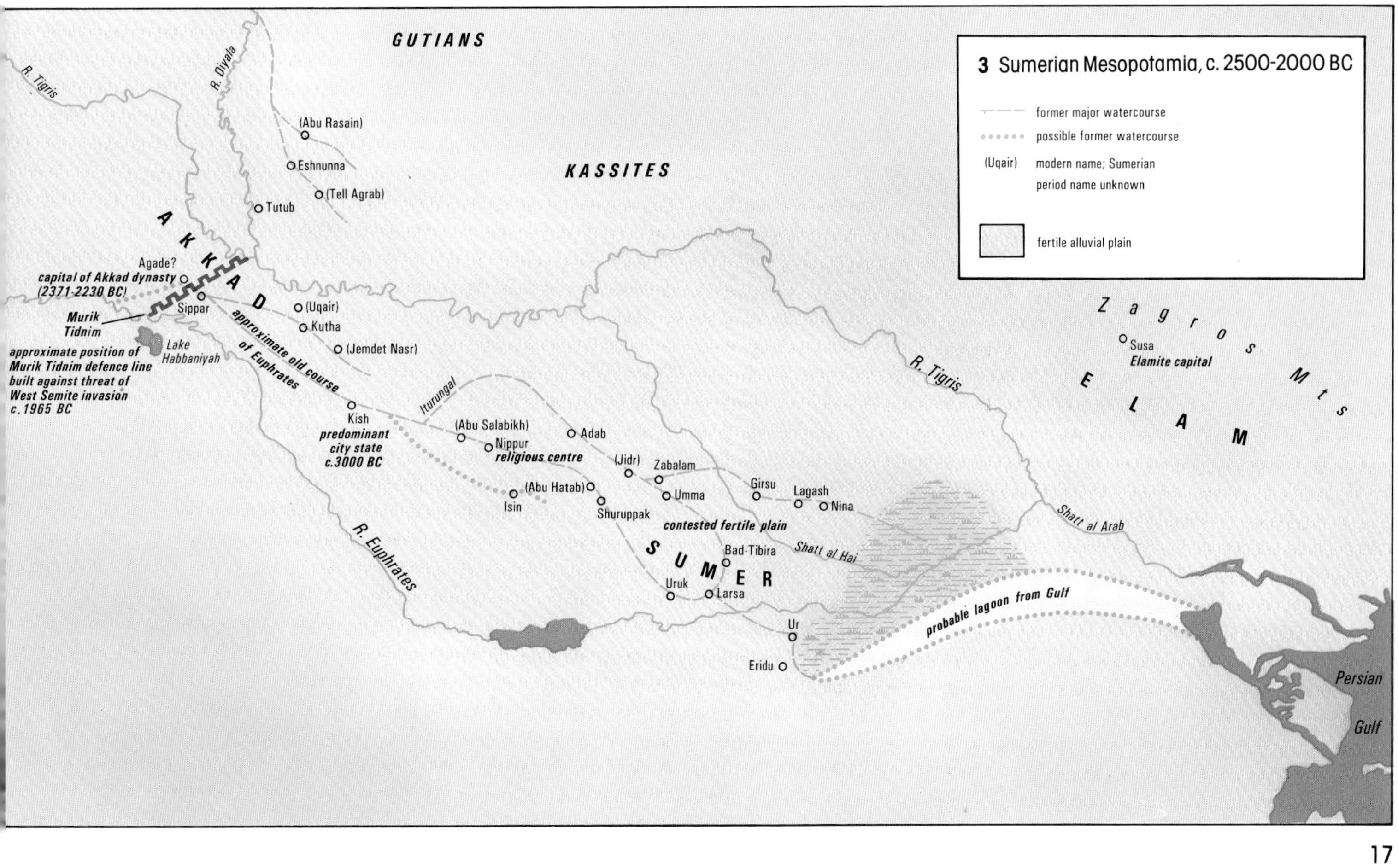
3 Sumerian Mesopotamia, c. 2500-2000 BC
former major watercourse
possible former watercourse
(Uqair) modern name; Sumerian period name unknown
fertile alluvial plain
GUTIANS
KASSITES
R. Tigris
R. Diyala
(Abu Rasain)
Eshnunna
(Tell Agrab)
Tutub
AKKAD
Agade?
capital of Akkad dynasty (2371-2230 BC)
Sippar
Murik Tidnim
approximate position of Murik Tidnim defence line built against threat of West Semite invasion c.1965 BC
Lake Habbaniyah
approximate old course of Euphrates
(Uqair)
Kutha
(Jemdet Nasr)
Kish
predominant city state c.3000 BC
Iturungal
(Abu Salabikh)
Nippur
religious centre
Adab
(Jidr)
Zabalam
(Abu Hatab)
Isin
Shuruppak
Umma
Girsu
Lagash
Nina
contested fertile plain
Shatt al Hai
Shatt al Arab
Bad-Tibira
SUMER
Uruk
Larsa
Ur
Eridu
probable lagoon from Gulf
R. Euphrates
Zagros Mts
Susa
Elamite capital
ELAM
Persian Gulf

The early Mediterranean world

The first European civilisation was that of Minoan Crete. The Cretans had bronze tools and weapons, systems of writing, and they were ruled by kings for whom they built spacious palaces at centres like Knossos. The earliest inhabitants of mainland Greece and the Aegean islands were probably related to the Cretans in speech and race, but shortly before 2000 BC the northern islands and parts of the mainland were overrun by peoples from Anatolia. A few centuries later groups from the north infiltrated the mainland and reached the Peloponnese.

Crete was unaffected by these movements and became exceedingly prosperous. Her rulers established colonies throughout the Aegean islands, of which the most important appears to have been Akrotiri on Thera. This period of expansion reached a climax about 1500 BC. Meanwhile powerful states arose on the mainland at Mycenae and elsewhere, some of which may have been tributary to Crete as later Greek legends hint. About 1450 BC invaders from the Greek mainland overran Crete, burning many of the towns and palaces, but preserving Knossos as their capital. In the fourteenth century a mixed civilisation, the Mycenaean, related to the Minoan, spread throughout the Aegean. Around 1300 BC the palace of Knossos was finally destroyed, and the whole Aegean probably became an empire ruled from Mycenae (map 1).

Shortly before 1200 BC Mycenae and other mainland centres were destroyed by invaders who may have been Greeks (map 2). Refugees escaping from them settled in islands like Naxos and Crete; some made their way to Italy, others to Cyprus and to Tarsus in Cilicia. Mean-while Armenians and Phrygians from the Balkans overthrew the Hittite empire in Anatolia. Groups expelled by them moved southwards and devastated Syria; some from coastal regions of Anatolia — the Sea Peoples of Egyptian records — occupied Enkomi in Cyprus and sailing against Egypt allied themselves with the Libyans to be defeated by the pharaoh Merneptah in 1232 BC. About fifty years later Ramesses III defeated another coalition of Sea Peoples; but some including the Philistines afterwards settled in Palestine.

About 1100 BC the last wave of Greeks, the Dorians, overran most of western Greece and the Peloponnese as the eventual distribution of Greek dialects shows. The Arcadians, however, maintained themselves in the centre of the Peloponnese, and Greeks speaking a dialect related to Arcadian reached Cyprus around 1050 BC. About a century later other non-Dorian Greeks, the Ionians, established settlements in the eastern Aegean and on the Anatolian coast (map 3).

Writing and many of the arts disappeared from the Aegean during this period of dislocation. But this was an age of technical advance, with iron replacing bronze for tools and weapons. The new Greek world was divided between hundreds of small independent communities or city-states linked by similar religions and dialects. Writing was eventually reintroduced using the Phoenician alphabet. In the eighth century BC a period of colonial expansion began. This epoch-making movement, caused by land-hunger, political oppression and the attraction of trade, changed the whole face of the Mediterranean and spread Greek civilisation as far as the Black Sea in the east and to Sicily and Spain in the west, where it was to come into conflict with outposts of the Phoenician city state of Carthage (map 4).

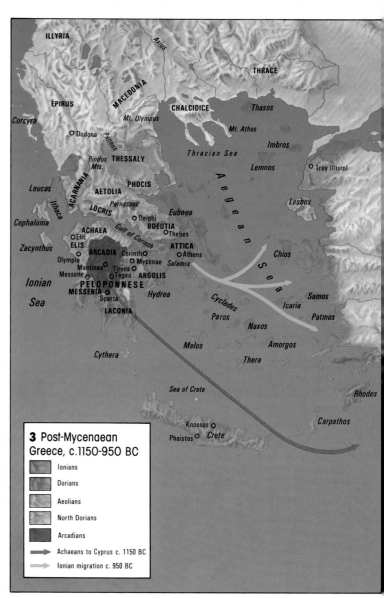

3 Post-Mycenaean Greece, c.1150-950 BC
- Ionians
- Dorians
- Aeolians
- North Dorians
- Arcadians
- → Achaeans to Cyprus c. 1150 BC
- → Ionian migration c. 950 BC

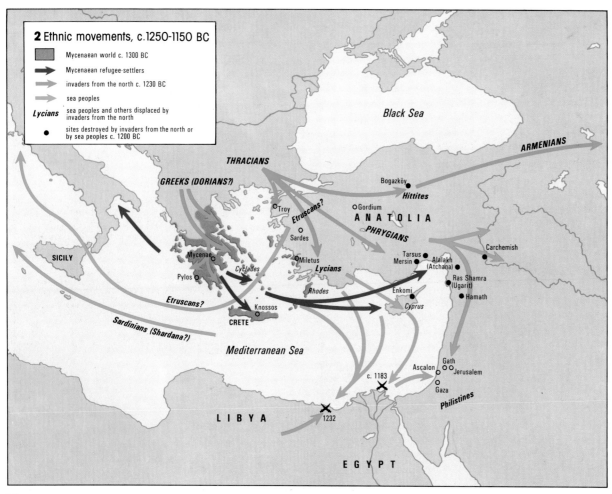

2 Ethnic movements, c.1250-1150 BC
- Mycenaean world c. 1300 BC
- → Mycenaean refugee-settlers
- → invaders from the north c. 1230 BC
- → sea peoples
- *Lycians* sea peoples and others displaced by invaders from the north
- ● sites destroyed by invaders from the north or by sea peoples c. 1200 BC

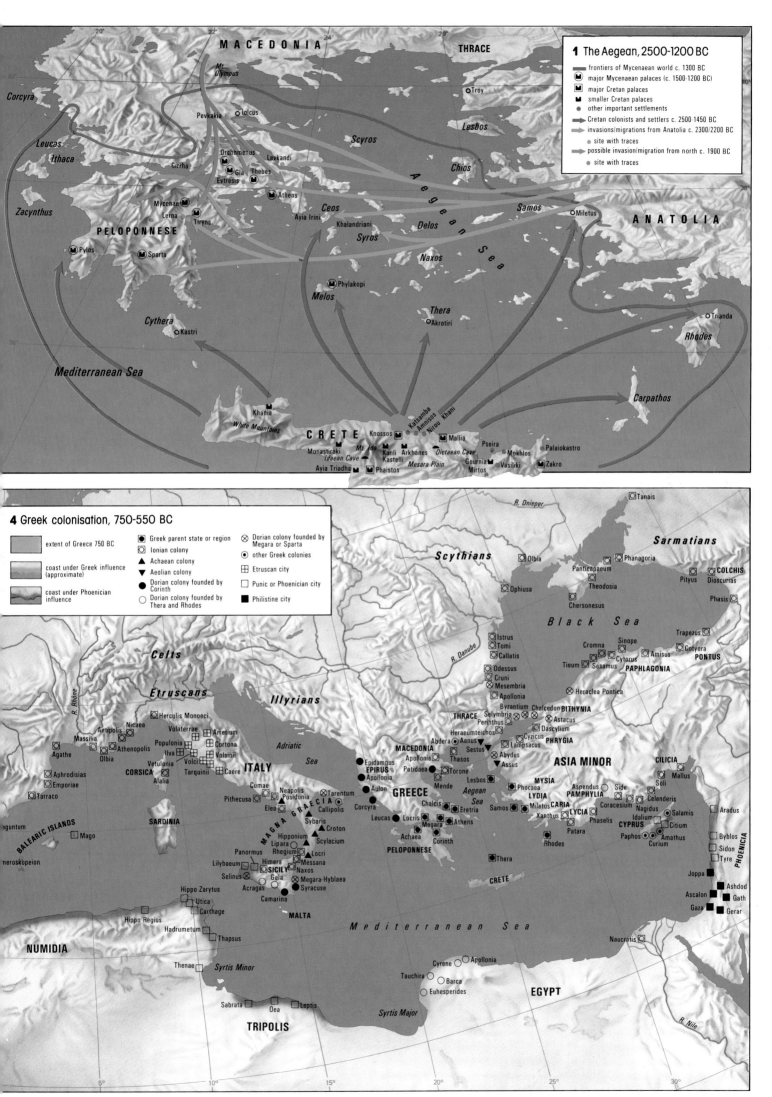

Egypt and the Near East, c.1600-330 BC

Because of their fabulous wealth the lands of the Fertile Crescent were always subject to assault from barbarian charioteers from adjoining steppes and mountains, jealous of their civilisation and greedy for their riches. Egypt alone was sheltered by the desert; but even Egypt fell prey about 1730 BC to an Asiatic people known as the Hyksos, who conquered the Delta and the Nile valley as far as Cusae, and ruled there until 1567 BC. By then Egypt's greatest age, marked by the pyramids of Cheops and Giza (c.2590 BC) and the artistic renaissance of the XIIth dynasty (1991–1786 BC), was over (map 1). But the Hyksos occupation stimulated a great revival and, under the XVIIIth dynasty (1570–1320 BC), a policy of expansion was initiated to preclude any further occupation. Egypt advanced through Palestine into Syria (map 2), and created an empire which extended almost to the Euphrates for the next thousand years.

Elsewhere the course of events was more involved as from 1600 to 500 BC one empire after another succumbed to the assaults of barbarian tribes armed, after 1100 BC, with iron weapons. The Hittite empire (map 2), predominant in Anatolia and Syria c.1350 BC, fell about 1250 to violent ethnic movements from the Aegean. The Mitanni and Hurri, after expanding towards the Mediterranean, were squeezed between the Hittites and Assyria, which threw off Mitannian overlordship c.1380 BC; into this gap infiltrated Semitic and other tribes, Philistines, Aramaeans, Hebrews, Phrygians, Chaldeans and Medes, who attempted to seize power in the older centres of civilisation. This power vacuum enabled the Israelites under David (c.1006–966 BC) to create a kingdom briefly controlling Palestine and Syria (map 4); but after Solomon (966–926 BC) the kingdom, inherently unstable because of its disparate tribal origins, quickly disintegrated. But change and fluidity, chaotic though their consequences were, had the effect of breaking down old geographical and cultural barriers and beginning the process of fusing the whole region into a single cosmopolitan society, over which, after 539 BC, Persia established hegemony.

The immediate beneficiary was As-

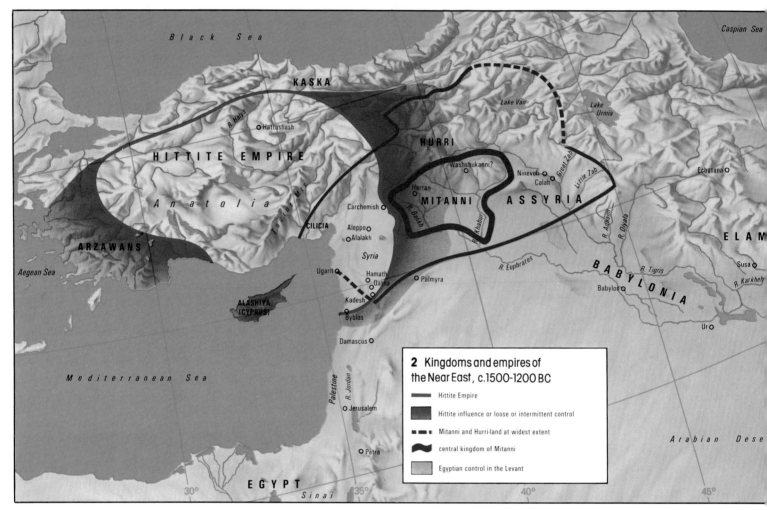

2 Kingdoms and empires of the Near East, c.1500-1200 BC

- Hittite Empire
- Hittite influence or loose or intermittent control
- Mitanni and Hurri-land at widest extent
- central kingdom of Mitanni
- Egyptian control in the Levant

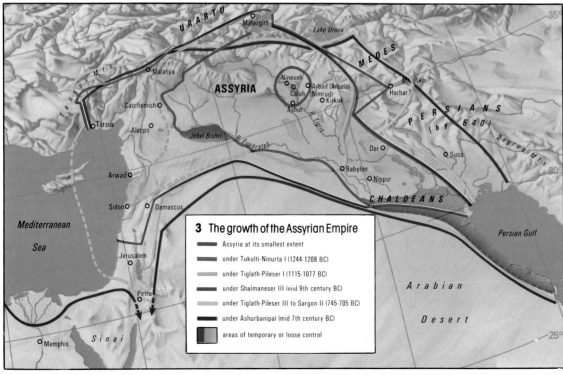

3 The growth of the Assyrian Empire

- Assyria at its smallest extent
- under Tukulti-Ninurta I (1244-1208 BC)
- under Tiglath-Pileser I (1115-1077 BC)
- under Shalmaneser III (mid 9th century BC)
- under Tiglath-Pileser III to Sargon II (745-705 BC)
- under Ashurbanipal (mid 7th century BC)
- areas of temporary or loose control

syria, the political successor of the Mitanni (map 3). But under Ashurbanipal (668–627 BC), the assault of Medes and Scythians, combined with domestic revolt in Babylonia, brought Assyrian power to ruin. The capital Nineveh was destroyed in 612 BC, and Assyria disappeared for ever in 605 BC. After an interlude in which Medes, Chaldeans and Egyptians divided the legacy, another semi-barbarian conqueror, Cyrus the Persian, rebelled against his Median overlord, captured the Median capital Ecbatana in 550 BC, and quickly overran most of the Middle East. When his son Cambyses (529–522

BC) conquered Egypt (525 BC), the Persian empire extended from the Nile to the Oxus (map 5). The ancient world was united under one administration, the barbarians were overawed. But now a new enemy arose in the west, where Persian attempts to subdue the Greek colonies in Asia Minor (page 18) brought conflict with European Greece. As early as 479 BC Persian attempts to subdue Athens were defeated. A century and a half later Alexander of Macedon destroyed the Persian empire (page 22), and the predominant role of Western Asia in history came to an end.

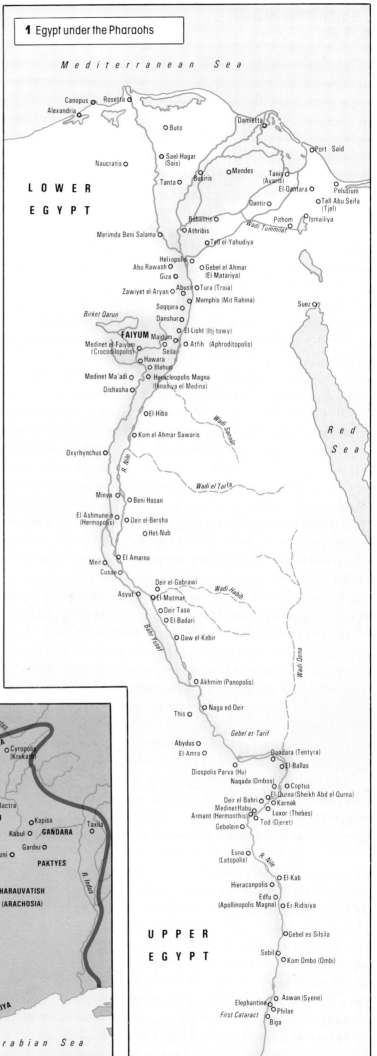

1 Egypt under the Pharaohs

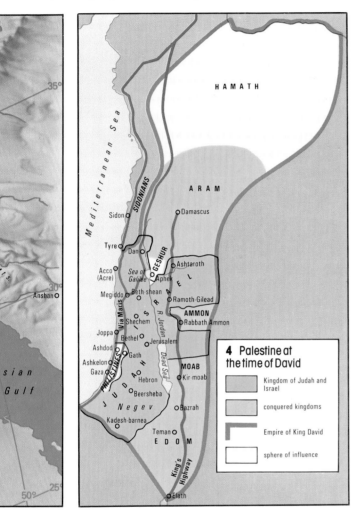

4 Palestine at the time of David

- Kingdom of Judah and Israel
- conquered kingdoms
- Empire of King David
- sphere of influence

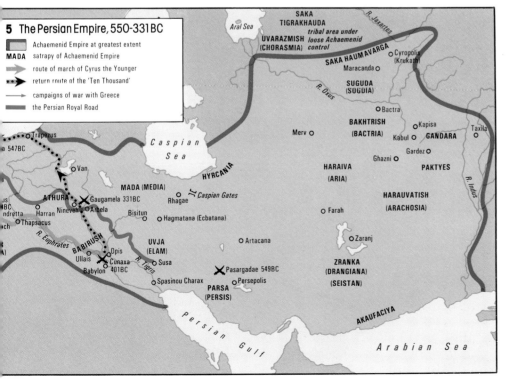

5 The Persian Empire, 550–331 BC

- Achaemenid Empire at greatest extent
- **MADA** satrapy of Achaemenid Empire
- route of march of Cyrus the Younger
- return route of the 'Ten Thousand'
- campaigns of war with Greece
- the Persian Royal Road

The Greek world
497-185 BC

The fifth century BC was the great age of Greece – the age of Pericles and Socrates, of Sophocles and Euripides, of the Parthenon and the sculptures of Phidias. It was also the century when internal strains (the growing conflict between oligarchy and democracy) and internecine war undermined the stability of the Greek city states and their ability to withstand external pressures. Colonisation had already carried Greek civilisation and Greek city life to Asia Minor (page 18). But here it came up against the Persian empire under Darius and Xerxes (page 20). Persian attempts to subdue Athens, which had been supporting the rebellious Ionians, were almost miraculously defeated at Marathon (490) and Salamis (480), (map 1). But thereafter the cities which had united against Persia fell apart, and the Peloponnesian war between Athens and Sparta and their allies (map 2) permanently weakened Greek resistance, and ensured the victory of Philip of Macedon (338). Under Philip's son, Alexander the Great, Macedonia became a world power, its dominion stretching from the Adriatic to India (map 3). Alexander's death in 323 BC at the age of 32 prevented the consolidation of his empire. In the succeeding struggles between his generals three major powers arose: Macedonia, shorn of its Asiatic conquests but still dominant in northern Greece; Egypt under the Ptolemies, with its capital at Alexander's newly founded city of Alexandria; and the Seleucid kingdom comprising the bulk of the Persian empire (map 4). To these were added in the east the Bactrian kingdom, extending over Afghanistan into northern India, and the Parthian empire, founded in 247 BC when a dissident provincial governor broke away from the Bactrian Greeks. This Parthian state eventually stretched from the Euphrates to the Indus and successfully withstood Roman expansion until it was displaced in AD 224 by a resurgent Persia under the Sasanian dynasty.

Although politically the empire of Alexander the Great proved ephemeral, in other respects its consequences were epoch-making. Alexander himself founded some 70 cities, not merely as military strongholds but as cultural centres – a policy continued by his Seleucid successors – and thus carried Greek civilisation far to the east. Greek culture was now no longer the preserve of separate city-states but infused and Hellenised the whole civilised world (*oikoumene*) as far as India and China. Greek itself became the *lingua franca* of the whole region, though more subtly the Greek world itself was permeated by oriental influences as its contacts with the ancient civilisations of the Near East intensified. When Rome asserted control over the Hellenistic world after its defeat of Macedon at Cynoscephalae in 197 and of the Seleucids at Magnesia in 190 BC, this was its inheritance; and the longer the Roman empire existed, the greater was the part played by the Hellenic and oriental elements in its civilisation.

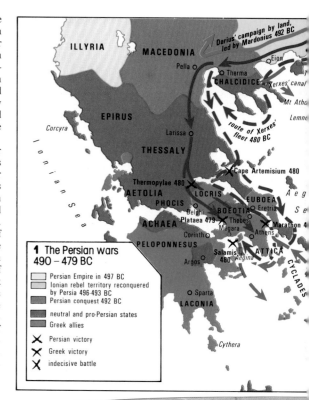

1 The Persian wars 490 – 479 BC

- Persian Empire in 497 BC
- Ionian rebel territory reconquered by Persia 496-493 BC
- Persian conquest 492 BC
- neutral and pro-Persian states
- Greek allies
- ✕ Persian victory
- ✕ Greek victory
- ✕ indecisive battle

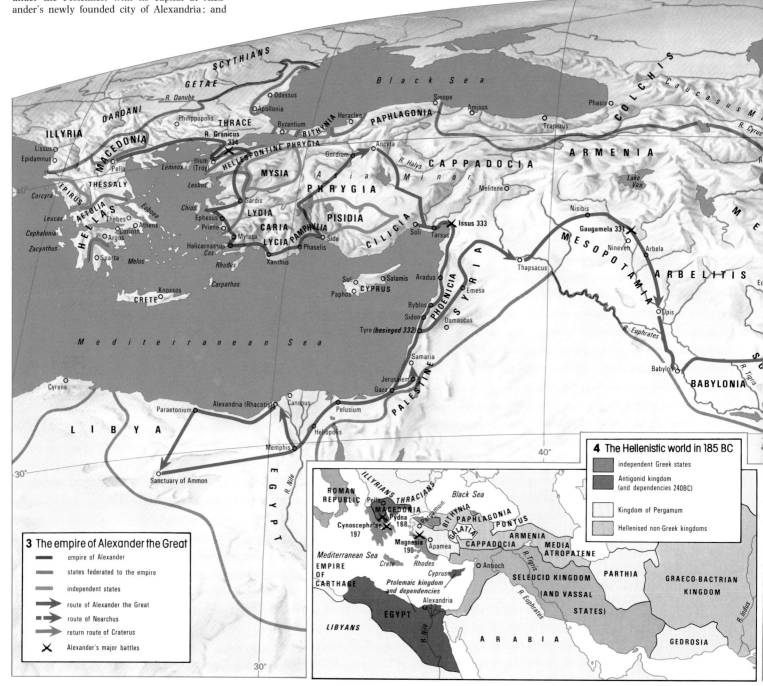

3 The empire of Alexander the Great

- empire of Alexander
- states federated to the empire
- independent states
- → route of Alexander the Great
- --→ route of Nearchus
- → return route of Craterus
- ✕ Alexander's major battles

4 The Hellenistic world in 185 BC

- independent Greek states
- Antigonid kingdom (and dependencies 240BC)
- Kingdom of Pergamum
- Hellenised non-Greek kingdoms

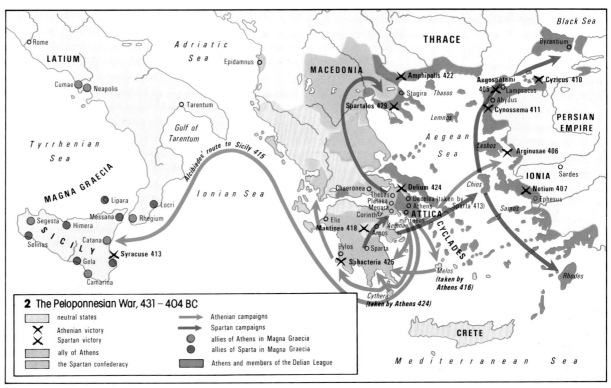

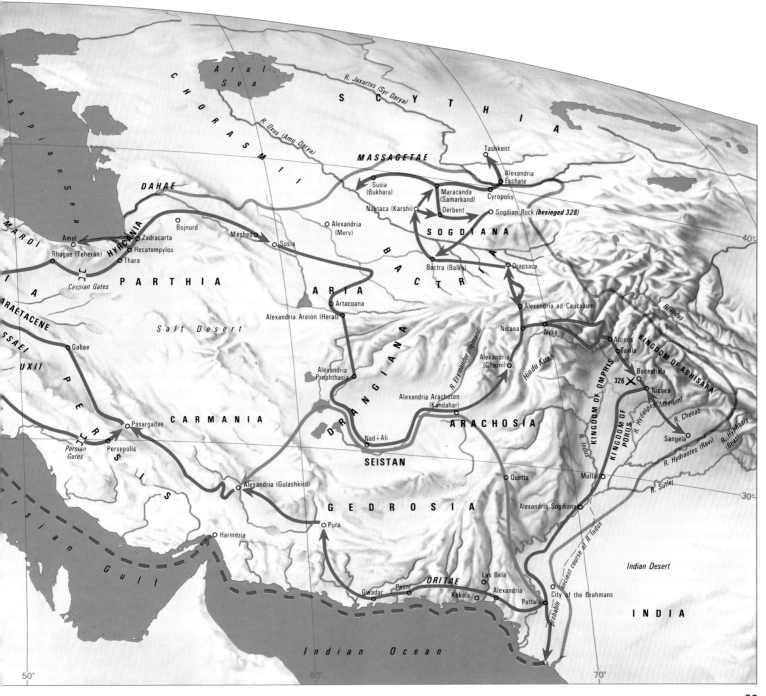

Trading links of the ancient world

Trade is as old as the beginning of settled urban life. Though ordinary needs were met by local agriculture and local manufacture, even the earliest cities had requirements that could not be satisfied locally. Jericho imported stone for tools from Anatolia (page 6); the Sumerians, who lacked timber, stone and minerals, developed trading links with Asia Minor and by sea with Dilmun on the Persian Gulf. But the formation of an intensive trading network spanning the whole Eurasian world only became possible after the rise of empires which could provide peace and security, build roads and maintain harbours. The Achaemenids made a beginning in sixth-century Persia, where Darius's Royal Road ran 1420 well-garrisoned miles (2300 km) from Sardis to Susa (page 20). But the decisive step forward was the rise, after 202 BC, of the Roman empire in the west and the Han empire in China. By the close of the first century BC Rome's conquests from the Atlantic to Syria formed a single vast trading area, gathered round a Mediterranean axis (map 2), and the expansion of Han China under Wu-ti (140–87 BC) created an economic bloc of similar

dimensions in the east (page 28). Both possessed an elaborate network of roads and a highly organised system of transport and marketing, which encouraged regional specialisation and an unprecedented interchange of goods and manufactures. In the west the requirements of the legions in the frontier provinces of Gaul and the Balkans were a further stimulus. Spain became a large-scale producer and exporter of wine and olive oil; but the most important export of all was grain from Egypt, North Africa and the Pontine provinces, upon which Rome itself and many cities of Greece and Asia Minor were dependent.

Nor did trade halt at the frontier. China sent a mission to Ferghana, Bukhara and Bactria in 128 BC, and shortly afterwards the famous Silk Route came into operation (map 1). It started at Tunhwang on China's far western boundary, and skirted north or south of the Takla Makan Desert to Kashgar, before crossing the Pamirs and debouching into Bactria, Persia and the Mediterranean coastal belt. But the Silk Route, spectacular though it was, was less important in economic terms than the sea route to India and the Far East, traffic along which increased greatly after the discovery of the monsoon around 100 BC. Previously there had been coastal traffic, mainly in Arab or Indian hands. Now up to 120 Greek vessels a year, some with a carry-

ing capacity of up to 500 tons, plied direct to the Indian ports of Barbaricum, Barygaza and Muziris, where they picked up eastern cargoes shipped by Indian merchants from Go Oc Eo in southern Cambodia, and carried them to Berenice and other Red Sea ports for transport on to Alexandria and thence to all parts of the Roman empire.

These far-flung trading links are impressive, but their economic importance should not be exaggerated. Both the Roman and the Han empires were self-sufficient in all essential commodities, and foreign trade was essentially a luxury trade, marginal to everyday needs. On the other hand, there is no doubt that foreign trade contributed directly to cultural interchange and to the spread of the great world religions (page 26). However, it also had other less happy consequences, particularly the spread of disease and pestilence (map 3). Earlier epidemics, like that which smote Athens in 430–29 BC, may have been transmitted by armies; but their incidence after about 100 BC leaves little doubt that, both in east and west, they were carried by caravans or merchant shipping from India or tropical Africa. Their precise character is not easily determined, though they seem to fall into two main groups, smallpox or measles, and bubonic plague; but there is no doubt about their devastating effects on vulnerable populations. 'One or two out of a hundred survived,' wrote the Chinese historian Ssu-ma Kuang of the epidemic of AD 317, and some later historians have attributed the failure both of China and of Rome to withstand the barbarian onslaughts of the fourth and fifth centuries to the sharp fall in manpower caused by imported pestilences.

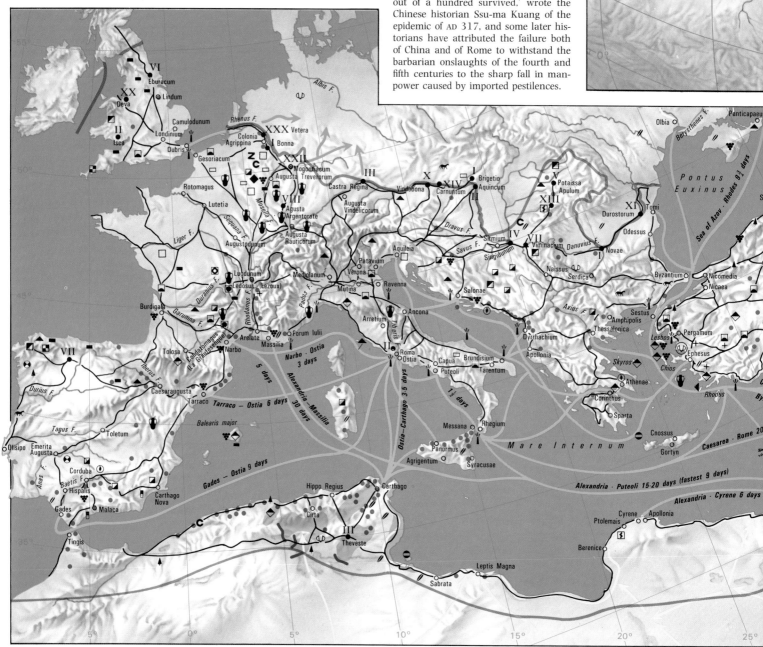

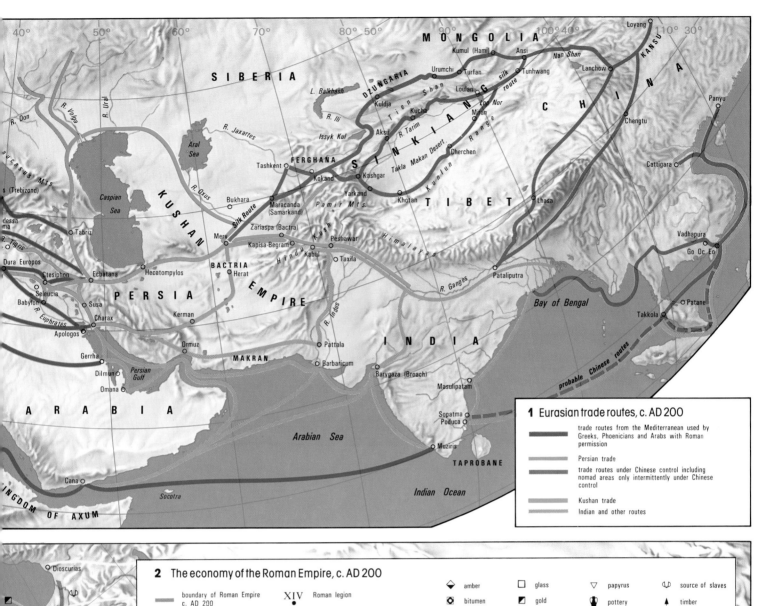

1 Eurasian trade routes, c. AD 200

- trade routes from the Mediterranean used by Greeks, Phoenicians and Arabs with Roman permission
- Persian trade
- trade routes under Chinese control including nomad areas only intermittently under Chinese control
- Kushan trade
- Indian and other routes

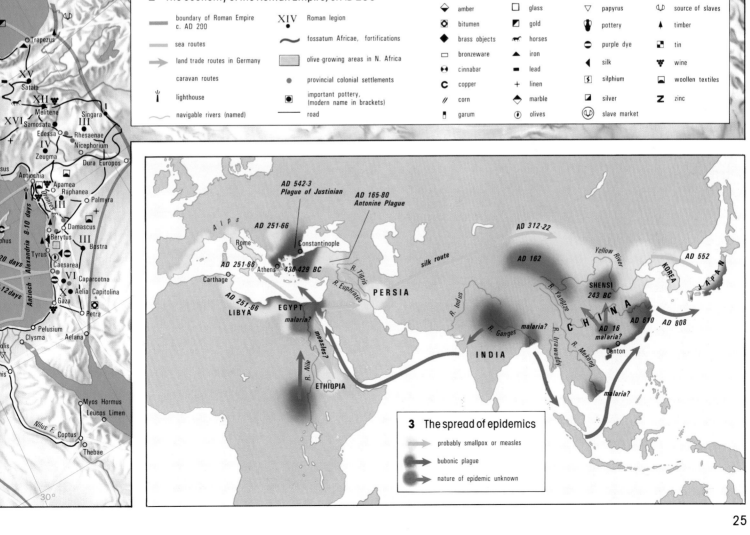

2 The economy of the Roman Empire, c. AD 200

- boundary of Roman Empire c. AD 200
- sea routes
- land trade routes in Germany
- caravan routes
- lighthouse
- navigable rivers (named)
- XIV Roman legion
- fossatum Africae, fortifications
- olive-growing areas in N. Africa
- provincial colonial settlements
- important pottery, (modern name in brackets)
- road

- amber
- bitumen
- brass objects
- bronzeware
- cinnabar
- copper
- corn
- garum
- glass
- gold
- horses
- iron
- lead
- linen
- marble
- olives
- slave market
- papyrus
- pottery
- purple dye
- silk
- silphium
- silver
- source of slaves
- timber
- tin
- wine
- woollen textiles
- zinc

3 The spread of epidemics

AD 542-3 Plague of Justinian
AD 165-80 Antonine Plague
AD 312-22
AD 162
AD 251-66
430-429 BC
AD 552
SHENSI 243 BC
AD 16 malaria?
AD 610
AD 808
malaria?
malaria?
malaria?
measles?

- probably smallpox or measles
- bubonic plague
- nature of epidemic unknown

The world religions
c.500 BC-AD 500

The period 550–500 BC saw the birth of great world religions in all the main centres of civilisation. Their appearance perhaps reflected a need in the rising empires of the old world for more universal creeds than the local tribal deities could provide, and their diffusion – particularly the spread of the great missionary religions, Buddhism and Christianity – was an important factor in linking together the different areas of civilisation (map 1). Their other major contribution – seen, for example, in the work of Anglo-Saxon missionaries in Germany or of Russian missionaries among the heathen tribes of the Urals (page 38) – was to carry civilisation to peoples outside the frontiers of the civilised world.

All the great religions shared, to one degree or another, a belief in a single spiritual reality. Not all were inspired by a missionary spirit. Hinduism, the oldest, was essentially the religion of the people of India, and Judaism, the religion of 'the chosen people of the Lord', was also exclusive. But Buddhism, originally a reformist movement within Hinduism, became perhaps the greatest of all missionary religions when it assumed its universalist, or Mahayana, form some 500 years after the death of its founder, Gautama (c.563–483 BC). Judaism also spread as a result of the persecution of the Jews by more formidable neighbours, beginning with the Babylonian exile (586 BC). After the Roman destruction of the temple in Jerusalem in AD 70 (map 3) the Jewish diaspora carried Judaism far and wide from its home in Palestine, until in time it became a worldwide religion. It also gave birth, directly or indirectly, to two of the world's great missionary religions, Christianity and Islam.

In the Far East the same period saw the rise of the ethical system of Kung Fu-tzu or Confucius (551–479 BC) and the mystical religion of the Tao, or 'the Way', associated with the shadowy figure of Lao-tzu. Later Buddhism spread eastward along the Silk Route through central Asia and with Taoism and Confucianism became one of the 'three religions' of traditional China. Buddhism also reached Japan in the sixth century AD, where it effectively displaced spirit-worship and

traditional Shinto until the revival of the latter in the nineteenth century.

The other great religion of the period was Zoroastrianism, which originated in Persia and is associated with another shadowy figure, Zarathustra. Zoroastrianism, which sees life as a battleground between the forces of good and the forces of evil, spread rapidly through the Roman world in the form of Mithraism, with shrines as far afield as northern Britain. It was one of the many oriental cults which permeated the Roman empire when, after the beginning of the Christian era, belief in the Greek pantheon and the household deities broke down. Until the end of the third century AD it was undecided which of the oriental mystery cults would prevail; but with the conversion of the emperor Constantine to Christianity and its recognition by the Edict of Milan (AD 313), still more after it became the official religion of the Roman empire under Theodosius (374–95), the die was cast. Heathen temples were uprooted; rival cults were condemned.

Christianity had begun as a Jewish splinter-movement; its founder, Jesus of Nazareth, saw himself as the Messiah, or Saviour, sent to liberate the Jews from the Roman yoke. But when, after Jesus's condemnation and crucifixion (AD 29), Jewish orthodoxy rejected his message, his disciples, notably Paul of Tarsus, turned instead to the conversion of the 'gentiles', or people outside the law. Paul's journeys (map 2) were a turning point. Thereafter Christianity spread rapidly, both in the Roman empire and also further east. Here the great Christian centres were Antioch and Edessa, the home of the Nestorian church which carried Christ's teaching to Persia and from there to China and India (page 38). This was the situation until the rise of Islam (page 40) changed the scene.

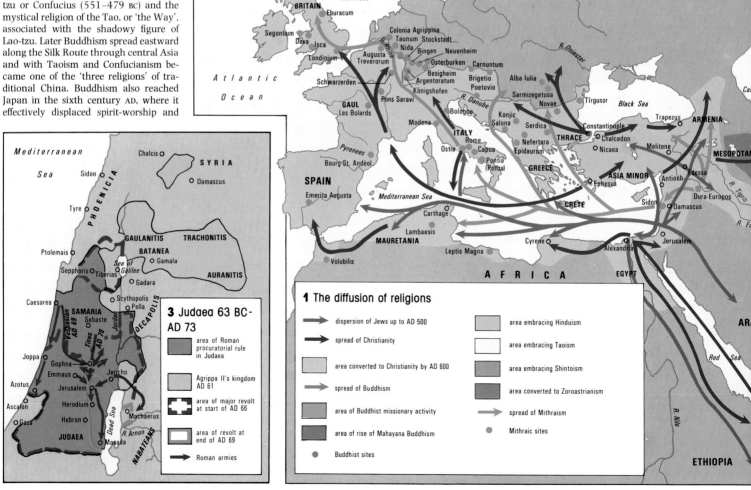

1 The diffusion of religions

→ dispersion of Jews up to AD 500

→ spread of Christianity

→ area converted to Christianity by AD 600

→ spread of Buddhism

area of Buddhist missionary activity

area of rise of Mahayana Buddhism

● Buddhist sites

area embracing Hinduism

area embracing Taoism

area embracing Shintoism

area converted to Zoroastrianism

→ spread of Mithraism

● Mithraic sites

3 Judaea 63 BC–AD 73

area of Roman procuratorial rule in Judaea

Agrippa II's kingdom AD 61

area of major revolt at start of AD 66

area of revolt at end of AD 69

→ Roman armies

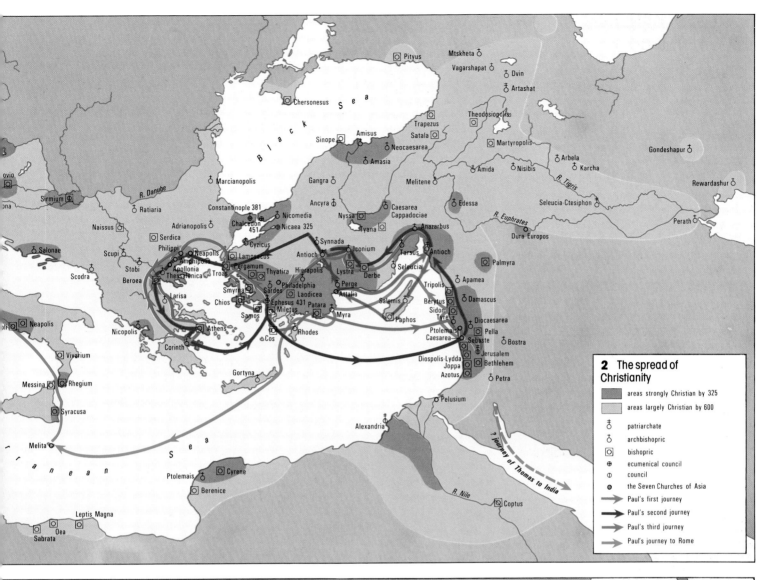

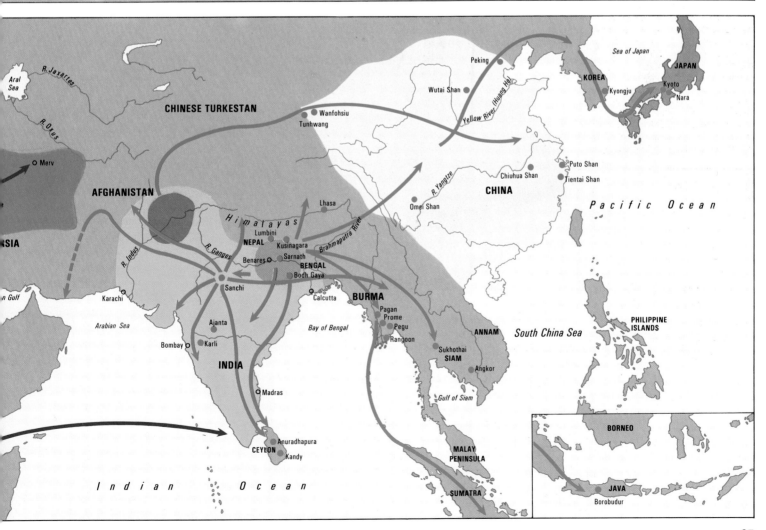

India and China: the first empires

The fifth and sixth centuries BC were a period of consolidation in India and China. In India by the end of the fifth century the 16 political units in existence in 600 BC had been reduced to four. In China, by 400 BC, instead of the multiple feudal principalities of the Chou period (page 8) seven major states were contending for supremacy. In both countries iron tools increased both agricultural productivity and the resources of the rising states. In China the area of civilisation had expanded from the Yellow river to the Yangtze valley and beyond. In India the deforestation of the north shifted the centre of power from the Indus, the seat of the earliest civilisations (page 8), to the fertile plain of the Ganges. Here the kingdom of Magadha emerged as the nucleus of the first Indian empire.

Politically, nevertheless, it was a period of continuous strife, and the resulting social tensions were a major factor in the emergence of the great religious and ethical systems, Buddhism, Taoism, Confucianism and Jainism (page 26), which, in various ways, expressed a yearning for a more stable world order. In India the turning point came in 320 BC when Chandragupta Maurya seized the Magadhan throne, annexed the lands east of the Indus, occupied large parts of central India north of the Narmada river, and in 303 BC annexed the Seleucid province of Trans-Indus. Chandragupta's grandson, Asoka (273–236), conquered Kalinga on the Bay of Bengal, and the greater part of the subcontinent was brought under one rule. His edicts, inscribed on pillars and rocks, evidence Asoka's conversion to Buddhism (map 4).

In China the turning point came with the rise of the state of Ch'in (328–308), which finally dominated China in 221 BC (map 1). But the ruthless centralising policy of the first Ch'in emperor, Shih Huang-ti (221–206), provoked a reaction, and after his death his empire collapsed. It was revived, after a period of civil war, by the Han dynasty, which compromised between centralising policies and the feudal principalities. In India, also, the death of Asoka introduced a long period of decentralisation, punctuated by invasion from the north, which was not overcome until AD 320 when the Guptas, based again on Magadha, imposed a new imperial rule (map 5). This classical age of Indian civilisation survived beyond the collapse of the Gupta empire caused by the barbarian invasions of the fifth century (page 32).

The barbarian invasions were also a turning point in China. The Ch'in and the Han built and extended the Great Wall against the nomad Hsiungnu in the north. Under the emperor Wu-ti (140–87) the Han extended their power to central Asia (map 2). With its efficient administration, a large export trade, and an extensive network of roads and canals, Han China, with its capital at Changan was extremely prosperous (map 3). But control over south China was tenuous, while in the north feudal magnates still exercised great power, which grew with the threat of war. Crisis came in AD 9, and although Han rule was restored, disintegration set in after c.AD 160. When in 304 the Hsiungnu broke through the Great Wall, China remained divided until 589.

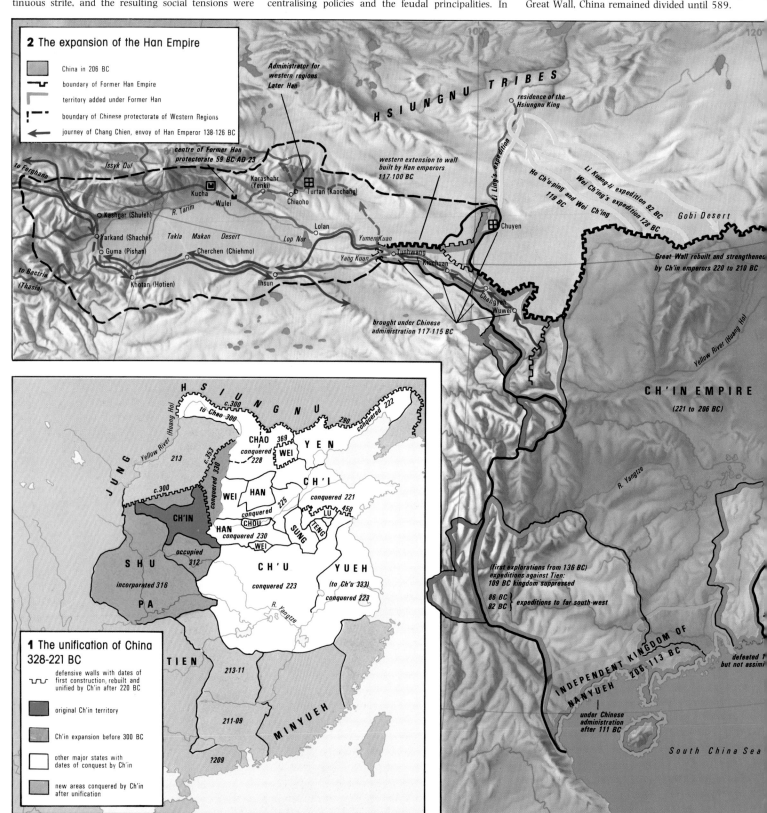

2 The expansion of the Han Empire

- China in 206 BC
- boundary of Former Han Empire
- territory added under Former Han
- boundary of Chinese protectorate of Western Regions
- journey of Chang Chien, envoy of Han Emperor 138-126 BC

1 The unification of China 328-221 BC

- defensive walls with dates of first construction, rebuilt and unified by Ch'in after 220 BC
- original Ch'in territory
- Ch'in expansion before 300 BC
- other major states with dates of conquest by Ch'in
- new areas conquered by Ch'in after unification

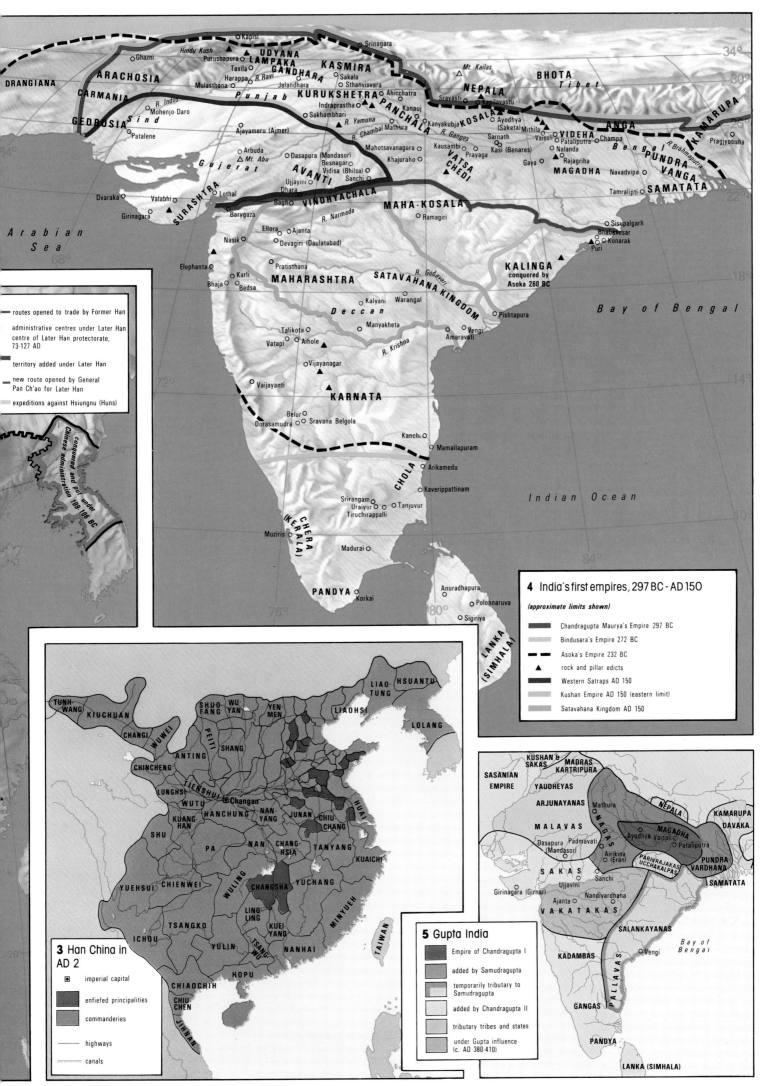

Kapisi
Srinagara
Hindu Kush
Ghazni
Purushapura
UDYANA
LAMPAKA
Mt. Kailas
BHOTA
KAMARUPA
ARACHOSIA
GANDHARA
KASMIRA
Tibet
DRANGIANA
Taxila
Sakala
Sthanvisvara
NEPALA
CARMANIA
Harappa
R. Ravi
Jalandhara
Sravasti
Kapilavastu
Mulasthana
Ahicchatra
Pragjyotisha
GEDROSIA
Sind
R. Indus
Punjab
KURUKSHETRA
Kanauj
PANCHALA
KOSALA
Ayodhya
Mithila
VIDEHA
ANGA
Mohenjo-Daro
Indraprastha
Kanyakubja
(Saketa)
Vaisali
Brahmaputra
Patalene
Sakhambhari
R. Yamuna
Kausambi
Sarnath
Pataliputra
Champa
Bengal
Ajayameru (Ajmer)
Chambal
Mathura
Prayaga
Kasi (Benares)
Nalanda
PUNDRA
Arbuda
Mahotsavanagara
VATSA
MAGADHA
Navadvipa
VANGA
Mt. Abu
Dasapura (Mandasor)
Besnagar
Khajuraho
CHEDI
Gaya
Rajagriha
Gujerat
Vidisa (Bhilsa)
Ujjayini
Sanchi
Tamralipti
SAMATATA
Dvaraka
Dhara
AVANTI
Valabhi
Lothal
VINDHYACHALA
MAHA-KOSALA
SURASHTRA
Baghor
R. Narmada
Ramagiri
Girinagara
Barygaza
Sisupalgarh
Arabian
Ellora
Ajanta
Bhabanesar
Sea
Nasik
Devagiri (Daulatabad)
Konarak
Puri
KALINGA
Elephanta
Pratisthana
conquered by
Karli
SATAVAHANA KINGDOM
Asoka 260 BC
Bhaja
Bedsa
MAHARASHTRA
R. Godavari
Bay of Bengal
Kalyani
Warangal
Pishtapura
Deccan
Manyakheta
Talikota
Amaravati
Vengi
Vatapi
Aihole
R. Krishna
Vijayanagar
Vaijayanti
KARNATA
Belur
Kanchi
Dorasamudra
Sravana Belgola
Mamallapuram
CHOLA
Arikamedu
Indian Ocean
Srirangam
Kaverippattinam
Uraiyur
Tanjuvur
Tiruchirappalli
CHERA
(KERALA)
Muziris
Madurai
PANDYA
Korkai
Anuradhapura
Polonnaruva
Sigiriya
LANKA
(SIMHALA)

4 India's first empires, 297 BC - AD 150

(approximate limits shown)

— Chandragupta Maurya's Empire 297 BC
— Bindusara's Empire 272 BC
- - - Asoka's Empire 232 BC
▲ rock and pillar edicts
— Western Satraps AD 150
Kushan Empire AD 150 (eastern limit)
Satavahana Kingdom AD 150

routes opened to trade by Former Han
administrative centres under Later Han
centre of Later Han protectorate, 73-127 AD
territory added under Later Han
new route opened by General Pan Ch'ao for Later Han
expeditions against Hsiungnu (Huns)

conquered and put under Chinese administration 109-106 BC

TUNH-WANG
KIUCHUAN
CHANGI
WUWEI
SHUO-FANG
WU-YEN
YEN-MEN
LIAO-TUNG
HSUANTU
LIAOHSI
CHINCHENG
ANTING
SHANG
PEITI
LOLANG
LUNGHSI
TIENSHUI
WUTU
HANCHUNG
Changan
NAN-YANG
JUNAN
CHIU-CHANG
HUAI
SHU
KUANG-HAN
PA
NAN
CHANG-HSIA
TANYANG
KUAICHI
YUEHSUI
CHIENWEI
WULING
CHANGSHA
YUCHANG
MINYUEH
TSANGKO
LING-LING
KUEI-YANG
NANHAI
TAIWAN
ICHOU
YULIN
TSANG-WU
CHIAOCHIH
HOPU
CHIU-CHEN
JIHNAN

3 Han China in AD 2

⊡ imperial capital
enfiefed principalities
commanderies
— highways
⌇⌇⌇ canals

KUSHAN & SAKAS
MADRAS
KARTRIPURA
SASANIAN
EMPIRE
YAUDHEYAS
ARJUNAYANAS
NEPALA
KAMARUPA
DAVAKA
MALAVAS
Mathura
NAGAS
MAGADHA
Ayodhya Vaisali
Dasapura
Padmavati
Pataliputra
(Mandasor)
Airikina (Eran)
PUNDRA
VARDHANA
SAKAS
PARIVRAJAKAS
UCCHAKALPAS
SAMATATA
Ujjayini
Sanchi
Girinagara (Girnar)
Ajanta
Nandivardhana
VAKATAKAS
SALANKAYANAS

5 Gupta India

Empire of Chandragupta I
added by Samudragupta
temporarily tributary to Samudragupta
added by Chandragupta II
tributary tribes and states
under Gupta influence (c. AD 380-410)

KADAMBAS
Vengi
Bay of Bengal
PALLAVAS
GANGAS
PANDYA
LANKA (SIMHALA)

29

The Roman Empire
264 BC–AD 565

Originally a collection of village-settlements of Latin shepherds, Rome developed into a city under Etruscan domination during the sixth century BC. She gradually united Italy under her leadership into a confederation which she controlled by establishing Roman and Latin colonies at strategic points and a network of roads (map 1). She owed her predominance above all to her disciplined military power, combined with skill and generosity in making wide grants of her own citizenship or in forming alliances.

Although her interests had hitherto been primarily agricultural, Rome soon clashed with Carthage, the dominant commercial power in the western Mediterranean in a series of three Punic Wars (map 2). The first (264–241 BC) compelled Rome to build a navy and was fought mainly at sea; in the second (218–201), provoked by Carthaginian expansion in Spain and Roman seizure of Sardinia, Hannibal invaded Italy (218) but was ultimately defeated in North Africa (202); some fifty years later war again erupted and the Romans destroyed Carthage itself. Thus Rome acquired an overseas empire: Sicily (241), Corsica and Sardinia (238), Spain (206) and Africa (roughly modern Tunisia, 146). Meanwhile she had been in conflict with the Hellenistic kingdoms of Macedon, Syria and Egypt, annexing Macedon (in 146) and Asia (i.e. western Turkey) in 133.

The strains involved in administering an em-pire with the hastily adapted constitutional machinery of a mere city-state, combined with the increasing ambitions of political leaders who gained the personal loyalty of armies while governing provinces, gradually overstrained the Republican constitution. Though Rome over-came any discontent in Italy by granting to all its free inhabitants full Roman citizenship (90–89 BC), she could not prevent civil war between Julius Caesar, who added Gaul to the Empire, and Pompey whose conquests were in the east. Thirteen years more of civil war after Caesar's murder in 44 BC led to the triumph of Augustus and the transformation of the Republican system into a principate with the emperor as the effective ruler.

This empire (map 3) brought the Mediterranean world an unparalleled period of peace, stability and economic prosperity, the predominantly Latin culture of the west complementing the Hellenism of the east. But after some two-and-a-half centuries, barbarian pressure on the frontiers increased, economic difficulties multiplied, and one ruler could no longer hold the whole empire together. So in AD 284 Diocletian reorganised the administration and with Constantine's establishment of a new capital, Constantinople, at Byzantium (330) the empire, though theoretically governed by joint rulers, gradually broke into two halves. Barbarian attacks increased and in the fifth century the Western Empire fell to the invaders. In the east the Byzantine Empire survived for another thousand years, though the efforts of Justinian in the mid-sixth century to re-unite the two halves of the old empire failed (map 4).

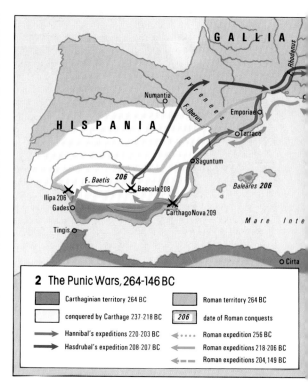

2 The Punic Wars, 264-146 BC

- Carthaginian territory 264 BC
- conquered by Carthage 237-218 BC
- Hannibal's expeditions 220-203 BC
- Hasdrubal's expedition 208-207 BC
- Roman territory 264 BC
- **206** date of Roman conquests
- Roman expedition 256 BC
- Roman expeditions 218-206 BC
- Roman expeditions 204, 149 BC

1 Roman expansion in Italy 510-264 BC

- Roman territory by 264 BC
- ■ Roman colonies
- ● Latin colonies
- allied states or tribal areas
- *VENETI* peoples

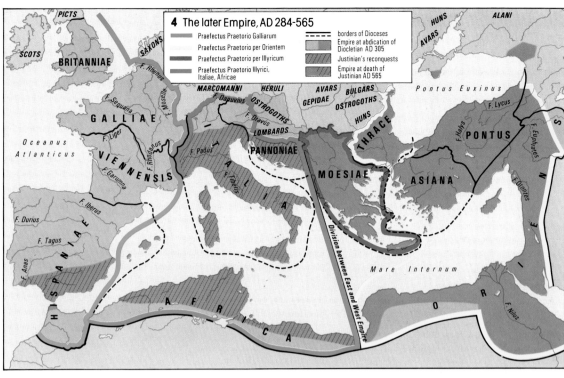

4 The later Empire, AD 284–565

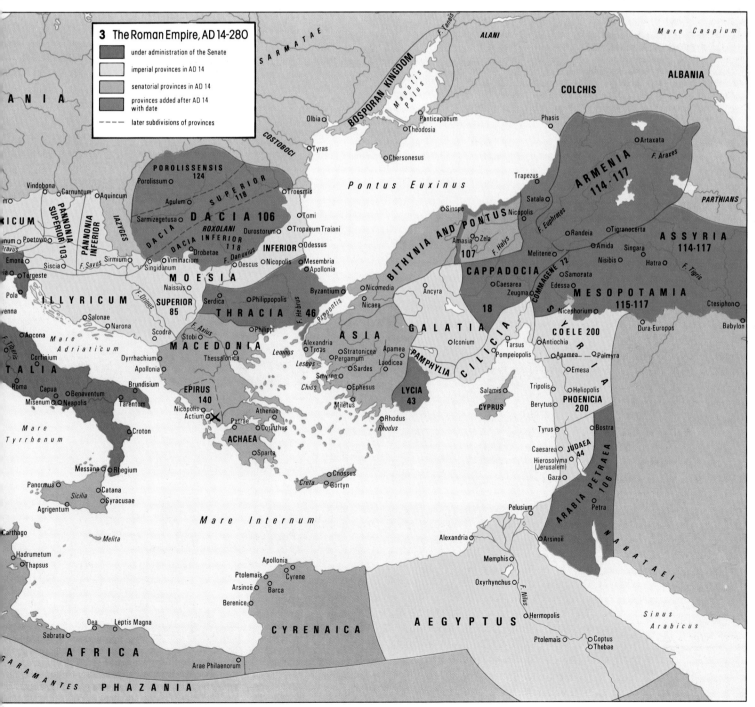

3 The Roman Empire, AD 14–280

The barbarian invasions

In the fourth and fifth centuries AD the irruption of nomadic peoples from central Asia threw the whole civilised world into disarray. The invading nomads were under no form of central control though their movements radiated from a common centre. They were mostly Mongoloid and their languages mostly of the Turkish family; they were pastoralists with mobile encampments of tents and they fought as mounted archers. All the established centres of civilisation were affected by them: China, the Gupta empire in India, Sasanian Persia and the Roman empire in the west (map 1). In 304 the Great Wall of China was breached by the Hsiung-nu, forbears of the Huns; in 367, in the far west, Picts and Scots broke through Hadrian's Wall into Britain. The setbacks were lasting, China remained disunited until 589, and western Europe (if we except the short-lived Carolingian revival) only began to recover from invasion around the middle of the eleventh century (page 36).

The appearance of the Huns in Europe c.370 immediately caused a great involuntary movement among the Germanic peoples who, centuries earlier, had moved down from Scandinavia and were settled on the northern confines of the Roman empire. The details, beginning with the Visigoths, who defeated the Roman emperor at Adrianople in 378, sacked Rome in 410 and passed over into Aquitaine in 418, can be followed on map 2. Behind the Visigoths followed other east and west Germanic peoples: Alans, Vandals, Sueves, Alemans, Franks, and finally the Ostrogoths who, having earlier been forced into subjection, liberated themselves after the defeat of the Huns in 451, and descended into Italy, where they were in control by 493. Only the Anglo-Saxon invasion of Britain, beginning c.440, followed a different course. Here scattered bands of warriors and settlers, moving by ship up the estuaries of the Humber, Thames and the Wash,

met with stubborn resistance, and it was almost two centuries before the invaders, following their victories at Deorham (577) and Chester (616), established control (map 3). Here there was little, if any, continuity.

In continental Europe continuity was more evident. Political control passed from Roman officials to German kings; but, except for the Anglo-Saxons and Franks, who could draw manpower from their homeland, the invaders were too few in number to change decisively the character of Roman society. Hence the success of the counter-offensive which Justinian launched in 533 (page 30). But Justinian's wars, and the havoc they wrought, left the way open for another wave of invasion from Asia, this time the Avars, and it was their onslaught, beginning c.560, that drove the Lombards into Italy (568). But they were too few in number to occupy the whole peninsula, and Italy remained divided between the Lombards, the Byzantine emperor and the Papacy (map 4). When the Lombard ruler Aistulf advanced south, seeking to establish his authority over the Lombard dukes of Spoleto and Benevento, occupied Ravenna in 751 and drove out the Byzantine exarch, the Pope, fearing for his independence, called on the Franks for aid. Thus was sealed the momentous alliance of the Carolingians and the Papacy, which resulted in Charles the Great's invasion, conquest and annexation of the Lombard kingdom in 774.

The appearance of the Avars also unsettled the Slav peoples who had expanded from their home in the region of the Pripet Marshes following the Germanic migration westwards. Beginning c.600 Slav warbands descended into Greece and the Balkans, while the Bulgars took control of the western shore of the Black Sea (map 5). The arrival of the Slavs, cutting the landbridge between Byzantium and the west, was a cardinal fact in European history. The rise of the Bulgarian Empire and the gradual consolidation of Serbia and Croatia left a permanent imprint on the demography and historical geography of Europe.

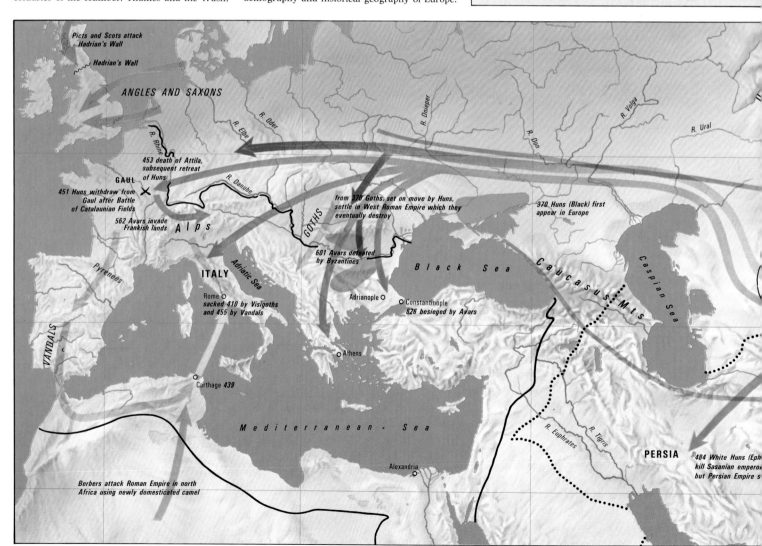

2 Germanic invasions of Europe

- Huns and campaigns of Attila
- Vandals, Alans, Sueves
- Visigoths
- Ostrogoths
- other Germanic peoples
- Scots and Britons
- Slavs
- boundary of Roman Empire AD395
- Anglo-Saxon settlement in England to AD626

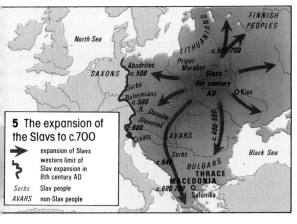

5 The expansion of the Slavs to c.700

→ expansion of Slavs
⌇ western limit of Slav expansion in 8th century AD

Sorbs Slav people
AVARS non-Slav people

North Sea
FINNISH PEOPLES
LITHUANIANS c.500-700
SAXONS c.500
Abodrites c.500
Pripet Marshes
Sorbs
Bohemians c.500
R. Danube
Slovenes c.600
Croats
Slavs 1st century AD
Kiev
c.400-500
c.640
Serbs
AVARS
BULGARS
THRACE
MACEDONIA c.600-700
Salonika
Black Sea

4 The Lombards in Italy

▢ Lombard Kingdom and duchies c.600
▢ Imperial territory c.600

Cividale
LOMBARDY
Verona
Pavia
ISTRIA
Parma
LIGURIA
Ravenna
Bologna
Rimini
EXARCHATE OF RAVENNA
TUSCANY
Siena
Adriatic Sea
DUCHY OF SPOLETO
Rome
DUCHY OF ROME
DUCHY OF BENEVENTO
CALABRIA
Brindisi
Naples
CAMPANIA
Amalfi
Tyrrhenian Sea
SICILY
Syracuse

3 Anglo-Saxon invasions of Britain, c.440-650

➤ lines of Anglo-Saxon advance
▨ forest
▨ fenland, swamp
· Anglo-Saxon burial places c.450-650
〃 British fortifications

LOTHIAN
STRATHCLYDE
BERNICIA
Bamburgh 547
REGED
Hexham 633
North Sea
DEIRA
York
R. Ribble
ELMEDSAETE (ELMET)
LINDSEY
Humber
PECSAETE
GWYNEDD
Chester 616
R. Dee
The Wash
MERCIANS
POWYS
WREOCENSAETE
MIDDLE ANGLES
EAST ANGLES
R. Wye
R. Severn
DYFED
BRYCHEINIOG
GWYNLLWG
R. Thames
Chiltern Hills
Bedcanford 571
EAST SAXONS
London
Crayford 457
Ebbsfleet 449
Deorham 577
WEST SAXONS
KENT
HÆSTINGAS
Old Sarum 552
ANDREDESWEALD
Cerdicesford 519
SOUTH SAXONS
Andredescester 491
WIHT
WEST WALES
Bindon 614
GAUL

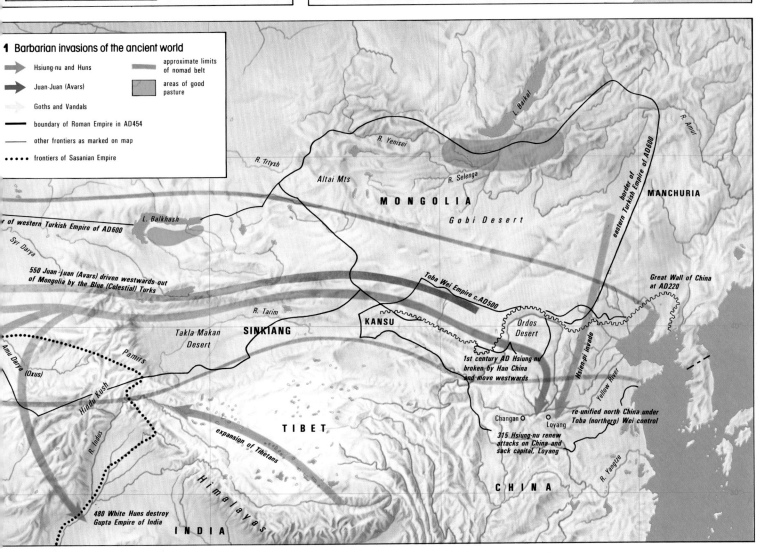

1 Barbarian invasions of the ancient world

➤ Hsiung-nu and Huns
➤ Juan-Juan (Avars)
➤ Goths and Vandals
━ boundary of Roman Empire in AD454
─ other frontiers as marked on map
⋯ frontiers of Sasanian Empire

▬ approximate limits of nomad belt
▨ areas of good pasture

L. Baikal
R. Amur
R. Yenisei
R. Trtysh
Altai Mts
R. Selenga
MONGOLIA
MANCHURIA
L. Balkhash
of western Turkish Empire of AD600
Syr Darya
Gobi Desert
border of eastern Turkish Empire of AD600
550 Juan-juan (Avars) driven westwards out of Mongolia by the Blue (Celestial) Turks
R. Tarim
Toba Wei Empire c.AD500
Great Wall of China at AD220
Amu Darya (Oxus)
Takla Makan Desert
SINKIANG
KANSU
Ordos Desert
Pamirs
Hsien-pi invade
Hindu Kush
R. Indus
1st century AD Hsiung-nu broken by Han China and move westwards
Yellow River
expansion of Tibetans
TIBET
Changan
Loyang
re-unified north China under Toba (northern) Wei control
315 Hsiung-nu renew attacks on China and sack capital, Loyang
Himalayas
480 White Huns destroy Gupta Empire of India
R. Yangtze
INDIA
CHINA

33

Germanic kingdoms of Western Europe

Within a century of the Germanic invasions there were settled kingdoms in western Europe, except in Britain where bands of invaders still met stubborn resistance. Among these (map 1) the Ostrogothic kingdom of Theodoric the Great (493–526) was outstanding. But the apparent stability proved short-lived. Monarchical institutions were still weak and religious differences divided the Arian rulers from their Catholic subjects. Justinian's attack on the Ostrogothic kingdom (page 30) destroyed the existing equilibrium in the west and opened the way for the advance of the Franks to the leading position (map 2).

The Franks also had appeared on the scene as scattered warbands, but Clovis (486–511) ruthlessly eliminated his rivals, made himself sole king, and reconciled the Gallo-Roman population by embracing the Catholic faith (497). He then turned against the neighbouring peoples, the Alemanni and Burgundians, defeated the Visigoths at Vouillé (507), near Poitiers, and forced them to withdraw to Spain and Septimania. But Theodoric's support for the other Germanic kingdoms checked further advance, and only after his death was a new phase of Frankish expansion possible. Deprived of Ostrogothic support, the Thuringians (531), Burgundians (532–4), and Alemanni (535) succumbed, and in 537 the Franks seized Provence.

Once the initial wave of conquest was spent, however, decline set in. Division of the royal patrimony, dynastic quarrels and alienation of the royal estates to buy aristocratic and ecclesiastical support, seemed after the death of Dagobert I (629–39) to presage the break-up of the kingdom. In Britain, on the other hand, the seventh century saw the emergence and consolidation of the kingdoms known as the Heptarchy. It seems that the kingdoms of the south-east (Sussex, Kent, Essex, East Anglia) were prevented from expanding by geographical obstacles, and leadership passed first to Northumbria and then to Mercia. The progress of Northumbria was helped by its early conversion to Christianity, but it was resisted by pagan Mercia under Penda (632–54), sometimes in alliance with the Britons, and by the time of Offa (757–96) the pre-eminence of Mercia, now Christian, was unquestionable. It controlled the four eastern kingdoms (map 3), and even Wessex recognised Mercian overlordship.

In the Frankish lands the turning point came with the battle of Tertry (687), when the leaders of the Austrasian aristocracy established their preponderance. This was the beginning of the rise of the Carolingian dynasty. Ruling at first indirectly, but after 751 with the royal title, the Carolingians restored Frankish fortunes and inaugurated a great surge of territorial expansion (map 4). Charles Martel (714–41) won a famous victory over the Arabs at Poitiers (732). His son Pepin (751–68) expelled them from Aquitania (752). Charles the Great, or Charlemagne (768–814), conquered Lombardy (774) and established Frankish rule in Italy. But his greatest victories were in the east, against the Bavarians (788), the Avars (796), and the Saxons (finally subdued in 804). His coronation as emperor by Pope Leo III in 800 marked the apogee of Frankish success.

However, Charlemagne's last ten years were beset by problems, the frontier marches never safe from attack; and after his death the inherent institutional weaknesses quickly became apparent. Civil war led to a first partition in 843. But the famous treaty of Verdun (map 5) was only a first step, and at Meersen (870) the 'Middle Kingdom' was eliminated (map 6) and the familiar outlines of Europe began to take shape. In 888 the Carolingian empire collapsed but its legacy to European civilisation remained.

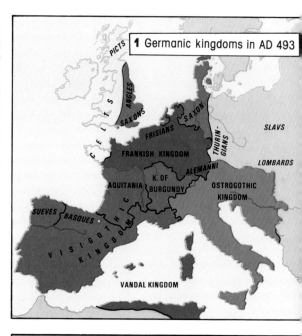

1 Germanic kingdoms in AD 493

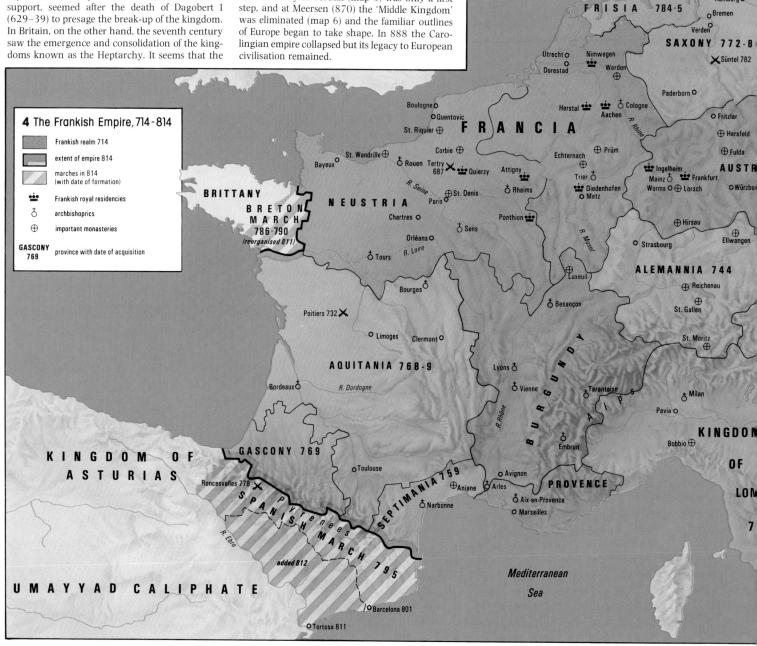

4 The Frankish Empire, 714–814

- Frankish realm 714
- extent of empire 814
- marches in 814 (with date of formation)
- 👑 Frankish royal residencies
- ⚲ archbishoprics
- ⊕ important monasteries

GASCONY 769 province with date of acquisition

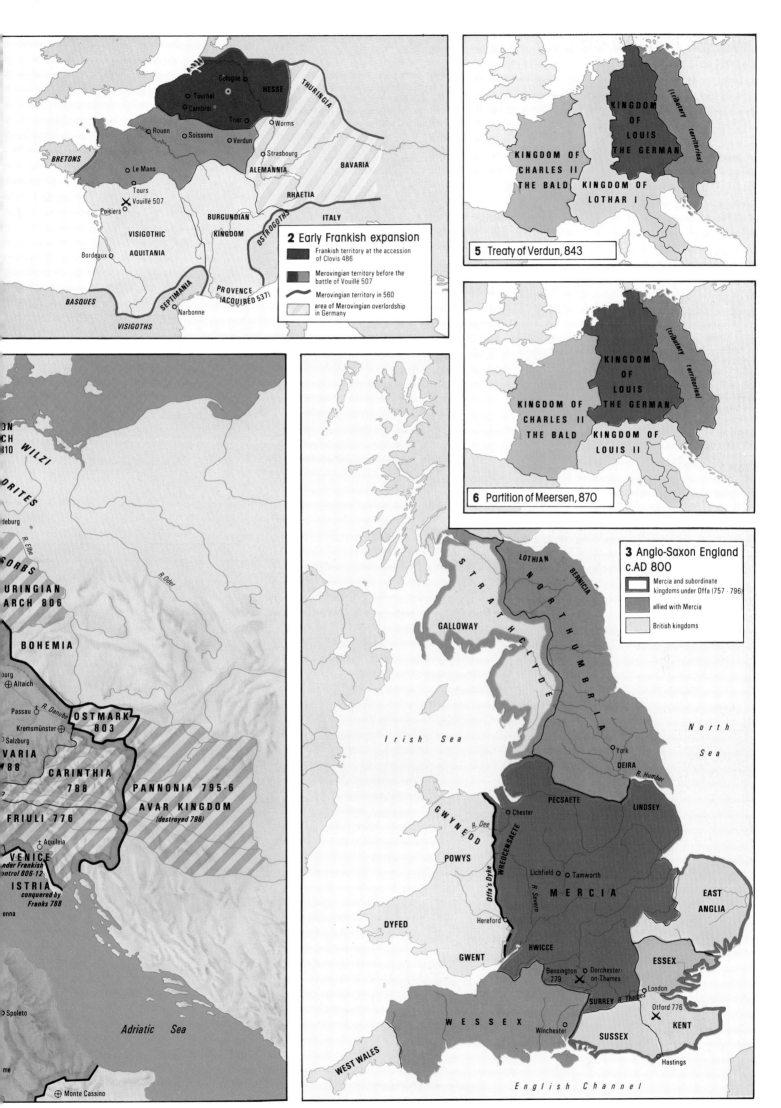

Invasion and recovery: Europe, 814-1149

The relative stability of western Europe under Charles the Great (Charlemagne) and of England under Offa of Mercia (page 34) was shattered in the ninth century by attacks by Saracens in the south, Magyars in the east, and Norwegians and Danes in the north and west (map 1). The Saracens pillaged Rome in 846, and after establishing a base at Fraxinetum in 890 raided deep into southern Gaul. Northern Italy and Germany were a prey to the Magyars who had moved into the Hungarian plain after Charlemagne's destruction of Avar power. The Vikings of Norway and Denmark also began as raiders; but in their case an initial phase of plunder was followed by settlement and colonisation, first in Orkney and Shetland, then in Ireland where Dublin was founded c.841, later (c.870) in Iceland and in England, where the Danish armies occupied the countryside round the Five Boroughs of the Midlands after 876. In France the West Frankish king conferred the lands at the mouth of the Seine — the later duchy of Normandy — on the Danish leader Rollo in 911.

The invasions were accompanied by widespread devastation and depopulation. Inevitably recovery was slow. In Germany (page 54) Otto I's defeat of the Magyars at the river Lech (955) was a turning point. In England only determined resistance by Alfred the Great (871-99) held the Danes at bay. After 909 his successors went over to the offensive and by 939 Scandinavian England had been subjugated. But after the death of Edgar (959-75) a second wave of Danish invasion began.

In southern Europe, where Spain had been in Arab hands for over two centuries, the Mediterranean was by 950 virtually a 'Muslim lake'. But the collapse of Arab unity after 936 (page 40) facilitated a Christian revival. After the fall of Fraxinetum in 972 the fleets of Pisa and Genoa went over to the offensive, attacking the Muslim bases in North Africa, while Venice cleared the Adriatic (map 2). After the First Crusade (1096-99) and the great Venetian naval victory off Ascalon in 1123, the Italian cities dominated Mediterranean trade. The period of the First Crusade also saw the beginning of the Christian reconquest of Spain under Alfonso VI (1065-1109), king of León and Castile, who actually advanced as far as Toledo in 1084 (map 4). But the first wave of reconquest was halted by the great Islamic revival under the Almoravid and Almohad dynasties. The Christian advance only resumed in the thirteenth century after the decisive victory at Las Navas de Tolosa (1212) which led rapidly to the conquest of Córdoba (1236), Valencia (1238), Murcia (1243), Seville (1248) and Cádiz (1262).

The ninth and tenth century invasions also disrupted royal authority and created political fragmentation. In Gaul the Frankish rulers virtually capitulated to the Vikings, leaving defence to the local magnates. The result was a great upsurge of feudalism. Peasant freemen virtually disappeared and society was polarised between nobles and serfs. In Germany power devolved into the hands of dukes and margraves who defended the frontiers, and in Italy only the walled cities could withstand the Magyar onslaught. The kingdom of Wessex was the exception, unique in tenth century Europe beyond the borders of Muslim Spain and Byzantium. Here the monarchy took control, creating during the reconquest of the Danelaw a system of shires and hundreds administered by sheriffs who were officials, not feudatories. But this royal government could not withstand the renewal of Danish attacks during the reign of Aethelred II (978-1016). By the beginning of the eleventh century England seemed destined to pass into a Scandinavian orbit (page 52). The Norman Conquest (map 3) decisively halted this development. William the Conqueror quickly established control in the south; but in the north, where Danish and Scottish intervention underpinned resistance, he only made his authority secure by systematic devastation (1069). Danish reconquest was still a threat until 1085; but after 1066 England was permanently aligned with the Christian and feudal civilisation of western Europe. The period of invasions had irrevocably changed the structure of Western society.

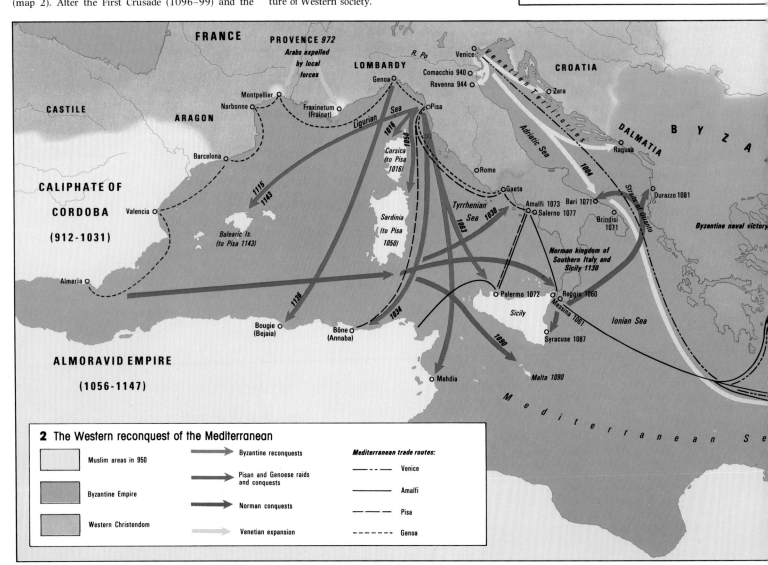

2 The Western reconquest of the Mediterranean

- Muslim areas in 950
- Byzantine Empire
- Western Christendom
- Byzantine reconquests
- Pisan and Genoese raids and conquests
- Norman conquests
- Venetian expansion

Mediterranean trade routes:
- ----- Venice
- ——— Amalfi
- — — Pisa
- - - - - Genoa

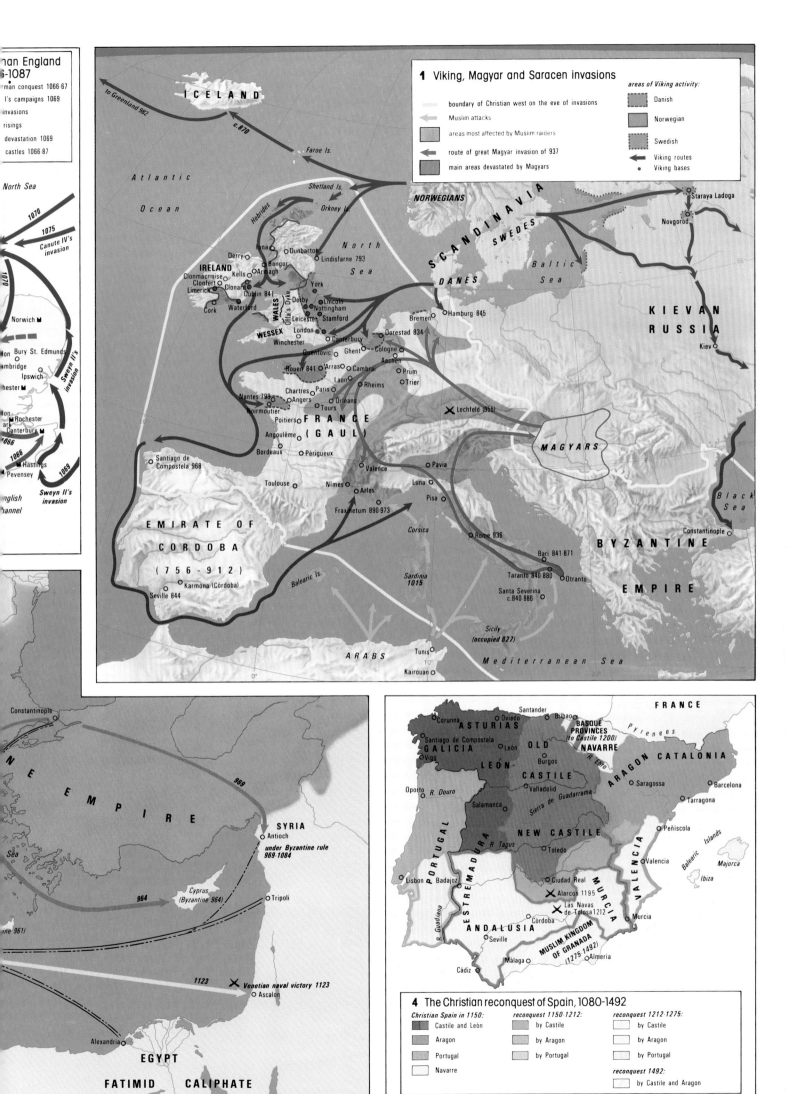

Norman England 1066-1087 (partial, left margin)

Norman conquest 1066-67

I's campaigns 1069

invasions

risings

devastation 1069

castles 1066-87

North Sea

1070

1075

Canute IV's invasion

1070

Norwich

Bury St. Edmunds

Cambridge

Ipswich

chester

Sweyn II's invasion

Rochester

Canterbury

1066

1066

Hastings

Pevensey 1069

Sweyn II's invasion

English

Channel

Map 1 — Viking, Magyar and Saracen invasions

1 Viking, Magyar and Saracen invasions

areas of Viking activity:

boundary of Christian west on the eve of invasions

Muslim attacks

Danish

areas most affected by Muslim raiders

Norwegian

route of great Magyar invasion of 937

Swedish

main areas devastated by Magyars

Viking routes

Viking bases

ICELAND

to Greenland 982

c.870

Faroe Is.

Atlantic Ocean

Shetland Is.

NORWEGIANS

Staraya Ladoga

SCANDINAVIA

SWEDES

Novgorod

Hebrides

Orkney Is.

North Sea

Baltic Sea

KIEVAN RUSSIA

Derry

Dunbarton

Iona

Lindisfarne 793

DANES

Bangor

IRELAND

Armagh

Kells

Clonmacnoise

Clonfert

York

Bremen

Hamburg 845

Kiev

Limerick

Clonard

Dublin 841

Lincoln

Waterford

Derby

Nottingham

Cork

WALES

Offa's Dyke

Leicester

Stamford

Dorestad 834

WESSEX

London

Winchester

Canterbury

Quentovic

Ghent

Cologne

Rouen 841

Arras

Cambrai

Aachen

Prüm

Nantes 799

Chartres

Paris

Laon

Rheims

Trier

Angers

Orléans

Noirmoutier

Tours

Lechfeld (955)

Poitiers

FRANCE (GAUL)

Angoulême

Santiago de Compostela 968

Bordeaux

Périgueux

MAGYARS

Valence

Pavia

Toulouse

Nîmes

Luna

Black Sea

Arles

Pisa

Fraxinetum 890-973

Corsica

EMIRATE OF CORDOBA (756-912)

Balearic Is.

Rome 936

BYZANTINE

Constantinople

Sardinia 1015

Bari 841-871

Karmona (Córdoba)

Taranto 840-880

Otranto

EMPIRE

Seville 844

Santa Severina c.840-886

Sicily (occupied 827)

ARABS

Tunis

Mediterranean Sea

Kairouan

Lower left map

Constantinople

NE EMPIRE

969

SYRIA

Antioch

under Byzantine rule 969-1084

964

Sea

Cyprus (Byzantine 964)

Tripoli

ine 961)

1123

Venetian naval victory 1123

Ascalon

Alexandria

EGYPT

FATIMID CALIPHATE

4 The Christian reconquest of Spain, 1080-1492

Santander

FRANCE

Corunna

Oviedo

Bilbao

ASTURIAS

BASQUE PROVINCES (to Castile 1200)

Pyrenees

Santiago de Compostela

León

OLD

NAVARRE

GALICIA

Vigo

Burgos

CASTILE

ARAGON

CATALONIA

LEÓN

R. Ebro

Oporto

R. Douro

Valladolid

Saragossa

Barcelona

Salamanca

Sierra de Guadarrama

Tarragona

PORTUGAL

NEW CASTILE

VALENCIA

Peñiscola

R. Tagus

Toledo

Valencia

Balearic Islands

Lisbon

Badajoz

Majorca

ESTREMADURA

Ciudad Real

MURCIA

Ibiza

R. Guadiana

Alarcos 1195

Las Navas de Tolosa 1212

ANDALUSIA

Córdoba

Murcia

Seville

MUSLIM KINGDOM OF GRANADA (1275-1492)

Almería

Cádiz

Málaga

4 The Christian reconquest of Spain, 1080-1492

Christian Spain in 1150:

reconquest 1150-1212:

reconquest 1212-1275:

Castile and León

by Castile

by Castile

Aragon

by Aragon

by Aragon

Portugal

by Portugal

by Portugal

Navarre

reconquest 1492:

by Castile and Aragon

Christianity and Judaism, c.600-1500

By the time of Pope Leo I (440–461) an organised Christian church existed with a hierarchy of bishops and a full-scale framework of patriarchates, provinces and dioceses. But the attempt to enforce orthodoxy, particularly at the Council of Chalcedon (451), caused serious internal conflict. The Monophysite or Coptic Christians of Egypt were alienated, the Nestorians driven into exile in Persia. Here they carried on great missionary work (map 1), only halted centuries later by the advance of Islam (page 40). In the west, however, where Christianity was the official religion of the Roman empire, the church suffered from the setbacks inflicted by the Germanic invasions of the western provinces (page 32), and subsequent rivalry between Rome and Constantinople resulted after 1054 in schism between Catholicism and Orthodoxy. A period of stagnation had set in, only ended by the Irish and later Anglo-Saxon missionaries (map 3), who converted the heathen tribes of Germany, reformed the Frankish church, and inaugurated a great missionary drive to Scandinavia and eastern Europe. In addition a counter-offensive against Islam was launched in a series of Crusades beginning in 1096. The general outline of the Christian thrust, north and east from the Rhine and Danube, can be followed on map 2.

The resurgence of Christianity, particularly marked after the pontificate of Leo IX (1048–54) was a disaster for the Jewish communities which had spread throughout Europe before and after the suppression of the Jewish revolts in Palestine by the Romans in AD 66 and 132. The Jews suffered no restrictions in the Roman empire and, with their widespread international connections, were welcomed as traders by the Carolingians and other early medieval kings. But the Crusades inaugurated a wave of intolerance, and the third and fourth Lateran Councils (1179, 1215) passed discriminatory legislation. The rise of a native merchant class also made Jews less indispensable to Christian rulers, and later they became the scapegoats for the economic setbacks of the fourteenth century (page 56). The result was the series of expulsions, beginning in England in 1290. In 1492 the Sephardic Jews were expelled from Spain, in 1497 from Portugal. The Ashkenazi in the German lands took refuge in Poland and Lithuania, where they formed tight communities in what later was called 'the Pale'. Only the eighteenth-century Enlightenment brought a beginning of reconciliation, but the Nazi experience was to show that it was far from complete.

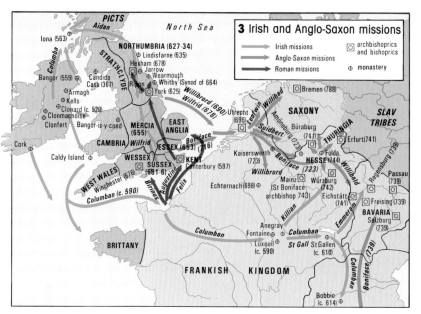

3 Irish and Anglo-Saxon missions
- Irish missions
- Anglo-Saxon missions
- Roman missions
- archbishoprics and bishoprics
- monastery

2 Christianity in Europe
- Monophysite Christians
- Orthodox Christians
- Catholic Christians
- original Catholic core
- Celtic churches
- Islam
- heathen peoples
- metropolitan see
- bishopric
- monastery/hermitage
- other churches
- routes of missionaries

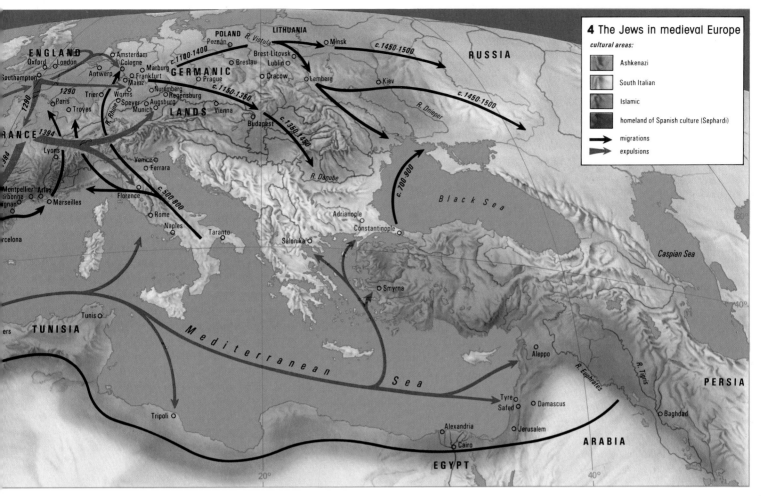

cultural areas:

Ashkenazi

South Italian

Islamic

homeland of Spanish culture (Sephardi)

→ migrations

⇒ expulsions

ENGLAND
Oxford London
Southampton

Amsterdam
Cologne
Antwerp
Marburg
Frankfurt
Mainz
GERMANIC

POLAND LITHUANIA
Poznán R. Vistula
Breslau Lublin
Prague Cracow

Minsk
c.1450-1500
RUSSIA

FRANCE
1290
Paris Troyes
1394
Lyons

Trier
Worms
Speyer Nuremberg
Munich Regensburg
Augsburg
R. Rhine
c.1100-1400
LANDS
c.1150-1360
Vienna

Lemberg Kiev
R. Dnieper
c.1450-1500

Montpellier
Narbonne
Arles
Marseilles

Florence
c.500-800

Venice
Ferrara

Budapest
c.1360-1450

R. Danube
c.700-900

Black Sea

Barcelona

Rome
Naples Taranto

Adrianople
Constantinople

Caspian Sea

TUNISIA
Tunis

Mediterranean Sea

Salonika

Smyrna

Aleppo
R. Euphrates
R. Tigris

PERSIA

Tripoli

Tyre Damascus
Safed

Baghdad

Alexandria
Cairo
Jerusalem

ARABIA

EGYPT

20° 40° 40°

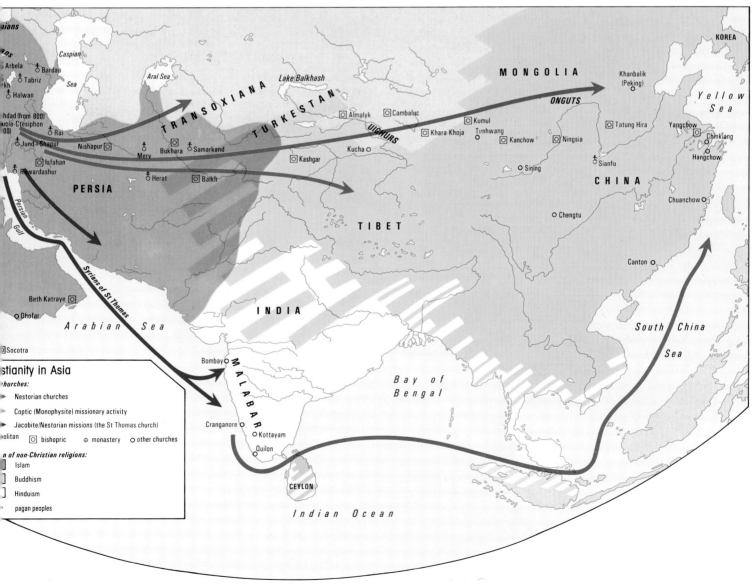

KOREA

Caspian
Sea
Arbela
Bardaa
Tabriz
Halwan

Aral Sea
Lake Balkhash

TRANSOXIANA

MONGOLIA
Khanbalik
(Peking)

Yellow
Sea

Baghdad (from 800)
Seleucia-Ctesiphon
(700)
Rai
Jund-i-Shapur
Isfahan
Rewardashur

Nishapur
Merv Bukhara Samarkand
Herat Balkh

TURKESTAN
Almalyk Cambaluc
UICHURS
Kashgar
Kucha

Khara-Khoja
Kumul
Tunhwang
Kanchow
Sining

ONGUTS

Tatung Hira
Ningsia
Sianfu

Yangchow
Chinkiang
Hangchow

PERSIA

CHINA
Chengtu

Chuanchow

Persian Gulf

TIBET

Canton

Beth Katraye

Syrians of St Thomas

Arabian Sea

INDIA

South China
Sea

Dhofar

Socotra

stianity in Asia

churches:

▶ Nestorian churches

▶ Coptic (Monophysite) missionary activity

▶ Jacobite/Nestorian missions (the St Thomas church)

olitan ▣ bishopric ⊕ monastery ○ other churches

n of non-Christian religions:

▯ Islam

▯ Buddhism

▯ Hinduism

▯ pagan peoples

Bombay
MALABAR

Cranganore
Kottayam
Quilon

Bay of
Bengal

CEYLON

Indian Ocean

The Islamic world
632-1517

The most important event in world history between the fall of Rome and the European voyages of discovery in the fifteenth century was the rise and expansion of Islam. Founded by Mohammed (born in Mecca c.AD 570), the new religion quickly captured the Arab world and became a major political force as well as the heir and transmitter of Hellenic civilisation. The speed of its advance after the Prophet's death in 632 was astounding. Palestine was occupied and the Byzantine army defeated by 636, Persia overrun by 643, and within a century the Arabs had conquered North Africa and Spain (712) and reached the western confines of China, where they defeated the T'ang army at the Talas river in 751. The stages of the advance, which also carried them to India, can be followed on map 1. The only serious setback was the failure, in 673 and again in 717, to reduce Constantinople, which left the Islamic world exposed to Byzantine counter-attack.

By then internal developments were bringing the Islamic thrust to a halt. After 750 the Umayyad caliphs, who had led the advance, were displaced by the Abbasid dynasty, and the centre of gravity moved from Damascus, the seat of empire since 661, to Baghdad (founded 762). In the west the Arabs, halted by the Franks at Poitiers in 732, withdrew behind the Pyrenees in 759, and a new, less active phase began. The Abbasid period was a time of great prosperity, magnificent building and cultural and intellectual vigour, but by the beginning of the tenth century the unity of the empire was dissolving under the impact of religious and political strife. When in 945 the Abbasid caliph was deprived of political power and confined to purely religious functions, control devolved into the hands of local dynasties. Among these (map 2) were the Fatimids of Egypt, the Almoravids and Almohads of North Africa and Spain, and the Ghaznavids who played a great part in the expansion of Islam into India (map 4).

The process of disruption was arrested in the eleventh century by nomads from Asia, the Seljuk Turks, who defeated Byzantium at the battle of Manzikert (1071) and established a new type of state based on a partnership between Turkish 'men of the sword' and the Arab and Persian ruling class. Seljuk authority was limited essentially to the heartland of the caliphate (Baghdad, Syria, Iran), but

the strengthening of government enabled the Arabs to withstand the Christian crusading offensive, and in 1187 Saladin, the founder of the new Ayyubid dynasty in Egypt, recaptured Jerusalem and destroyed the Christian principalities in Palestine and Syria which had been founded after the First Crusade (map 3). But the Christian advance in Spain and the Norman conquest of Sicily (page 36) shifted the axis of the Islamic world to the east, and here the balance was once again changed by the appearance of a new wave of Asiatic peoples, the Mongols and the Ottoman Turks. From the end of the thirteenth century the dominant fact in the political history of the Muslim world was the victorious Ottoman advance (page 48), but both in India and in

Indonesia (maps 4 and 5), and also in sub-Saharan Africa (page 60), Islam continued to gain adherents, until today its believers comprise about one-seventh of the world's population. A new and powerful force in history had arrived on the scene.

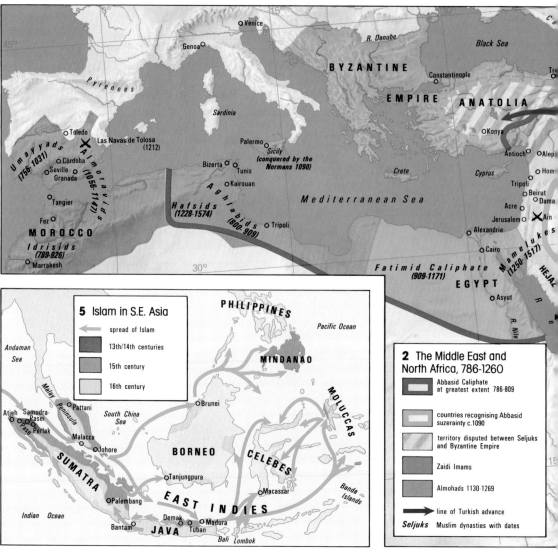

5 Islam in S.E. Asia
→ spread of Islam
▮ 13th/14th centuries
▮ 15th century
▮ 16th century

2 The Middle East and North Africa, 786-1260
▮ Abbasid Caliphate at greatest extent 786-809
▮ countries recognising Abbasid suzerainty c.1090
▨ territory disputed between Seljuks and Byzantine Empire
▮ Zaidi Imams
▮ Almohads 1130-1269
→ line of Turkish advance
Seljuks Muslim dynasties with dates

3 The Muslim reconquest of Palestine
— boundary of Crusader states
▮ Byzantine Empire
conquests of Saladin:
— before 1171
— before 1187
— 1187 to 1189

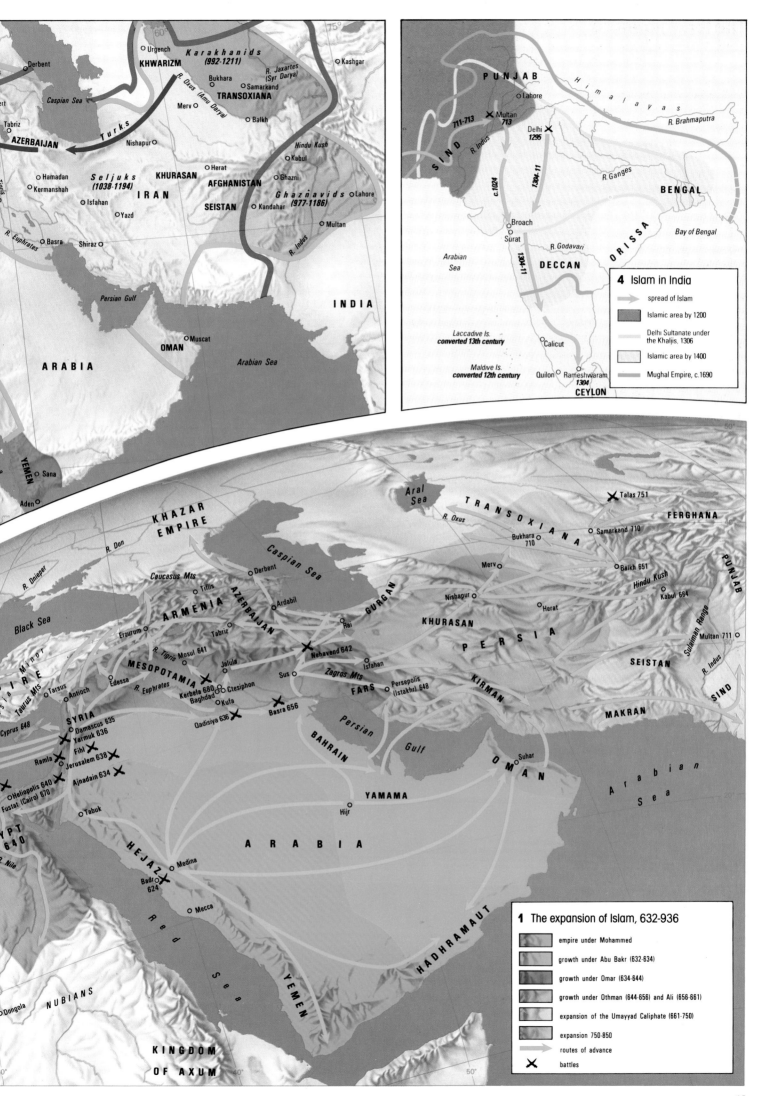

KHWARIZM
Urgench
Karakhanids (992-1211)
R. Jaxartes (Syr Darya)
Kashgar
Derbent
Bukhara
Samarkand
TRANSOXIANA
Caspian Sea
Merv
Balkh
Tabriz
AZERBAIJAN
Turks
Nishapur
Hindu Kush
Kabul
Hamadan
Seljuks (1038-1194)
Herat
KHURASAN
Ghazni
Kermanshah
IRAN
AFGHANISTAN
Ghaznavids (977-1186)
Lahore
Isfahan
Yazd
SEISTAN
Kandahar
R. Euphrates
R. Tigris
Basra
Shiraz
Multan
INDIA
Persian Gulf
Muscat
OMAN
Arabian Sea
ARABIA
YEMEN
Sana
Aden

4 Islam in India

PUNJAB
Lahore
Himalayas
Multan 711-713, *713*
SIND
R. Indus
Delhi *1295*
R. Brahmaputra
R. Ganges
BENGAL
1304-11
c.1024
R. Godavari
ORISSA
Broach
Surat
Arabian Sea
Bay of Bengal
DECCAN
1304-11
Laccadive Is. **converted 13th century**
Calicut
Maldive Is. **converted 12th century**
Quilon Rameshwaram *1304*
CEYLON

→ spread of Islam
▓ Islamic area by 1200
▬ Delhi Sultanate under the Khaljis, 1306
░ Islamic area by 1400
▬ Mughal Empire, c.1690

KHAZAR EMPIRE
R. Don
R. Dnieper
Aral Sea
R. Oxus
TRANSOXIANA
Talas 751 ✕
FERGHANA
Caspian Sea
Caucasus Mts
Derbent
Tiflis
Bukhara 710
Samarkand 710
Erzurum
ARMENIA
AZERBAIJAN
Ardabil
GURGAN
Merv
Balkh 651
Hindu Kush
Black Sea
Tabriz
Rai
Nishapur
KHURASAN
PUNJAB
Herat
PERSIA
Kabul 664
Asia Minor
R. Tigris
Mosul 641
Nehavend 642
Sulaiman Range
Taurus Mts
Tarsus
MESOPOTAMIA
Jalula
Isfahan
R. Indus
Antioch
Edessa
R. Euphrates
Kerbela 680 ✕
Ctesiphon
Sus
Persepolis (Istakhr) 648
KIRMAN
Multan 711
SIND
Baghdad
Kufa
FARS
Zagros Mts
SEISTAN
Cyprus 648
SYRIA
Damascus 635
Basra 656 ✕
Qadisiya 636 ✕
MAKRAN
Yarmuk 636 ✕
Fihl ✕
Ramla ✕
Jerusalem 638 ✕
Ajnadain 634 ✕
BAHRAIN
Persian Gulf
OMAN
Suhar
Arabian Sea
Heliopolis 640 ✕
Fustat (Cairo) 670
EGYPT 640
YAMAMA
Tabuk
Hijr
ARABIA
R. Nile
HEJAZ
Medina
NUBIANS
Dongola
Red Sea
Badr 624 ✕
Mecca
YEMEN
HADHRAMAUT
KINGDOM OF AXUM

1 The expansion of Islam, 632-936

▓ empire under Mohammed
▓ growth under Abu Bakr (632-634)
▓ growth under Omar (634-644)
▓ growth under Othman (644-656) and Ali (656-661)
▓ expansion of the Umayyad Caliphate (661-750)
▓ expansion 750-850
→ routes of advance
✕ battles

The Byzantine world, 610-1453

The history of the Roman empire was marked almost from the outset by a shift of focus to the east. The original cause was the lure of the wealth of the older oriental civilisations and the economic strength of the great commercial centres of Egypt and western Asia (page 24). Later, the loss of the western provinces to Germanic invaders (page 34) hastened the trend. Simultaneously the great Persian revival under the Sasanians forced Rome to concentrate its efforts on defence of its eastern frontier. After Justinian (page 30) the west was neglected, the Roman empire became an eastern, Greek-speaking dominion. The change is conventionally placed in the reign of Heraclius (610–641). From this time it is customary to speak of a Byzantine rather than a Roman empire.

Heraclius brought the long contest with Persia to a victorious close at Nineveh (628), but almost immediately was confronted by an even more redoubtable foe: Islam. The struggle with Islam (page 40) and with the Slavs, pressing against the European frontier in the Balkans (page 32), now became the dominant fact in Byzantine history. What is remarkable is Byzantine resilience. To meet the Arab threat, Asia Minor was reorganised into military districts, or 'themes', manned by a peasant militia (map 2). After two long Arab sieges of Constantinople had been repelled (674–8, 717–8), the new Macedonian dynasty (867–1056) launched a vigorous counter-offensive. By the death of Basil II (976–1025) the frontiers had been pushed back almost to their earlier limits. The Arabs were driven back to Jerusalem (976), and Bulgaria was finally reduced to a group of Christian provinces. Even later Manuel I (1143–80) still planned to recover the former Byzantine territories in Italy. But constant war imposed heavy financial strains, as well as profound and debilitating social change, and in spite of phases of aggressive counter-offensive

and expansion, the frontiers steadily shrank (map 1).

After Basil I, the decisive fact was the appearance of a new foe, the Seljuk Turks (page 40). The crushing Seljuk victory at Manzikert (1071) induced Alexios I (1081–1118) to call on the west for help, thus initiating the sequence of events that led to the First Crusade. In retrospect, it was a disastrous move. The Franks were less concerned to aid Byzantium than to set up their own principalities in Palestine and Asia Minor. The Normans, by now in control of Sicily and Byzantine Italy, were greedy for Byzantine territory in the Morea (Peloponnese) and further east. The Italian cities, Venice to the fore, were striving to engross the oriental trade (page 36). The outcome, after a century of vicissitudes, was the Fourth Crusade (1202–4), the conquest and pillage of Constantinople, the partition of the Byzantine empire, and the establishment in its place of a Latin empire (map 3). But the Latin empire proved short-lived. The Greek-speaking population resented it, and a new dynasty, the Paleologues, restored the Greek empire in 1261.

It was, nevertheless, only a shadow of the former Byzantine empire; and when a new Turkish people, the Ottomans, established itself in Anatolia, and then, outflanking Constantinople, advanced into Byzantium's European territories (page 48), its fate was sealed (map 4). The rest of the story is an epilogue, ending with the fall of Constantinople in 1453. Nevertheless the story of Byzantium is not without greatness and lasting achievements. For centuries it was ahead of the west in government and in the arts of civilisation. It also passed on its culture and its religion to the Balkan peoples and to Russia. 'Two Romes have fallen,' a Russian monk wrote shortly after 1453, 'but the third is standing, and there shall be no fourth.' He was speaking of Moscow. Russia, gradually consolidated under its Varangian rulers and their Muscovite successors (page 44), now emerged as heir to the Byzantine inheritance. This was to be a fact of lasting importance in world history.

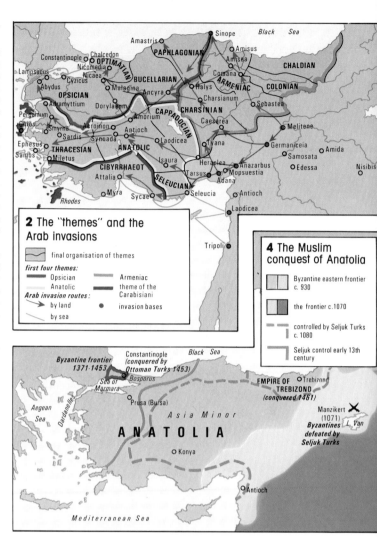

2 The "themes" and the Arab invasions

final organisation of themes

first four themes:

Opsician
Anatolic

Armeniac
theme of the Carabisiani

Arab invasion routes:

→ by land
by sea

● invasion bases

4 The Muslim conquest of Anatolia

Byzantine eastern frontier c. 930

the frontier c.1070

controlled by Seljuk Turks c. 1080

Seljuk control early 13th century

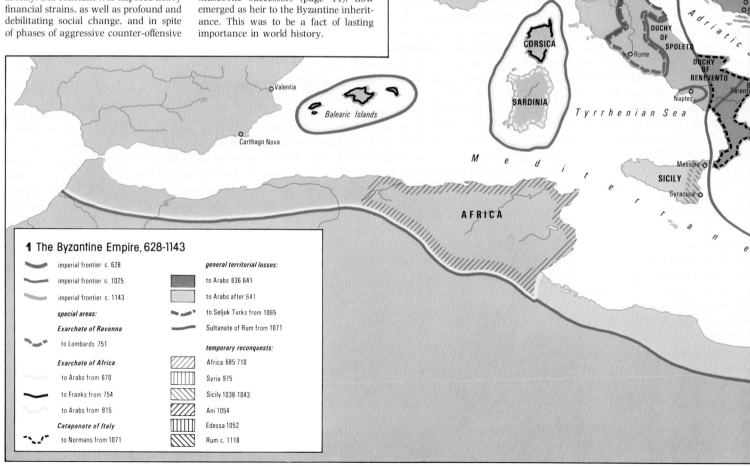

1 The Byzantine Empire, 628-1143

imperial frontier c. 628
imperial frontier c. 1025
imperial frontier c. 1143

special areas:

Exarchate of Ravenna
to Lombards 751

Exarchate of Africa
to Arabs from 670
to Franks from 754
to Arabs from 815

Catapanate of Italy
to Normans from 1071

general territorial losses:

to Arabs 636-641
to Arabs after 641

to Seljuk Turks from 1065
Sultanate of Rum from 1071

temporary reconquests:

Africa 685-710
Syria 975
Sicily 1038-1043
Ani 1054
Edessa 1052
Rum c. 1118

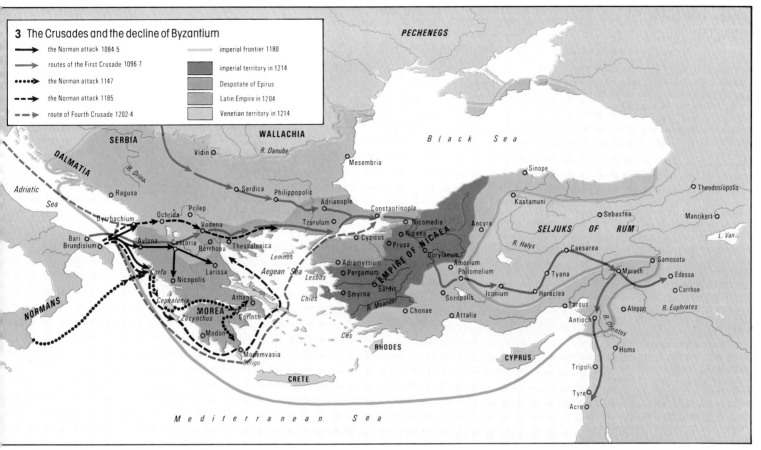

3 The Crusades and the decline of Byzantium

- ➡ the Norman attack 1084-5
- ➡ routes of the First Crusade 1096-7
- ●●●➡ the Norman attack 1147
- – – ➡ the Norman attack 1185
- – – ➡ route of Fourth Crusade 1202-4
- ▬▬ imperial frontier 1180
- ▨ imperial territory in 1214
- ▨ Despotate of Epirus
- ▨ Latin Empire in 1204
- ▨ Venetian territory in 1214

PECHENEGS

Black Sea

SERBIA
WALLACHIA
Adriatic Sea
DALMATIA

Vidin
R. Danube
Mesembria
Theodosiopolis

Ragusa
R. Drina
Serdica
Philippopolis
Adrianople
Constantinople
Sinope
Kastamuni
Sebastea
Manzikert

Dyrrhachium
Ochrida
Prilep
Vodena
Tzurulum
Nicomedia
Ancyra
SELJUKS OF RUM
L. Van

Bari
Brundisium
Avlona
Castoria
Berrhoea
Thessalonica
Cyzicus
Nicaea
Prusa
R. Halys
Caesarea
Samosata

NORMANS
Corfu
Nicopolis
Larissa
Lemnos
Aegean Sea
Negroponte
Adramyttium
Pergamum
EMPIRE OF NICAEA
Dorylaeum
Amorium
Philomelium
Tyana
Marash
Edessa

Cephalonia
Zacynthus
MOREA
Athens
Corinth
Lesbos
Chios
Smyrna
Sardis
R. Meander
Chonae
Sozopolis
Iconium
Heraclea
Tarsus
Antioch
Aleppo
Carrhae
R. Euphrates

Modon
Cos
Attalia
RHODES
CYPRUS
Tripoli
Homs

Monemvasia
Cerigo
CRETE
Tyre
Acre

Mediterranean Sea

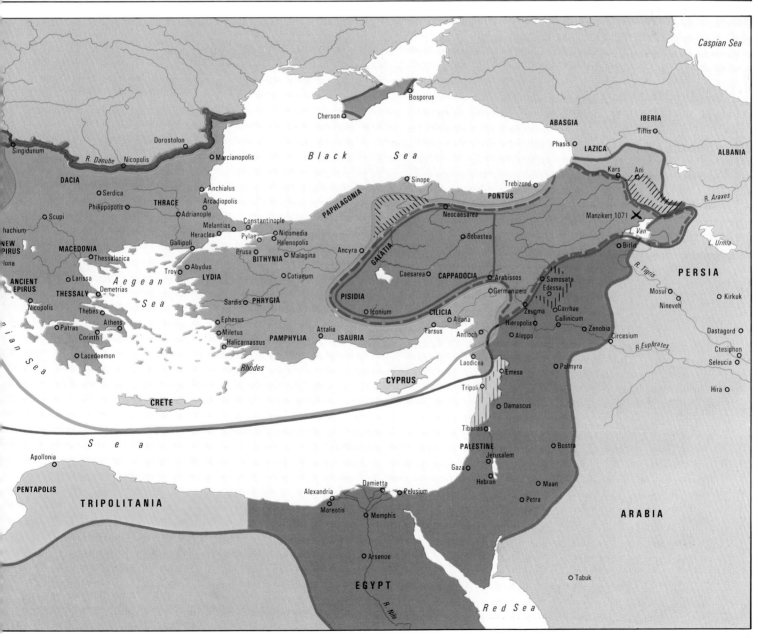

Caspian Sea

Singidunum
R. Danube
Nicopolis
Dorostolon
Marcianopolis
Black Sea
Cherson
Bosporus
ABASGIA
IBERIA
Tiflis

DACIA
Serdica
Anchialus
Arcadiopolis
Sinope
Trebizond
Phasis
LAZICA
ALBANIA
Kars
Ani

hachium
Scupi
Philippopolis
THRACE
Adrianople
Melantias
Constantinople
PAPHLAGONIA
PONTUS
Neocaesarea
Manzikert 1071
R. Araxes

NEW EPIRUS
MACEDONIA
Thessalonica
Heraclea
Gallipoli
Pylae
Nicomedia
Helenopolis
BITHYNIA
Prusa
Malagina
Ancyra
Sebastea
L. Van
Bitlis
L. Urmia

ANCIENT EPIRUS
Larissa
Troy
Abydus
LYDIA
Cotiaeum
GALATIA
Caesarea
CAPPADOCIA
Arabissos
Samosata
Edessa
Mosul
Nineveh
Kirkuk
PERSIA

THESSALY
Demetrias
Aegean Sea
Sardis
PHRYGIA
PISIDIA
Iconium
Germanicea
Zeugma
Carrhae
Callinicum
R. Tigris

Nicopolis
Thebes
Athens
Ephesus
Miletus
Attalia
ISAURIA
CILICIA
Adana
Tarsus
Antioch
Hieropolis
Aleppo
Zenobia
Circesium
R. Euphrates
Dastagord

Patras
Corinth
Lacedaemon
Halicarnassus
PAMPHYLIA
Rhodes
CYPRUS
Laodicea
Emesa
Palmyra
Ctesiphon
Seleucia

ian Sea
Apollonia
Sea
Tripoli
Damascus
Hira

PENTAPOLIS
Tiberias
PALESTINE
Bostra
ARABIA

TRIPOLITANIA
Gaza
Jerusalem
Hebron
Maan

Alexandria
Damietta
Pelusium
Petra

Mareotis
Memphis

Arsinoe
Tabuk

EGYPT
R. Nile
Red Sea

Early Russia
862-1245

Three factors shaped the early history of Russia: the movement eastward of Slav tribal settlers; the impact of the Vikings or Varangians, seafaring raiders and traders from Sweden who entered northern Russia c.850 (page 36) and imposed tribute on the neighbouring Slavs and Finns; the basic geography of the region, particularly the division between the forests of central and northern Russia and the treeless steppes of the south through which successive waves of invaders from Asia poured into Europe. Fierce Pechenegs controlled the fertile steppelands. To avoid them Slav colonists moved into central Russia, where they settled in the river basins, clearing the forests and living by agriculture, hunting, trapping and by the fur trade.

At first the Slavs resisted the Varangians. But in 862 they called in 'Rurik the Viking' to restore order and protect them from Pecheneg raiders. Rurik occupied Novgorod, but the Varangians immediately pushed south to Smolensk and then along the Dnieper to Kiev (882). They thus controlled the trade route from the Baltic to the Black Sea. At the same time they imposed their rule over the Slav tribes on both sides of the river (map 1). It was nevertheless only a loose tributary overlordship, and it was not until the time of Vladimir I (980–1015) that the

tribal regions were welded together into a single state.

The reign of Vladimir's son, Yaroslav I (1019–54) was the high point of Kievan Russia. Converted to Christianity under Vladimir and in close contact with Constantinople, Kiev ranked high among European cities. But the new state had grown too quickly and after 1054 its decline was rapid. Dynastic conflict was incessant, and the administration ineffective. At the same time the destruction of the Khazar empire by Svyatoslav (965) opened the way for a new wave of Asiatic nomads, the Polovtsy, who broke through the defences erected by Vladimir I and sacked Kiev in 1093. The result was a great exodus of peasants northwards to the region between the Oka and the Volga, where many new towns were founded including Vladimir, Suzdal, Rostov, Moscow and Tver. Novgorod-Seversk, and in the west, Galich and Vladimir-Volynsk broke away from Kiev. After 1125 the axis of Russian life shifted north and the state broke up into warring principalities (map 2), among which Vladimir-Suzdal was outstanding.

The final blow to the old order was the Mongol invasions, which fell upon the Volga region before turning south against Kiev which was sacked in 1240 (map 3), while Novgorod was exposed simultaneously to German and Swedish attack. Mongol control was only indirect, but its results were far-reaching. Kievan Russia, already debilitated, disappeared for ever, and the way was open for the rise of Moscow.

1 Varangian Russia, 862-1054

- Varangian territory c.980
- *Ulichi* — East Slav tribes
- **KHAZARS** — Finno-Ugrian and Asiatic peoples
- Varangian (Viking) trade routes
- Varangian raids on Constantinople 907, 944
- Svyatoslav's campaigns 964-71
- Pecheneg raids

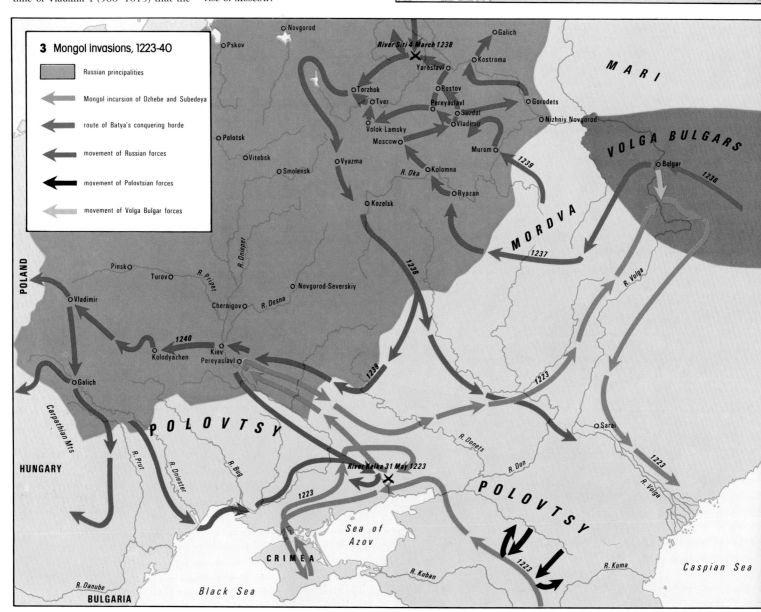

3 Mongol invasions, 1223-40

- Russian principalities
- Mongol incursion of Dzhebe and Subedeya
- route of Batya's conquering horde
- movement of Russian forces
- movement of Polovtsian forces
- movement of Volga Bulgar forces

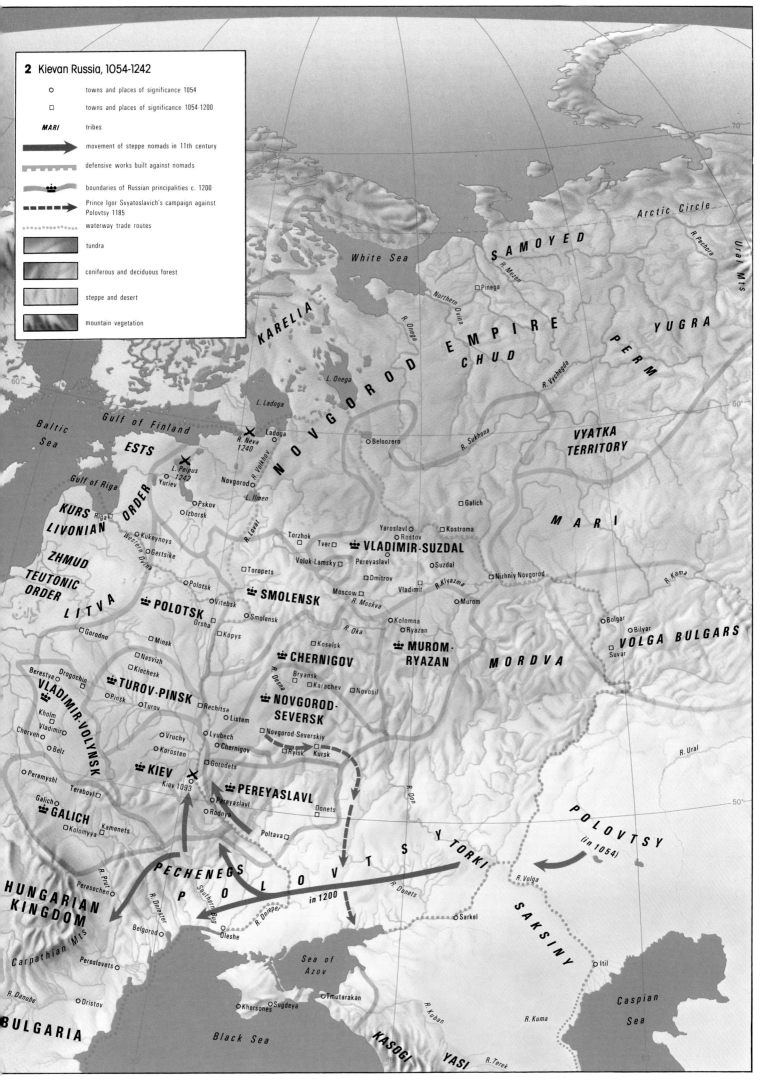

2 Kievan Russia, 1054–1242

○   towns and places of significance 1054

□   towns and places of significance 1054-1200

MARI   tribes

➤   movement of steppe nomads in 11th century

▬   defensive works built against nomads

♔   boundaries of Russian principalities c. 1200

┅➤   Prince Igor Svyatoslavich's campaign against Polovtsy 1185

⋯⋯   waterway trade routes

    tundra

    coniferous and deciduous forest

    steppe and desert

    mountain vegetation

Arctic Circle

White Sea

SAMOYED

R. Mezen

R. Pechora

Ural Mts

○ Pinega

Northern Dvina

YUGRA

KARELIA

R. Onega

N O V G O R O D   E M P I R E

CHUD

R. Vychegda

PERM

L. Onega

L. Ladoga

Gulf of Finland

Baltic Sea

ESTS

✕ Ladoga

R. Neva 1240

R. Volkhov

□ Beloozero

R. Sukhona

VYATKA TERRITORY

60°

60°

L. Peipus 1242 ✕

○ Yuriev

Novgorod ○

L. Ilmen

□ Galich

M A R I

Gulf of Riga

KURS

Riga ○

LIVONIAN ORDER

○ Kukeynos

○ Gertsike

R. Lovat

□ Toropets

Torzhok □

Tver □

Yaroslavl □

○ Rostov

□ Kostroma

Western Dvina

○ Pskov

○ Izborsk

ZHMUD

TEUTONIC ORDER

LITVA

□ Volok-Lamsky

Pereyaslavl □

♔ **VLADIMIR-SUZDAL**

□ Suzdal

□ Nizhniy Novgorod

R. Kama

♔ **POLOTSK**

□ Polotsk

Vitebsk ○

○ Dmitrov

Vladimir □

R. Klyazma

□ Gorodno

Minsk □

Orsha ○

Smolensk □

□ Kopys

♔ **SMOLENSK**

Moscow □

R. Moskva

□ Murom

VOLGA BULGARS

□ Bolgar

Bilyar □

○ Nesvizh

○ Klechesk

R. Oka

□ Kolomna

○ Ryazan

Suvar □

Berestye ○

Drogochin ○

♔ **TUROV-PINSK**

○ Pinsk

□ Koselsk

♔ **MUROM-RYAZAN**

M O R D V A

○ Turov

□ Rechitsa

♔ **CHERNIGOV**

R. Desna

Bryansk □

○ Karachev

□ Novosil

VLADIMIR-VOLYNSK

♔ □ Listem

♔ **NOVGOROD-SEVERSK**

○ Kholm

○ Vladimir

○ Cherven

○ Belz

○ Vruchy

Lyubech ○

□ Novgorod-Severskiy

□ Chernigov

○ Korosten

□ Rylsk

Kursk □

○ Peremyshl

Terebovl ○

♔ **KIEV**

□ Gorodets

✕ Kiev 1093

♔ **PEREYASLAVL**

○ Galich

♔ **GALICH**

Kolomyya □

Kamenets □

○ Pereyaslavl

○ Rodnya

R. Don

R. Ural

50°

50°

R. Prut

Peresechen ○

P E C H E N E G S

Poltava □

Donets

P O L O V T S Y   *T O R K I*

POLOVTSY (in 1054)

R. Volga

HUNGARIAN KINGDOM

Belgorod ○

R. Dniester

Southern Bug

P O L O V T S Y

in 1200

R. Dnieper

R. Donets

○ Sarkel

SAKSINY

Oleshe ○

Carpathian Mts

Pereslavets ○

Sea of Azov

○ Itil

BULGARIA

R. Danube

○ Dristov

○ Khersones

○ Sugdeya

Tmutarakan ○

KASOGI

R. Kuban

YASI

R. Kuma

Caspian Sea

Black Sea

R. Terek

45

The Mongol Empire, 1206-1696

The Mongols, a primitive nomadic people from the depths of Asia, had tremendous influence on the course of world history. Few in number, but augmented by Turcoman auxiliaries, they threw themselves against the old centres of civilisation in east and west (map 1). After overrunning the Ch'in empire in north China between 1211 and 1234, they defeated the Sung army and ruled over the whole of China from 1280 to 1367 (page 50). They even launched seaborne expeditions against Java and Japan, though neither was successful. In the west their first victim was the Muslim empire of Khwarizm (1220), after which they turned against the Abbasid caliphate, sacking Baghdad in 1258. But the decisive Mameluke victory at Ain Jalut (1260) halted their advance in this direction. Meanwhile, they had thrown themselves against Christian Europe, overrunning the northern Russian principalities in 1237–8 and sacking Kiev in 1240 (page 44), before advancing into Hungary and Poland and destroying a German-Polish army at Legnica in 1241 (map 2).

The architect of these amazing victories was a certain Temujin, known to history as Genghis Khan, son of a Mongol chief, who united the different Mongol tribes under his leadership (1206) and subdued other neighbouring, mainly Turcoman tribes, before turning against China in 1211. Genghis died in 1227, but his wars of conquest were continued by his sons and grandsons, among whom Ogedei, elected Great Khan in 1229, and Möngke, who succeeded in 1251, were outstanding. But the vast empire lacked coherence and stability, and the Mongols failed to develop appropriate institutions. Genghis himself divided his empire among his four sons, like earlier Frankish rulers in the west (page 34), and with similar results. Already on the death of Ogedei (1241), Genghis' grandson Batu, commander-in-chief in the west, withdrew his army from Poland to the base on the lower Volga, in order to take part in the choice of a successor. It never returned and western Europe was spared, though Russia remained a Mongol tributary for over two centuries. Finally, on the death of Möngke (1259), the brittle unity dissolved. Kublai (d. 1294) was elected Great Khan, but instead of a general overlordship, his authority was confined to the east, and the western khanates (Chagatai, Il-Khan and the Golden Horde) went their own way (map 3). By the sixteenth century only the eastern khanate survived: in Persia the Ilkhanids were displaced by a local Turcoman dynasty in 1353, and later the successors of the Golden Horde, which had broken up into a number of smaller khanates at the time of Tamerlane the Great, were mopped up by a resurgent Russia.

It was, paradoxically, Timur, or Tamerlane (1336–1405), traditionally the last great Mongol conqueror (though he was in fact a Turcoman from Transoxiana), whose victorious career initiated the decline. Timur's vast empire (map 4) fell apart rapidly after his death while leading an expedition against China; but in the course of his conquests he destroyed the Chagatai khanate, which ceased to exist in 1405, and dislocated the

Golden Horde. Henceforward the Mongols were under attack from all sides, increasingly at a disadvantage as the introduction of firearms weighed the balance on their adversaries' side. In the west Russia absorbed the former territories of the Golden Horde (page 84). In the east, the Mongols threw back a major Chinese assault in 1449 (page 50) and resumed their offensive under Altan Khan (1507–82); but in the end Mongolia itself was brought under Chinese dominion in 1696 by the new Ch'ing dynasty (page 106). Nevertheless the Mongol impact had lasting results. All the older civilisations were affected; faced by the Mongol challenge, their history took a new course.

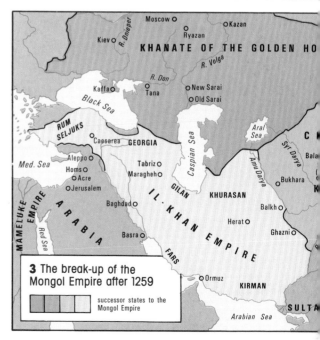

1 The Mongol Empire before 1259

- the Mongol Empire before 1259
- → campaigns under Genghis Khan
- → campaigns of his successors
- |||||| incursions and loose Mongol control
- *OIROTS* Mongol tribes around 1220

2 The Mongol invasion of Europe, 1237-42

3 The break-up of the Mongol Empire after 1259

- successor states to the Mongol Empire

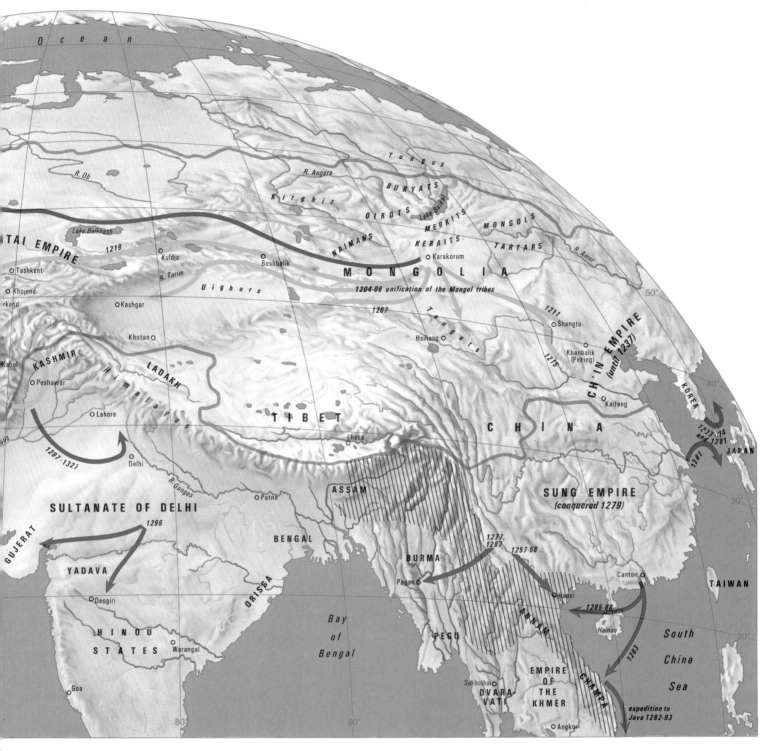

Ocean

R. Ob

TAI EMPIRE 1219
Tashkent
Khojend
Kuldja
R. Tarim
Beshbalik
Kashgar
Khotan

R. Angara

Kirghiz

OIROTS
NAIMANS
MERKITS
KERAITS

Lake Baikal

BURYATS

Tungus

MONGOLS
TARTARS
R. Amur

Karakorum

MONGOLIA

1204-06 unification of the Mongol tribes

1207

Tanguts

Hsiliang

1211

Shangtu

1215

CH'IN EMPIRE
(until 1237)

Khanbalik
(Peking)

Kaifeng

KOREA

1273-74
and 1281

1281

JAPAN

50°

40°

30°

Kabul
KASHMIR
Peshawar
Lahore

LADAKH

Himalayas

1297-1327

Delhi

R. Ganges

TIBET

Lhasa

CHINA

SUNG EMPIRE
(conquered 1279)

SULTANATE OF DELHI

1296

GUJERAT

YADAVA

Deogiri

HINDU
STATES

Warangal

Goa

Patna

BENGAL

ASSAM

ORISSA

Bay
of
Bengal

BURMA

Pagan

PEGU

Sukhothai

DVARA-
VATI

EMPIRE
OF
THE
KHMER

Angkor

1277,
1287

1257-58

Hanoi

ANNAM

CHAMPA

1285-86

Haiman

1283

Canton

TAIWAN

South
China
Sea

expedition to
Java 1292-93

80°

90°

20°

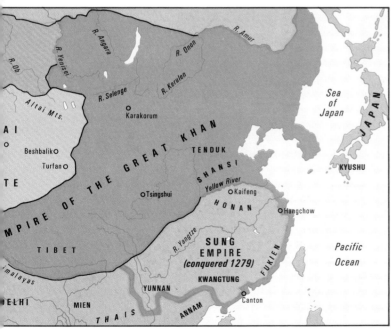

R. Ob
R. Yenisei
Altai Mts.
R. Angara
R. Selenge
R. Onon
R. Kerulen
R. Amur

Beshbalik
Turfan

Karakorum

TENDUK

SHANSI
Tsingshui
Yellow River
Kaifeng
HONAN

EMPIRE OF THE GREAT KHAN

Sea
of
Japan

JAPAN

KYUSHU

TIBET

R. Yangtze

Hangchow

SUNG
EMPIRE
(conquered 1279)

FUKIEN

Pacific
Ocean

DELHI

MIEN

THAIS

YUNNAN

KWANGTUNG

ANNAM

Canton

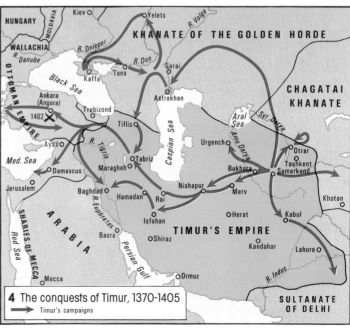

HUNGARY
WALLACHIA
MOLDAVIA

Kiev

R. Dnieper
R. Danube

Yelets

R. Volga

KHANATE OF THE GOLDEN HORDE

R. Don

Kaffa
Tana

Sarai

Astrakhan

Black
Sea

OTTOMAN EMPIRE

Ankara
(Angora)

1402

Trebizond

Ayas
Med. Sea

Tiflis

Caspian
Sea

Aral
Sea

Syr Darya

CHAGATAI
KHANATE

Urgench

Amu Darya

Otrar

Tashkent
Samarkand

Tabriz

Maragheh

Bukhara

Merv

Nishapur

Khotan

Damascus

Jerusalem

Baghdad

Hamadan

Rai

Isfahan

Herat

Kabul

Kandahar

Lahore

ARABIA

Basra

R. Euphrates

R. Tigris

Shiraz

TIMUR'S EMPIRE

SHARIFS OF MECCA

Red Sea

Mecca

Persian Gulf

Ormuz

R. Indus

SULTANATE
OF DELHI

4 The conquests of Timur, 1370-1405

→ Timur's campaigns

47

The Muslim resurgence
1301-1639

The revival of Islam after 1300 and the great wave of Muslim expansion that followed, dominated the next four centuries, far more so than European expansion, which had only marginal effects before 1700. After 1354 the Christian west stood on the defensive, while the Turks conquered the whole of Europe east of the Adriatic and south of the Danube. The progress of Islam in the east was equally remarkable. By 1500 northern India was under Muslim rule, and most of the south after 1565 when the last surviving Hindu state, Vijay-anagar, succumbed. It prevailed also in the oases of central Asia, in the outlying provinces of Ming China, and was making rapid headway in Java.

This amazing revival was the more remarkable because in 1258, when the Mongols sacked Baghdad and overthrew the caliphate (page 46), the Muslim world was in disarray. The Seljuk sultanate (page 40) had broken up after half a century, and only the Mamelukes of Egypt and Syria maintained any sort of political stability. Two factors transformed the situation. One was the revitalisation of Islam itself under the impact of Sufi mysticism. The other was the infiltration, with or in the wake of the Mongols, of Turkic peoples from central Asia, who, after conversion and assimilation, became the spearhead of Muslim advance. It was they who, in 1206, set up the Delhi Sultanate, the leading Indian state until the appearance in 1526 of Babur, another warrior from Inner Asia. In the west Turkish warriors settled around 1265 in the Anatolian borderlands, and here in 1301 their leader, Osman, founded a state which became the core of the future Ottoman empire (map 1). By 1354 the Turks had crossed the Dardanelles to Gallipoli, and their victory at Kosovo (1389) and repulse of a Christian counter-offensive at Nicopolis (1396) left them masters of the Balkans. Only the invasion of Timur (page 46) and his destruction of the Turkish army at Ankara (1402) gave hard-pressed Byzantium respite. But the renewal of expansion under Murad II (1421–51) and Mehemmed II (1451–81) sealed its fate. In 1453 Constantinople fell, and Mehemmed went on to extend control over Moldavia, the Crimea and Trebizond, turning the Black Sea into an Ottoman lake.

By the time that Suleiman the Magnificent (1520–66) succeeded to the throne, the Ottoman empire was one of the world's leading powers, comparable with Ming China or Charles V's empire in the west. But now two other empires arose to share pre-eminence in the Muslim world. The one was the Mughal empire, founded by Babur in 1526, but only consolidated by his grandson, Akbar (1556–1605). The other was Persia, which had been in a state of chaos ever since it was overrun by Timur. Here, in 1500, the leader of a fanatical Shi'a sect, Ismail Safavi, seized Tabriz, crowned himself shah as Ismail I (1500–24), and quickly reunited the country. Safavid Persia reached its peak under Abbas I (1587–1629), by which time the three Muslim empires controlled a wide belt of territory from the frontiers of Austria and Morocco to the borders of China, the foothills of the Himalayas and the Bay of Bengal (map 2). But their divisions and rivalries, particularly the clash between Sunnite Turkey and Shi'ite Persia, drove a wedge into the Muslim world, comparable to the conflict between Catholics and Protestants in western Europe. Shi'ism had originated centuries earlier over the question of the true succession to the Prophet Mohammed; but wider issues, religious and political, were involved. In Persia a resurgent nationalism certainly played a part. The Safavids were the first native Persian dynasty since Sasanian times, and Ismail I's decision to make Shi'ism the Persian state religion was a challenge to the orthodox Turkish sultan. The Ottoman reaction was swift. In 1514 Ismail's armies were defeated near Tabriz. In 1516, to prevent the heresy from spreading, Syria and Egypt were taken over. These successes enabled Suleiman to resume the Ottoman advance in Europe. After the battle of Mohács (1526) Hungary was overrun and Vienna was besieged (1529). But Persia remained a thorn in the Ottoman side. The long wars against the Safavids (1534–35, 1554–55, 1577–90, 1603–19) were not the only reason for the Muslim decline which became apparent after 1560, but they certainly hastened it. This was a great age of Islamic art and architecture, particularly in Persia and India. But in a changing world Islam remained static. All three Muslim empires were essentially land-based; but now hegemony was passing to the sea, and to the peoples on the fringe – the Dutch, the French, the English – who knew how to master and exploit it.

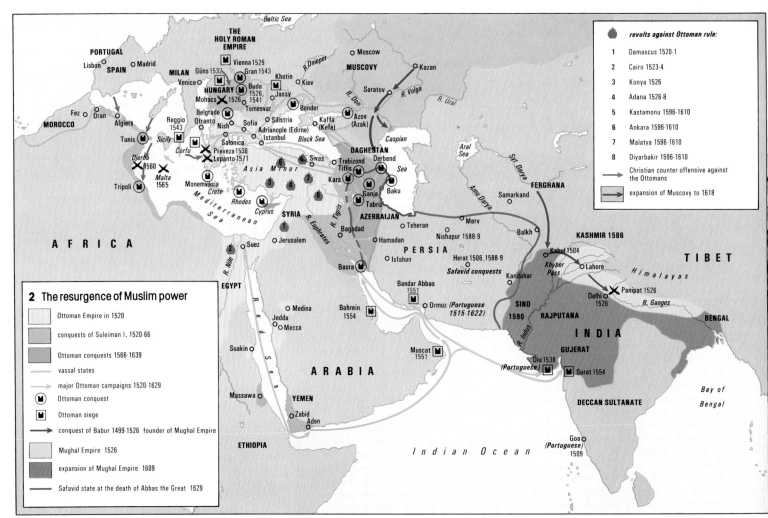

2 The resurgence of Muslim power

- Ottoman Empire in 1520
- conquests of Suleiman I, 1520-66
- Ottoman conquests 1566-1639
- vassal states
- major Ottoman campaigns 1520-1629
- Ottoman conquest
- Ottoman siege
- conquest of Babur 1499-1526 founder of Mughal Empire
- Mughal Empire 1526
- expansion of Mughal Empire 1609
- Safavid state at the death of Abbas the Great 1629

revolts against Ottoman rule:

1. Damascus 1520-1
2. Cairo 1523-4
3. Konya 1526
4. Adana 1526-8
5. Kastamonu 1596-1610
6. Ankara 1596-1610
7. Malatya 1596-1610
8. Diyarbakir 1596-1610

- Christian counter-offensive against the Ottomans
- expansion of Muscovy to 1618

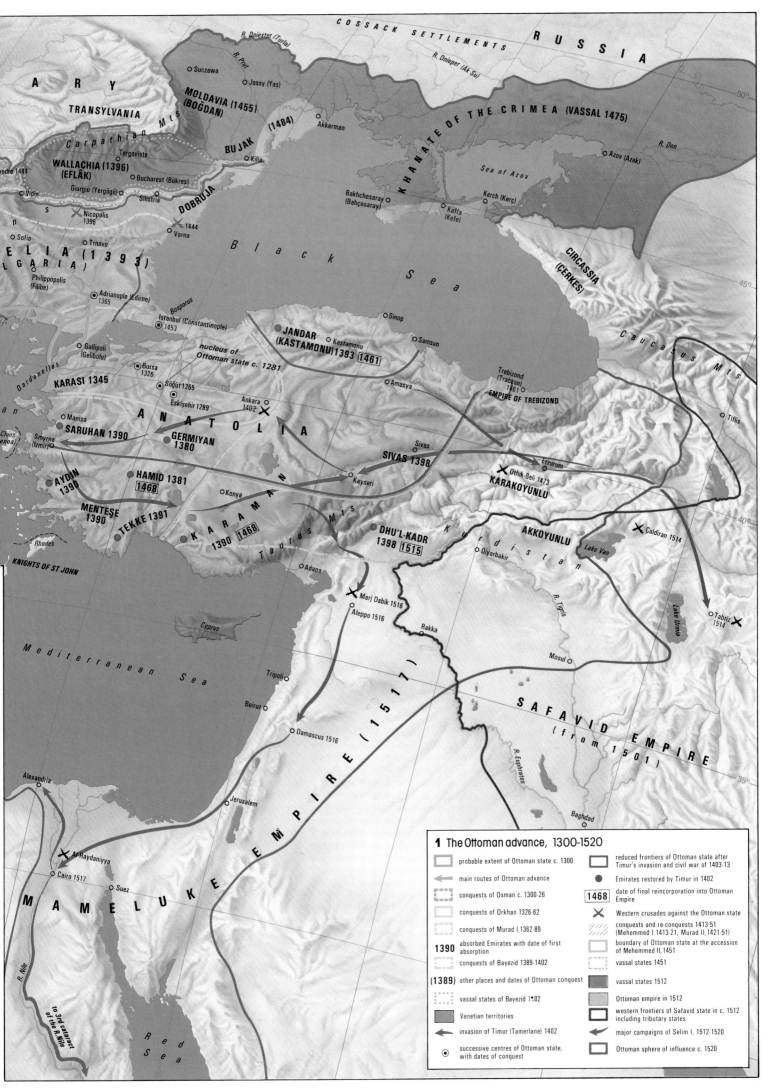

R U S S I A

COSSACK SETTLEMENTS

R. Dniester (Turla)

o Suczawa

R. Prut

o Jassy (Yaş)

MOLDAVIA (1455)
(BOĞDAN)

(1484)

o Akkerman

KHANATE OF THE CRIMEA (VASSAL 1475)

R. Dnieper (Ak Su)

R. Don

o Azov (Azak)

A R Y

TRANSYLVANIA

Carpathian Mts

Tergoviste o

WALLACHIA (1396)
(EFLÂK)

o Bucharest (Bükreş)

o Giurgiu (Yergöğü)

o Vidin

S

o Nicopolis 1396

BUJAK

o Kilia

DOBRUJA

Silistria

Sea of Azov

Bakhchesaray (Bahçesaray) o

Kerch (Kerç) o

o Kaffa (Kefe)

CIRCASSIA
(ÇERKES)

endre 1444

o 1444

Varna

ELIA (1393)
LGARIA)

o Sofia

o Trnovo

o Philippopolis (Filibe)

◉ Adrianople (Edirne) 1365

B l a c k   S e a

o Sinop

o Samsun

C a u c a s u s   M t s

Bosporus

Istanbul (Constantinople) 1453

Bursa 1326

JANDAR
(KASTAMONU) 1393 [1461]

Kastamonu

nucleus of Ottoman state c. 1281

o Amasya

o Trebizond (Trabzon) 1461

EMPIRE OF TREBIZOND

o Tiflis

o Gallipoli (Gelibolu)

KARASI 1345

Söğüt 1265

Eskişehir 1289

Ankara 1402 ✕

A N A T O L I A

o Manisa

SARUHAN 1390

Smyrna (Izmir) o

GERMIYAN 1380

o Sivas

SIVAS 1398

o Erzurum

Otluk-Beli 1473 ✕

KARAKOYUNLU

o Çaldıran 1514 ✕

Chios enoa) o

AYDIN 1390

HAMID 1381 [1468]

o Kayseri

o Konya

K A R A M A N

AKKOYUNLU

Lake Van

MENTEŞE 1390

TEKKE 1391

1390 [1468]

Taurus Mts

DHU'L-KADR 1398 [1515]

o Diyarbakir

K u r d i s t a n

o Tabriz 1514 ✕

Lake Urmia

o Rhodes

KNIGHTS OF ST JOHN

o Adana

✕ Marj Dabik 1516

Aleppo 1516 o

o Rakka

R. Tigris

o Mosul

o Cyprus

M e d i t e r r a n e a n   S e a

o Tripoli

o Beirut

S A F A V I D   E M P I R E
(f r o m   1 5 0 1)

M A M E L U K E   E M P I R E   (1 5 1 7)

o Damascus 1516

o Alexandria

✕ Al-Raydaniyya

o Cairo 1517

o Suez

o Jerusalem

o Baghdad

R. Euphrates

R. Nile

R e d   S e a

to 3rd cataract of the R. Nile

1 The Ottoman advance, 1300-1520

▭ probable extent of Ottoman state c. 1300	▭ reduced frontiers of Ottoman state after Timur's invasion and civil war of 1403-13
← main routes of Ottoman advance	● Emirates restored by Timur in 1402
▭ conquests of Osman c. 1300-26	[1468] date of final reincorporation into Ottoman Empire
▭ conquests of Orkhan 1326-62	✕ Western crusades against the Ottoman state
▭ conquests of Murad I, 1362-89	⟋⟋ conquests and re-conquests 1413-51 (Mehemmed I.1413-21, Murad II, 1421-51)
1390 absorbed Emirates with date of first absorption	▭ boundary of Ottoman state at the accession of Mehemmed II, 1451
▭ conquests of Bayezid 1389-1402	▭ vassal states 1451
(1389) other places and dates of Ottoman conquest	▓ vassal states 1512
▭ vassal states of Bayezid 1402	▓ Ottoman empire in 1512
▓ Venetian territories	▭ western frontiers of Safavid state in c. 1512 including tributary states
← invasion of Timur (Tamerlane) 1402	◄ major campaigns of Selim I, 1512-1520
◉ successive centres of Ottoman state, with dates of conquest	▭ Ottoman sphere of influence c. 1520

49

China and its neighbours
618-1644

The recovery of China from the barbarian invasions of the fourth and fifth centuries (page 32) was the work of the Sui dynasty (581–617). But it was the T'ang (618–907) who ushered in one of the great ages of Chinese history. Under the T'ang and their successors, the Sung (960–1279), China attained a level of prosperity, social stability and civilisation far ahead of contemporary Europe; and it was only another wave of invasion from inner Asia, this time the Mongols (page 46), that brought this era of wellbeing to a temporary halt. During the period of Mongol domination (1280–1368) much of the land was devastated, particularly in the north, and the population, which in 1280 probably topped 100 million, was reduced by 1393 to 60 million. The Ming dynasty (1368–1644) reversed these setbacks and put China back on the course charted by its T'ang predecessors.

T'ang China (map 1) was a centralised empire with a uniform administrative organisation of prefectures, in which the old ruling aristocracy was replaced by officials recruited by an examination system which lasted into the twentieth century. A massive movement of population into the fertile Yangtze valley and southern China produced large agricultural surpluses which stimulated trade and urban development. The T'ang also embarked on an ambitious programme of external expansion which carried them in the north-west to the Tarim Basin before they were halted by the Arabs at the Talas river in 751. By 649, the end of the reign of T'ai-tsung, 88 Asiatic peoples recognised Chinese overlordship. But the widespread military expeditions over-extended the empire's resources, many of the gains proved only temporary, and after 1127 even north China was lost and only recovered after the fall of the Mongol dynasty in 1386. Their successors, the Ming, also engaged in an active foreign policy, particularly against the Mongols in the north (map 4), but these ventures proved too costly and sparked off a series of rebellions which, coupled with external pressures from the Manchus in Liaotung and Japanese raiders, toppled the dynasty.

Military and political reverses did not impede the expansion of Chinese culture and political institutions to all her neighbouring states. Those most directly affected were Korea, under Chinese rule from 668 to 676 and a vassal state after 1392, Japan and South-East Asia, though in the latter region, where they came into contact with Indian and (from about AD 1300) Islamic influences, they were largely confined to north Vietnam. In South-East Asia the small temple states of the ninth to twelfth centuries (Prambanan, Angkor, Pagan), established under Hindu and Buddhist influence, gave way after the thirteenth century to new political centres (Ava, Pegu, Phnom Penh), while in Vietnam, where Chinese attempts at reconquest failed, a new kingdom of Dai Viet arose. But behind the fluctuating political fortunes the outstanding fact was the formative influence of Hinduism, Buddhism and Confucianism; their assimilation defined the distinctive character of South-East Asian civilisation (map 2).

In Japan Chinese influence was more direct. As early as AD 645 the whole administration had been re-modelled on the pattern of T'ang China. The two capitals, Nara (710) and Kyoto (794), were copied from the T'ang capital of Changan, and Buddhism was introduced from China. But after 1192 the bureaucratic state was displaced by a feudalised society, until finally, between 1467 and 1590, the country broke up into a series of warring Daimyo clans (map 3). It was the work of Oda Nobunaga (1534–82) and Hideyoshi Toyotomi (1535–98) to bring the anarchy under control, and prepare the way for the Tokugawa shogunate which gave Japan 250 years of internal peace and prosperity until, in the middle of the nineteenth century the western powers forced Japan into the modern world (page 126).

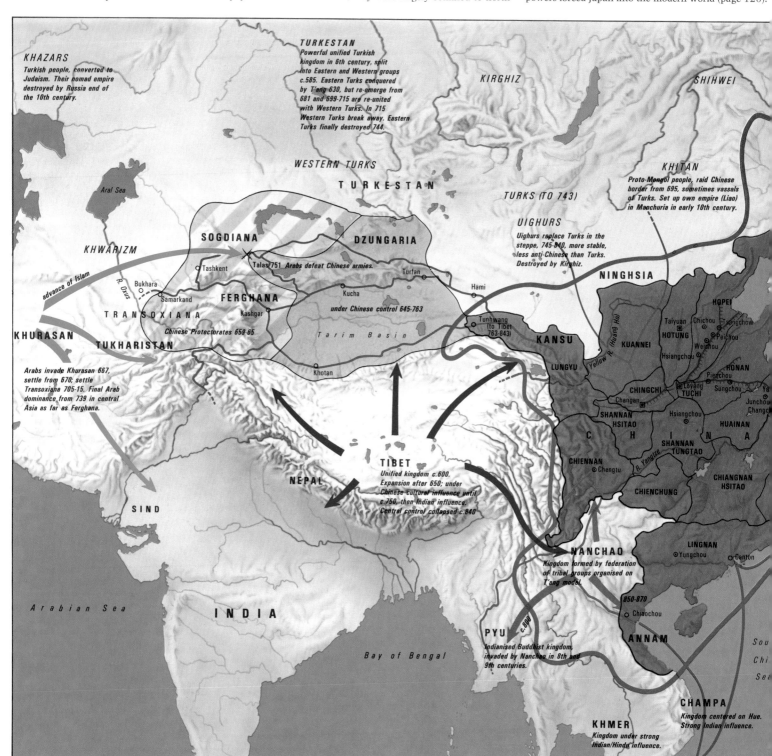

3 Civil war in Japan 1467-1590

spheres of influence of the most powerful Daimyo clans

——— boundaries of Daimyo domains

Uesugi
Hojo
Takeda
Imagawa
Oda
Kyoto
Nara
Mori
Segabe
Otomo
Shimazu

Sea of Japan

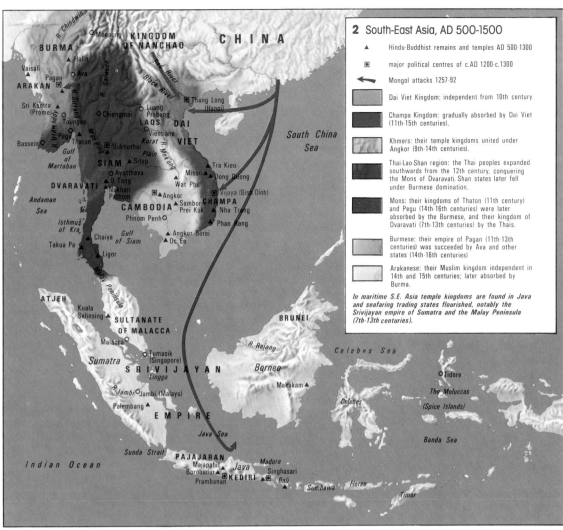

2 South-East Asia, AD 500-1500

▲ Hindu-Buddhist remains and temples AD 500-1300

⊞ major political centres of c.AD 1200-c.1300

← Mongol attacks 1257-92

▢ Dai Viet Kingdom: independent from 10th century

▢ Champa Kingdom: gradually absorbed by Dai Viet (11th-15th centuries)

▢ Khmers: their temple kingdoms united under Angkor (9th-14th centuries).

▢ Thai-Lao-Shan region: the Thai peoples expanded southwards from the 12th century, conquering the Mons of Dvaravati. Shan states later fell under Burmese domination.

▢ Mons: their kingdoms of Thaton (11th century) and Pegu (14th-16th centuries) were later absorbed by the Burmese, and their kingdom of Dvaravati (7th-13th centuries) by the Thais.

▢ Burmese: their empire of Pagan (11th-13th centuries) was succeeded by Ava and other states (14th-16th centuries)

▢ Arakanese: their Muslim kingdom independent in 14th and 15th centuries; later absorbed by Burma.

In maritime S.E. Asia temple kingdoms are found in Java and seafaring trading states flourished, notably the Srivijayan empire of Sumatra and the Malay Peninsula (7th-13th centuries).

C H I N A

KINGDOM OF NANCHAO

BURMA
Moaung
Halin
Vaisali
Pagan
Ava
Sri Ksetra (Prome)
ARAKAN
Toungoo
Chiengmai
Bassein
Pegu
Thaton
Sukhothai
Gulf of Martaban
SIAM
DVARAVATI
Ayutthaya
U Tong
Nakhon Pathom
Andaman Sea
ATJEH
Kuala Selinsing
Chaiya
Takua Pa
Ligor
Isthmus of Kra
Gulf of Siam
Malay Peninsula
Kuala
Malacca
SULTANATE OF MALACCA
Sumatra
Tumasik (Singapore)
Lingga
R. Jambi
Jambi (Malayu)
Palembang
S R I V I J A Y A N
E M P I R E
Sunda Strait
Java Sea
PAJAJARAN
Majapahit
Borobudur
Prambanan
Java
KEDIRI
Singhasari
Madura
Bali
Sumbawa
Flores
Timor

Luang Prabang
LAOS
Vientiane
Korat
DAI VIET
Thang Long (Hanoi)
Tra Kieu
Misoi
Dong Duong
Wat Phu
Vijaya (Binh Dinh)
Angkor
Sambor
CHAMPA
Prei Kuk
Nha Trang
Phnom Penh
Angkor Borei
Oc Eo
Phan Rang
CAMBODIA
R. Chindwin
R. Salween
Black River
Red River
R. Sittang
R. Irrawaddy
R. Mekong
Mekong Plain
Sitep
South China Sea
BRUNEI
R. Rajang
Makakam
Celebes Sea
Borneo
Celebes
Tidore
The Moluccas (Spice Islands)
Banda Sea
Indian Ocean

Still occupied by Ainu aboriginal peoples.

...AE (POHAI) kingdom on the Chinese ... set up by remnants of Korean ... of Koguryo. Independent ... Destroyed by Khitan 934.

Sea of Japan

...ILLA

JAPAN Independent politically: increasing Chinese cultural influence from 6th century. In 7th century a strong centralised kingdom based on Chinese institutions.

Before 660 there were three states in Korea - Koguryo, Paekche and Silla. The T'ang destroyed Paekche in 660, Koguryo in 668 and occupied N. Korea. Strong resistance led to Chinese withdrawal in 676, leaving all Korea under Silla, a powerful, centralised state on Chinese lines.

The T'ang Empire of China

▢ under permanent T'ang civil administration

▢ temporary Chinese occupation in 7th century

▢ under Chinese military control (protectorate)

▢ zone of Chinese cultural dominance

——— roads and trade routes

⊥⊥⊥⊥ canals

⊞ metropolitan prefectures

⊙ principal prefectures

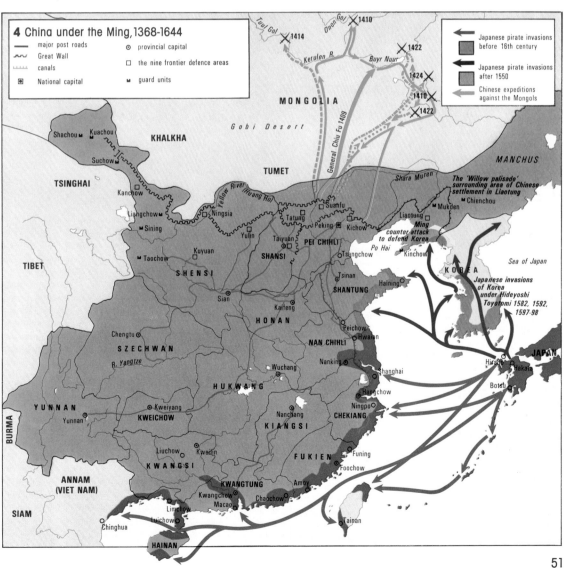

4 China under the Ming, 1368-1644

——— major post roads

〰 Great Wall

⊥⊥⊥ canals

⊡ National capital

⊙ provincial capital

□ the nine frontier defence areas

◼ guard units

← Japanese pirate invasions before 16th century

← Japanese pirate invasions after 1550

← Chinese expeditions against the Mongols

Tuul Gol
Onon Gol
×1410
×1414
Kerulen R.
Buyr Nuur
×1422
×1424
×1410
×1422
General Chiu Fu 1409
MONGOLIA
Gobi Desert
KHALKHA
Shachou
Kuachou
Suchow
TSINGHAI
Kanchow
Liangchow
Ningsia
Sining
TUMET
Shara Muren
MANCHUS
The 'Willow palisade' surrounding area of Chinese settlement in Liaotung
Mukden
Chienchou
Liaotung
Suanfu
Tatung
Yulin
Kichow
Peking
Ming counter-attack to defend Korea
KOREA
Sea of Japan
Japanese invasions of Korea under Hideyoshi Toyotomi 1582, 1592, 1597-98
TIBET
Kuyuan
Taochow
SHENSI
Taiyuan
SHANSI
PEI CHIHLI
Tsangchow
Po Hai
Kinchow
Sian
Tsinan
SHANTUNG
Haining
Kaifeng
HONAN
Peichow
Hwaian
NAN CHIHLI
Chengtu
SZECHWAN
R. Yangtze
Wuchang
Nanking
Shanghai
HUKWANG
Kweiyang
KWEICHOW
Nanchang
Hangchow
Ningpo
CHEKIANG
Hiraq...
JAPAN
Hakata
Botsh...
BURMA
YUNNAN
Yunnan
KIANGSI
Liuchow
Kwedin
KWANGSI
Funing
FUKIEN
Foochow
Amoy
SIAM
ANNAM (VIET NAM)
Kwangchow
KWANGTUNG
Macao
Chaochow
Limchow
Luichow
Tainan
Chinghua
HAINAN
Yellow River (Huang Ho)

Northern and Western Europe, 930-1314

Two features marked the period following the Viking and Magyar invasions in northern and western Europe: the emergence of settled states and the spread of Christianity. The two went hand in hand. Both in Scandinavia and in the Slavonic east the Christian church, introduced in Denmark by Harold Bluetooth in 965, in Norway by Olaf Tryggveson (995–1000), in Bohemia by Boleslav II (967–99), and in Poland by Miesko I (960–92), contributed substantially to political cohesion. The rise of powerful kingdoms in Poland and Denmark was also in part a response to German pressure. In Poland (map 1) the Piast dynasty united the tribes of Great (or northern) Poland. Boleslav Chrobry (992–1025) not only added Little Poland, Silesia and Lausitz but also temporarily Bohemia and Moravia. In Denmark Harold Bluetooth (940–86) defended Slesvig from German attack, strengthening and extending the fortified Danevirke (map 3). In Norway and Sweden development was hampered by formidable geographical obstacles (map 5). Under Sweyn I, who also became king of England in 1013, both countries were under Danish control; and Sweyn's son Canute the Great (1014–35) ruled a great but short-lived Anglo-Scandinavian empire (map 4). Following an interlude under Edward the Confessor (1042–66) England passed under Norman rule (page 36). Norway achieved independence and was united under Magnus the Good (1033–47). Sweden (except for the southern provinces which remained under Danish rule) was welded together by the kings of Uppland, and Denmark itself settled down within its frontiers after the death of Sweyn II (1047–74).

Nevertheless all countries were plagued by dynastic conflict and aristocratic resistance. In Poland Boleslav Chrobry's ambitious foreign policy provoked a sharp reaction after his death. In England William the Conqueror was faced by baronial unrest as early as 1074. But it was France that suffered most from feudal disruption. The Capetian kings, who displaced the Carolingians in 987, were confined to the Ile de France, and even here royal authority was insecure until the reign of Louis VI (1108–37). Even then the Capetians lagged behind the feudal princes. The continental possessions of Henry II of England (the so-called Angevin Empire) far outmatched the French royal domain (map 2). When Philip Augustus (1180–1223) conquered Normandy (1204) and the Angevin Empire collapsed, English rule was confined to Gascony, and the Capetians embarked on a policy of expansion which carried them to the Mediterranean by 1229.

In England expansion had begun on the morrow of the Conquest when Norman barons invaded Wales and set up extensive marcher lordships. A century later they moved on to Ireland. By 1250 two-thirds of the country had been occupied, but Ireland remained divided and rebellious. So also did Wales which had seen a remarkable national resurgence under Llewellyn the Great (1197–1240). But Edward I (1272–1307) would not brook Welsh independence. After a first campaign (1276), followed by systematic castle building to enforce English control, a second campaign in 1283 (map 7) placed the principality directly under royal administration in 1284. Edward's attempt in 1296 to repeat the process in Scotland was a costly failure, culminating in the English defeat at Bannockburn in 1314. Like his French contemporary, Philip the Fair (1285–1314), defeated by the Flemings in 1302, Edward had overreached himself. The great baronial families, still firmly ensconced (map 6), forced him in 1297 to confirm the charters wrested from King John in 1215. It was a prelude to the aristocratic reaction and the setbacks of the fourteenth century.

1 The rise of Poland

- Polish territory 960-92
- lands added by Boleslav Chrobry 992-1025
- lands temporarily in Polish occupation
- Hungarian territory
- German territory
- bishoprics with foundation
- archbishoprics
- wasteland (forest and swamp)

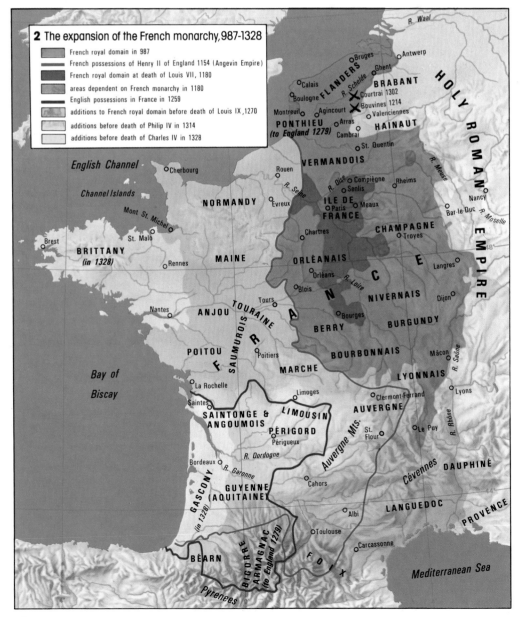

2 The expansion of the French monarchy, 987-1328

- French royal domain in 987
- French possessions of Henry II of England 1154 (Angevin Empire)
- French royal domain at death of Louis VII, 1180
- areas dependent on French monarchy in 1180
- English possessions in France in 1259
- additions to French royal domain before death of Louis IX, 1270
- additions before death of Philip IV in 1314
- additions before death of Charles IV in 1328

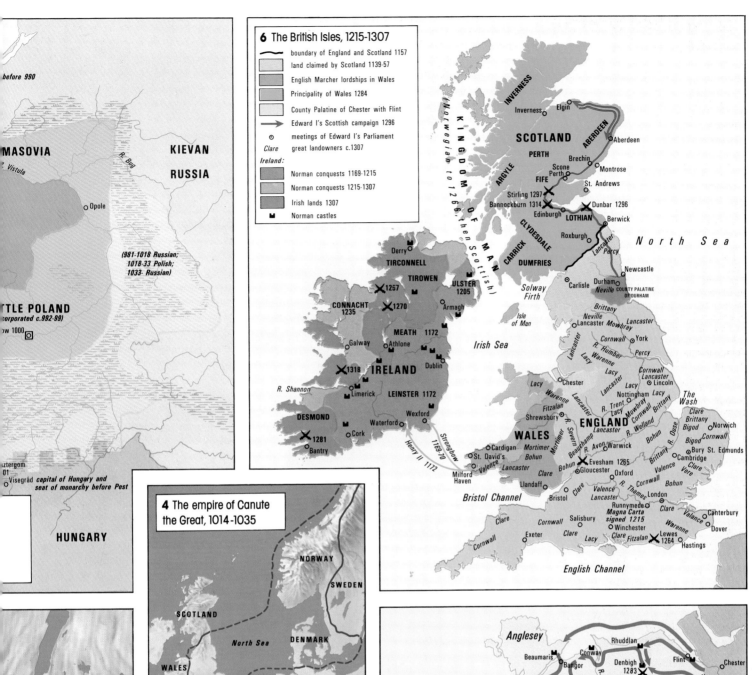

6 The British Isles, 1215-1307

- ⌇⌇ boundary of England and Scotland 1157
- land claimed by Scotland 1139-57
- English Marcher lordships in Wales
- Principality of Wales 1284
- County Palatine of Chester with Flint
- → Edward I's Scottish campaign 1296
- ⊙ meetings of Edward I's Parliament
- *Clare* great landowners c.1307

Ireland:
- Norman conquests 1169-1215
- Norman conquests 1215-1307
- Irish lands 1307
- ▟ Norman castles

before 990

MASOVIA

R. Vistula

KIEVAN

RUSSIA

○ Opole

(981-1018 Russian;
1018-33 Polish;
1033- Russian)

TTLE POLAND
corporated c.992-99)
ow 1000 ⊡

R. Bug

tergom
01
○ Visegrád *capital of Hungary and*
seat of monarchy before Pest

HUNGARY

KINGDOM OF MAN
(Norwegian to 1266, then Scottish)

SCOTLAND
INVERNESS
○ Inverness
○ Elgin
ABERDEEN
○ Aberdeen
PERTH
Brechin ○
Montrose ○
Scone
Perth ○
St. Andrews ○
FIFE
✕ Stirling 1297
✕ Bannockburn 1314
Edinburgh
LOTHIAN
Berwick
ARGYLE
CARRICK
CLYDESDALE
DUMFRIES
Roxburgh ○
Lanc Percy
Solway Firth
○ Carlisle
Durham ○ *Neville* COUNTY PALATINE OF DURHAM
Newcastle ○
North Sea

Derry ○
TIRCONNELL
TIROWEN
ULSTER 1205
✕ 1257
CONNACHT 1235
✕ 1270
Armagh ○
MEATH 1172
Galway ○
Athlone ○
○ Dublin
IRELAND
✕ 1318
R. Shannon
▟ Limerick
LEINSTER 1172
DESMOND
✕ 1281
Bantry
▟ Cork
Waterford ○
Wexford ○
Irish Sea
Isle of Man

Brittany
Neville *Mowbray* *Lancaster*
Lancaster *Cornwall* ○ York
Lacy *R. Humber*
Chester *Lacy* *Lancaster* ○ Lincoln
Lacy *Cornwall*
Nottingham *Lancaster* *Lacy*
Shrewsbury *R. Trent* *Mowbray* *Brittany* *The Wash*
Fitzalan *Lacy* *Clare*
WALES ENGLAND *Lancaster* *Brittany* *Bigod*
Mortimer *R. Severn* *Bohun* *Bigod* ○ Norwich
○ Cardigan *Mortimer* *Beauchamp* *R. Welland* *Cornwall*
St. David's ○ *Bohun* Warwick *Brittany* Cambridge ○ Bury St. Edmunds
Valence *Lancaster* ✕ Evesham 1265 *Valence* *Vere*
Llandaff ○ *Clare* Gloucester ○ Oxford *Cornwall* *Clare*
Bohun *Valence* *R. Thames* *Bohun* London ○
Bristol ○ Runnymede Clare ✕ *Valence* Canterbury ○
Lancaster Magna Carta *Warenne* Dover ○
Cornwall signed 1215
Salisbury ○ Winchester ○
Exeter ○ *Clare* *Clare* *Clare* *Fitzalan* ✕ Lewes 1264 Hastings ○
Cornwall *Lacy*
Bristol Channel
English Channel

○ St. David's
Milford Haven
Henry II 1172
Strongbow 1169-70

---

4 The empire of Canute the Great, 1014-1035

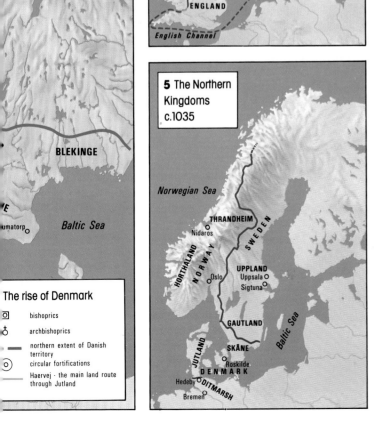

NORWAY
SWEDEN
SCOTLAND
North Sea
DENMARK
WALES
ENGLAND
English Channel

---

5 The Northern Kingdoms c.1035

Norwegian Sea
THRANDHEIM
Nidaros ○
SWEDEN
NORWAY
Oslo ○
HORTHALAND
UPPLAND
Uppsala ○
Sigtuna ○
GAUTLAND
Baltic Sea
SKÅNE
JUTLAND
DENMARK
Roskilde ○
Hedeby ○ DITMARSH
Bremen ○

Blekinge
Baltic Sea
BLEKINGE
umatorp ○

The rise of Denmark

- ⊡ bishoprics
- ⚲ archbishoprics
- — northern extent of Danish territory
- ⊙ circular fortifications
- — Haervej - the main land route through Jutland

---

7 The conquest of Wales, 1283-4

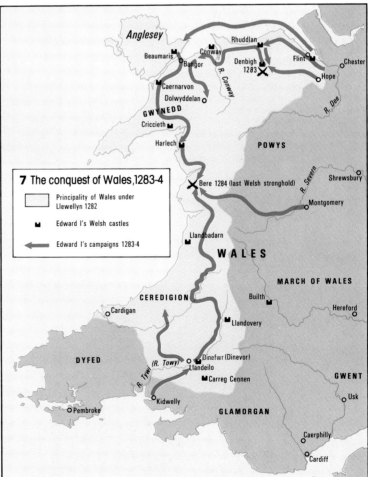

- Principality of Wales under Llewellyn 1282
- ▟ Edward I's Welsh castles
- → Edward I's campaigns 1283-4

Anglesey
Rhuddlan
Beaumaris ▟
Conway
Denbigh 1283 ✕
Flint ▟
○ Chester
Bangor ▟
R. Conway
Hope
Caernarvon ▟
Dolwyddelan ▟
R. Dee
GWYNEDD
Criccieth ▟
POWYS
Harlech ▟
✕ Bere 1284 (last Welsh stronghold)
Shrewsbury ○
R. Severn
Llandbadarn ▟
Montgomery ○
WALES
CEREDIGION
MARCH OF WALES
○ Cardigan
Builth ▟
Hereford ○
Llandovery ○
DYFED
R. Tywi
(R. Towy)
Dinefwr (Dinevor)
Llandeilo ○
Carreg Cennen ▟
GWENT
Usk ○
Kidwelly ○
Pembroke ○
GLAMORGAN
Caerphilly ○
Cardiff ○

The medieval German Empire
962-1356

Germany, or the eastern half of the Frankish empire, was the first country in Europe to recover from the setbacks of the ninth century invasions (page 36). This fact assured its predominance for upward of three centuries. German rulers never sought to assert control over the West Frankish lands, but, as heirs to the Carolingians, they claimed the imperial title and the right to rule over Italy and the lands of the former 'Middle Kingdom.' Germany's control of the Alpine passes between Lombardy and the Rhinelands assured not only its political preponderance but also gave it a leading place in the cultural exchange between Mediterranean and northern Europe.

There was, at first, no sense of a common German, or East Frankish, identity, and the effective control of the first German ruler, Henry I of Saxony (919–936), scarcely extended beyond Saxony and Franconia (map 1). But his son, Otto I (936–973), brought the other German duchies under royal control. Also, by defeating the Magyars at the battle of Lechfeld (955), he freed Germany from external threats and was able, in 951 and 961, to intervene effectively in Italy. His coronation as emperor (962) sealed the historic connexion between Germany and Italy. As heir to the Carolingian tradition, he also inaugurated a Christian drive against the pagan Slavs on the eastern frontier. But the great Slav revolt of 983 halted this advance until the twelfth century, and German efforts were concentrated instead on the south and south-west. The result, in 1034, was the addition of Burgundy to the imperial domains.

In spite of these successes, aristocratic resistance to royal centralisation was never overcome, and an opportunity to renew it came in 1075, when the outbreak of conflict between the emperor Henry IV (1056–1106) and the papacy, which saw imperial power in Italy as a threat to its independence, played into the German princes' hands. The ensuing civil war (1076–1122) was a turning point in German history. Although the monarchy emerged successful, its position was permanently weakened. German power was apparently restored during the reign of Frederick I (1152–1190), but it depended increasingly on the riches of Italy, and this embroiled Frederick not only with the papacy but also with the Italian cities. The marriage of his son, Henry VI, with Constance, the heiress of Sicily (1186), held out new possibilities. But the prospect of the union of Sicily and the empire alarmed the papacy, which saw itself being encircled, and led to the final struggle between Frederick II (1212–1250), and Pope Innocent IV (1243–1254).

Meanwhile Germany was being overtaken by the western monarchies (page 52). The empire under Frederick II was still the most imposing political body in Europe (map 3), but by 1200 Paris was the intellectual and cultural centre of Europe, and by comparison with England and Sicily Germany's financial organisation was antiquated. Eastward expansion had begun again after 1138 (map 2). It added two-thirds to the German territories and shifted the seat of power from Rhine to Elbe. But the beneficiaries were the princes on the eastern frontier, not the monarchy. Later, the Teutonic Knights conquered heathen Prussia (map 4), but within the empire the tendency was to fragmentation rather than expansion, and gains in the east were offset by loss of control over Italy which now went its own way (page 56). In default of royal authority local leagues were formed to resist princely encroachments and to preserve the peace. The most famous and enduring was the Swiss Confederation, formed in 1291 (map 5). The Golden Bull of 1356, formally recognising the autonomy of the princes, marked the beginning of a new era in German history; but the age of German preponderance in Europe had already ended a century earlier.

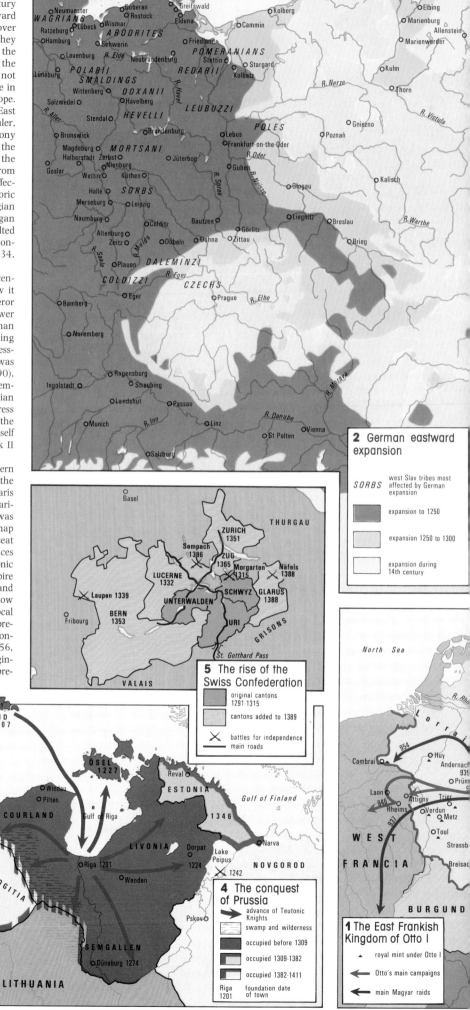

2 German eastward expansion

SORBS — west Slav tribes most affected by German expansion

expansion to 1250

expansion 1250 to 1300

expansion during 14th century

5 The rise of the Swiss Confederation

original cantons 1291-1315

cantons added to 1389

✕ battles for independence

main roads

4 The conquest of Prussia

→ advance of Teutonic Knights

swamp and wilderness

occupied before 1309

occupied 1309-1382

occupied 1382-1411

Riga 1201 — foundation date of town

1 The East Frankish Kingdom of Otto I

▲ royal mint under Otto I

← Otto's main campaigns

← main Magyar raids

Baltic Sea

North Sea

Holstein
Bornhöved 1227
Lübeck
Hamburg
Schwerin
Cammin
Gdansk (Danzig)
Bremen
Lüneburg
Havelberg
Stettin
Pomerania
Saxony
Altmark
DUCHY OF BRUNSWICK
(after 1235)
Brandenburg
Gniezno
Poznań
Utrecht
Münster
Magdeburg
Lusatia
Silesia
Lower
Lorraine
Dortmund
DUCHY OF
WESTPHALIA
(after 1180)
Paderborn
Goslar
ANHALT
(After 1180)
Meissen
Freiberg
Wrocław (Breslau)
Bruges
Ghent
Brussels
Aachen
Cologne
Thuringia
Naumburg
Altenburg
Brabant
Liège
Hersfeld
Erfurt
Eger
Prague
KINGDOM
OF BOHEMIA
Bouvines 1214
Hainaut
Cambrai
KINGDOM
Frankfurt
Mainz
Gelnhausen
Würzburg
Bamberg
Regensburg
Moravia
Trier
Worms
Nuremberg
Kaiserslautern
Franconia
Speyer
Trifels
Hagenau
Hohenstaufen
Ulm
Augsburg
Austria
Strassburg
OF
Swabia
Munich
Vienna
Upper
Lorraine
Verdun
Metz
Toul
Alsace
GERMANY
Salzburg
Styria
Semmering
Besançon
Basel
Constance
Zurich
Burgundy
Tyrol
Brixen
Carinthia
Brenner
Pontebba
Bozen
St. Gotthard
Septimer
A
L
P
S
Trient
Friuli
Carniola
Lyons
St. Bernard
Como
Verona
Aquileia
Bergamo
Vicenza
Treviso
Padua
KINGDOM
Mont Cenis
Novara
Milan
Brescia
Crema
Verona
Venice
Vercelli
Lodi
Cremona
Pavia
Piacenza
Mantua
VENETIAN TERRITORIES
OF
Turin
Asti
Alessandria
Tortona
Parma
Reggio
Modena
Ferrara
Savoy
KINGDOM
Genoa
Bologna
Imola
Ravenna
ARLES
Lombardy
expansion of Papal States under Innocent III
Faenza
Rimini
Pistoia
Lucca
Florence
Ancona
Adriatic Sea
Provence
Pisa
ITALY
Arles
Arezzo
Marseilles
Siena
Tuscany
Perugia
Assisi
Orvieto
Spoleto
Viterbo
Rieti
Tagliacozzo 1268
PAPAL
PATRIMONY
Tivoli
1190
Apricena
Rome
Ostia
Tusculum
Anagni
San Germano
1193
Lucera
Foggia
1191, 1194
Troia
Benevento
Barletta
Gaeta
Capua
1194
Melfi
Bari
Naples
Salerno
KINGDOM
Brindisi
Amalfi
Taranto
Lecce
Cosenza
OF
Palermo
Monreale
Messina
Reggio
Trapani
Cefalù
SICILY
Catania
Syracuse

3 The Hohenstaufen Empire
1152–1250

eastward spread of German
peasant settlement 12th century

German settlement by 1200-1250

city with over 10,000 inhabitants

member of Lombard Leagues
of 1167 and 1226

member of 1167 League only

member of 1226 League only

German invasions 1190-94

Henry VI's Genoese and Pisan fleet
1194

main Hohenstaufen palaces
and castles

mountain pass

Inset map:

Baltic Sea

Hedeby
Oldenburg 948
WAGRIANS
ABODRITES
WARNABI
c. 937-82
POLABI
REDARII
Pomerania
936
Lenzen
929
VELETIANS
Nordmark
Havelberg 948
HEVELLI
Gniezno 1000
Magdeburg 967
Brandenburg 948
Poznań 968
Werla
Quedlinburg
Lusatia
POLAND
Merseburg 968
LUSIZZI
Wallhausen
SORBS
Meissen 968
MILIZI
Erfurt
Zeitz 968
Mark
Zeitz
DALEMINZI
933
938
Fulda
Salz
950
Bohemia
(tributary from 950)
937
938
954
Prague 975
Regensburg
955
Augsburg
955
Ostmark
Pressburg
955
Bavaria
Wels 943
Pitten
HUNGARY
951
961
Styria
Carinthia
(Duchy 976)

new bishopric with
date of foundation

bishopric destroyed in
Slav rising of 983

visited more than
once by Henry I

MILIZI Slav tribes

frontier c.950

55

Fourteenth century Europe

After the rise and consolidation of national monarchies in Spain, France and England in the thirteenth century (page 52), the fourteenth century was a period of setbacks on all fronts in western Europe. In part, this may be attributed to a sudden climatic deterioration (the onset of the 'little ice age') which brought to an end the agricultural boom that had been virtually continuous since 1150. Already in 1315–17 Europe experienced a 'great famine', and the weakening of human powers of resistance induced by inadequate nourishment may have been one factor accounting for the rapid spread of the Black Death, or bubonic plague, which first appeared in the Crimea in 1346 and spread from there first by ship to Italy and then to the west (map 1). But there were also other factors. All the western monarchies had over-extended themselves financially, and the economic setback accentuated their difficulties. Philip IV's unsuccessful attempts to subdue Flanders played after his death (1314) into the hands of the aristocracy; so also

did the involvement of Catalonia in Italy after the death of James II (1285–1327); and in England the attempt to subdue Scotland (map 4) proved to be a running sore. Ireland also virtually went its own way until Tudor times (page 72), and Wales, conquered but not subdued by Edward I (page 52), had a great national revival under Owain Glyndwr (1400–1409). Germany broke apart into rival principalities after the extermination of the Hohenstaufen dynasty (page 54), and Italy went the same way once Hohenstaufen rule was removed, breaking up into a number of local lordships or *signorie* (map 3). In the end, even the Catholic church was affected by the economic and fiscal stringency. From 1378 to 1417 it was divided by schism (map 6), which undermined its authority, while its financial extortions gave impetus to the anti-papal, reformatory movements of Hus in Bohemia and Wyclif in England.

Eastern Europe, on the other hand, was in process of recovery from the Mongol incursions of the thirteenth century (page 46). Bohemia under Charles IV (1333–78), Poland under Casimir III (1339–70), and Hungary

under Louis the Great (1342–82), all made rapid stride helped perhaps by the fact that the impact of the Bla Death was less severe in the east than in the west, an also by exploitation of their natural resources, such the silver mines of Kutna Hora (map 2). In the west, the other hand, the setback was lasting. Two Engli kings, Edward II (1327) and Richard II (1399) we murdered. The Hundred Years' War between Englan and France (map 5) resulted in widespread devastatio Overall, the Black Death reduced the population Europe by roughly one-third. Further, the misery cause by economic recession and military ravages sparked a series of popular risings, the Jacquerie in France an the Peasants' Revolt in England being best known (ma 1), although urban discontent – the weavers' rising Flanders under Artevelde, or the Ciompi in Florence was no less significant in the long run. It was not un after c.1450 that recovery began (page 82); but eve then under-currents of popular resentment persiste which found their outlet in the messianic movements the Reformation (page 74).

3 Italy, c.1310

- Papal states
- ● Republican communes
- ○ cities under Signorial domination c.1310

the Signorie:

1 Avvocati	5 Da Camino	9 Este	13 Malatesta
2 Bonacolsi	6 Da Correggio	10 Fissiraga	14 Robert of Anjou
3 Brusati	7 Da Polenta	11 Langosco	15 Scotti
4 Cavalcabo	8 Della Scala	12 Maggi	16 Visconti

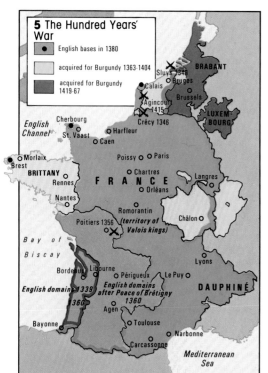

5 The Hundred Years' War

- ● English bases in 1380
- acquired for Burgundy 1363-1404
- acquired for Burgundy 1419-67

2 Eastern Europe 1278-1389

growth of Lithuania 1300-1377:

- to 1300
- under Gedymin 1316-41
- under Olgierd 1345-77
- Lithuania under Jagiello and Witold from 1377
- Poland-Lithuania after union of 1386
- Habsburg lands
- Bohemian lands

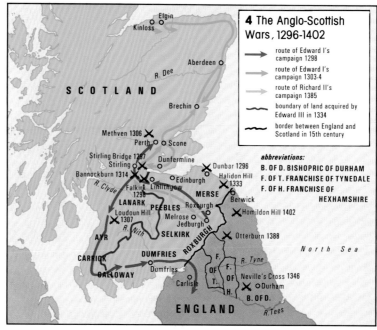

4 The Anglo-Scottish Wars, 1296-1402

- route of Edward I's campaign 1298
- route of Edward I's campaign 1303-4
- route of Richard II's campaign 1385
- boundary of land acquired by Edward III in 1334
- border between England and Scotland in 15th century

abbreviations:
B. OF D. BISHOPRIC OF DURHAM
F. OF T. FRANCHISE OF TYNEDALE
F. OF H. FRANCHISE OF HEXHAMSHIRE

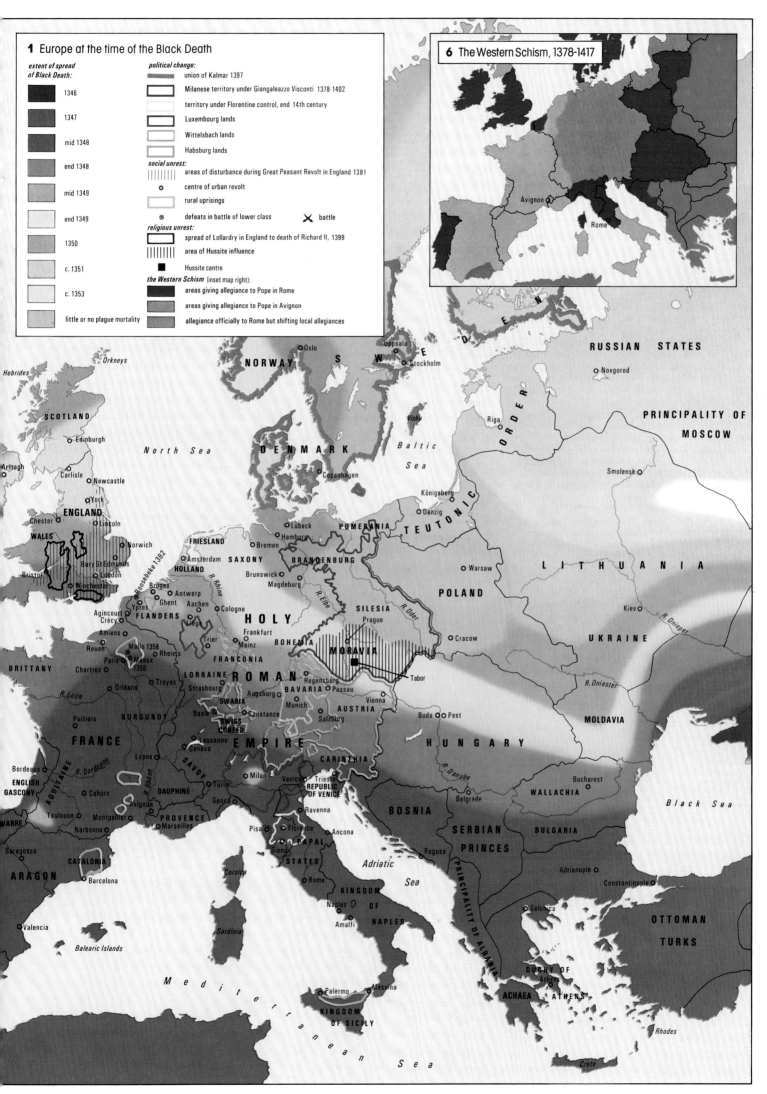

1 Europe at the time of the Black Death

extent of spread
of Black Death:

- 1346
- 1347
- mid 1348
- end 1348
- mid 1349
- end 1349
- 1350
- c. 1351
- c. 1353
- little or no plague mortality

political change:

- union of Kalmar 1397
- Milanese territory under Giangaleazzo Visconti 1378-1402
- territory under Florentine control, end 14th century
- Luxembourg lands
- Wittelsbach lands
- Habsburg lands

social unrest:

- areas of disturbance during Great Peasant Revolt in England 1381
- ⊙ centre of urban revolt
- rural uprisings
- ⊗ defeats in battle of lower class   ✕ battle

religious unrest:

- spread of Lollardry in England to death of Richard II, 1399
- area of Hussite influence
- ■ Hussite centre

the Western Schism (inset map right):

- areas giving allegiance to Pope in Rome
- areas giving allegiance to Pope in Avignon
- allegiance officially to Rome but shifting local allegiances

6 The Western Schism, 1378-1417

RUSSIAN STATES

PRINCIPALITY OF MOSCOW

Orkneys
Hebrides
SCOTLAND
Edinburgh
Armagh
Carlisle Newcastle
York
ENGLAND
Chester Lincoln
WALES
Norwich
Bury St Edmunds
Bristol
London
Winchester
Roosebeke 1382
Bruges
Antwerp
Ghent
Ypres
FLANDERS Liège
Agincourt Aachen
Crécy
Amiens
Rouen
Mello 1358
Rheims
Paris
Chartres
Meaux 1358
BRITTANY
Orléans
Troyes
LORRAINE
FRANCE
Poitiers
BURGUNDY
Strasbourg
SWABIA
Basle
SWISS
CONFED.
Lausanne
Geneva
Lyons
SAVOY
Bordeaux
AQUITAINE
ENGLISH
GASCONY
Cahors
DAUPHINÉ
Avignon
Toulouse
PROVENCE
Marseilles
NAVARRE
Narbonne
Saragossa
CATALONIA
ARAGON
Barcelona
Valencia
Balearic Islands

Oslo
NORWAY
Uppsala
Stockholm
DENMARK
Copenhagen
Lübeck
Hamburg
Bremen
FRIESLAND
Amsterdam
SAXONY
HOLLAND
Brunswick
Magdeburg
BRANDENBURG
R. Rhine
Cologne
HOLY
Frankfurt
BOHEMIA
Mainz
Trier
FRANCONIA
ROMAN
Regensburg
BAVARIA
Passau
Augsburg
Munich
EMPIRE
Constance
Salzburg
AUSTRIA
Vienna
CARINTHIA
Milan
Turin
Genoa
Venice
Trieste
REPUBLIC
OF VENICE
Ravenna
Pisa
Florence
Ancona
PAPAL
Siena
STATES
Corsica
Rome
Sardinia
KINGDOM
OF
NAPLES
Naples
Amalfi
Palermo Messina
KINGDOM
OF SICILY

North Sea
Baltic Sea
Visby
Riga
ORDER
Königsberg
Danzig
POMERANIA
TEUTONIC
Warsaw
LITHUANIA
POLAND
Prague
SILESIA
R. Oder
MORAVIA
Cracow
Tabor
R. Elbe
Kiev
R. Dnieper
UKRAINE
Buda Pest
MOLDAVIA
HUNGARY
R. Dniester
R. Danube
Bucharest
WALLACHIA
Belgrade
Black Sea
BOSNIA
SERBIAN
PRINCES
BULGARIA
Ragusa
Adrianople
Constantinople
PRINCIPALITY OF ALBANIA
Salonica
OTTOMAN
TURKS
DUCHY OF
Athens
ACHAEA ATHENS
Rhodes
Adriatic Sea
Crete

Smolensk
Novgorod

Mediterranean Sea

Avignon
Rome

57

Medieval trade routes
c.1000-1500

Trading connexions had been remarkably widespread during late antiquity, and they had brought with them important cultural interchanges (page 24). The barbarian invasions, beginning c.300 AD and lasting some 200 years, had disastrous results. The Silk Route from Rome to China was cut, and even within the Roman empire communications broke down. There was a short-lived recrudescence in Carolingian times, involving trade in the North Sea, centred on Dorestad and Quentovic; but it was only after c.1000, with the restoration of relatively stable conditions, that trade picked up. In particular, the Italian cities, already in contact with the Near East (page 36), established connexions with north-west Europe, where the fairs of Champagne were becoming clearing-houses for trade between Italy and the rising industrial centres of Flanders (map 1).

The consolidation of the German empire under the Saxon and Salian dynasties (page 54) gave impetus to trade from west to east, along a line running from the Low Countries via Cologne to Magdeburg, and along the Main valley to Bamberg and Prague. Its control of the Alpine passes, particularly after the opening of the Septimer and St. Gotthard passes during the Hohenstaufen period, stimulated trade with Italy, which contributed to the growing wealth of the south German cities, among them Augsburg, which later became a major commercial and financial centre after the rise of the Fugger merchant family in the fifteenth century. In the north the most important city was Lübeck (founded 1158), the key point controlling trade between the North Sea and the Baltic and the seat of the Hanseatic League, an association of German merchants which took shape in 1259 and was formally constituted in 1358. With its far-flung network of associated cities and its branches in London, Bruges and Bergen, the Hansa dominated the trade of northern Europe in the fourteenth and fifteenth centuries. It also had connexions with Venice and Genoa, the cities which dominated Mediterranean and Levantine commerce (map 2).

Levantine trade fell into two broad categories: the spice trade, in which Venice predominated, and the silk trade, largely in the hands of Genoa and its merchant colonies in Constantinople and at Kaffa, Tana and Trebizond. The latter profited greatly from the restoration of order and settled government in central Asia by the Mongols (page 46), which allowed a resumption of overland trade, and for a time there was extensive east–west traffic, exemplified by the famous journeys of Marco Polo between 1271 and 1295 (map 3). But the roads opened by the rise of the Mongol empire in the thirteenth century were closed by its decline in the mid-fourteenth century. The important spice trade from Ormuz to the Black Sea was also badly affected; but the trade via the Red Sea and Alexandria to Venice continued without interruption until the Ottoman conquest of Egypt in 1517 (page 48).

Spices were indispensable, easy to handle and highly profitable, and they were the staple of intercontinental trade in this period. Both Europe and China were dependent for supplies on the spice-producing regions of Asia, particularly the Moluccas and the Malay archipelago, and the resultant transactions, largely in the hands of Arab and Indian middlemen, created a complicated network of sea routes, hinging on Malacca, which stretched from the Red Sea and the Persian Gulf to the South China Sea (map 3). In the early fifteenth century, between 1405 and 1433, the Chinese sent seven expeditions through the Strait of Malacca to the Indian Ocean and beyond; but this enterprise ceased abruptly after 1440. Meanwhile, Portugal was probing down the west coast of Africa (page 64) in search of gold; but later, when Genoa, which had lost its eastern markets after the fall of Constantinople in 1453, provided financial backing for the Portuguese ventures, the main objective became the search for an alternative route to the east, to cut out Genoa's rival, Venice. When the Portuguese reached India in 1498, and Columbus, despatched by Portugal's rival, Spain, reached America, a new era had begun. The thousand-year-old pattern, centred on the Mediterranean, gave way to an Atlantic economy (page 82), and the whole economic and political balance in Europe shifted dramatically.

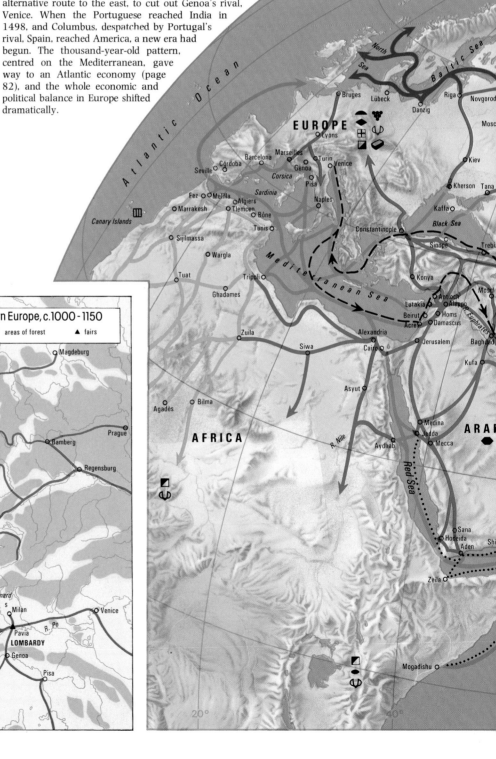

3 Eurasian trade routes, c.1000 - 1500

principal Eurasian routes

principal Eurasian sea routes

area of Muslim domination in the mid-15th century

principal Hanseatic routes

trans-Saharan trade routes

– – – Marco Polo's routes (1271-95)

· · · · · Chinese Admiral Cheng-ho's routes (1405-33)

major commodities:

● camphor

cottons

drugs

dyestuffs

gold

ivory

◆ linen

⊞ metalware

pepper

◆ perfumes

porcelain

◇ precious stones

◀ silks

silver

slaves

soap

spices

sugar

wine

woollens

1 Trade routes in Western Europe, c.1000 - 1150

—— trade routes   areas of forest   ▲ fairs

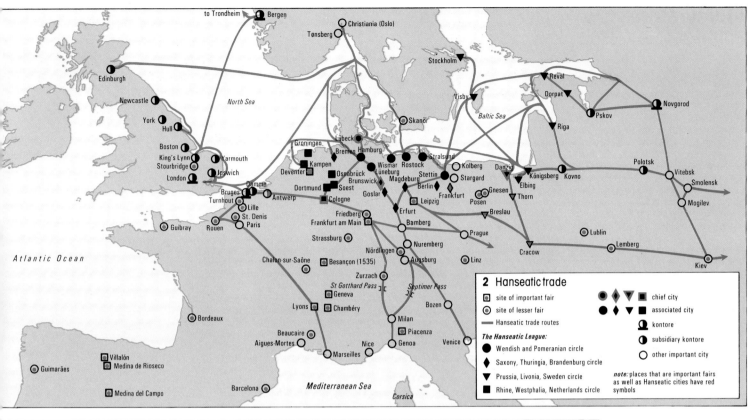

2 Hanseatic trade

- ▣ site of important fair
- ◉ site of lesser fair
- — Hanseatic trade routes

The Hanseatic League:
- ● Wendish and Pomeranian circle
- ◆ Saxony, Thuringia, Brandenburg circle
- ▼ Prussia, Livonia, Sweden circle
- ■ Rhine, Westphalia, Netherlands circle

- ◑◆▼■ chief city
- ●◆◆▼■ associated city
- ⬯ kontore
- ◐ subsidiary kontore
- ○ other important city

note: places that are important fairs as well as Hanseatic cities have red symbols

Atlantic Ocean

North Sea

Baltic Sea

to Trondheim · Bergen
Tønsberg · Christiania (Oslo)
Stockholm · Reval · Dorpat · Novgorod
Visby · Pskov
Skanör · Riga · Polotsk · Vitebsk · Smolensk
Edinburgh
Newcastle · York · Hull
Boston · King's Lynn · Stourbridge · Ipswich · Yarmouth
London · Bruges · Damme · Antwerp · Turnhout · Lille · St. Denis · Paris
Groningen · Lübeck · Hamburg · Bremen · Wismar · Rostock · Stralsund · Kolberg · Danzig · Königsberg · Kovno · Mogilev
Deventer · Kampen · Osnabrück · Lüneburg · Stettin · Stargard · Elbing · Thorn · Kiev
Dortmund · Brunswick · Magdeburg · Berlin · Gnesen · Posen · Breslau · Lublin
Soest · Goslar · Leipzig · Frankfurt · Lemberg
Cologne · Erfurt
Guibray · Rouen · Friedberg · Bamberg · Prague
Frankfurt am Main · Nuremberg · Linz
Strassburg · Nördlingen · Augsburg · Cracow
Chalon-sur-Saône · Besançon (1535) · Bozen
Zurzach
St Gotthard Pass · Septimer Pass
Geneva · Milan
Lyons · Chambéry · Piacenza · Venice
Bordeaux · Beaucaire · Nice · Genoa
Aigues-Mortes · Marseilles
Guimarães · Villalón · Medina de Rioseco · Barcelona
Medina del Campo

Mediterranean Sea

Corsica

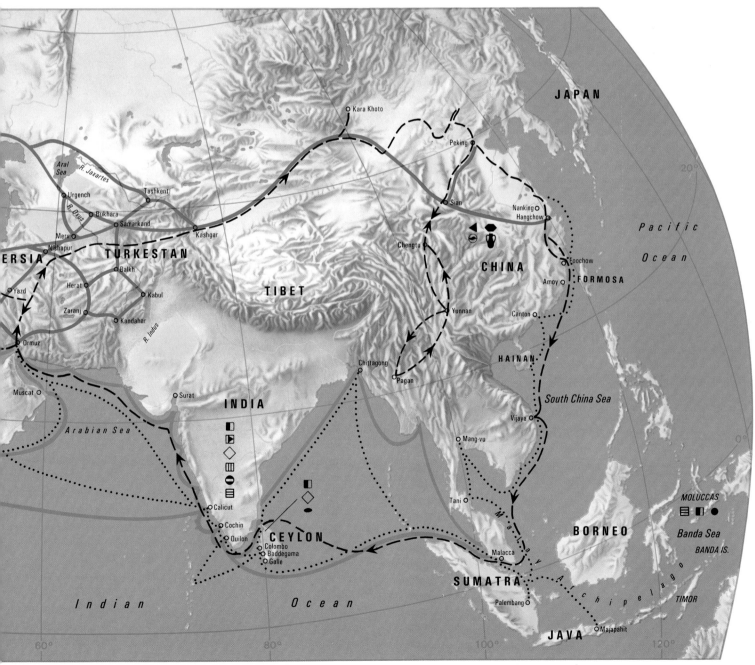

JAPAN
Kara Khoto · Peking
Aral Sea · R. Jaxartes
Urgench · Tashkent · Sian · Nanking · Hangchow · Pacific Ocean
Bukhara · Samarkand · Kashgar · Chengtu · CHINA · Foochow · FORMOSA
Merv · Nishapur · Amoy
ERSIA · TURKESTAN · Balkh · Yunnan · Canton
Yazd · Herat · Kabul · TIBET · HAINAN
Zaranj · Kandahar · R. Indus
Ormuz · Chittagong · South China Sea
Muscat · Surat · Pagan · Vijaya
Arabian Sea · INDIA · Mang-vu
Calicut · MOLUCCAS
Cochin · Tani · BORNEO · Banda Sea
Quilon · CEYLON · BANDA IS.
Colombo · Baddegama · Galle · Malacca
SUMATRA · TIMOR
Indian Ocean · Palembang
JAVA · Majapahit

African states and empires, c.900-1800

By the end of the first millennium AD great changes had taken place in Africa. The rise of a culture based on iron-working (page 10) led to a large-scale displacement of Khoisan-speaking Bushmen and Hottentots by settled Bantu-speaking agriculturalists (map 3) and to the appearance of extensive states and empires based on trade. In the south, Zimbabwe, with its monumental stone buildings, exported gold and copper to the Orient via the port of Sofala, and the impressive Kongo state on the west coast had an important trade in ivory. Further north, the Arab conquest of the Maghreb and the rise of the Almoravid and Almohad empires (page 40) marked a watershed. The Arabs, great traders, developed and extended the trans-Saharan caravan routes, and there is no doubt that trade was an important factor in the development of the great empires which arose in the sub-Saharan savanna. The early history of Ghana (some 500 miles north-west of the modern state with the same name) precedes the Islamic era; but its successors, Mali and Songhay, owed much of their wealth and civilisation, described in glowing terms

by Arab travellers, to the Islamic impact. So also did the Kanem-Borno empire around Lake Chad and, after the fifteenth century, the city states of Hausaland (map 1). Arab merchant colonies also spread far down the east coast from Mogadishu to Kilwa. The staples of trade in all cases were gold, ivory and slaves. According to a conservative estimate, the trans-Saharan slave trade before the coming of the Europeans amounted to almost 5 million.

The arrival of the Portuguese on the African coast and the building in 1448 of a first European fort and warehouse at Arguin, followed (1482) by a second at Elmina on the Gold Coast, had at first little impact on Africa. The immediate objective was to share directly in the gold trade, hitherto dominated by Muslim middlemen, and the slave trade was a secondary by-product. But with the development of sugar plantations in Brazil (page 68) and later in the West Indies, the slave trade became a major source of profit, particularly after Dutch and British traders ousted the Portuguese. Along the length of the Gold and Slave Coasts, from Axim to the Niger Delta, fortified trading stations (or 'factories') were set up as bases for this trade (map 2, inset), and the Portuguese continued to export slaves further south in Angola. Of some 15 million Africans shipped aboard between 1450 and 1870, some 90 per cent

went to South America and the Caribbean, most of them between 1700 and 1800. The effects on Africa of this appalling trade in human beings are not easy to quantify, though the effects on the victims themselves need no description. Furthermore, the loss of population was not evenly divided and some areas suffered disproportionately. Others profited from the trade. After the invasion and destruction of the great Songhay empire by Morocco in 1591, the forest states of Asante, Dahomey and Benin, having direct access to the Atlantic and to European trade, increased in importance and political power (map 2). Elsewhere, however, much of the interior remained unexplored and virtually unknown. In the far south the Dutch were established in the Cape Colony; but, in a continental perspective, its extent was still minimal. In the north-east Islam was spreading; but the Christian kingdom of Ethiopia, despite a serious setback in the 1520s, still held its own. By 1800, with the exception of the Ottomans in the north (and even their power was more nominal than real), Africa remained independent of foreign control. Nevertheless there is little sign that it was ready to meet the European challenge that developed in the nineteenth century (page 102). It was a world unto itself, but in no position to compete with the technological dynamism of the West.

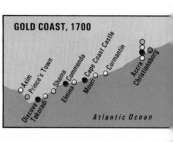

GOLD COAST, 1700

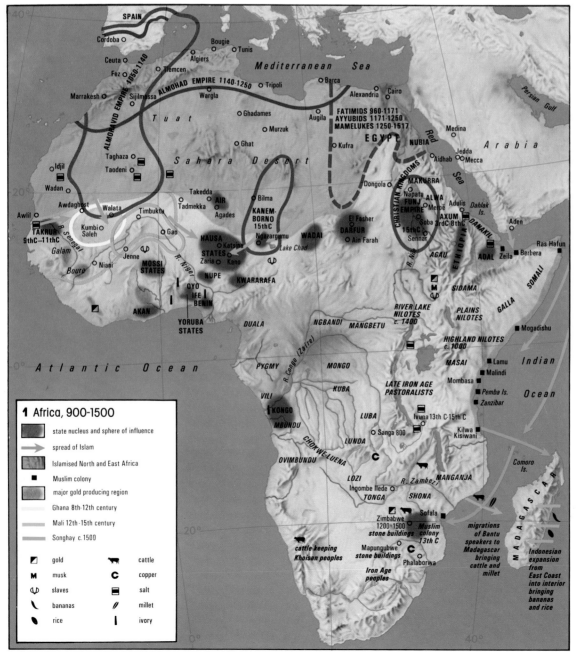

1 Africa, 900-1500

- state nucleus and sphere of influence
- spread of Islam
- Islamised North and East Africa
- Muslim colony
- major gold producing region
- Ghana 8th-12th century
- Mali 12th-15th century
- Songhay c.1500

gold		cattle	
musk		copper	
slaves		salt	
bananas		millet	
rice		ivory	

3 African languages

c.3000-2000 BC (right):

- Niger-Kordofanian
- Nilo-Saharan
- Afro-Asiatic
- Khoisan
- unoccupied

c.AD 1000 (above):

- Niger-Kordofanian (including Bantu)
- Nilo-Saharan
- Afro-Asiatic
- Khoisan
- Malayo-Polynesian

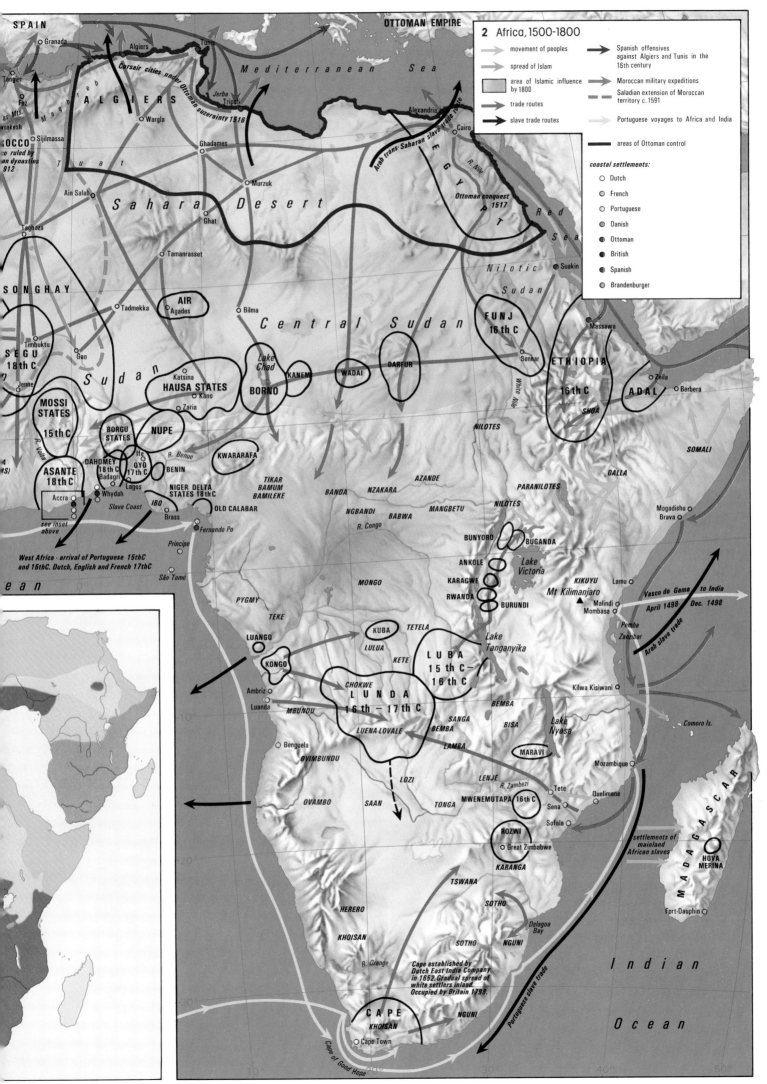

SPAIN

OTTOMAN EMPIRE

2 Africa, 1500-1800

→ movement of peoples
→ spread of Islam
▨ area of Islamic influence by 1800
→ trade routes
→ slave trade routes

→ Spanish offensives against Algiers and Tunis in the 16th century
→ Moroccan military expeditions
- - - Saladian extension of Moroccan territory c. 1591
→ Portuguese voyages to Africa and India
━━ areas of Ottoman control

coastal settlements:
○ Dutch
◔ French
○ Portuguese
◑ Danish
◕ Ottoman
● British
◖ Spanish
◗ Brandenburger

o Granada
Tangier
Fez
as Mts.
ROCCO
Morocco ruled by
an dynasties
912
SONGHAY
Taghaza
Ain Salah
SEGU
18th C
Jenne
MOSSI
STATES
15th C
R. Volta
S)
ASANTE
18th C
Accra
see inset
above

West Africa · arrival of Portuguese 15thC and 16thC. Dutch, English and French 17thC

Corsair cities under Ottoman suzerainty 1516

Algiers
ALGIERS
Wargla
o Sijilmassa

Tunis
Maghreb
Ghadames
Murzuk
Ghat
Tamanrasset

Jerba
Tripoli

Mediterranean Sea

Alexandria
Cairo
Arab trans-Saharan slave trade route
Ottoman conquest 1517

Sahara Desert

Bilma

Central Sudan

AIR
Agades

Tadmekka

Timbuktu
Gao

Sudan

Katsina
HAUSA STATES
Kano
Zaria

BORGU
STATES
NUPE
DAHOMEY
18th C
Badagri
OYO
17th C
Ife
BENIN
Lagos
Whydah
Slave Coast
IBO
Brass

Lake
Chad
KANEM
BORNO

WADAI
DARFUR

NIGER DELTA
STATES 18th C
OLD CALABAR
Fernando Po
Principe
São Tomé

KWARARAFA

TIKAR
BAMUM
BAMILEKE
BANDA
NGBANDI
R. Congo

NZAKARA
BABWA

AZANDE
MANGBETU

FUNJ
16th C
Senhar

Nilotic Sudan
Massawa

White Nile
NILOTES

ETHIOPIA
16th C
SHOA

ADAL
Zeila
Berbera

SOMALI

GALLA

PARANILOTES
NILOTES

BUNYORO
ANKOLE
KARAGWE
RWANDA
Lake
Victoria
BUGANDA
BURUNDI

KIKUYU
Mt Kilimanjaro ▲
Lamu
Malindi
Mombasa
Pemba
Zanzibar

Mogadishu
Brava

Vasco da Gama to India
April 1498   Dec. 1498

Arab slave trade

MONGO
PYGMY
TEKE

LUANGO
KONGO
Ambriz
Luanda
MBUNDU
Benguela
OVIMBUNDU
OVAMBO

KUBA
LULUA
KETE
CHOKWE
LUNDA
16th – 17th C
LUENA-LOVALE
SAAN

TETELA
LUBA
15th C –
16th C
Lake
Tanganyika
SANGA
BEMBA

BISA
BEMBA

LOZI
LENJE
TONGA

LAMBA

MARAVI

Lake
Nyasa

Kilwa Kisiwani

Comoro Is.

Mozambique

MWENEMUTAPA 16th C
R. Zambezi
Tete
Sena
Quelimane

ROZWI
Great Zimbabwe
KARANGA
Sofala

settlements of mainland African slaves

MADAGASCAR
HOVA
MERINA

Fort-Dauphin

HERERO
KHOISAN
TSWANA
SOTHO
NGUNI
Delagoa
Bay
SOTHO
NGUNI

R. Orange

Cape established by Dutch East India Company in 1652. Gradual spread of white settlers inland. Occupied by Britain 1798.

CAPE
KHOISAN
Cape Town

Cape of Good Hope

NGUNI

Portuguese slave trade

Indian Ocean

61

America on the eve of European conquest

Two great and wealthy civilisations confronted the Spaniards when they arrived in America at the beginning of the sixteenth century: the Aztec empire in Mexico and the Inca empire in Peru. The former had a population of 10–12 millions, the latter 6 millions or possibly considerably more. A few other centres of civilisation existed, such as the Chibcha state in modern Colombia; but the remainder of the continent was sparsely inhabited (perhaps 1 million north of the Rio Grande and 1 million in the rest of South America) and divided among more than a thousand small tribal societies, with distinct, often unrelated languages (map 1). Few regions, particularly in the north, had reached the stage of settled agriculture (map 4).

The Aztec and Inca empires were different in character, but there is no evidence of any contact between them. The Aztecs, like the Toltecs who controlled much of Mexico in the eleventh and twelfth centuries, were raw warriors from the north who entered Mexico during the thirteenth century and settled on islands in Lake Texcoco, where c.1325 they founded the town of Tenochtitlán, which was to become their capital. The Inca empire was created by one of the numerous tribes of Quechua stock inhabiting the central Andes, which established itself in the Cuzco valley in the twelfth century. The expansion of both came late and only reached its full extent on the eve of the Spanish conquest. In the case of the Aztecs (map 2) the first step was to ally with the neighbouring tribes in Texcoco and Tlacopán against their overlords in Azcapotzalco, and then to turn against their allies. This aggressive policy began c.1427 under Itzcoatl and was continued by Montezuma I. It reached its peak under Montezuma II (1502–20), when the Aztecs, in control of the greater part of Mexico, were beginning to enter Maya territory in Yucatán. Inca expansion began under the eighth emperor, Viracocha, and his son Pachacuti (1438–63), whose son Topa subdued the coastal civilisation of Chimú (1470), and then, after his accession as emperor (1471), pushed south into Chile and northern Argentina (map 3). Huayna Capac (1493–1525) advanced north into modern Ecuador, where he founded a second capital at Quito. By now the Inca empire was some 200 miles wide and 2500 miles long, held together by an impressive system of highways and post-stations, with relays of runners who conveyed imperial orders to all parts of the empire.

The Incas created a genuine imperial system, with an hereditary dynasty, a Quechua aristocracy and a highly trained bureaucracy. All land was state-owned, and there was a complex system of irrigation. The ordinary Indian spent nine months of the year working for the state, but in return was protected from famine by large state-owned food repositories and provided for in sickness and old age. The Aztec empire, on the other hand, rather like that of the Mongols in Europe (page 46), was essentially a harsh military dominion over vassal peoples, who were left to rule themselves on condition that they paid heavy tribute to Tenochtitlán in food, textiles, pottery and other goods, but increasingly in human beings for sacrifice to the Aztec gods. The number of sacrificial victims rose from 10,000 a ye to 50,000 a year at the time of the Spanish conques This was certainly one reason why the Totonacs ar Tlaxcalans welcomed the Spanish invaders of Mexic (page 68), and resentment against Inca oppressic probably played a similar role in Peru. Neither empi was as stable as it seemed. Nevertheless their collaps at the hands of small bands of adventurers (Cortés ha only 600 men, a few small cannon, 13 muskets ar 16 horses when he invaded Mexico in 1519, ar Pizarro had only 180 men, 27 horses and 2 cannc when he attacked the Inca empire in 1531) is not easi explained.

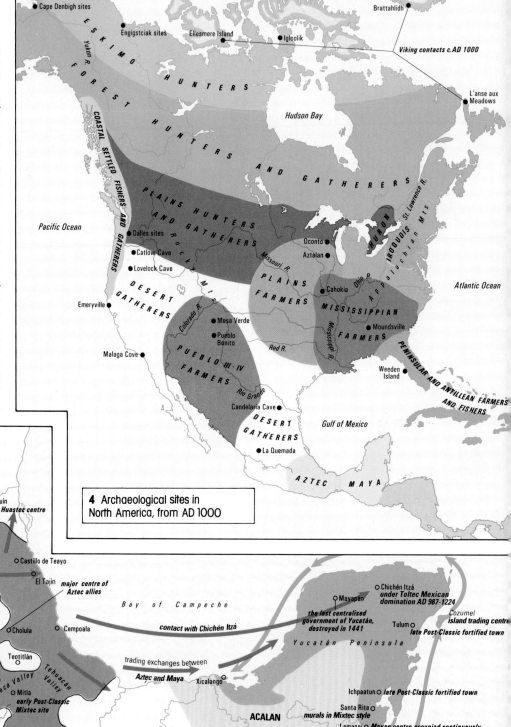

4 Archaeological sites in North America, from AD 1000

2 The Aztec Empire in Mexico

- Maya cultural area
- Post-Classic Maya kingdoms
- area of Aztec domination 1519
- spread of Toltec influence from 9th century AD
- Post-Classic trading routes

La Quemada *NW outpost of Mexican culture*

centre of Toltec military state

late Post-Classic Tarascan site

R. Pánuco

Tamuín *late Huastec centre*

Aztec capital founded AD 1325

Tula *800-1000*

Azcapotzalco

Castillo de Teayo

Tzintzuntzan

El Tajín *major centre of Aztec allies*

Ortices

Tenochtitlán

Texcoco

Aztec period temple carved in rock

Tlacopán

Malinalco

Tlaxcala

Xochicalco

Cholula

Cempoala

R. Balsas

Teotitlán

early Post-Classic site 800-1000 with Maya contacts

Monte Albán *tombs in old Zapotec ceremonial centre*

Mitla

early Post-Classic Mixtec site

Guiengola

Tehuacán Valley

Oaxaca Valley

Bay of Campeche

contact with Chichén Itzá

trading exchanges between

Aztec and Maya

Xicalango

ACALAN

Mayapán

Chichén Itzá *under Toltec Mexican domination AD 987-1224*

the last centralised government of Yucatán, destroyed in 1441

Tulum

Cozumel *island trading centre*

late Post-Classic fortified town

Yucatán Peninsula

Ichpaatun *late Post-Classic fortified town*

Santa Rita *murals in Mixtec style*

Lamanai o *Mayan centre occupied continuously until mid 17th century*

Gulf of Honduras

XOCONUSCO

rich province supplying cacao to the Aztec capital

Zaculeu

Xoconocho

highland Mayan kingdoms under central Mexican influence

Wild Cane Cay island trading centre

Iximché

Pacific Ocean

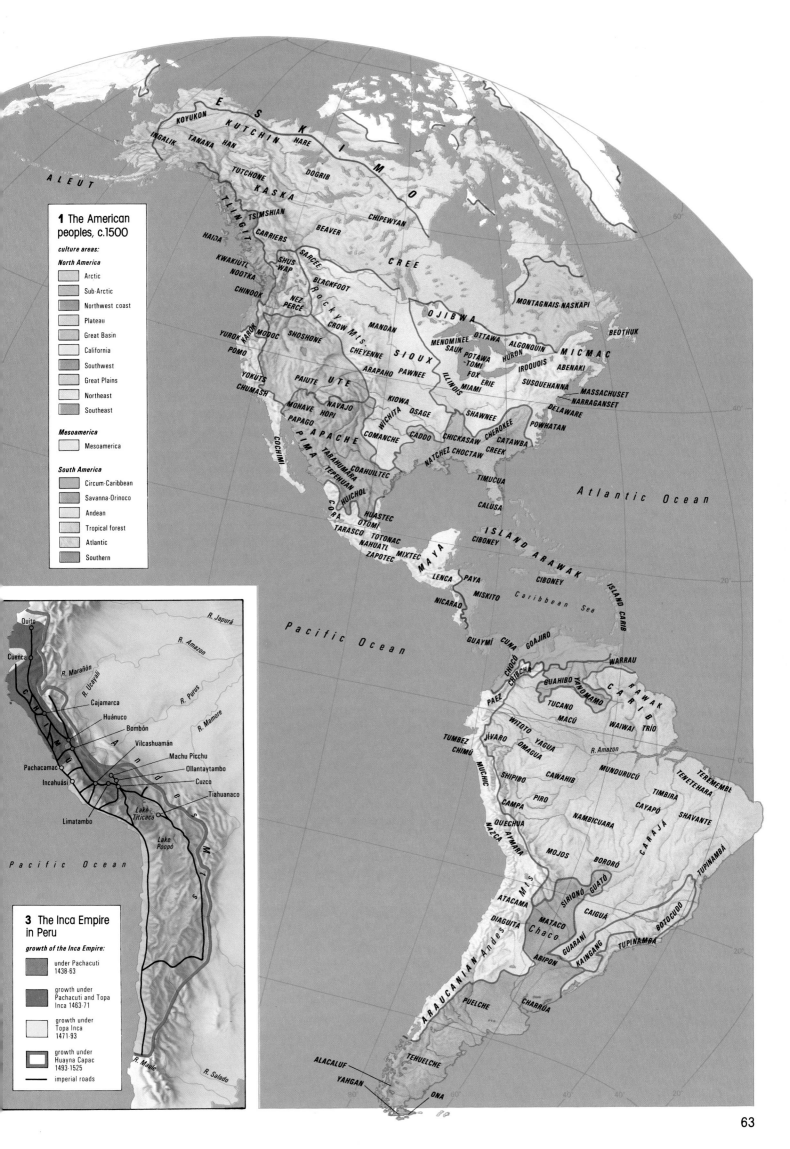

1 The American peoples, c.1500

culture areas:

North America
- Arctic
- Sub-Arctic
- Northwest coast
- Plateau
- Great Basin
- California
- Southwest
- Great Plains
- Northeast
- Southeast

Mesoamerica
- Mesoamerica

South America
- Circum-Caribbean
- Savanna-Orinoco
- Andean
- Tropical forest
- Atlantic
- Southern

3 The Inca Empire in Peru

growth of the Inca Empire:
- under Pachacuti 1438-63
- growth under Pachacuti and Topa Inca 1463-71
- growth under Topa Inca 1471-93
- growth under Huayna Capac 1493-1525
- imperial roads

Map 1 labels

ALEUT
KOYUKON
INGALIK
TANANA
HAN
KUTCHIN
HARE
E S K I M O
TUTCHONE
DOGRIB
KASKA
TLINGIT
TSIMSHIAN
CHIPEWYAN
HAIDA
CARRIERS
BEAVER
CREE
KWAKIUTL
SHUS-WAP
SARCEE
NOOTKA
BLACKFOOT
MONTAGNAIS-NASKAPI
CHINOOK
NEZ PERCÉ
ROCKY MTS
OJIBWA
BEOTHUK
MANDAN
OTTAWA
MENOMINEE
ALGONQUIN
MICMAC
YUROK KAROK MODOC
CROW MTS
SAUK POTAWA-TOMI
HURON
ABENAKI
POMO
SHOSHONE
CHEYENNE
SIOUX
FOX ERIE
IROQUOIS
SUSQUEHANNA
YOKUTS
PAIUTE
UTE
ARAPAHO
PAWNEE
ILLINOIS
MIAMI
MASSACHUSET
NARRAGANSET
CHUMASH
KIOWA
WICHITA OSAGE
SHAWNEE
DELAWARE
POWHATAN
MOHAVE HOPI
NAVAJO
PAPAGO
APACHE
COMANCHE
CADDO
CHICKASAW
CHEROKEE
CATAWBA
COCHIMI
PIMA
TARAHUMARA
COAHUILTEC
NATCHEZ CHOCTAW
CREEK
TEPEHUAN
HUICHOL
TIMUCUA
CORA
HUASTEC
CALUSA
TARASCO
OTOMÍ
TOTONAC
ISLAND ARAWAK
NAHUATL
MIXTEC
MAYA
CIBONEY
ZAPOTEC
LENCA
PAYA
CIBONEY
ISLAND CARIB
NICARAO
MISKITO
Caribbean Sea
GUAYMÍ
CUNA
GOAJIRO
CHOCÓ
CHIBCHA
WARRAU
PAEZ
GUAHIBO
YANOMAMO
ARAWAK
TUMBEZ
CHIMÚ
JIVARO
OMAGUA
TUCANO
WITOTO
YAGUA
MACÚ
WAIWAI
TRÍO
CARIB
MUCHIC
SHIPIBO
CAWAHIB
MUNDURUCÚ
TEREMEMBE
PIRO
TIMBIRA
TENETEHARA
CAMPA
NAMBICUARA
CAYAPÓ
SHAVANTE
NAZCA
QUECHUA
AYMARA
MOJOS
CARAJÁ
BORORÓ
SIRIONÓ
GUATÓ
ATACAMA
MATACO
CAIGUÁ
DIAGUITA
Chaco
GUARANÍ
KAINGANG
TUPINAMBA
ABIPON
TUPINAMBA
ABAUCANIAN Andes
PUELCHE
CHARRÚA
ALACALUF
TEHUELCHE
YAHGAN
ONA

Map 3 labels

Quito
Cuenca
R. Japurá
R. Amazon
R. Marañón
R. Ucayali
R. Purus
Cajamarca
Huánuco
R. Mamore
Bombón
Vilcashuamán
Machu Picchu
Ollantaytambo
Pachacamac
Cuzco
Incahuási
Tiahuanaco
Limatambo
Lake Titicaca
Lake Poopó
Pacific Ocean
R. Maule
R. Salado
CHIMU
ANDES
Mts

Atlantic Ocean

Pacific Ocean

R. Amazon

63

European voyages of discovery
1487-1780

The European voyages of discovery opened a new era in world history. They began early in the fifteenth century when Portuguese navigators advanced southward, round the coast of Africa, in search of gold, slaves and spices, until in 1487 Dias and de Covilhã, brought them into the Indian Ocean (map 1). Thenceforth voyages of exploration multiplied, particularly after the resurgence of Islam made the old route to the east via Alexandria and the Red Sea precarious.

While the Portuguese explored the eastern route to Asia, the Spaniards sailed west. Once in the Indian Ocean the former quickly reached their goal: Malabar (1498), Malacca (1511), and the Moluccas (1512). The Spanish search for a western route to the Spice Islands was less successful. Its unintended but momentous result was Columbus' discovery of the New World in 1492 (map 2), followed by the Spanish conquest of America (page 68). But it was not until after 1524, when Verrazzano traced the coastline of North America as far north as Nova Scotia, that the existence of a new continent was generally accepted, and meanwhile the search for a western route to Asia continued, leading to extensive exploration of the Caribbean (map 3). Finally, in 1521, Magellan rounded South America, entered the Pacific, and reached the Philippines, but the route was too long and hazardous for commercial purposes. In 1557 the Portuguese occupied Macao, and after 1564 Spanish galleons traded between Manila and Acapulco in Mexico; but otherwise the exploration of the Pacific was delayed until the eighteenth century (map 4). This was the work of British, Dutch and Russians seeking a navigable passage via the Arctic between the Atlantic and the Pacific, and hoping also to locate a hypothetical southern continent. Both proved illusory; but the result was the charting of New Zealand and the eastern coast of Australia, both in a few years opened to European colonisation (page 112).

Meanwhile England and France, unwilling to recognise the monopoly claimed by Spain and Portugal in the Treaty of Tordesillas (1494), had embarked on a series of voyages intended to reach Asia by a northern route (map 2). All these proved abortive and were abandoned after 1632, but they resulted in the opening of North America to European settlement. The English, French and Dutch were also unwilling to abandon the profitable trade with South and South-East Asia to the Portuguese and Spaniards, and the later years of the sixteenth and first half of the seventeenth centuries saw a determined and ultimately successful effort to breach their privileged position (page 66). After 1500 direct sea contact was established between continents and regions which hitherto had gone their own way in isolation. It was necessarily a slow process, and for long the European footholds in Asia and Africa remained tenuous and precarious. But by the time of the death of the last great explorer, James Cook, in 1779, the worldwide network of relationships had been formed which characterises the modern era and differentiates it from all preceding times.

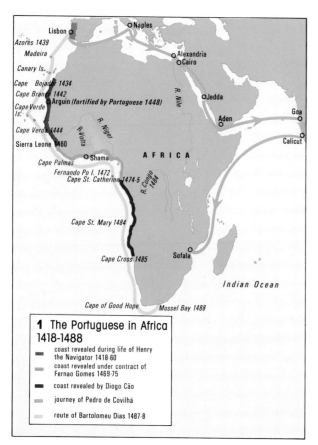

1 The Portuguese in Africa 1418-1488

- coast revealed during life of Henry the Navigator 1418-60
- coast revealed under contract of Fernao Gomes 1469-75
- coast revealed by Diogo Cão
- journey of Pedro de Covilhã
- route of Bartolomeu Dias 1487-8

Voyages intended for S. Asia by S.E. Route:
1/Dias 1487/88 (outward) discovered open water S. of Cape Agulhas; entered Indian Ocean;

reached Great Fish River.
2/Vasco da Gama 1487-99 (outward) discovered best use of Atlantic winds on way to Cape of Good Hope; reached India,

navigated by local pilot.
3/Cabral 1500 (outward) the second Portuguese voyage to India, sighted coast of Brazil at Monte Pascoal, probably acciden

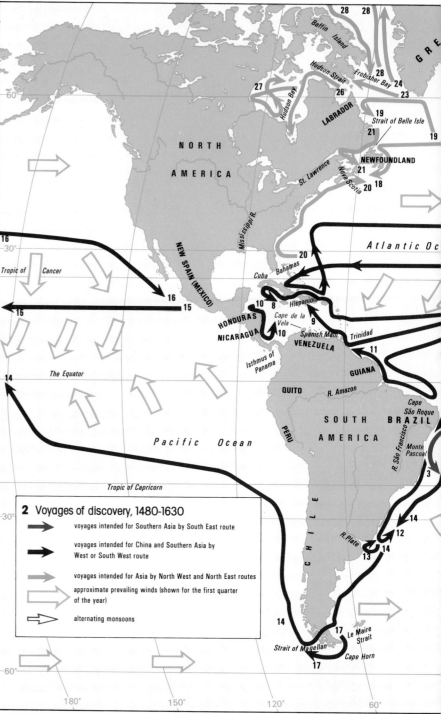

2 Voyages of discovery, 1480-1630

- → voyages intended for Southern Asia by South East route
- → voyages intended for China and Southern Asia by West or South West route
- → voyages intended for Asia by North West and North East routes
- ⇨ approximate prevailing winds (shown for the first quarter of the year)
- ⇨ alternating monsoons

Voyages in the Caribbean:
29/Bastidas & La Cosa 1501-02 explored coast from Gulf of Maracaibo to Gulf of Urabá.
30/Pinzón & Solís 1508 sent from Spain to find strait to Asia, coasted E. coast of Yucatán.
31/Ponce de León 1512-13 sailed from Puerto Rico, explored coast of Florida from N. of Cape Canaveral to (possibly) Pensacola. May have sighted Yucatán on return. First explorer to note force of Gulf Stream.
32/Hernández de Córdoba 1516 sailed from Cuba, explored N. and W. coasts of Yucatán. First report of Mayan cities.
33/Grijalva 1517 followed S. and W. coasts of Gulf of Mexico as far as Pánuco River.
34/Pineda 1519 explored N. and W. coasts of Gulf of Mexico from Florida to Pánuco River. Finally ended hope of strait to Pacific in that region.

Voyages in the Pacific:
35/Roggeveen 1721-22 discovered Easter Island and some of the Samoan group. Circumnavigation.
36/Bering 1728 sailed from Kamchatka, discovered strait separating N.E. Asia from N.W. America.
37/Wallis 1766-68 discovered Society Islands (Tahiti), encouraged hope of habitable southern continent. Circumnavigation.
38/Cook 1768-71 charted coasts of New Zealand, explored E. coast of Australia, confirmed existence of Torres Strait. Circumnavigation.
39/Cook 1772-75 made circuit of southern oceans in high latitude, charted New Hebrides, ended hope of habitable southern continent. Circumnavigation.
40/Cook & Clerke 1776-80 discovered Sandwich Islands (Hawaii), explored coast of N. America from Vancouver to Unimak Pass, sailed through Bering Strait to edge of pack ice, ended hope of passage through Arctic to Atlantic.

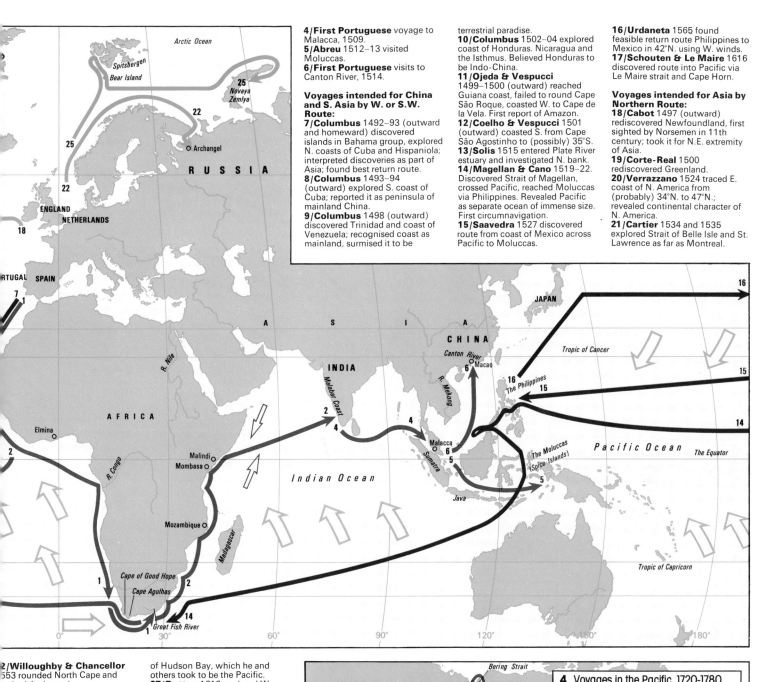

4/First Portuguese voyage to Malacca, 1509.
5/Abreu 1512–13 visited Moluccas.
6/First Portuguese visits to Canton River, 1514.

Voyages intended for China and S. Asia by W. or S.W. Route:
7/Columbus 1492–93 (outward and homeward) discovered islands in Bahama group, explored N. coasts of Cuba and Hispaniola; interpreted discoveries as part of Asia; found best return route.
8/Columbus 1493–94 (outward) explored S. coast of Cuba; reported it as peninsula of mainland China.
9/Columbus 1498 (outward) discovered Trinidad and coast of Venezuela; recognised coast as mainland, surmised it to be

terrestrial paradise.
10/Columbus 1502–04 explored coast of Honduras. Nicaragua and the Isthmus. Believed Honduras to be Indo-China.
11/Ojeda & Vespucci 1499–1500 (outward) reached Guiana coast, failed to round Cape São Roque, coasted W. to Cape de la Vela. First report of Amazon.
12/Coelho & Vespucci 1501 (outward) coasted S. from Cape São Agostinho to (possibly) 35°S.
13/Solís 1515 entered Plate River estuary and investigated N. bank.
14/Magellan & Cano 1519–22. Discovered Strait of Magellan, crossed Pacific, reached Moluccas via Philippines. Revealed Pacific as separate ocean of immense size. First circumnavigation.
15/Saavedra 1527 discovered route from coast of Mexico across Pacific to Moluccas.

16/Urdaneta 1565 found feasible return route Philippines to Mexico in 42°N. using W. winds.
17/Schouten & Le Maire 1616 discovered route into Pacific via Le Maire strait and Cape Horn.

Voyages intended for Asia by Northern Route:
18/Cabot 1497 (outward) rediscovered Newfoundland, first sighted by Norsemen in 11th century; took it for N.E. extremity of Asia.
19/Corte-Real 1500 rediscovered Greenland.
20/Verrazzano 1524 traced E. coast of N. America from (probably) 34°N. to 47°N.; revealed continental character of N. America.
21/Cartier 1534 and 1535 explored Strait of Belle Isle and St. Lawrence as far as Montreal.

2/Willoughby & Chancellor 1553 rounded North Cape and reached Archangel.
23/Frobisher 1574 reached Frobisher Bay in Baffin Island, which he took for a 'strait'.
24/Davis 1587 explored W. coast of Greenland to the edge of the ice in 72°N.
25/Barents 1596–97 discovered Bear Island and Spitsbergen and wintered in Novaya Zemlya.
26/Hudson 1610 sailed through Hudson Strait to the S. extremity

of Hudson Bay, which he and others took to be the Pacific.
27/Button 1612 explored W. coast of Hudson Bay, concluded Bay land-locked on the W.
28/Baffin & Bylot 1616 explored whole coastline of Baffin Bay and decided that no navigable N.W. passage existed in that area.

4 Voyages in the Pacific, 1720-1780

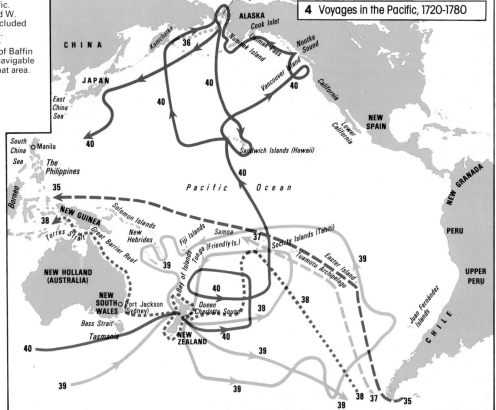

3 Voyages in the Caribbean, 1493-1519

→ voyages intended for China and Southern Asia by West or South West route

→ voyages exploring the Caribbean

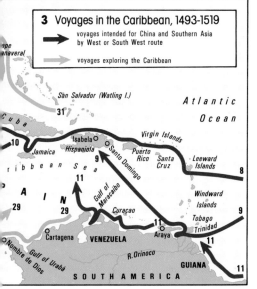

European expansion overseas, 1493-1713

The Portuguese were the first to exploit the European voyages of discovery. Theirs was essentially a trading empire, and by the middle of the sixteenth century they had more than fifty forts and factories reaching from Sofala on the Zambezi to Nagasaki in Japan (map 1). In 1557 they occupied Macao on the Chinese mainland. The Spaniards, on the other hand, set out on a deliberate policy of conquest and settlement, first in Hispaniola and, a decade or so later, in Mexico and Peru. The result was the foundation of the great Spanish colonial empire (page 68). But the Iberian preponderance did not go unchallenged. Particularly after the foundation of the English and Dutch East India Companies, in 1600 and 1602 respectively, Portuguese trade came under attack (map 2). With the acquisition of Batavia (1619) as an eastern headquarters and of the Cape of Good Hope (1652) as a station on the route to the east, Dutch commercial pre-eminence was assured.

While there was no direct attack on Spain's mainland empire the islands of the Caribbean, coveted as a prime source of sugar for the European market, became an object of intense rivalry and competition, in which all the leading powers engaged (map 4). Furthermore, whatever Spanish pretensions may have been, it was unable to make its presence felt much north of the Rio Grande. There was a slow advance in the west into California; but on the east coast Spanish power was limited to a tenuous foothold in Florida. Here the states of northern Europe, led by England and France, took the lead. France, in particular, advancing down the St. Lawrence estuary, penetrated deep into the interior, exploring the whole Mississippi valley (1682) and establishing fortified posts all the way to the Gulf of Mexico (map 3). The English, on the other hand, established a series of settlements along the eastern coast, beginning with Virginia in 1607. The clash of commercial and colonial interests which ensued ushered in the first age of imperial rivalry and conflict (page 86). Its prelude was the Anglo-Dutch wars of 1652–73 (page 80) which resulted in the British seizure (1664) of the Dutch settlement of New Amsterdam, subsequently renamed New York. It marked the decline of the Netherlands and the rise of England and France to the paramount position in the overseas world.

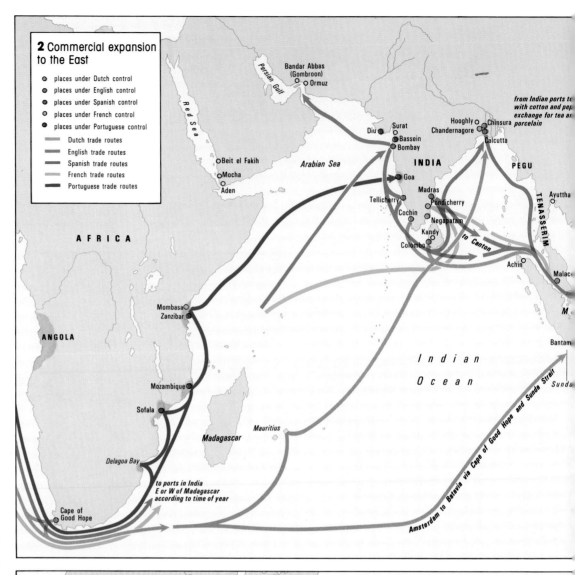

2 Commercial expansion to the East

- places under Dutch control
- places under English control
- places under Spanish control
- places under French control
- places under Portuguese control
- Dutch trade routes
- English trade routes
- Spanish trade routes
- French trade routes
- Portuguese trade routes

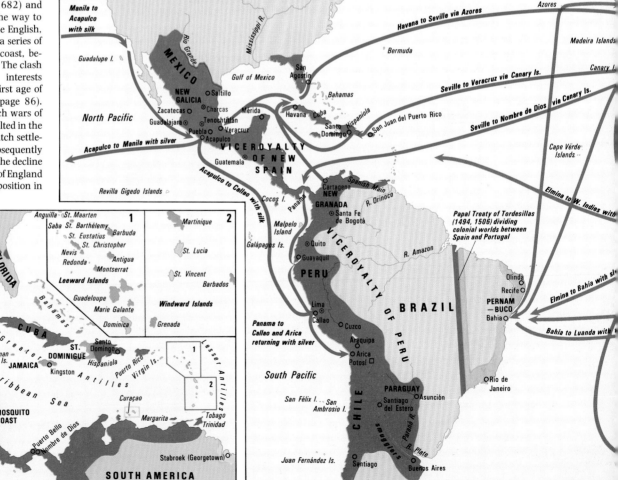

4 The West Indies

- Spanish settlements
- French settlements
- English settlements
- Dutch settlements

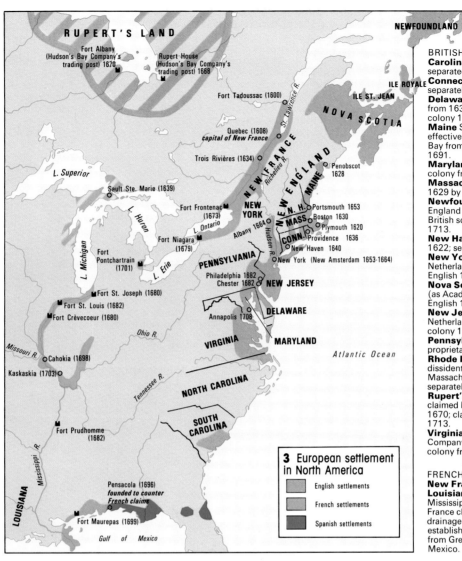

BRITISH TERRITORIES
Carolina Settled from 1663; separated into two colonies 1713.
Connecticut Settled 1635–38; separately incorporated 1662.
Delaware Settled by Swedes from 1638; separate proprietary colony 1704.
Maine Settled from 1622; effectively part of Massachusetts Bay from 1651, formally annexed 1691.
Maryland Settled as proprietary colony from 1632.
Massachusetts Bay Settled 1629 by Massachusetts Bay Co.
Newfoundland Claimed for England by John Cabot 1497; British sovereignty recognised 1713.
New Hampshire Part of Maine 1622; separate province from 1698.
New York Settled as New Netherland from 1623. Seized by English 1664.
Nova Scotia Settled by French (as Acadia) 1604; ceded to English 1713.
New Jersey Part of New Netherland; English proprietary colony 1664.
Pennsylvania Settled as proprietary colony from 1681.
Rhode Island Settled by dissident groups from Massachusetts Bay from 1636; separately incorporated from 1644.
Rupert's Land Fur trading area claimed by Hudson Bay Co. from 1670; claim recognised by France 1713.
Virginia Settled by Virginia Company from 1607; crown colony from 1624.

FRENCH TERRITORIES
New France Settled from c.1608.
Louisiana After exploration of Mississippi by La Salle (1682), France claimed whole Mississippi drainage. Fortified trading posts established at strategic points from Great Lakes to Gulf of Mexico.

3 European settlement in North America

☐ English settlements
☐ French settlements
☐ Spanish settlements

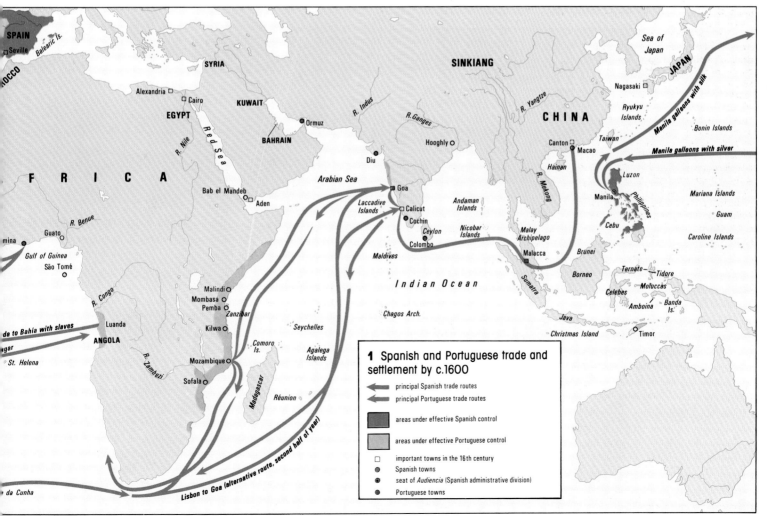

1 Spanish and Portuguese trade and settlement by c.1600

→ principal Spanish trade routes
→ principal Portuguese trade routes

☐ areas under effective Spanish control
☐ areas under effective Portuguese control

☐ important towns in the 16th century
● Spanish towns
◉ seat of *Audiencia* (Spanish administrative division)
● Portuguese towns

Colonial America
1519-1783

The conquest of Mexico by Hernán Cortés in 1519–20 (map 1), and of Peru by Francisco Pizarro in 1531–33 (map 2), laid the foundations of the Spanish colonial empire in America. With the help of rebellious tribes, oppressed by their Aztec and Inca conquerors (page 62), both were amazingly successful. By 1535, when vice-regal government was set up in Mexico and Lima was founded as the capital of Peru, the first dramatic phase of conquest was over. By 1550 all the chief centres of settled population were in Spanish hands, though the task of pushing forward frontiers into unexplored territory continued until the end of the colonial period (map 3). New vice-royalties were set up in New Granada (1739) and Rio de la Plata (1776), and new military governments in Texas (1718) and California (1767). But none of the later, sparsely inhabited conquests compared with Mexico and Peru in wealth and importance. Potosí in Upper Peru and Guanajuato in Mexico became the biggest sources of silver in the world, and by 1560 silver was the chief export from the American colonies to Spain.

Elsewhere on the American mainland colonisation was slower to take effect. The Portuguese, on the eastern coast of South America, were only goaded into action by fear of the French. But in 1549 they founded Bahía as an administrative capital, and sugar plantations and mills, worked by slaves from Africa, were introduced. Between 1575 and 1600 coastal Brazil became the foremost sugar-producing territory in the western world, and attracted many land-hungry immigrants from Portugal and the Azores. But the vast Brazilian interior remained largely unexplored and in the hands of native Indian tribes (map 4). The same was true of the whole of North America at this date, beyond the frontier of New Spain. With its harsh climate and poor soil, the eastern seaboard of North America was uninviting territory, and for the first century after its discovery the great Newfoundland fisheries were its main attraction. There was also a fur trade with the natives, and by 1535 French explorers had penetrated far up the St. Lawrence river in the quest of skins and furs. When, after 1670, the English also built up a fur-trading empire, based on Hudson Bay (map 5), the result was a rivalry which erupted in the colonial wars of the eighteenth century (page 86). Nevertheless, fish and furs were the original staple of North America, and settlement, strongly opposed by fishing interests, only began in the seventeenth century, with the foundation of Acadia, or Nova Scotia, by the French in 1604, of Virginia (1607) and Massachusetts Bay (1629) by the English, and of New Netherland, later New York, by the Dutch in 1623. Even so, progress was slow. As late as the end of the seventeenth century, the total population of the twelve English colonies was a mere 250,000.

The pattern of settlement was also different in the north. The English colonists wanted land for farms and plantations, expelling or exterminating the native population. The history of the British colonies in the eighteenth century is punctuated by savage Indian wars. In Virginia, and later in the Carolinas, where tobacco was introduced as a cash-crop from Guiana, the plantations were worked by Negro slaves, numbering well over 100,000 by the time of the American War of Independence. The Spaniards, on the other hand, relied on Indian labour, both in ranching and mining, and readily intermarried; hence the extensive *mestizo* population, particularly in Mexico and Peru. At the same time, all the colonies were firmly administered in the interests of the mother country. This inevitably provoked resentment on the part of the colonial élites, and lay behind the demand for independence which erupted in the north in 1775 (page 92) and in Latin America in 1808 (page 96).

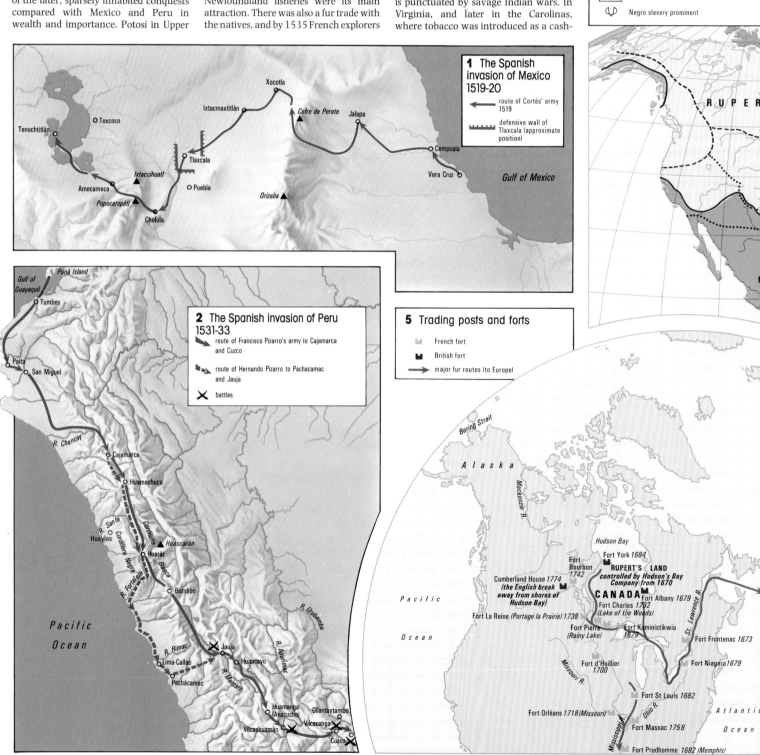

4 Population and settlement

- United States
- frontier of European settlement
- international boundary
- provincial boundary
- 1763 Proclamation Line
- Indian territory
- Negro slavery prominent

1 The Spanish invasion of Mexico 1519-20

- route of Cortès' army 1519
- defensive wall of Tlaxcala (approximate position)

2 The Spanish invasion of Peru 1531-33

- route of Francisco Pizarro's army to Cajamarca and Cuzco
- route of Hernando Pizarro to Pachacamac and Jauja
- battles

5 Trading posts and forts

- French fort
- British fort
- major fur routes (to Europe)

3 The development of colonial America

French territory
Spanish territory
Portuguese territory
Dutch territory
Russian territory
British by 1763
ceded by France to Britain 1763
ceded by France to Spain 1763
United States 1783
international boundary
provincial boundary
major exports
colonisation routes:
Spanish
Portuguese
British
Russian
French

Arctic Ocean

unexplored

GREENLAND

RUPERT'S LAND
(Hudson's Bay Company)

Hudson Bay

disputed by Russia and Spain

NEWFOUNDLAND

furs

ceded to Britain 1763

QUEBEC

St. Lawrence R.

Quebec
Montreal

NOVA SCOTIA

whale products, fish

UNITED
STATES
OF
AMERICA
1783

Boston
New York
Philadelphia

naval stores, furs, fish, grain

San Francisco

LOUISIANA

Ohio R.

THE
THIRTEEN
COLONIES

Jamestown

tobacco, grain

INTERIOR
PROVINCES

Los Angeles (1780)

Mississippi R.

Rio Grande

WEST FLORIDA

skins

New Orleans

EAST FLORIDA
(Br. 1763-83)

NEW

Gulf of Mexico

BAHAMA
ISLANDS
(Br. 1783)

sugar, tobacco

WEST

SPAIN

silver

CUBA

INDIES

Atlantic

Guanajuato

Mexico

JAMAICA
(Br. 1655)

SANTO DOMINGO

SAINT-
DOMINGUE

GUADELOUPE (Fr.)

MARTINIQUE (Fr.)

silver

Belize
(Br. 1683)

Caribbean Sea

CURAÇAO (Dutch 1634)

CENTRAL AMERICA

cochineal, gold

gold

Caracas

VENEZUELA

tobacco, cocoa beans, hides

QUEBEC

R. Orinoco

Paramaribo

Cayenne

GUIANA

Panama

Pacific

Santa Fé
de Bogotá

NEW

GRANADA

drugs, rare plants

*slave trade
from
Africa*

Venezuela

Quito

Ocean

*gold,
naval stores*

R. Amazon

NEW
GRANADA

BRAZIL

BRAZIL

PERU

*silver,
drugs*

Lima

Cuzco

Potosí

PERU

UPPER
PERU

R. São Francisco

*dyewoods,
sugar,
tobacco,
cotton*

Bahia

Treaty of Tordesillas 1494, 1506

CHILE

RIO
DE LA
PLATA

*copper,
grain*

R. Paraná

Paraguay R.

gold, diamonds

Rio de Janeiro

beef

CHILE

RIO
DE LA
PLATA
1776

hides, silver

Buenos Aires

Indian frontier

South

FALKLAND IS.

Atlantic

Ocean

*Spanish American
population in 1800*
(total 16.9 millions)

Whites 3.3

Indians 7.5

Negros 0.8

Mestizos 5.3

*Population of the
United States and Canada,
1820*
(total 11.6 millions)

Whites 9.0

Mulattos 0.1

Negroes 1.9

Indians 0.6

69

South-East Asia, 1511-1826

When European traders and adventurers broke through into the Indian Ocean at the close of the fifteenth century (page 64), the great prize, drawing them forward, was the spices of South-East Asia. Here was untold wealth to be tapped. But here also, at one of the world's main crossroads, where cultural influences from China and India intermingled, they found themselves in a region of great complexity, divided in religion between Buddhism, Hinduism and Islam, and politically fragmented and unstable (map 1). On the mainland, rival peoples and dynasties competed for hegemony. In the Malayan archipelago the empires of Srivijaya and Majapahit (page 50) had disappeared, leaving behind scores of petty states, with little cohesion. This was the situation when Albuquerque conquered the great international emporium of Malacca for the king of Portugal in 1511.

The Portuguese presence changed little at first. Albuquerque and his successors were there to dominate the spice trade through a chain of fortified trading-stations, linked by naval power. Provided this was accepted, they had no wish to interfere with the native potentates. Far more important, after the arrival on the scene of the Dutch and English (page 66), was the challenge to their trading monopoly by their European rivals. For most of the seventeenth century this rivalry was the dominant factor (map 3). The Dutch, in particular, began a systematic conquest of the Portuguese settlements, capturing Malacca in 1641, and then turned against the British. But in doing so, they were inevitably drawn into local politics. After establishing a base at Batavia in 1619, they interfered in succession disputes among the neighbouring sultans, to ensure their own position, and in this way gradually extended control over Java, expelling the British from Bantam in 1682 (map 4). Already earlier they had driven them out of the Spice Islands by the 'massacre of Amboina' (1623) and the seizure of Macassar (1667), in this way forcing the English East India Company to turn instead to the China trade. With this in view the British acquired Penang on the west coast of Malaya in 1786, the first step in a process which was ultimately to make them masters of the Malay peninsula.

But this was still exceptional. European activities encroached on the out-lying islands, but had little impact on the mainland monarchies, which had no direct interest in European trade and were mainly concerned with extending their power at the expense of their neighbours. This is a complicated story, because all the main centres were also under pressure from the hill peoples of the interior, always waiting to assert their independence; but the main lines of development are indicated on map 2. They include the advance of Annam at the expense of Cambodia, the rise of a new Burmese empire under Alaungpaya (1735–60), after a Mon rebellion in 1740, and successful Siamese resistance to Burmese encroachment, in spite of Burmese conquest in 1767. These events occurred for the most part without European involvement, but during the struggle for empire between England and France in the eighteenth century (page 86) some states were implicated. Already under Louis XIV France had intervened in Siam against the Dutch. During the Anglo-French war in India after 1746 it supported the Mon rebellion in Burma, and in reply the English East India Company seized the island of Negrais at the mouth of the Bassein river. Later, when the Burmese, foiled in their attempt to conquer Siam, switched their efforts to the north, the British, fearing for the security of Bengal, again intervened. The result was the first Anglo-Burmese war (1824–26) and the British annexation of Assam, Arakan and Tenasserim.

In Malaya there was similar encroachment on the independent rulers when the British, after acquiring Penang in 1786, established Singapore in 1819 as a free trade port after its acquisition by Raffles. This led to a conflict of interests with Holland which was only settled by the Anglo-Dutch treaty of 1824 when the British withdrew from Sumatra in return for Dutch withdrawal from Malacca (map 5). The future Dutch and British colonial empires in South-East Asia were taking shape. But their control was still loose and indirect. Only after the Industrial Revolution in Europe, and the expanding demand for raw materials and markets, were the lives and fortunes of the peoples of the region seriously affected.

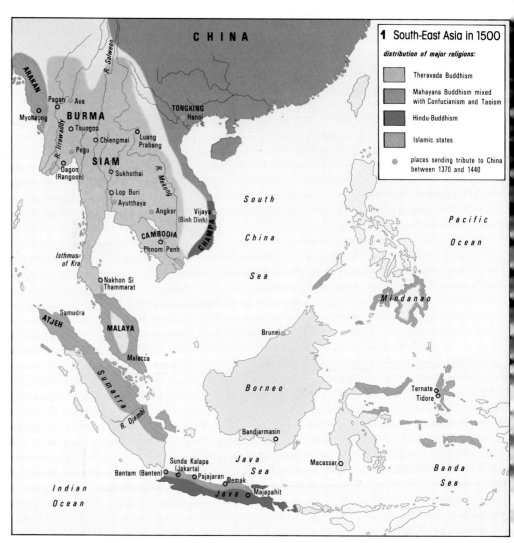

1 South-East Asia in 1500

distribution of major religions:

- Theravada Buddhism
- Mahayana Buddhism mixed with Confucianism and Taoism
- Hindu-Buddhism
- Islamic states
- places sending tribute to China between 1370 and 1440

3 European rivalries 1511-1682

- English expeditions
- Dutch expeditions
- Spanish expeditions
- Portuguese expeditions

first Dutch voyage to Bantam and Batavia 1595

English East India Company's first voyage to Atjeh and Bantam 1601-2

Portuguese expedition to Malacca 1511; to Bandas 1512; to Moluccas 1513

Malacca 1511 captured by Portuguese 1641 captured from Portuguese by Dutch

1571 Spanish capital Manila

abortive Spanish expedition to Tidore 1524

Francis Drake calls at Ternate 1579

Spanish expeditions from Manila to aid the Portuguese against Ternate begin 1582; against the Dutch from 1606

1513 Portuguese arrive at Ternate and Tidore.

1602-82 English factory

Batavia 1619 founded by Dutch

1667 captured by Dutch.

Amboina 1623 massacre of English factors by Dutch

low Farm Woes
nt Nightmares

with winter coming, the Election Day cash payments are the bigger concern, and political unknown.

Mr. Stenholm's own survival rests very much on his farm background and the ties he has nurtured with agricultural interests over his 20 years in Congress. From agribusiness giants to small ranchers and growers, his campaign finance reports testify to this support, and, even more than in his election two years ago, rural co-ops and hospitals are organizing on his behalf.

Matched against him are Christian conservatives he once counted as allies, and from Marilyn Quayle to Sen. John Ashcroft (R., Mo.), national GOP figures are stumping the district with his opponent, Rudy Izzard, this week. A 41-year-old dentist, Mr. Izzard came within a few points of winning in 1996 and hopes the tough economic times and Republican Gov. George Bush's own barnstorming re-election campaign will push him over the top.

The match reflects the perils that face even conservative Democrats in today's steadily more urbanized, more partisan Republican South. Because of his party, Mr. Stenholm is being attacked by the Christian right; because of his staunch conservatism, he's attacked by outside groups on the left.

ow Many Hits'

"They have been in this race with all our feet," says the farmer-legislator, belying his rural roots. "You wonder how many hits you can take."

Having voted for years against abortion, Mr. Stenholm was stunned to find himself targeted this week by the National Right to Life Political Action Committee having supported a campaign-finance-rehaul bill opposed by that PAC. At the

Asian-American Is in Close Race Against Boxer

By John Harwood
Staff Reporter of The Wall Street Journal

PALO ALTO, Calif.—Two years ago, the election campaign ended in disappointment for Albert Chin. A Clinton supporter, he watched a late-breaking campaign-finance scandal cast a shadow over the new prominence of Asian-Americans in politics.

But this fall, Mr. Chin has reason to celebrate: the very real prospect that his fellow Chinese-American, Matt Fong, a Republican, could unseat Democratic Sen. Barbara Boxer in Tuesday's election. "It's very important," says Mr. Chin, a businessman who serves on the board of San Francisco's Chinese Hospital. "For all these years we really didn't have any representation."

His excitement, like that of the other Asian-Americans who packed a recent Fong fund-raiser here at Ming's Restaurant, suggests that the 1996 campaign-money controversy may prove to have had virtually no impact

Matt Fong

on the rising political participation of Asian-Americans. Moreover, their enthusiasm for Mr. Fong could become a critical factor in one of the nation's key Senate races. A Field Poll released yesterday shows Ms. Boxer pulling out to a nine-percentage-point lead after a barrage of

Chile's Pinochet Fo⋯

Chilean Gen. Augusto Pinochet Ugarte, now under arrest in London pending judgments on his case by the British House of Lords and Spain's National Court, neither sought power nor exercised it in a manner we normally associate with dictators. Ultimately, he relinquished control of the Chilean government voluntarily and conducted a smooth restoration of civilian rule. To evaluate his actions, you must understand the circumstances of the attempted Marxist takeover of Chile in the 1970s.

Salvador Allende reached the presidency of Chile in 1970 with only 36% of the vote, barely 40,000 votes ahead of the can-

The Americas

By James R. Whelan

didate of the right. In Mr. Allende's 1,000 days of rule, Chile degenerated into what the much-lionized former Chilean president Eduardo Frei Montalva (father of the current president) called a "carnival of madness." Eleven months before the fall of President Allende, Mr. Frei said: "Chile is in the throes of an economic disaster: not a crisis, but a veritable catastrophe. . . ."

Shortly after those remarks were made, the legal ground beneath the Allende presidency began to crumble. The Chilean Supreme Court, the Bar Association and the leftist Medical Society, along with the Chamber of Deputies and provincial heads of the Christian Democrat Party, all warned that Allende was systematically trampling the law and constitution. By August 1973, more than a million Chileans—half the work force—were on strike, demanding that Allende go. Transport and industry were paralyzed. On Sept. 11, 1973, the armed forces acted

to oust Allende, going into battle against his gunslingers. Six hours after the fighting erupted, Allende blew his head off in the presidential palace with an AK 4⁷ given to him by Fidel Castro.

By the time the generals had complete⋯ their takeover, they were heroes to at leas⋯ two-thirds of the Chilean population. Bu⋯ they came under a heavy propaganda a⋯ tack from abroad. Much of the vilificatio⋯ emanated from Moscow. But it also cam⋯ from the then-powerful left in Western Eu⋯ rope. Part of the fury stemmed from a mi⋯ reading among European socialists ⋯ what Chilean "socialism" was all about. ⋯ Chile, the Socialist Party was the party ⋯ Maoist-style violence.

After the coup, Mr. Frei again spok⋯ out. In a moving letter to the head of th⋯ World Union of Christian Democrac⋯ Italy's Premier Mariano Rumor, the fc⋯ mer Chilean president wrote: "The mi⋯ tary have saved Chile. . . .Civil war wa⋯ fully planned by the Marxists. . . the eco⋯ omy of Chile was headed for disaster. ⋯ this country is destroyed." In those sen⋯ ments, he was joined by Chile's then tw⋯ other living ex-presidents. One of the⋯ Gabriel González Videla, said he "did ⋯ have words to thank the armed forces ⋯ having liberated us from the Marx⋯ claws." Looking ahead, he said he ⋯ pected "the best, because they have sav⋯ us and will permit us to live in dem⋯ racy. . . the totalitarian apparatus whi⋯ had been prepared to destroy us has its⋯ been destroyed. . . ."

Such judgments—expressed by m⋯ Chileans—would not, however, spare ⋯ military the wrath of leftist political eli⋯ around the world. To counter the still ex⋯ ing well-armed and well-funded guerr⋯ and urban terrorist forces, the embatt⋯ government created, in 1974, a military⋯ telligence agency which—before ⋯ Pinochet disbanded it in 1978—would

t Marxist Violence

e a rogue elephant responsible for of the human rights abuses. What is om spoken of is that most of the victims e terrorists. Before Fidel Castro sen- ed him to 30 years in prison in 1989, an Gen. Patricio de la Guardia ged at his "trial" of his service in Chile ng the Allende years. He said he had art of an international para-military ade—one that the Chilean government nated to number about 15,000.

n June 1974, the Communist Party in e reiterated its doctrine that the right se violence was "non-negotiable." But alk of violence was muted for a time as arty attempted to gain political allies.)76, however, party ideologue Volodia elboim in a Radio Moscow broadcast e of the need to "rethink the military lem," adding that Communists could be "Gullivers bound hand and foot by lity."

n April 5, 1977, a group of cashiered ean military men in London an- nced the formation of a "Front of De- ratic Armed Forces of Chile in Exile." cond such group was formed the same in Brussels and a third shortly after- ds in Communist East Berlin. On April spokesman named Jaime Estevez said Radio Moscow broadcast that the pur- e of these Soviet-backed entities was to the fight "for the overthrow of the fas- junta." In August of that year, the Cen- Committee of the Chilean Communist ty constituted itself as "The General f of Revolution."

n 1979, one month after the Sandinistas their way into power in Nicaragua, ean Communist Party Secretary Gen- Luis Corvalan said Chile "could be- e the second Nicaragua." A month r, he warned that "if fascism is not dicated... terrorism would find in Chile ide open field for its action." A year r, from his Moscow refuge, Corvalan proclaimed a new era of "acute violence." Corvalan endorsed guerrilla warfare, ter- rorism and a massive armed uprising.

By 1986, increasingly legalized political activity in Chile was gathering momentum in preparation for what would be free elec- tions in 1988. Early that year, the military stumbled onto part of one of the largest clandestine arms shipments in the history of the hemisphere, enough to arm 5,000 men. It was traced to Cuba. That same year, a meticulously planned assassina- tion plot involving 70 terrorists narrowly missed killing Gen. Pinochet; five of his es- corts were murdered.

In the aftermath of each of these inci- dents, the government cracked down on the terrorist groups. Inevitably, innocent people were affected. The armed under- ground responded with stepped-up sabo- tage—and a campaign of assassinations of police officers. Among many examples: On April 2, 1988 three youths murdered police Corp. Alfredo Rivera Rojas, a 35-year-old father of two, while he was carrying gro- ceries home in Santiago.

There were innocent victims on both sides of this civil war, but the fact is that far fewer died in Chile than did in most other Latin conflicts in this century. The Rettig Commission—named by the first post-military government to investigate human rights abuses and headed by a for- mer Allende minister—counted a total of 2,279 dead and missing on both sides. The first three months of fighting claimed 1,261 of the victims.

What the Chilean military—arguably the most professional and disciplined in all of Latin America—left behind was a nation incomparably better off than the wreckage they inherited. But General Pinochet's op- ponents have never forgotten their defeat.

Mr. Whelan is the author of six books on Latin America, including a history of Chile.

Texas Legislator's Battle Shou
Are Turning Races Into Incun

By David Rogers
Staff Reporter of The Wall Street Journal

MERKEL, Texas—Stoop-shouldered, with his plowman arms by his side, Rep. Charles Stenholm comes politicking on the brick-paved streets of this small West Texas town.

"Working on that three-inch rain," he grins, surprising drought-stricken merchants and farmers at their morning drugstore coffee. Leaving the flower shop minutes later, he shouts over his shoulder: "We need the votes. They're after us this time."

Bad weather and low cotton prices have knocked the pins out of the farm economy here. Next Tuesday, Republicans hope to do the same to Mr. Stenholm, a thorn in their side as the top Democrat on the House Agriculture Committee and last remnant of the rural conservative Democrats who once dominated the South.

The 60-year-old cotton farmer is in the fight of his political life, as agriculture's troubles here are replicated in rural districts across the country. Amid Asia's economic turmoil, grain prices have tumbled across the Upper Midwest and wheat-growing counties in Rocky Mountain states. And what looks like an incumbent-friendly election elsewhere can be an incumbent's nightmare, making farm issues pivotal to a half dozen other races for Congress.

"It will make the difference," Idaho Democrat Richard Stallings says of agriculture's influence in the campaign. As an outsider, low wheat and cattle prices have boosted his own comeback bid for an open seat in his Republican-dominated state. In the House district next door, the same combination of low commodity prices has put GOP Rep. Helen Chenowith, a member of

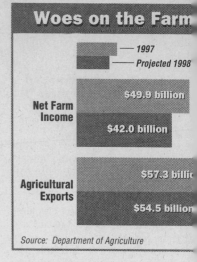

Woes on the Farm

— 1997
— Projected 1998

Net Farm Income
$49.9 billion
$42.0 billion

Agricultural Exports
$57.3 billic
$54.5 billion

Source: Department of Agriculture

vainly in May to derail a popular Se‚ passed crop-insurance and agricultura search bill.

As prices fell this year, Democrats Mr. Stenholm tried to amend the 1996 f‚ reform law. Republicans refused, anc standoff led Congress simply to put ch in the mail. Annual market-transition ments to farmers, which were meant t‚ cline over time under the GOP's orig plan, will be bigger by half this fall— paid early.

The Agriculture Department nounced yesterday that the first $2.8(lion in payments will begin to go out T day, Election Day. In Texas alone, t payments could total about $248 mil the largest amount to cotton producers

'A Godsend'

"This money is going to be a godse Mr. Stenholm says. "The bad news is in none of this was the‚ ‚‚‚ ‚‚‚‚‚‚‚

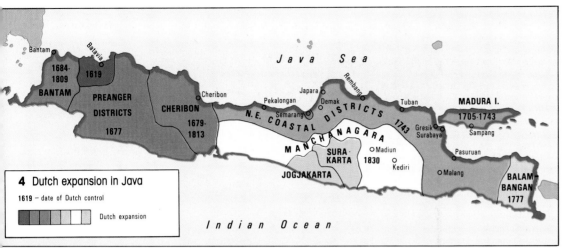

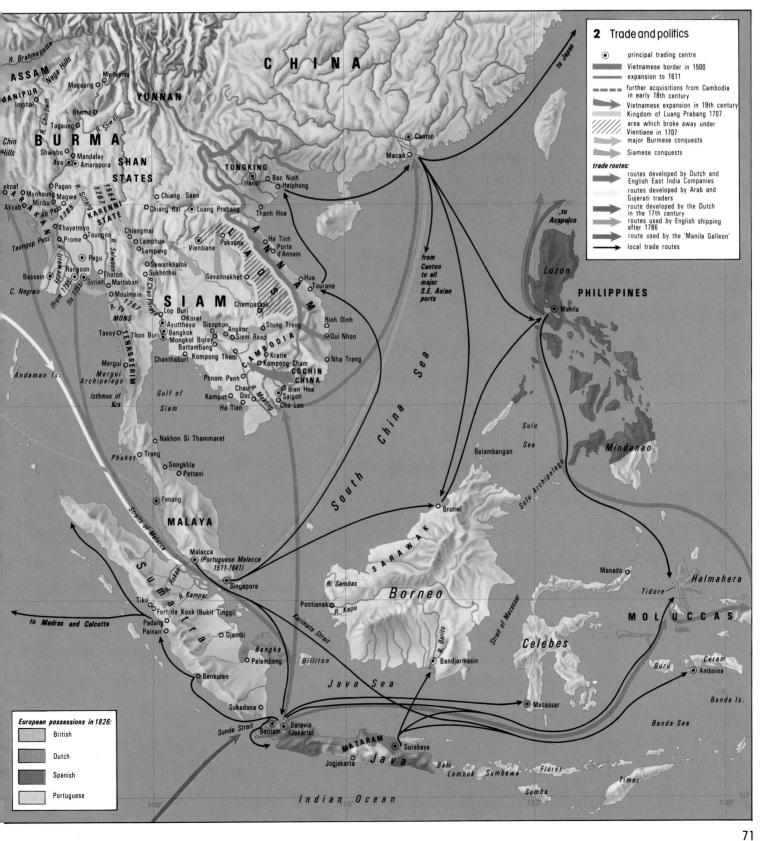

New monarchy in Europe, 1453-1547

In Europe revival after the setbacks of the fourteenth century (page 56) began around 1450. The whole continent was affected. In the east Ivan III (1462–1505) profited from the decline of the Mongol khanates (page 46) to inaugurate a rapid expansion of the territory of Muscovy (page 84) and to attack the independence of Tver, Novgorod and the landowning aristocracy. In the west endemic civil war in Spain was ended after the union of Castile and Aragon in 1479. The ending of the Hundred Years' War between England and France (1453) and the expulsion of the English from French territory saw a rapid extension of the area controlled by the French monarchy (map 2), while in England Edward IV (1461–83) began a restoration of royal power which was carried further by the new Tudor dynasty after 1485. Through the Council in the North with its seat at York, and the Council in the March of Wales, with its seat at Ludlow, the turbulent outlying regions were brought under control, while Wales itself and the palatinates of Chester and Durham wcrc integrated into the parliamentary and judicial systems from 1536 (map 4). But an attempt to integrate Ireland by Poynings' Law (1494) had little effect, and although Henry VIII was proclaimed King of Ireland (1541), English power was effectively limited to the Pale around Dublin. Scotland also resisted successfully.

Not all attempts at state-building were a success. The efforts of the dukes of Burgundy to erect an independent state in the rich lands between France and the Empire collapsed when the ambitious Charles the Bold was killed at Nancy in 1477 (map 3). The empire of Matthias

Corvinus of Hungary (1458–90) also proved ephemeral. Italy remained divided, in spite of a marked strengthening of government under rulers such as Lorenzo de' Medici (1469–92) at Florence and Ludovico Sforza (1460–99) at Milan (map 5), and after the French invasion of 1494 internal divisions left Italy a prey to foreign intervention. The main legatee in all instances was the house of Habsburg, which succeeded to the Spanish possessions in 1516 and emerged, under Charles V (1519–56) as the preponderant power in western Europe (map 1). But the diversified Habsburg empire lacked cohesion, and when the Ottoman advance, halted on the middle Danube since 1456, was resumed after 1520 (page 48), and at the same time the emperor was involved in the religious wars in Germany (page 74), the strain was too great. In 1556 Charles V abdicated and the empire was divided between the Austrian and Spanish Habsburgs. Only ten years later the Dutch revolt began.

The Dutch revolt, although the most formidable uprising (page 76), was not exceptional. In England, from Henry VII to Elizabeth I, the Tudors were faced by repeated rebellions, and elsewhere, even in Russia, resistance to centralisation became a powerful force after 1550. The rise of the new monarchies was less a new beginning than the culmination of the long struggle of aristocracy and monarchy. Their financial and administrative machinery was not adequate enough to raise a new, modern system of government in place of the old feudal order, and the decisive change from the old to the new was not made until after another century of strife and turmoil.

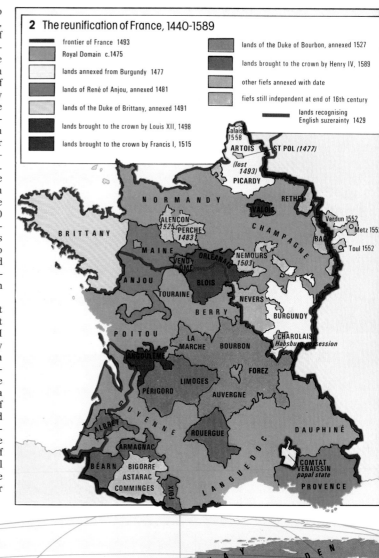

2 The reunification of France, 1440-1589

- frontier of France 1493
- Royal Domain c.1475
- lands annexed from Burgundy 1477
- lands of René of Anjou, annexed 1481
- lands of the Duke of Brittany, annexed 1491
- lands brought to the crown by Louis XII, 1498
- lands brought to the crown by Francis I, 1515
- lands of the Duke of Bourbon, annexed 1527
- lands brought to the crown by Henry IV, 1589
- other fiefs annexed with date
- fiefs still independent at end of 16th century
- lands recognising English suzerainty 1429

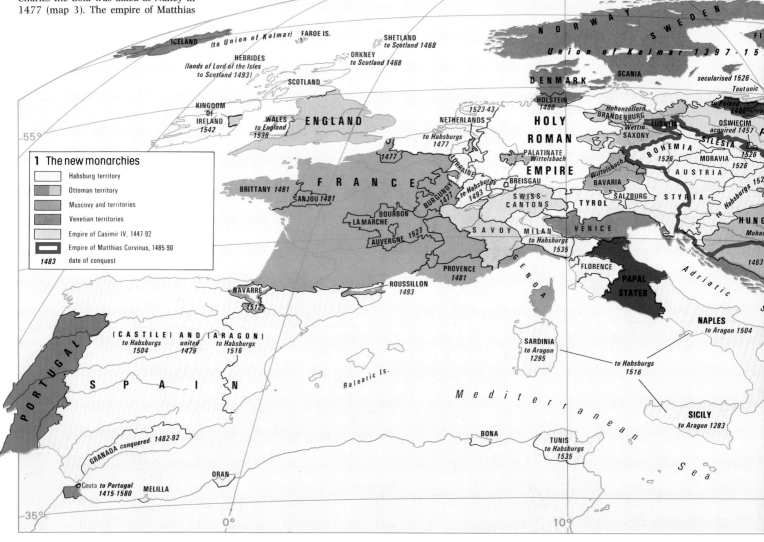

1 The new monarchies

- Habsburg territory
- Ottoman territory
- Muscovy and territories
- Venetian territories
- Empire of Casimir IV, 1447-92
- Empire of Matthias Corvinus, 1485-90
- *1483* date of conquest

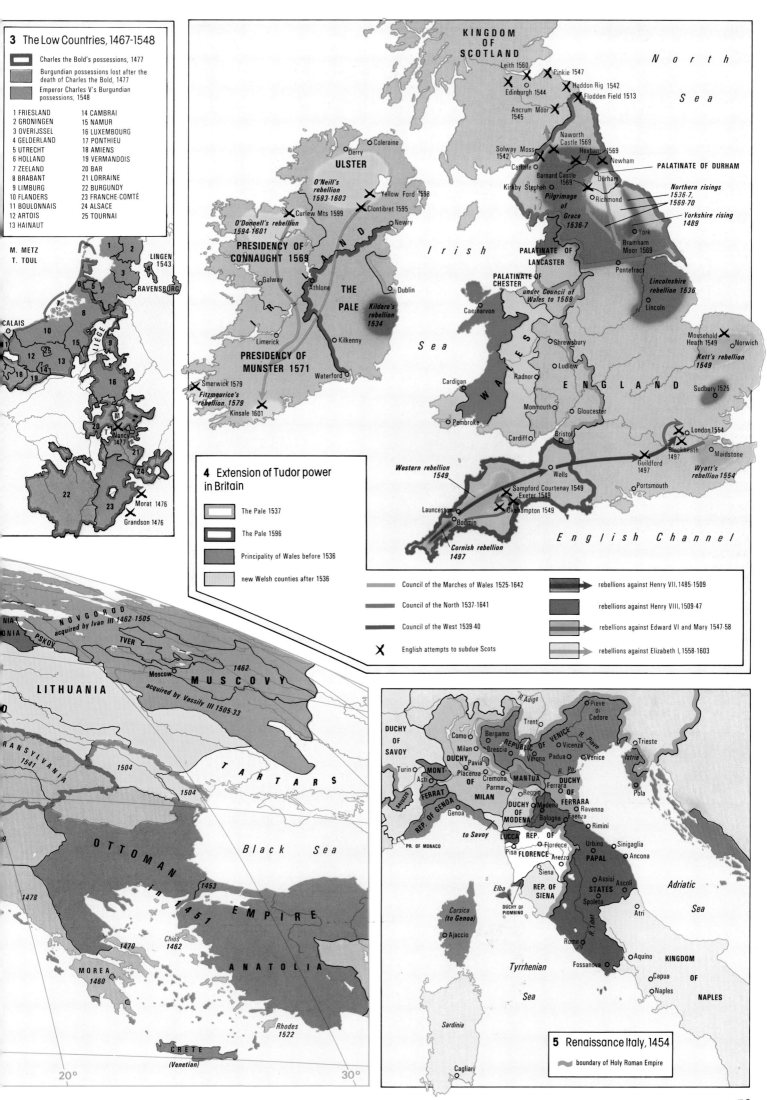

3 The Low Countries, 1467-1548

- Charles the Bold's possessions, 1477
- Burgundian possessions lost after the death of Charles the Bold, 1477
- Emperor Charles V's Burgundian possessions, 1548

1 FRIESLAND
2 GRONINGEN
3 OVERIJSSEL
4 GELDERLAND
5 UTRECHT
6 HOLLAND
7 ZEELAND
8 BRABANT
9 LIMBURG
10 FLANDERS
11 BOULONNAIS
12 ARTOIS
13 HAINAUT
14 CAMBRAI
15 NAMUR
16 LUXEMBOURG
17 PONTHIEU
18 AMIENS
19 VERMANDOIS
20 BAR
21 LORRAINE
22 BURGUNDY
23 FRANCHE-COMTÉ
24 ALSACE
25 TOURNAI

M. METZ
T. TOUL

LINGEN 1543
RAVENSBURG
CALAIS
LIÈGE
Nancy 1477
Morat 1476
Grandson 1476

4 Extension of Tudor power in Britain

- The Pale 1537
- The Pale 1596
- Principality of Wales before 1536
- new Welsh counties after 1536

- Council of the Marches of Wales 1525-1642
- Council of the North 1537-1641
- Council of the West 1539-40
- ✕ English attempts to subdue Scots
- rebellions against Henry VII, 1485-1509
- rebellions against Henry VIII, 1509-47
- rebellions against Edward VI and Mary 1547-58
- rebellions against Elizabeth I, 1558-1603

KINGDOM OF SCOTLAND
North Sea
Leith 1560
Pinkie 1547
Haddon Rig 1542
Edinburgh 1544
Flodden Field 1513
Ancrum Moor 1545
Naworth Castle 1569
Solway Moss 1542
Hexham 1569
Newham
Carlisle
PALATINATE OF DURHAM
Barnard Castle 1569
Durham
Kirkby Stephen
Pilgrimage of Grace 1536-7
Richmond
Northern risings 1536-7, 1569-70
Yorkshire rising 1489
York
Bramham Moor 1569
Pontefract
Coleraine
Derry
ULSTER
O'Neill's rebellion 1593-1603
Yellow Ford 1598
Clontibret 1595
Curlew Mts 1599
Newry
O'Donnell's rebellion 1594-1601
PRESIDENCY OF CONNAUGHT 1569
Galway
Athlone
THE PALE
Dublin
Kildare's rebellion 1534
IRELAND
Irish Sea
PALATINATE OF LANCASTER
PALATINATE OF CHESTER
under Council of Wales to 1569
Lincolnshire rebellion 1536
Lincoln
Mousehold Heath 1549
Norwich
Kett's rebellion 1549
Caernarvon
Shrewsbury
WALES
ENGLAND
Limerick
Kilkenny
PRESIDENCY OF MUNSTER 1571
Waterford
Cardigan
Ludlow
Radnor
Monmouth
Gloucester
Sudbury 1525
Pembroke
Cardiff
Bristol
London 1554
Blackheath 1497
Maidstone
Guildford 1497
Wyatt's rebellion 1554
Smerwick 1579
Fitzmaurice's rebellion 1579
Kinsale 1601
Western rebellion 1549
Wells
Sampford Courtenay 1549
Exeter 1549
Launceston
Okehampton 1549
Bodmin
Cornish rebellion 1497
Portsmouth
English Channel

LITHUANIA
NOVGOROD acquired by Ivan III 1462-1505
PSKOV
TVER
Moscow 1462
MUSCOVY
acquired by Vassily III 1505-33
TARTARS
TRANSYLVANIA 1541
1504
1504
OTTOMAN EMPIRE in 1451
Black Sea
1478
1453
Chios 1462
1470
MOREA 1460
ANATOLIA
Rhodes 1522
CRETE (Venetian)
20°
30°

5 Renaissance Italy, 1454

- boundary of Holy Roman Empire

R. Adige
Pieve di Cadore
Trent
R. Piave
DUCHY OF SAVOY
Como
Bergamo
REPUBLIC OF VENICE
Vicenza
Trieste
Milan
Brescia
Verona
Padua
Venice
Istria
Turin
DUCHY OF
Pavia
Mantua
R. Po
Pola
MONT-FERRAT
Asti
Piacenza
Cremona
DUCHY OF MANTUA
Parma
Reggio
Ferrara
DUCHY OF FERRARA
Ravenna
SALUZZO
DUCHY OF MILAN
DUCHY OF MODENA
Modena
Faenza
Rimini
REP. OF GENOA
Genoa
to Savoy
Bologna
PR. OF MONACO
LUCCA
REP. OF
Pisa
FLORENCE
Florence
Arezzo
Urbino
Sinigaglia
Ancona
PAPAL STATES
Siena
Assisi
Ascoli
Elba
REP. OF SIENA
Spoleto
Adriatic Sea
DUCHY OF PIOMBINO
Corsica (to Genoa)
Ajaccio
Rome
R. Tiber
Atri
Tyrrhenian Sea
Fossanova
Aquino
KINGDOM OF NAPLES
Capua
Naples
Sardinia
Cagliari

73

The Reformation in Europe, 1517-1648

The closing years of the fifteenth century saw a great revival of popular religion in Europe, but the established church, which never fully recovered from the effects of the schism of 1378–1417 (page 56), was ill equipped to satisfy its needs. Except in Bohemia and Moravia, where the Hussites comprised over half the population, and in England, where small groups of Lollards survived, heresy was virtually dead by 1500; but the materialism of the Renaissance popes and the self-seeking of the higher clergy discredited the hierarchy in the eyes of many laymen. Some, like Erasmus of Rotterdam (1466–1536) and Sir Thomas More (1478–1535), still pinned their hopes on spiritual renewal; but elsewhere, particularly in Germany and German-speaking Switzerland, financial and other abuses fired revolt. In 1517 Martin Luther (1483–1546) posted his 95 theses on the church door at Wittenberg. In 1520, under the impulse of Huldreich Zwingli (1484–1531), Zurich renounced allegiance to Rome. Their denunciations of the clergy and the supremacy of the pope and their demand for a return to the standards of early Christianity exercised a vast appeal. By 1560 (map 1) seven out of ten of the Emperor's subjects were Protestants, and the reformed faith prevailed in Scandinavia, Baltic Europe and England. Further impetus came from the teaching of John Calvin (1509–64). In France over one hundred Calvinist churches existed by 1559 and perhaps 700 by 1562, and Calvinism also made rapid progress in Poland, Hungary and Scotland, where it became the official religion in 1560. In addition, a number of more radical sects

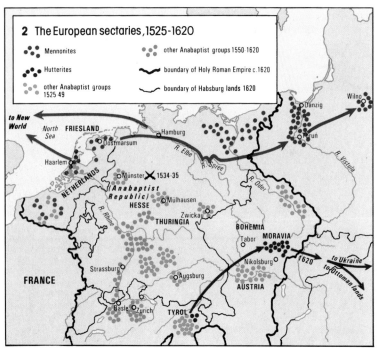

2 The European sectaries, 1525-1620

- Mennonites
- Hutterites
- other Anabaptist groups 1525-49
- other Anabaptist groups 1550-1620
- boundary of Holy Roman Empire c.1620
- boundary of Habsburg lands 1620

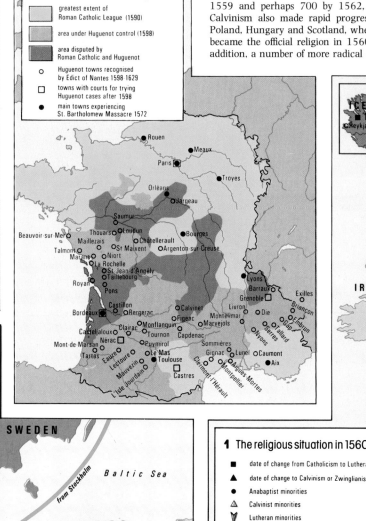

3 The French wars of religion

- greatest extent of Roman Catholic League (1590)
- area under Huguenot control (1598)
- area disputed by Roman Catholic and Huguenot
- ○ Huguenot towns recognised by Edict of Nantes 1598-1629
- □ towns with courts for trying Huguenot cases after 1598
- ● main towns experiencing St. Bartholomew Massacre 1572

4 The Thirty Years' War in Germany 1618-48

- route of the Spanish Army 1634
- route of Gustavus Adolphus 1631-2
- ✕ imperial (Catholic) victory
- ✕ imperial (Catholic) defeat
- boundary of Holy Roman Empire
- areas affected by Edict of Restitution 1629
- ■ date region became Lutheran
- ▲ date region became Calvinist

the religious position in 1640:

- Lutheran
- Calvinist
- Catholic
- regained by Roman Catholics

1 The religious situation in 1560

- ■ date of change from Catholicism to Lutheranism
- ▲ date of change to Calvinism or Zwinglianism
- ● Anabaptist minorities
- △ Calvinist minorities
- ▽ Lutheran minorities
- ◐ Roman Catholic minorities
- □ Muslim minorities

there were scattered Jewish communities in the Ottoman Empire, Hungary, Poland, Portugal, Bohemia and Italy

- Roman Catholic
- Calvinist
- Lutheran
- Anglican
- Hussite
- Orthodox
- Muslim

rang up, Anabaptists, Mennonites and others (map 2), which rejected theology, ritual and clerical order in favour of biblical simplicity and often combined evangelism with social protest. They even proclaimed an Anabaptist republic at Münster in 1534, but it was brutally suppressed the next year.

However, the reformation was soon entangled in politics. Princes and kings, including Henry VIII of England, saw an opportunity to despoil the church of its wealth. Some German princes espoused protestantism out of fear of imperial power. Luther himself, dependent on princely support, turned against the more radical sectaries and condemned the peasants' revolt of 1525. Foreign policy

also played a part. The Valois kings of France, though combating the protestant Huguenots at home, supported the German Protestant princes against the Habsburg emperor. Although the French Huguenots won toleration by the Edict of Nantes (1598), their numbers were severely reduced during the religious wars between 1562 and 1589 (map 3), and elsewhere in Europe the second half of the sixteenth century saw a great Catholic revival, led by the Jesuit order, founded in 1534 by St. Ignatius Loyola (1491–1556), and inspired by the reforms of the Council of Trent between 1545 and 1563. Using the Jesuits as their spearhead, Catholic rulers went over to the offensive. Protestants were expelled

from Bavaria (1579) and Styria (1600), and in Poland the number of Protestant churches decreased from 560 in 1572 to 240 in 1650.

The decisive phase of the struggle between Protestants and Catholics, the Thirty Years' War, took place in the Holy Roman Empire (map 4). It began in 1618–21 when the emperor Ferdinand II defeated the Bohemian Protestants at the battle of the White Mountain (1620) and won back Bohemia and Moravia for Catholicism. When he turned against the Protestant princes of Germany, Denmark, England and the Dutch intervened on the Protestant side, but the imperial forces were initially successful and in 1629 an Edict of Restitution was promulgated

which reclaimed large areas of church lands held by Protestant princes. Only the intervention of Gustavus Adolphus of Sweden saved the Protestant cause from collapse. But the Swedish victories at Breitenfeld (1631) and Lützen (1632) brought in Spain on the imperial side, while France allied with Sweden and declared war on Spain (1635). The war was now a European war, but by 1644 it was evident that neither side could hope for outright victory, and in 1648 the Peace of Westphalia brought a compromise solution. Lutherans and Calvinists retained the lands they held in 1624, and the wars of religion were over. But Germany, the scene of battle, suffered a lasting setback.

Western Europe, 1558-1648

The second half of the sixteenth and the first half of the seventeenth centuries were a time of turbulence throughout Europe. In Russia the 'time of troubles' after the death of Ivan the Terrible (1584) lasted until 1613. Northern Europe was embroiled in almost continuous war from 1561 to 1658, as Sweden, independent since the time of Gustavus Vasa (1523–60), struggled with Denmark, Russia, Poland and Brandenburg for control of the Baltic and its important trade. The rise of the Swedish empire (map 3), leading to Gustavus Adolphus' intervention in the Thirty Years' War (page 74) and the Swedish acquisition of western Pomerania, Wismar and the bishoprics of Bremen and Verden at the Peace of Westphalia, vitally affected the balance of power in Europe and was one of the most significant developments of the period. In western Europe progress was more chequered. The new monarchies of the preceding period (page 72) had over-reached themselves, and from around 1536 reaction set in, particularly when rising prices, recession and widespread unemployment reinforced existing discontents. The Elizabethan Poor Law and other legislation of 1563 was no remedy; indeed, the reign of Elizabeth I (1558–1603), was less auspicious than often painted, and Elizabeth, whose relations with parliament deteriorated sharply at the end of her reign, left her Stuart successors on the English throne a legacy of unsolved problems with which they failed to cope.

From around 1530, sometimes earlier, the history of France and England was punctuated by revolts. As in Germany (page 74), they reflected a combination of religious, social and political grievances. In England the northern risings of 1536 and 1569 (page 72) were Catholic protests against the suppression of the old faith, but they also embodied the resistance of the northern gentry to centralisation and control from London. On the other wing the unrest of radical dissenters combined dissatisfaction with Henry VIII's and Elizabeth's conservative church settlements with resistance to the enclosure of common lands for the benefit of grasping landlords. A similar mixture of motives permeated the frequent uprisings, 500 in all, in France (map 2). These were largely revolts of the common people, driven to extremes by economic hardship; but in the end the most influential factor, visible in France in the revolt of the judges and nobility which drove the king from Paris in 1649, was resistance to autocracy, centralisation and taxation. The Dutch revolt, beginning in 1566, which effectively secured independence in 1609 (map 1),

was inspired by fear that the central government, controlled from Spain, intended to override the traditional liberties of the Netherlands. Similar motives underlay the Catalan and Portuguese revolts against Castile (1640). The problem of the central governments was that inflation and other economic difficulties, together with the expense of war, were eating into their resources. Hence the attempt of Charles I (1625–49) to levy tonnage and poundage, collect forced loans and impose ship money (1634), levies which were the antecedent causes of the English civil war (map 4). When civil war finally broke out in 1642, it was a defence of traditional English liberties against a thrusting monarchy, a fact which explains the conservatism of the subsequent settlement. When, after the defeat of the monarchy, the Lord Protector, Oliver Cromwell, beat down the radical Levellers in 1647, the future outlines of a conservative England, dominated by the gentry, were drawn. After the Restoration in 1660, still more after 1688, power was shared between parliament, representing landowners and merchants, and the crown, with the former gradually asserting its preponderance.

In continental Europe the sequel was different. In France the failure of the Fronde broke the power of the aristocracy and cleared the way for the absolutism of Louis XIV (page 80). Only in Germany was the disarray caused by a century of religious and political conflict enduring. Here the devastation of the Thirty Years' War resulted in a decline of population from some 21 millions in 1618 to around 13 millions in 1648 (map 5), and though some regions were spared, the setback was undeniable. The outcome was a major shift in the European balance. The Habsburgs, who had dominated the previous period, were in retreat, and the future was in the hands of a resurgent France and its rivals, the maritime powers.

The English Civil War (below)

1/Edinburgh 1638: National Covenant signed.

2/Newcastle 1640: Scottish Covenanters invade England and force Charles I to buy them off.

3/Kilkenny 1641: centre of rebellion by Irish Catholics (to 1649).

4/Antrim 1641: massacre of Catholics by Protestants.

5/Westminster 1642: English Parliament raises army against Charles I.

6/Edgehill 1642: first battle of English Civil War, indecisive.

7/Westminster 1643: alliance of English Parliament and Scottish Covenanters against Charles I (to 1648).

8/Nantwich 1644: Parliamentary army defeats Irish Catholic invasion in support of Charles I.

9/Marston Moor 1644: Scots and Parliamentary army defeat Charles I and occupy N. England.

10/Lostwithiel 1644: Parliamentary army loses control of SW England to King.

11/Tippermuir 1644: Montrose and Scottish royalists defeat Covenanters.

12/Philiphaugh 1645: Montrose defeated by Covenanters and forced to flee.

13/Naseby 1645: Parliamentary army defeats Charles I and wins control of all England.

14/Burford 1647: Oliver Cromwell suppresses mutiny of Parliamentary troops (the 'Levellers').

15/Preston 1648: Cromwell defeats Covenanters' invasion of England in support of Charles I.

16/Whitehall 1649: Parliament tries and executes Charles I.

17/Drogheda and Wexford 1649: Cromwell overruns Ireland and ends rebellion there; occupied to 1660.

18/Dunbar 1650: Cromwell defeats Covenanters and occupies Scotland (to 1660).

19/Scone 1651: Charles II crowned king of Scotland by Covenanters.

20/Worcester 1651: Cromwell defeats invasion of Covenanters in support of Charles II who is forced to flee abroad (to 1660).

21/Whitehall 1658: death of Oliver Cromwell (Head of State since 1654).

22/Westminster 1660: coronation of Charles II as king of England.

1 The Dutch revolt, 1559-1

- boundary of Netherlands 1548
- rebel areas in 1572 (December)
- furthest extent of Dutch revolt (July 1577)
- rebel areas December 1588
- rebel areas December 1606
- Dutch conquests 1621-48
- the Dutch Republic 1648

English Channel

Dunkir

KINGD
OF
DENM

North Sea

Hamburg

DUTCH
REPUBLIC

Bremen

Hano

R. Weser

Münster

Göttin

Cologne

R. Rhine

Coblenz

R. Mosel

Frankfur

Mainz

Trier

Würzbur

Heidelberg

Strassburg

Breisach

Basle

SWISS
CONFEDERATION

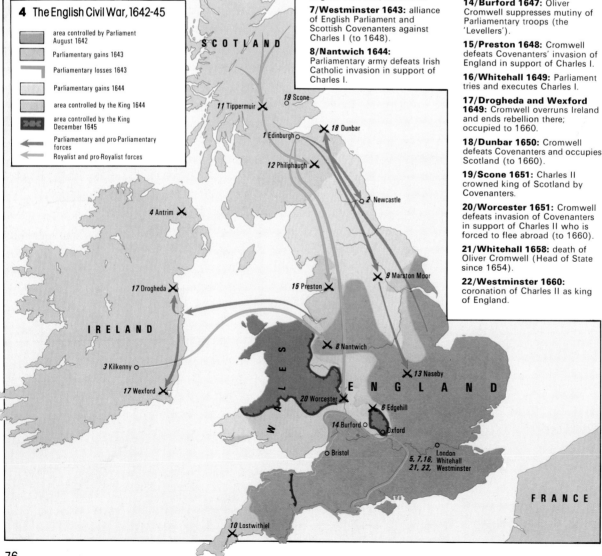

4 The English Civil War, 1642-45

- area controlled by Parliament August 1642
- Parliamentary gains 1643
- Parliamentary losses 1643
- Parliamentary gains 1644
- area controlled by the King 1644
- area controlled by the King December 1645
- Parliamentary and pro-Parliamentary forces
- Royalist and pro-Royalist forces

SCOTLAND

19 Scone

11 Tippermuir

18 Dunbar

1 Edinburgh

12 Philiphaugh

2 Newcastle

4 Antrim

9 Marston Moor

17 Drogheda

15 Preston

IRELAND

8 Nantwich

3 Kilkenny

13 Naseby

17 Wexford

WALES

20 Worcester

ENGLAND

6 Edgehill

14 Burford

Oxford

Bristol

London
5, 7, 16, Whitehall
21, 22, Westminster

FRANCE

10 Lostwithiel

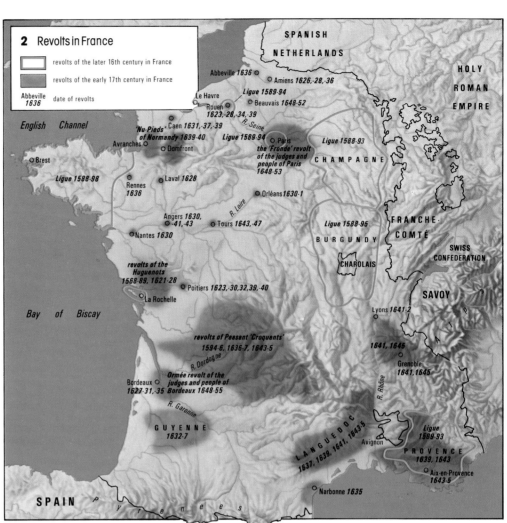

2 Revolts in France

□ revolts of the later 16th century in France

▨ revolts of the early 17th century in France

Abbeville 1636 date of revolts

Abbeville 1636
Amiens 1626,-28,-36
Le Havre
Ligue 1589-94
Beauvais 1648-52
Rouen 1623,-28,-34,-39
Caen 1631,-37,-39
'Nu-Pieds' of Normandy 1639-40
Ligue 1589-94
Paris the 'Fronde' revolt of the judges and people of Paris 1648-53
Ligue 1588-93
CHAMPAGNE
Avranches
Domfront
Brest
Ligue 1588-98
Laval 1628
Orléans 1630-1
Rennes 1636
R. Loire
FRANCHE-COMTÉ
Angers 1630,-41,43
Tours 1643,-47
Ligue 1588-95
BURGUNDY
SWISS CONFEDERATION
Nantes 1630
CHAROLAIS
revolts of the Huguenots 1588-89, 1621-28
Poitiers 1623,-30,32,39,-40
SAVOY
La Rochelle
Bay of Biscay
Lyons 1641-2
revolts of Peasant 'Croquants' 1594-6, 1636-7, 1643-5
R. Dordogne
1641, 1645
Grenoble 1641, 1645
Bordeaux 1627-31,-35
Ormée revolt of the judges and people of Bordeaux 1648-55
R. Garonne
GUYENNE 1632-7
LANGUEDOC 1637, 1639, 1641, 1643-5
Avignon
Ligue 1569-93
PROVENCE 1639, 1643
Aix-en-Provence 1643-5
Narbonne 1635
SPAIN
Pyrenees

5 Depopulation during the Thirty Years' War

~ boundary of Holy Roman Empire 1648

population decrease:

| 0-15% | 15-33% | 33-66% | over 66% |

3 The rise of the Swedish Empire

▨ Sweden at the death of Gustavus Vasa 1560

▨ conquests 1561-1645

□ conquests 1645-1658

~ Swedish Empire at its greatest extent 1658

77

Germany and its neighbours
1648-1806

The Peace of Westphalia (1648), besides bringing to a close the wars of religion (page 74), was a milestone in German history. The failure of the emperor to impose his will on the Protestant princes confirmed the political fragmentation which had gathered pace since the fourteenth century (page 54). After 1648 Germany was a patchwork of some 300 small, petty states and free cities (map 1). In addition, the independence of Holland and Switzerland was formally recognised. Theoretically the rights of the princes were limited by the rights of the Holy Roman Empire, but in practice every prince was emperor in his own lands, with full sovereign powers including the right to make foreign alliances. Political disruption was also compounded by a sharp economic setback, due partly to the devastation and depopulation resulting from the Thirty Years' War, but also to a long-term shift in the European economy. The great south German banking houses of Welser and Fugger went bankrupt in 1614 and 1627 respectively. The Hanseatic League, in disarray since the closing years of the sixteenth century, was dissolved in 1669. Everywhere the towns were in decline, particularly in Austria, Prussia and Bavaria, but even worse was the plight of the peasantry. In Bohemia and Moravia their legal rights were abolished; in the north and north-east they were ejected from their holdings to permit the consolidation of Junker estates, and reduced to serfdom (page 82). Impoverishment and stagnation were the result. A modest economic recovery occurred after 1750; but with its resources dissipated on ostentatious building and the upkeep of princely households Germany was an economic and social backwater. It was also a pawn in great power politics. Divided among themselves and fearful of Habsburg ambitions, the princes were clients of foreign powers, including England and Sweden, but particularly of France, which used its position to make inroads on German territories in the west (page 80), annexing Strasbourg (1681), most of Alsace (1697), the free county of Burgundy (1714), and Bar and Lorraine (1766).

After 1648, apart from Austria, only Saxony, Bavaria and Brandenburg could claim even the status of second-rate powers. Saxony, with the mineral resources of the Erzgebirge and its varied industries, was the most advanced, while Bavaria was falling behind; but Brandenburg-Prussia was beginning, under the Great Elector (1640–88) the long climb which made it by 1786 the second German power and the rival of Austria. The rise of Prussia (map 2) is a story of tenacity, unscrupulous diplomacy, but above all of single-

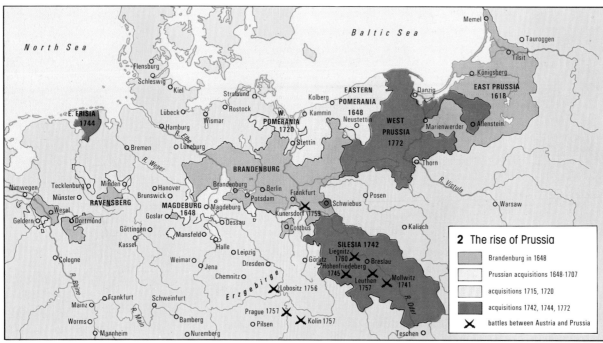

2 The rise of Prussia
- Brandenburg in 1648
- Prussian acquisitions 1648-1707
- acquisitions 1715, 1720
- acquisitions 1742, 1744, 1772
- ✕ battles between Austria and Prussia

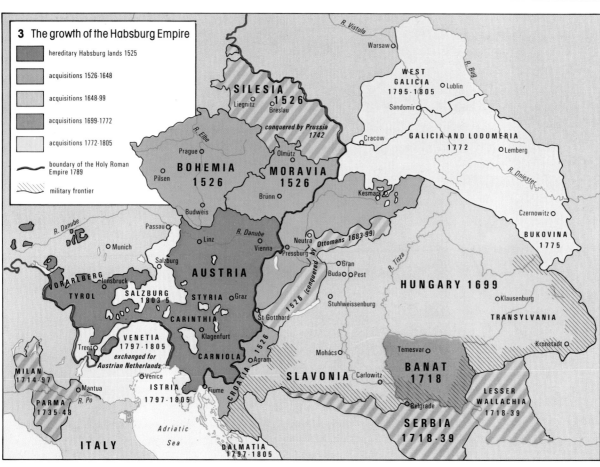

3 The growth of the Habsburg Empire
- hereditary Habsburg lands 1525
- acquisitions 1526-1648
- acquisitions 1648-99
- acquisitions 1699-1772
- acquisitions 1772-1805
- boundary of the Holy Roman Empire 1789
- military frontier

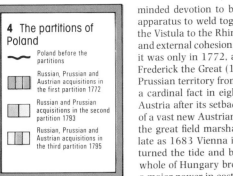
minded devotion to building a strong military and administrative apparatus to weld together the scattered territories stretching from the Vistula to the Rhine. The Hohenzollern domains lacked internal and external cohesion. Prussia itself was until 1657 a Polish fief; and it was only in 1772, after the first partition of Poland (map 4) that Frederick the Great (1740–86) succeeded in creating a continuous Prussian territory from Memel to Magdeburg. More impressive, and a cardinal fact in eighteenth-century history, was the recovery of Austria after its setbacks in the Thirty Years' War and the creation of a vast new Austrian empire (map 3). This was largely the work of the great field marshal, Prince Eugene of Savoy (1663–1736). As late as 1683 Vienna itself was besieged by Turkish armies. Eugene turned the tide and by 1699 they had been thrown back and the whole of Hungary brought under Habsburg rule. Austria was now a major power in eastern Europe, while in the west the peace settle-

ment of 1714 brought it the Spanish Netherlands and the Spanish inheritance in Italy. But it was a giant with feet of clay, with weak finances and an inadequate army. Serbia and Belgrade, acquired in 1718, were lost again in 1739, Lombardy and southern Italy in 1734–5. When, on the death of Charles VI (1711–40) and the accession of Maria Theresa (1740–80), Frederick II of Prussia seized Silesia, Austria's inherent weaknesses were exposed. Although the struggle went on until 1763, it proved impossible to dislodge the Prussians. Later both Prussia and Austria took advantage of the disarray of Poland to enlarge their territories in the east. But in the three partitions (map 4) they had to share the spoils with Russia, and their mutual suspicions and rivalry left the west exposed to France. When the French revolutionary armies marched into Germany in 1793 the old order was doomed, and in 1806 the Holy Roman Empire passed unmourned from the map of Europe.

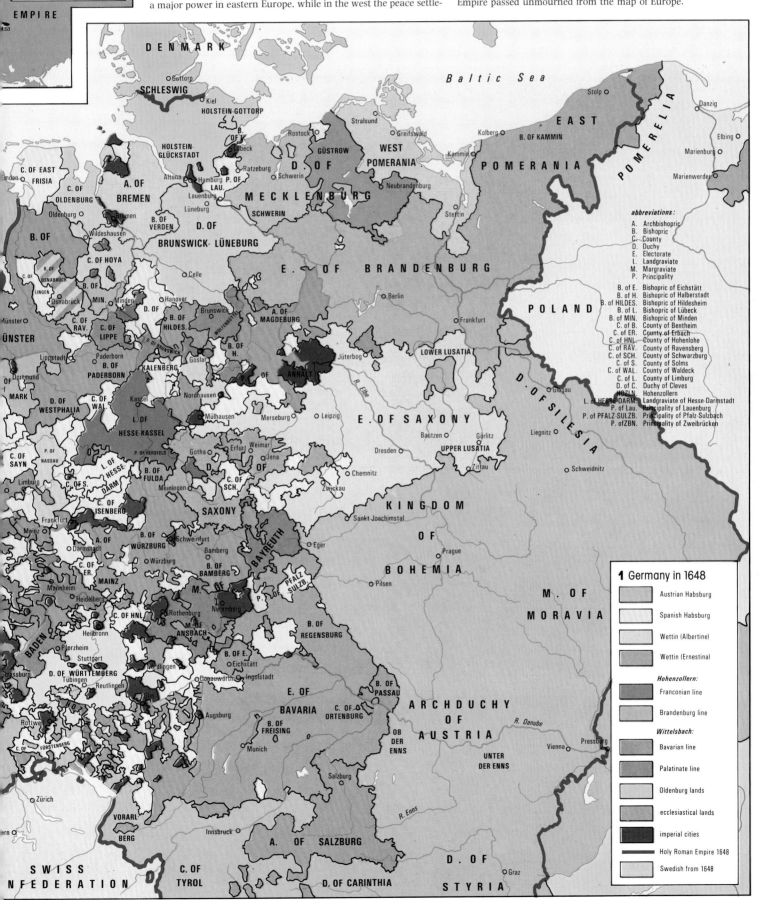

1 Germany in 1648

- Austrian Habsburg
- Spanish Habsburg
- Wettin (Albertine)
- Wettin (Ernestina)

Hohenzollern:
- Franconian line
- Brandenburg line

Wittelsbach:
- Bavarian line
- Palatinate line
- Oldenburg lands
- ecclesiastical lands
- imperial cities
— Holy Roman Empire 1648
- Swedish from 1648

abbreviations:

A.	Archbishopric
B.	Bishopric
C.	County
D.	Duchy
E.	Electorate
L.	Landgraviate
M.	Margraviate
P.	Principality
B. of E.	Bishopric of Eichstätt
B. of H.	Bishopric of Halberstadt
B. of HILDES.	Bishopric of Hildesheim
B. of L.	Bishopric of Lübeck
B. of MIN.	Bishopric of Minden
C. of B.	County of Bentheim
C. of ER.	County of Erbach
C. of HNL	County of Hohenlohe
C. of RAV.	County of Ravensberg
C. of SCH.	County of Schwarzburg
C. of S.	County of Solms
C. of WAL.	County of Waldeck
C. of L.	County of Limburg
D. of C.	Duchy of Cleves
HOZLN.	Hohenzollern
L. of HESSE-DARM.	Landgraviate of Hesse-Darmstadt
P. of Lau.	Principality of Lauenburg
P. of PFALZ-SULZB.	Principality of Pfalz-Sulzbach
P. ofZBN.	Principality of Zweibrücken

France and Europe
1648 – 1715

Under Louis XIV who succeeded to the throne in 1643, France became the leading country of Europe. His long minority, during Cardinal Mazarin's rule, saw the last major revolts of the aristocracy in defence of its prescriptive rights. When in 1661 Louis became effective ruler, the ground had been prepared for a new regime of centralisation and absolutism. This was the work of Mazarin, who had broken the aristocratic revolts and who turned the *intendants* into permanent representatives of the royal will in the provinces; of Louvois, who reformed the army; and particularly of Colbert's programme of financial reform. At the same time Vauban encircled France with a chain of defensive fortresses (map 1). All this was accompanied by great public works,

including the Languedoc canal, connecting the Atlantic and the Mediterranean, the palace of Versailles, and much building in Paris which became the centre of the cosmopolitan civilisation of Europe.

But Louis XIV's wars, inspired by an almost neurotic fear of the revival of the empire of Charles V and the encirclement of France by Habsburg power, seriously damaged this solid achievement. Beginning with his attack on the Spanish Netherlands in 1667, they imposed a growing burden of taxation and gradually united Europe against him (map 4). England and Holland, maritime and colonial rivals since 1652 (map 3), settled their differences by the Treaty of Breda (1667) and in alliance with Sweden compelled Louis to make peace at Aix-la-Chapelle in 1668. Thereupon Louis detached England from the anti-French alliance by the Secret Treaty of Dover (1670), won over Sweden, and turned against Holland in 1672; but he was halted by an alliance between Austria, Spain and Brandenburg (which

defeated his Swedish allies at Fehrbellin in 1675), an at the Peace of Nimwegen (1678) Holland emerge unscathed.

These inconclusive results convinced Louis that ther was little hope of major territorial acquisitions by direc conquest, and after 1679 he turned to a policy of indirec aggression, nibbling away at German territory in th east, particularly in Alsace (map 2), the object being t absorb the remainder of the Burgundian territorie which had been partitioned between France and Austri after the death of Charles the Bold in 1477 (page 72 Strasbourg was annexed in 1681, the Palatinate burn and ravaged in 1689. But these provocative and ofte brutal actions united German opinion against him, an the revocation of the Edict of Nantes (1685) and th persecution of the French Huguenots incensed th Protestant powers. The result was the formation of th Grand Alliance (1689), led by William of Orange, wh had succeeded to the English throne after the revolutio

f 1688 and the deposition of James II. Louis' attempts to foment
ebellion in Ireland failed after the defeat of the French navy at La
ogue (1692), but fighting continued inconclusively on the con-
nent until 1697, when the Peace of Ryswick registered Louis' first
erious setback.

A new phase opened with the death without heirs of Charles II of
pain in 1700. This event had long been anticipated, but plans to
ivide the Spanish dominions in such a way as to maintain the
alance of power were thwarted not only by the rivalry of France
nd Austria, but also by the maritime powers (England and Holland),
vhich feared French ascendancy in overseas trade if it acquired the
panish overseas empire. The result was the long War of the Spanish
uccession (map 5), ended, in spite of the victories of Prince Eugene
f Savoy and the Duke of Marlborough, by the compromise Peace of
trecht in 1713. The French candidate retained the Spanish throne
s Philip V, and France kept most of its gains on its eastern frontier
map 2). But the ruinous expense of Louis' wars left France in a
esperate situation, with a legacy of financial disorder and internal
iscontent from which his successors never fully recovered.

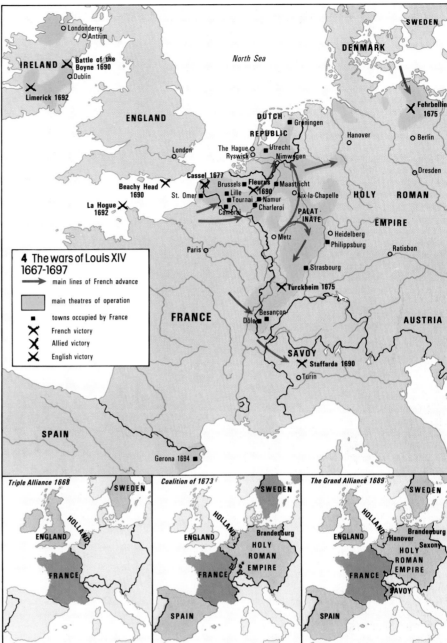

4 The wars of Louis XIV 1667-1697
→ main lines of French advance
■ main theatres of operation
■ towns occupied by France
✕ French victory
✕ Allied victory
✕ English victory

Triple Alliance 1668
Coalition of 1673
The Grand Alliance 1689

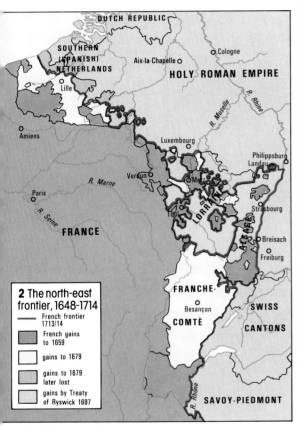

2 The north-east frontier, 1648-1714
— French frontier 1713/14
French gains to 1659
gains to 1679
gains to 1679 later lost
gains by Treaty of Ryswick 1697

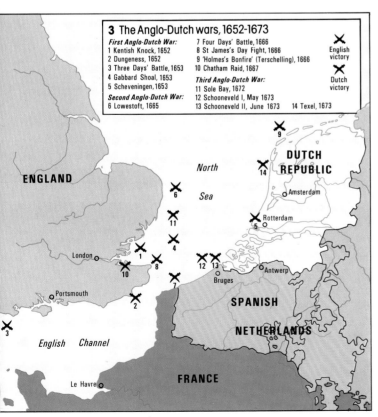

3 The Anglo-Dutch wars, 1652-1673

First Anglo-Dutch War:
1 Kentish Knock, 1652
2 Dungeness, 1652
3 Three Days' Battle, 1653
4 Gabbard Shoal, 1653
5 Scheveningen, 1653
Second Anglo-Dutch War:
6 Lowestoft, 1665
7 Four Days' Battle, 1666
8 St James's Day Fight, 1666
9 'Holmes's Bonfire' (Terschelling), 1666
10 Chatham Raid, 1667
Third Anglo-Dutch War:
11 Sole Bay, 1672
12 Schooneveld I, May 1673
13 Schooneveld II, June 1673
14 Texel, 1673

✕ English victory
✕ Dutch victory

5 The War of the Spanish Succession 1702-1713
to Spanish House of Bourbon
to Great Britain
to Austria
to Savoy
to France
to Prussia
✕ Allied victory
✕ Bourbon victory
✕ indecisive

The European economy
c.1500-1815

Recovery from the economic setbacks of the fourteenth century (page 56) began around 1450, and Europe's population expanded rapidly, though the fast growth of the sixteenth century was interrupted by war, rebellion, famine and plague in the seventeenth century and not resumed until the middle of the eighteenth century. Overall it increased from an estimated 69 million in 1500 to 188 million in 1800, but the increase was uneven and most marked in Britain and the Netherlands, by 1700 the greatest textile producers of Europe, the most active traders, with the largest merchant fleets and rapidly growing shipbuilding and metalware industries. The result was a shift in the economic axis. In 1500 industry was concentrated in the narrow corridor running north-south from Antwerp and Bruges through Ulm and Augsburg to Milan and Florence. By 1700 the axis ran west-east from England and Holland through the metal and woollen districts of the lower Rhine to the industrial concentrations of Saxony, Bohemia and Silesia, and thence to Russia, now beginning to build up an industrial base (map 4). The great expansion of overseas trade, particularly after 1700, also favoured the maritime powers (map 5). A consequence was the decline of the great trading cities of northern Italy, dominant two centuries earlier. In 1500 only four cities — Paris, Milan, Naples and Venice — had more than 100,000 inhabitants. By 1700 this number had trebled, and the majority of the rising urban centres lay west of the Rhine. London and Paris had already passed the half-million mark.

Significant as these developments were, agriculture was still Europe's most important industry. As late as 1815 three-quarters of its population were employed on the land, though here again there were sharp regional differences. In most of Europe farmers were subsistence peasants, whose smallholdings of 2–10 hectares produced only about 20 per cent more than their immediate needs. But in the west the need to feed growing urban populations led, first in Holland and then in Britain, to an agricultural revolution. The Dutch poured capital into land reclamation, recovering some 180,000 hectares between 1540 and 1715 (map 3), and developed intensive cultivation, eliminating the need to leave land fallow by means of a rotation of crops, which was later taken over in England. The growing population was also sustained by the introduction of new, more productive crops, mainly from America, including maize, which gave a far higher yield than the old regional cereals of southern Europe, and the potato, introduced in 1525, which spread slowly until it became a key field crop after 1700 (map 2). Urban demand also stimulated specialisation (Holland was exporting 90 per cent of its cheese by 1700), and generated a massive demand in western Europe for wheat and rye from Pomerania, Prussia, Poland and Russia, greatly to the profit of Holland which virtually monopolised the Baltic carrying trade in the sixteenth and seventeenth centuries.

The profitable grain-export trade of eastern Europe adversely affected the position of the peasant population which had enjoyed relative freedom before 1500 but now was reduced to a state of abject serfdom on large commercial estates. Only on the frontiers (e.g. in Hungary and on the Volga) where they performed military service, did the peasants retain freedom. Otherwise emancipation (postponed in Russia until 1861) only came slowly after the French Revolution, and the same was true in western Germany where, following the savage repression of the great peasant revolt of 1525, feudal relationships persisted (map 1). A few rulers, notably the emperor Joseph II (1780–90) realised that improvement of productivity depended on breaking the old feudal relationships; but they were frustrated by landed interests. The European position in north-west Europe was very different. Serfdom had disappeared in the Low Countries by 1300. In France and England feudal services had been replaced, even before 1500, by money rents; and although, when prices rose after 1700, French lords sought to recoup themselves by reviving ancient dues (only abolished in 1793), peasant ownership was protected by the courts. Rising prices led, in England, to enclosure of the common fields, a precondition for agricultural improvement. Rich peasants benefited, but poor peasants, driven off the land, flocked to the towns, where they provided the labour force for the new industries.

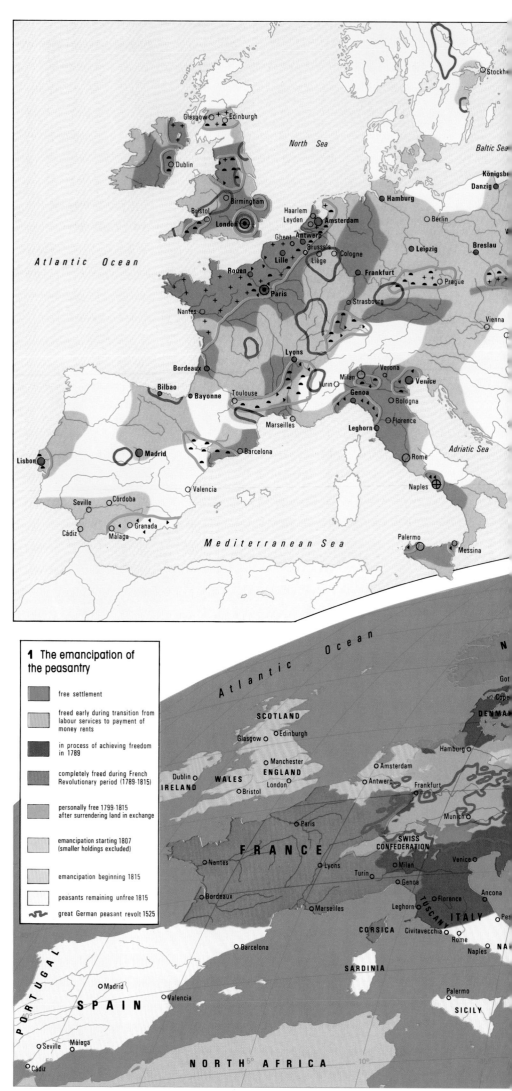

1 The emancipation of the peasantry

- free settlement
- freed early during transition from labour services to payment of money rents
- in process of achieving freedom in 1789
- completely freed during French Revolutionary period (1789-1815)
- personally free 1799-1815 after surrendering land in exchange
- emancipation starting 1807 (smaller holdings excluded)
- emancipation beginning 1815
- peasants remaining unfree 1815
- great German peasant revolt 1525

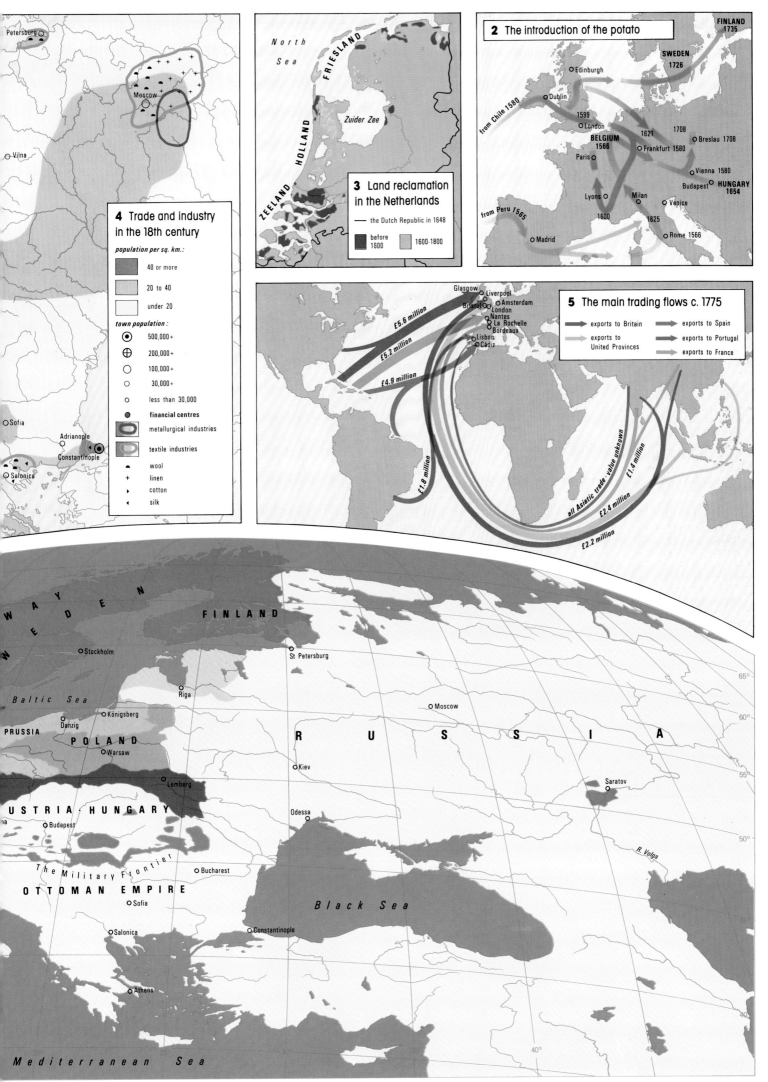

4 Trade and industry in the 18th century

population per sq. km.:

- 40 or more
- 20 to 40
- under 20

town population:

- ⊙ 500,000+
- ⊕ 200,000+
- ○ 100,000+
- ○ 30,000+
- ○ less than 30,000
- ● **financial centres**
- metallurgical industries
- textile industries
- wool
- + linen
- cotton
- silk

3 Land reclamation in the Netherlands

— the Dutch Republic in 1648

- before 1600
- 1600-1800

North Sea

FRIESLAND
HOLLAND
Zuider Zee
ZEELAND

2 The introduction of the potato

FINLAND 1735
SWEDEN 1726
○ Edinburgh
○ Dublin
from Chile 1580
1599
London
1621
1708
○ Breslau 1708
BELGIUM 1566
Frankfurt 1580
Paris ○
Vienna 1580
Budapest ○ HUNGARY 1654
from Peru 1565
Lyons ○
Milan ○
Venice ○
1600
1625
○ Madrid
Rome 1566

5 The main trading flows c. 1775

- → exports to Britain
- → exports to United Provinces
- → exports to Spain
- → exports to Portugal
- → exports to France

Glasgow ○
Liverpool ○
Bristol ○
Amsterdam ○
London ○
Nantes ○
La Rochelle ○
Bordeaux ○
Lisbon ○
Cádiz ○

£5.6 million
£5.2 million
£4.9 million
£1.8 million
all Asiatic trade: value unknown
£1.4 million
£2.4 million
£2.2 million

N O R W A Y
S W E D E N
FINLAND
○ Stockholm
Baltic Sea
○ Riga
○ St Petersburg
○ Moscow
PRUSSIA
○ Königsberg
Danzig ○
POLAND
Warsaw ○
○ Kiev
Saratov ○
○ Lemberg
USTRIA - HUNGARY
○ Budapest
Odessa ○
The Military Frontier
OTTOMAN EMPIRE
○ Sofia
Black Sea
○ Bucharest
R. Volga
○ Salonica
○ Constantinople
○ Athens
Mediterranean Sea

65°
60°
55°
50°
40°

○ Petersburg
○ Moscow
○ Vilna
○ Sofia
Adrianople
Constantinople
○ Salonica

The expansion of Russia, 1462-1905

The rise of modern Russia dates from the reign of Ivan III (1462–1505). During the preceding century the principality of Moscow had expanded at the expense of its immediate neighbours; but it was still a tributary of the Mongols (page 46), and in the west it was hemmed in by the great Polish-Lithuanian state, which extended deep into the Ukraine (page 56). Ivan III threw off the Mongol overlordship (1480), and in the west his conquest of the ancient republic of Novgorod (1478) opened the way to Livonia and the White Sea. Under his son Vassily (1503–33) and his grandson Ivan IV (1533–84) the advance continued. The subjection of the Khanate of Kazan (1552) opened the way across the Urals into Siberia; the conquest of the Khanate of Astrakhan (1556) gave Moscow control of the Volga to the Caspian Sea. But in the west Lithuania and Poland, joined after 1560 by Sweden, fought back vigorously, and during the 'time of troubles' following the death of Ivan IV made substantial gains at Russian expense (map 1). This, on the other hand, was the time of the great Russian thrust across Siberia, which, beginning in 1582, reached the Sea of Okhotsk by 1639 (map 2).

Siberia, where the population in 1720 was only about 400,000, still counted for little. The axis of Russian expansion was in the west, its thrust symbolised by Peter the Great's foundation of the new capital, St. Petersburg (1703). His long Swedish wars, concluded by the Peace of Nystad (1721), brought him Estonia, Livonia and part of Karelia. Russia now had free access to the Baltic. Under Catherine II (1762–96) it won control of the northern shore of the Black Sea, where Odessa (founded 1794) became a main outlet for Russian exports. But the question of secure access from the Black Sea to the Mediterranean remained unsolved. It was to be a central concern of Russian policy in the nineteenth century, and when it was thwarted by the other European powers in 1856 and again in 1878 Russia turned from

Europe to Asia, securing control of the Caucasus (1857–64) and then of the Khanates of Tashkent (1865), Samarkand (1868), Bukhara (1868), Khiva (1873) and Kokand (1876), while in the Far East it conquered the Amur and Ussuri regions at the expense of China (map 3). But defeat in the Crimean War (1854–56) convinced Russia of its backwardness, and in 1861, as a first step to modernisation, the serfs were liberated. Some went to Siberia, far more to the towns, where they provided a working force for industrialisation which began in the 1870s and was especially rapid 1893–1904 and 1909–13, when it exceeded the American growth rate. A metallurgical industry was developed in the Ukraine (map 4) producing mainly rails for the expanding railways. But it was also unstable. Russian ambitions in the Far East excited British and Japanese fears, and the result was the Anglo-Japanese alliance (1902) and the Russo-Japanese war of 1904–5 (page 126), which halted Russian expansion until 1945. At home the consequences were even more ominous. An urban proletariat had been formed which became the mainstay of the revolution of 1905 and more fatefully still in 1917.

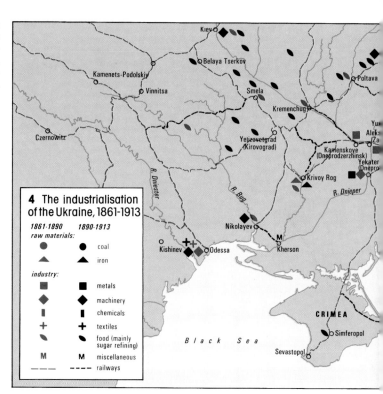

4 The industrialisation of the Ukraine, 1861-1913

1861-1890	1890-1913	
raw materials:		
●	●	coal
▲	▲	iron
industry:		
■	■	metals
◆	◆	machinery
❙	❙	chemicals
✛	✛	textiles
◗	◗	food (mainly sugar refining)
M	M	miscellaneous
———	-----	railways

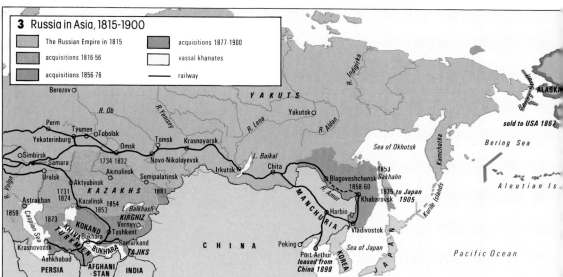

3 Russia in Asia, 1815-1900

▢ The Russian Empire in 1815		▢ acquisitions 1877-1900	
▢ acquisitions 1816-56		▢ vassal khanates	
▢ acquisitions 1856-76		—— railway	

2 Russian expansion in Siberia, 1581-1800

	Russian territory in 1581
	territory added 1581-98
	territory added 1598-1618
	territory added 1618-89
	territory added in 1650s; returned to China 1689
	territory added 1689-1725
	territory added 1725-62
	territory added 1762-1800

YAKUTS native peoples
○ Bratsk 1630 forts and trading posts (with date of foundation)

1 Muscovy and the Russian Empire, 1462-1815

Map labels (geographic):

Inset (top left): Chertkovo, Millerovo, Lisichansk, Kramatorsk, zhkovka, Lugansk, R. Donets, Kadiyevka, Gorlovka, Makiyevka (Makeyevka), Aleksandrovsk-Grushevskiy, Yuzovka (Donetsk), Novocherkassk, R. Don, Taganrog, Rostov, Mariupol (Zhdanov), Yekaterinodar (Krasnodar), vorossiysk, ea of zov, nsk

Barents Sea, Kola Peninsula, White Sea, Obdorsk 1595, PECHORA, R. Pechora, R. Mezen, R. Ob, Berezov 1593, 1501, Ural Mts, YUGRA, 1472, R. Kama, R. Vychegda, Solvychegodsk, Ustyug, 1393-1425, R. Sukhona, Solikamsk, Perm 1724, Nizhniy Tagil 1724, Yekaterinburg 1725, Kungur

FINLAND 1809, 1743, 1721, L. Ladoga, Vyborg, Kronstadt 1704, St. Petersburg 1703, Narva, Gulf of Finland, KARELIA, L. Onega, 1478, Archangel 1584, Kholmogory, NOVGOROD TERRITORY, 1478, Kargopol, 1478, 1362-89, Vologda, Soligalich, 1364, Galich, 1489, Vyatka, R. Vyatka, UDMURTY, MARI, KHANATE OF KAZAN 1552, Kazan, R. Belaya, Ufa 1586, SIBERIA, BASHKIRS

ESTONIA 1721, LIVONIA 1478, Pskov, L. Peipus, Novgorod, L. Ilmen, R. Lovat, 1478, 1393-1425, 1364, Yaroslavl, Kostroma, 1451, 1364, R. Oka, CHUVASHI, Baltic Sea, Riga, COURLAND, Western Dvina, 1510, 1772, LITHUANIA, Memel, R. Niemen, Kovno, Vilna, Polotsk, Vitebsk, 1503, Velikiye Luki, 1514-21, 1389-1425, Tver, R. Volga, Dmitrov, 1302, Vyazma, 1494, Mozhaysk, Moscow, Vladimir, 1364, Murom, Nizhniy Novgorod, Arzamas, 1393, MESHCHERA, MORDVA, Penza 1650, R. Sura, Simbirsk 1648, Samara 1586, Syzran 1683

Minsk, Mogilev, Smolensk, 1634, 1772, Serpukhov, 1301, Kolomna, 1353-59, Kaluga, 1425-62, Tula, Ryazan, 1521, Tambov 1636, R. Khoper, Saratov 1590, R. Volga, NOGAI TARTARS, Orenburg 1743, R. Ural, KALMUKS

Grodno, R. Vistula, Kalish, Warsaw, 1807, 1795, POLAND, 1793, Pinsk, R. Pripet, Gomel, 1503, R. Desna, Chernigov, Bryansk, Orel 1564, 1494, Yelets 1592, Kursk 1586, 1503, Belgorod 1593, 1634, Voronezh 1586, R. Don, Kamyshin, Tsaritsyn 1589, KHANATE OF ASTRAKHAN 1556, Guryev 1645

Lublin, Lemberg, Novograd-Volynskiy, Kiev, Pereyaslavl, 1793, R. Dnieper, 1667, Kharkov 1654, Poltava, Kamenets, R. Dniester, R. Prut, Bratslav, AUSTRIA, MOLDAVIA, BESSARABIA, ZAPOROZHYE, Sech, 1791, Kishinev, Nikolayev 1789, Ochakov, 1774, Kherson 1774, 1783, Yekaterinoslav (Kodak) 1786, DON COSSACKS, 1739, Cherkassk, R. Don, Taganrog, Azov, KALMUKS, Astrakhan, Caspian Sea

Akkerman 1812, Odessa 1794, R. Danube, KHANATE OF CRIMEA, Yevpatoriya, Karasubazar, Kerch, Feodosiya (Kaffa), Sevastopol 1783, Simferopol 1784, Bakhchisaray, Sea of Azov, 1783, KUBAN COSSACKS, Stavropol, R. Kuma, Yekaterinodar 1792

OTTOMAN EMPIRE, Black Sea, Pyatigorsk, R. Terek, 1784, DAGHESTAN, Derbent, 1810, Sukhum-Kale, 1806, Vladikavkaz, 1804, Kutaisi, 1801, Poti, Tiflis, GEORGIA, R. Kura, 1805, AZERBAIJAN, Baku, 1813, Sea, ceded temporarily by Persia 1723-32

Legend:

- boundary of Russian territories in 1462
- boundary of Lithuania in 1462

the expansion of Muscovy:

- Moscow territory at end of 13th century
- *1478* date of acquisition by Muscovy
- acquisitions to 1462
- acquisitions under Ivan III, 1462-1505
- acquisitions during 16th century (1505-86)
- acquisitions during 17th century

- acquisitions during 18th century
- acquisitions 1801-15
- territory ceded to Sweden 1617 and Poland 1618
- recovered from Poland 1634
- recovered from Poland 1667
- area affected by Pugachev uprising 1773-4
- route of Pugachev rebels
- Orel 1564 date of foundation of new town

The struggle for empire
1713-1805

The Treaty of Utrecht (1713), which ended the War of Spanish Succession (page 80), sought to establish stability in Europe and overseas on the basis of a balance of power. But owing to commercial disputes and colonial rivalries, particularly in America, peace remained precarious. In 1739 war broke out between England and Spain; in 1740 Frederick II of Prussia, supported by France, seized Silesia (page 78); and when France, supporting Spain, declared war on England in 1744, the European and overseas wars were fused into a single global conflict. It also quickly turned into a duel between England and France, particularly when, after the inconclusive Treaty of Aix-la-Chapelle (1748), fighting again broke out in North America in 1754. Here the French, with their strategically situated forts, were initially successful. But the whole situation changed when William Pitt the Elder, later Earl of Chatham became British prime minister in 1756. By allying with and subsidising Prussia, struggling to retain Silesia against an overwhelming French-Austrian-Russian coalition, Pitt compelled France to concentrate on the continental war. Naval victories at Quiberon Bay and Lagos in 1759 assured British control of the Atlantic and prevented reinforcements reaching Canada (map 1). The result was the loss of the French and, when Spain entered the war on the French side in 1761, of the

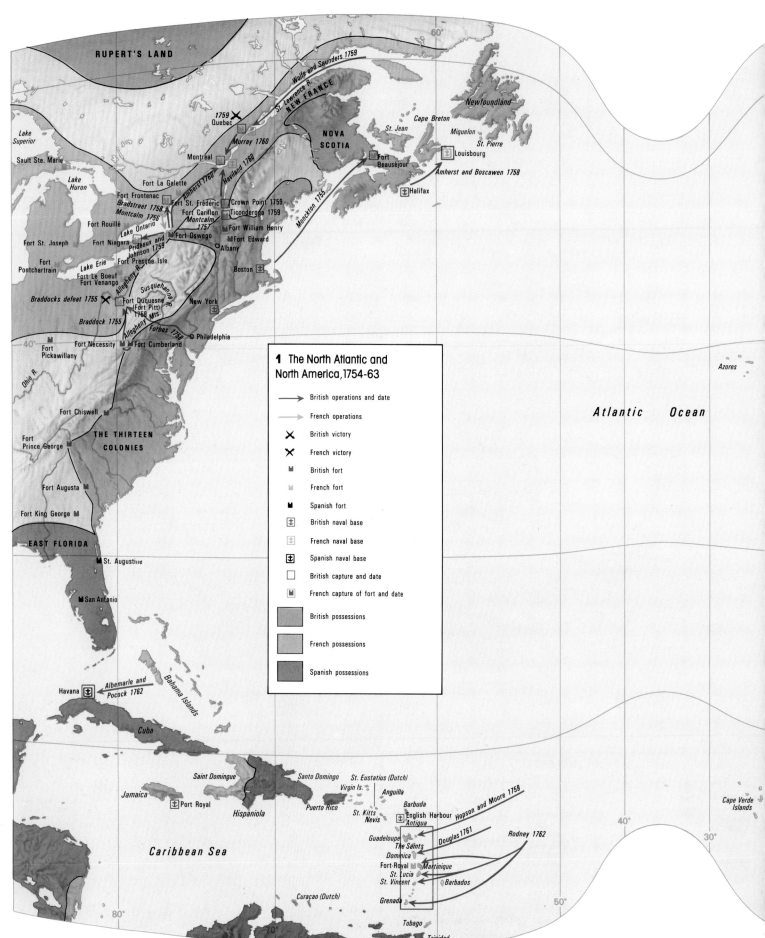

1 The North Atlantic and North America, 1754-63

- → British operations and date
- → French operations
- ✕ British victory
- ✕ French victory
- ◾ British fort
- ◾ French fort
- ◾ Spanish fort
- ⊞ British naval base
- ⊞ French naval base
- ⊞ Spanish naval base
- ☐ British capture and date
- ◾ French capture of fort and date
- British possessions
- French possessions
- Spanish possessions

spanish colonial empires in North America. At the Peace of Paris (1763) the French and Spanish possessions in the West Indies were restored, but England retained the North American mainland east of the Mississippi, including Florida which was ceded by Spain.

The British triumph was nevertheless short-lived. When the thirteen colonies rebelled in 1776 (page 92), France, which had rebuilt its navy, supported the rebels and by naval action compelled Great Britain to recognise American independence in the Treaty of Versailles (1783). In India, on the other hand, Britain built an empire which lasted until 1947. Here again, sea-power was decisive, enabling the English East India Company to checkmate the ambitions of the able French governor, Joseph Dupleix, to build a French empire in the Carnatic (map 2). By 1761 France was eliminated as a rival in India. But the decisive fact was the decline of the Mughal empire (page 48). After the death of Aurangzeb (1707) Maratha chiefs and Mysore asserted their independence. The resulting conflicts forced the British East India Com-

pany to take action (map 3). Clive's victory at Plassey (1757) brought Bihar, Orissa and Bengal under British rule. The fall of Tipu in Mysore (1799) ensured their ascendancy in the south. By the end of the governor-generalship of Richard Wellesley (1797–1805). British supremacy was an acknowledged fact. Revolutionary France attempted a comeback, and Napoleon planned an invasion of India (page 90). But once again sea-power was decisive, and in 1815 Great Britain occupied an unrivalled position in the colonial world.

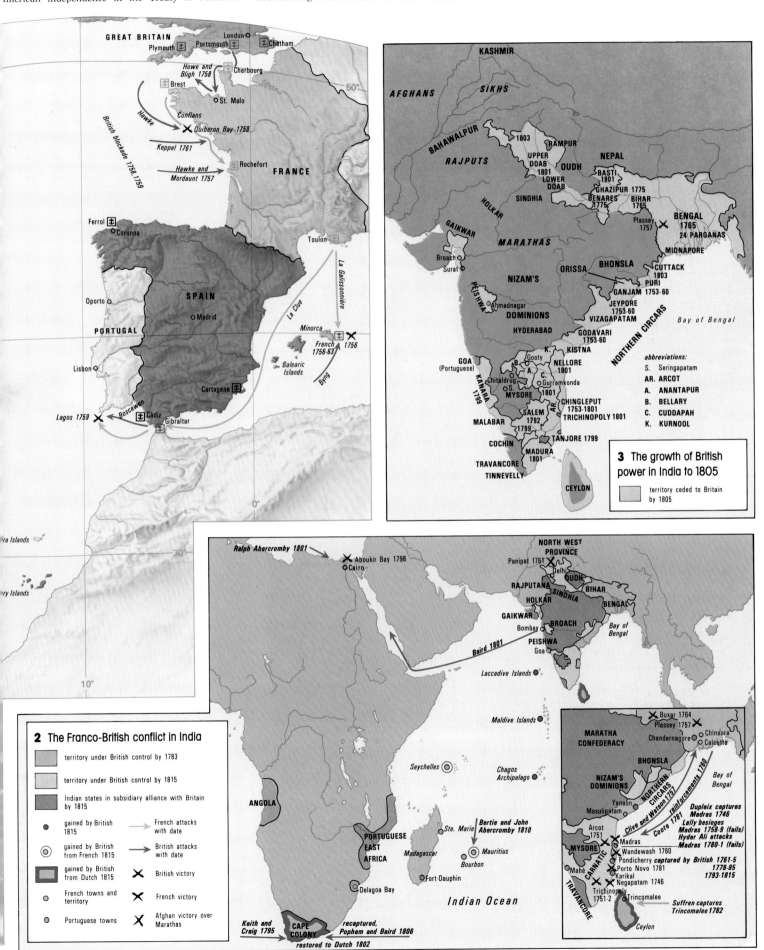

The age of revolution
1773-1810

1755, 1793 Corsica Local clans led by Paoli rebelled against Genoese rule and established independent democratic government. France bought island from Genoa in 1768, crushed revolt. Second attempt by Paoli to secure independence from (revolutionary) France, 1793, resulted in brief British occupation; rise of Bonaparte, himself a Corsican, put an end to separatist movement.

1768 Geneva Middle-class citizens of small city-state rebelled against domination by few patrician families; with French support the latter stayed in control.

1773 South-East Russia Serfs, Cossacks and Asiatic tribes rebelled in Volga and Ural region under leadership of Pugachev, a Don Cossack. Russian army put down revolt in 1774.

1775 America Resistance by Britain's Thirteen Colonies to her financial policies resulted in open warfare and Declaration of Independence, 1776.

1784 Dutch Netherlands Three-cornered struggle for power between Stadtholder, patrician families who controlled Estates General, and middle class Patriot party which aimed to democratise government. In 1787 Prussian troops defeated Patriot army and restored Stadtholder with greater powers.

1787 Austrian Netherlands (Belgium) Revolt against centralising policy of Emperor Joseph II, leading to proclamation of the Republic of the United Belgian Provinces (1790). Fights broke out between aristocratic and middle-class rebels; Austrian Emperor reconquered area, 1790.

1789 France (See main text). Risings by peasantry and Parisians overthrew feudal social and political order; Louis XVI's opposition and attempted flight led to abolition of monarchy (1792). King and Queen were guillotined as traitors (1793). Threat of invasion led to Jacobin 'reign of terror', ended by fall and execution of Robespierre (1794). Following weak and corrupt rule of Directory (1795–99) power passed to Napoleon Bonaparte.

1789 Liège Middle-class citizens supported by workers and peasants expelled prince-bishop and abolished feudalism. Bishop restored by Austrian troops, 1790.

1790 Hungary Magyar nobles rejected edicts of Austrian emperor and demanded greater independence for Hungary within Habsburg Empire; later, frightened by peasant disturbances, accepted compromise with the monarchy.

1791 Poland King, supported by lesser nobles, adopted new constitution designed to strengthen Poland against Russian encroachment. Catherine II of Russia, at invitation of greater nobles, invaded, destroyed constitution and divided large areas of Polish territory between Russia and Prussia. Attempt by Kościuszko and lesser nobles to strengthen surviving Polish state (1794) crushed by Russia and Prussia; Poland partitioned and ceased to exist as a separate state.

1791 Haiti Slave rising in western (French) part of island (Saint Domingue) resulted in rise of black leader, Toussaint l'Ouverture; by 1801 had conquered rest of island from Spaniards and secured virtual independence. Island then seized by the French, rising suppressed, and independence not fully secured until 1825.

1793 Sardinia In return for expelling French revolutionary invaders, islanders demanded autonomy within combined kingdom of Piedmont-Sardinia. King reasserted his authority when French threat subsided in 1796.

1798 Ireland Rebellion of United Irishmen seeking independence from England, put down by British army. Suicide of Wolfe Tone.

1804 Serbia Peasant rising against local garrison developed into demand for autonomy within Ottoman Empire. Under Karageorge Serbs fought fiercely for three years before revolt crushed by Turks.

1808 Spain After Napoleon placed his own brother, Joseph, on throne, a peasant rebellion gave assistance to British expeditionary force under Wellington. Middle-class intellectuals proclaimed constitution, but it did not survive restoration of Bourbon king in 1814.

1809 Tyrol After Austria renewed war against Napoleon, the peasants of Tyrol, whose territory had been taken from Austria by Napoleon in 1805 and given to Bavaria, rebelled under Hofer against new rulers. Revolt was crushed by Bavarian and French troops.

1810 Spanish America (See page 96).

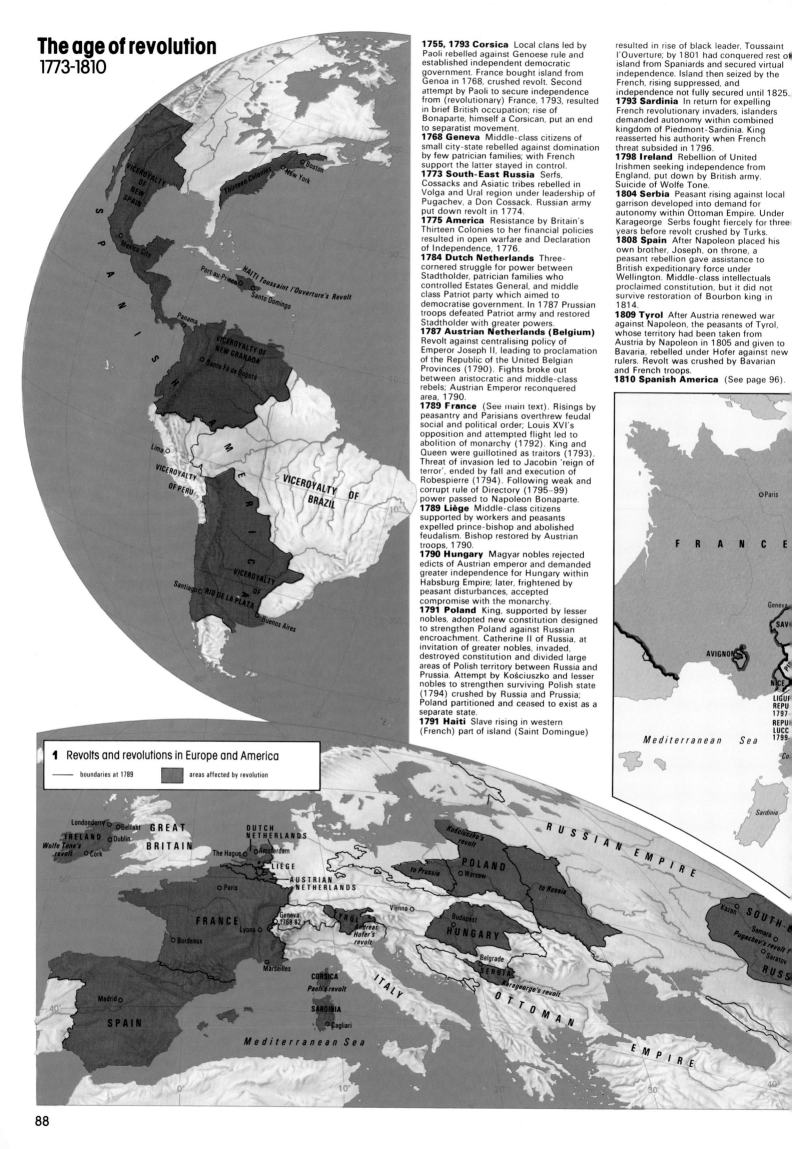

1 Revolts and revolutions in Europe and America

— boundaries at 1789   ▓ areas affected by revolution

The second half of the eighteenth century was a time of revolutionary ferment throughout the western hemisphere, from the Volga, where a great peasant insurrection under Pugachev in 1773 took Kazan and threatened Moscow, to Haiti, where the black population rose in rebellion in 1791 under Toussaint l'Ouverture and won control of the island by 1801. The character of the many rebellions of the period (map 1) was varied, but all derived, directly or indirectly, from the Enlightenment, with its assertion of the rights of man, its rationalism and rejection of traditional authority. Paradoxically, it was enlightened rulers, such as Catherine II of Russia (1762–96) and Joseph II of Austria (1780–90), searching for more modern and efficient foundations for government, who gave practical expression to the new ideas, thus provoking the opposition of vested interests, aristocratic and provincial. Provinces like the Austrian Netherlands (1787) and Hungary (1790) rose in rebellion against the centralising policies and reforming edicts of progressive rulers; colonial peoples resisted dictation by the home government and demanded autonomy or

at least no taxation without consent, as in North America in 1775 (page 92) and in South America after 1808 (page 96). The demand for independence was the commonest motive for revolt, and lay behind the risings in Ireland (1798), Corsica (1755, 1793), Sardinia (1793), Spain (1808), Serbia (1804), and the Tyrol (1809). Sometimes they were underpinned by social unrest; but this was exceptional. Serfdom was abolished in Savoy (1771), Austria (1781), Baden (1783) and Denmark (1788), and peasants had more to hope for from reforming monarchs than from nobles who were their oppressors. Hence their failure to support the gentry in the Polish revolts of 1791 and 1794. Revolts against patrician oligarchies occurred in Geneva (1768) and the Netherlands (1784–87); but usually it was only when concerted aristocratic opposition to the monarchy opened the flood-gates that the peasants and the labouring class took a hand. This was what happened in France after 1787.

The immediate cause of the French revolution was the financial crisis arising from the American war (page 86). By

1786 the government was faced with bankruptcy, and after a vain attempt to persuade an Assembly of Notables to tax the privileged classes, Louis XVI was forced by a rebellious aristocracy to summon the Estates-General which had not met since 1614. When the Estates-General turned itself into a National Assembly on June 17, 1789, the revolution had begun, but it was still a middle-class revolution, and the constitution drawn up in 1791 showed their distrust of the masses by limiting the right to vote. But they counted without the workers, exasperated by a serious economic crisis and by fear of counter-revolution. In Paris, a popular rising stormed the Bastille (July 14, 1789); in the provinces peasants burned châteaux and murdered landlords. Matters now proceeded apace (map 2), particularly when Austria and Prussia threatened invasion. This sealed the fate of constitutional monarchy. In 1792 a republic was proclaimed; in 1793 Louis XVI was executed and a Committee of Public Safety set up, first under Danton and then under Robespierre, which instituted a reign of terror against enemies at home, while Carnot mobilised an army

of 770,000 men against enemies abroad.

By 1795 the French armies were victorious and the revolution had spent itself. Spain and Prussia made peace; French troops held Belgium and the left bank of the Rhine, while William V of Holland was deposed and his country turned into a Batavian republic, closely bound to France, forerunner of other similar republics from Naples to Switzerland (map 3). French influence was spreading far and wide, a victory not simply for French arms but for the ideas and achievements of the revolution, equality before the law, the abolition of feudalism, and the 'rights of man' as defined in the famous declaration of October 2, 1789. When French troops entered the Rhineland in 1792 they were welcomed as liberators and 'brothers' by the educated middle classes. Except among the conservative peasantry, who fought the revolution in France itself from 1793 to 1802, the principles of the French revolution had immense appeal; and though their appeal was later dimmed, they lighted a torch which was never extinguished, even during the reaction which set in after 1815.

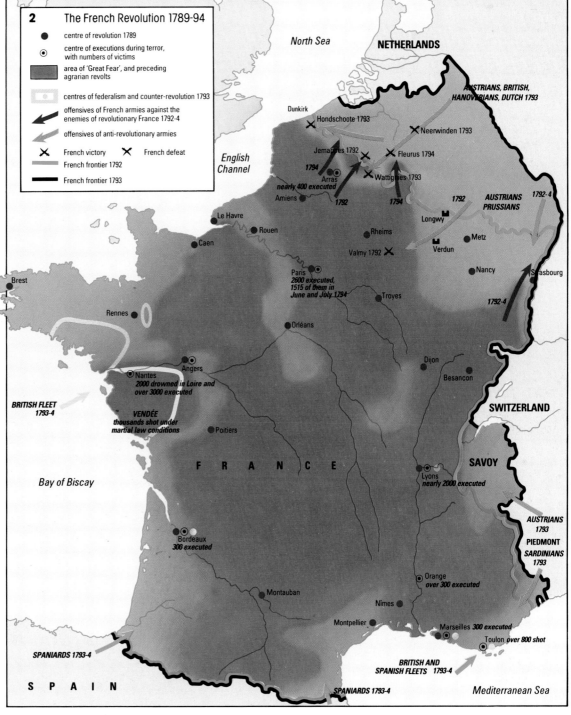

2 The French Revolution 1789-94

- centre of revolution 1789
- centre of executions during terror, with numbers of victims
- area of 'Great Fear', and preceding agrarian revolts
- centres of federalism and counter-revolution 1793
- offensives of French armies against the enemies of revolutionary France 1792-4
- offensives of anti-revolutionary armies
- ✕ French victory   ✕ French defeat
- French frontier 1792
- French frontier 1793

3 The expansion of revolutionary France, 1793-99

- frontier of France 1789
- frontier of France 1799
- areas annexed by France
- areas occupied by France
- Venetian territory given by France to Austria 1797
- states established by revolutionary France

Napoleonic Europe

In 1799 the 31-year-old general Napoleon Bonaparte seized power in France and was to rule until 1814, first as First Consul and then, after 1804, as emperor. His reign was a watershed in the history not only of France but of the whole of Europe. Napoleon had won his reputation by his spectacular victories over Sardinia and Austria in the Italian campaign of 1796; but after 1799, particularly during the Consulate, he proved as brilliant a statesman and administrator as a general. In 1799 Frenchmen, particularly the urban and rural middle classes, wanted peace and security. Napoleon gave them both. The wars were ended by the treaties of Lunéville (1801) and Amiens (1802); for the first time in ten years there was general peace in Europe. At home he gave the citizens who had supported the 'Thermidorian reaction' of 1794 the stability which the Directory (1795–99) had

failed to provide. But he was no reactionary. He made it his task to mould the essential achievements of the revolution into permanent institutions. In 1800 the 83 *départements* into which France had been divided in 1789 were reorganised under prefects responsible to the First Consul. The new civil code of 1804 confirmed the property rights created by the revolution and won him the lasting support of the peasant proprietors who were the backbone of the country. At the same time a career open to talents was provided for men of ability rising through the system of state schools and universities established in 1802.

These achievements outlived Napoleon himself, but peace proved elusive. A durable settlement might have been reached with the continental powers, Prussia and Austria; but the issues between France and England were too deep-seated for compromise, and in 1803 Great Britain declared war on France.

Thereafter war continued almost without interruption until 1815. In essence it was a continuation of the Anglo-French conflict of the eighteenth century (page 86), complicated by the traditional British fear, ever since the French occupation of the Austrian Netherlands in 1792, of a hostile great power on the Scheldt. From that time Great Britain was the moving spirit behind the anti-French coalitions which it kept going, as in the Seven Years' War, by subsidies. France, on the other hand, had not abandoned the hope of recovering the overseas empire lost in 1763. Napoleon's expedition to Egypt (1798–99) was intended to open the back door to India, and there were other plans for recuperating France's position in the Caribbean and on the American mainland. They were foiled by British control of the sea. Nelson's destruction of the French fleet at Aboukir sealed the fate of the Egyptian expedition (map 2), and elsewhere the French navy was no

match for the British, which thwarte French attempts to intervene in Irelan (1797–98) and a projected invasion England in 1804 (map 3). After Nelson victory at Trafalgar (1805), British con trol of the seas was assured, and Na poleon had no alternative except to tur against Britain's continental allies, hopin in this way to seal off Europe and brin Britain to heel by economic pressure.

Napoleon's campaigns against Au tria, Prussia and Russia in 1806 an 1807 were brilliantly successful, an 1810 saw him at the peak of his powe directly controlling the whole of wester Europe from Catalonia to Lübeck as we as Italy west of the Apennines, with sate lite kingdoms and duchies in Spain, th remainder of Italy and Westphalia (ma 1). But so long as Britain held out, Na poleon's position was insecure. Control the sea enabled the British to land a expeditionary force under the future Duk of Wellington in Spain (1808). His a

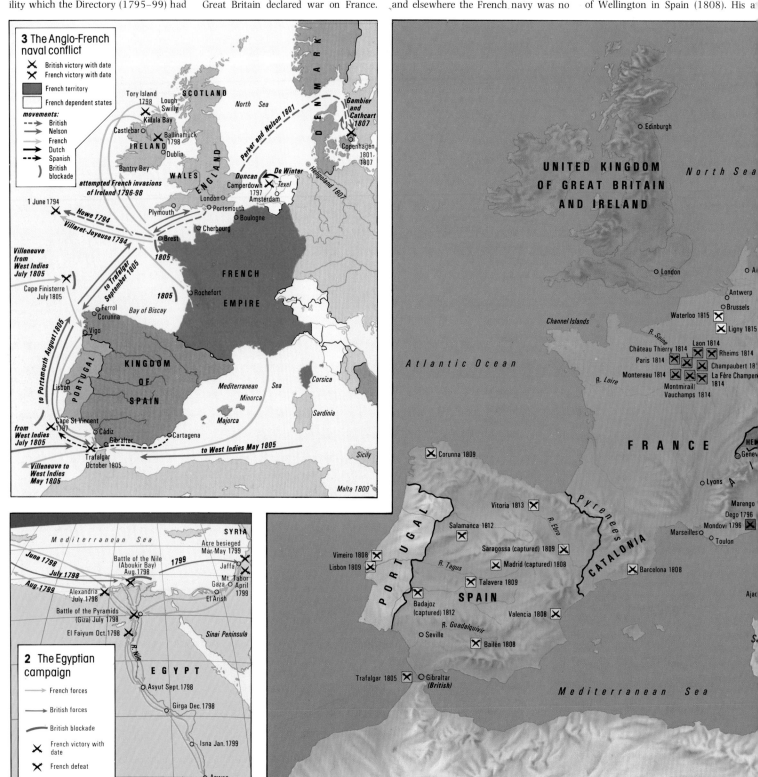

90

mpt to close the continent to British
ade led to his breach with Russia. The
vasion of Russia (1812) was an act of
esperation, a gamble which failed, and
ter the retreat from Moscow and the
attle of Leipzig (1813) Napoleon's fate
as sealed. In the reaction which fol-
wed much, but not all, of his system
erished. In Germany, in particular, the
apoleonic settlements of 1797–98 and
803 reduced the 234 territories of the
d empire to 40 (map 4), and after 1815
ere was no going back. Equally im-
ortant were the institutional changes
troduced on the French model. A
ociety based on wealth and merit rather
an prescription and privilege was intro-
uced in the Netherlands, the Rhinelands
nd north-east Italy, and even countries
ke Prussia reformed to meet the French
hallenge. The political geography of
urope was rationalised and the modern
ational state was born, fragile at first
ut destined to command the future.

4 Napoleonic Germany 1806

— Confederation of the Rhine 1806

1 Württemberg
2 Baden
3 Würzburg
4 Thuringian states
5 Electorate of Hesse
6 Swedish Pomerania
7 Oldenburg
8 Hesse
9 Berg

1 The empire of Napoleon

French territories ruled directly from Paris c. 1810

states ruled by members of Napoleon's family c. 1810

other dependent states c. 1810

British or British occupied territory

✗ French victory   ✗ French defeat

⊠ battles of the Italian campaign

⊠ battles of the War of the Second Coalition

⊠ battles of the War of the Third Coalition

⊠ battles in the Austrian War of 1809

⊠ battles in the Peninsular War

⊠ battles of the Russian campaign

⊠ battles of the War of Liberation from French Rule

⊠ battles in the defence of France

⊠ battles in the War of the 100 Days

The United States
1783-1865

The disputes and difficulties leading to the American War of Independence and the foundation of the United States began almost immediately after the English victory over France and the acquisition of Canada at the Peace of Paris in 1763 (page 86). When the British government reorganised its vastly expanded North American possessions, establishing a huge Indian reserve west of the Alleghenies (1763) and extending the boundaries of Quebec to the Mississippi and Ohio rivers (1774), its measures were bitterly resented by the colonists in New England, Virginia and Pennsylvania as a check to westward expansion. This resentment, combined with resistance to English tax demands and trade controls, was one of the factors behind the revolt of the American colonies. The War of Independence (map 1) began at Lexington and Concord in Massachusetts in April 1775 and was ended, after the British surrender at Yorktown (October 1781), by the Treaty of Versailles (1783), which extended the frontiers of the newly independent United States to the Great Lakes in the north and the Mississippi in the west.

Once independence was achieved, expansion proceeded rapidly. In 1783 the new republic comprised some 800,000 square miles of territory. The purchase of Louisiana from France (1803) more than doubled its extent. Thereafter expansion in the south and west was largely by conquest at the expense of Mexico (map 2), though the Oregon question, finally settled in 1846, looked for a moment as though it might bring war with Great Britain. In the north settlers moved into the 'back country' in increasing numbers after 1800, but it was the arrival of a new wave of European immigrants, predominantly German and Irish, which populated the Midwest. By 1860 the frontier of settlement had reached the 98th meridian, the dividing line between sparse and adequate rainfall.

This vast territorial expansion, which raised the population from approximately 3,000,000 in 1783 to 31,000,000 on the eve of the Civil War, had important political consequences. By 1860 the original 13 states had increased to 34. The result was a deterioration in the relative position of the Southern states with their plantation economy and black slave population, as a result of which the plantation aristocracy saw itself being swamped by the industrialising North and the growing Midwest. This, rather than the simple issue of slavery, was the underlying cause of the American Civil War, but the issues were in fact inseparable because, with over 90 per cent of the black population living in the South (map 3), the moral question was also a regional question. Abraham Lincoln, elected President in 1860 by a northern vote, was right when he said that the nation could not permanently remain 'half-slave and half-free.'

The North fought at first to preserve the Union; but, significantly, it was over the question of whether slavery should be permitted in Kansas and Nebraska that the conflict came to a head. Soon after Lincoln's election South Carolina seceded from the Union and was quickly joined by ten other states (map 4) which came together as the Confederate States of America with their capital at Richmond, Virginia. The course of the war, which opened with an attack on Fort Sumter in April 1861, can be followed on map 5. Northern strategy was to deny the South vital resources by a naval blockade, to gain control of key river routes and forts in the west and to capture the Confederate capital of Richmond. In spite of the preponderance of the North in manpower and resources, the South held out for four years, a fact which heightened the bitterness and resentment during the subsequent period of Reconstruction. The outcome has been called 'the Second American Revolution'; by crippling the Southern ruling class and liberating its labour force, it determined that the thrusting, urban, industrialised North, with its creed of competitive capitalism, would stamp its pattern – for good or ill – on post-bellum America.

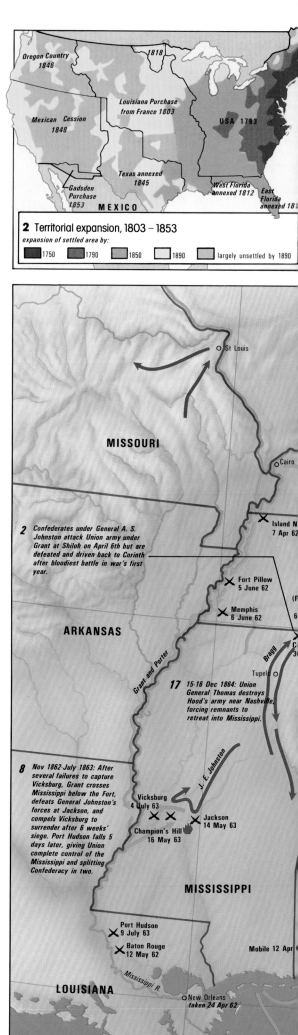

2 Territorial expansion, 1803 – 1853
expansion of settled area by:
1750 | 1790 | 1850 | 1890 | largely unsettled by 1890

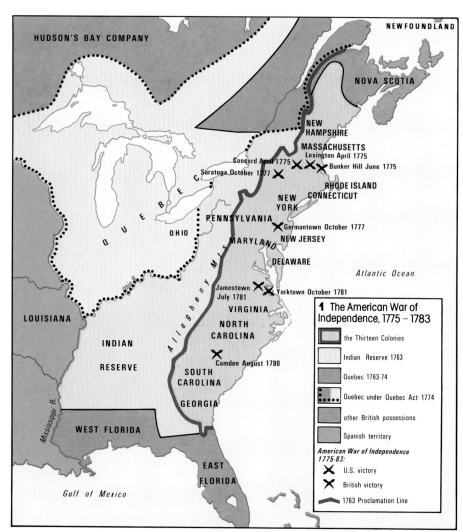

1 The American War of Independence, 1775 – 1783
- the Thirteen Colonies
- Indian Reserve 1763
- Quebec 1763-74
- Quebec under Quebec Act 1774
- other British possessions
- Spanish territory

American War of Independence 1775-83:
- ✕ U.S. victory
- ✕ British victory
- ▬ 1763 Proclamation Line

2 Confederates under General A. S. Johnston attack Union army under Grant at Shiloh on April 6th but are defeated and driven back to Corinth after bloodiest battle in war's first year.

17 15-16 Dec 1864: Union General Thomas destroys Hood's army near Nashville, forcing remnants to retreat into Mississippi.

8 Nov 1862-July 1863: After several failures to capture Vicksburg, Grant crosses Mississippi below the Fort, defeats General Johnston's forces at Jackson, and compels Vicksburg to surrender after 6 weeks' siege. Port Hudson falls 5 days later, giving Union complete control of the Mississippi and splitting Confederacy in two.

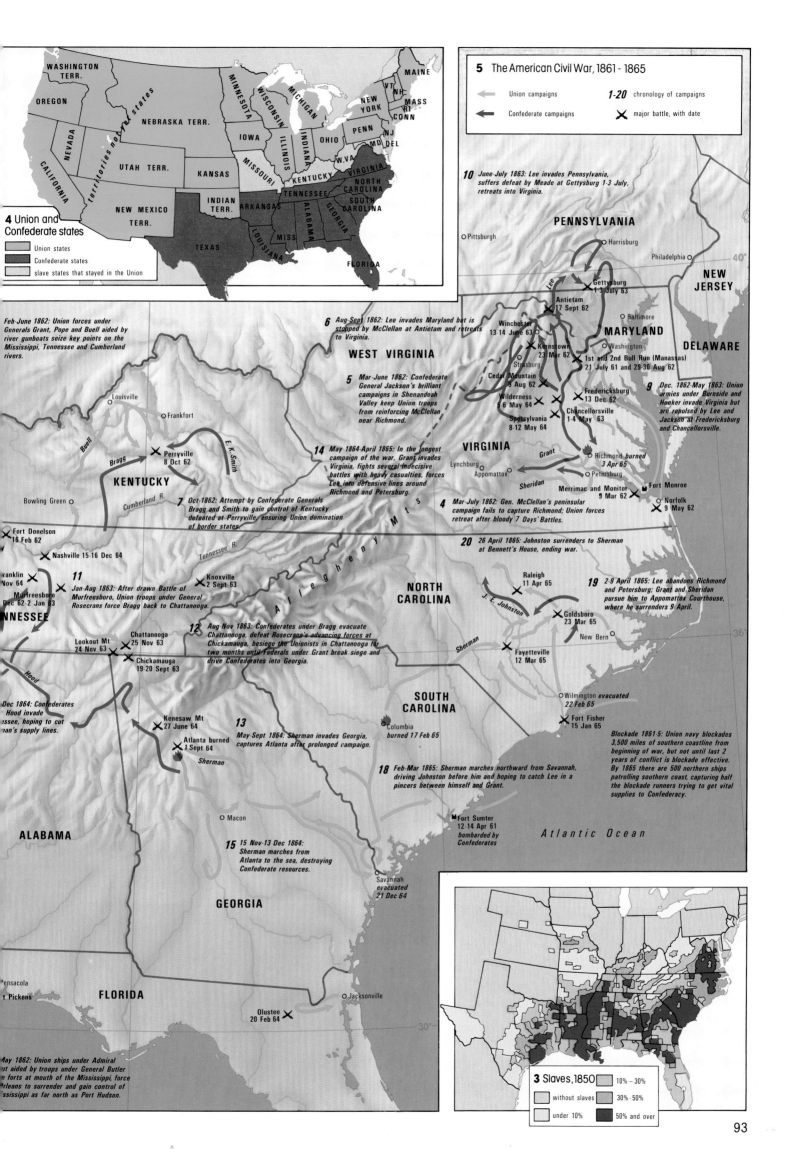

4 Union and Confederate states

Union states
Confederate states
slave states that stayed in the Union

5 The American Civil War, 1861 - 1865

Union campaigns   *1-20* chronology of campaigns
Confederate campaigns   ✗ major battle, with date

10 *June-July 1863: Lee invades Pennsylvania, suffers defeat by Meade at Gettysburg 1-3 July, retreats into Virginia.*

6 *Aug-Sept 1862: Lee invades Maryland but is stopped by McClellan at Antietam and retreats to Virginia.*

5 *Mar-June 1862: Confederate General Jackson's brilliant campaigns in Shenandoah Valley keep Union troops from reinforcing McClellan near Richmond.*

14 *May 1864-April 1865: In the longest campaign of the war, Grant invades Virginia, fights several indecisive battles with heavy casualties, forces Lee into defensive lines around Richmond and Petersburg.*

9 *Dec. 1862-May 1863: Union armies under Burnside and Hooker invade Virginia but are repulsed by Lee and Jackson at Fredericksburg and Chancellorsville.*

7 *Oct 1862: Attempt by Confederate Generals Bragg and Smith to gain control of Kentucky defeated at Perryville, ensuring Union domination of border states.*

4 *Mar-July 1862: Gen. McClellan's peninsular campaign fails to capture Richmond; Union forces retreat after bloody 7 Days' Battles.*

Feb-June 1862: Union forces under Generals Grant, Pope and Buell aided by river gunboats seize key points on the Mississippi, Tennessee and Cumberland rivers.

20 *26 April 1865: Johnston surrenders to Sherman at Bennett's House, ending war.*

19 *2-9 April 1865: Lee abandons Richmond and Petersburg; Grant and Sheridan pursue him to Appomattox Courthouse, where he surrenders 9 April.*

11 *Jan-Aug 1863: After drawn Battle of Murfreesboro, Union troops under General Rosecrans force Bragg back to Chattanooga.*

12 *Aug-Nov 1863: Confederates under Bragg evacuate Chattanooga, defeat Rosecrans's advancing forces at Chickamauga, besiege the Unionists in Chattanooga for two months until Federals under Grant break siege and drive Confederates into Georgia.*

Dec 1864: Confederates Hood invade [Tenn]essee, hoping to cut [Sherm]an's supply lines.

13 *May-Sept 1864: Sherman invades Georgia, captures Atlanta after prolonged campaign.*

18 *Feb-Mar 1865: Sherman marches northward from Savannah, driving Johnston before him and hoping to catch Lee in a pincers between himself and Grant.*

15 *15 Nov-13 Dec 1864: Sherman marches from Atlanta to the sea, destroying Confederate resources.*

Fort Sumter 12-14 Apr 61 bombarded by Confederates

Blockade 1861-5: Union navy blockades 3,500 miles of southern coastline from beginning of war, but not until last 2 years of conflict is blockade effective. By 1865 there are 500 northern ships patrolling southern coast, capturing half the blockade runners trying to get vital supplies to Confederacy.

May 1862: Union ships under Admiral [Farragu]t aided by troops under General Butler [seize th]e forts at mouth of the Mississippi, force [New Or]leans to surrender and gain control of [the Missis]sippi as far north as Port Hudson.

3 Slaves, 1850

without slaves
under 10%
10% – 30%
30% – 50%
50% and over

The expansion of the United States
1803-1898

The dominant fact in the history of the United States during the nineteenth century was the opening of the continent. In 1783 the effective frontier of the new Republic was the Allegheny Mountains (page 92). The Louisiana Purchase (1803) opened vast new areas for explorers, led by the famous expedition of Lewis and Clark (1804–8), and for settlers who quickly followed in their wake (map 1). After the Mexican wars (1846–8) and the discovery of gold in California (1848) prospectors, miners, speculators and settlers pushed west across the mountain chains from Salt Lake City and Santa Fe or by the Overland Trail from San Antonio. The great westward movement, bolstered by a confident belief in America's 'manifest destiny', could not, however, proceed without brutal disregard for the native population. The destruction of the North American Indians had begun much earlier in New England in the Pequot war of 1636, and the Delaware Indians were uprooted and driven west before the end of the eighteenth century; but it was in the 1830s, when the land-hunger of the white planters and settlers became insatiable, that the expulsion of whole tribes, Cherokee, Chocktaw, Creek and Chickasaw, and their deportation to the Midwest (and later to Indian reservations) got underway. By 1840 the frontier had reached the 100th meridian, and it was here, in the Midwest and West, that the great battles of the 1860s and 1870s took

place, which reduced the Indian population to scarcely more than 200,000 by the end of the nineteenth century (map 2).

In their place, and usurping their lands, poured in a flood of immigrants, mainly from Europe, which reached its peak in the last decade of the century (diagram 4). In the later phases most of the immigrants (from southern and eastern Europe) remained in the cities on the eastern seaboard, where they swelled the industrial proletariat; but by mid-century Germans and Scandinavians had formed a preponderant element on the farming frontier of Wisconsin, Iowa and Minnesota, and in the last quarter of the century British and Irish settlers, as well as native Americans, played an important part in the development of cattle ranching

and stock raising in Texas, Wyoming and New Mexico. British capital and British land companies also contributed. But the most important area of European investment before 1914 was the financing of American railways, particularly the transcontinental lines. Railroads in operation in 1840 were confined to a few industrial regions in the east. British capital provided the finance to double the mileage between 1866 and 1873 and to carry it west, and this westward shift of transport and population was accompanied by a similar shift of agricultural production (map 3). The effects were dramatic. By 1890, when the rail network was larger than that of the whole of Europe, including the British Isles and Russia, a population moving onto virgin lands, with improved mechanisation, such as the steel plough, new strains of cotton, wheat and maize, and the ubiquitous barbed wire fence, had made the United States the world's leading agricultural producer.

By 1890 the frontier was closed, the prospect of indefinite opportunities within the boundaries of the United States becoming a thing of the past. West of the 100th meridian population was still sparse, and urban and industrial development negligible (page 110); the great upsurge in the colonisation and development of California and the Pacific seaboard was still to come. Nevertheless 1890 marked a turning point, registered in 1898 when the United States, denying its own past refusal to involve itself in other continents, turned from the American continent to the wider world of Asia. In 1898 American history merged into world history, with incalculable consequences for the future.

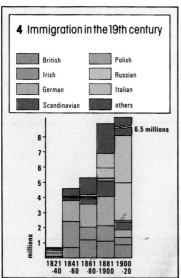

4 Immigration in the 19th century

British	Polish
Irish	Russian
German	Italian
Scandinavian	others

6.5 millions

8
7
6
5
4
3
2
1
millions

1821 1841 1861 1881 1900
-40   -60   -80 -1900 -20

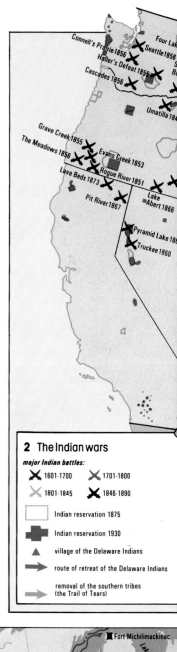

2 The Indian wars

major Indian battles:
- ✗ 1601-1700
- ✗ 1701-1800
- ✗ 1801-1845
- ✗ 1846-1890

☐ Indian reservation 1875

✚ Indian reservation 1930

▲ village of the Delaware Indians

➡ route of retreat of the Delaware Indians

➡ removal of the southern tribes (the Trail of Tears)

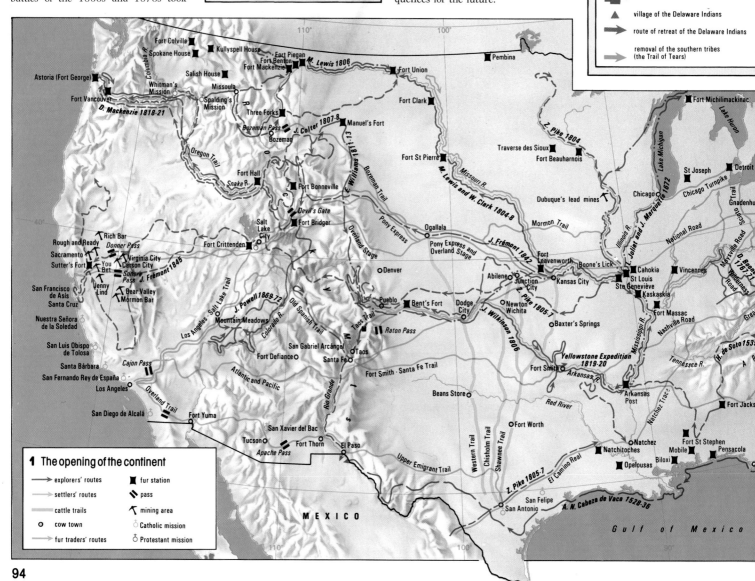

1 The opening of the continent

- ➡ explorers' routes
- ➡ settlers' routes
- ▬ cattle trails
- ○ cow town
- ➡ fur traders' routes
- ■ fur station
- ◥ pass
- ⅄ mining area
- ⌂ Catholic mission
- ⌂ Protestant mission

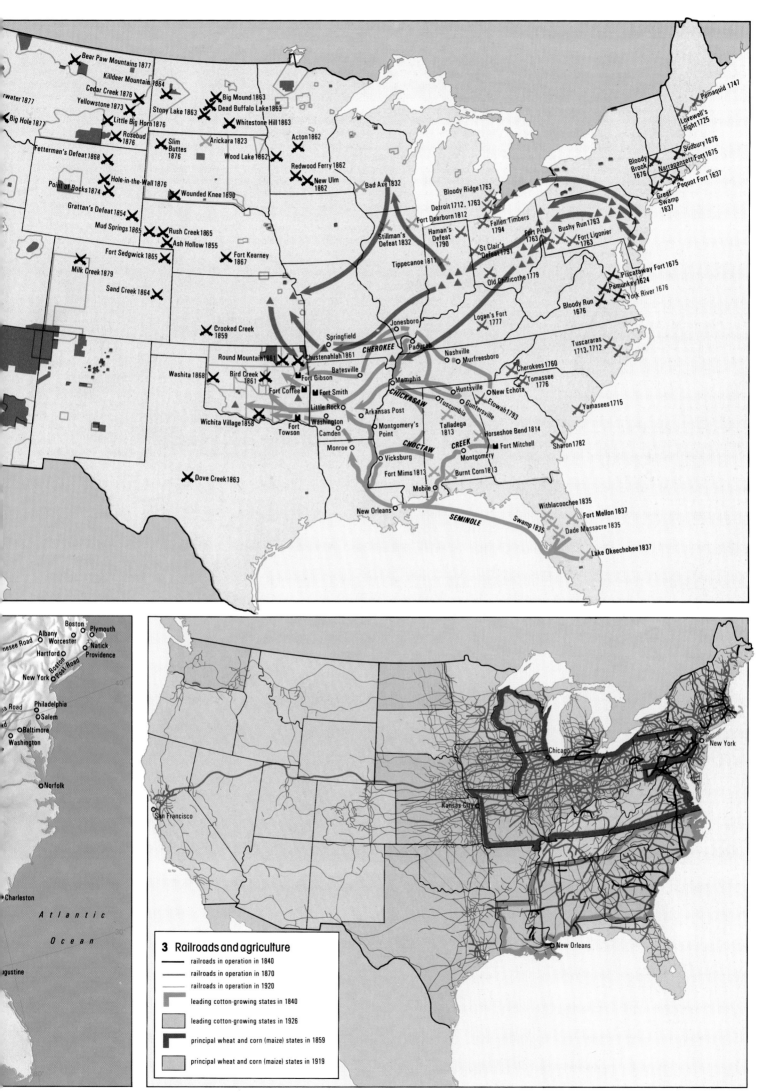

Bear Paw Mountains 1877
Killdeer Mountain 1864
Cedar Creek 1876
water 1877
Yellowstone 1873
Big Mound 1863
Big Hole 1877
Little Big Horn 1876
Stony Lake 1863
Dead Buffalo Lake 1863
Rosebud 1876
Whitestone Hill 1863
Fetterman's Defeat 1868
Slim Buttes 1876
Arickara 1823
Acton 1862
Hole-in-the-Wall 1876
Wood Lake 1862
Point of Rocks 1874
Wounded Knee 1890
Redwood Ferry 1862
New Ulm 1862
Grattan's Defeat 1854
Bad Axe 1832
Bloody Ridge 1763
Pemaquid 1747
Lovewell's Fight 1725
Mud Springs 1865
Rush Creek 1865
Detroit 1712, 1763
Fort Dearborn 1812
Fallen Timbers 1794
Sudbury 1676
Ash Hollow 1855
Stillman's Defeat 1832
Haman's Defeat 1790
Fort Pitt 1763
Bushy Run 1763
Fort Ligonier 1763
Bloody Brook 1676
Narragansett Fort 1675
Fort Sedgwick 1865
Fort Kearney 1867
St Clair's Defeat 1791
Pequot Fort 1637
Milk Creek 1879
Tippecanoe 1811
Old Chillicothe 1779
Great Swamp 1637
Sand Creek 1864
Logan's Fort 1777
Piscataway Fort 1675
Pamunkey 1624
Bloody Run 1676
York River 1676
Crooked Creek 1859
Springfield
Jonesboro
CHEROKEE
Paducah
Nashville
Tuscararas 1713, 1712
Round Mountain 1861
Chustenahlah 1861
Batesville
Murfreesboro
Cherokees 1760
Washita 1868
Bird Creek 1861
Fort Gibson
Memphis
Tomassee 1776
Fort Coffee
Fort Smith
Huntsville
New Echota
Little Rock
CHICKASAW
Tuscumbia
Etowah 1793
Yamasees 1715
Arkansas Post
Guntersville
Wichita Village 1858
Washington
Montgomery's Point
Talladega 1813
Horseshoe Bend 1814
Camden
Sharon 1782
Fort Towson
CHOCTAW
CREEK
Fort Mitchell
Monroe
Montgomery
Vicksburg
Burnt Corn 1813
Dove Creek 1863
Fort Mims 1813
Mobile
New Orleans
SEMINOLE
Withlacoochee 1835
Fort Mellon 1837
Swamp 1835
Dade Massacre 1835
Lake Okeechobee 1837

Boston
Albany
Plymouth
nesee Road
Worcester
Hartford
Natick
Providence
New York
Boston Post Road
Philadelphia
Salem
Baltimore
Washington
Norfolk
San Francisco
Chicago
New York
Kansas City
Charleston
Atlantic
Ocean
New Orleans
ugustine

3 Railroads and agriculture
— railroads in operation in 1840
— railroads in operation in 1870
— railroads in operation in 1920
leading cotton-growing states in 1840
leading cotton-growing states in 1926
principal wheat and corn (maize) states in 1859
principal wheat and corn (maize) states in 1919

Independent Latin America
1808-1910

Napoleon's invasion of Spain and Portugal in 1808 (page 90) enabled their colonies to assert their independence. The revolt began in Argentina in 1810 and Venezuela in 1811, and was later helped by Great Britain and the United States which prevented intervention by the Holy Alliance. After the fall of Lima (1821) and Bolívar's victory at Ayacucho (1824) Spain's fate in South America was sealed. In the north, early revolts in Mexico were suppressed, but in 1823 a republic was proclaimed, and a last Spanish attempt at reconquest in 1829 was defeated by Santa Ana. Only Brazil made the transition to nationhood peacefully. Here Portugal agreed to a constitution, and in 1822 the Portuguese king's eldest son became ruler of an independent Brazilian empire, as Pedro I. Only in 1889 when, following the abolition of slavery (1888), disgruntled plantation-owners rose in revolt, was the empire replaced by a federal republic.

Independence essentially was a political movement in the hands of the colonial aristocracy, who wanted a transfer of authority but a minimum of social upheaval. After 1826 the old colonial division between a privileged minority, monopolising land and office, and a barely subsisting mass of peasants, grew sharper. Though the period was rarely without civil strife, the *caudillos*, or military dictators, who dominated the scene during the 50 years following independence, ruled in the interests of the privileged classes, and there was only marginal reform before the Indian, Benito Juárez, took over in Mexico in 1861 (map 1). There were also repeated territorial disputes between the different republics, the fiercest being the War of the Pacific for control of the Atacama Desert nitrate deposits (map 4), to say nothing

of the wars with the United States (page 92) which deprived Mexico of 40 per cent of its territory. Bolívar had plans for an all-encompassing South American Union, but they came to nothing at the Congress of Panama (1826). Instead, such federations as existed (e.g. Great Colombia, 1819–30) quickly fell apart into their constituent elements, usually representing former Spanish administrative units.

For most of the century there was virtually a subsistence economy in most republics. Brazil, with its coffee plantations based on slave labour, was an exception. Elsewhere the *hacendados* treated their estates more or less as self-supporting and self-sufficient, and had little interest in production for the market. Change only came after about 1880 when foreign investment, hitherto modest, increased rapidly (map 3). Even so, it was highly selective, concentrated mainly in Argentina, Brazil, Mexico and Chile. Except in Mexico, where the United States predominated, Britain had the lion's share,

much of it in railways. The stimulus was undoubte[d] but it also shifted the economy sharply to the export [of] primary products. Argentina's 'revolution on the pam[pas'] made it a main supplier of grain and meat; Chi[le] was the world's leading producer of nitrates; Bra[zil] exported coffee and rubber, and American food corpo[r]ations invested heavily in the so-called 'banana repu[b]lics.' The economic 'take off' also attracted a new wa[ve] of European, mainly Italian and Spanish, settlers, no[t]ably in Argentina, which greatly altered the populatio[n] profile (map 2). Urbanisation increased apace, and wi[th] it came the beginning of a new urban and industri[al] proletariat and a middle class growing rich on the expo[rt] trade. But unbalanced growth also produced new pro[b]lems. The dictatorship of Porfirio Díaz (1877–191[1]) brought spectacular economic progress to Mexico, b[ut] the mass of the people were left in abject poverty. Th[e] result was the Mexican revolution of 1911, the ha[r]binger of a new era in the history of Latin America.

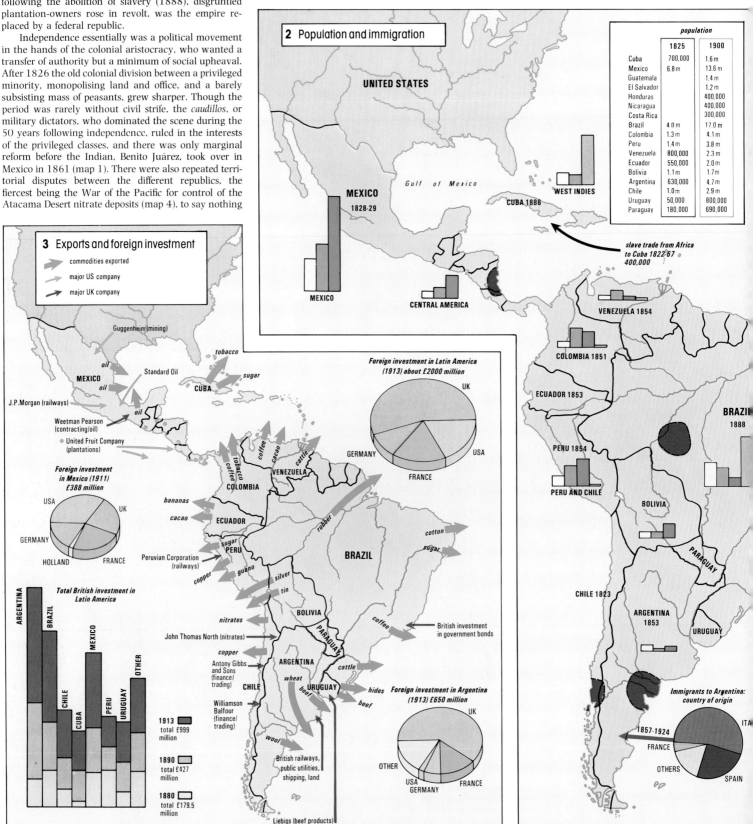

2 Population and immigration

	population	
	1825	1900
Cuba	700,000	1.6 m
Mexico	6.8 m	13.6 m
Guatemala		1.4 m
El Salvador		1.2 m
Honduras		400,000
Nicaragua		400,000
Costa Rica		300,000
Brazil	4.0 m	17.0 m
Colombia	1.3 m	4.1 m
Peru	1.4 m	3.8 m
Venezuela	800,000	2.3 m
Ecuador	550,000	2.0 m
Bolivia	1.1 m	1.7m
Argentina	630,000	4.7 m
Chile	1.0 m	2.9 m
Uruguay	50,000	800,000
Paraguay	180,000	690,000

slave trade from Africa to Cuba 1822-67 400,000

3 Exports and foreign investment

commodities exported
major US company
major UK company

Foreign investment in Latin America (1913) about £2000 million
UK
GERMANY
USA
FRANCE

Foreign investment in Mexico (1911) £388 million
USA
UK
GERMANY
HOLLAND
FRANCE

Total British investment in Latin America
1913 total £999 million
1890 total £427 million
1880 total £179.5 million

Foreign investment in Argentina (1913) £650 million
UK
OTHER
USA
GERMANY
FRANCE

British investment in government bonds

Immigrants to Argentina: country of origin
1857-1924
FRANCE
ITALY
OTHERS
SPAIN

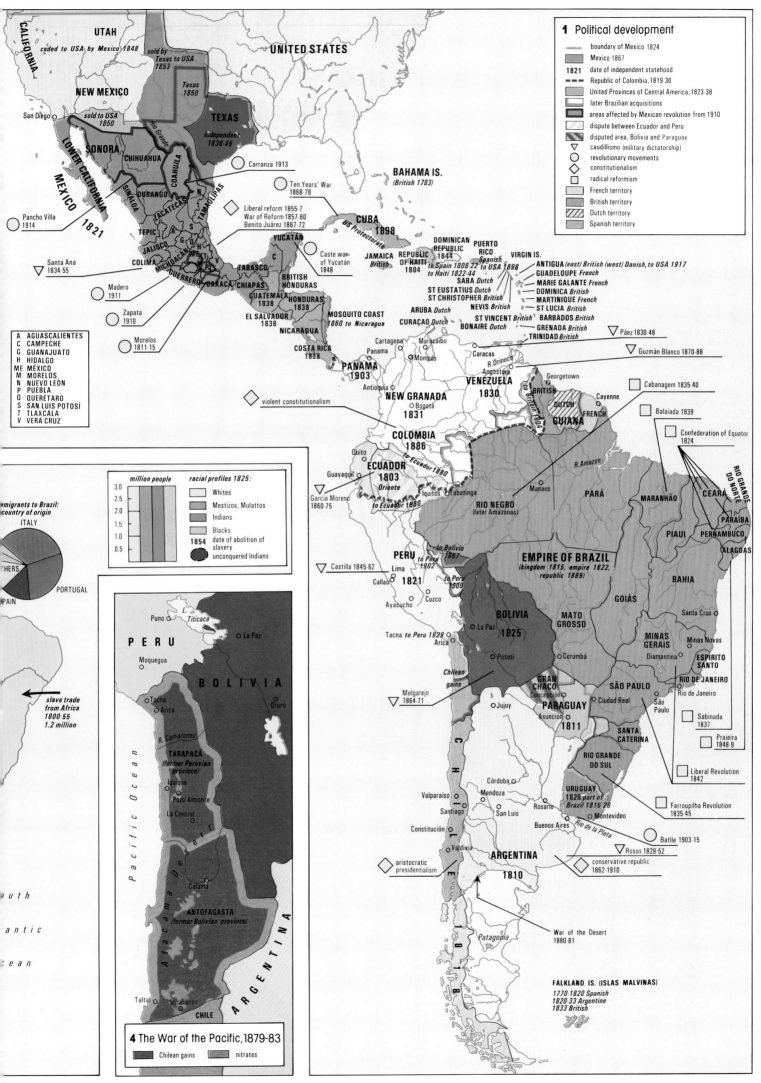

The Industrial Revolution in Europe, 1760-1914

The Industrial Revolution, which began in England in the reign of George III (1760–1820), was the catalyst of the modern world. Nevertheless the speed of change should not be exaggerated. Even in continental Europe its impact was limited before 1850 to a few industrial enclaves, and it was not until the last quarter of the nineteenth century – in the case of France, Italy and Russia only after 1890 – that the great surge forward occurred. Outside Europe, with the sole exception of the United States, its impact was delayed for much longer (page 108). Even in Germany 35 per cent of the population was engaged in agriculture in 1895, and most of eastern Europe (Poland, Romania, Bulgaria) and mu[ch] of southern Europe (Spain, Greece, southern Italy) w[ere] virtually untouched by industry. Until 1900, when [it] began to be challenged by Germany and the Unit[ed] States, the United Kingdom was the workshop of t[he] world, and its industrial strength, which enabled it [to] dominate world markets, accounts for its pre-eminen[ce] in the age of imperialism (page 100).

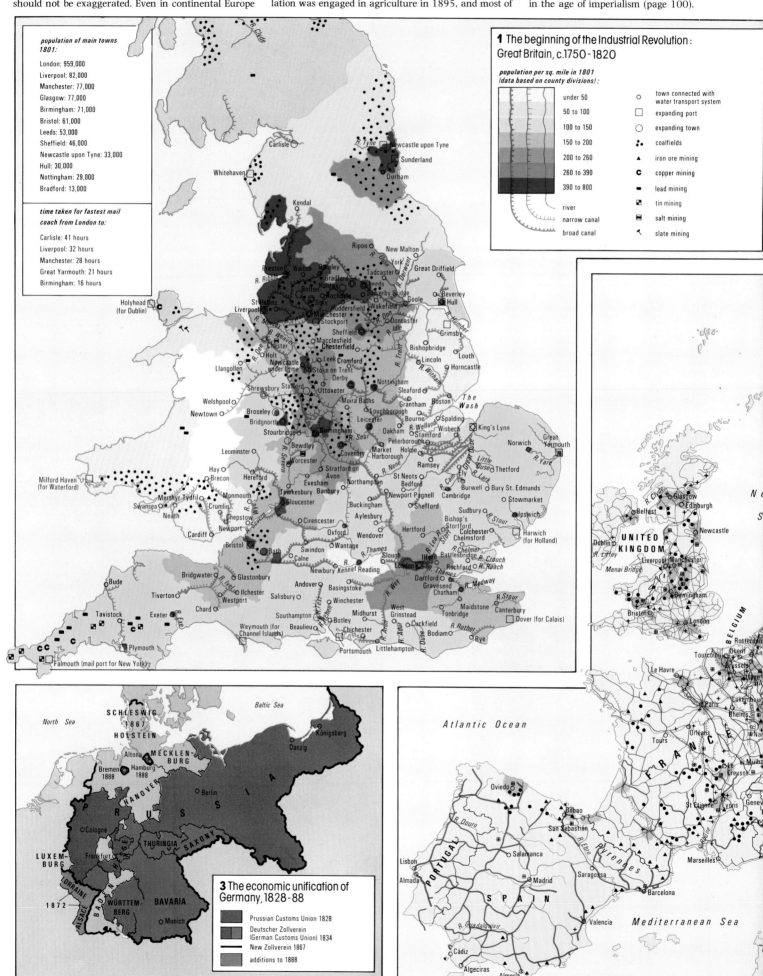

population of main towns 1801:

London: 959,000
Liverpool: 82,000
Manchester: 77,000
Glasgow: 77,000
Birmingham: 71,000
Bristol: 61,000
Leeds: 53,000
Sheffield: 46,000
Newcastle upon Tyne: 33,000
Hull: 30,000
Nottingham: 29,000
Bradford: 13,000

time taken for fastest mail coach from London to:

Carlisle: 41 hours
Liverpool: 32 hours
Manchester: 28 hours
Great Yarmouth: 21 hours
Birmingham: 16 hours

1 The beginning of the Industrial Revolution: Great Britain, c.1750-1820

population per sq. mile in 1801 (data based on county divisions):

under 50
50 to 100
100 to 150
150 to 200
200 to 260
260 to 390
390 to 800

river
narrow canal
broad canal

○ town connected with water transport system
□ expanding port
◯ expanding town
⁙ coalfields
▲ iron ore mining
C copper mining
▬ lead mining
⊡ tin mining
⊟ salt mining
⌃ slate mining

3 The economic unification of Germany, 1828-88

Prussian Customs Union 1828
Deutscher Zollverein (German Customs Union) 1834
New Zollverein 1867
additions to 1888

Many factors account for the precedence of Great Britain. It was not only that it was well endowed with coal, iron, and other basic materials; so were many other countries. It was also spared the almost continuous warfare which plagued continental Europe, particularly the French revolutionary and Napoleonic wars (pages 88, 90). Unlike France and Germany, where markets and trade were limited by a multiplicity of customs barriers and internal and external frontiers, Great Britain after the union of England and Scotland in 1707 was a single economic unit, where men and goods moved freely. It also enjoyed an advantageous position in Atlantic trade, from which capital flowed into industry. In an age of sailing ships, ports like Liverpool, Glasgow and Bristol had obvious advantages over Hamburg and Bremen. The English social structure was also favourable. In contrast to continental Europe, where most peasants were still tied to the soil (page 82), the early disappearance of serfdom in England meant that the surplus labour released by the enclosure of common land during the eighteenth century could move, without legal obstacles, to the growing industrial centres. Finally, England had a unique network of navigable rivers and canals (map 1), which was of inestimable importance before the railway age for moving both raw materials and finished goods.

In its earliest phase English manufacture had relied on water power; hence the location of the early cotton and woollen mills on the slopes of the Pennines. But essentially the Industrial Revolution, in the century to 1870, was a revolution of coal and iron. Its basis was the application of steam power to machinery, and a series of technical innovations – Watt's rotative engine (1782) and Cartwright's power loom (1792) among others – quickly demonstrated the superiority of steam-power driven machines. In continental Europe, apart from Belgium, where industrialisation proceeded rapidly after 1820, the use of steam power came more slowly. The famous German steel firm of Krupp, later to be a giant of German industry, was founded in 1810 in green fields outside Essen, where a stream provided water power; it had only 7 employees in 1826 and 122 in 1846. Here, and elsewhere, large-scale industry was held back by political fragmentation, lack of capital, and, above all, by poor communications, which severely limited markets. What changed this, above all else, was railway development, beginning in the 1830s. By 1860 the railway networks of Britain, Belgium and Germany were virtually complete, although in Austria-Hungary and Russia large-scale construction was only beginning (map 2). With their demand for rails, sleepers, engines and carriages, railways also provided immense impetus to heavy industry. A second factor was the dismantling of obstructions to trade. In France internal tariffs had been demolished in 1790 as part of the revolutionary reorganisation. In 1818 Prussia followed suit, setting up free trade between its provinces, followed by a Prussian Customs Union (1828) including other smaller German territories, and finally (1834) the German Customs Union, or Zollverein, comprising 17 states and some 26 million people (map 3). Here was a solid basis for the development of German industry.

A new period, sometimes called the Second Industrial Revolution, opened after 1870. The new German Empire, founded in 1871, was in the forefront. Coal and iron were still basic, and here Germany forged ahead, increasing its coal output from 38 million tons in 1871 to 279 million tons in 1913 and its iron output from 1.5 million tons to 15 million tons. But it was in the new branches of industry – steel, electricity and chemicals – that Germany outpaced all other nations. German steel production leapt from 1.5 million tons in 1880 to over 13 million tons in 1910, by which time Krupps was employing 70,000 men. Steel, electricity and chemicals were the index of the new industrial society, and at a time of growing international tension (page 116) Germany's headstart was bound to produce a defensive reaction among its rivals. The intensive industrialisation which occurred in France after 1895 and in northern Italy after 1905 represented a deliberate national effort not to be left behind. The same was true of the great upsurge of Russian industry after 1890, particularly the massive development of the iron and steel industry of the Donets basin (page 84). By now much of heavy industry was keyed to armaments. Industrialisation had changed the face of Europe by 1914; but it had also made it more dangerous and more explosive.

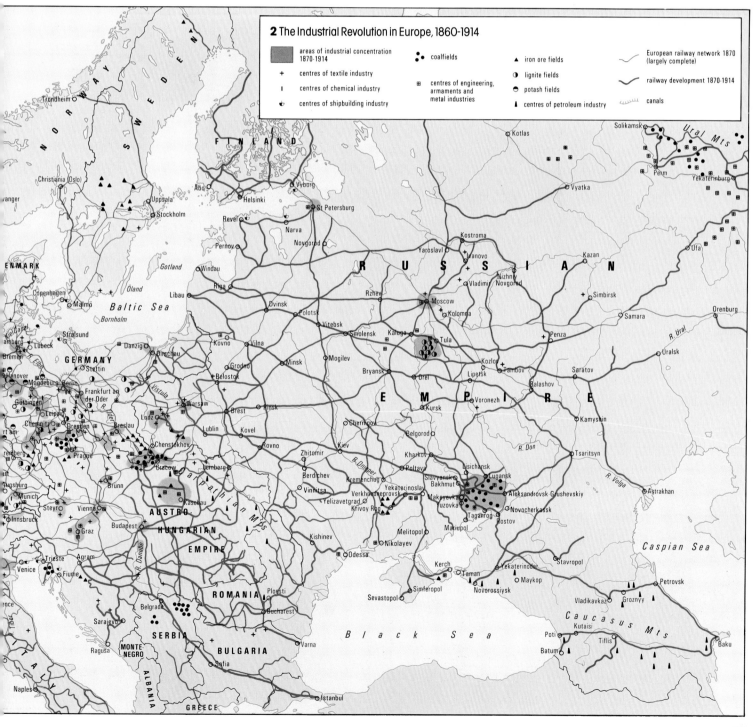

2 The Industrial Revolution in Europe, 1860-1914

areas of industrial concentration 1870-1914

+ centres of textile industry

I centres of chemical industry

centres of shipbuilding industry

coalfields

centres of engineering, armaments and metal industries

▲ iron ore fields

lignite fields

potash fields

centres of petroleum industry

European railway network 1870 (largely complete)

railway development 1870-1914

canals

European imperialism
1815-1914

Between 1815 and 1914, under the impact of the Industrial Revolution, the character of European imperialism changed. Earlier the motivating force had been the search for the riches of the Orient, and the European stake in Asia and Africa was confined to trading stations and the strategic outposts necessary to protect the trade. In 1815, with the important exception of India, this was still the situation. But in the nineteenth century two new factors came into play. The first was the enforced opening of the world – Turkey and Egypt (1838), Persia (1841), China (1842), even Japan (1858) – to European, particularly British, commerce; in short, the breaking down of barriers to European penetration. The second, setting in around 1880, when a new phase of the Industrial Revolution got under way (page 98), was the search for the raw materials without which industry, in its new form, could not exist. Tin and rubber from Malaya, nickel from Canada, copper from Australia and South America were now the sinews of European industry; and so the scramble for natural resources began, providing a new impetus for colonial expansion. Between 1880 and 1914 Europe added over 8½ million square miles, or one-fifth of the land area of the globe, to its overseas colonial possessions.

Nevertheless no clear line divides the period before and the period after 1880. Criticism of imperialism was certainly strong in the first half of the century. Free traders of the so-called 'Manchester School' argued cogently that empire was unnecessary, even detrimental,

to commerce, and the burgeoning trade with the ex-colonial countries of North and South America seemed to prove their point. Nevertheless imperial expansion was continuous after 1815. Both Great Britain and France – particularly France, which had lost its first empire in 1815 and was determined to constitute a new empire – steadily advanced (map 1). The French conquered Algeria in the 1830s, annexed Tahiti and the Marquesas in the 1840s, expanded their colony in Senegal in the 1850s, and began the conquest of Indo-China in 1859. Great Britain, which had retained the Cape of Good Hope, the maritime provinces of Ceylon and other strategically important footholds (Malta, Mauritius, the Seychelles) in 1815, also continued to expand. Fearing a French challenge, it claimed sovereignty over Australia and New Zealand (page 112). It built up its power in India (page 104), acquired Singapore (1819), Malacca (1824), Hong Kong (1842), Natal (1843), Lower Burma (1852) and Lagos (1861). Many of these acquisitions were defensive reactions against France; most were intended to secure its position in India which, with its army of 150–200,000, made Britain the strongest territorial power in the east. Even so, except for India, imperialism still only touched the outer fringes of Asia and Africa. Even the Russian empire, which by 1886 was to engross much of central Asia (page 84), still only affected the periphery.

After 1880 a fundamental change came about. Its causes were partly economic, but still more important were the rivalries of the European powers, each of which feared that its competitors would steal a march on it. Comparison of maps 1 and 2 points out the difference. Even as late as 1870 colonial penetration was

marginal. By 1914 the European powers had engross nine-tenths of Africa and a large part of Asia. Betwe 1871 and 1914 the French empire grew by nearly million square miles and 47 million people, mainly north and west Africa and Indo-China, but also in t Pacific islands and Madagascar. But a significant fac was the entry of new claimants, particularly Germa and Italy, challenging the old imperial powers. G many acquired an empire of 1 million square miles a 14 million colonial subjects in South-West Afri Togoland, the Cameroons, Tanganyika and the Pac Islands. Italy obtained Tripoli and Libya, Eritrea a Italian Somaliland, but failed in 1896 to conquer Ab sinia. But the greatest gains of all were made by Gr Britain, which secured control over Nigeria, Ken Uganda, Northern and Southern Rhodesia, Egypt a the Sudan, as well as areas in the Pacific including and parts of Borneo and New Guinea. The keystone the British empire was India, and its acquisitions we made with a view to bolstering British control o access to India and the Indian Ocean via the Su Canal and East Africa, but also via Singapore and south Pacific (map 3). So long as it was assured of c trol of the Indian Ocean, the British imperial positi was secure.

In retrospect, the fragility of the European empi so hastily assembled between 1884 and 1914, is obvio None of the imperial powers had the resources to gove them adequately. European imperialism was m ephemeral than anyone, at the close of the ninetee century, could have believed; and yet it left an indeli impression on the peoples of Asia and Africa, propelli them willingly or unwillingly into the twentieth centu

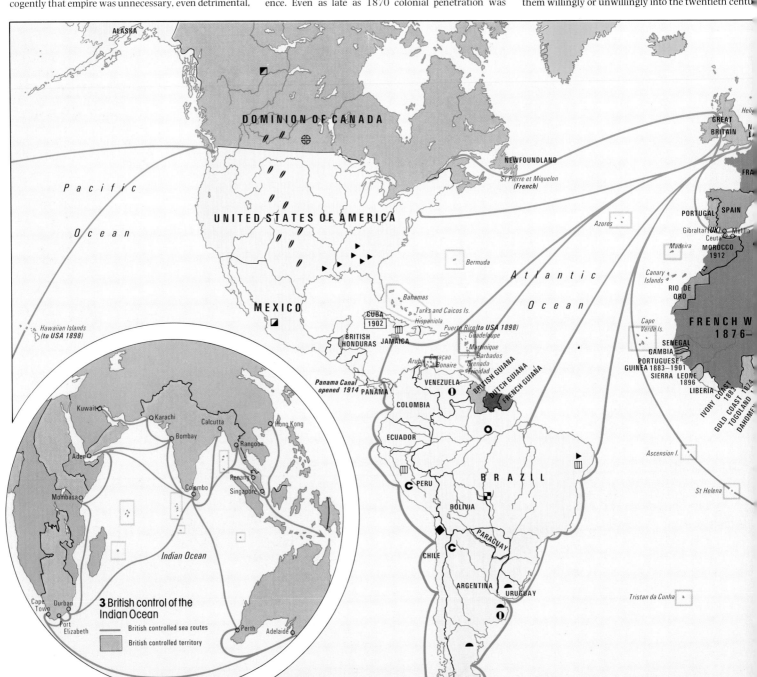

3 British control of the Indian Ocean
— British controlled sea routes
▨ British controlled territory

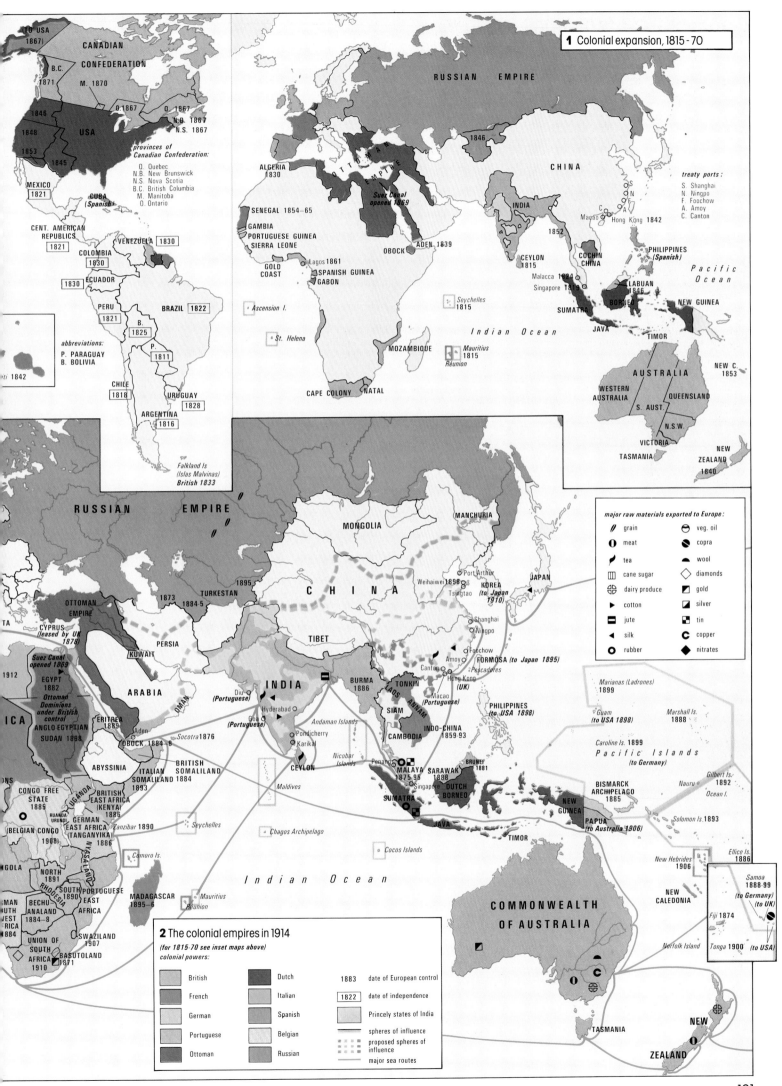

Nineteenth century Africa

Although European exploration began in the eighteenth century (map 1), its impact on Africa was limited until after 1870, except in the far south where Dutch settlers, or Boers, in Cape Colony, who had been brought under British rule in 1806, moved north in the Great Trek (1835) in search of land and freedom, and founded settlements which eventually became the republics of the Orange Free State and Transvaal (map 2). The only other area of European settlement was Algeria, conquered by France between 1830 and 1847 after fierce resistance under Abd al Kadir. Nevertheless this was a period of great change and instability in Africa. In the north-east the dominating fact was the advance of Egypt under Mohammed Ali, who conquered northern Sudan in 1820, founded Khartoum as its capital in 1830, and inaugurated the attempt to build a great Egyptian empire reaching the length of the Nile and east to the Horn of Africa. In the north-west a great Muslim religious revival, beginning around 1804 under Uthman dan Fodio, carried the Fulani south into Hausaland, where they founded the Sultanate of Sokoto. Later, another empire was carved out further west, between the Ivory Coast and the Upper Niger, by a Mandingo Muslim leader, Samory. In the south, the outstanding event was the rise of the Zulus, which resulted in a great political and demographic revolution (the so-called *Mfecane* or 'time of troubles'), as the local tribes were driven west and north into Rhodesia, Malawi and Zambia.

This was the situation when the European 'scramble for Africa' got under way after 1882 (page 100), and the countries named above were leaders of African resistance (map 3). The Zulus, hard pressed between British and Boers after the British annexation of Natal (1845), held out fiercely until the war of 1879–81, when their country was annexed (map 2). Resistance elsewhere was

equally strong. Samory was only defeated by the French in 1898; Sokoto only fell to the British in 1903. In the north the British established a *de facto* protectorate over a bankrupt Egypt after 1882 (turned into a full-scale protectorate in 1914); but they were only able to secure control of the Sudan in 1898 after the slaughter of some 20,000 Sudanese. Nowhere was occupation unchallenged, as the great Herero and Maji-Maji revolts of 1904–6 against German colonialism showed. But the only lasting success was the Ethiopian defeat of Italy at Adowa in 1896. Morocco kept a precarious independence until 1912 before being divided between France and Spain, and Libya and Cyrenaica were occupied by Italy in the same year. By 1914 the European powers were in full control (map 5). Apart from Ethiopia, only Liberia could claim independence.

The position of the Boer republics in the south was different. Transvaal also had been annexed by Great Britain in 1877 and then restored to independence in 1881. But the discovery of diamonds at Kimberley and of gold on the Witwatersrand (1886) sealed their fate. The entry of foreign speculators (*Uitlanders*) sparked Boer hostility, and when an attempt by Cecil Rhodes (Prime Minister of Cape Colony, 1890–96) to stage a take-over failed dismally (Jameson Raid, 1895), the outcome was the Boer War (1899–1902), in which, after initial Boer successes, ruthless British suppression forced the Boers to capitulate (map 4). Nevertheless the Afrikaners secured favourable terms after the Peace of Vereeniging (May 31, 1902), including the use of their own language and the exclusion of blacks from the franchise, and this compromise made possible the formation (1910) of the Union of South Africa as a dominion of the British Commonwealth. It was nevertheless a betrayal of black Africans by Britain which led step by step to the policy of *Apartheid* (1948) and to the radical conflicts which bedevilled South Africa after the rest of the continent had won its independence.

5 Africa after partition, 1914

- French
- British
- German
- Portuguese
- Belgian
- Spanish
- Italian
- Anglo-Egyptian Condominium

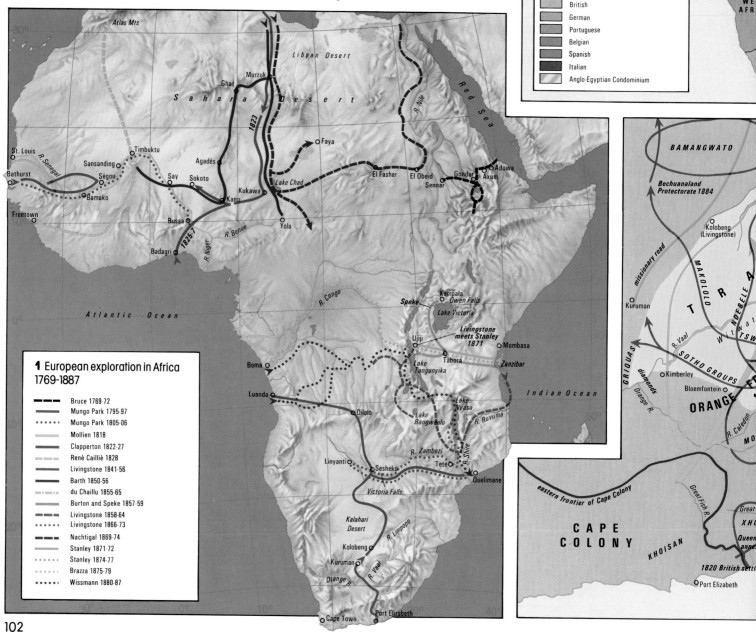

1 European exploration in Africa 1769-1887

- Bruce 1769-72
- Mungo Park 1795-97
- Mungo Park 1805-06
- Mollien 1818
- Clapperton 1822-27
- René Caillié 1828
- Livingstone 1841-56
- Barth 1850-56
- du Chaillu 1855-65
- Burton and Speke 1857-59
- Livingstone 1858-64
- Livingstone 1866-73
- Nachtigal 1869-74
- Stanley 1871-72
- Stanley 1874-77
- Brazza 1875-79
- Wissmann 1880-87

Partial map (left edge):

GYPT
n dominion
itish control
882)

O-EGYPTIAN
SUDAN

ERITREA

FRENCH
SOMALILAND

BRITISH
SOMALILAND

ETHIOPIA

UGANDA

ITALIAN
SOMALILAND

BRITISH
EAST
AFRICA
(KENYA)

*Indian
Ocean*

GERMAN
EAST
AFRICA

RN
RHODESIA

NYASALAND

OUTHERN
RHODESIA

MOZAMBIQUE

MADAGASCAR

SWAZILAND

BASUTOLAND

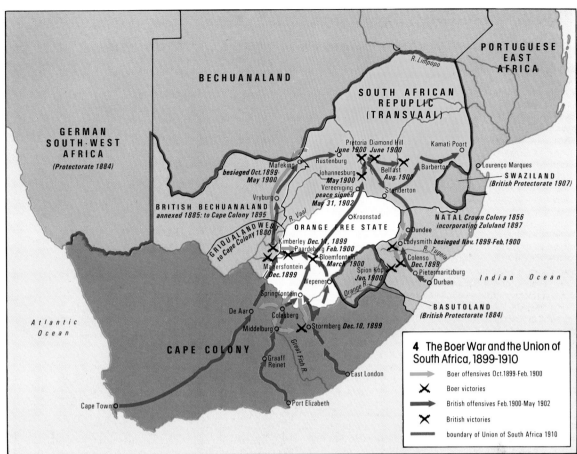

4 The Boer War and the Union of South Africa, 1899-1910

→ Boer offensives Oct.1899-Feb. 1900
✕ Boer victories
➤ British offensives Feb.1900-May 1902
✕ British victories
▬ boundary of Union of South Africa 1910

BECHUANALAND

GERMAN
SOUTH-WEST
AFRICA
(Protectorate 1884)

SOUTH AFRICAN
REPUBLIC
(TRANSVAAL)

PORTUGUESE
EAST
AFRICA

R. Limpopo

Pretoria — Diamond Hill June 1900 / June 1900
Rustenburg — Kamati Poort
Mafeking *besieged Oct.1899-May 1900*
Johannesburg — Belfast Aug. 1900 — Barberton
May 1900
Vereeniging *peace signed May 31, 1902* — Standerton
Lourenço Marques
SWAZILAND *(British Protectorate 1907)*

BRITISH BECHUANALAND *annexed 1885: to Cape Colony 1895*

Vryburg
R. Vaal
Kroonstad
NATAL *Crown Colony 1856 incorporating Zululand 1897*

GRIQUALAND WEST *to Cape Colony 1880*
ORANGE FREE STATE
Kimberley *Dec. 11, 1899* Paardeberg *Feb. 1900*
Bloemfontein *March 1900*
Ladysmith *besieged Nov. 1899-Feb. 1900*
Colenso *Dec.1899*
Dundee
R. Tugela
Magersfontein *Dec.1899*
Spion Kop *Jan. 1900*
Pietermaritzburg
Wepener
Orange R.
Durban
Indian Ocean

Springfontein
BASUTOLAND *(British Protectorate 1884)*

Atlantic Ocean

De Aar — Colesberg
Middelburg — Stormberg *Dec. 10, 1899*
Graaff Reinet
Great Fish R.
East London

CAPE COLONY

Cape Town
Port Elizabeth

R. Limpopo

NGUNI

A L

1852

annexed by Britain 1877-81

SOSHANGANE

KAZI
Boers defeat British 1881
Majuba Hill

SWAZI

R. Buffalo
ZULU
Ulundi 1881
ZULULAND *annexed by Britain 1879-81*
R. Tugela
Isandhlwana
✕ 1879

by Britain 1845 (Boers migrated here in 1830s, after British annexation)

ASUTOLAND
Port Natal
by Cape 1871-84 thereafter stered by Britain

PONDO
nexed by Cape
1-94

ir War

ed 1836

an Ocean

2 South Africa 1818-81

⬭ African nations or tribal groups
ZULU African peoples
➤ African migrations
▨ land partially emptied by African migrations
➤ the Great Trek - Boer migration
➤ Boer Republics
battles of Zulu Wars:
✕ British victories
✕ Zulu victory

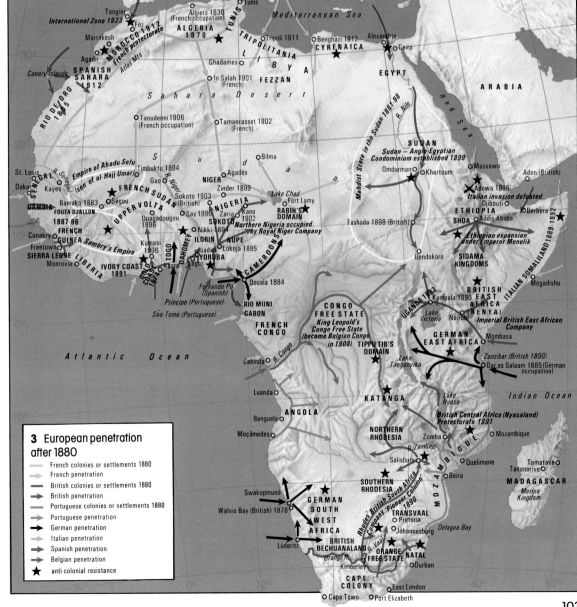

3 European penetration after 1880

▬ French colonies or settlements 1880
➤ French penetration
▬ British colonies or settlements 1880
➤ British penetration
▬ Portuguese colonies or settlements 1880
➤ Portuguese penetration
➤ German penetration
➤ Italian penetration
➤ Spanish penetration
➤ Belgian penetration
★ anti-colonial resistance

Mediterranean Sea

Tangier
International Zone 1923 ★ Fez — MOROCCO 1912 *French protectorate*
Algiers 1830 *(French occupation)*
ALGERIA 1870
Tunis
TUNIS 1881
Tripoli 1911
TRIPOLITANIA
Benghazi 1912
CYRENAICA
Alexandria
Cairo

Marrakesh
Agadir
SPANISH SAHARA 1912
Atlas Mts
Ghadames
L I B Y A
FEZZAN

Canary Islands
RIO DE ORO 1885
In Salah 1901 *(French)*
EGYPT
ARABIA

Sahara Desert

Taoudenni 1906 *(French occupation)*
Tamanrasset 1902 *(French)*
Bilma

Su da n

Mahdist State in the Sudan 1881-98
R. Nile
SUDAN *Sudan – Anglo-Egyptian Condominium established 1899*
Omdurman
Khartoum
Massawe
Aden (British)

St. Louis
R. Senegal
SENEGAL
Empire of Ahadu Sefu *(son of al-Hajj Umar)*
Timbuktu 1894
Gao
Agadès
NIGER
Zinder 1899
Lake Chad
Fort Lamy
★ Adowa 1896 *Italian invasion defeated*
ETHIOPIA
SHOA
Djibouti
Berbera 1884

Dakar
Kayes
Ségou
FRENCH SUDAN
R. Niger
Sokoto 1903 (British)
NIGERIA
Kano 1902
RABIH'S DOMAIN
Addis Ababa
Ethiopian expansion under Emperor Menelik
SIDAMA KINGDOMS
ITALIAN SOMALILAND 1889-1892

GAMBIA
Bamako 1883
FOUTA DJALLON 1887-96
UPPER VOLTA
Ouagadougou 1896
Say 1896
SOKOTO
Zaria
Northern Nigeria occupied by Royal Niger Company
Fashoda 1898 (British)
Gondokoro
Mogadishu

Conakry
FRENCH GUINEA
Samory's Empire
Nikki 1894
ILORIN
NUPE
CAMEROONS
Douala 1884

Freetown
SIERRA LEONE
LIBERIA
Kumasi 1896
TOGO
DAHOMEY
Ibadan
YORUBA
Lokoja 1885

Monrovia
IVORY COAST 1891
GOLD COAST
Accra
Lagos
Fernando Po *(Spanish)*
RIO MUNI
GABON
CONGO FREE STATE
King Leopold's Congo Free State (became Belgian Congo in 1908)
TIPPU TIB'S DOMAIN
UGANDA 1893
Kampala 1890
Lake Victoria
Nairobi
BRITISH EAST AFRICA (KENYA)
Imperial British East African Company

Príncipe *(Portuguese)*
São Tomé *(Portuguese)*
FRENCH CONGO
Cabinda
R. Congo
Lake Tanganyika
GERMAN EAST AFRICA
Mombasa
Zanzibar (British 1890)
Dar es Salaam 1885 (German occupation)

Atlantic Ocean

Luanda
KATANGA
Lake Nyasa
Indian Ocean

Benguela
ANGOLA
NORTHERN RHODESIA
British Central Africa (Nyasaland) Protectorate 1891
Zomba
Mozambique

Moçâmedes
R. Zambezi
Salisbury
MOZAMBIQUE
Quelimane
Tamatave
MADAGASCAR
Merina Kingdom

Swakopmund
GERMAN SOUTH WEST AFRICA
Rhodes's British South Africa Company 'Pioneer Column' 1890
SOUTHERN RHODESIA
Beira
Tananarive

Walvis Bay (British) 1878
BRITISH BECHUANALAND
TRANSVAAL
Pretoria
Johannesburg
Delagoa Bay

Lüderitz
Orange R.
R. Vaal
ORANGE FREE STATE
NATAL
Durban
CAPE COLONY
Kimberley
Cape Town
Port Elizabeth
East London

India under British rule, 1805-1947

By 1805 the hegemony of the English East India Company in the Indian sub-continent was an established fact. With the conquest of Sind (1843) and the Sikh kingdom of the Punjab (1849) its dominion became co-terminous with the country's natural frontier in the north-west, while in the north a war with Nepal (1814–16) extended it to the Himalayan foothills (map 1). To the east the British clashed with the Burmese empire and in 1826 and 1852 annexed most of its territories, including Assam. Upper Burma itself was brought under British rule in 1886 (map 2). Within India Dalhousie's Doctrine of Lapse led to the absorption of dependent states like Oudh and several Maratha kingdoms into the directly administered territories. Not surprisingly, this policy provoked disaffection among dispossessed rulers and the rural propertied classes, and the pent-up discontent found a violent outlet in the rebellion of 1857. Beginning as a mutiny of the Company's Indian sepoys, the revolt soon involved princes, landlords and peasants throughout northern India, but the loyalty of the Sikhs and the passivity of the Deccan and southern India enabled the British to crush it after fourteen months of bitter fighting.

The mutiny was a watershed in the history of British India. It discredited the Company and in 1858 the British government assumed direct control, though the autonomy of the Indian princes was respected. The impetus to economic development was immediate. First-class roads were built, totalling 57,000 miles by 1927, but it was the railways, planned by Dalhousie in 1853, which opened the country and made possible the exploitation of raw materials and the profitable introduction of export crops, such as tea. Between 1869 and 1929 India's foreign trade increased sevenfold. How far this benefited the rural masses is a moot question; but the development of modern industries brought into existence an Indian entrepreneurial class. After 1921, when protective tariffs were introduced, industrial expansion made further progress (map 3).

With the rise of a new middle class, partly through industry but more through the recruitment of educated Indians into the colonial administration, came a reawakened political consciousness. The Indian National Congress (1885) accepted British rule, though in 1905 an extremist wing under Bal Gangadhar Tilak turned to violence. But it was only after 1919 that Congress, under Gandhi's leadership, fought actively for Home Rule and, after 1929, for independence (map 4). Gandhi's civil disobedience campaigns galvanised the Indian masses; but Congress's claim to represent all Indians, Hindu and Muslim alike, alienated the Muslim minority and led to conflicts which resulted in 1947 in partition (map 5). Faced by mounting unrest and the naval mutiny of 1946, the Labour government in England realised that a transfer of power could not be delayed; but the event that forced its hand was the communal rioting of 1946–47. Plans for partition were hastily drawn up. But the boundary award in Kashmir, Punjab and Bengal resulted in large-scale disturbances in which some 500,000 lost their lives, and left a tense situation which erupted in the India-Pakistan war of 1965.

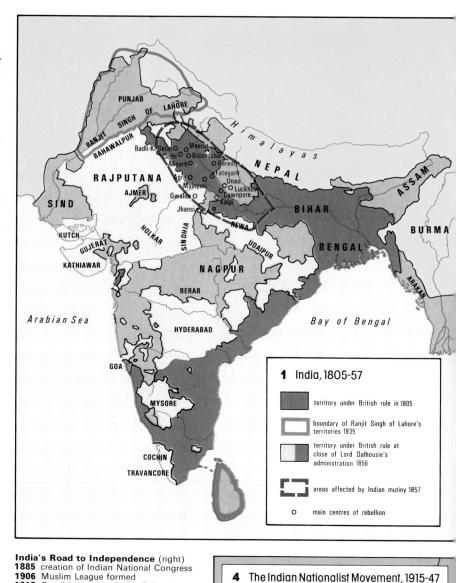

1 India, 1805-57

territory under British rule in 1805

boundary of Ranjit Singh of Lahore's territories 1835

territory under British rule at close of Lord Dalhousie's administration 1856

areas affected by Indian mutiny 1857

○ main centres of rebellion

2 The annexation of Burma, 1826-86

British India

area annexed by British 1826

area annexed by British 1852

area annexed by British 1886

— boundary of modern Burma

India's Road to Independence (right)
1885 creation of Indian National Congress
1906 Muslim League formed
1915 Gandhi returns to India. Following death of Gokhale (1915) and Tilak (1920) emerges as leader of Congress
1916 Lucknow Pact: Congress and Muslim League agree to co-operate in demand for home rule (*swaraj*)
1917 Montagu Declaration: Britain's goal is 'responsible government for India as an integral part of the British Empire.' But
1919 Government of India Act leaves central administration and police powers in hands of Viceroy
1919 Amritsar Massacre: troops fire on demonstrators and kill 379 Indians
1920 Khilafat Committee of Hindus and Muslims adopts Gandhi's programme of peaceful non-cooperation (*satyagraha*)
1920 First Civil Disobedience campaign
1922 after violence at Chauri Chaura and Moplah rising in South India
1922-29 Gandhi (in prison 1922–24) withdraws from active politics
1928 Revival of political activity; rise of Jawaharlal Nehru (President of Lahore Congress, 1929). Widening rift between Congress and Muslim League
1929 Lahore Congress demands immediate independence
1930 Gandhi's march to the sea opens Second Civil Disobedience campaign, 90,000 arrests
1930-32 Round Table Conference breaks down over question of separate electorates for Muslims, Sikhs and Untouchables
1935 Government of India Act. Denounced by Nehru as 'satanic', but main provisions accepted by Bombay Congress which agrees to participate in provincial elections
1937 Congress wins 8 out of 11 provinces in elections, but at cost of alienating Muslims
1938 Jinnah reorganises Muslim League
1939 resignation of Congress ministries after Viceroy declares war without consulting Indian leaders
1940 Lahore resolution of Muslim League in favour of independent Pakistan
1942 Congress rejects British offer of Dominion Status after war. Gandhi launches 'Quit India' campaign. 'August Revolt' suppressed and Congress leaders imprisoned
1946 Second British Cabinet Mission fails. Communal violence in Calcutta, E. Bengal, Bihar and Punjab; half-million deaths
1947 partition and independence

4 The Indian Nationalist Movement, 1915-47

British India and Ceylon

Princely States

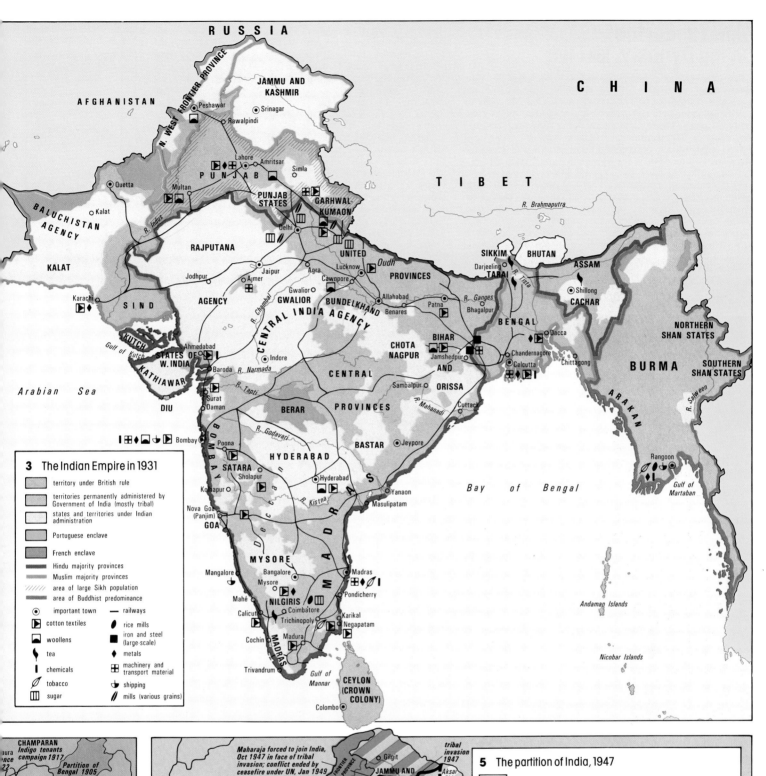

3 The Indian Empire in 1931

5 The partition of India, 1947

China under the Ch'ing Dynasty, 1644-1911

A new era in Chinese history opened in 1644 when the Ming dynasty, beset for a century by Mongol invasions, Japanese raids and civil war, was displaced by a line of foreign, Manchurian, emperors which ruled China until 1911. The Ch'ing, or Manchu, dynasty was resisted in south China for half a century but it quickly established good relations with the dominant Chinese gentry (shen-chin) and with its support began a successful policy of territorial expansion which went on until late in the eighteenth century (map 1).

At the same time there was a great economic upsurge (map 2) and a huge increase in population, from 100 million in 1650 to 300 million in 1820 and 420 million in 1850. There was also a considerable export trade in tea, silk and porcelain with the West from Canton and with Russia from Kyakhta. But the financial strain of the wars of expansion and the pressure of the growing population on the land imposed hardships which led to recurrent unrest and revolts, not only among the minority peoples who were harshly exploited by Chinese and Manchus alike, but also in the heart of China itself. Of these the most serious was the White Lotus rebellion between 1795 and 1804. Meanwhile the export surplus was converted after 1825 into a net outflow as a result of the opium trade. Manchu China was still the world's largest and most populous empire. But its growing economic difficulties, coupled with the failure to expand the administration to match the rapid growth of population, and the pressures of the Western powers, seeking to open the China market for their manufactures, resulted in a crisis which came to a head after Chinese attempts to halt the illicit opium trade were decisively defeated by the British in the Opium War of 1839-42.

The Opium War had two major consequences. First, it resulted in the cession of Hong Kong to the British and in the opening of the first five Treaty Ports (their number was thereafter steadily in-creased) in which foreigners enjoyed extra-territorial rights. Secondly, it weakened imperial authority and led to the great Taiping rebellion (1850-64), the most serious but only one of many rebellions which shook Manchu power to its foundations (map 3). The Taiping and Nien rebellions alone left 25 million dead and vast areas, including the wealthy region around Nanking, were devastated. They also convinced the Western powers that Ch'ing China was on the point of collapse and inaugurated a scramble for concessions (map 4).

The response of the Manchu court and bureaucracy was hesitant and half-hearted, more intent on maintaining traditional institutions and Confucian values than on modernisation. Foreign powers had taken advantage of the situation: the British and French occupied Peking in 1856 and forced open more treaty ports, the Russians occupied the Amur region in 1858 and the Maritime Province in 1860 and China was defeated by France in a war over Indo-China in 1884-85. But it was the overwhelming success of Japan in the war of 1894-95 that convinced a section of the Chinese intelligentsia that only a break with the past could save China, and they secured the support of the young emperor Kuang-su. But the reform movement of 1898 was defeated by the dowager empress Tzu-hsi whose reaction was to turn the popular discontent against the foreigners. The result was the Boxer Rising of 1900, an outburst of xenophobia savagely suppressed by the Western powers, who imposed a heavy indemnity and wrung still further concessions from China. By now even the imperial government realised that modernisation was imperative; but, in spite of a number of reforms, its attitude was still essentially conservative. Convinced that the imperial government was the main obstacle to change, revolutionary groups sprang up everywhere after 1901, and when in 1911 a small-scale army mutiny broke out in Wuchang, disaffection spread throughout the whole country (page 122). The imperial government fell, almost without fighting; but China had still to undergo more than forty years of tribulation before it finally made the transition to the modern world.

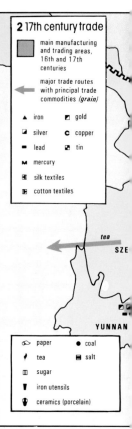

2 17th century trade

- main manufacturing and trading areas, 16th and 17th centuries
- ← major trade routes with principal trade commodities *(grain)*
- ▲ iron
- ▱ silver
- ▬ lead
- M mercury
- ▣ silk textiles
- ▣ cotton textiles
- ◘ gold
- C copper
- tin

- ⟳ paper
- ♦ tea
- ▥ sugar
- ▼ iron utensils
- ⬡ ceramics (porcelain)
- ● coal
- ▱ salt

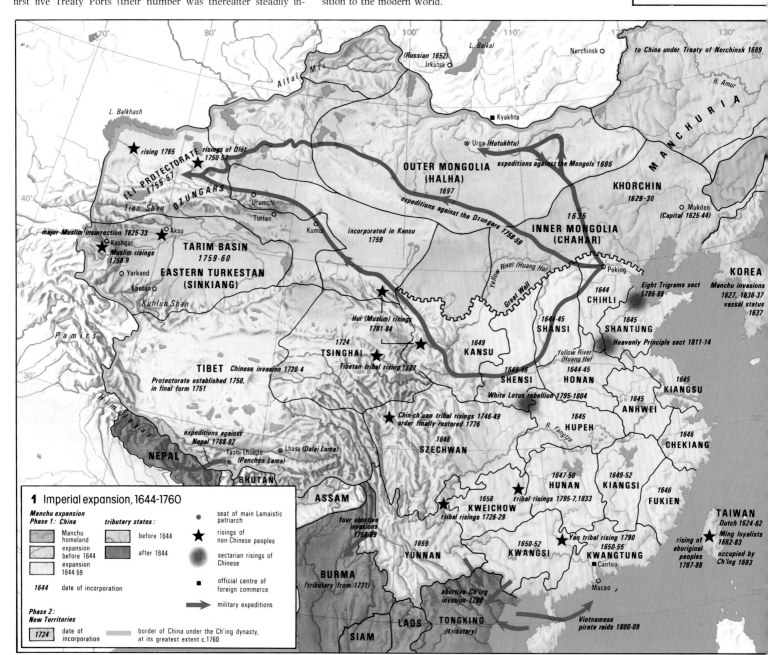

1 Imperial expansion, 1644-1760

Manchu expansion
Phase 1: China

- Manchu homeland
- expansion before 1644
- expansion 1644-59

1644 date of incorporation

tributary states:
- before 1644
- after 1644

⊗ seat of main Lamaistic patriarch

★ risings of non-Chinese peoples

sectarian risings of Chinese

▪ official centre of foreign commerce

→ military expeditions

Phase 2:
New Territories
1724 date of incorporation

border of China under the Ch'ing dynasty, at its greatest extent c.1760

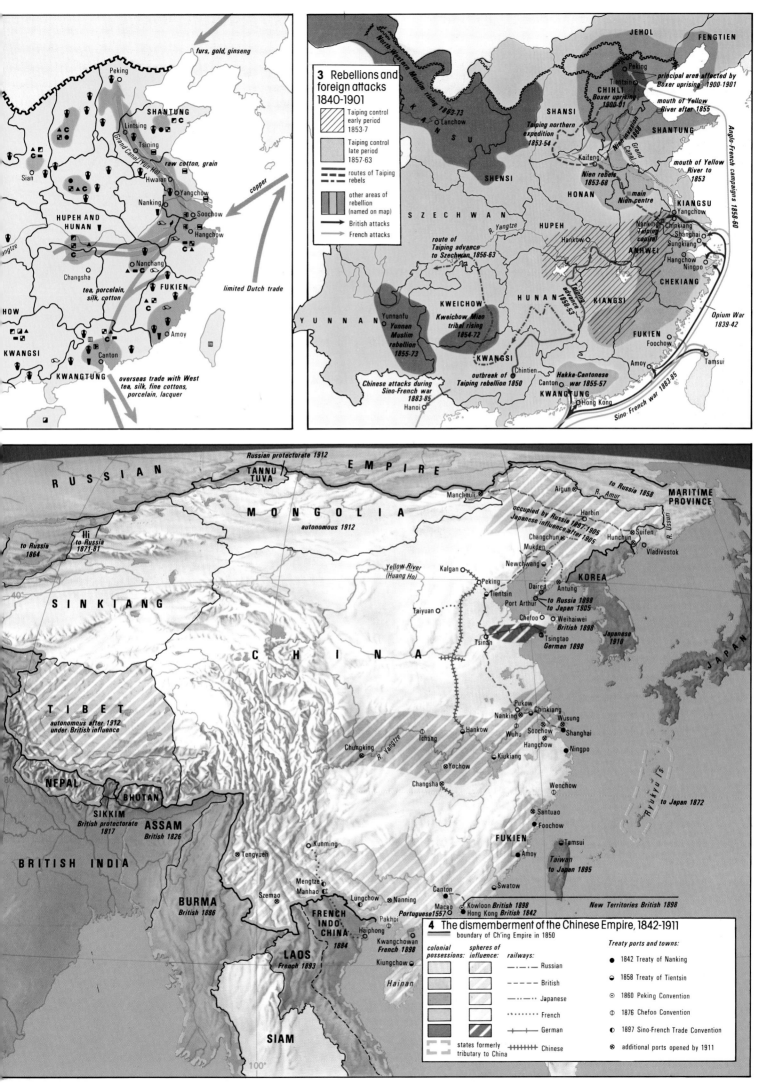

The world economy, 1850-1929

After the middle of the nineteenth century the Industrial Revolution, which had radiated from Great Britain to north-west Europe and the eastern seaboard of the United States, spread to the rest of the world. The result, by 1914, was the formation of a single interdependent world economy. But the impact was extremely varied. Though the United States after 1890 was becoming an important subsidiary centre, the focus throughout was on Europe, and most of the development was keyed to the needs of European industry for raw materials and fed by European capital. In 1914 Great Britain was the largest source of foreign investment, with overseas assets totalling nearly £4,000 million, while the United States, like Russia, was still a net borrower (map 3); but in world trade it was losing the predominance it had enjoyed in 1860 to Germany and the United States (diagram 5).

One factor behind these developments was the vast, unprecedented flow of population, mainly from Europe to the New World, but also from China and India to South-East Asia and East Africa (map 2). Between 1850 and 1920 over 40 million Europeans emigrated overseas or to Siberia, carrying with them European institutions and skills which they used to exploit the vast overseas territories. Much foreign investment went into building the infrastructure of railways, ports and shipping and creating the network of communications upon which the functioning of the world economy depended. Outside Europe and the United States there were only 9,100 miles of railroad track in 1870. By 1911 it had increased

to 175,000 miles. Equally important was the expansion of world shipping and the replacement of sailing ships by ocean-going steamships of large capacity. The opening of the Suez Canal (1869) and the Panama Canal (1914) gave a great fillip to world trade (diagram 4). Traffic via Suez rose from 437,000 tons in 1870 to over 20 million tons in 1913, and foreign trade increased threefold in volume during the same period.

Nevertheless the effects of industrialisation were distinctly one-sided. The main shipping routes (map 3) were between the advanced countries and the white dominions, or between them and the producers of raw materials. Even as late as 1929 the world was still a white man's world. A few countries such as India (page 104) and China had begun to develop their own industries; but, with the exception of Japan, they were small enclaves in a vast rural population. In 1914 there were still only 900,000 factory workers in the whole of India, and 69 per cent of cotton operatives in 1919 were in Bombay province. Nowhere outside the United States and Europe was the income produced by manufacturing substantial in 1930 (map 1) and in most cases it accrued to foreign investors. This was true of Malaya, which by 1900 was producing nearly half the world's tin and by 1910 was a major exporter of rubber, and of Katanga, where copper production rose from nothing in 1900 to 305,000 tons (including Northern Rhodesia) in 1930. Here, as elsewhere, the bulk of the population benefited only marginally, and per capita income in most countries seems actually to have declined. This was the situation which led, a generation later, to the conflict of rich nations and poor nations (page 150) and the demand for a New International Economic Order.

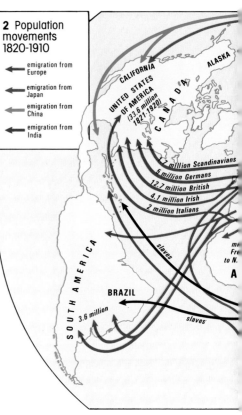

2 Population movements 1820-1910

- → emigration from Europe
- → emigration from Japan
- → emigration from China
- → emigration from India

1.7 million Scandinavians
5 million Germans
12.7 million British
4.1 million Irish
2 million Italians

3.6 million

slaves

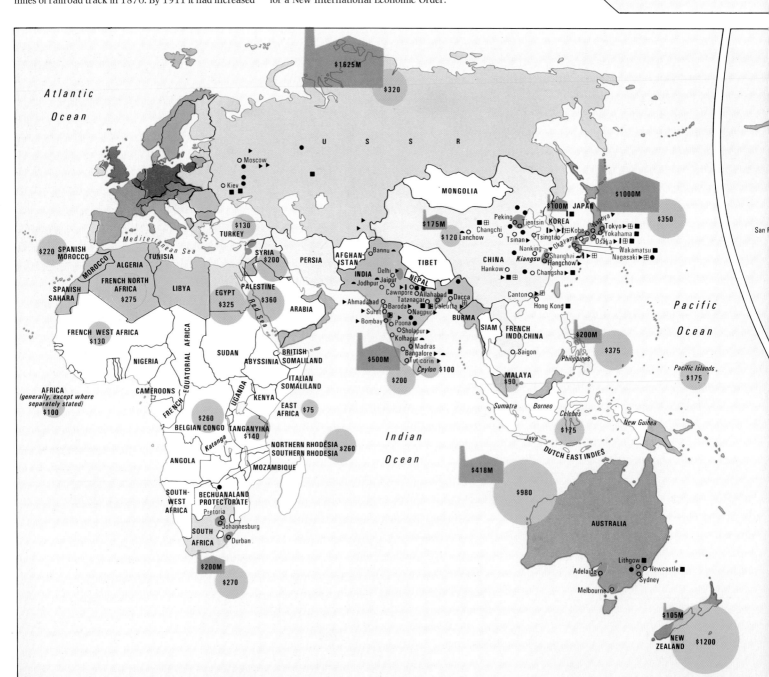

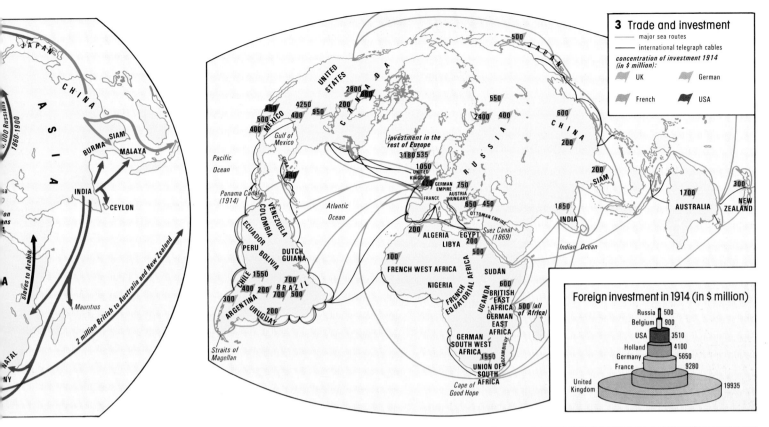

3 Trade and investment

major sea routes
international telegraph cables

concentration of investment 1914 (in $ million):

UK
German
French
USA

JAPAN

CHINA

ASIA

BURMA SIAM
MALAYA

INDIA
CEYLON

slaves to Arabia

Mauritius

2 million British to Australia and New Zealand

NATAL

NY

2,000 Russians 1860-1900

UNITED STATES

CANADA

2800 480

4250 950
500 400
MEXICO
400

Gulf of Mexico

Pacific Ocean

Panama Canal (1914)

COLOMBIA
VENEZUELA
ECUADOR
PERU BOLIVIA
DUTCH GUIANA
CHILE 1550
400 200
BRAZIL
700 500
300
ARGENTINA
URUGUAY 200

Straits of Magellan

Atlantic Ocean

investment in the rest of Europe
3180 535

1050
UNITED KINGDOM
GERMAN EMPIRE 750
AUSTRIA HUNGARY
FRANCE
OTTOMAN EMPIRE 650 450

ALGERIA EGYPT 200
LIBYA 500

100
FRENCH WEST AFRICA
NIGERIA
FRENCH EQUATORIAL AFRICA
SUDAN
UGANDA 600
BRITISH EAST AFRICA
GERMAN EAST AFRICA 500 (all of Africa)

GERMAN SOUTH WEST AFRICA 1550

MOZAMBIQUE

UNION OF SOUTH AFRICA

Suez Canal (1869)

Indian Ocean

Cape of Good Hope

RUSSIA

500

JAPAN

550
2400 400
600
CHINA 200
200 SIAM

200

1850
INDIA

1700 AUSTRALIA

300

NEW ZEALAND

Foreign investment in 1914 (in $ million)

Russia 500
Belgium 900
USA 3510
Holland 4100
Germany 5650
France 9280
United Kingdom 19935

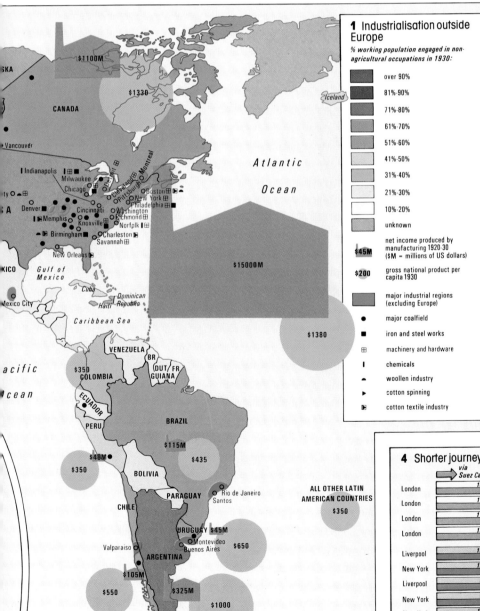

1 Industrialisation outside Europe

% working population engaged in non-agricultural occupations in 1930:

over 90%
81%-90%
71%-80%
61%-70%
51%-60%
41%-50%
31%-40%
21%-30%
10%-20%
unknown

$45M — net income produced by manufacturing 1920-30 ($M = millions of US dollars)

$200 — gross national product per capita 1930

major industrial regions (excluding Europe)

● major coalfield
■ iron and steel works
⊞ machinery and hardware
ꟷ chemicals
▲ woollen industry
▶ cotton spinning
▣ cotton textile industry

$1100M

$1330

CANADA

Vancouver

Iceland

Atlantic Ocean

Indianapolis
Milwaukee
Chicago
Detroit
Cleveland
Montreal
Pittsburgh
Boston
New York
Philadelphia
Washington
Richmond
Norfolk
Denver
Cincinnati
Memphis
Knoxville
Birmingham
Charleston
Savannah
New Orleans

$15000M

MEXICO
Gulf of Mexico
Mexico City
Cuba
Dominican Republic
Haiti
Caribbean Sea

VENEZUELA
COLOMBIA $350
BR
DUT/FR GUIANA
ECUADOR
PERU
$48M
$350
BRAZIL
$115M
$435

$1380

BOLIVIA
PARAGUAY
Rio de Janeiro
Santos

CHILE
URUGUAY $45M
Montevideo
Buenos Aires $650
Valparaiso
ARGENTINA
$105M
$550
$325M
$1000

ALL OTHER LATIN AMERICAN COUNTRIES
$350

Pacific Ocean

5 Balance of world trade, 1860 and 1913

		Europe	N. America	S. America	Asia	Africa
UNITED KINGDOM	imports 1860	419	252	96	143	80
	exports	358	132	74	139	36
	imports 1913	1,548	848	393	458	220
	exports	917	265	272	620	248
USA	imports 1860	217	–	80	29	–
	exports	249	–	46	11	–
	imports 1913	893	199	381	298	26
	exports	1,479	469	294	140	29
FRANCE	imports 1860	234	47	41	16	34
	exports	293	49	53	3	45
	imports 1913	880	187	183	192	148
	exports	937	89	94	36	181
HOLLAND	imports 1860	92	5	3	32	–
	exports	87	2	1	14	–
	imports 1913	624	190	87	274	14
	exports	1,131	57	9	73	14
GERMANY	imports 1913	1,402	423	290	250	118
	exports	1,828	184	183	130	50
RUSSIA	imports 1913	556	–	–	–	–
	exports	719	–	–	–	–

figures in million dollars US

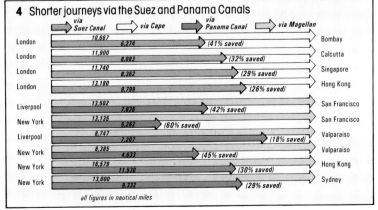

4 Shorter journeys via the Suez and Panama Canals

via Suez Canal | via Cape | via Panama Canal | via Magellan

London	10,667 / 6,274 (41% saved)		Bombay
London	11,900 / 8,083 (32% saved)		Calcutta
London	11,740 / 8,362 (29% saved)		Singapore
London	13,180 / 9,799 (26% saved)		Hong Kong
Liverpool	13,502 / 7,836 (42% saved)		San Francisco
New York	13,135 / 5,262 (60% saved)		San Francisco
Liverpool	8,747 / 7,207 (18% saved)		Valparaiso
New York	8,385 / 4,633 (45% saved)		Valparaiso
New York	16,579 / 11,530 (30% saved)		Hong Kong
New York	13,000 / 9,332 (29% saved)		Sydney

all figures in nautical miles

The United States and Canada, 1865-1920

The rise of the modern United States dates effectively from the Civil War, but development was very uneven. For the defeated South the period of Reconstruction (1865–77) was a bitter experience. South Carolina had ranked third in the nation in per capita wealth in 1860; ten years later it was fortieth, and Mississippi, Alabama and Georgia fared no better. Worst of all was the position of the 4 million liberated slaves, who found themselves (as the black leader Frederick Douglass said) without money, property or friends. The great upsurge in population, from 31 million in 1860 to 92 million in 1910, by-passed the South and concentrated wealth and power in the north-east where, with the exploitation of the rich ore reserves of the Mesabi Range in Minnesota and the vast coal reserves of the Appalachians, industry spread rapidly from the original manufacturing belt between Boston and New Jersey to Pitts-

burgh, Detroit and Chicago. Only around 1920 did cheap labour attract the textile industry from New England to the South (map 2).

The Civil War itself had stimulated Northern industry. After 1865 it forged ahead. But the most striking achievement of the immediate post-war period was the opening of the Great Plains, made possible by the railroad boom after 1870. In 1860 some 30,000 miles of railway were in operation, but few lines extended beyond the Great Lakes. By 1870 the mileage had reached 53,000, by 1880 93,000 and by 1890 163,000 miles (page 94). Land grants of more than 132 million acres encouraged railway promoters, and homestead grants of 285 million acres attracted settlers. The number of farms rose from 2 million in 1860 to 6 million in 1910, and grain exports, which the rail network made possible, were an important source of capital for industrial development. The population west of the Mississippi rose from 6 million in 1870 to 26 million in 1910. Nevertheless the bulk of the population was concentrated

in the north-east (map 5), and most of the 25 million immigrants between 1870 and 1914 remained there, providing cheap labour for American industry. Their miserable conditions, and those of the southern blacks, lay behind the unrest which erupted in the 1890s (map 2).

In Canada railway development was even more important than in the United States. Hitherto the 'small and unimportant' eastern colonies (as Lord Durham described them in his famous Report of 1839) had gone their separate ways, more closely linked to the United States, which made no secret of its hope to absorb them, than with each other. After the acquisition of Alaska from Russia (map 4), United States' pressure grew, and to meet it the Canadian Federation was formed in 1867 and completed by the adhesion of Manitoba (1870) and British Columbia (1871). The great transcontinental railways – the Great Western and Canadian Pacific (completed 1885), followed by the Canadian Northern and Grand Trunk Pacific – were the lifeblood of the new Dominion and

changed the axis of Canadian life. Railway development opened Manitoba and Saskatchewan, and made Canada into one of the world's leading wheat producers (map 1). It also led to the discovery of rich mineral deposits, particularly copper and nickel (1883). The other major industry in 1914 was lumber and the manufacture of paper and newsprint. In general, however, industrialisation was only beginning, though the value of Canada's industrial output increased from $190 million in 1890 to over $500 million in 1914.

In the United States, on the other hand, the 1880s and 1890s saw an astounding industrial upsurge. Output of coal and iron increased twenty times between 1870 and 1913, by which date steel production exceeded that of Britain and Germany combined. But the 'Gilded Age' was also a time of gross inequalities and speculation and over-production caused serious economic setbacks, particularly in 1873 and 1893, which led not only to industrial unrest but also to a search for new markets, particularly in

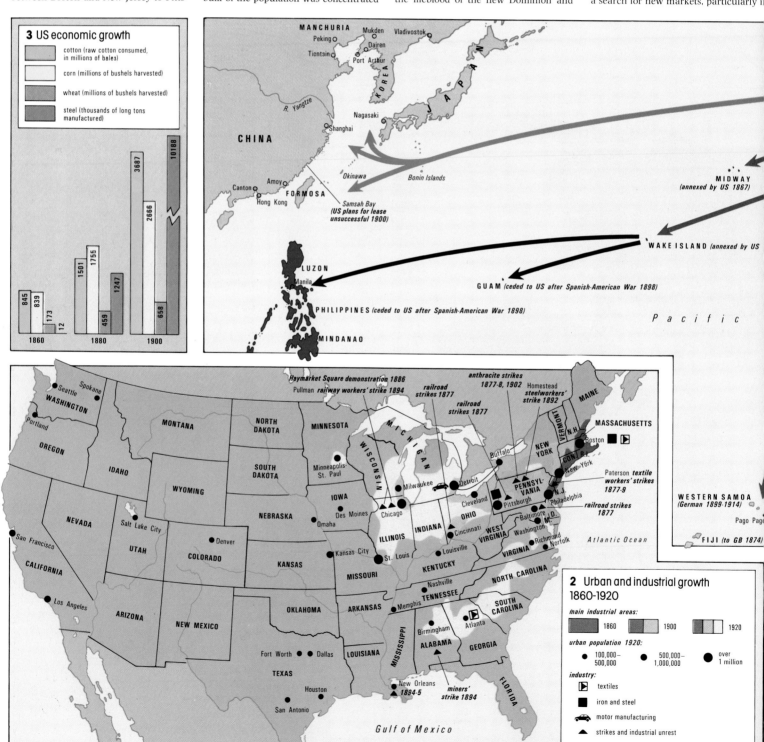

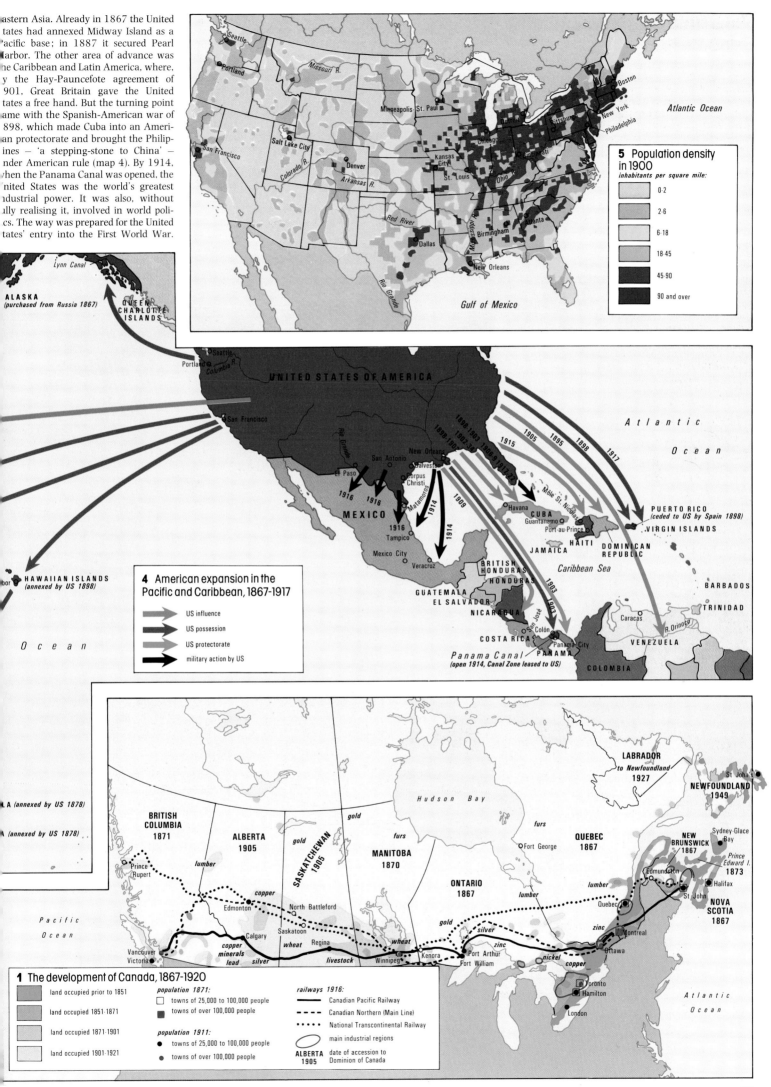

eastern Asia. Already in 1867 the United
States had annexed Midway Island as a
Pacific base; in 1887 it secured Pearl
Harbor. The other area of advance was
the Caribbean and Latin America, where,
by the Hay-Pauncefote agreement of
1901, Great Britain gave the United
States a free hand. But the turning point
came with the Spanish-American war of
1898, which made Cuba into an American protectorate and brought the Philippines – 'a stepping-stone to China' –
under American rule (map 4). By 1914,
when the Panama Canal was opened, the
United States was the world's greatest
industrial power. It was also, without
fully realising it, involved in world politics. The way was prepared for the United
States' entry into the First World War.

5 Population density
in 1900

inhabitants per square mile:

0-2

2-6

6-18

18-45

45-90

90 and over

ALASKA
(purchased from Russia 1867)

4 American expansion in the
Pacific and Caribbean, 1867-1917

US influence

US possession

US protectorate

military action by US

HAWAIIAN ISLANDS
(annexed by US 1898)

1 The development of Canada, 1867-1920

land occupied prior to 1851

land occupied 1851-1871

land occupied 1871-1901

land occupied 1901-1921

population 1871:
☐ towns of 25,000 to 100,000 people
■ towns of over 100,000 people

population 1911:
● towns of 25,000 to 100,000 people
● towns of over 100,000 people

ALBERTA
1905
date of accession to
Dominion of Canada

railways 1916:
—— Canadian Pacific Railway
- - - Canadian Northern (Main Line)
· · · National Transcontinental Railway
⬭ main industrial regions

111

Australia and New Zealand from 1788

Although Australia and New Zealand were discovered by the Dutch explorer Tasman in 1642, colonisation only began after Cook hoisted the British flag at Botany Bay in 1770 (page 64). New South Wales served as a penal colony from 1788 to 1839, Van Diemen's Land (later Tasmania) from 1804 to 1853, and in 1829 the British government, fearing to be forestalled by the French, claimed the whole Australian continent. Fear of France also led to the annexation of New Zealand in 1840. But in both lands geographical obstacles, lack of exportable products, and, in the case of New Zealand, the bitter Maori wars between 1860 and 1871, made the early years of colonisation difficult. New South Wales was hemmed in by the Blue Mountains. Beyond the Great Dividing Range the country soon became arid and inhospitable. Coastal settlements at Perth (1829), Melbourne (1835), and Adelaide (1836) established

bridgeheads for exploration in the west (map 5), but as late as 1850 the total white population was only around 350,000, while in New Zealand it was still below 100,000 in 1860. Inducements to settle were few. Neither country was self-supporting, and early trade (chiefly seal products and sandalwood) was insufficient to pay for imports (map 4), and was further hampered by the East India Company's monopoly in the area.

The discovery of gold in New South Wales and Victoria in 1851 and in Otago (South Island) in 1861 initiated a new phase. Even more important was the rapid growth of sheep farming. In 1850 Australia sent 39 million lb. of wool to Great Britain. By 1879 the quantity had increased to 300 million lb. In New Zealand, where wool was largely a South Island product, exports rose from £67,000 in value in 1853 to £2,700,000 twenty years later. The development of the North Island, held back by the Maori wars, came later, after the introduction of refrigeration. Refrigeration made possible the large-scale export of frozen lamb from the South Island, but it also lay behind the growth of dairy farming in the

north, which now, stimulated by the exports trade [in] butter and cheese, drew ahead of the south in population.

Political development kept pace with econom[ic] growth. In 1855 New South Wales, Victoria, South Au[s]tralia and Tasmania became self-governing colonie[s,] followed by Queensland in 1859, and in 1901 joined to[-] gether to form the Commonwealth of Australia. Ne[w] Zealand, which had been divided in 1852 into six pro[-] vinces, each with an elected council, became a unite[d] Dominion in 1876, after measures had been taken t[o] safeguard the rights of the Maori population. Both dom[-] inions remained heavily dependent on primary export[s.] For long they enjoyed preferential treatment in th[e] British market; but developments after 1945, particu[-] larly the British retreat from Asia, brought importan[t] changes. In 1952 both dominions joined for securit[y] with the United States in the ANZUS Pact, and whe[n] Great Britain entered the European Common Marke[t] (1973) and dismantled imperial preference, they wer[e] forced to diversify their economies and seek new ma[r]kets. The process of reorientation is still continuing.

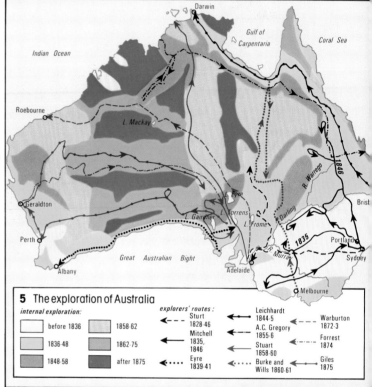

5 The exploration of Australia

internal exploration:

before 1836	1858-62
1836-48	1862-75
1848-58	after 1875

explorers' routes:

Sturt 1828-46	Leichhardt 1844-5
Mitchell 1835, 1846	A.C. Gregory 1855-6
Eyre 1839-41	Stuart 1858-60
	Burke and Wills 1860-61
	Warburton 1872-3
	Forrest 1874
	Giles 1875

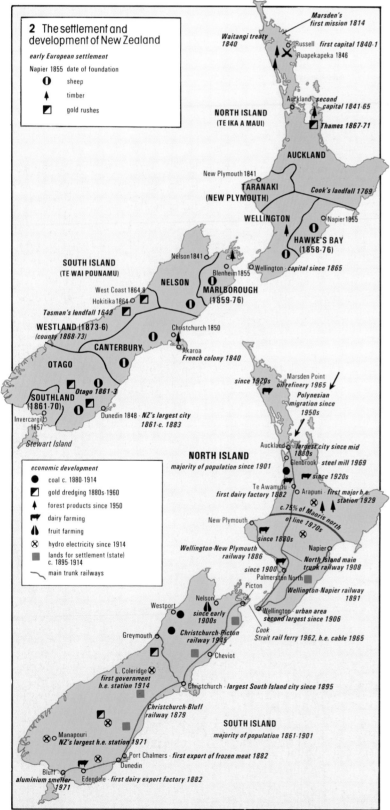

2 The settlement and development of New Zealand

early European settlement

Napier 1855 date of foundation

- **O** sheep
- **▲** timber
- **◪** gold rushes

economic development

- **●** coal c. 1880-1914
- **◪** gold dredging 1880s-1960
- **▲** forest products since 1950
- **🐄** dairy farming
- **◖** fruit farming
- **⊗** hydro electricity since 1914
- **■** lands for settlement (state) c. 1895-1914
- main trunk railways

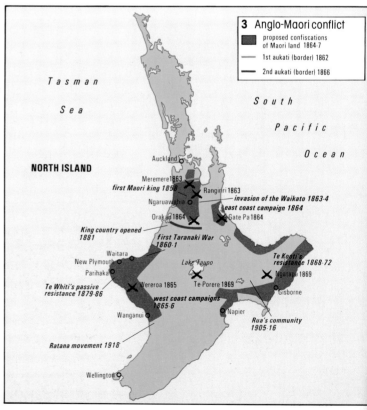

3 Anglo-Maori conflict

- proposed confiscations of Maori land 1864-7
- 1st aukati (border) 1862
- 2nd aukati (border) 1866

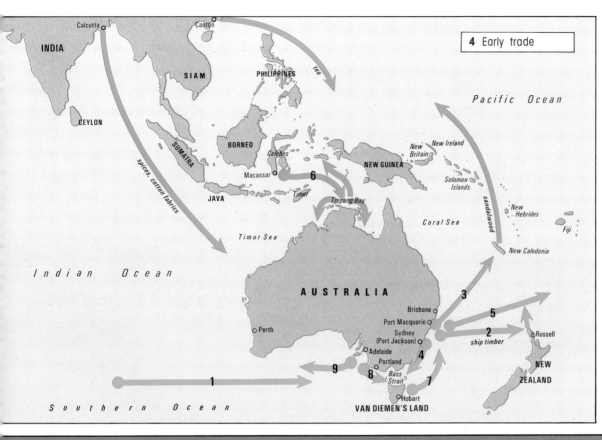

4 Early trade

Early trade (left)

1/Main route from Europe via Cape of Good Hope. First colonisation fleet to New South Wales 1788, mainly convicts and marines. By 1790, with arrival of second fleet, it was clear that the colonies would be reliant upon regular supplies from Europe.

2/Convict transport ships return to U.K. via New Zealand for timber, and Canton for tea or Calcutta for oriental goods.

3/Sydney-based ships to Pacific islands for sandalwood to trade for tea at Canton.

4/Sydney-based ships to Bass Strait islands for seal skins and oil (first major exports to U.K.). Seal fields soon exhausted. Eastern colony ports used as bases for American and British whaling ships, an industry developed by colonists from 1820s.

5/Sydney to Tahiti for pork for provisioning convicts.

6/Macassan fishermen to northern Australian coast to collect trepang (sea cucumbers) to trade with Chinese merchants.

7/Van Diemen's land grain to Sydney.

8/South Australian grain to eastern colonies.

9/South Australian grain to Europe. From 1840s wool and minerals, the basis of late nineteenth century trade with Europe.

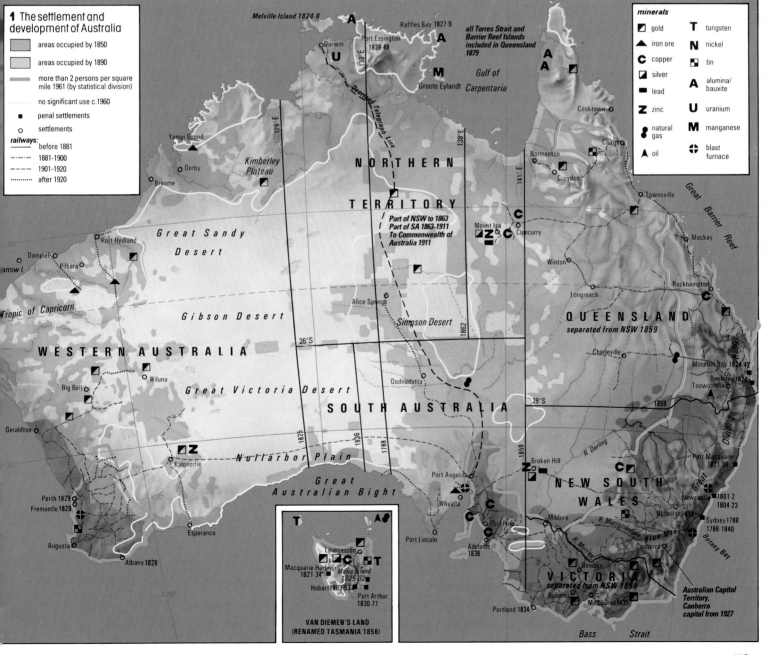

1 The settlement and development of Australia

- areas occupied by 1850
- areas occupied by 1890
- more than 2 persons per square mile 1961 (by statistical division)
- no significant use c.1960
- ■ penal settlements
- ○ settlements

railways:
- —·—·— before 1881
- —··—··— 1881-1900
- — — — 1901-1920
- ········· after 1920

minerals

gold		T	tungsten
iron ore		N	nickel
C copper		tin	
silver		A	alumina/bauxite
lead		U	uranium
Z zinc		M	manganese
natural gas		blast furnace	
A oil			

European nationalism
1815-1914

The flame of nationalism was kindled in Europe by the French revolution. In France itself the revolution forged a sense of national unity, and elsewhere, notably in Spain and Prussia, the humiliation of defeat and French occupation after 1807 produced a short-lived national reaction. For the most part, however, nationalism was confined to a narrow segment of the middle class. It was anathema to the ruling classes, and rarely touched working people. Polish peasants held aloof from the insurrections of 1831, 1846 and 1863; in Ireland only acute agrarian distress after 1877 lined them up behind the nationalists. Down to 1848 liberal and constitutional reform was the main demand, and it was against this, rather than nationalism, that the victorious powers set their faces after the fall of Napoleon at the Congress of Vienna in 1815. Their other main objective was to erect a barrier against a resurgence of revolutionary France. Hence their decision to transfer the Austrian Netherlands (later Belgium) to Holland, to install Prussia in West-phalia and most of the Rhineland, and to hand over the ancient republic of Genoa to Sardinia-Piedmont. As compensation for the loss of the Netherlands, Austria received the Venetian republic and the duchy of Milan, as well as indirect control of Parma, Modena and Tuscany. Sweden, which had to surrender Finland to Russia, was compensated with Norway.

The overriding objective of the great powers after 1815 was to uphold the Vienna settlement and to combat the threat of liberalism and nationalism, but by 1830, when a new wave of liberal and nationalist agitation broke out, the eastern and western powers were drawing apart. By destroying a common front, their divergence of interests enabled Greece (page 116) and Belgium to obtain independence, although in the latter case the territorial settlement, including the disposal of Limburg and Luxembourg was postponed until 1839 (map 5).

In Norway the forced union with Sweden aroused resentment similar to that felt in Belgium towards Holland. There was friction, but little active resistance, and eventually a Norwegian declaration of independence was accepted by Sweden (map 4). The course of events in Poland (1831, 1846) and in Italy, Germany and Hungary in 1848–49 was more eventful. Here nationalist agitation erupted in full-scale war; but the solidarity of the conservative powers and divisions among the nationalists themselves brought all to nothing.

What changed this situation was the rise of a new generation of statesmen. Louis Napoleon, emperor of France since 1852, Cavour, who became prime minister of Sardinia-Piedmont in the same year, and Bismarck, minister-president of Prussia after 1862, all toyed with nationalism, confident of their ability to use it for their own ends. These were not the ends of the liberals who had led the nationalist movements of 1848–49. Cavour's purpose was to ensure that Italian unification was carried out by and in the interests of Sardinia; hence his opposition to the famous Sicilian expedition of the patriot Garibaldi (1807–82) in 1860. Bismarck was determined to ensure that Germany was merged in Prussia, not Prussia in Germany. Both also realised that their objectives could only be achieved by war and diplomacy. Hence Cavour's alliance with France against Austria (1858) and Bismarck's wars of 1864, 1866 and 1870. The result was the unification of Italy (except for Venetia and the Papal State) in 1861 (map 3) and the unification of Germany in 1871 (map 2). Both were retrospectively endorsed by liberal nationalists, but neither satisfied the nationalism they aroused. Italy still laid claim to the Alto Adige, Fiume and Trieste. Bismarck's 'small German' solution, excluding Austria, disappointed those who hankered after a Greater Germany. Indeed, it was after 1870, when the problems of the multi-national Austro-Hungarian state came to the fore, that nationalist claims became loudest. The confusion of peoples and languages in eastern Europe (map 1) defied easy solutions and exacerbated the conflicts which led, step by step, to war in 1914.

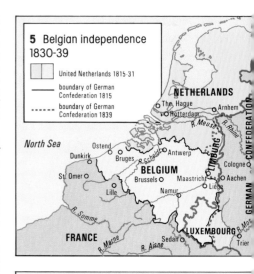

5 Belgian independence 1830-39

United Netherlands 1815-31
—— boundary of German Confederation 1815
----- boundary of German Confederation 1839

4 The Scandinavian kingdoms

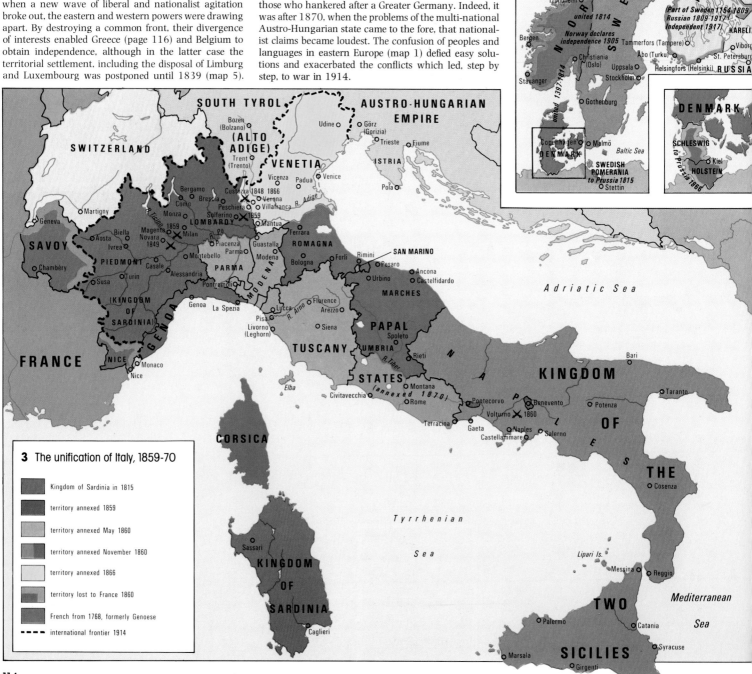

3 The unification of Italy, 1859-70

Kingdom of Sardinia in 1815
territory annexed 1859
territory annexed May 1860
territory annexed November 1860
territory annexed 1866
territory lost to France 1860
French from 1768, formerly Genoese
----- international frontier 1914

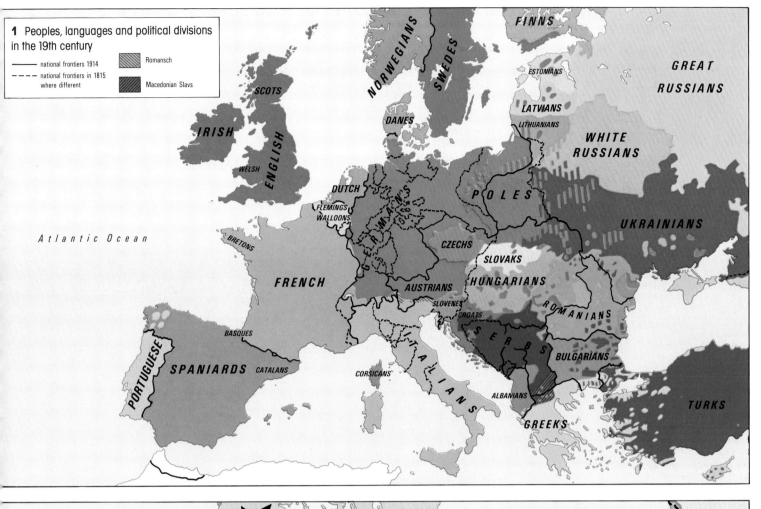

1 Peoples, languages and political divisions in the 19th century

national frontiers 1914
national frontiers in 1815 where different

▨ Romansch
▨ Macedonian Slavs

Atlantic Ocean

SCOTS
IRISH
WELSH
ENGLISH
BRETONS
FRENCH
PORTUGUESE
SPANIARDS
BASQUES
CATALANS
CORSICANS
DUTCH
FLEMINGS
WALLOONS
G E R M A N S
DANES
NORWEGIANS
SWEDES
FINNS
ESTONIANS
LATVIANS
LITHUANIANS
WHITE RUSSIANS
GREAT RUSSIANS
P O L E S
UKRAINIANS
CZECHS
SLOVAKS
AUSTRIANS
HUNGARIANS
SLOVENES
CROATS
R O M A N I A N S
S E R B S
BULGARIANS
I T A L I A N S
ALBANIANS
GREEKS
TURKS

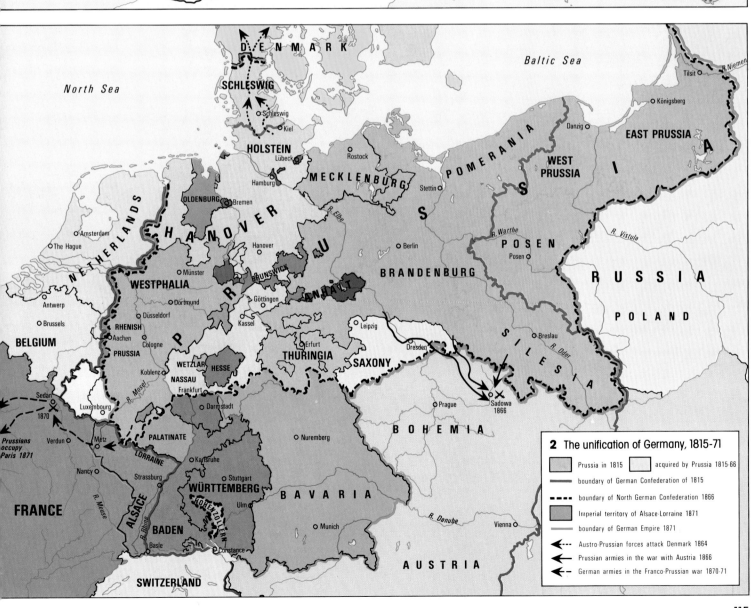

2 The unification of Germany, 1815-71

▨ Prussia in 1815
☐ acquired by Prussia 1815-66
── boundary of German Confederation of 1815
---- boundary of North German Confederation 1866
▨ Imperial territory of Alsace-Lorraine 1871
── boundary of German Empire 1871
◄--- Austro-Prussian forces attack Denmark 1864
◄── Prussian armies in the war with Austria 1866
◄-- German armies in the Franco-Prussian war 1870-71

North Sea
Baltic Sea

DENMARK
SCHLESWIG
Schleswig
Kiel
HOLSTEIN
Lübeck
Rostock
MECKLENBURG
Stettin
P O M E R A N I A
WEST PRUSSIA
Danzig
Königsberg
R. Niemen
Tilsit
EAST PRUSSIA
P R U S S I A
Hamburg
Bremen
OLDENBURG
H A N O V E R
Amsterdam
The Hague
NETHERLANDS
Münster
BRUNSWICK
Hanover
R. Elbe
Berlin
BRANDENBURG
R. Warthe
POSEN
Posen
R. Vistula
R U S S I A
POLAND
P R U S S I A
WESTPHALIA
Antwerp
Brussels
BELGIUM
Dortmund
Düsseldorf
RHENISH
Aachen
Cologne
PRUSSIA
Koblenz
WETZLAR
HESSE
NASSAU
Frankfurt
ANHALT
Göttingen
Kassel
Erfurt
THURINGIA
Leipzig
Dresden
SAXONY
Breslau
R. Oder
S I L E S I A
Prague
Sadowa 1866
B O H E M I A
Sedan
1870
Prussians occupy Paris 1871
Verdun
Metz
Luxembourg
PALATINATE
LORRAINE
Nancy
Strassburg
ALSACE
R. Meuse
R. Rhine
FRANCE
Darmstadt
Karlsruhe
Stuttgart
WÜRTTEMBERG
BADEN
HOHENZOLLERN
Basle
Constance
Nuremberg
B A V A R I A
Ulm
R. Danube
Munich
Vienna
AUSTRIA
SWITZERLAND
R. Mosel

115

The European powers
1878-1914

After the unification of Germany and of Italy (page 114), it seemed for a time as though the major questions which had disturbed the peace of Europe since 1848 had been resolved. Bismarck, the architect of German unification, concentrated his efforts after 1871 upon building a system of alliances which would ensure the future of the new German Reich. The 'wild Junker' had become a conservative, anxious only to preserve what had been won; and his alliances were defensive. But the history of the next forty years is the story of how alliances, originally defensive and stabilising in intent, turned into an aggressive and destabilising system. Furthermore, the unification of Germany and of Italy, far from marking a halting place, opened up a hornet's nest of nationalist revindications. After 1870 the nationalist

movement which had agitated western Europe for forty years, spilled over into the Balkans; and the struggles of the Balkan peoples for independence inevitably involved the powers who were their supporters or adversaries, particularly Russia and Austria-Hungary, which, after its exclusion from Germany and Italy after 1866, was essentially an eastward-looking Balkan power.

The evolution of the relations between the great powers between 1879, when Bismarck tried to reconcile his sympathies with a conservative Russia with support for Austria-Hungary, and 1914, when the whole precarious balance fell apart, is indicated diagrammatically on maps 2(a) to 2(f). Until the beginning of the new century the system worked reasonably well. Revolts in the Balkans between 1875 and 1878, culminating in Russian intervention and war with Turkey, thoroughly alarmed the powers; and after the Congress of Berlin (1878) Balkan affairs took a secondary place. Checked in Europe, Russia turned to central Asia and the Far

East, and during the first half of the period the dominant themes were Anglo-Russian rivalry in Asia and Anglo-French rivalry in Africa. What changed this situation was the decision of Germany under William II, particularly after Bülow became chancellor in 1900, to seek 'a place in the sun'. This was not unreasonable; but by now most places in the sun had been occupied, and German policy was seen as a threat by the established imperial powers. The result was the Anglo-French reconciliation (1904) and the Anglo-Russian reconciliation (1907). German 'world policy' also required a navy, resulting in the naval competition which soured Anglo-German relations between 1906 and 1912. After 1907 the Triple Entente with France and Russia became the lynch-pin of British policy, the only firm assurance against the German 'threat'. Germany, on the other hand, saw itself being 'encircled' by a hostile ring constructed by Great Britain.

The result was that the lines between the Triple Alliance and the Triple Entente were drawn tighter. Also

1 The Balkans, 1878-1913

- - - frontier of Ottoman Empire 1800

――― proposed Bulgaria under Treaty of San Stefano 1878

━━━ national frontiers after the Balkan wars 1912-13

ermany was driven closer to its only dependable ally, Austria-Hungary. When Austria annexed Bosnia-Herzegovina in 1908, Bülow lent full support, and Austro-Russian antagonism in the Balkans, hitherto suppressed, was rekindled. The climax was postponed until the outbreak of the Balkan wars in 1912. The aggrandisement of Serbia which resulted was viewed by Austria as an intolerable threat. Russia, on the other hand, could not leave Serbia in the lurch without losing credibility. The result was the stupendous build-up of armaments (diagram 3) as the grinding logic of the system came into play. When in 1914 the murder of the Austrian archduke Franz Ferdinand brought matters to a head, the combustible material was piled up which exploded in the First World War.

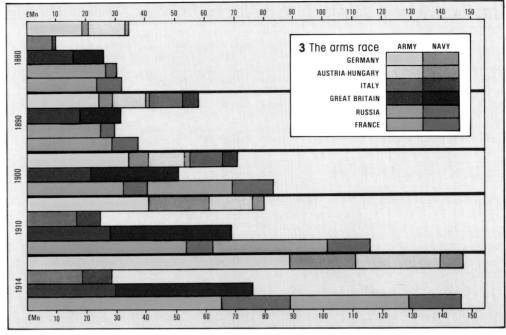

2 European alliances

† Austro-German Alliance (the Dual Alliance) 1879-1918

♔ Three Emperors' Alliance 1881-87

▨ Austro-Serbian Alliance 1881-95

▲ Triple Alliance 1882-1915

■ Austro-German-Romanian Alliance 1883-1916

○ Franco-Russian Alliance 1894-1917

✎ Russo-Bulgarian military convention 1902-13

stripes, similar and identical colours indicate an entente or community of interests

2a/The Dual Alliance: October 1879, resulted from the Balkan upheavals of 1875-8. When Russia attacked Turkey and imposed the Treaty of San Stefano, the Austro-Russian understanding of 1873 broke down. Bismarck's purpose in the Dual Alliance was to stabilise the situation. Germany could not afford to let Austria-Hungary succumb to a Russian attack; but the alliance was strictly defensive. It did not imply a common front against Russia, understanding with which was still a basic element in Bismarck's policy, still less a German commitment to underwrite Austrian ambitions in the Balkans. Nevertheless the Dual Alliance marked a turning point: the era of formal alliances had begun.

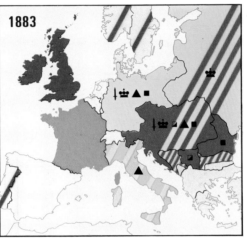

2b/Bismarck's system at its zenith: 1883. The formation of the Three Emperors' Alliance (1881) appeared to have restored stability in Eastern Europe. But the smouldering Austro-Russian antagonism continued, brought to a head again by the Bulgarian crisis of 1886-7. Alliances with Serbia (1881) and Romania (1883) sought to limit Russian influence in the Balkans. The Triple Alliance of Germany, Austria and Italy (1882) insured Austria against Italian attack in case of war with Russia. After the Three Emperors' Alliance broke down, Bismarck sought security by his Reinsurance Treaty with Russia (1887), while Austria joined in a 'Mediterranean agreement' with Britain, Italy and Spain against France and Russia.

2c/The 'New Course' in Germany: 1891. Even before Bismarck's fall in 1890, it was evident that his complicated system of alliances was running into difficulties. Russo-German relations deteriorated sharply after 1887 as a result of tariff and loan disputes. When the new German chancellor, Caprivi, dropped Bismarck's Reinsurance Treaty, renewed the Triple Alliance, and lined up with the 'Mediterranean entente', Russia replied by a military convention and alliance with France (1894). But the 'new course' was short-lived. After 1895 Germany saw more profit in co-operation with France and Russia in the Far East, while Austria-Hungary and Russia agreed (1897) to put Balkan problems on ice.

2d/The Anglo-French entente: 1904. The decision of William II and Bülow after 1897 to move from a continental, European to a 'world' policy challenged all three established imperial powers and brought about a major realignment. In 1902 France settled its long-standing dispute with Italy; in 1904 it reached a similar settlement with Great Britain. Germany's attempt to exploit Russia's weakness after the Russo-Japanese war and the 1905 revolution to prise apart the Franco-Russian alliance misfired. Franco-British ties were strengthened; Russia and England settled their colonial differences in 1907, and the three powers joined in the Triple Entente to counter and contain Germany.

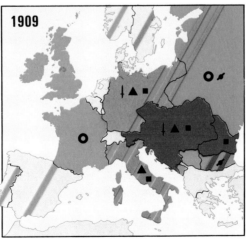

2e/Europe after the Bosnian crisis: 1909. The Austrian annexation of Bosnia and Herzegovina, a response to the Turkish revolution of 1908, ended the Austro-Russian Balkan entente of 1897 and caused a major crisis in international relations. When Russia protested, Germany gave Austria full support, reversing Bismarck's defensive interpretation of the Dual Alliance, and forced Russia to back down. Henceforward Austria-Hungary and Russia were at loggerheads in the Balkans. Anglo-German relations also were at their nadir, a consequence of growing naval rivalry. The result was to consolidate the Triple Entente, particularly after the second Morocco crisis (1911), when Britain took the lead in opposing Germany.

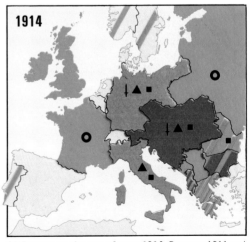

2f/Europe on the eve of war: 1914. Between 1911 and 1914 the front between the Triple Alliance and the Triple Entente hardened. During the Balkan wars (1912-13), when Serbia, Greece and Bulgaria combined to drive Turkey out of Europe, the two groups still co-operated. But Austria was aghast at the consequent enlargement of Serbia and feared pro-Serb irredentism in its Slav provinces, and Germany was haunted by the spectre of encirclement. When, after the assassination of Franz Ferdinand at Sarajevo on 28 June 1914, Austria decided to punish Serbia and Berlin threw itself unreservedly behind Vienna, the system of alliances almost automatically led to general war.

The First World War
1914-1918

When the assassination of the Austrian heir-presumptive, Archduke Franz Ferdinand, by Bosnian terrorists at Sarajevo on June 28, 1914, sparked off the immediate sequence of events that led to the First World War, the European powers were already divided into heavily armed camps (page 116), and neither was prepared to risk diplomatic defeat. Germany already had its battle plan prepared: the famous Schlieffen Plan, drawn up in 1905, to trap and annihilate the French army by a great encircling movement through Belgium before France's Russian ally had time to mobilise. The expectation everywhere was for a short war, over by Christmas 1914, and only after this expectation proved false did the search for allies begin in earnest. Germany and

Austria were joined by the Ottoman Empire and Bulgaria, the Entente powers by Italy, Romania and Greece, and eventually by the United States (map 1).

The German strategy was very nearly successful and brought the German armies within 40 miles of Paris (map 2). It was frustrated by the unexpectedly rapid mobilisation of Russia, which invaded East Prussia and defeated the German 8th Army at Gumbinnen (August 20, 1914). Although the Russians were repulsed at Tannenberg (August 26–29), their offensive drew off German reserves, which helped the French and British armies in the west to halt the German advance in the battle of the Marne (September 5–8), while the Russians simultaneously inflicted a crushing defeat on Austria at Lemberg. The Schlieffen Plan had failed, Germany was forced to despatch troops to the east to prop up the Austrian front, and in the west the war

became a war of trenches, artillery, barbed wire and machine guns. Each side launched offensives, with sickening casualties, but without succeeding in advancing more than a few thousand yards. Railways could bring up reinforcements to the front before slow-moving advancing troops could make good any advantage they might have created. The question for both, by the end of 1915, was how to break the stalemate. The answer of the Entente, sponsored by Winston Churchill, was to attack Germany from the rear by campaigns in the Dardanelles and Mesopotamia (page 124), at Salonika, and, after Italy entered the war on May 23, 1915, against Austria on the Isonzo. All were failures. The German answer was to bring Great Britain to its knees by crippling losses at sea. The submarine campaign, initiated on February 1, 1917, was nearly successful, and only defeated when Lloyd George introduced the con-

voy system in May. But its result was t bring the United States into the war o the Entente side on April 6, 1917.

Even so, the German position wa not hopeless. Huge losses in the Brusilo offensive of 1916 and economic chaos a home had broken the Russian fightin spirit, and the Russian revolutions c March and October 1917 (page 12C enabled Germany to transfer troops fron the Eastern to the Western Front in th hope of victory before the United State could mobilise. On March 21, 1918

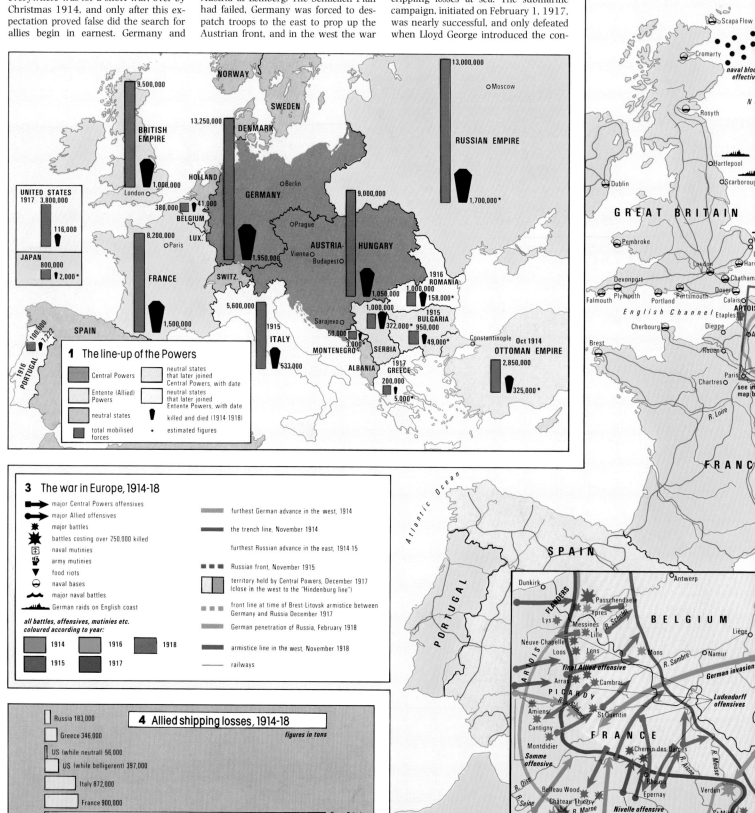

1 The line-up of the Powers

- Central Powers
- Entente (Allied) Powers
- neutral states
- neutral states that later joined Central Powers, with date
- neutral states that later joined Entente Powers, with date
- killed and died (1914-1918)
- total mobilised forces
- * estimated figures

3 The war in Europe, 1914-18

- major Central Powers offensives
- major Allied offensives
- major battles
- battles costing over 250,000 killed
- naval mutinies
- army mutinies
- food riots
- naval bases
- major naval battles
- German raids on English coast
- furthest German advance in the west, 1914
- the trench line, November 1914
- furthest Russian advance in the east, 1914-15
- Russian front, November 1915
- territory held by Central Powers, December 1917 (close in the west to the "Hindenburg line")
- front line at time of Brest-Litovsk armistice between Germany and Russia December 1917
- German penetration of Russia, February 1918
- armistice line in the west, November 1918
- railways

all battles, offensives, mutinies etc. coloured according to year:

1914 1916 1918
1915 1917

4 Allied shipping losses, 1914-18

figures in tons

- Russia 183,000
- Greece 346,000
- US (while neutral) 56,000
- US (while belligerent) 397,000
- Italy 872,000
- France 900,000
- Great Britain 7,800,000

indenburg and Ludendorff launched
heir great offensive in the west (map 3).
nce again it was a near success, but the
llied line held, and on July 18 the French
ommander Foch launched the counter-
ffensive which was to be the decisive
ampaign of the war. On September 29
udendorff acknowledged defeat. By now
ar weariness was rampant. Austria and
ulgaria were near to collapse; the
ritish blockade had brought Germany
o the edge of starvation; and the Ger-
an government, fearful of a Bolshevik

revolution, sued for an armistice. On
November 11, 1918, fighting ceased.
Over 8 million men had perished, as had
three empires, the Tsarist, the Austro-
Hungarian and the Ottoman. In retrospect the war of 1914–18 was the great
European civil war, which destroyed the
old European order, squandered Europe's
human and material resources, and
jeopardised its future. Few people realised
in 1918 what had happened; but the age
of European predominance was over and
a new age of global politics had begun.

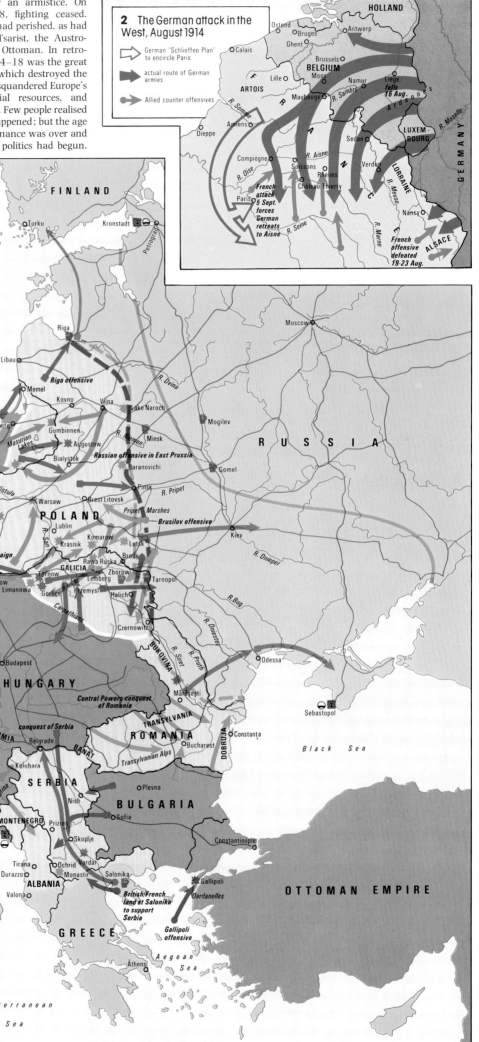

2 The German attack in the West, August 1914

German "Schlieffen Plan" to encircle Paris

actual route of German armies

Allied counter offensives

119

The Russian Revolution
1905-1925

Revolution came to Russia suddenly, but not unexpectedly, in the wake of the unsuccessful Russo-Japanese war of 1904–05 (page 126). Intensive industrialisation since 1890 had created a large, profoundly discontented urban proletariat, and it was they who spearheaded the revolution of 1905, although their revolt sparked off widespread unrest in the countryside (map 1). The Tsar was forced to grant a constitution, including a *duma*, or parliament, but by 1907 the government was back in full control. Nevertheless the 1905 revolution irreparably weakened the old order, and after 1912, following the shooting of strikers in the Lena goldfields in Siberia, a great new wave of social unrest swept the empire. Internally, Russia was in no position in 1914 to meet the challenge of the First World War; and when in the winter of 1916–17 economic dislocation, hunger and sheer incompetence brought the crisis to a head, the government capitulated almost without resistance. This was the February revolution of 1917, which placed power in the hands of liberal Duma politicians. But the Provisional Government's authority was circumscribed by the powerful Petrograd Council (or Soviet) of Soldiers' and Workers' Deputies, and it was also compromised by its commit-

ment to continue the war. When, in April, Lenin returned from exile in Switzerland, promising peace, land and bread, and demanding all power for the Soviets, its days were numbered. An attempt in September by the Commander-in-Chief, General Kornilov, to seize the capital miscarried when his troops rebelled, and on November 7 (October 25 by the old calendar) the Bolsheviks struck, arrested the Provisional Government, and assumed power in the name of the Soviets. This was the October, or Bolshevik, revolution.

The odds were weighted heavily against the new government. The overriding need was peace, and Lenin insisted, against strong opposition, on accepting the onerous terms imposed by Germany in the Treaty of Brest-Litovsk (March 1918). But immediately the Bolsheviks were faced with civil war and foreign intervention, as White Russian armies with British, French, Czech and other support, attacked the new republic (map 2). Lenin pinned his hope on war-weariness and revolution in the west (map 3) and on uprisings among subject peoples in the east (map 4), but to little avail. In Europe, particularly in Germany, revolutionary currents were strong between 1919 and 1923, but they were met by counter-revolutionary forces, including Hitler's National Socialists. However, foreign intervention and the threat of a White Tsarist restoration rallied support for the Reds, and by 1920 the civil war had been won. But the devastation was immense. Industrial production

in 1920 was down to one-seventh of the 1913 leve[l] and shortages provoked a wave of strikes and riots, cu[l]minating in the Kronstadt naval mutiny (Februar[y] 1921). Lenin's answer was the 'New Economic Policy' (NEP), in effect a relaxation of requisitioning and con[-]trols. The new policy worked: by the end of 1925 indus[-]trial production had regained its pre-war level. Further[-]more, the overt hostility of the West relaxed. War wit[h] Poland, which had invaded Russia in 1920, was ende[d] by the Treaty of Riga (March 1921), and at the sam[e] time a treaty of friendship was signed with Turkey. [It] was followed by the Rapallo Treaty with German[y] (1922) and in 1924 by diplomatic recognition fro[m] Britain, France and other European countries.

After Lenin's death in 1924 and a period of dispute[d] succession Lenin's eventual successor, Stalin, ouste[d] Trotsky, with his policy of 'permanent revolution'. Stalin's policy of 'socialism in one country', implyin[g] large-scale industrialisation and a re-shaping of in[-]efficient agriculture, placed Russia, at a terrible huma[n] cost, in the first rank of industrial and internationa[l] powers. Inaugurated by the first Five Year Plan of 192[8] in many respects it marked a sharp break with th[e] revolution of 1917. But it was also a fulfilment o[f] Lenin's work. Even at the time of Lenin's death Russi[a] was backward and under-developed. By 1939, as Leni[n] foresaw, Bolshevism had become 'a world force' changing the course of history.

3 Red star over Europe

NORWAY
FINLAND
Helsinki
civil war, Jan.-May 1918. Marxists defeated
SWEDEN
ESTONIA
Communists control Riga, Jan.-May 1918
Riga
LATVIA
DENMARK
LITHUANIA
EAST PRUSSIA
Bremen *Hamburg unsuccessful Communist uprising, Oct.1923*
Soviet Republic, Jan. 1919. Lasts 4 weeks
GERMANY
German revolution overthrows Kaiser, brings Socialists to power, Nov.1918
Berlin
unsuccessful Communist insurrection, March 1921
Leipzig
Warsaw
Communist (Spartakist) uprising crushed, Jan.1919
Red Army, attacking Poland after Polish invasion of the Ukraine, defeated outside Warsaw, Aug.1920
Bavarian Soviet Republic, April 1919. Lasts 4 weeks
CZECHOSLOVAKIA
POLAND
Munich
AUSTRIA
Hungarian Soviet Republic, headed by Bela Kun, March-Aug. 1919
Slovakian Soviet Republic, July 1919. Lasts 3 weeks
HUNGARY
ROMANIA
YUGOSLAVIA
ITALY
Communist uprising crushed, Sept. 1923
Sofia
BULGARIA
Adriatic Sea
Baltic Sea

FINLAND
Helsinki
Vyborg
Abo
Sveaborg
St. Petersburg
Kronstadt
Narva
Revel
Vyatka
Motovilikhinskiy
Nizhnetagilskiy
Alapayevskiy
Votkinskiy
Yekaterinburg
Izhevskiy
Zlatoust
Riga
Dvinsk
Ivanovo-Voznesensk
Yaroslavl
Kostroma
Kazan
Vladimir
Bogorodsk
Sormovo
Orekhovo-Zuyevo
Nizhny Novgorod
Moscow
Kaluga
Kolomna
Penza
Samara
Tula
Ryazan
Tambov
Smolensk
R. Dvina
RUSSIAN EMPIRE
Grodno
Lomzha
Bobruysk
Baranovichi
Belostok
Kursk
Voronezh
Saratov
Lugansk
Warsaw
R. Don
R. Ural
Lodz
Dombrova
Rovno
Kiev
Kharkov
Kadiyevka
Tsaritsyn
Ostrog
Berdichev
Poltava
Debaltsevo
Kremenchug
Yenakiyevo
R. Dnieper
Yekaterinoslav
Yuzovka
Makeyevka
Sulin
R. Dniester
Aleksandrovsk
Rostov-on-Don
R. Volga
Odessa
Nikolayev
Mariupol
Taganrog
Yekaterinodar
Stravropol
Feodosiya
Novorossiysk
Sochi
Sevastopol
Black Sea
Kutaisi
Vladikavkaz
Baku
Batum
Tiflis
Kars
Caspian Sea

4 Red star over Asia

SOVIET UNION
Samara
Comintern Congress of Peoples of the East, attended by Arabs, Chinese, Kurds, Persians, Turks. Sept.1920
Trans Siberian Railway
seat of Kolchak's 'All Russian' Government, 1918-19
Omsk
Tomsk
Krasnoyarsk
capital of independent pro-Bolshevik Far Eastern Republic, established April 1920, merged with Soviet Russia, Nov.1922
North Sakhalin regained from Japan, 1925
Sakhalin
FAR EASTERN REPUBLIC
Baku
Caspian Sea
Aral Sea
Khiva
centre of Bolshevik activity in Soviet Central Asia from Nov 1917, though cut off from Moscow for 2 years
Tannu Tuva People's Republic established Aug. 1921, incorporated into Soviet Union 1944
L. Balkhash
L. Baikal
Chita
Blagoveshchensk
Khabarovsk
TANNU TUVA
Irkutsk
Harbin
Independent Soviet Peoples Republics of Bukhara and Khiva established 1920, incorporated into Soviet Union 1925
Bukhara
Tashkent
Mongolian People's Republic established under Soviet protection, July 1921
Ulan Bator
MANCHURIA
Vladivostok
JAPAN
SINKIANG
CHINA
Peking
May 4th Movement of radical intelligentsia and workers 1919, leading to formation of Chinese Communist Party, July 1921

1 The first Russian revolution, 1905

● major strikes and armed workers' uprisings

▬ peasant unrest and land seizures

▲ workers' soviets

■ army mutinies

⊞ naval mutinies

〰 voyage of the battleship Potemkin

2 Russia in war and revolution

boundary of the Russian Empire, 1914

front between Russia and Central Powers, March 1917

★ principal towns where Bolsheviks took power, Nov. 1917-Feb. 1918 (dates in new calendar)

boundary of Russian territory occupied by Central Powers following the Treaty of Brest-Litovsk, March 1918

boundary of area controlled by the Bolsheviks, August 1918

eastern boundary of area controlled by the Bolsheviks, April 1919

area controlled by the Bolsheviks, October 1919

boundary of Soviet Territory, March 1921

boundary of areas controlled by anti-Bolshevik forces, May 1920

White Russian armies

non-Russian anti-Bolshevik forces

Barents Sea

Entente fleet

Murmansk
**BRITISH
FRENCH
CANADIANS
ITALIANS
SERBS**

White Sea

**CANADIANS
AMERICANS**

Archangel
17 Feb 1918

**BRITISH
FRENCH**

NORWAY

SWEDEN

FINLAND

independence of Finland recognised December 1917

FINNS

Helsinki

Petrozavodsk
17 Jan 1918

L. Ladoga

L. Onega

BOLSHEVIK RUSSIA

Kronstadt

Petrograd (Lenigrad)
7 Nov 1917

Revel (Tallinn)
8 Nov 1917

British fleet

Kornilov's attack on Petrograd September 1917

Vologda
8 Feb 1918

Vyatka
8 Dec 1917

Perm
14 Nov 1917

Nicholas II and family shot by Bolsheviks July 1918

Yekaterinburg (Sverdlovsk)
8 Nov 1917

ESTONIA

Yudenich

LETTS

Riga

Pskov
15 Nov 1917

Novgorod
27 Nov 1917

Kostroma
15 Dec 1917

Izhevsk
9 Nov 1917

LATVIA

BALTIC GERMANS

Vitebsk
9 Nov 1917

Yaroslavl *9 Nov 1917*

Ivanovo
7 Nov 1917

Kazan
8 Nov 1917

Kolchak 1918-19

Baltic Sea

LITHUANIA

Smolensk
12 Nov 1917

Tver (Kalinin)
10 Nov 1917

Nizhny Novgorod (Gorkiy)
10 Nov 1917

Ufa
8 Nov 1917

GERMANY (E.PRUSSIA)

Minsk
7 Nov 1917

Moscow
15 Nov 1917

Kaluga
11 Dec 1917

CZECHS

Mogilev
1 Dec 1917

Tula
20 Dec 1917

Trans-Siberian Railway

Warsaw

Brest-Litovsk

Orel
14 Nov 1917

Samara
9 Nov 1917

Penza
4 Jan 1918

Orenburg
31 Jan 1918

POLES

Gomel
12 Nov 1917

Tambov
13 Feb 1918

POLAND

Voronezh
12 Nov 1917

Saratov
9 Nov 1917

CZECHOSLOVAKIA

Zhitomir
22 Jan 1918

Kiev
8 Feb 1918

Denikin 1919

HUNGARY

ROMANIANS

Poltava
19 Jan 1918

Kharkov
24 Dec 1917

**Don Cassacks
1917-19**

Tsaritsyn (Stalingrad) (Volgograd)
27 Nov 1917

Ural Cossack Army 1918-20

BESSARABIA

Yekaterinoslva (Dnepropetrovsk)
11 Jan 1918

R. Don

R. Volga

ROMANIA

Kishinev
10 Dec 1917

Niklnlayev
27 Jan 1918

Novocherkassk
25 Feb 1918

Rostov-on-Don
10 Nov 1917

Astrakhan
7 Feb 1918

Odessa
31 Jan 1918

Wrangel 1920

Cossacks

Caspian Sea

Sevastopol
29 Dec 1917

Simferopol
26 Jan 1918

Novorossiysk
14 Dec 1917

BULGARIA

FRENCH

Black Sea

BRITISH

Georgians

1919-20

Mensheviks

Baku
15 Nov 1917

Krasnovodsk

Entente fleet

BRITISH

Batum

Tiflis (Tbilisi)

BRITISH

TURKEY

Kars

BRITISH

Tabriz
1918-19

PERSIA

121

The Chinese Revolution
1911-1949

By 1911 the imperial government of China was thoroughly discredited, and it only needed an army mutiny at Wuchang to repudiate its authority (map 1). But the republic proclaimed in 1912, with Sun Yat-sen as its first president, was overwhelmed by its inherited problems, and within weeks Sun was displaced by Yuan Shih-k'ai, the most powerful general of the old regime. After Yuan's death in 1916 the government in Peking lost control and power passed into the hands of provincial warlords, whose armies caused untold damage

and millions of casualties. Compounding this misery were the expansionist policies of Japan, which had secured control of Shantung and Manchuria in 1915 (page 126), as well as the presence of foreign powers, based in the Treaty Ports, who interfered in Chinese politics and exploited the struggling Chinese economy.

In 1919, when the Paris Peace Conference refused to abrogate Japanese and other foreign privileges, this desperate situation exploded in a massive upsurge of Chinese nationalism, which found vent in the 4 May Movement of 1919, a spontaneous uprising of students and urban workers, which was the real starting point of the Chinese revolution. It provided a new constituency for Sun Yat-sen, who had taken refuge at Canton,

and in 1923 Sun reorganised his Nationalist (Kuomintang, KMT) Party, allied with the Chinese Communist Party (CCP, founded in 1921), and prepared to reunite the country. But Sun died in 1925, and it was Chiang Kai-shek, the Moscow-trained general of the KMT army, who led the great Northern Expedition of 1926 which aimed at the elimination of the warlords and the unification of the country (map 2). Helped by peasant and workers' uprisings along its route, it was astonishingly successful, and by April 1927 Chiang established his capital at Nanking. But the uneasy alliance of KMT and CCP could not hold, and in 1927 Chiang turned on his allies, massacring the Communists in Shanghai. Furthermore, the warlords were not entirely eliminated, an

1 The revolution of 1911

● 8 Nov. 1911 revolt, with date of province's independence

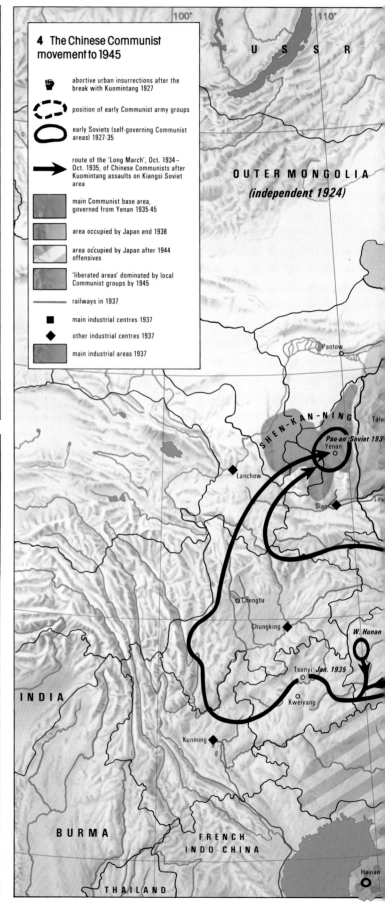

4 The Chinese Communist movement to 1945

abortive urban insurrections after the break with Kuomintang 1927

position of early Communist army groups

early Soviets (self-governing Communist areas) 1927-35

route of the 'Long March', Oct. 1934–Oct. 1935, of Chinese Communists after Kuomintang assaults on Kiangsi Soviet area

main Communist base area, governed from Yenan 1935-45

area occupied by Japan end 1938

area occupied by Japan after 1944 offensives

'liberated areas' dominated by local Communist groups by 1945

railways in 1937

■ main industrial centres 1937

◆ other industrial centres 1937

main industrial areas 1937

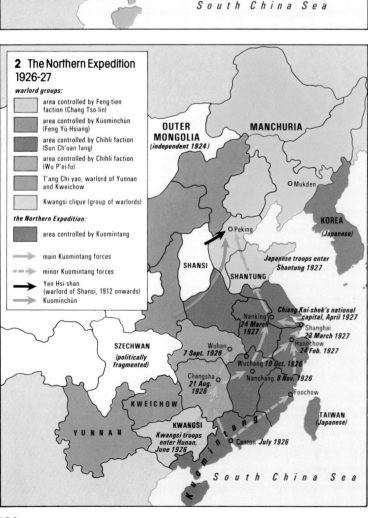

2 The Northern Expedition 1926-27

warlord groups:

area controlled by Feng-tien faction (Chang Tso-lin)

area controlled by Kuominchün (Feng Yü-Hsiang)

area controlled by Chihli faction (Sun Ch'uan-fang)

area controlled by Chihli faction (Wu P'ei-fu)

T'ang Chi-yao, warlord of Yunnan and Kweichow

Kwangsi clique (group of warlords)

the Northern Expedition:

area controlled by Kuomintang

→ main Kuomintang forces

⇢ minor Kuomintang forces

→ Yen Hsi-shan (warlord of Shansi, 1912 onwards)

→ Kuominchün

Chiang's direct rule was limited effectively to the lower Yangtze (map 3). Finally, the Japanese, fearing the potential challenge from a reunited China, decided to reinforce their hold in the north. After 1931, when Japan overran Manchuria, Chiang had to meet simultaneously the Japanese threat from without and the Communist threat at home.

Chiang's purge had virtually eliminated the Communists in the cities, but peasant disaffection, arising from his failure to carry out land reform, provided them with new possibilities in the countryside. It was Mao Tse-tung who realised this, and his base at Chingkang Shan in a remote mountainous area was the main, though not the only, seedbed of the revitalised Com-

munist movement. KMT attacks drove Mao to Kiangsi where the most important Soviet was established and where the Communists ruled an area of several million people developing reform programmes as a peasant-based party rather than an urban, proletarian party on the Russian model. Further KMT attacks forced the Communists to abandon Kiangsi and it was on the famous Long March, to Yenan (map 4), where Mao gathered widespread support by his reform programmes and by spearheading resistance to the Japanese invasion, that his peasant-based wing of the party gained ascendancy. The result was that large areas of China passed under Communist control, while Chiang's government, which had withdrawn under Japanese

pressure to the remote fastness of Chungking, was unpopular and out of touch. This was the situation in 1945 after the defeat of Japan, though other factors, particularly the growing Soviet-American involvement, played a part. Negotiations for a political settlement broke down and in 1947 open civil war broke out. The Communists defeated the Nationalists in Manchuria and took Peking in January 1949 (map 5). The great battle around Suchow (November 1948–January 1949) opened the way south. On October 1, 1949, the People's Republic was proclaimed, and the Nationalists fled to Taiwan. But the civil war compounded the devastation of the previous decades and China's new rulers were left with a formidable task of reconstruction.

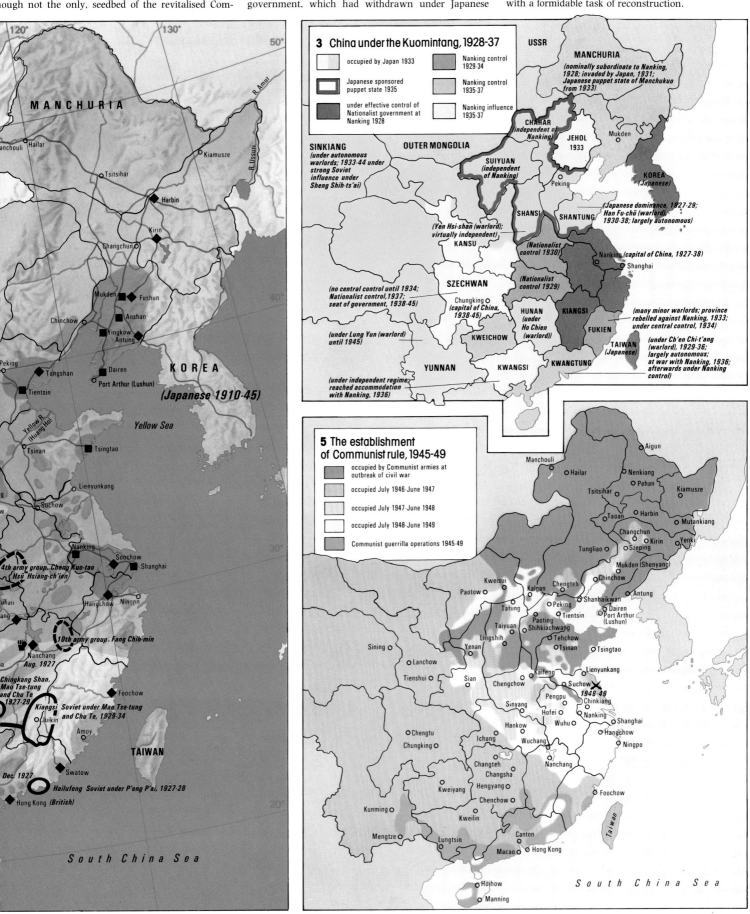

3 China under the Kuomintang, 1928-37

occupied by Japan 1933
Japanese sponsored puppet state 1935
under effective control of Nationalist government at Nanking 1928
Nanking control 1929-34
Nanking control 1935-37
Nanking influence 1935-37

5 The establishment of Communist rule, 1945-49

occupied by Communist armies at outbreak of civil war
occupied July 1946-June 1947
occupied July 1947-June 1948
occupied July 1948-June 1949
Communist guerrilla operations 1945-49

The Ottoman Empire
1805-1923

The decline of the Ottoman Empire, after its revival under the Kuprülü grand-viziers (1656–91), had begun with the Treaty of Carlowitz (1699), when Hungary passed from Ottoman to Habsburg rule (page 78). Under Catherine the Great it came under Russian pressure (page 84). But disintegration only set in seriously during the nineteenth century. An early intimation was Mohammed Ali's establishment of a virtually independent government in Egypt after 1805. But the main factor was Western pressure, political and economic. In 1838 an Anglo-Turkish Commercial Convention forced the empire to open its doors to Western commerce and exploitation, and by 1881 the Turkish state was bankrupt. Nevertheless it was kept alive until 1914 because the European powers feared to create a power vacuum which their rivals could exploit. But there was steady

encroachment. France occupied Algeria (1830) and Tunisia (1881); Italy seized Libya and the Dodecanese (1912); and the British occupied Egypt (1882) and controlled Aden and much of the Persian Gulf (map 1). An Armenian bid for independence was savagely repressed (1895), but the Balkan wars of 1912–13 dealt a fatal blow to Turkey's position in Europe, and by 1914 disaffected Arab dynasties were on the edge of revolt.

Turkey's entry into the 1914 war on the side of the Central Powers completed the process of disintegration. The Turks fought well and held the initiative until 1917. An Allied attempt to land at Gallipoli and advance on Constantinople (April 1915) was abandoned with heavy losses (January 1916), and an advance towards Baghdad ended in defeat at Kut el Amara (April 29, 1916). Only the Russians made progress, occupying Turkish Armenia (July 1916), until the Russian revolution restored initiative to the Ottoman armies (map 2). Meanwhile, the British had begun negotiations with dissident Arabs, holding out the prospect of an independent Arab

kingdom. The result was the Arab revolt of 1916, which made possible the two-pronged attack which carrie British and Arab forces in 1917 to Baghdad and Jeru salem, and eventually to Damascus, Beirut and Aleppo But now complications set in. While negotiating wit the Arabs, the Allied powers had entered into secre agreements for the partition of the Ottoman empire, in cluding the establishment of a Jewish National Home i Palestine (map 3). In October 1918 the French lande troops at Beirut as a preliminary to occupying Syria; i May 1919 Greece occupied Smyrna. In Turkey th humiliating peace terms imposed by the Allied power produced a strong nationalist reaction under Mustaph Kemal (Atatürk), who fought a long and bitter wa against the Greeks (map 4) and liberated Anatolia. Th Treaty of Lausanne (1923) acknowledged his succes and marked the birth of the new secular Turkish re public. Elsewhere in the Middle East disillusion with th peace settlement laid up a store of anti-Western resent ment which boded ill for the future.

The Middle East and North Africa 1800–1923 (below)

Aden Occupied by British from India 1839.
Afghanistan Independent sultanate. Durrani dynasty to 1835, then invasions and influence from British India.
Albania Ottoman province; independent princedom 1912, kingdom 1928.
Algeria French conquest 1830–47.
Armenia Western part in Ottoman Empire, eastern occupied by Russia 1804; independent republic 1918–20, divided between USSR and Turkey.
Azerbaijan Persian until beginning of 19th century; partly under Russian occupation 1803–28; independent republic 1918–20, incorporated into USSR thereafter.
Bahrain Independent sheikdom since late 18th century; British protection since 1820, formalised 1892.
Bessarabia Ottoman province; Russian from 1812; southern part ceded by Russia to Moldavia 1856, taken back by Russia 1878; linked with Romania 1918.
Bosnia-Herzegovina Austrian administration from 1878, annexed 1908; incorporated in Yugoslavia after 1918.
Bukhara Independent khanate; Russian protectorate 1868, full incorporation 1924.
Bulgaria Autonomous Ottoman province 1878; united with Eastern Rumelia, 1885; independent kingdom 1908.
Crete Ottoman province; Egyptian rule 1822–40; autonomous 1898; incorporated in Greece 1913.
Cyprus Ottoman province; British occupation 1878.

Daghestan Persian; Russian occupation completed by 1859.
Dodecanese Ottoman province; Italian occupation 1912.
Eastern Rumelia Ottoman province 1878; incorporated in Bulgaria 1885.
Egypt Ottoman province under Mohammed Ali from 1805; British occupation 1882, protectorate 1914.
Georgia Independent kingdom under intermittent Persian control; incorporated in Russia 1801; independent republic 1918–20, incorporated into USSR 1920.
Greece Ottoman rule until 1821; independent state from 1833; enlarged by additions, in particular Crete (1913) and Macedonia (1913). Smyrna (Izmir) and hinterland briefly occupied 1920–22.
Hejaz Local rulers (Sharifs of Mecca) under Ottoman sovereignty until 1916. Sharifs as independent rulers 1916–24 (see Nejd).
Iraq Ottoman provinces, unified in 1921 as kingdom (Hashimite family) under British mandate.
Kars and Ardahan Ottoman until 1878; Russian from 1878; in Armenian republic 1918–20; re-occupied by Turkey 1920.
Khiva Independent khanate; Russian occupation 1873.
Kokand Independent khanate; Russian occupation 1876.

Kuwait Autonomous sheikdom (Al Sabah family), with Ottoman claim to sovereignty. British protection formalised after 1899.
Lebanon Local princes under Ottoman rule 1861–1914; French occupation from 1918, then mandate.
Libya Local rulers under Ottoman sovereignty until 1835; direct Ottoman rule from 1835; Italian conquest 1911.
Macedonia Ottoman province; divided between Greece, Serbia and Bulgaria 1913.
Montenegro Autonomous region within Ottoman Empire; independent 1878; kingdom 1910; incorporated in Yugoslavia after 1918.
Morocco Independent sultanate; French and Spanish protectorates after 1912.
Muscat and Oman Local rulers from 18th century (Al Bu Said family); British protection formalised in 1891.
Nejd Local rulers (professing Wahabi version of Islam); Egyptian control 1818–40; conflict of Ibn Saud and Ibn Rashid dynasties, with Saudi victory 1921. By 1932, Asir, Hasa, Hejaz and Nejd incorporated in kingdom of Saudi Arabia.
Palestine British occupation from 1917, then mandate with obligation of facilitating creation of Jewish national home.

Persia (Iran) Independent kingdom, British and Russian penetration; agreement on spheres of influence 1907.
Qatar Sheikdom; British protection formalised in 1916.
Romania Ottoman provinces of Moldavi and Wallachia under local rulers; united 1859; independent kingdom 1878.
Serbia Autonomous from early 19th century; independent kingdom 1878; incorporated in Yugoslavia after 1918.
Sudan Under Egyptian rule from 1821; indigenous rule (Mahdiya) early 1880s to 1898; British occupation and Anglo-Egyptian condominium from 1898.
Syria Ottoman province; brief bid for independence under Hashimites 1918–20; French occupation in 1920, then mandate
Transjordan Part of Ottoman province of Damascus; from 1921 Hashimite princedom under British mandate for Palestine.
Trucial Oman Small sheikdoms under British protection, 1820s onwards.
Tunisia Virtually autonomous province o Ottoman Empire; French protectorate 1881
Turkey Core of Ottoman Empire, then independent republic 1922.
Yemen Local rulers, holding Zaidi versior of Islam, under Ottoman sovereignty; independent after 1918.

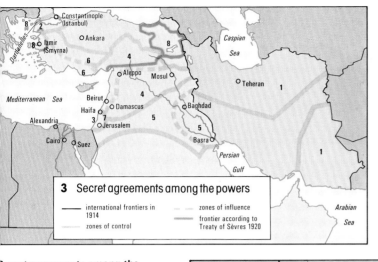

3 Secret agreements among the powers

— international frontiers in 1914
‥‥ zones of control
‥‥ zones of influence
━━ frontier according to Treaty of Sèvres 1920

4 The Greco-Turkish War, 1920-22

▨ area under Greek control 1920
━ limit of Greek advance 1921
▷ direction of Greek offensive 1921
▨ boundary of Greek control 1921-22
▶ direction of Turkish offensive 1922

Secret agreements among the powers (above)

1/Britain and Russia divided Persia (1907) into spheres of influence, with a neutral zone in between

2/France, Britain and Russia agreed (1915) that Constantinople and the Straits should be Russian

3/The Sykes-Picot Agreement (1916) internationalised Palestine

4/France would control the Syrian coast, and influence the interior

5/Britain would similarly control Iraq

6/Italy would similarly control south-west Asia Minor

7/Britain promised Mecca Arab independence (Husain-McMahon letters 1915–16) and agreed to set up a Jewish national home in Palestine (Balfour Declaration 1917)

8/Treaty of Sèvres (1920) made modifications; Constantinople and the Straits would become international. Greece would take Smyrna and its hinterland; an independent Armenia would occupy eastern Asia Minor

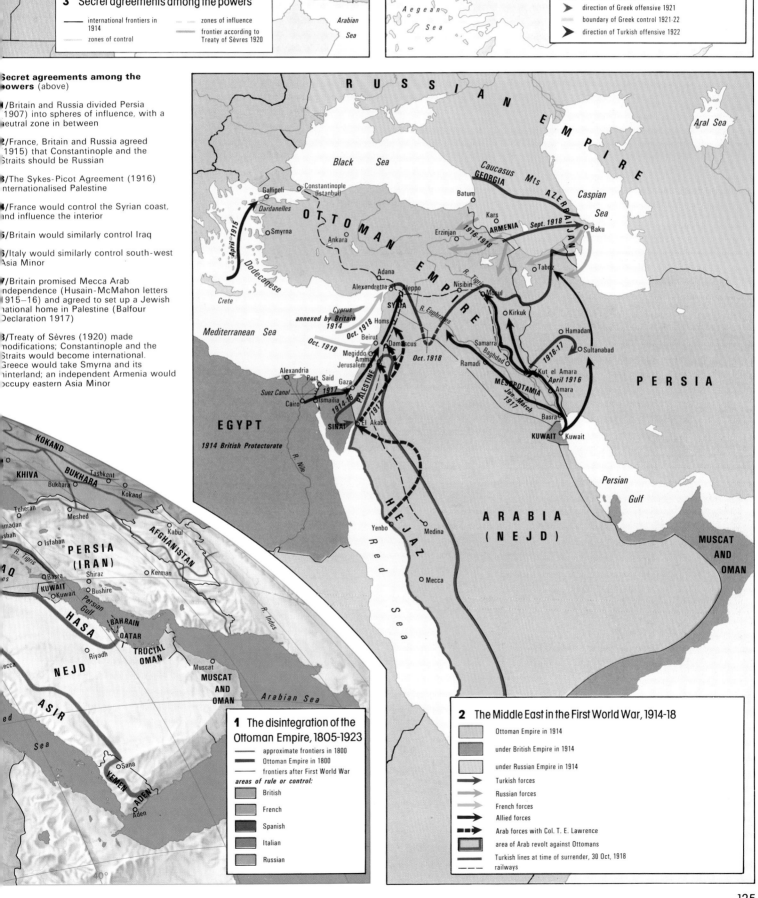

1 The disintegration of the Ottoman Empire, 1805-1923

— approximate frontiers in 1800
━ Ottoman Empire in 1800
— frontiers after First World War
areas of rule or control:
British
French
Spanish
Italian
Russian

2 The Middle East in the First World War, 1914-18

Ottoman Empire in 1914
under British Empire in 1914
under Russian Empire in 1914
→ Turkish forces
→ Russian forces
→ French forces
→ Allied forces
▶▶ Arab forces with Col. T. E. Lawrence
▢ area of Arab revolt against Ottomans
━ Turkish lines at time of surrender, 30 Oct, 1918
--- railways

Modern Japan, 1868-1941

The Tokugawa shogunate, established in 1609 (page 50), gave Japan two hundred years of peace and prosperity. But a generation before 1868 it was evident that internal tensions were building up and that the *bakufu* (or Shogun's government) in Edo was losing control. Peasant unrest and discontent among impoverished *samurai*, whose position had been undermined by the growth of a money economy, was compounded by British, Russian, French and American pressure for the opening of Japan to foreign trade. A period of complicated manoeuvring ensued, in which the four western feudal domains (*han*), Satsuma, Choshu, Tosa and Hizen, took the lead (map 1). The outcome was the so-called Meiji restoration, when the emperor, supported by dissident elements, moved from Kyoto to Edo, now re-named Tokyo (or eastern capital), displaced the Shogun, and took direct control of government.

The Meiji restoration of 1868 was in reality a revolution, carried out with the definite aim of modernisation and westernisation. The old feudal structure was replaced in 1871 by a modern system of prefectures. Samurai privileges were abolished (1873), though samurai from Choshu had a leading place in the new conscript army. A western style peerage (1884), cabinet government (1885) and a two-chamber parliament (1889) laid the foundations of political stability; a national education system was instituted (1872) providing teaching for 90 per cent of children by 1900. At the same time economic development was taken in hand (map 2). The first railway was opened in 1872, and by 1906 the main network was completed. Industrialisation proceeded more slowly, beginning effectively only at the end of the 1800s. By 1889 the number of

cotton mills had risen from 3 in 1877 to 83, and by 1913 Japanese production dominated the home market and had a substantial foothold abroad, particularly in China. Nevertheless agriculture remained the main employment until after the First World War. The number employed in agriculture fell from 70 per cent of the population in the 1870s to 57 per cent in 1914, but still provided almost all the foodstuffs for a population which rose from 39 million in 1868 to 56 million in 1918.

International recognition of Japan's new status was nevertheless slow in coming. It had been forced in the 1850s to negotiate unequal treaties with the western powers, and it was not until 1894 that foreign consular jurisdiction was abolished and only in 1911 that Tokyo regained tariff autonomy. These concessions were a tribute to Japan's military successes, seen above all in the war with China (1894–95) and in the Russo-Japanese war (map 4). The first overseas ventures, in the Bonin and Ryukyu islands and in Taiwan, were undertaken primarily to still unrest at home, but in 1894 Japan embarked on a full-scale imperialist policy (map 3). Even so, it was forced by the European powers to return all its conquests except Taiwan; but the Anglo-Japanese treaty of 1902, inspired by mutual fear of Russia, was a turning point. In the war with Russia (1904–05), Japan's forces achieved a series of victories culminating in the fall of Port Arthur (January 1905), the battle of Mukden (February–March), and the destruction of the Russian Baltic fleet in the Tsushima Straits (May). After the war the two combatants rapidly reached agreement over a division of spheres of interest, which allowed Japan to annex Korea in 1910. It had embarked on the creation of a Japanese empire on the Asian mainland, and the war of 1914–18 and the Russian revolution (page 120) enabled it to gain a foot-

hold in Shantung and Manchuria. Although onc again western pressure compelled it to withdraw, Japa was recognised at the Peace Conference in 1919 as major power with a permanent seat on the Council o the League of Nations.

During the 1920s Japanese policy veered betwee cooperation with the west and an inherent anti-foreig feeling, fed by a sense of discrimination. Until 193 cooperation prevailed, but the impact of the Grea Depression (page 130) swung the balance in the oppo site direction, and, beginning with the advance int Manchuria in 1931, Japan set out to carve out an em pire in East Asia. After the Japanese attack on th Chinese mainland in 1937, tension grew with the Unite States. The lines of the Second World War were alread being drawn. When Germany defeated France an Holland in 1940, Japan's moment seemed to hav arrived, and the advance into South-East Asia bega (map 5). In spite of astounding initial successes (pag 134), it was a gamble that failed. But paradoxically th failure, and the subsequent American occupation, pro pelled Japan even more decisively into the modern worl than the Meiji restoration, socially authoritarian an backward-looking, had done.

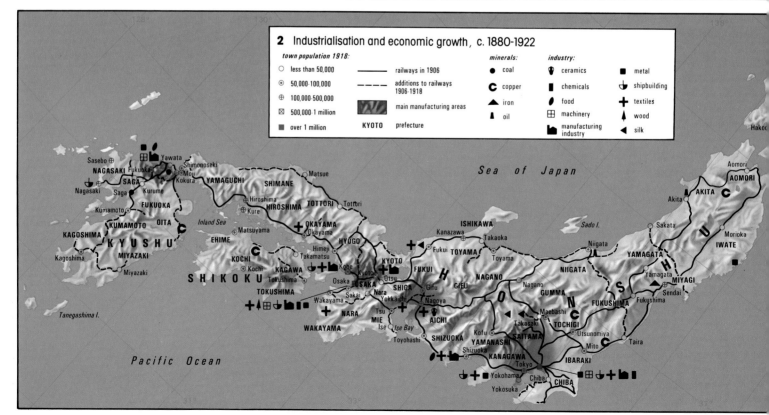

1 Japan in 1868

- provincial borders
- Five highways
- extensions to the Five Highways
- secondary roads
- sea-routes
- important castle towns
- *feudal territories:*
- major Tokugawa domains
- major anti-Bakufu domains
- American, Russian, British and other naval visits

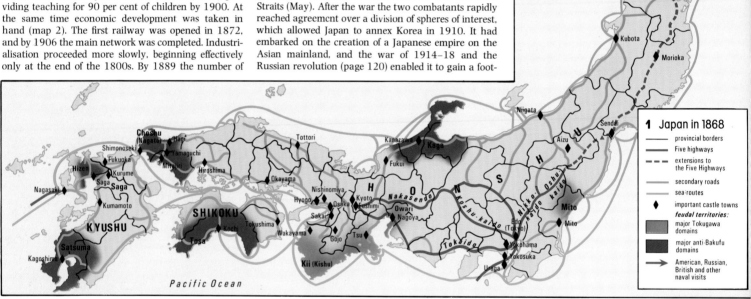

2 Industrialisation and economic growth, c. 1880-1922

town population 1918:
- ○ less than 50,000
- ◉ 50,000-100,000
- ⊕ 100,000-500,000
- ⊠ 500,000-1 million
- ■ over 1 million

- railways in 1906
- additions to railways 1906-1918
- main manufacturing areas
- KYOTO prefecture

minerals:
- coal
- copper
- iron
- oil

industry:
- ceramics
- chemicals
- food
- machinery
- manufacturing industry

- metal
- shipbuilding
- textiles
- wood
- silk

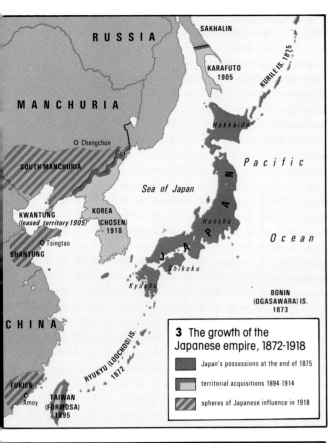

3 The growth of the Japanese empire, 1872-1918

- Japan's possessions at the end of 1875
- territorial acquisitions 1894-1914
- spheres of Japanese influence in 1918

4 The Russo-Japanese War 1904-05

← movements of Japanese forces 1904-05

— railways in 1918

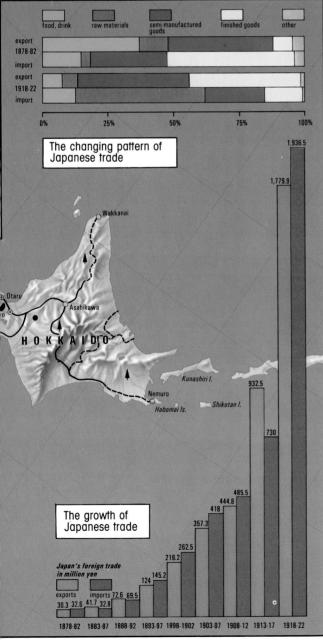

food, drink   raw materials   semi-manufactured goods   finished goods   other

export 1878-82
import

export 1918-22
import

0%   25%   50%   75%   100%

The changing pattern of Japanese trade

The growth of Japanese trade

Japan's foreign trade in million yen

exports   imports

	exports	imports
1878-82	30.3	32.6
1883-87	41.7	32.8
1888-92	72.6	69.5
1893-97	124	145.2
1898-1902	219.2	262.5
1903-07	357.3	418
1908-12	444.8	485.5
1913-17	730	932.5
1918-22	1,779.9	1,936.5

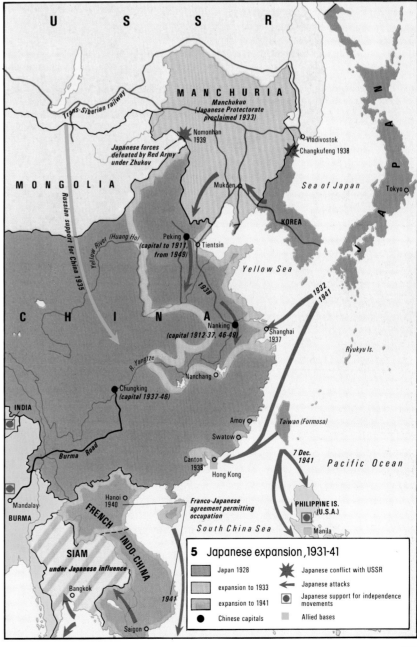

5 Japanese expansion, 1931-41

- Japan 1928
- expansion to 1933
- expansion to 1941
- ● Chinese capitals
- ✳ Japanese conflict with USSR
- ← Japanese attacks
- ◉ Japanese support for independence movements
- Allied bases

European political problems, 1919-1939

The First World War shattered the equipoise of 1914. The long-term goal after 1918 was a return to 'normalcy', but it was always an illusion. Not merely had the collapse of the Habsburg Empire, the defeat of Germany, and the Bolshevik Revolution completely altered the balance of power in Europe, but the pre-war economic equilibrium also was destroyed. All the victorious powers were in debt to the United States, and Great Britain, which had largely financed its allies, never fully recovered. These facts weighed heavily at the Paris Peace Conference in 1919, but the dominant fact was probably fear of the spread of revolution from Russia. This accounts for the relatively lenient treatment of Germany, which suffered only minor territorial losses, except for the restoration to the newly independent Poland of the lands seized in the partitions at the end of the eighteenth century. The real problem facing the peacemakers was the tangle of nationalities in Europe. Finland, Estonia, Latvia and Lithuania were detached as independent republics from Russia, which was not represented at the Conference, and Russia also lost Bessarabia to Romania and a large part of White Russia to Poland after the Russo-Polish war of 1920. However, the independent republics of White Russia, Georgia, Armenia and Azerbaijan were brought back into the Soviet Union in 1921 (map 2). The main beneficiary of the peace settlement was Romania, which, in addition to Bessarabia, acquired the Dobruja from Bulgaria and Transylvania from Hungary. But the projected dismemberment of Turkey was thwarted by the national revival under Mustapha Kemal Atatürk (page 124), and in 1923 the new republic was recognised by the Treaty of Lausanne.

The peace treaties left dissatisfied minorities everywhere, and there were widespread movements of refugees, the most extreme case being the wholesale exchange of populations negotiated after the Greco-Turkish war of 1920-22 (map 3). More important politically, they also created a lasting sense of injustice and discrimination. It was inconceivable that either Germany or Russia, once they recovered their strength, would accept a position of inferiority. In addition, there was the irredentism of Hungary, the country which had suffered most from the peace settlement, which was exploited, after 1927, by Mussolini's Fascist Italy, which

hoped in this way to build up for itself a dominant position in the Danubian basin. Thus Europe was divided between revisionists and anti-revisionists, and the only hope for the latter was to support the status quo by a system of military pacts. France, with its alliances with Poland (1921) and Czechoslovakia (1924), underpinning the 'Little Entente' between Czechoslovakia, Yugoslavia and Romania (1921), was the heart and soul of this security system (map 1). It operated effectively until the Great Depression (page 130) and the instability it engendered in France, which undercut France's credibility among its East European clients. When Poland signed a Neutrality Pact with Germany in 1934, it marked the beginning of the collapse of the French security system.

The Locarno treaties (1925), whereby Germany recognised the post-war frontier settlements with France and Belgium, marked the end of the long years of frustration, civil disorder and conflict which had bedevilled Europe since 1918. Germany was welcomed back into the community of nations; so also, after 1925, was Soviet Russia. But the stabilisation of 1925–29 was more apparent than real. With the exception of Czechoslovakia, none of the new states of eastern Europe was economically viable, and the onset of the Depression exposed their weaknesses and left them a prey to German infiltration. Spain also, where the monarchy had been superseded by a republic in 1931, was caught up in its repercussions, which brought a confrontation of left and right and undermined the republican government. The result, in 1936, was civil war (map 4), in which eventually the rebels under General Franco, supported by Italy and Germany, were successful. The failure of France and England to aid the republic discredited them in the eyes of their allies and encouraged Italian and German aggression. Hitler's repudiation of the Locarno treaties, followed by the annexation of Austria (1938) was a clear sign of his intentions; but the destruction of Czechoslovakia, abetted by Poland and Hungary, and the Italian annexation of Albania (1939), further exposed the ambivalence of the western powers (map 5). Whether an alliance with the Soviet Union would have halted the aggressors is a matter of dispute. However, when negotiations between the Soviet Union and the Western powers broke down in 1939, and the Russians, fearing a war of two fronts with Germany and Japan, signed the notorious Nazi-Soviet Non-Aggression Pact, the collapse of the unstable European balance of 1919–39 was inevitable.

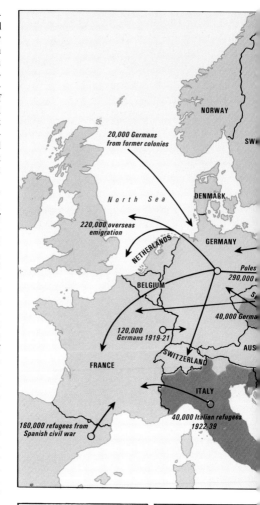

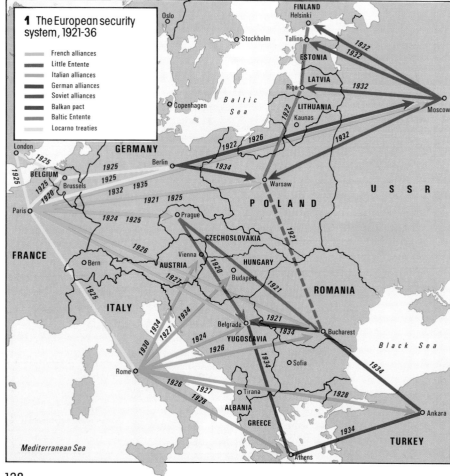

1 The European security system, 1921-36

- French alliances
- Little Entente
- Italian alliances
- German alliances
- Soviet alliances
- Balkan pact
- Baltic Entente
- Locarno treaties

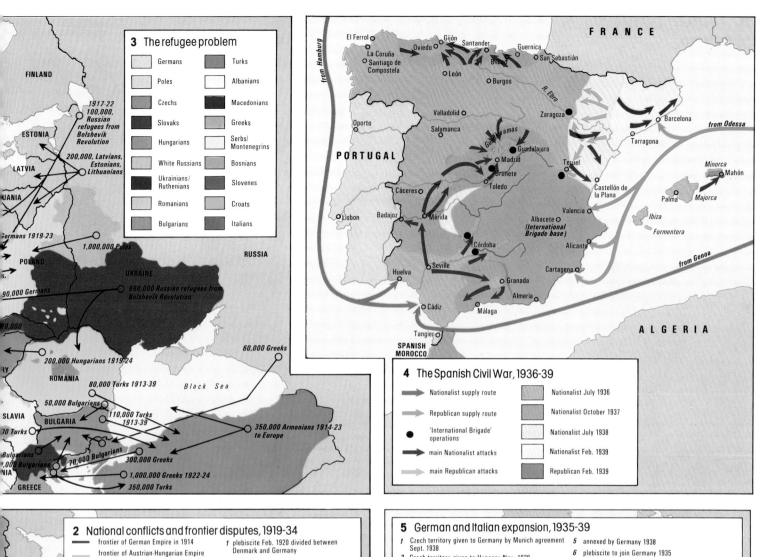
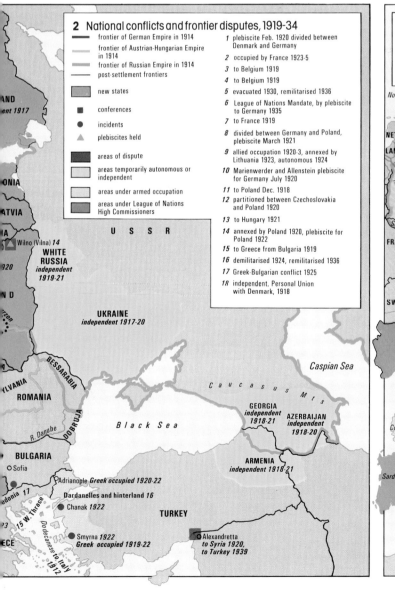

3 The refugee problem

Germans · Turks
Poles · Albanians
Czechs · Macedonians
Slovaks · Greeks
Hungarians · Serbs/Montenegrins
White Russians · Bosnians
Ukrainians/Ruthenians · Slovenes
Romanians · Croats
Bulgarians · Italians

1917-22 100,000, Russian refugees from Bolshevik Revolution
200,000, Latvians, Estonians, Lithuanians
Germans 1919-23
1,000,000 Poles
650,000 Russian refugees from Bolshevik Revolution
200,000 Hungarians 1919-24
80,000 Turks 1913-39
50,000 Bulgarians
110,000 Turks 1913-39
350,000 Armenians 1914-23 to Europe
70,000 Bulgarians
300,000 Greeks
60,000 Greeks
1,000,000 Greeks 1922-24
350,000 Turks

4 The Spanish Civil War, 1936-39

→ Nationalist supply route
→ Republican supply route
● 'International Brigade' operations
→ main Nationalist attacks
→ main Republican attacks

Nationalist July 1936
Nationalist October 1937
Nationalist July 1938
Nationalist Feb. 1939
Republican Feb. 1939

2 National conflicts and frontier disputes, 1919-34

— frontier of German Empire in 1914
— frontier of Austrian-Hungarian Empire in 1914
— frontier of Russian Empire in 1914
— post-settlement frontiers

new states
■ conferences
● incidents
▲ plebiscites held
areas of dispute
areas temporarily autonomous or independent
areas under armed occupation
areas under League of Nations High Commissioners

1 plebiscite Feb. 1920 divided between Denmark and Germany
2 occupied by France 1923-5
3 to Belgium 1919
4 to Belgium 1919
5 evacuated 1930, remilitarised 1936
6 League of Nations Mandate, by plebiscite to Germany 1935
7 to France 1919
8 divided between Germany and Poland, plebiscite March 1921
9 allied occupation 1920-3, annexed by Lithuania 1923, autonomous 1924
10 Marienwerder and Allenstein plebiscite for Germany July 1920
11 to Poland Dec. 1918
12 partitioned between Czechoslovakia and Poland 1920
13 to Hungary 1921
14 annexed by Poland 1920, plebiscite for Poland 1922
15 to Greece from Bulgaria 1919
16 demilitarised 1924, remilitarised 1936
17 Greek-Bulgarian conflict 1925
18 independent, Personal Union with Denmark, 1918

Wilno (Vilna) 14
WHITE RUSSIA independent 1919-21
UKRAINE independent 1917-20
GEORGIA independent 1918-21
AZERBAIJAN independent 1918-20
ARMENIA independent 1918-21
Adrianople Greek occupied 1920-22
Dardanelles and hinterland 16
Chanak 1922
Smyrna 1922 Greek occupied 1919-22
Alexandretta to Syria 1920, to Turkey 1939

5 German and Italian expansion, 1935-39

1 Czech territory given to Germany by Munich agreement Sept. 1938
2 Czech territory given to Hungary Nov. 1938
3 occupied by Hungary March 1939
4 Czech territory taken by Poland Sept. 1939
5 annexed by Germany 1938
6 plebiscite to join Germany 1935
7 Italian expansion
8 annexation of Memel March 1939

(reoccupied by Germany 1936)
Saar 6
ALBANIA (annexed by Italy 1939)
ETHIOPIA (conquered by Italy 1935-36)

→ Italian campaigns 1935-36

The Great Depression
1929-1939

After 1925 it appeared that the disorders of the post-war world had been overcome and a period of relative stability and prosperity had begun. The Great Depression quickly dispelled this illusion. Conventionally its starting point was the financial crash on Wall Street in October 1929; but this was only the manifestation of deeper weaknesses in the world economy. In the United States business was in trouble long before the crash. Worldwide, commodity prices had been falling since 1926, impairing the capacity of exporters such as Australia to buy products from Europe and the United States. The German economy also was faltering by 1928. However, more important than the causes of the depression were its consequences. These were almost instantaneous, although it was only after 1930 that dislocation reached its peak. Its most arresting manifestation was unemployment which reached record heights in 1932. In many industrial countries over a quarter of the labour force was thrown out of work. Industrial production fell to 53 per cent of its 1929 level in Germany and the United States, and world trade sank to 35 per cent of its 1929 value. Attempts to solve the problem only made things worse. As early as 1930 the United States imposed the Hawley-Smoot Tariff, the highest in its history. The United Kingdom responded in 1932 by negotiating the Ottawa Agreements, a series of preferential tariffs for the Commonwealth. Another expedient was competitive devaluation. After England left the Gold Standard in 1931, country after country followed suit and the result was the development of closed currency blocs (map 1), which inhibited international trade still further.

Economic nationalism fostered political nationalism, just as unemployment and the erosion of middle-class living standards fostered political extremism. The fall of the Hamaguchi government in Japan in 1931 marked the end of constitutional democracy and the beginning of Japanese aggression in Manchuria (page 126). In Germany, Brüning's deflationary policies, raising unemployment from under 3 million in 1930 to 6 million two years later, paved the way for Hitler. Hitler's accession to power in January 1933 was followed by Dollfuss's dictatorship in Austria, and eastern Europe, with the exception of Czechoslovakia, quickly followed suit (map 3). France remained precariously democratic until 1940, and in the United Kingdom, where a right-wing 'national' government won a huge majority in 1931, Mosley's fascist movement made little headway. But even here and in the United States, where F. D. Roosevelt was elected president in 1932 with a promise of a 'New Deal', fascist movements exercised considerable pressure (map 2). Only the Soviet Union, isolated from the world economy, was able to sustain economic growth (map 1) – a fact which was to be of cardinal importance after 1941. Roosevelt's New Deal made initial progress, but faltered after 1936 when a new phase of economic down-turn began. By 1939 the United States had not regained the level of industrial output of 1929, and only the Second World War, and the boost it gave to production pulled it out of depression.

The effects of the depression also hit the primary producing countries of Asia, Africa and Latin America. Here, as the crisis radicalised peasants and workers, nationalist and revolutionary movements gained new bases of support. In this respect, as in many others, the Great Depression was the catalyst of the modern world.

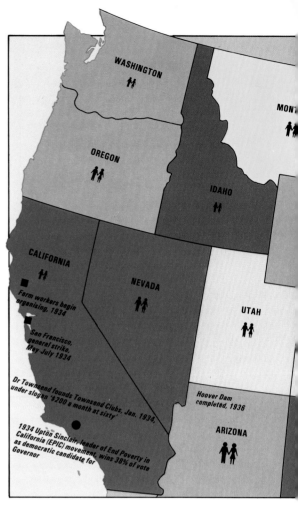

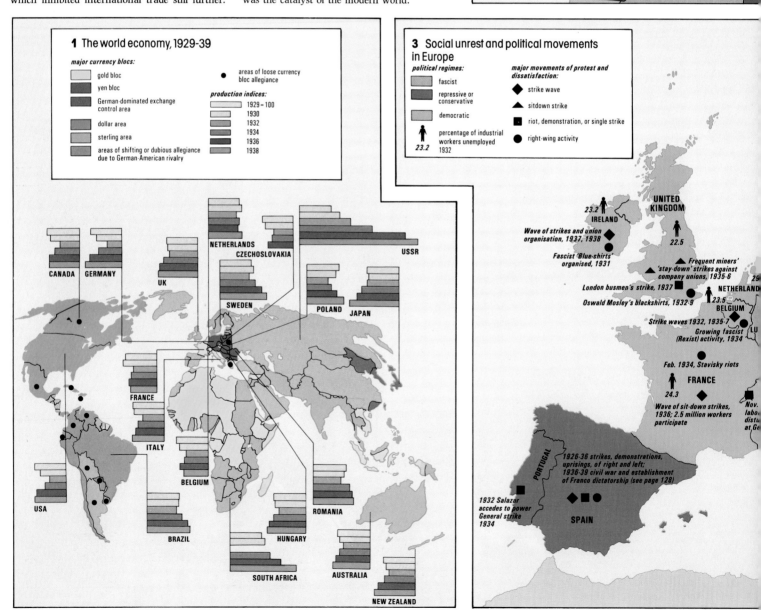

1 The world economy, 1929-39

major currency blocs:
- gold bloc
- yen bloc
- German-dominated exchange control area
- dollar area
- sterling area
- areas of shifting or dubious allegiance due to German-American rivalry
- ● areas of loose currency bloc allegiance

production indices:
- 1929 = 100
- 1930
- 1932
- 1934
- 1936
- 1938

3 Social unrest and political movements in Europe

political regimes:
- fascist
- repressive or conservative
- democratic
- 👤 percentage of industrial workers unemployed 1932 (23.2)

major movements of protest and dissatisfaction:
- ◆ strike wave
- ▲ sitdown strike
- ■ riot, demonstration, or single strike
- ● right-wing activity

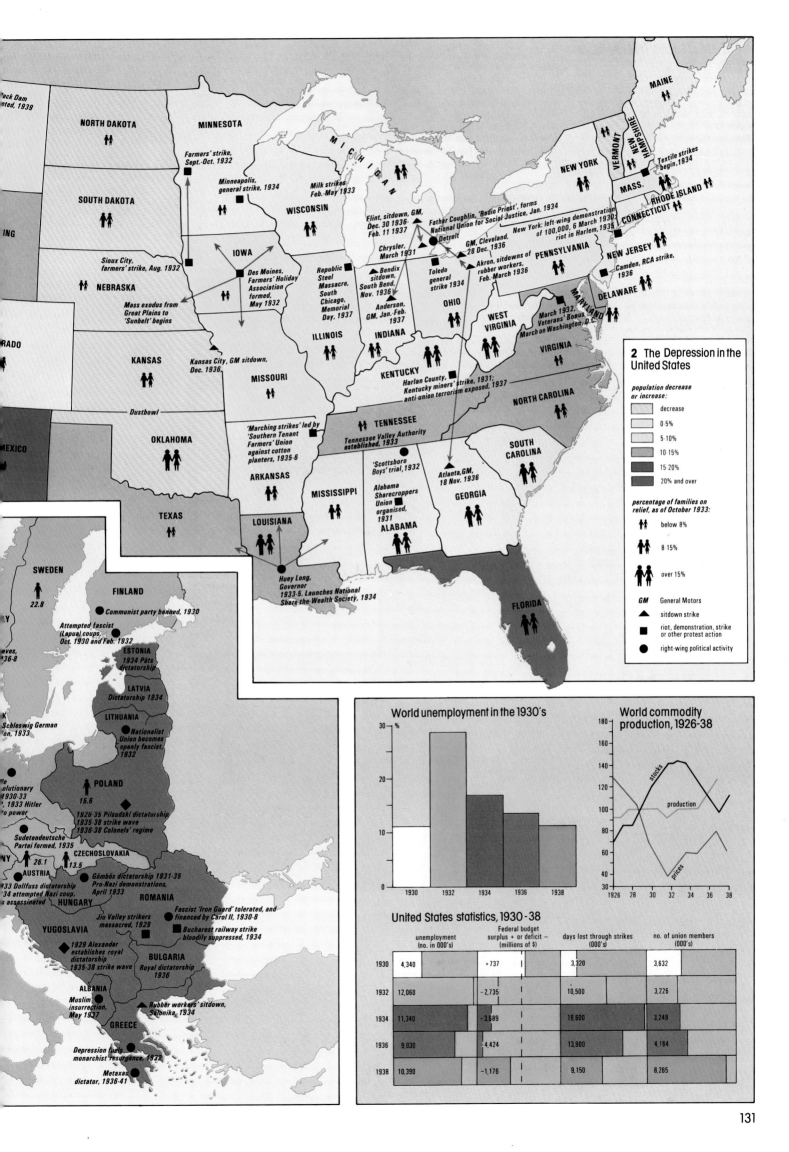

NORTH DAKOTA

MINNESOTA

MICHIGAN

MAINE

VERMONT
NEW HAMPSHIRE

NEW YORK

MASS.

RHODE ISLAND

CONNECTICUT

SOUTH DAKOTA

WISCONSIN

Peck Dam ...ted, 1939

Farmers' strike, Sept.-Oct. 1932

Minneapolis, general strike, 1934

Milk strikes Feb.-May 1933

Flint, sitdown, GM, Dec. 30 1936-Feb. 11 1937

Father Coughlin, 'Radio Priest', forms National Union for Social Justice, Jan. 1934

New York: left-wing demonstration of 100,000, 6 March 1930; riot in Harlem, 1935

Textile strikes begin, 1934

Chrysler, March 1931

GM, Cleveland, 28 Dec. 1936

Detroit

PENNSYLVANIA

NEW JERSEY

DELAWARE

ING

IOWA

Sioux City, farmers' strike, Aug. 1932

NEBRASKA

Des Moines, Farmers' Holiday Association formed, May 1932

Mass exodus from Great Plains to 'Sunbelt' begins

Republic Steel Massacre, South Chicago, Memorial Day, 1937

Bendix sitdown, South Bend, Nov. 1936

Toledo general strike 1934

Anderson, GM, Jan.-Feb. 1937

OHIO

Akron, sitdowns of rubber workers, Feb.-March 1936

WEST VIRGINIA

Camden, RCA strike, 1936

MARYLAND

March 1932, Veterans' Bonus March on Washington, D.C.

VIRGINIA

RADO

MEXICO

KANSAS

Kansas City, GM sitdown, Dec. 1936

MISSOURI

ILLINOIS

INDIANA

KENTUCKY

Harlan County, Kentucky miners' strike, 1931; anti-union terrorism exposed, 1937

NORTH CAROLINA

Dustbowl

OKLAHOMA

'Marching strikes' led by 'Southern Tenant Farmers' Union against cotton planters, 1935-6

TENNESSEE

Tennessee Valley Authority established, 1933

SOUTH CAROLINA

ARKANSAS

'Scottsboro Boys' trial, 1932

Atlanta, GM, 18 Nov. 1936

GEORGIA

TEXAS

MISSISSIPPI

Alabama Sharecroppers Union organised, 1931

ALABAMA

LOUISIANA

Huey Long, Governor 1933-5. Launches National Share-the-Wealth Society, 1934

FLORIDA

2 The Depression in the United States

population decrease or increase:

- decrease
- 0-5%
- 5-10%
- 10-15%
- 15-20%
- 20% and over

percentage of families on relief, as of October 1933:

below 8%

8-15%

over 15%

GM General Motors

▲ sitdown strike

■ riot, demonstration, strike or other protest action

● right-wing political activity

SWEDEN
22.8

FINLAND

Communist party banned, 1930

Attempted fascist (Lapua) coups, Oct. 1930 and Feb. 1932

ESTONIA
1934 Päts dictatorship

LATVIA
Dictatorship 1934

LITHUANIA

Nationalist Union becomes openly fascist, 1932

Schleswig German ...on, 1933

POLAND
15.6

1926-35 Pilsudski dictatorship 1935-38 strike wave 1936-38 Colonels' regime

...olutionary ...930-33 ..., 1933 Hitler ...o power

Sudetendeutsche Partei formed, 1935

CZECHOSLOVAKIA
26.1   13.5

...NY

AUSTRIA

...33 Dollfuss dictatorship ...34 attempted Nazi coup, ...s assassinated

HUNGARY

Gömbös dictatorship 1931-35 Pro-Nazi demonstrations, April 1933

ROMANIA

Fascist 'Iron Guard' tolerated, and financed by Carol II, 1930-8

YUGOSLAVIA

Jiu Valley strikers massacred, 1929

Bucharest railway strike bloodily suppressed, 1934

1929 Alexander establishes royal dictatorship 1935-38 strike wave

BULGARIA
Royal dictatorship 1936

ALBANIA
Muslim insurrection, May 1937

Rubber workers' sitdown, Salonika, 1934

GREECE

Depression fuels monarchist resurgence, 1932

Metaxas dictator, 1936-41

World unemployment in the 1930's

%

30

20

10

0

1930   1932   1934   1936   1938

World commodity production, 1926-38

180
160
140
120
100
80
60
40
30

1926 28 30 32 34 36 38

stocks

production

prices

United States statistics, 1930-38

	unemployment (no. in 000's)	Federal budget surplus + or deficit − (millions of $)	days lost through strikes (000's)	no. of union members (000's)
1930	4,340	+ 737	3,320	3,632
1932	12,060	− 2,735	10,500	3,226
1934	11,340	− 3,689	19,600	3,249
1936	9,030	− 4,424	13,900	4,164
1938	10,390	− 1,176	9,150	8,265

The War in the West
1939-1945

Hitler's accession to power in 1933 added a new dimension to international politics. He was held back at first by Germany's diplomatic isolation and by the need to put the shattered economy back on its feet. But by 1936 this phase was over. The re-occupation of the Rhineland, the denunciation of the Locarno treaties (page 128), the Rome-Berlin axis, and the anti-Comintern Pact with Japan, demonstrated the new thrust of German policy. Nevertheless Hitler hoped to get his way by threats and bluster rather than by war, and the unopposed annexation of Austria and the dismemberment of Czechoslovakia in 1938 seemed to prove him right. When in the following year he turned against Poland he expected that England and France would once again give way, and believed that the notorious Nazi-Soviet pact of August 23, 1939, would deter the Western powers from intervention. But this time Hitler miscalculated. When German

troops invaded Poland (September 1, 1939), England and France declared war, though they did nothing to aid the Poles.

For the first three years the German armies, with their *Blitzkrieg* strategy, were extraordinarily successful (map 1). After the fall of Poland Hitler halted, hoping that the Western powers would negotiate a compromise peace. Then, in April 1940, he launched his attack in the west, overran Denmark and Norway, and turned against France, which was knocked out of the war before the end of June. But the new Churchill government in London refused to concede defeat, and Hitler launched a major air offensive, intended to prepare the way for invasion. The victory of the Royal Air Force in the Battle of Britain forced him on September 17, 1940, to call off the projected invasion. Instead, Hitler decided to attack Soviet Russia. The directive for 'Operation Barbarossa' was issued in December 1940, the invasion of Russia launched on June 22, 1941. It nearly succeeded. Before the tide turned, German armies were outside Moscow and Leningrad and had overrun southern Russia to the

Black Sea and the Caucasus.

Meanwhile two other events intervened. One was the lack of success of Italy, which had entered the war in 1940, which forced Hitler, in 1941, to divert troops to conquer Yugoslavia and Greece and to reinforce the African front. Secondly the United States, entering the war in 1941 (page 134), supplied Britain and Russia with much needed arms and equipment, and also helped to defeat the German submarine campaign in the Atlantic (map 3). The British victory at El Alamein (October 1942), the subsequent capitulation of the Italian and German armies in Africa (May 1943), the Anglo-American invasion of Sicily and then Italy, and the fall of Mussolini (July 1943), were major Allied successes. But it was the great Russian victory at Stalingrad (January 1943) that was decisive. The Germans' last major offensive in the east at Kursk failed in July 1943. Thereafter they fought a stubborn defensive war (map 2), but after the Anglo-American landings in northern France (June 1944) and the opening of the Second Front, the ring was closed,

and the bases were lost for the 'secre[t] weapons' which Hitler hoped would forc[e] the British to capitulate. The Ardenne[s] offensive (December 1944) was a fina[l] attempt to break out in the west; but b[y] now the Allies held the initiative. [A] major Soviet offensive against Eas[t] Prussia opened in January 1945, and b[y] April Berlin was under assault. On Apr[il] 30 Hitler committed suicide, and o[n] May 7 his successor, Admiral Doenit[z,] surrendered unconditionally. The cos[ts] were appalling: 15 million military an[d] 35 million civilians had perished, 2[0] million of whom were Soviet citizen[s.] Some 6 million Jews were exterminate[d] in concentration camps or otherwise[;] Anglo-American saturation bombing re[-] duced many German cities to rubble, an[d] 25 million Russians were left homeles[s.] Europe was in ruins, and already the di[f]-ferences between the victorious power[s,] which were to darken the post-war year[s] (page 136), were visible.

1 The German advance, 1939-43

- Axis territory 1 September 1939
- Axis satellites
- Axis occupied
- German advances 1939-41
- Italian advances
- Axis attack on USSR 1941
- Axis advances in USSR 1942
- Allied forces
- airborne landings
- Allied withdrawals
- cities severely damaged by bombing
- Soviet occupied territory 1939-40
- British Empire
- neutral powers

principal German concentration and extermination camps: ●

1 Auschwitz-Birkenau	7 Flossenbürg	14 Ravensbrück
2 Belzec	8 Gross Rosen	15 Sachsenhausen
3 Bergen-Belsen	9 Majdanek	16 Sobibor
4 Buchenwald	10 Mauthausen	17 Stutthof
5 Chelmno	11 Mittelbau	18 Theresienstadt
6 Dachau	12 Natzweiler	19 Treblinka
	13 Neuengamme	

The War in Asia and the Pacific, 1941-1945

In 1941 the war in the Far East, which had begun in 1937 (page 126), merged with the war in Europe, and the Second World War began. This had been foreseen as early as 1936 by the Chinese Communist leader, Mao Tse-tung, when he warned the West that Japanese policy was directed not only against China but also against all countries with interests in the Pacific. But England and France, preoccupied with the threat from Nazi Germany, had few forces to spare for the Far East, and in the United States isolationism was still powerful. The decisive turning point came with the German victory in Europe in May, 1940, which placed the French, British and Dutch colonies at the mercy of Japan. A Tripartite Pact with Germany and Italy (1940) and a Neutrality Pact with the Soviet Union (1941) prepared the way for a Japanese advance south. The only question was whether the United States could be neutralised. When this proved impossible, the surprise attack on Pearl Harbor was prepared. It took place on December 7, 1941, bringing the United States into the war.

Pearl Harbor temporarily crippled the American Pacific Fleet, and the Japanese advanced in three major directions: against the Philippines and the Dutch East Indies to secure essential war materials, against continental Asia (Malaya, Burma, India), and into Oceania (Guam, New Guinea, the Bismarck Archipelago and the Solomon Islands) to protect the central thrust. Japan's successes were spectacular (map 1). Singapore, the British base, fell on February 15, 1942, and Burma was overrun in March and April (map 2). The Dutch capitulated in March and the U.S. base at Corregidor on May 6. Within six months Japan had made itself master of virtually the whole of South-East Asia. But by the autumn of 1942 the United States had recovered. On August 7, 1942, American forces under General Mac-Arthur landed at Guadalcanal (Solomon Islands), and the attack on the Japanese perimeter began. It was an arduous slogging match, leapfrogging from island to island, and it was not until April 1944 that the Japanese abandoned their southern base at Rabaul. More decisive were the great naval battles which cut Japanese supply lines and prevented reinforcement, as well as winning new forward bases for American ground and air forces. The battle of the Coral Sea (May 1942) was indecisive, though it halted the Japanese advance; but the American victories at Midway (June 1942) and Leyte Gulf (October 1944) eliminated the Japanese navy as an effective fighting force. They also enabled the United States to re-occupy the Gilbert and Marshall Islands, Saipan and Guam, and to begin the reconquest of the Philippines (October 1944–February 1945).

By the middle of 1944 it was evident that Japan had

lost the war. In May 1944 British and Indian troops, advancing from Imphal, began the reconquest of Burma (map 2), and American aircraft based in China began attacks on the Japanese mainland. After the American occupation of Iwo Jima (February 1945) and of Okinawa (April–May 1945) the air offensive was stepped up (map 3). Three-quarters of Tokyo and many other industrial cities were destroyed, but the Japanese fighting spirit remained unbroken. It was in these circumstances that President Truman, who had succeeded President Roose-velt, decided to use the atom-bomb. On August 6, 1945, the first atom-bomb was dropped on Hiroshima, a second three days later on Nagasaki. Simultaneously Russia declared war on Japan. The next day an Imperial Conference declared for peace, and on September 2 Japan capitulated. Nevertheless the consequences of the Pacific War were epoch-making. By exposing the fragility of the colonial regimes, Japan gave new impetus to the anti-imperial revolt of Asia, which would be a dominant feature of the post-war world.

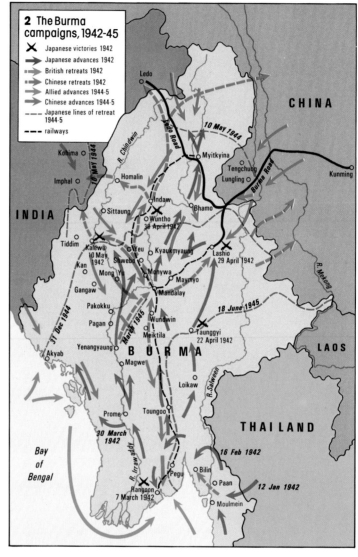

2 The Burma campaigns, 1942-45

✕ Japanese victories 1942
→ Japanese advances 1942
⇢ British retreats 1942
⇢ Chinese retreats 1942
→ Allied advances 1944-5
→ Chinese advances 1944-5
- - Japanese lines of retreat 1944-5
– – railways

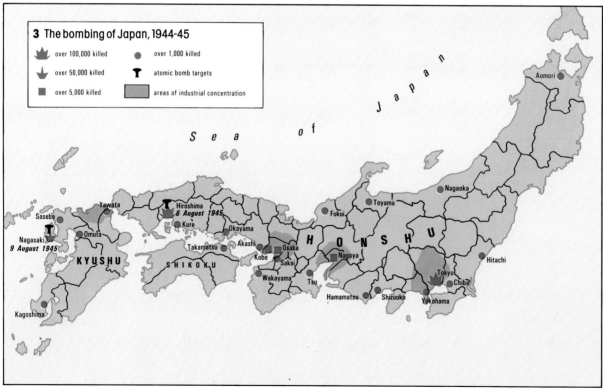

3 The bombing of Japan, 1944-45

- over 100,000 killed
- over 50,000 killed
- over 5,000 killed
- over 1,000 killed
- atomic bomb targets
- areas of industrial concentration

1 The Japanese advance, and the Allied counter-offensive, 1941-45

↘ Japanese advance or strike
↘ Allied advance
✈ Allied air attack
● Japanese base
■ Allied base
◉ Japanese base bypassed or neutralised
✳ atomic bomb target

SOVIET UNION

Chita

9 Aug 1945 Soviet Army attacks

Sea of Okhotsk

Kamchatka

Bering Sea

60°

Commander Is

Aleutian Is

Adak I

Attu I Kiska I Amchitka I

Dutch Harbor

Khabarovsk

Sakhalin

MANCHURIA (MANCHUKUO)

INNER MONGOLIA

Mukden

Peking

Japanese perimeter Nov 1941

Kaifeng

Tientsin

Dairen

Gensan

Keijo

KARA FUTO

Hokkaido

Kurile Is

Japanese perimeter Aug 1945

Japanese perimeter March 1944

Japanese perimeter July 1942

planned Japanese perimeter

40°

KOREA

Fusan

Sea of Japan

JAPAN

Japanese perimeter 1868 and Sept 1945

Honshu

Tokyo

Tsingtao

Nanking

Hiroshima

Shikoku

Nagasaki

Kyushu

Shanghai

East China Sea

Japanese perimeter Oct 1944

Japanese perimeter July 1937

Midway

3/5 June 1942 Japanese forces repulsed

Amoy

Okinawa

17 May-14 Aug 1945 direct air attack on Japan from Okinawa

Bonin Is

Iwo Jima

Volcano Is

Oahu

Hawaiian Is

20°

Pearl Harbor

7 Dec 1941 U.S. Fleet sunk by Japanese air attack on Pearl Harbor

Formosa

Hong Kong

1941

24 Nov 1944-14 Aug 1945 20th Air Force maintains direct air attack on Japan

Wake I

South China Sea

7 Dec 1941 Japanese attack Philippines

Luzon

Philippine Is

Manila

25 Oct 1944 heavy Japanese naval losses

Marianas

Saipan

Tinian

Mindoro

20 Oct 1944 Leyte landing

Guam

May 1942 regidor renders

Caroline Is

Eniwetok

Marshall Is

Pacific Ocean Area Forces

Sulu Sea

Mindanao

Zamboanga

Kwajalein

Majuro

Makin I

Gilbert Is

Christmas I

runei Tarakan

Palau

Pacific   Ocean

Truk

Tarawa

Abemama

0°

Balikpapan

Morotai

Manado

Halmahera

Celebes

Sorong

Schouten Is

Manus I

Admiralty Is

Bismarck Arch

New Ireland

Green Is

Ellice Is

masin

Ceram

Hollandia

Wewak

Rabaul

Amboina

New Guinea

New Britain

Bougainville

7 Aug 1942-9 Feb 1943 Guadalcanal Japanese repulsed

Makassar

Banda Sea

Aroe Is

New Guinea

Solomon Is

Russell Is

25/26 Oct 1942 Japanese forces repulsed

D I E S

Flores

Tanimbar Is

Port Moresby

Buna

Tulagi

Santa Cruz Is

Lombok

Soemba

Timor

17-25 Sept 1942 Japanese ground forces repulsed

4/8 May 1942 Battle of the Coral Sea, Japanese forces repulsed

South Pacific Area Forces

Espiritu Santo

Fiji Is

Cape York

26 Aug 1942 Battle of Milne Bay, Japanese repulsed

South West Pacific Area Forces

New Hebrides

9 Feb 1942 U.S. forces land

Timor Sea

Darwin

Coral Sea

New Caledonia

12 March 1942 U.S. forces land

A U S T R A L I A

130°

170°

40°

Sydney

Melbourne

Europe after 1945

Europe emerged from the war of 1939–45 devastated and politically divided. Major territorial changes in the east, where Soviet frontiers were advanced approximately to the former Tsarist boundary and Poland was compensated with German territory up to the Oder-Neisse line, were accompanied by a vast movement of displaced persons, including over 12 million Germans (map 1). Germany and Austria were divided into occupation zones and placed under four-power control. But growing Soviet-American conflict after the abortive Potsdam conference (July–August 1945) undermined four-power cooperation, and the consolidation of the Soviet hold in eastern Europe (map 4) accelerated the division of the continent into two armed camps, completed by the establishment of the North Atlantic Treaty Organisation (1949) and the Warsaw Pact Organisation (1955) (map 3). In 1949 the three western zones of Germany became the German Federal Republic, while Moscow established the German Democratic Republic in the east. Both were reorganised into new modern administrative systems (map 5).

Economic recovery in the West was stimulated by American aid under the Marshall Plan (1947), and after 1950 western Europe experienced an unprecedented economic boom (diagram 2). Simultaneously, the process of economic integration was initiated which led in 1957 to the creation of the European Economic Community (EEC), though at first Great Britain remained outside, founding a rival organisation, EFTA (European Free Trade Association), and only joining the EEC with Denmark and Ireland in 1973 (map 3). In eastern Europe, Soviet reparations drained the economy and recovery scarcely began until after the death of Stalin in 1953. Harsh conditions led to widespread strikes and demonstrations in eastern Germany in 1953 (map 5) and to national uprisings in Poland and Hungary in 1956, the latter, like the experiment in national communism in Czechoslovakia in 1968, brutally suppressed

by Soviet troops. Nevertheless, after 1957 there was considerable economic progress. East Germany and Romania forged ahead. Elsewhere, progress was sluggish and uneven, notably in Poland where the formation, in 1979, of an active trade union movement, Solidarity, resulted in the imposition of martial law by 1981.

Politically, by 1970 Europe had settled on its new course. Austria had recovered sovereignty in 1955. The German question still remained. The decision of the new West German chancellor, Brandt, reversing earlier policies, to recognise the post-war Polish western frontier (1970) and the separate existence of two German states (1972) stabilised the situation. Confirmed in 1975 at the European Security Conference at Helsinki, it removed old tensions and inaugurated a period of détente and peaceful co-existence. Trade between eastern and western Europe increased rapidly. Much of this was financed by Western loans. There was much discussion of economic reform, with Hungary leading the way. In Western Europe there was an upsurge of prosperity following the formation of the EEC, although member

states remained divided over exchange rates, the Common Agricultural Policy and hidden protectionism. Between 1958 and 1962 trade between member states increased by 130 per cent, and in seven years Italian industrial production rose by 107 per cent. But the benefits were uneven and accrued mainly to the core countries. Spain, Portugal and other countries on the periphery remained backward, and elsewhere there were regional pockets of persistent depression. Northern Ireland, prosperous in the immediate post-war years, suffered a sharp setback after 1970, and economic distress coupled with longstanding religious and racial grievances, fanned by a series of bloody incidents in 1972, gave rise to a situation bordering on civil war (map 6). In Spain, Basques and Catalans obtained only a measure of autonomy. Left-wing terrorism, with the Red Brigade in Italy, the Red Army Faction in West Germany and others, brought bomb outrages to Western capitals. In the early 1980s, as recession and competition hit the older industries, there was much industrial turmoil and unemployment everywhere was high.

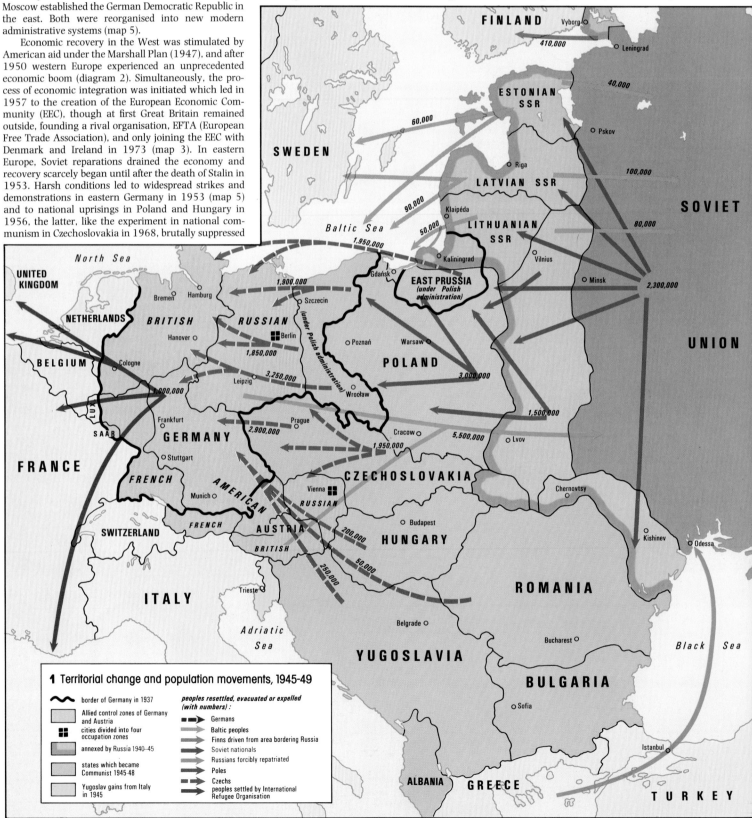

1 Territorial change and population movements, 1945-49

- 〰 border of Germany in 1937
- ▢ Allied control zones of Germany and Austria
- ▣ cities divided into four occupation zones
- ▨ annexed by Russia 1940–45
- ▢ states which became Communist 1945-48
- ▢ Yugoslav gains from Italy in 1945

peoples resettled, evacuated or expelled (with numbers):
- ▰▶ Germans
- → Baltic peoples
- → Finns driven from area bordering Russia
- → Soviet nationals
- → Russians forcibly repatriated
- → Poles
- ▰▰▶ Czechs
- → peoples settled by International Refugee Organisation

136

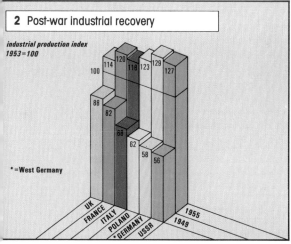

2 Post-war industrial recovery

industrial production index
1953=100

100 | 114 | 120 | 118 | 123 | 129 | 127
88 | 82 | 68 | 62 | 58 | 56

1955
1949

* = West Germany

UK
FRANCE
ITALY
POLAND
*GERMANY
USSR

ICELAND
EFTA 1970

UNITED STATES
AND CANADA

Atlantic

Ocean

North
Sea

SWEDEN

NORWAY

FINLAND
associate member
of EFTA 1961

DENMARK

SOVIET UNION

IRISH
REP.
EEC 1973

UK

NETHERLANDS

BELG.

LUX.

WEST
GERMANY

EAST
GERMANY

POLAND

GERMANY

CZECHOSLOVAKIA

FRANCE

SWITZ.

AUSTRIA

HUNGARY

ROMANIA

ITALY

YUGOSLAVIA
limited involvement
in COMECON
from 1964

BULGARIA

PORTUGAL
joined
EEC 1986

SPAIN
joined NATO 1982
joined EEC 1986

Corsica

Sardinia

Mediterranean Sea

Sicily

ALBANIA

GREECE
(joined EEC 1981)

withdrew from
Warsaw Pact, 1968

TURKEY

3 Military and economic blocs, 1980

military partition :

● NATO 1949-55

● Warsaw Pact Organisation

economic blocs :

original members of EEC

subsequent members of EEC

Benelux Customs Union 1947 (and EEC)

Council for Mutual Economic Assistance (Comecon) 1949

subsequent members of Comecon

members of European Free Trade Association (EFTA) 1960

Denmark and UK leave EFTA Dec. 1972, join EEC Jan. 1973

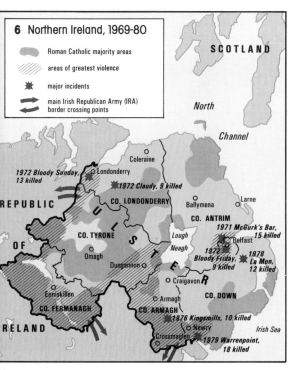

6 Northern Ireland, 1969-80

Roman Catholic majority areas

areas of greatest violence

major incidents

main Irish Republican Army (IRA)
border crossing points

SCOTLAND

North

Channel

Coleraine

Londonderry
1972 Bloody Sunday,
13 killed

1972 Claudy, 9 killed

CO. LONDONDERRY

Ballymena

Larne

CO. ANTRIM

REPUBLIC

CO. TYRONE

Lough
Neagh

1971 McGurk's Bar,
15 killed

Belfast

1972
Bloody Friday,
9 killed

1978
La Mon,
12 killed

OF

Omagh

Dungannon

Craigavon

CO. DOWN

Enniskillen

Armagh

CO. ARMAGH

IRELAND

CO. FERMANAGH

1976 Kingsmills, 10 killed

Newry

Crossmaglen

1979 Warrenpoint,
18 killed

Irish Sea

4 The Soviet Union and Eastern Europe, 1945-49

Soviet territorial gains
since 1939

Warsaw Pact allies

Polish gains from Germany

air corridors for Western
access to Berlin

Western autobahn to Berlin

ESTONIA

LATVIA

LITHUANIA

Kaliningrad

EAST
PRUSSIA

USSR

Berlin

EAST
GERMANY

POLAND
opposition parties
dissolved Nov. 1947

formation of Socialist Unity Party, April 1946
German Democratic Republic established Oct. 1949
Berlin blockade June 1948–May 1949

Prague

Communist coup in Prague
Feb. 1948

CZECHOSLOVAKIA

NORTHERN
BUKOVINA

Vienna

RUTHENIA

BESSARABIA

AUSTRIA

Budapest

HUNGARY
opposition parties dissolved
Nov. 1947

ROMANIA
king abdicated Dec. 1947

Belgrade

YUGOSLAVIA

Tito breaks
with
Moscow,
June 1948

Bucharest

BULGARIA
Dimitrov takes over as
prime minister,
Nov. 1946

ALBANIA

GREECE
civil war 1946
communists suppressed, 1949

5 Post-War Germany

border of Germany in 1937

border of German Democratic Republic 1949

borders of German post-war administrative regions

● administrative capital

🔥 centres of the June Uprising 1953

DENMARK

North Sea

Baltic Sea

Königsberg
to Russia 1945

SCHLESWIG-
HOLSTEIN

Rügen

Danzig
to Poland
1945

E. PRUSSIA
to Poland 1945

BREMEN AND
BREMERHAVEN
(joint city state)

HAMBURG
(city state)

Kiel

MECKLENBURG

GERMAN

Schwerin

R. Elbe

POMERANIA

Stettin

R. Oder

AND

SILESIA

Bremen

LOWER SAXONY

DEMOCRATIC

NETHERLANDS

GERMAN

Hanover

REPUBLIC

BRANDENBURG

Berlin (E. Berlin capital
of Democratic Republic,
W. Berlin separate state of
Federal Republic, 1951)

POLAND

FEDERAL

R. Rhine

NORTH

Düsseldorf

RHINE-WESTPHALIA

REPUBLIC

SAXONY-
ANHALT

Potsdam

Halle

HESSE

Bonn (capital of
Federal Republic,
1949)

Leipzig

Dresden

to Poland 1945

R. Neisse

Coblenz
(temporary
capital)

Wiesbaden

Weimar

SAXONY

THURINGIA

LUX.

Mainz

Frankfurt am Main

RHINELAND
PALATINATE

CZECHOSLOVAKIA

SAARLAND
French occupied;
to Germany 1957

WÜRTTEMBERG
BADEN (1945-52)

BADEN
Stuttgart

BAVARIA

WÜRTTEMBERG
(3 Länder united,
1952)

FRANCE

BADEN
(1945-52)

WÜRTTEMBERG
HOHENZOLLERN
(1945-52)

Munich

SWITZERLAND

AUSTRIA

137

Retreat from empire after 1947

The European empires of the nineteenth century (page 100) were still intact in 1939, though most German and Ottoman possessions had passed as 'mandates' to Great Britain and France. What was remarkable was the speed of their collapse. In Asia weaknesses were exposed by Japanese victories in 1941. In Africa, the Suez War of 1956 signalled a nationalist upsurge, which gathered momentum after the Gold Coast (Ghana) became independent in 1957.

None of the European powers surrendered its colonies voluntarily. After the Japanese defeat, France fought stubbornly to restore control in Indo-China, and the Netherlands struggled to contain the nationalists in Java, who had proclaimed an Indonesian republic in 1945. Neither was successful. Vietnamese victory at Dien Bien Phu (1954) forced France to give way (page 148). In Indonesia the nationalists advanced step by step into Kalimantan, Celebes and the Moluccas, until by 1956 they controlled the whole of the former Dutch East Indies except West Irian, which they annexed in

1963 (map 2). The British, also, had no intention of abdicating their imperial position, but continual unrest forced their hand and in 1947 India and Pakistan became independent (page 104), followed by Burma and Ceylon. Nevertheless Britain still clung to its base at Singapore, fought a long war against Malayan insurgents and resisted Indonesian attempts to annex Sarawak and Brunei. Only after 1967, when Aden was evacuated, did Britain abandon its presence east of Suez, except in Hong Kong, to be retained until 1997, its economic success being of great benefit to China.

Resistance to independence was strongest in colonies with a white settler population, or where there was substantial European investment. This was the situation in the Belgian Congo (Zaire) where, within days of independence, the province of Katanga, with its rich copper and uranium resources, seceded, resulting in prolonged civil war, only halted in 1965 when a government favourable to Western mining interests was set up (map 4). In Algeria, with a white population of one million, the bloodiest war of liberation was fought between 1954 and 1962, first in the countryside and then in the cities (map 3). But

conflict was scarcely less bitter in Rhodesia, Kenya and the Portuguese colonies of Angola, Mozambique and Guinea-Bissau. The British attempted to save the situation in the Rhodesias and Nyasaland by creating a Central African Federation (1953); but when Zambia and Malawi rejected this compromise (1964), Southern Rhodesia declared unilateral independence (1965) in order to ensure white predominance. But the collapse of the Portuguese empire in 1974 forced the Rhodesian government, now surrounded by black states, to begin negotiations with the black leadership in Rhodesia. In 1980 Rhodesia, now renamed Zimbabwe, became an independent black republic.

By now the formal structures of European imperialism had been dismantled (map 1). After 1960, except where special interests were involved, direct rule was seen as a liability and by 1980, apart from a few small islands, only South Africa and Namibia remained as bastions of white rule. But political emancipation did not remove economic dependence. As the Ghanaian leader, Kwame Nkrumah, said in 1965, colonisation had only been replaced by 'neo-colonialism', and it was debt, particularly in black Africa, which became a great problem.

3 The Algerian Civil War 1954-62

☐ French administrative and military territories

〰 French defensive frontier lines

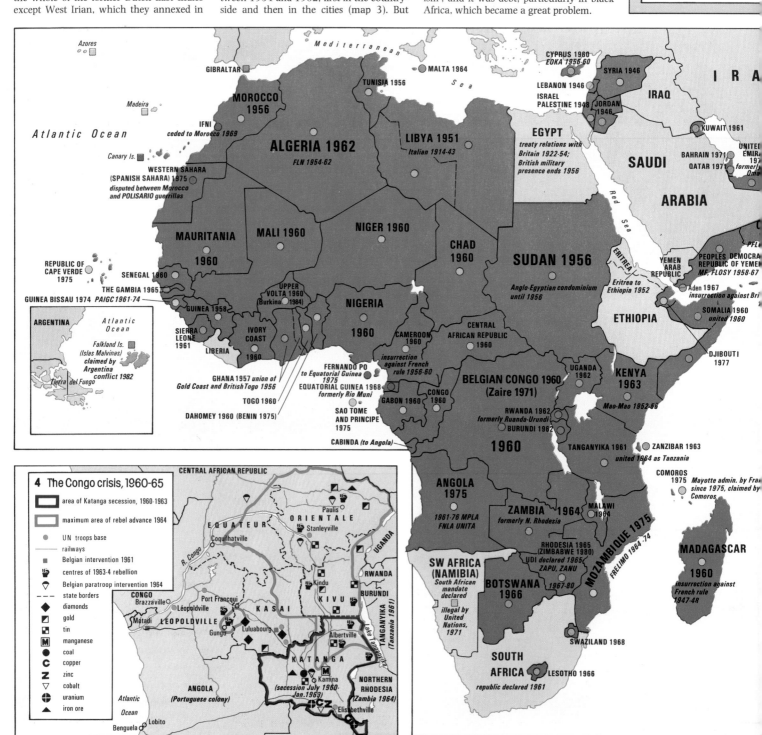

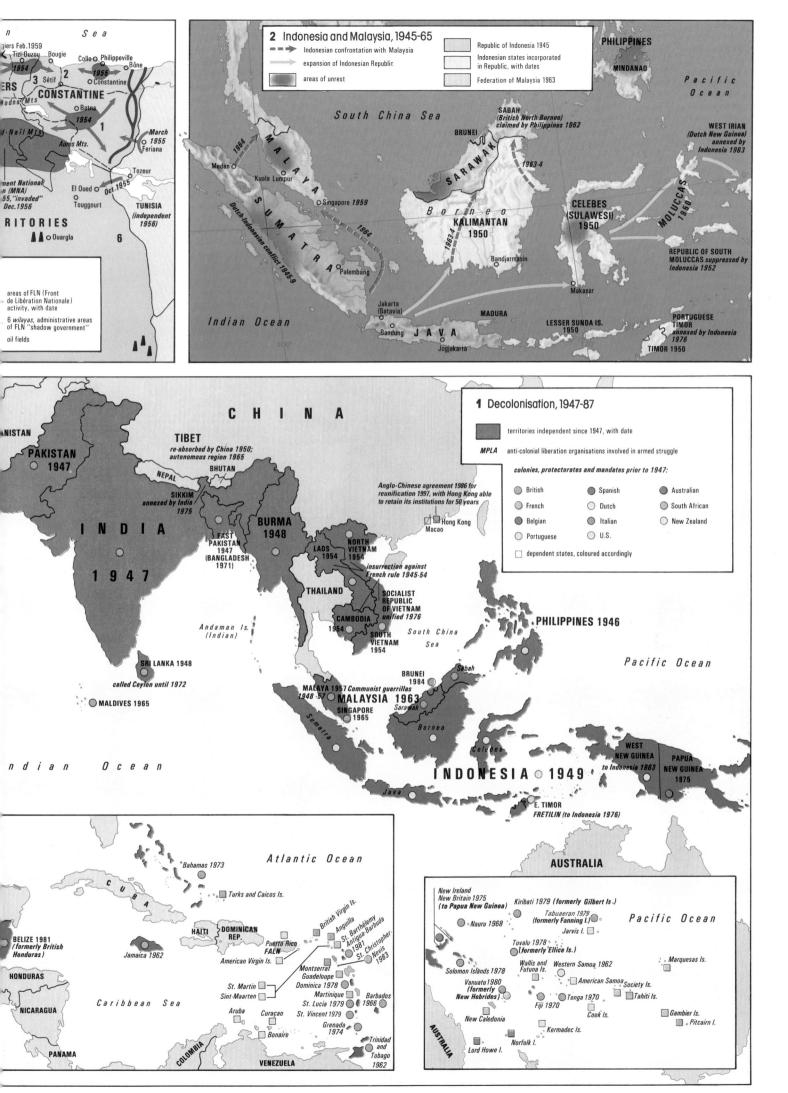

Asia and Africa after independence

The history of Asia and Africa since independence is one of chronic instability. Three factors stand out: first, the seizure of power by military leaders (Egypt 1952, Pakistan 1958, Ghana 1966, Indonesia 1967), with the aim (rarely successful) of abolishing corruption and stabilising the economy; second, the resurgence of long-standing regional, tribal and religious conflicts (Naga unrest in India, Kurdish revolts in northern Iraq, Turkey and Iran, nationalist uprisings among the Kachins, Mons, Shans and other 'hill peoples' in Thailand and Burma); finally persistent intervention by the great powers, particularly in the Middle East. Sino-Soviet rivalry lay behind the Vietnamese invasion of Cambodia and the Chinese invasion of Vietnam (1979). In Africa the United States and the Soviet Union inter-

vened in the Somali-Ethiopian war (1976–78), and France sent troops to Chad, and, with other Western powers, helped to quell the insurrection in Zaire in 1978. The attempted secession of Biafra (map 2), essentially a revolt of the Ibo people in eastern Nigeria against northern domination, was defeated by the federal government, with broad international backing. On the other hand, the secession of Bangladesh from Pakistan (1971) was successful, though only achieved with massive Indian military support.

Two countries alone were exceptions from the general pattern. Japan's progress, after the recovery of independence in 1951, was phenomenal. Maintaining close relations with the United States, successive governments concentrated on industrial development and new technology until in the 1970s Japan emerged as the world's third industrial nation (diagram 4). The case of China is more equivocal. Reconstruction after the Revolution (page 122) proceeded apace; but the

'Great Leap Forward' (1958–60) and the 'Cultural Revolution' (1966–68) brought not only political strife but also severe economic disruption and widespread massacre. After the death of Mao Tsetung (1976) stability returned and there was wide-ranging economic reform, particularly in agriculture. China also became an industrial power, and the inequalities of the period before 1949 were largely eliminated. Elsewhere, per-

sistent poverty and gross disparities of income fomented discontent. A few countries (South Korea, Taiwan, Singapore) made considerable economic progress despite recession in the later 1970s, and the countries of the 'Pacific rim' took a high share of trade in new technology. Elsewhere, even in the oil-rich nations, poverty was endemic. Average income in Nigeria in 1975 was under $500; in Iran, at the time of the revolution against the

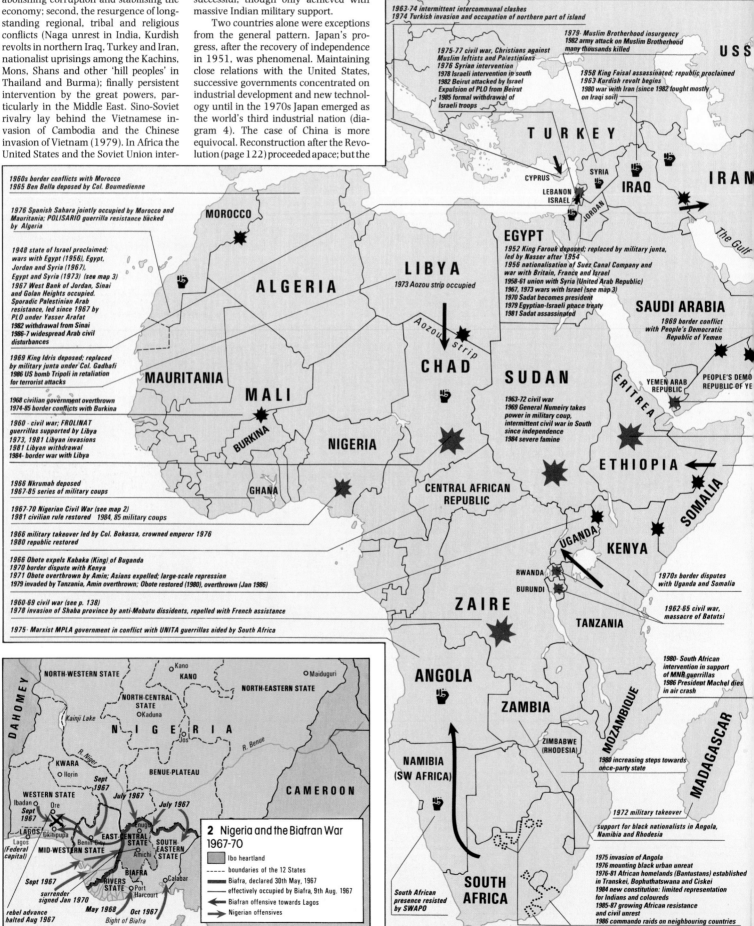

1963-74 intermittent intercommunal clashes
1974 Turkish invasion and occupation of northern part of island

1975-77 civil war, Christians against Muslim leftists and Palestinians
1976 Syrian intervention
1978 Israeli intervention in south
1982 Beirut attacked by Israel
Expulsion of PLO from Beirut
1985 formal withdrawal of Israeli troops

1979- Muslim Brotherhood insurgency
1982 army attack on Muslim Brotherhood many thousands killed

1958 King Faisal assassinated; republic proclaimed
1963 Kurdish revolt begins
1980 war with Iran (since 1982 fought mostly on Iraqi soil)

USSR

TURKEY

CYPRUS

SYRIA

LEBANON
ISRAEL

JORDAN

IRAQ

IRAN

The Gulf

1960s border conflicts with Morocco
1965 Ben Bella deposed by Col. Boumedienne

1976 Spanish Sahara jointly occupied by Morocco and Mauritania; POLISARIO guerrilla resistance backed by Algeria

MOROCCO

1948 state of Israel proclaimed; wars with Egypt (1956), Egypt, Jordan and Syria (1967), Egypt and Syria (1973) (see map 3)
1967 West Bank of Jordan, Sinai and Golan Heights occupied. Sporadic Palestinian Arab resistance, led since 1967 by PLO under Yasser Arafat
1982 withdrawal from Sinai
1986-7 widespread Arab civil disturbances

ALGERIA

LIBYA

1973 Aozou strip occupied

EGYPT

1952 King Farouk deposed; replaced by military junta, led by Nasser after 1954
1956 nationalisation of Suez Canal Company and war with Britain, France and Israel
1958-61 union with Syria (United Arab Republic)
1967, 1973 wars with Israel (see map 3)
1970 Sadat becomes president
1979 Egyptian-Israeli peace treaty
1981 Sadat assassinated

SAUDI ARABIA

1969 border conflict with People's Democratic Republic of Yemen

1969 King Idris deposed; replaced by military junta under Col. Gadhafi
1986 US bomb Tripoli in retaliation for terrorist attacks

MAURITANIA

MALI

Aozou strip

CHAD

SUDAN

ERITREA

YEMEN ARAB REPUBLIC

PEOPLE'S DEMO REPUBLIC OF YE

1968 civilian government overthrown
1974-85 border conflicts with Burkina

1960 - civil war; FROLINAT guerrillas supported by Libya
1973, 1981 Libyan invasions
1981 Libyan withdrawal
1984- border war with Libya

BURKINA

NIGERIA

1963-72 civil war
1969 General Numeiry takes power in military coup, intermittent civil war in South since independence
1984 severe famine

ETHIOPIA

1966 Nkrumah deposed
1967-85 series of military coups

GHANA

SOMALIA

1967-70 Nigerian Civil War (see map 2)
1981 civilian rule restored 1984, 85 military coups

CENTRAL AFRICAN REPUBLIC

1966 military takeover led by Col. Bokassa, crowned emperor 1976
1980 republic restored

UGANDA

KENYA

1970s border disputes with Uganda and Somalia

1966 Obote expels Kabaka (King) of Buganda
1970 border dispute with Kenya
1971 Obote overthrown by Amin; Asians expelled; large-scale repression
1979 invaded by Tanzania, Amin overthrown; Obote restored (1980), overthrown (Jan 1986)

RWANDA

BURUNDI

1962-65 civil war, massacre of Batutsi

1960-69 civil war (see p. 138)
1978 invasion of Shaba province by anti-Mobutu dissidents, repelled with French assistance

ZAIRE

TANZANIA

1975- Marxist MPLA government in conflict with UNITA guerrillas aided by South Africa

ANGOLA

1980- South African intervention in support of MNR guerrillas
1986 President Machel dies in air crash

ZAMBIA

MOZAMBIQUE

MADAGASCAR

NAMIBIA (SW AFRICA)

ZIMBABWE (RHODESIA)

1980 increasing steps towards once-party state

1972 military takeover

support for black nationalists in Angola, Namibia and Rhodesia

South African presence resisted by SWAPO

SOUTH AFRICA

1975 invasion of Angola
1976 mounting black urban unrest
1976-81 African homelands (Bantustans) established in Transkei, Bophuthatswana and Ciskei
1984 new constitution: limited representation for Indians and coloureds
1985-87 growing African resistance and civil unrest
1986 commando raids on neighbouring countries

Map 2 — Nigeria and the Biafran War

DAHOMEY

NORTH-WESTERN STATE

Kano
KANO

Maiduguri

NORTH-EASTERN STATE

NORTH-CENTRAL STATE
Kaduna

Kainji Lake

N I G E R I A

R. Niger

Jos

R. Benue

KWARA
Ilorin

BENUE-PLATEAU

WESTERN STATE
Ibadan
Ore
Sept 1967

Sept 1967
July 1967

July 1967

CAMEROON

LAGOS
Lagos (Federal capital)
Okitipupa

Benin City
EAST-CENTRAL STATE
Enugu

SOUTH-EASTERN STATE

MID-WESTERN STATE
Sept 1967

Amichi

BIAFRA

RIVERS STATE

Calabar

surrender signed Jan 1970

Port Harcourt

rebel advance halted Aug 1967

May 1968

Oct 1967

Bight of Biafra

2 Nigeria and the Biafran War 1967-70
- Ibo heartland
- - - - boundaries of the 12 States
- Biafra, declared 30th May, 1967
- effectively occupied by Biafra, 9th Aug. 1967
- Biafran offensive towards Lagos
- Nigerian offensives

Shah in 1978, it was under $2500.

Faced by the threat of internal disruption, governments everywhere looked to the great powers for support. Inevitably they were drawn into great power politics. Iran, where the United States covertly helped the Shah's supporters to oust the nationalist Mossadeq in 1953, was one bastion of American influence in the Middle East until 1979 when Ayatollah Khomeini introduced revolutionary Islamic fundamentalism and a long war with Iraq ensued. The Jewish state of Israel, at war with its Arab neighbours ever since its foundation in 1948 (map 3) received US support. The Soviet Union supported Syria and Egypt until the latter, after the Egyptian-Israeli war of 1973, turned to the United States for financial backing. This diplomatic revolution inaugurated a new phase. At Camp David (1978) Egypt and Israel came to terms and in March 1979 a peace treaty was signed, according to which Israel agreed to evacuate Sinai and give 'full autonomy' to the West Bank and Gaza. But Israel still refused to recognise the Palestine Liberation Organisation, which itself refused to recognise Israel. Here, as elsewhere in the under-developed world, the situation by the mid-1980s remained explosive, with potentially dangerous consequences for the peace of the world.

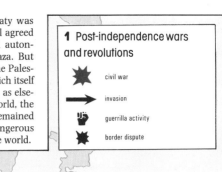

1 Post-independence wars and revolutions

- civil war
- invasion
- guerrilla activity
- border dispute

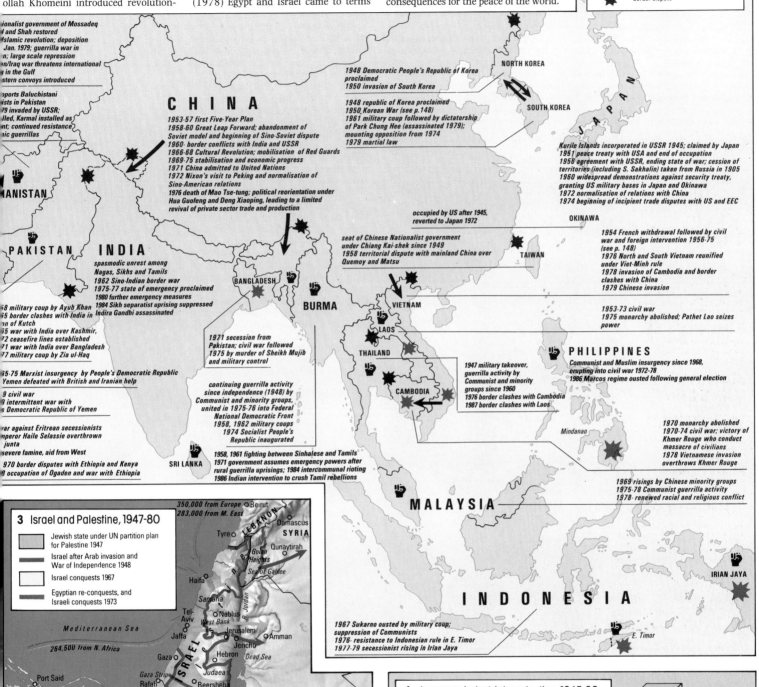

Left margin entries:
[...]ionalist government of Mossadeq [...]and Shah restored
[...]Islamic revolution; deposition [...] Jan. 1979; guerrilla war in [...]n; large scale repression [...]n/Iraq war threatens international [...] in the Gulf [...]stern convoys introduced

[...]pports Baluchistani [...]ists in Pakistan
[...]79 invaded by USSR; [...]lled, Karmal installed as [...]nt; continued resistance [...]ic guerrillas

[...]8 military coup by Ayub Khan
[...]5 border clashes with India in [...]n of Kutch
[...]5 war with India over Kashmir,
[...]2 ceasefire lines established
[...]1 war with India over Bangladesh
[...]7 military coup by Zia ul-Haq

[...]5-75 Marxist insurgency by People's Democratic Republic [...]Yemen defeated with British and Iranian help

[...]9 civil war
[...]9 intermittent war with [...] Democratic Republic of Yemen

[...]war against Eritrean secessionists
[...]mperor Haile Selassie overthrown [...] junta
[...]severe famine, aid from West

[...]970 border disputes with Ethiopia and Kenya
[...]8 occupation of Ogaden and war with Ethiopia

CHINA
1953-57 first Five-Year Plan
1958-60 Great Leap Forward; abandonment of Soviet model and beginning of Sino-Soviet dispute
1960- border conflicts with India and USSR
1966-68 Cultural Revolution; mobilisation of Red Guards
1969-75 stabilisation and economic progress
1971 China admitted to United Nations
1972 Nixon's visit to Peking and normalisation of Sino-American relations
1976 death of Mao Tse-tung; political reorientation under Hua Guofeng and Deng Xiaoping, leading to a limited revival of private sector trade and production

NORTH KOREA
1948 Democratic People's Republic of Korea proclaimed
1950 invasion of South Korea

SOUTH KOREA
1948 republic of Korea proclaimed
1950 Korean War (see p.148)
1961 military coup followed by dictatorship of Park Chung Hee (assassinated 1979); mounting opposition from 1974
1979 martial law

JAPAN / OKINAWA
Kurile Islands incorporated in USSR 1945; claimed by Japan
1951 peace treaty with USA and end of occupation
1956 agreement with USSR, ending state of war; cession of territories (including S. Sakhalin) taken from Russia in 1905
1960 widespread demonstrations against security treaty, granting US military bases in Japan and Okinawa
1972 normalisation of relations with China
1974 beginning of incipient trade disputes with US and EEC

occupied by US after 1945, reverted to Japan 1972

TAIWAN
seat of Chinese Nationalist government under Chiang Kai-shek since 1949
1958 territorial dispute with mainland China over Quemoy and Matsu

PAKISTAN / INDIA
spasmodic unrest among Nagas, Sikhs and Tamils
1962 Sino-Indian border war
1975-77 state of emergency proclaimed
1980 further emergency measures
1984 Sikh separatist uprising suppressed Indira Gandhi assassinated

BANGLADESH / BURMA
1971 secession from Pakistan; civil war followed 1975 by murder of Sheikh Mujib and military control

continuing guerrilla activity since independence (1948) by Communist and minority groups, united in 1975-76 into Federal National Democratic Front 1958, 1962 military coups 1974 Socialist People's Republic inaugurated

VIETNAM
1954 French withdrawal followed by civil war and foreign intervention 1956-75 (see p. 148)
1976 North and South Vietnam reunified under Viet-Minh rule
1978 invasion of Cambodia and border clashes with China
1979 Chinese invasion

LAOS
1953-73 civil war
1975 monarchy abolished; Pathet Lao seizes power

THAILAND
1947 military takeover, guerrilla activity by Communist and minority groups since 1960
1976 border clashes with Cambodia
1987 border clashes with Laos

PHILIPPINES
Communist and Muslim insurgency since 1968, erupting into civil war 1972-78
1986 Marcos regime ousted following general election

CAMBODIA
1970 monarchy abolished
1970-74 civil war; victory of Khmer Rouge who conduct massacre of civilians
1978 Vietnamese invasion overthrows Khmer Rouge

Mindanao

SRI LANKA
1958, 1961 fighting between Sinhalese and Tamils
1971 government assumes emergency powers after rural guerrilla uprisings; 1984 intercommunal rioting
1986 Indian intervention to crush Tamil rebellions

MALAYSIA
1969 risings by Chinese minority groups
1975-78 Communist guerrilla activity
1978- renewed racial and religious conflict

IRIAN JAYA

INDONESIA
1967 Sukarno ousted by military coup; suppression of Communists
1976- resistance to Indonesian rule in E. Timor
1977-79 secessionist rising in Irian Jaya

E. Timor

3 Israel and Palestine, 1947-80
- Jewish state under UN partition plan for Palestine 1947
- Israel after Arab invasion and War of Independence 1948
- Israel conquests 1967
- Egyptian re-conquests, and Israeli conquests 1973

350,000 from Europe — Beirut
283,000 from M. East
264,500 from N. Africa

Tyre
Damascus
LEBANON
SYRIA
Golan Heights
Quanytirah
Sea of Galilee
Haifa
Samaria
R. Jordan
Tel-Aviv
Nablus
West Bank
Jaffa
Jerusalem
Amman
Gaza
Jericho
Gaza Strip
Hebron
Dead Sea
Rafah
Judaea
Beersheba
JORDAN
El Arish
Negev
Port Said
Suez Canal
Ismailia
Giddi Pass
Suez
Mitla Pass
Mediterranean Sea

Sinai Peninsula
returned to Egypt 1981
Elat
Aqaba
SAUDI ARABIA
Abu Rudeis oilfield
Gulf of Aqaba
Gulf of Suez
Strait of Tiran

EGYPT

population movements:
- Jewish immigration 1948-64
- Arab emigration 1948 (total 726,000)
- Arab emigration 1967 (total 400,000)

Sharm el Sheikh
Red Sea
Ras Muhammad

4 Japanese industrial production, 1945-80

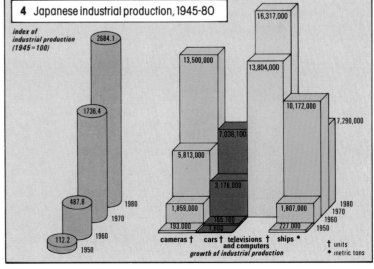

index of industrial production (1945=100)

2684.1
1736.4
487.8
112.2

16,317,000
13,500,000
13,804,000
10,172,000
7,290,000
7,038,100
5,813,000
3,178,000
1,859,000
1,807,000
227,000
193,000
165,100
1,600

cameras † | cars † | televisions and computers † | ships *
growth of industrial production

† units
* metric tons

1950 1960 1970 1980

Latin America since 1930

The world depression of 1930 (page 130) was a watershed in the history of Latin America. Heavily dependent on primary exports (map 2), all the republics were hit by the drop in world trade. Chile's exports fell by over 80 per cent between 1929 and 1933; those of Bolivia and Peru by 75 per cent. In Brazil coffee was burnt. Only oil-exporting Venezuela more or less weathered the storm. The result was widespread disillusion with the middle-class liberal or radical parties which seemed helpless. In 1930 and 1931 11 of the 20 republics south of the Rio Grande experienced revolutionary changes of government. In Mexico, where Cárdenas (1934–40) revived the land distribution policies of 1911, the shift was to the left, and a few other countries (e.g. Colombia) had progressive regimes; but the swing was mainly to the right, though not back to nineteenth century *caudillismo* (page 96), the social bases of which were being eroded by urbanisation and population movements (map 3). The new dictators were populists, appealing directly to the masses and cooperating with organised labour and the trade unions. They also introduced programmes of industrialisation, following Soviet (or more often) fascist models, to reduce dependence on overseas markets and hasten economic development.

Manufacturing industry was given a further boost by the Second World War which cut off imported consumer goods and stimulated the industrial sector. But industrialisation made Latin America de-pendent upon imported capital goods, raw materials, technology and finance, creating enormous foreign debts. New forms of foreign penetration such as the multi-national corporation exploited the cheap labour markets of Latin America without stimulating economic development. Social tensions arose from income concentration, unemployment, lack of opportunities and the presence of foreign interests. Social revolutions were attempted but frustrated in Guatemala, Bolivia and Chile (map 1), and this underlined the obstacles to change when economies are too narrowly based to sustain welfare programmes and when local élites are prepared to collaborate with the United States. Cuba from 1959 attempted to achieve social change, economic growth, and freedom from the United States simultaneously. The revolution led to greater social equality and an improvement in the prospects of rural workers but it also involved a commitment to a repressive government and a dependence on the Soviet Union.

In the face of revolutionary change many regimes closed their ranks, and in the course of the 1970s the military governments of the south combined political repression with economic liberalism and enjoyed some support from the upper and middle sectors. But world recession hit their economies and, with the exception of Chile, drove the military back to the barracks in the mid-1980s. Democracies such as Mexico and Venezuela offered an alternative model and with the rise of oil revenues from 1973 could claim economic and social gains. But the end of the oil boom and excessive state expenditure cast a shadow over their future development.

☐	Mexican Revolution 1910-40
☐	Guatemalan Revolution 1944-54
▽ ⬡	Military Junta 1979 (Romero overt...
☐	Sandinista revolt 1979 (Somoza overthr...
◯	Figueres 1948
◯	Liberal-Conservative Pact, 1957
▽	Intermittent militarism to 1978
◯	Election of reformist government 1978

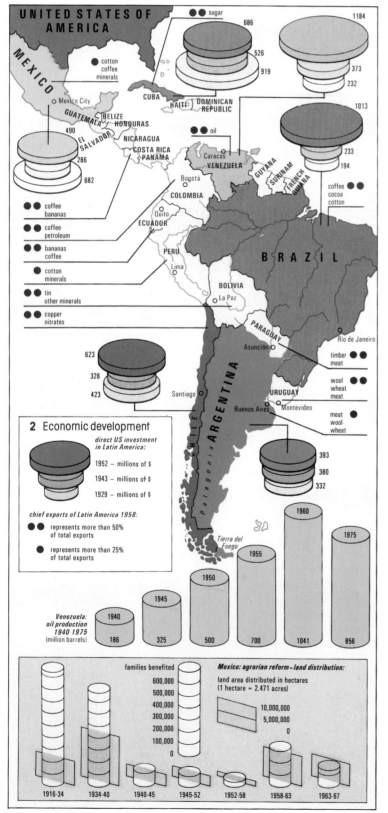

2 Economic development

direct US investment in Latin America:

- 1952 — millions of $
- 1943 — millions of $
- 1929 — millions of $

chief exports of Latin America 1958:

- ●● represents more than 50% of total exports
- ● represents more than 25% of total exports

Venezuela: oil production 1940 1975 (million barrels)

1940	1945	1950	1955	1960	1975
186	325	500	700	1041	856

families benefited

600,000
500,000
400,000
300,000
200,000
100,000
0

| 1916-34 | 1934-40 | 1940-45 | 1945-52 | 1952-58 | 1958-63 | 1963-67 |

Mexico: agrarian reform - land distribution:

land area distributed in hectares
(1 hectare = 2.471 acres)

10,000,000
5,000,000
0

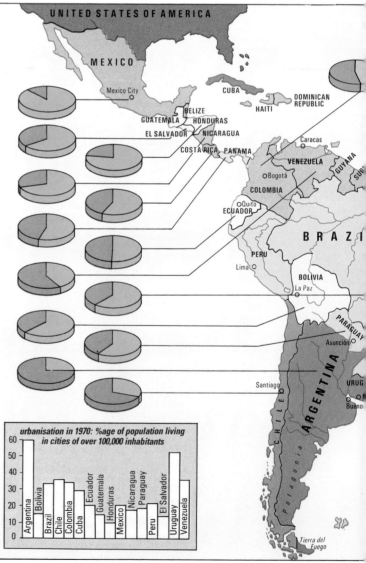

urbanisation in 1970: %age of population living in cities of over 100,000 inhabitants

Argentina, Bolivia, Brazil, Chile, Colombia, Cuba, Ecuador, Guatemala, Honduras, Mexico, Nicaragua, Paraguay, Peru, El Salvador, Uruguay, Venezuela

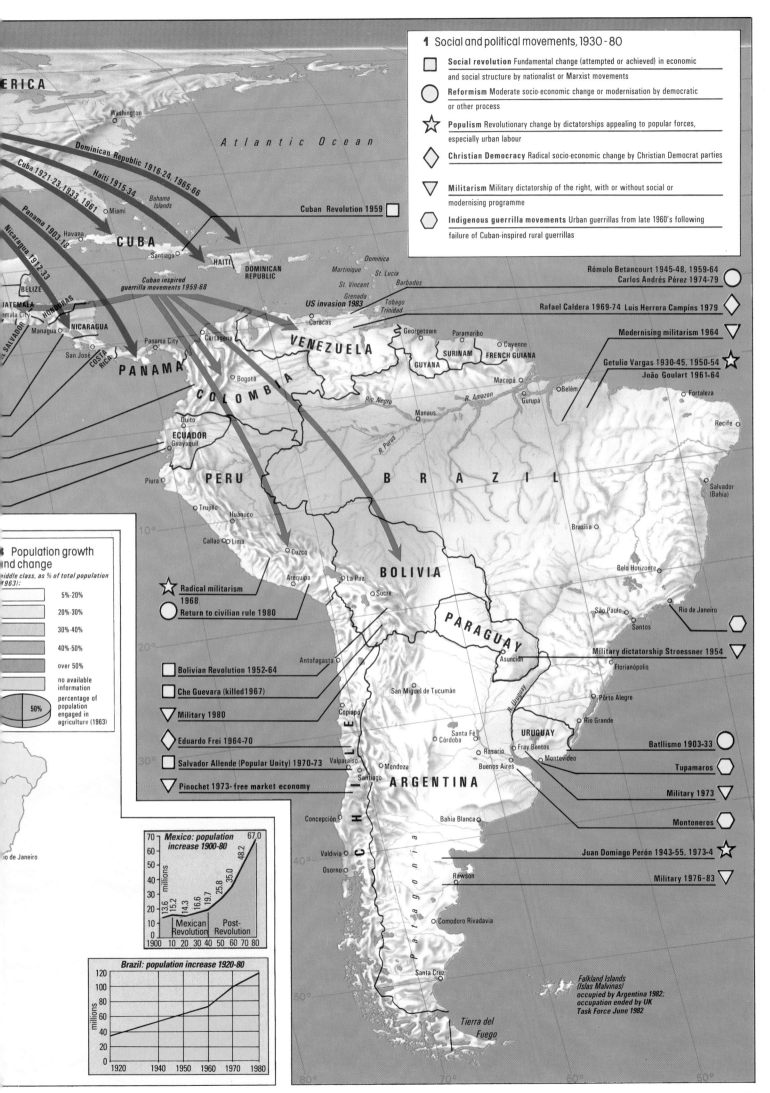

1 Social and political movements, 1930-80

☐ **Social revolution** Fundamental change (attempted or achieved) in economic and social structure by nationalist or Marxist movements

○ **Reformism** Moderate socio-economic change or modernisation by democratic or other process

☆ **Populism** Revolutionary change by dictatorships appealing to popular forces, especially urban labour

◇ **Christian Democracy** Radical socio-economic change by Christian Democrat parties

▽ **Militarism** Military dictatorship of the right, with or without social or modernising programme

⬡ **Indigenous guerrilla movements** Urban guerrillas from late 1960's following failure of Cuban-inspired rural guerrillas

Atlantic Ocean

Washington

Dominican Republic 1916-24, 1965-66

Cuba 1921-23, 1933, 1961

Haiti 1915-34

Panama 1903-18

Nicaragua 1912-33

Bahama Islands

Miami

Cuban Revolution 1959 ☐

Havana

CUBA

Santiago

HAITI

DOMINICAN REPUBLIC

Dominica

Martinique

St. Lucia

St. Vincent

Barbados

Grenada

Tobago

Trinidad

Cuban inspired guerrilla movements 1959-68

US invasion 1983

Caracas

BELIZE

GUATEMALA

HONDURAS

SALVADOR

Managua

NICARAGUA

San José

COSTA RICA

Panama City

PANAMA

Cartagena

VENEZUELA

Georgetown

Paramaribo

Cayenne

SURINAM

FRENCH GUIANA

GUYANA

Bogotá

COLOMBIA

Quito

ECUADOR

Guayaquil

Macapá

Belém

Rio Negro

R. Amazon

Gurupá

Fortaleza

Manaus

Rómulo Betancourt 1945-48, 1959-64
Carlos Andrés Pérez 1974-79 ○

Rafael Caldera 1969-74 Luis Herrera Campins 1979 ◇

Modernising militarism 1964 ▽

Getulio Vargas 1930-45, 1950-54 ☆
João Goulart 1961-64

PERU

Piura

Trujillo

Huánuco

R. Purus

B R A Z I L

Recife

Salvador (Bahia)

Callao Lima

Cuzco

Brasília

10°

Arequipa

La Paz

BOLIVIA

Sucre

Belo Horizonte

São Paulo

Rio de Janeiro

Santos

⬡

Population growth and change

iddle class, as % of total population 1963):

- 5%-20%
- 20%-30%
- 30%-40%
- 40%-50%
- over 50%
- no available information

percentage of population engaged in agriculture (1963)

50%

☆ **Radical militarism 1968**

○ **Return to civilian rule 1980**

☐ **Bolivian Revolution 1952-64**

☐ **Che Guevara (killed 1967)**

▽ **Military 1980**

◇ **Eduardo Frei 1964-70**

☐ **Salvador Allende (Popular Unity) 1970-73**

▽ **Pinochet 1973- free market economy**

Antofagasta

P A R A G U A Y

Asunción

Military dictatorship Stroessner 1954 ▽

Florianópolis

San Miguel de Tucumán

Pôrto Alegre

Copiapó

R. Uruguay

Rio Grande

URUGUAY

Santa Fé
Córdoba

Fray Bentos

Rosario

Montevideo

Buenos Aires

Batllismo 1903-33 ○

Tupamaros ⬡

Valparaíso

Santiago

C H I L E

Mendoza

A R G E N T I N A

Military 1973 ▽

Montoneros ⬡

Concepción

Bahía Blanca

Juan Domingo Perón 1943-55, 1973-4 ☆

Valdivia

Osorno

Rawson

Military 1976-83 ▽

20°

30°

40°

io de Janeiro

```
70  Mexico: population          67.0
60    increase 1900-80
50                              48.2
40
30              25.8  35.0
20  13.6 14.3 16.6 19.7
10  15.2
 0  Mexican  Post-
    Revolution Revolution
1900 10 20 30 40 50 60 70 80
```
millions

Comodoro Rivadavia

Falkland Islands (Islas Malvinas) occupied by Argentina 1982; occupation ended by UK Task Force June 1982

```
Brazil: population increase 1920-80
120
100
 80
 60
 40
 20
  0
 1920 1940 1950 1960 1970 1980
```
millions

Tierra del Fuego

50°

60°

The United States from 1945

The years from 1940 to 1980 saw economic, demographic, and social changes in the United States that dramatically transformed the lives of its people. During these decades the agricultural, industrial, and service sectors of the economy reached unprecedented levels of scale and productivity. Fewer farmers provided not only ample sustenance to a population which, by 1980, was overwhelmingly urban, but also a significant proportion of the world's production of major staples such as wheat, corn, and soya beans (diagram 5, A–C). Mechanisation (under 10 per cent of the cotton crop was harvested by machine in 1949, 96 per cent in 1969), greater yields from improved seed and fertilisers, and an intensely market-oriented and government subsidised system of sales and distribution made this possible. The economy at large grew at a comparable pace until the 1970s. The gross national product (in constant 1958 dollars) was $227.2 billion in 1940, $722.5 billion in 1970. The service sector expanded more rapidly than did manufacturing, and cities such as Atlanta and Houston in the South and Southwest, and Los Angeles, San Francisco, and Denver in the West, became major centres of economic activity (map 4).

This economic growth was accompanied by massive flows of people both within and into the country. With the end of large-scale immigration in the 1920s and the relative immobility of the 1930s, it seemed as though the mobility of American life was over. But the armament build-up during the Second World War attracted many people to the old industrial centres of the Northeast and the Midwest, and to new plants elsewhere. Economic expansion after the war sustained these flows. Millions of blacks and whites left the Southern countryside for the East, the Midwest, and the far West: many more agricultural, industrial, and professional families moved to the

West, the Sun Belt of the South and Southwest, and to burgeoning cities around the nation (map 1). An interstate system of highways totalling about 40,000 miles by 1980 facilitated the long-distance movement of people, and the rise of complex networks of residence and work (map 2). By 1980 only a third of the population lived in non-metropolitan areas.

The flow of people into the US also grew. About 10 million recorded immigrants came between 1950 and 1980 (plus millions more illegally). Larger numbers arrived from Asia and Latin America than ever before (map 1). Perhaps the most dramatic social change was in the realm of race relations. Between 1940 and 1980 a centuries-old structure of formal, explicit racial discrimination against blacks and Asians all but disappeared. Minorities made major gains in education, income, and social acceptance. But this revolution in race relations was not without strains. The massive black and Hispanic migration to American cities exploded in substantial urban riots during the troubled years of the 1960s (map 3). A further strain was imposed by the war in Vietnam, particularly after President Johnson's decision in 1965 to commit ground troops on a massive scale (page 148). By 1968 opposition to the war had become a further divisive factor in American society.

Vietnam also imposed serious strains on the American economy. After 1967 the United States entered a period of inflation and deficits, abandoning the Gold Standard and depreciating the dollar in 1971. Competition from the EEC and Japan brought US industrial predominance to an end; by 1980 unemployment, particularly among blacks and other minorities, became a serious problem. In 1980 a Republican president, Ronald Reagan, was elected on a programme of tax-cuts and rearmament. He was triumphantly re-elected in 1984 after high economic growth, but budgetary strains and the Wall Street crash of Oct. 1987 set a question mark on his achievements.

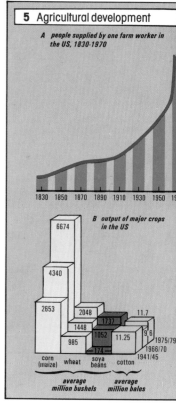

5 Agricultural development

A *people supplied by one farm worker in the US, 1830-1970*

1830 1850 1870 1890 1910 1930 1950 19

B *output of major crops in the US*

6674
4340
2653   2048   11.7
1448   1737
         1052   9.6   1975/79
985   174   11.25   1966/70
                         1941/45

corn (maize)   wheat   soya beans   cotton

average million bushels   *average million bales*

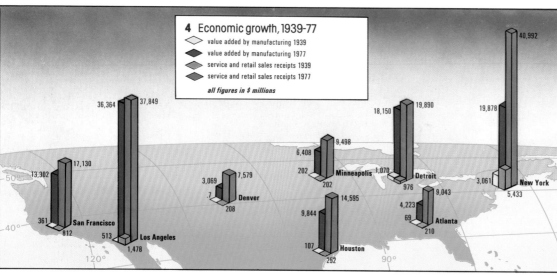

4 Economic growth, 1939-77

◇ value added by manufacturing 1939
◆ value added by manufacturing 1977
◈ service and retail sales receipts 1939
◈ service and retail sales receipts 1977

all figures in $ millions

40,992
37,849 36,364
19,890 18,150 19,878
13,302 17,130
9,498
6,408
7,579 3,069
3,061
976
9,043
4,223
14,595
9,844
812 361
513
1,478
252 107
208 .7
202 202 1,070
69 210
5,433

San Francisco
Los Angeles
Denver
Minneapolis
Detroit
New York
Houston
Atlanta

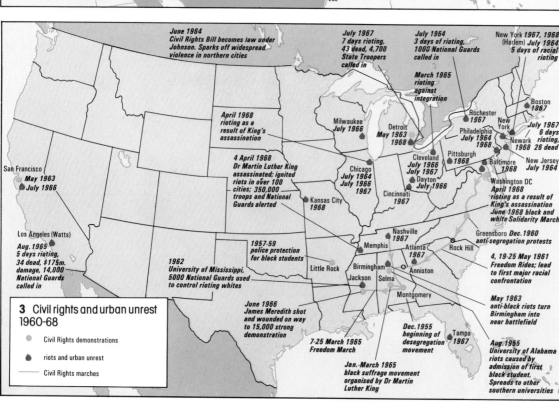

3 Civil rights and urban unrest 1960-68

● Civil Rights demonstrations
🔥 riots and urban unrest
— Civil Rights marches

June 1964 Civil Rights Bill becomes law under Johnson. Sparks off widespread violence in northern cities

July 1967 7 days rioting, 43 dead, 4,700 State Troopers called in

July 1964 3 days of rioting, 1000 National Guards called in

New York 1967, 1968 (Harlem) **July 1964** 5 days of racial rioting

March 1965 rioting against integration

April 1968 rioting as a result of King's assassination

4 April 1968 Dr Martin Luther King assassinated; ignited riots in over 100 cities; 350,000 troops and National Guards alerted

Milwaukee **July 1966**

Detroit **May 1963 1968**

Rochester **1967**

Boston **1967**

New York **July 1967** 6 days rioting, Newark **1968** 26 dead

Philadelphia **July 1964 1968**

Cleveland **July 1966 July 1967**

Pittsburgh **1968**

Baltimore **1968**

New Jersey **July 1964**

Chicago **July 1964 July 1966 1967**

Dayton **July 1966**

Cincinnati **1967**

Washington DC **April 1968** rioting as a result of King's assassination **June 1968** black and white Solidarity March

Kansas City **1968**

1957-59 police protection for black students

1962 University of Mississippi, 5000 National Guards used to control rioting whites

San Francisco **May 1963 July 1966**

Los Angeles (Watts) **Aug. 1965** 5 days rioting, 34 dead, $175m. damage, 14,000 National Guards called in

Nashville **1967**

Memphis

Atlanta **1967**

Rock Hill

Greensboro **Dec.1960** anti-segregation protests

4, 19-25 May 1961 Freedom Rides; lead to first major racial confrontation

Little Rock

Birmingham

Anniston

Jackson

Selma

May 1963 anti-black riots turn Birmingham into near battlefield

Montgomery

June 1966 James Meredith shot and wounded on way to 15,000 strong demonstration

7-25 March 1965 Freedom March

Jan.-March 1965 black suffrage movement organised by Dr Martin Luther King

Dec.1955 beginning of desegregation movement

Tampa **1967**

Aug.1955 University of Alabama riots caused by admission of first black student. Spreads to other southern universities

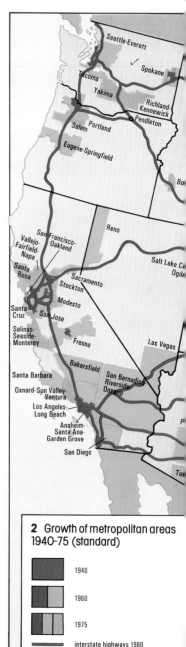

Seattle-Everett
Spokane
Tacoma
Yakima
Richland-Kennewick
Pendleton
Salem Portland
Eugene-Springfield
Reno
San Francisco-Oakland
Vallejo-Fairfield-Napa
Santa Rosa
Salt Lake City Ogde
Sacramento
Stockton
Modesto
Santa Cruz San Jose
Salinas-Seaside-Monterey
Fresno
Las Vegas
Bakersfield
Santa Barbara
San Bernadino Riverside Ontario
Oxnard-Sun Valley-Ventura
Los Angeles-Long Beach
Anaheim-Santa Ana-Garden Grove
San Diego

2 Growth of metropolitan areas 1940-75 (standard)

■ 1940
■ 1960
▦ 1975
— interstate highways 1980

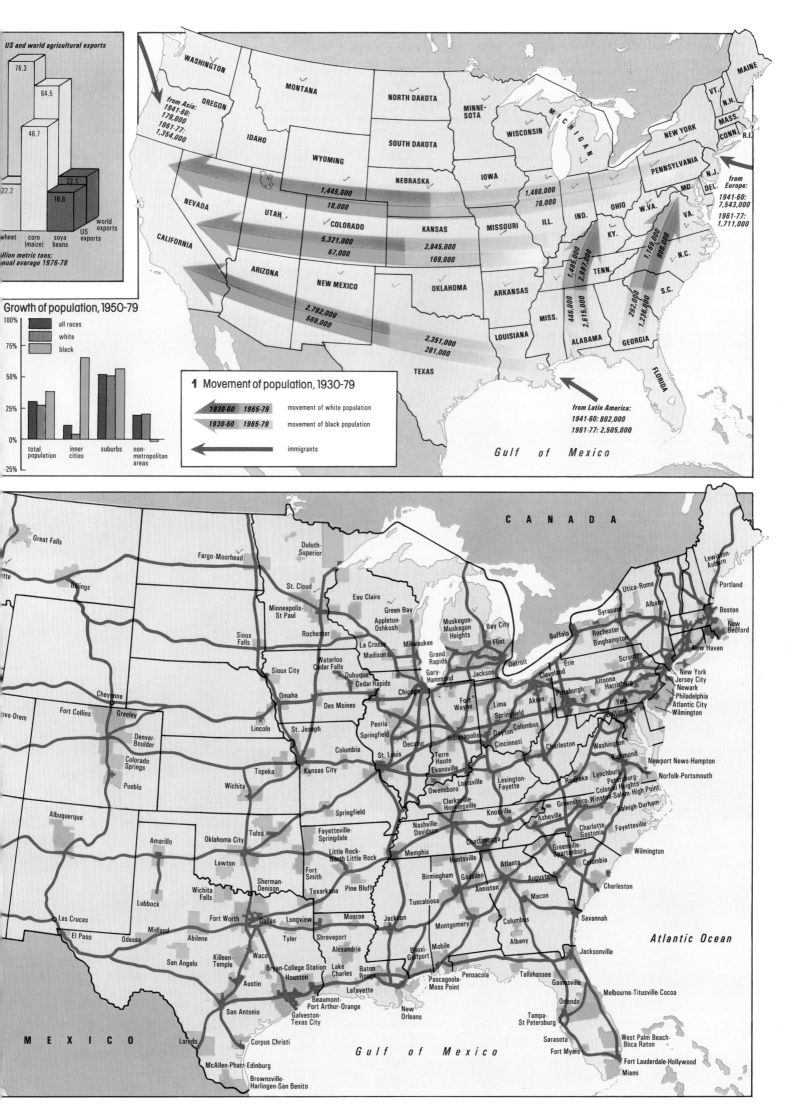

US and world agricultural exports

76.3
64.5
48.7
22.2
22.1
18.6

wheat | corn (maize) | soya beans | US exports | world exports

million metric tons; annual average 1976-78

Growth of population, 1950-79

all races
white
black

100%
75%
50%
25%
0%
-25%

total population | inner cities | suburbs | non-metropolitan areas

1 Movement of population, 1930-79

| 1930-60 | 1965-79 | movement of white population |
| 1930-60 | 1965-79 | movement of black population |

immigrants

from Asia:
1941-60: 179,000
1961-77: 1,354,000

from Europe:
1941-60: 7,543,000
1961-77: 1,711,000

from Latin America:
1941-60: 802,000
1961-77: 2,505,000

WASHINGTON
OREGON
MONTANA
IDAHO
WYOMING
NEVADA
UTAH
CALIFORNIA
ARIZONA
NEW MEXICO
COLORADO
NORTH DAKOTA
SOUTH DAKOTA
NEBRASKA
KANSAS
OKLAHOMA
TEXAS
MINNESOTA
IOWA
MISSOURI
ARKANSAS
LOUISIANA
WISCONSIN
MICHIGAN
ILL.
IND.
OHIO
KY.
TENN.
MISS.
ALABAMA
GEORGIA
FLORIDA
NEW YORK
PENNSYLVANIA
W.VA.
VA.
N.C.
S.C.
MAINE
VT.
N.H.
MASS.
CONN.
R.I.
N.J.
DEL.
MD.

1,445,000
18,000
5,321,000
67,000
2,792,000
569,000
1,480,000
78,000
2,845,000
169,000
2,351,000
281,000
1,495,000
2,987,000
446,000
2,615,000
1,169,000
900,000
282,000
1,236,000

Gulf of Mexico

CANADA

Great Falls
Butte
Billings
Fargo-Moorhead
Duluth-Superior
St. Cloud
Minneapolis-St Paul
Rochester
Eau Claire
Green Bay
Appleton-Oshkosh
Muskegon-Muskegon Heights
Bay City
Flint
La Crosse
Milwaukee
Madison
Sioux Falls
Sioux City
Waterloo-Cedar Falls
Dubuque
Cedar Rapids
Grand Rapids
Gary-Hammond
Jackson
Detroit
Cleveland
Erie
Buffalo
Rochester
Binghamton
Syracuse
Utica-Rome
Albany
Lewiston-Auburn
Portland
Boston
New Bedford
New Haven
Cheyenne
Omaha
Des Moines
Chicago
Fort Wayne
Lima
Springfield
Akron
Pittsburgh
Altoona
Harrisburg
Scranton
New York
Jersey City
Newark
Philadelphia
Atlantic City
Wilmington
York
Baltimore
Provo-Orem
Fort Collins
Greeley
Denver-Boulder
Colorado Springs
Pueblo
Lincoln
St. Joseph
Peoria
Springfield
Decatur
St. Louis
Indianapolis
Dayton
Columbus
Cincinnati
Charleston
Washington
Richmond
Newport News-Hampton
Norfolk-Portsmouth
Topeka
Kansas City
Columbia
Terre Haute
Evansville
Louisville
Lexington-Fayette
Roanoke
Lynchburg
Petersburg-Colonial Heights
Albuquerque
Wichita
Owensboro
Clarksville-Hopkinsville
Knoxville
Asheville
Greensboro-Winston-Salem-High Point
Raleigh-Durham
Springfield
Nashville-Davidson
Charlotte-Gastonia
Fayetteville
Amarillo
Oklahoma City
Tulsa
Fayetteville-Springdale
Little Rock-North Little Rock
Memphis
Chattanooga
Greenville-Spartanburg
Columbia
Wilmington
Lawton
Fort Smith
Huntsville
Atlanta
Charleston
Wichita Falls
Sherman-Denison
Texarkana
Pine Bluff
Birmingham
Gadsden
Anniston
Augusta
Lubbock
Macon
Las Cruces
El Paso
Odessa
Midland
Abilene
Fort Worth
Dallas
Longview
Tyler
Monroe
Jackson
Tuscaloosa
Montgomery
Columbus
Savannah
San Angelo
Killeen-Temple
Waco
Bryan-College Station
Austin
Shreveport
Alexandria
Biloxi-Gulfport
Mobile
Albany
Charleston
San Antonio
Houston
Beaumont-Port Arthur-Orange
Galveston-Texas City
Lake Charles
Baton Rouge
Lafayette
New Orleans
Pascagoola-Moss Point
Pensacola
Tallahassee
Gainesville
Jacksonville
Melbourne-Titusville-Cocoa
Orlando
Tampa-St Petersburg
Sarasota
Fort Myers
West Palm Beach-Boca Raton
Fort Lauderdale-Hollywood
Miami
Corpus Christi
Laredo
McAllen-Pharr-Edinburg
Brownsville-Harlingen-San Benito

MEXICO

Gulf of Mexico

Atlantic Ocean

145

The Soviet Union after 1926

The history of the Soviet Union, as we know it today, dates less from the revolution of 1917 than from the collectivisation of agriculture and the first Five Year Plan in 1928. By the time of Lenin's death in 1924 the new Bolshevik state had survived the perils of civil war and foreign intervention (page 120). But its future shape and character were undecided. What determined them were the policies introduced by Stalin after 1928. They have been called, not inappropriately, 'the second Bolshevik revolution.' Both the collectivisation of agriculture and the first Five Year Plan were implemented with massive brutality. Collective farming claimed, on a conservative estimate, at least 2–3 million victims. Nevertheless, by 1939 a much reduced agricultural population was tilling a larger area than in 1929 and getting a harvest 20 per cent bigger; and the surplus population had moved into industry. Between 1926 and 1940 the industrial labour force grew by 30 millions, and the output of steel, coal, electricity and oil increased by leaps and bounds (diagram 3B), providing the Soviet Union with the industrial basis to withstand the German onslaught in 1941.

The war against Germany (page 132), in which some 20 million Russians perished, caused immense devastation; 1,700 towns and 70,000 villages were destroyed. But major new industrial centres, such as Magnitogorsk in the southern Urals and Stalinsk (Novokuznetsk) on the Kuzbass coalfield, which had been developed during the 1930s (map 1), were beyond the reach of the German armies, and during the war more than 1,000 important factories were evacuated from western Russia to the Urals and beyond. Nevertheless the setback was undeniable. Industrial production was down by over 30 per cent in 1946 as compared with 1940. What was remarkable was the speed of recovery. By 1953 the pre-war level was reached and passed, but at immense human cost. Massive reparations, particularly from eastern Germany, accounted in part for the recovery, but more important was the large-scale use of forced labour, drafted into the hitherto barren north and north-east. The result was a shift in the centre of economic gravity, the foundation of new towns far away from the old industrial centres, and a corresponding movement of population (map 2). But the onset of the Cold War (page 148) necessitated a diversion of productive capacity to armaments and, as in the pre-war period, heavy industry had its first priority. The improvement of living standards lagged far behind. Agriculture was neglected. In 1953, as Khrushchev later pointed out, grain production still hovered around its 1913 level. In addition,

Stalin's last years saw increasing regimentation by an inflated police apparatus and a top-heavy bureaucracy.

Stalin's death in 1953 brought an immediate reaction against his heavy-handed rule, even more marked after Khrushchev's famous denunciation of Stalinism at the 20th Party Congress in 1956. Under Khrushchev (1955–64) there was genuine relaxation, both abroad, where the reduction of Cold War tension seemed to open new prospects, and at home. At the 21st and 22nd Party Congresses (1959, 1961) Khrushchev held out glowing promises of a future of plenty, based on an upswing in agriculture and a switch to consumer products. In fact, Khrushchev's crash programme to open up the 'virgin lands' of Siberia and Kazakhstan produced bumper crops in 1956 and 1958, but subsequently failed to live up to expectations, and in 1963 it was necessary to import from Canada. Simultaneously, re-

newed tension with the United States, culminating in the Cuban missile crisis (page 148), once again enforced a shift of productive capacity back to armaments. In addition, Soviet industrial growth, which had been over 10 per cent per annum during the preceding decade, slowed significantly after 1958. These setbacks sealed Khrushchev's fate. Under Brezhnev and Kosygin, who succeeded in 1964, there was no abrupt reversal of direction. The Soviet Union steadily increased its industrial capacity, and even agriculture advanced quite rapidly (diagrams 3C, 3D). But its image had changed. Sixty years after 1917 it was just another big industrial power, struggling with problems that seemed intractable. The planning system now looked clumsy and incapable of reform: widespread discontent brought a reforming leader, M.S. Gorbachov, to power in 1984 with promises of reconstruction and a new openness.

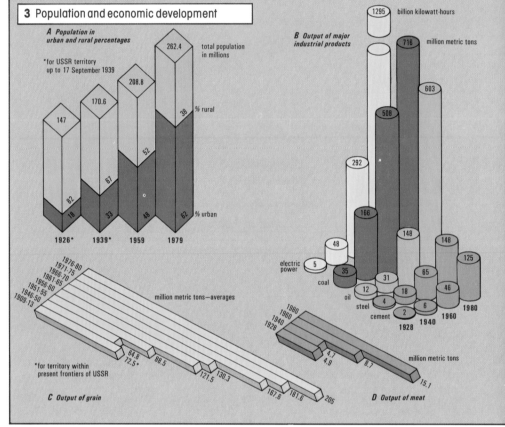

3 Population and economic development

A Population in urban and rural percentages

*for USSR territory up to 17 September 1939

total population in millions

% rural / % urban

1926* 147 (82/18)
1939* 170.6 (67/33)
1959 208.8 (52/48)
1979 262.4 (38/62)

B Output of major industrial products

1295 billion kilowatt-hours
716 million metric tons
603 / 508 / 292 / 166 / 148 / 148 / 125 / 65 / 48 / 46 / 35 / 31 / 18 / 12 / 6 / 5 / 4 / 2

electric power / coal / oil / steel / cement

1928 / 1940 / 1960 / 1980

C Output of grain

million metric tons—averages

1909-13 / 1946-50 / 1951-55 / 1956-60 / 1961-65 / 1966-70 / 1971-75 / 1976-80

*for territory within present frontiers of USSR

72.5* / 64.8 / 88.5 / 121.5 / 130.3 / 167.6 / 181.6 / 205

D Output of meat

million metric tons

1928 / 1940 / 1960 / 1980

4.9 / 4.7 / 8.7 / 15.1

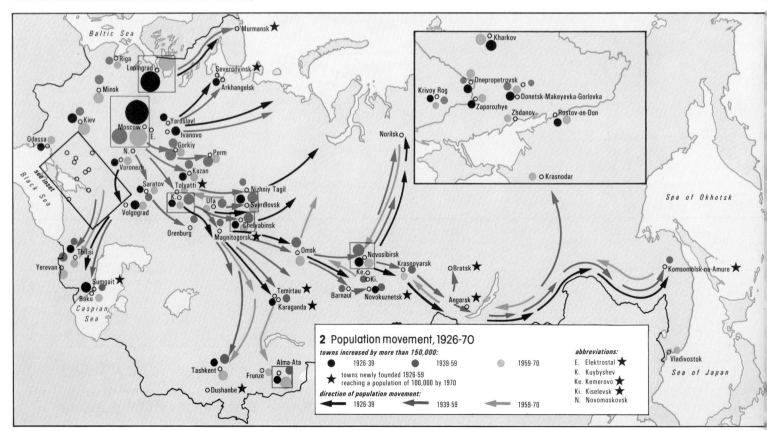

2 Population movement, 1926-70

towns increased by more than 150,000:
- ● 1926-39
- ● 1939-59
- ○ 1959-70
- ★ towns newly founded 1926-59 reaching a population of 100,000 by 1970

direction of population movement:
- ← 1926-39
- ← 1939-59
- ← 1959-70

abbreviations:
- E. Elektrostal ★
- K. Kuybyshev
- Ke. Kemerovo ★
- Ki. Kiselevsk ★
- N. Novomoskovsk

1 Industrial expansion 1926-80

- ● coal mining
- ◑ lignite mining
- ◖ petroleum extraction
- ✚ natural gas extraction
- ⏚ oil shale mining
- ▲ iron ore mining
- ⊗ electricity generation
- ■ integrated iron and steel industry
- ⊠ steel making
- ◆ non-ferrous metal industry
- ⊞ metal working and machine building industry
- ▮ chemical industry

periods of industrial expansion:
- ■ 1926-1940
- ■ 1941-1945
- ■ 1946-1980

forced labour camps operated in Siberia during Stalin's rule 1928-1953

The Cold War from 1947

With the elimination of Germany, Japan and Italy and the weakening of Great Britain and France in the Second World War, the USA and the USSR emerged as the two 'super-powers'. The Cold War was the expression of their political and ideological confrontation. Conflict was already visible before the end of the war. In view of the US monopoly of the atom-bomb and the potential threat it implied for the USSR, Stalin decided, after the failure of the Potsdam Conference (July–Aug. 1945), to consolidate Soviet control in Eastern Europe (page 136). In reply, the USA built up the defence of Western Europe, with the formation of the North Atlantic Treaty Organisation (NATO) in 1949.

Starting as a conflict over central Europe and divided Germany, the Cold War soon developed into a global confrontation. For the United States the Korean War (1950) was evidence of a world-wide Communist conspiracy, although, in fact, the Chinese only intervened when the American advance to the Yalu river seemed to threaten their security (map 2); but American policy hereafter was to 'contain' the Communist powers by a series of encircling alliances. NATO was followed by SEATO (South-East Asia Treaty Organisation, 1954) and the Baghdad Pact (1955), converted into CENTO (Central Treaty Organisation) in 1959. By this time the USA had over 1400 foreign bases, including 275 bases for nuclear bombers, in 31 countries around the Soviet perimeter (map 1). Meanwhile the USSR had acquired nuclear weapons (A-bomb 1949, H-bomb 1953), and when it launched the first space satellite (Sputnik) in 1957, a new dimension was added. Although the intercontinental ballistic missile (ICBM) did not make the American bases obsolete, it meant that, in the event of nuclear war, each of the two super-powers could attack the other's cities directly. The resulting 'nuclear stalemate' enforced a gradual reappraisal.

There were other contributory factors. The monolithic blocs were showing signs of strain, evidenced on the Soviet side by Polish and Hungarian uprisings (1956) and growing signs of a Sino-Soviet rift. In Western Europe, France under General de Gaulle rejected American political leadership after 1958. Furthermore, the Baghdad Pact, far from increasing security in the Middle East, divided it into hostile camps, opening it, after America declined to finance the Aswan high dam and after the Suez War (1956), to Soviet influence (map 4). For the USA the

Cuban revolution (1959) posed more immediate problems. When, after an unsuccessful attempt by US-supported dissidents to unseat Fidel Castro, the USSR sent nuclear missiles to Cuba, war seemed imminent, until Khrushchev agreed (Oct. 26, 1962) to their removal (map 5). But in Indo-China, where the US had refused in 1954 to endorse the settlement of the long anti-colonial war against France (page 138) and had set up a counter-revolutionary regime in Saigon, the situation remained tense. In the end the US was forced to intervene directly, and by 1968 some 543,000 American ground troops, as well as substantial naval and air forces, were committed. But this failed to defeat the guerrilla tactics of the Vietnamese National Liberation Front (map 3), and in 1973, with the US economy under severe pressure, President Nixon called a halt. After 1972, when Nixon visited Peking and Moscow and signed the first SALT treaty limiting nuclear armaments, Cold War gave way to détente, though after the Soviet invasion of Afghanistan (1979), a new arms race began, culminating in the controversial US 'Star Wars' programme. Under M.S. Gorbachov, Soviet diplomacy and internal policies became more flexible, a new Intermediate Nuclear Forces (INF) treaty being signed (Dec. 1987) with the promise of further reduction of missiles.

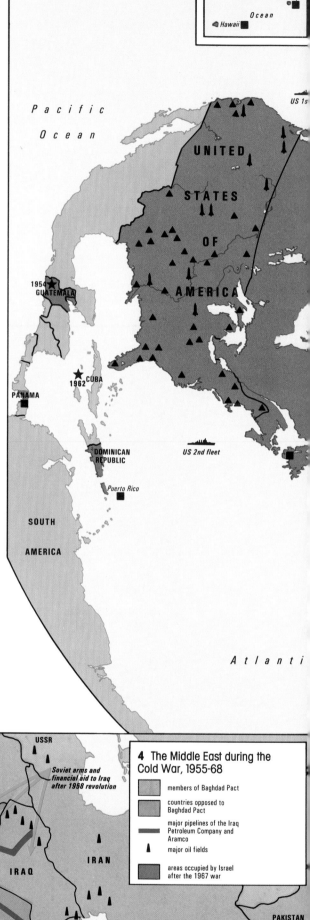

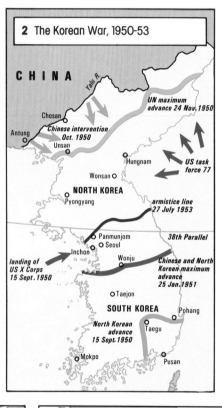

2 The Korean War, 1950-53

CHINA

Yalu R.

Chosan

Antung · **Chinese intervention Oct. 1950**

Unsan

UN maximum advance 24 Nov. 1950

Hungnam

US task force 77

Wonsan

NORTH KOREA

Pyongyang

armistice line 27 July 1953

Panmunjom
Seoul
Inchon
38th Parallel

Wonju

landing of US X Corps 15 Sept. 1950

Chinese and North Korean maximum advance 25 Jan.1951

Taejon

SOUTH KOREA

Pohang

North Korean advance 15 Sept. 1950

Taegu

Mokpo

Pusan

CHINA

Dien Bien Phu · Haiphong
Hanoi · **Gulf of Tongking**

NORTH VIETNAM
Thanh Hoa

LAOS

7th US fleet 1964

HAINAN

Vinh

Dong Hoi
Vinh Linh

Udon Thani

Hue
Phu Bai
Da Nang

THAILAND

Nakhon Ratchasima

Chu Lai

Bangkok

Qui Nhon

CAMBODIA

SOUTH VIETNAM

Phnom Penh

3 The war in Vietnam, 1957-73

Saigon

- controlled by the NLF
- controlled by the Saigon government
- contested areas

4 The Middle East during the Cold War, 1955-68

TURKEY

USSR

Soviet arms and financial aid to Iraq after 1958 revolution

Soviet aid to Syria 1955-8

US 6th fleet

SYRIA

American landings in Lebanon 1958

American aid to Israel

JORDAN

(2)
(3)

IRAQ

IRAN

(1)

EGYPT

SAUDI ARABIA

PAKISTAN

Soviet aid to build Aswan dam

- members of Baghdad Pact
- countries opposed to Baghdad Pact
- major pipelines of the Iraq Petroleum Company and Aramco
- ▲ major oil fields
- areas occupied by Israel after the 1967 war

decline of British influence:
(1) evacuation of Canal Zone 1954
(2) dismissal of General Glubb 1956
(3) Iraqi revolution, assassination of Nuri es-Said 1958
(4) withdrawal from Aden 1968

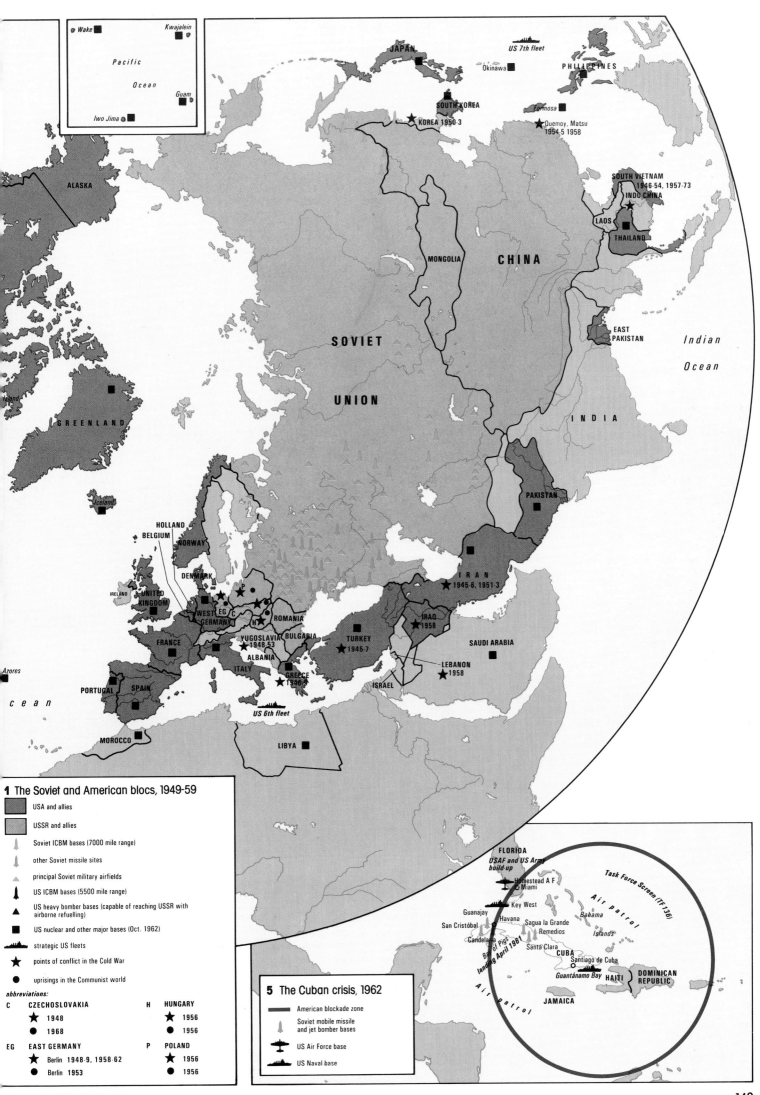

Pacific
Ocean
● *Wake*
Kwajalein
Guam
Iwo Jima

US 7th fleet
JAPAN
Okinawa
PHILIPPINES
SOUTH KOREA
KOREA 1950-3
Formosa
Quemoy, Matsu
1954-5 1958

ALASKA

SOUTH VIETNAM
1946-54, 1957-73
INDO-CHINA
LAOS
THAILAND

MONGOLIA
CHINA

SOVIET

UNION

EAST
PAKISTAN
*Indian
Ocean*

Island
GREENLAND

I N D I A

Iceland

HOLLAND
BELGIUM
NORWAY
DENMARK
IRELAND
UNITED
KINGDOM
WEST
GERMANY
EG
C
H
P
ROMANIA
YUGOSLAVIA
1948-53
BULGARIA
ALBANIA
ITALY
GREECE
1946-9
ISRAEL
FRANCE
TURKEY
1945-7
US 6th fleet
Azores
PORTUGAL
SPAIN
cean
MOROCCO
LIBYA

PAKISTAN

IRAN
1945-6, 1951-3
IRAQ
1958
LEBANON
1958
SAUDI ARABIA

1 The Soviet and American blocs, 1949-59

USA and allies

USSR and allies

Soviet ICBM bases (7000 mile range)

other Soviet missile sites

principal Soviet military airfields

US ICBM bases (5500 mile range)

US heavy bomber bases (capable of reaching USSR with airborne refuelling)

US nuclear and other major bases (Oct. 1962)

strategic US fleets

points of conflict in the Cold War

uprisings in the Communist world

abbreviations:

C	CZECHOSLOVAKIA	H	HUNGARY
★	1948	★	1956
●	1968	●	1956
EG	EAST GERMANY	P	POLAND
★	Berlin 1948-9, 1958-62	★	1956
●	Berlin 1953	●	1956

5 The Cuban crisis, 1962

American blockade zone

Soviet mobile missile and jet bomber bases

US Air Force base

US Naval base

FLORIDA
USAF and US Army build-up
Homestead A F
Miami
Key West
Task Force Screen (TF 136)
Air patrol
*Bahama
Islands*
Guanajay
Havana
San Cristóbal
Candelaria
Sagua la Grande
Remedios
*Bay of Pigs
landing April 1961*
Santa Clara
CUBA
Santiago de Cuba
Guantánamo Bay
HAITI
DOMINICAN
REPUBLIC
JAMAICA
Air patrol

The world in the 1980s

Changes came so rapidly in the late twentieth century that traditional expectations became unreliable guides to actual experience. Economic growth faltered in the 1970s and 1980s, bringing the post-war decades of extraordinary expansion to at least a temporary halt. In the rich countries of the West, unemployment and inflation persisted. No one had a ready cure, since official policies that checked inflation were liable to increase unemployment, and vice versa. Economic difficulties in Russia and Eastern Europe took the form of recurrent shortages of goods and foodstuffs, often compounded by defects of quality.

Harsher dilemmas confronted the poor nations. In innumerable villages, the rural peasant majority of humankind faced an unacceptable choice between impoverishing the rising generation, or sending children who were not needed at home to some distant city to compete for whatever jobs there were. Population growth underlay this crisis (diagram 2). Current political ideologies had no real answer. Communist China, socialist India, together with dictatorial (largely military) regimes in Latin America and Africa all found that their most energetic efforts at urban and industrial development fell short of a solution.

Exchanges of skill, capital and labour between rich and poor countries became sticky as one government after another began to face intractable internal problems. When oil-exporting governments agreed to a radical increase in the price of what had become the world's principal fuel in 1973, they introduced a major disturbance to the world economy. By 1985 the effort to restrict oil production so as to maintain high prices had broken down, yet, ironically, cheaper oil created new dislocations which were only sometimes beneficial.

Loans from rich to poor nations had expanded rapidly in the decades of prosperity. Their usefulness was uncertain and they became crippling burdens to many debtor countries by the 1980s (map 4). The world's financial system therefore came under extraordinary strain, which was only partially relieved by rescheduling payments for the principal debtors.

Migration from poor to rich countries was another sort of exchange that ran into difficulties in the 1980s. Cheap immigrant labour had been welcomed in the rich countries during the post-war boom. But when unemployment became troublesome, racial and ethnic frictions mounted and boiled over into sporadic riots in the leading industrial cities of the Western world.

Japan remained immune to such difficulties, having no significant immigrant population. In other respects, too, Japan's economy suffered less than that of other industrialised nations, and Western nations even began trying to import Japanese managerial techniques, reversing the pattern of imitation that had carried Japan to the forefront of the world economy. If Japan and other Far Eastern nations (Korea, Singapore, Taiwan and above all, China) continue to outstrip the rest of the world in one line of economic activity after another, Western world leadership will presumably be supplanted by a new era of Far Eastern primacy. But indications of such a shift remain ambiguous as long as the success of China's massive effort at modernisation remains uncertain.

Each human community remains unique. Yet all of them faced fundamental uncertainties in the mid-1980s simply because persistence in traditional ways of behaviour no longer achieved accustomed and expected results. This made the last decades of the twentieth century more nerve-wracking than usual, even among the not inconsiderable fraction of humankind whose access to material goods far exceeded anything known to former generations.

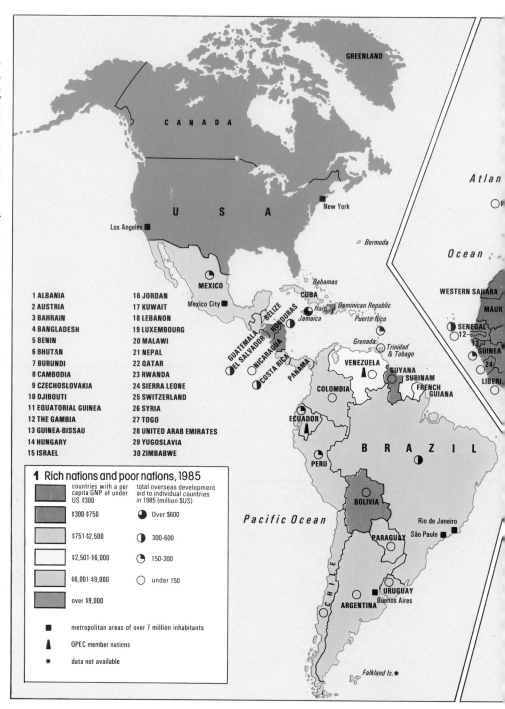

1 ALBANIA	16 JORDAN
2 AUSTRIA	17 KUWAIT
3 BAHRAIN	18 LEBANON
4 BANGLADESH	19 LUXEMBOURG
5 BENIN	20 MALAWI
6 BHUTAN	21 NEPAL
7 BURUNDI	22 QATAR
8 CAMBODIA	23 RWANDA
9 CZECHOSLOVAKIA	24 SIERRA LEONE
10 DJIBOUTI	25 SWITZERLAND
11 EQUATORIAL GUINEA	26 SYRIA
12 THE GAMBIA	27 TOGO
13 GUINEA-BISSAU	28 UNITED ARAB EMIRATES
14 HUNGARY	29 YUGOSLAVIA
15 ISRAEL	30 ZIMBABWE

1 Rich nations and poor nations, 1985

countries with a per capita GNP of under US $300

$300-$750

$751-$2,500

$2,501-$6,000

$6,001-$9,000

over $9,000

total overseas development aid to individual countries in 1985 (million $US)

Over $600

300-600

150-300

under 150

■ metropolitan areas of over 7 million inhabitants

▲ OPEC member nations

✳ data not available

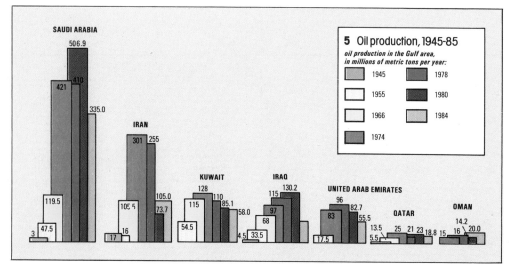

SAUDI ARABIA
3 47.5 119.5 421 506.9 410 335.0

IRAN
17 16 105.5 301 255 105.0 73.7

KUWAIT
54.5 115 128 110 85.1 58.0 4.5 33.5

IRAQ
17.5 68 97 115 130.2 55.5

UNITED ARAB EMIRATES
83 96 82.7

QATAR
5.5 13.5 25 21 23 18.8

OMAN
15 16 14.2 20.0

5 Oil production, 1945-85

oil production in the Gulf area, in millions of metric tons per year:

1945	1978
1955	1980
1966	1984
1974	

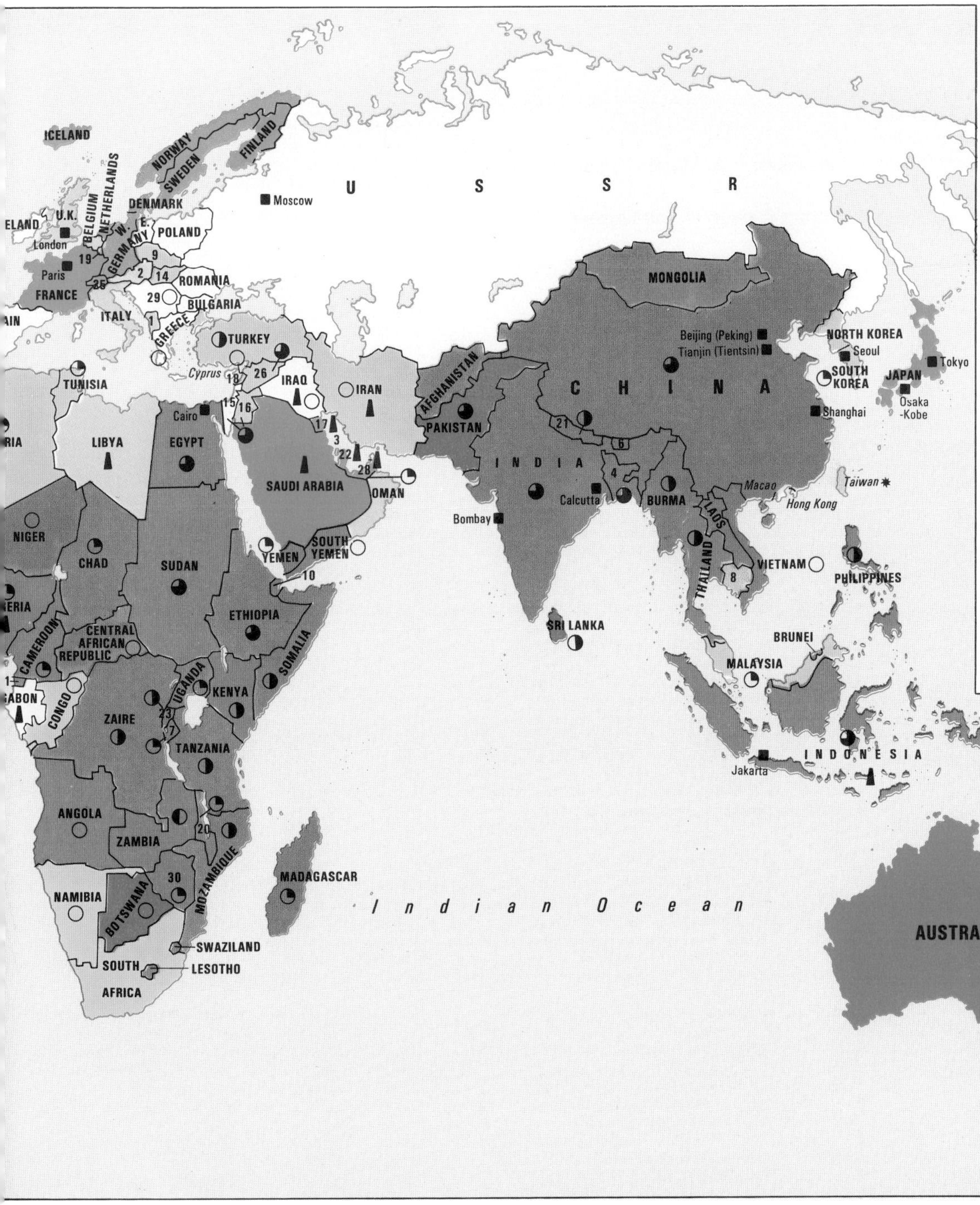
ICELAND
U.K.
London
Paris
FRANCE
BELGIUM
NETHERLANDS
DENMARK
NORWAY
SWEDEN
FINLAND
W. GERMANY
POLAND
ROMANIA
BULGARIA
ITALY
GREECE
TURKEY
Cyprus
TUNISIA
LIBYA
Cairo
EGYPT
IRAQ
IRAN
SAUDI ARABIA
OMAN
YEMEN
SOUTH YEMEN
NIGER
CHAD
SUDAN
ETHIOPIA
SOMALIA
CENTRAL AFRICAN REPUBLIC
CAMEROON
GABON
CONGO
ZAIRE
UGANDA
KENYA
TANZANIA
ANGOLA
ZAMBIA
NAMIBIA
BOTSWANA
MOZAMBIQUE
MADAGASCAR
SWAZILAND
LESOTHO
SOUTH AFRICA
U S S R
Moscow
MONGOLIA
AFGHANISTAN
PAKISTAN
C H I N A
Beijing (Peking)
Tianjin (Tientsin)
Shanghai
NORTH KOREA
Seoul
SOUTH KOREA
JAPAN
Tokyo
Osaka -Kobe
I N D I A
Calcutta
Bombay
BURMA
LAOS
THAILAND
VIETNAM
Macao
Hong Kong
Taiwan
PHILIPPINES
SRI LANKA
BRUNEI
MALAYSIA
I N D O N E S I A
Jakarta
PAPUA NEW GUINEA
Solomon Is.
Pacific Ocean
Vanuatu (New Hebrides)
Fiji
New Caledonia
Indian Ocean
AUSTRALIA
NEW ZEALAND

2 World population, 1985

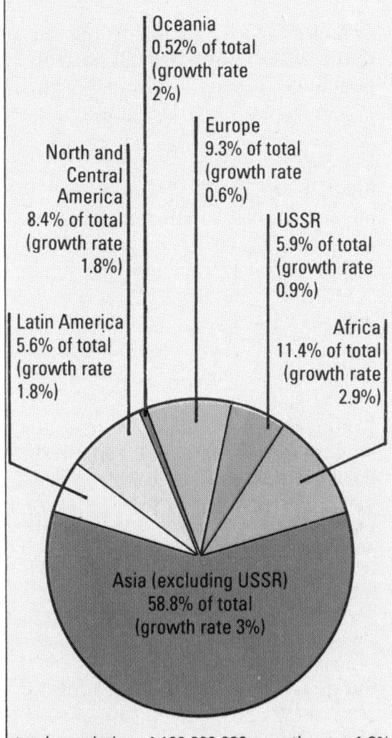
Oceania
0.52% of total
(growth rate
2%)
Europe
9.3% of total
(growth rate
0.6%)
North and
Central
America
8.4% of total
(growth rate
1.8%)
USSR
5.9% of total
(growth rate
0.9%)
Latin America
5.6% of total
(growth rate
1.8%)
Africa
11.4% of total
(growth rate
2.9%)
Asia (excluding USSR)
58.8% of total
(growth rate 3%)

total population: 4,160,000,000 growth rate: 1.8%

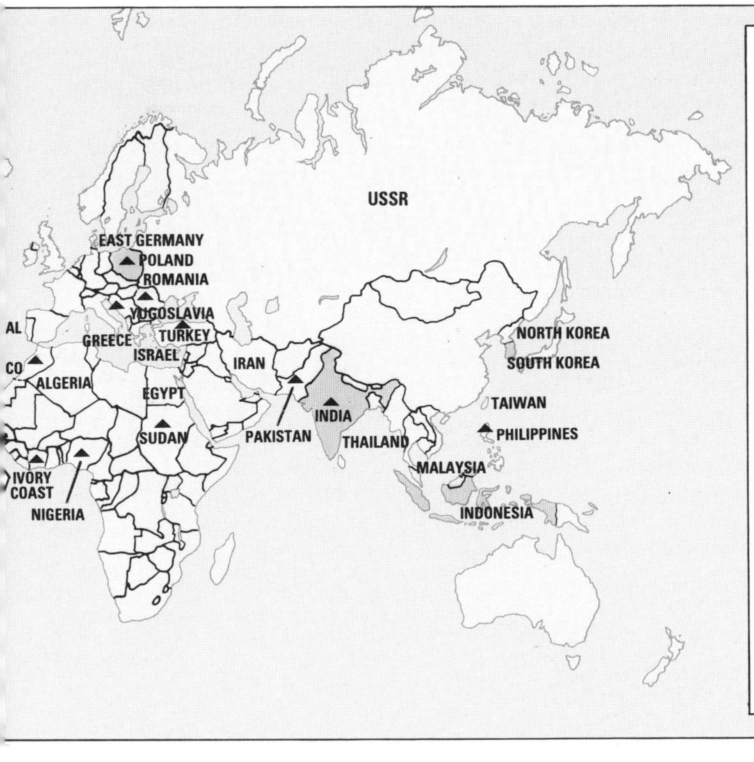
USSR
EAST GERMANY
POLAND
ROMANIA
YUGOSLAVIA
GREECE
TURKEY
ISRAEL
IRAN
ALGERIA
EGYPT
SUDAN
PAKISTAN
INDIA
THAILAND
IVORY COAST
NIGERIA
NORTH KOREA
SOUTH KOREA
TAIWAN
PHILIPPINES
MALAYSIA
INDONESIA

4 International debt

external debts 1982 (excluding short-term debts)

- US $5-20 billion
- US $20-50 billion
- over US $50 billion
- ▲ debts requiring rescheduling 1975-83 (more than US $5 billion)

The world recession of the 1970s left many developing countries attempting, with decreasing earnings, to service increased interest payments on loans. By 1983 many were forced to reschedule these loans, and to introduce austere economic programmes which would nevertheless avoid severe social and political upheavals.

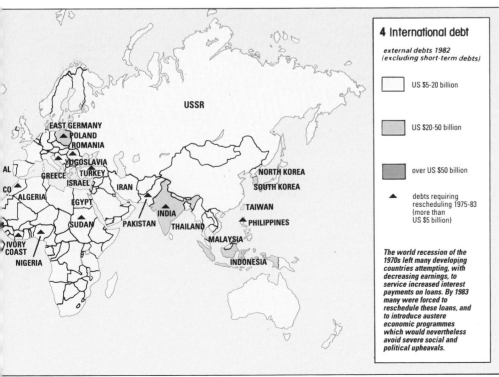

3 The gap between nations

- life expectancy at birth
- infant mortality (deaths per 1000 live births)
- literacy % of population

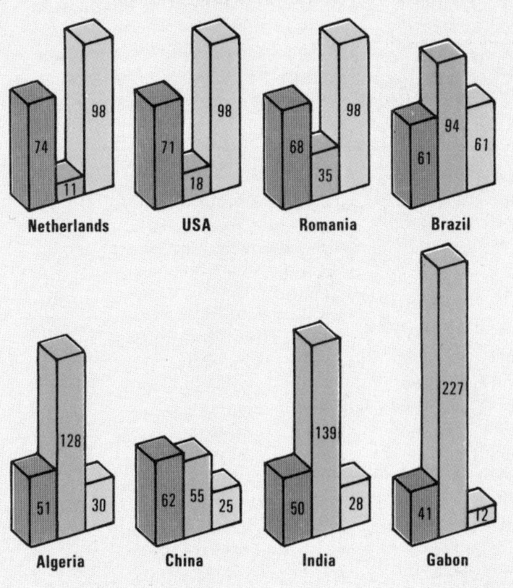
74
11
98
Netherlands
71
18
98
USA
68
35
98
Romania
61
94
61
Brazil
51
128
30
Algeria
62
55
25
China
50
139
28
India
41
227
12
Gabon

Acknowledgements

ACKNOWLEDGEMENTS AND BIBLIOGRAPHY
We have pleasure in acknowledging the following:
Map 3, page 5, is based, with kind permission, on Professor P.A. Martin, *American Population Explosion* Science Magazine 1973
Map 5, page 76, is based, with kind permission, on map 2, page 107 in *Grosser Atlas Zur Weltgeschichte*, Westermann
Map 5, page 111, is based, with the kind permission of George Philip & Son Ltd, on page 215 of *The New Cambridge Modern History Atlas* H.C. Darby, H. Fullard (eds.)

Among the large number of works consulted by contributors, the following contain valuable maps and other data that have been particularly useful:

I. History Atlases

Atlas zur Geschichte 2 vols. Leipzig 1976
Bazilevsky, K.V., Golubtsov, A., Zinoviev, M.A. *Atlas Istorii SSR*, Moscow 1952
Beckingham, C.F. *Atlas of the Arab World and the Middle East*, London 1960
Bertin, J. (et al) *Atlas of Food Crops*, Paris 1971
Bjørklund, O., Holmboe, H., Røhr, A. *Historical Atlas of the World*, Edinburgh 1970
Cappon, L. (et al) *Atlas of Early American History*, Chicago 1976
Darby, H. C., Fullard, H. (eds.) *The New Cambridge Modern History* vol. XIV: Atlas, Cambridge 1970
Davies, C.C. *An Historical Atlas of the Indian Peninsula*, London 1959
Engel, J. (ed.) *Grosser Historischer Weltatlas* 3 vols. Munich 1953–81
Fage, J.D. *An Atlas of African History*, London 1958
Gilbert, M. *Russian History Atlas*, London 1972
Gilbert, M. *Recent History Atlas 1860–1960*, London 1966
Gilbert, M. *First World War Atlas*, London 1970
Gilbert, M. *Jewish History Atlas*, London 1969
Hazard, H.W. *Atlas of Islamic History*, Princeton 1952
Herrmann, A. *Historical and Commercial Atlas of China*, Havard 1935
Herrmann, A. *An Historical Atlas of China*, Edinburgh 1966
Jedin, H., Latourette, K.S., Martin, J. *Atlas zur Kirchengeschichte*, Freiburg 1970
Joppen, C., Garrett, H.L.O. *Historical Atlas of India*, London 1938
Kinder, H., Hilgermann, W. *DTV Atlas zur Weltgeschichte* 2 vols. Stuttgart 1964
Matsui and Mori *Ajiarekishi chizu*, Tokyo 1965
May, H.G. (ed.) *Oxford Bible Atlas*, Oxford 1974
Nelson's Atlas of the Early Christian World, London 1959
Nelson's Atlas of World History, London 1965
Nihon rekishi jiten Atlas vol., Tokyo 1959
Palmer, R.R. (ed.) *Atlas of World History*, Chicago 1965
Paullin, C.O. *Atlas of the Historical Geography of the United States*, Washington 1932
Ragi al Faruqi, I. *Historical Atlas of the Religions of the World*, New York 1974
Roolvink, R. *Historical Atlas of the Muslim Peoples*, London 1957
Schwartzberg, J.E. (ed.) *A Historical Atlas of South Asia* Chicago 1978
Shepherd, W.R. *Historical Atlas*, New York 1964
Toynbee, A.J., Myers, E.D. *A Study of History, Historical Atlas and Gazetteer*, Oxford 1959
Treharne, R.F., Fullard, H. (eds.) *Muir's Historical Atlas*, London 1966
Van der Heyden, A.M., Scullard, H.H. *Atlas of the Classical World*, London 1959
Wesley, E.B. *Our United States . . . . its History in Maps*, Chicago 1977
Westermann *Grosser Atlas zur Weltgeschichte*, Brunswick 1978
Whitehouse, D. & R. *Archaeological Atlas of the World*, London 1975
Wilgus, A.C. *Latin America in Maps*, New York 1943

II. General Works

Ahzweiler, H. *L'Asie Mineure et les Invasions Arabes*, Revue Historique 1962
Ajayi, J.F.A., Crowder, M. *History of West Africa* vols. 1 & 2 London 1974
Allchin, B. & R. *The Birth of Indian Civilisation*, London 1968
Australia, Commonwealth of, Department of National Development, *Atlas of Australian Resources*
Barraclough, G. *Medieval Germany*, Oxford 1938
Basham, A.L. *The Wonder that was India*, London 1967
Beresford, M. *New Towns of the Middle Ages*, London 1967

Berney, M. (ed.) *Australia*, Sydney 1965
Bloch, M. *Les Caractères Originaux de l'Histoire Rurale Française*, Oslo 1931
Boisselier, J. *La Statuaire du Champa*, Paris 1963
Bury, J.B., Cook, S.A., Adcock, F.E. (eds.) *The Cambridge Ancient History*, Cambridge 1923–
Bury, J.B., Gwatkin, H.M., Whitney, J.P. (eds.) *The Cambridge Medieval History*, Cambridge 1911
Chang, K.C. *The Archaeology of Ancient China*, New Haven & London 1968
Cheng Te-k'un *Archaeology in China*, Cambridge 1959
Churchill, Winston S. *The Second World War*, London 1948–53
Coedès, G. *Les Etats Hindouisés de l'Indochine et d'Indonésie*, Paris 1964
Cook, M.A. (ed.) *A History of the Ottoman Empire to 1730*, Cambridge 1974
Cresswell, K.A.C. *A Short Account of Early Muslim Architecture*, Oxford 1958
Crowder, M. *West Africa under Colonial Rule*, London 1968
Cumberland, K.B. *Aotearoa Maori: New Zealand about 1780*, Geographical Review no. 39
Curtin, P. de A. *The Atlantic Slave Trade*, Wisconsin 1969
Dalton, B.J. *War and Politics in New Zealand 1855–1870*, Sydney 1967
Darby, H.C. (ed.) *An Historical Geography of England before AD 1800*, Cambridge 1936 & 1960
Despois, J., Raynal, R. *Géographie de l'Afrique du Nord*, Paris 1967
Dyos, H.J., Aldcroft, D.H. *British Transport*, Leicester 1969
East, W.G. *The Geography behind History*, London 1965
East, W.G. *An Historical Geography of Europe*, London 1966
Edwardes, M. *A History of India*, London 1961
Evans, B.L. *Agricultural and Pastoral Statistics of New Zealand 1861–1954*, Wellington 1956
Ferguson, J. *The Heritage of Hellenism*, London 1973
Fisher, C.A. *South-East Asia*, London 1964
Fletcher, A. *Tudor Rebellions*, London 1968
Fowler, K. *The Age of Plantagenet and Valois*, New York 1967
Fourquin, G. *Histoire Economique de l'Occident Médiéval*, Paris 1969
Ganshof, F.L. *Etude sur le Développement des Villes entre Loire et Rhin au Moyen Age*, Paris–Brussels 1943
Geelan, P.J.M., Twitchett, D.C. (eds.) *The Times Atlas of China*, London 1974
Gernet, J. *Le Monde Chinois*, Paris 1969
Grousset, R. *The Empire of the Steppes: A History of Central Asia*, New Brunswick N.J. 1970
Guillermaz, J. *Histoire du Parti Communiste Chinois*, Paris 1968
Hall, D.G.E. *A History of South-East Asia*, London 1968
Harlan, J.R. *The Plants and Animals that Nourish Man*, Scientific American 1976
Harlan, J.R., Zohary, D. *The Distribution of Wild Wheats and Barleys*, Science 1966
Hatton, R.M. *Europe in the age of Louis XIV*, London 1969
Henderson, W.O. *Britain and Industrial Europe 1750–1870*, Liverpool 1954
Hopkins, A.G. *Economic History of West Africa*, London 1973
Inalcik, H. *The Ottoman Empire: The Classical Age 1300–1600*, London 1973
Jeans, D.N. *An Historical Geography of New South Wales to 1901*, Sydney 1972
Kennedy, J. *A History of Malaya 1400–1959*, London 1962
Kjölstad, T., Rystad, G. *5000 år: Epoker och utvecklingslinjer*, Lund 1973
Konigsberger, H., Mosse, G.L. *Europe in the sixteenth century*, London 1968
Langer, W.L. *An Encyclopedia of World History*, London 1972

La Roncière (et al) *L'Europe au Moyen Age*, Paris 1969
Lattimore, O. *Inner Asian Frontiers of China*, New York 1951
Lyashchenko, P.I. *History of the National Economy of Russia to the 1917 Revolution*, New York 1949
Majumdar, R.C. *The Vedic Age*, Bombay 1951
Majumdar, R.C. *History and Culture of the Indian People, Age of Imperial Unity*, Bombay 1954
Macmillan's Atlas of South-East Asia, London 1964
McBurney, C.B.M. *Proceedings of the British Academy LXI* 1975
McIntyre, W.D., Gardner, W.J. *Speeches and Documents on New Zealand History*, Oxford 1970
McNeill, W.H. *A World History*, New York 1971
Meinig, D.W. *On the Margins of the Good Earth*, New York 1962, London 1963
Mellaart, J. *The Neolithic of the Near East*, London 1975
Ministry of Works *A Survey of New Zealand Population*, Wellington 1960
Miquel, A. *L'Islam et sa Civilisation*, Paris 1968
Morrell, W.P., Hall, D.O.W. *A History of New Zealand Life*, Christchurch 1957
Moss, H. St. L.B. *The Birth of the Middle Ages*, Oxford 1935
Mulvaney, D.J. *The Prehistory of Australia*, London 1975
Mussett, L *Les Invasions: Les Vagues Germaniques*, Paris 1965
Mussett, L. *Les Invasions: Le Second Assaut contre l'Europe Chrétienne*, Paris 1971
The National Atlas of the United States of America, Washington DC 1970
Neatby, H. *Quebec, The Revolutionary Age 1760–1791*, London 1966
New Zealand Official Yearbook, Wellington 1893–
Ogot, B.A. (ed.) *Zamani, A Survey of East African History*, London 1974–1976
Oliver, R., Fagan, B. *Africa in the Iron Age c.500 BC–AD 1400*, Cambridge 1975
Oliver, R., Atmore, A. *Africa since 1800*, Cambridge 1972
Ostrogorsky, G. *History of the Byzantine State*, Oxford 1956
Parker, W.H. *An Historical Geography of Russia*, London 1968
Piggott, S. *Prehistoric India to 1000 BC*, London 1962
Pitcher, D.E. *An Historical Geography of the Ottoman Empire*, Leiden 1973
Sanders, W.T., Marino, J. *New World Prehistory: Archaeology of the American Indian*, Englewood Cliffs, N.J. 1970
Saum, L.O. *The Fur Trader and the Indian*, London 1965
Seltzer, L.E. (ed.) *The Columbia Lippincott Gazetteer of the World*, New York 1952
Simkin, C.F. *The Traditional Trade of Asia*, Oxford 1968
Smith, C.T. *An Historical Geography of Western Europe before 1800*, London & New York 1960
Smith, W.S. *The Art and Architecture of Ancient Egypt*, London 1965
Snow, D. *The American Indians: their Archaeology and Prehistory*, London 1976
Stavrianos, L.S. *The World to 1500*, Englewood Cliffs, N.J. 1975
Stein, Sir Aurel *Travels in Central Asia*, London 1935
Stratos, A.N. *Byzantium in the seventh century*, Athens 1965
Tarn, W.W. *Alexander the Great*, Cambridge 1948
Tate, D.J.M. *The Making of South-East Asia*, Kuala Lumpur 1971
Thapar, R. *A History of India*, London 1967
The Times Atlas of the World, Comprehensive Edition, London 1980
Toynbee, A.J. (ed.) *Cities of Destiny*, London 1967
Toynbee, A.J. *Mankind and Mother Earth*, Oxford 1976
U.S. Strategic Bombing Survey, Summary Report (Pacific War), Washington 1946
Van Alstyne, R.W. *The Rising American Empire*, Oxford 1960
Van Heekeren, H.R. *The Stone Age of Indonesia*, The Hague 1957
Wadham, S., Wilson, R.K., Wood, J. *Land Utilization in Australia*, Melbourne 1964
Watters, R.F. *Land and Society in New Zealand*, Wellington 1965
Wheatley, P. *The Golden Khersonese*, Kuala Lumpur 1961
Wheeler, M. *Early India and Pakistan to Ashoka*, London 1968
Willey, G. *An Introduction to American Archaeology* vols. 1 & 2 Englewood Cliffs, N.J. 1970
Williams, M. *The Making of the South Australian Landscape*, London 1974
Wilson, M., Thompson, L. *Oxford History of South Africa* vols. 1 & 2 Oxford 1969, 1971

INDEX

1 HISTORICAL PLACE NAMES

Geographical names vary with time and with language, and there is some difficulty in treating them consistently in an historical atlas, especially for individual maps within whose time span the same place has been known by different names. We have aimed at the simplest possible approach to the names on the maps, using the index to weld together the variations.

On the maps forms of names will be found in the following hierarchy of preference:
a English conventional names or spellings, in the widest sense, for all principal places and features, e.g., Moscow, Vienna, Munich, Danube (including those that today might be considered obsolete when these are appropriate to the context, e.g. Leghorn).

b Names that are contemporary in terms of the maps concerned. There are here three broad categories:
i names in the ancient world, where the forms used are classical, e.g., Latin or latinized Greek, but extending also to Persian, Sanskrit, etc.
ii names in the post-medieval modern world, which are given in the form (though not necessarily the spelling) current at the time of the map (e.g., St. Petersburg before 1914, not Leningrad).
iii modern names where the spelling generally follows that of *The Times Atlas of the World*, though in the interests of simplicity there has been a general omission of diacritics in spellings derived by transliteration from non-roman scripts, e.g., Sana rather than Şan'ā'.

2 THE INDEX

The index does not include every name shown on the maps. In general only those names are indexed which are of places, features, regions or countries where 'something happens', i.e., which carry a date or symbol or colour explained in the key, or which are mentioned in the text.

Where a place is referred to by two or more different names in the course of the atlas, there will be a corresponding number of main entries in the index. The variant names in each case are given in brackets at the beginning of the entry, their different forms and origins being distinguished by such words as *now*, *later*, *formerly* and others included in the list of abbreviations (*right*).

'Istanbul (*form.* Constantinople, *anc.* Byzantium)' means that the page references to that city on maps dealing with periods when it was known as Istanbul follow that entry, but the page references pertaining to it when it had other names will be found under those other names.

Places are located generally by reference to the country in which they lie (exceptionally by reference to island groups or sea areas), this being narrowed down where necessary by location as E(ast), N(orth), C(entral), etc. The reference will normally be to the modern state in which the place now falls unless (a) there is a conventional or historical name which conveniently avoids the inevitably anachronistic ring of some modern names, e.g., Anatolia rather than Turkey, Mesopotamia rather than Iraq, or (b) the modern state is little known or not delineated on the map concerned, e.g., many places on the Africa plates can only be located as W., E., Africa, etc.

Reference is generally to page number/map numbers (e.g., 118/1) unless the subject is dealt with over the plate as a whole, when the reference occurs as 118-9 (i.e., pages 118 and 119). All entries with two or more references have been given sub-headings where possible, e.g., Civil War 129/4. Battles are indicated by the symbol ✕. References to names of persons, treaties, etc. occurring in the text are followed by the abbreviation T. e.g. 'Alexander the Great 22T.'

Though page references are generally kept in numerical order, since this corresponds for the most part with chronological order, they have been rearranged occasionally where the chronological sequence would be obviously wrong, or in the interests of grouping appropriate references under a single sub-heading.

All variant names and spellings are cross-referenced in the form 'Bourgogne (Burgundy)', except those which would immediately precede or follow the main entries to which they refer. The bracketed form has been chosen so that such entries may also serve as quick visual indications of equivalence. Thus Bourgogne (Burgundy) means not only 'see under Burgundy' but also that Burgundy is another name for Bourgogne.

3 ABBREVIATIONS

a/c	also called
Alb.	Albanian
anc.	ancient
Ar.	Arabic
a/s	also spelled
Bibl.	Biblical
Bulg.	Bulgarian
C	Century (when preceded by 17, 18 etc.)
C	Central
Cat.	Catalan
Chin.	Chinese
Cz.	Czech
Dan.	Danish
Dut.	Dutch
E	East(ern)
Eng.	English
Est.	Estonian
f/c	formerly called
Finn.	Finnish
form.	former(ly)
Fr.	French
f/s	formerly spelled
Ger.	German
Gr.	Greek
Heb.	Hebrew
Hung.	Hungarian
Indon.	Indonesian
Ir.	Irish
Is.	Island
It.	Italian
Jap.	Japanese
Kor.	Korean
Lat.	Latin
Latv.	Latvian
Lith.	Lithuanian
Mal.	Malay
med.	medieval
mod.	modern
Mong.	Mongolian
N	North(ern)
n/c	now called
Nor.	Norwegian
n/s	now spelled
NT	New Testament
obs.	obsolete
OT	Old Testament
Pers.	Persian
Pol.	Polish
Port.	Portuguese
Rom.	Romanian
Russ.	Russian
S	South(ern)
s/c	sometimes called
Som.	Somali
Sp.	Spanish
S. Cr.	Serbo-Croat
SSR	Soviet Socialist Republic
Sw.	Swedish
Turk.	Turkish
Ukr.	Ukrainian
US(A)	United States (of America)
var.	variant
W	West(ern)
Wel.	Welsh
WW1	The First World War
WW2	The Second World War

Chaeronea - Colón

Chaeronea C Greece 23/2
Chagar Bazar (*a/c* Shubat-Enlil) Mesopotamia 16/1
Chagatai Khanate C Asia 47/3, 4
Chagos Archipelago Indian Ocean British control 101/2
Chahar former province of N China 106/1; independent of Nanking 123/3
Chaiya S Thailand Hindu-Buddhist remains 51/2
Chakipampa C Andes early site 12/5
Chak Purbane Syal NW India early settlement 9/5
Chalcedon (*mod.* Kadiköy) NW Anatolia centre of early Christianity 26/1; Dorian colony 19/4; Council 38T
Chalcidice (*mod.* Khalkidhiki) region of N Greece Persian War 22/1
Chalcis C Greece parent state 19/4
Chaldeans people of Mesopotamia 20/3
Chaldian Theme Byzantine province of E Anatolia 42/2
Chaldiran (Çaldiran)
Chalon-sur-Saône S France medieval fair 59/2
Châlons-sur-Marne N France bishopric 117/1; seat of intendant 80/1; WW1 118/3; WW2 132/1
Chambéry SE France medieval fair 59/2
Champa Hindu-Buddhist kingdom of Indo-China 50/1, 51/2, 70/1; under Mongol control 47/1
Champagne region of NE France French Royal domain 52/2
Champaubert NE France 90/1
Champion's Hill S USA ⚔93/5
Chanak (*Turk.* Çanakkale) W Turkey 1922 incident 129/2
Chancelade France site of early man 3/3
Chancellorsville SE USA ⚔93/5
Chandernagore E India French settlement 67/2, 87/2
Chandoli W India site 9/1
Chandragupta I Indian king 29/5
Chandragupta II Indian king 29/5
Chandragupta Maurya Indian emperor 28T, 29/4
Changan N China Han capital 29/3; T'ang city 50/1
Changchou E China T'ang prefecture 50/1
Changchun Manchuria treaty port 107/4; railway 127/4
Changi NW China Han commanderie 29/3
Changkufeng Manchuria Russo-Japanese conflict 127/5
Changsha C China Han principality 29/3; treaty town 107/4; captured by Kuomintang 122/2; captured by Japanese 135/1
Chang Tso-lin Chinese warlord 122/2
Changyeh NW China conquered by Han 28/2
Chanhu-Daro N India Harappan site 9/1, 5
Chansen N Thailand Iron Age site 8/3
Chao early state of N China 28/1
Charax early port on Persian Gulf 24/1
Chard SW England Industrial Revolution 98/1
Chardzhou (*until 1940* Chardzhuy) Russ. C. Asia industry 147/1
Charlemagne Frankish king 34T
Charles the Bold, of Burgundy, 35/5, 6; 72T
Charles Martel King of Franks 34T
Charles Town Path SE USA settlers' route 94/1
Charles V Holy Roman Emperor 72T
Charolais region of E France Habsburg possession 72/2
Charrúa Indian tribe of Argentina 63/1
Charsinian Theme Byzantine province of C Anatolia 42/2
Charsinianum C Anatolia Byzantine Empire 42/2
Château-Thierry N France ⚔90/1; WW1 118/3 (inset)
Chatham SE England Dutch naval raid 81/3; naval base 87/1; Industrial Revolution 98/1; WW1 119/3
Chattanooga SE USA ⚔93/5
Chatti Germanic tribe of Roman Empire 30/3
Chauci Germanic tribe of Roman Empire 30/3
Chavín C Andes site 13/1
Chedi early kingdom of N India 29/4
Chekiang province of E China Ming economy 51/4; Manchu expansion 106/1; Taiping control 107/3
Chełm (Kholm)
Chelmno Poland concentration camp 132/1
Chelmsford (*anc.* Caesaromagus) E England Industrial Revolution 98/1
Chelyabinsk C Russia industry 147/1; urban growth 146/2
Chemin des Dames NE France WW1 118/3 (inset)
Chemnitz (*since 1953* Karl-Marx-Stadt) E Germany WW1 119/3
Chemulpo (Inchon)
Ch'en N China Chou domain 9/6
Chengchow N China Shang site 8/4; on railway 123/4
Cheng-ho early Chinese navigator 59/3
Chengtu W China on trade route 25/1, 59/3; Ming provincial capital 51/4
Chepstow W England Industrial Revolution 98/1
Chera (*mod.* Kerala) region of S India 29/4
Cherbourg N France English base in Hundred Years' War 56/5; French naval base 80/1, 87/1; WW2 132/2
Cherchell (Caesarea)
Cherchen Chin. C Asia silk route 25/1, 28/2
Cheremkhovo S Siberia industry 147/1
Cherepovets NW Russia industry 147/1
Cheribon (*Dut.* Tjeribon *n/s* Ceribon) district of Java Dutch control 70/4
Chernigov Ukraine bishopric 38/2; principality 45/2
Chernovtsy (Czernowitz)
Cherokee Indian tribe of SE USA 63/1
Cherokees SE USA ⚔95/2
Chersonesus Crimea Ionian colony 19/4; bishopric 27/2
Cherusci Germanic tribe of Roman Empire 30/3
Chester (*anc.* Deva) C England castle 36/3; ⚔33/3; county palatine 73/4; Industrial Revolution 98/1
Cheyenne plains Indian tribe of C USA 63/1
Ch'i NE China Chou domain 9/6; state 28/1
Chia NW China Western Chou domain 9/6
Chiang Kai-shek Chinese statesman 122T
Chiangling C China Western Chou site 9/6
Chiang Mai (Chiengmai)
Chiangnan Hsitao S China T'ang province 50/1
Chiangnan Tung E China Sung province 50/1
Chiangnan Tungtao SE China T'ang province 50/1
Chiao N China Western Chou domain 9/6
Chiaochih China/Vietnam Han commanderie 29/3
Chiaoho Chin. C Asia Han expansion 28/2
Chiapa de Corzo C Mexico early site 12/2
Chiapas province of S Mexico 97/1
Chiba C Japan city and prefecture 126/2, 134/3
Chibcha Andean Indian tribe 63/1
Chicago N USA industry 109/1, 110/2; population 111/5; civil unrest 144/3
Chichén Itzá Mexico Toltec domination 62/2
Chichester S England castle 36/3; Industrial Revolution 98/1
Chichou NE China T'ang prefecture 50/1
Chichun C China Western Chou site 9/6
Chickamauga SE USA ⚔93/5
Chickasaw Indian tribe of SE USA 95/2
Chienchou NE China Ming military post 51/4
Chienchung SW China T'ang province 50/1
Chiengmai (*n/s* Chiang Mai) N Thailand early political centre 51/2
Chiennan W China T'ang province 50/1
Chientao district of Manchuria occupied by Russia 127/4
Chienwei W China Han commanderie 29/3
Chieti (Teate)
Chihli former province of N China Boxer uprising 107/3
Chihuahua province of N Mexico 97/1; US military action 111/4
Chile Spanish colony 69/4; independence from Spain 97/1; War of the Pacific 97/4; exports and foreign investment 96/3; population 96/2; economy 142/2, 3; political development 143/1
Chilia-Nouă (Kilia)
Chimkent Russ. C Asia industry 147/1
Chimú Andean Indian tribe 63/1, 2
Chin N China Chou domain 9/6; empire conquered by Mongols 46/1
Ch'in NW China Chou domain 9/6; empire 28/1, 2; 47/1
China agricultural origins 7/4; beginnings of civilisation 8/2, 4; Chou dynasty 9/6; early trade routes 59/3; Buddhism 27/1; unification 28/1; Han expansion 28/2, 29/3; early Christianity 39/1; T'ang Empire 50/1; Mongol conquests 47/1; Ming Empire 51/4; early trade 51/4; Ch'ing 106-107; Manchu expansion 106/1; Manchu Empire 107/4; Russo-Japanese war 127/4; European spheres of influence 107/4; Boxer rebellion 107/3; Empire overthrown 122/1; Communist Party founded 123/4, 5; Japanese occupation 127/3, 5; Cold War 149/1; political development 141/1
Chingchi N China T'ang province 50/1
Chinghai (Tsinghai)
Chingkang Shan SE China early Communist soviet 123/4
Chingleput SE India ceded to Britain 87/3
Chinkiang E China treaty port 107/4
Chinnampo N Korea Russo-Japanese war 127/4
Chinook coast Indian tribe of W Canada 63/1
Chinsura Bengal Dutch settlment 66/2; 87/2
Chios (*mod. Gk.* Khios) island of E Aegean bishopric 27/2; to Genoa 48/1; ceded to Greece 116/1
Chipewyan sub-arctic Indian tribe of N Canada 63/1
Chirand NE India site 9/1
Chishima-retto (Kurile Islands)
Chisholm Trail C USA cattle trail 94/1
Chişinău (Kishinev)
Chita E Siberia Trans-Siberian railway 84/3; capital of Far Eastern Republic 120/4; industry 147/1
Chittagong SE Bangladesh trade 59/3
Chiuchang E China Han commanderie 29/3
Chiuchen N Indo-China Han commanderie 29/3
Chiuhua Shan mountain of E China Buddhist site 27/1
Chiusi (Clusium)
Chkalov (Orenburg)
Chocó Indian tribe of S America 63/1
Choctaw Indian tribe of S USA 95/2
Choga Mami Mesopotamia site 7/2
Chola ancient country of S India 29/4
Cholula C Mexico early site 12/2; on Cortés' route 68/1
Chorasmii people of C Asia 23/3
Chosen (Korea)
Chota Nagpur region of N India 105/3
Chotin (Khotin)
Chou NC China Western Chou domain 9/6; warring state 28/1
Choukoutien N China site 3/3, 5/2, 8/2
Christchurch S Island, New Zealand founded 112/2
Christiania (Oslo)
Christianity, spread of 26-27, 38-9
Christiansborg Gold Coast early Danish settlement 60/2 (inset)
Chu N China Western Chou domain 9/6
Ch'u C China Chou domain 9/6; warring state 28/1
Ch'u NE China Western Chou domain 9/6
Chud (*a/c* Chudi) early tribe of N Russia 45/2
Chudskoye Ozero (Lake Peipus)
Chukchi tribe of NE Siberia 84/2
Chumash Indian tribe of W USA 63/1
Chün C China Western Chou domain 9/6
Chün N China Western Chou site 9/6
Chungking C China treaty town 107/4; capital during WW2 127/5
Chustenahlah C USA ⚔95/2
Chuvashi tribe of C Russia, conquered 85/1
Chuyen NW China administrative centre of later Han 28/2
Ciboney Indian tribe of the Caribbean 63/1
Cibyrrhaeot Theme Byzantine province of S Anatolia 42/2
Cieszyn (Teschen)
Cilicia (*Hittite name* Kizzuwadna) region of S Anatolia 19/4; Hittite Empire 20/2; Alexander's Empire 22/3; Achaemenid Empire 20/5; Roman province 31/3; Byzantine Empire 43/1
Cincinnati N USA industry 109/1, 110/2; civil unrest 144/3
Circassia (*Turk.* Çerkes) region of Caucasus 49/1
Circeii C Italy Latin colony 30/1
Cirencester (*anc.* Corinium) W England Industrial Revolution 98/1
Cirene (Cyrene)
Cirrha C Greece early site 19/1
Cirta (*mod.* Constantine) N Algeria Roman Empire 24/2, 30/2, 3; early bishopric 26/2
Cisalpine Republic N Italy state established by French Revolution 89/2
Citium (*OT* Kittim) Cyprus Phoenician colony 19/4
Ciudad de México (Mexico City)
Civil War England 76/4
Civil War Spain 129/4
Civil War USA 92/5
Civita Castellana (Falerii)
Claudy N Ireland IRA 136/6
Clearwater NW USA ⚔95/2
Cleveland N USA industry 109/1, 110/2; civil unrest 144/3
Cleves (*Ger.* Kleve) NW Germany Reformation 75/1; duchy 79/1
Clonard Ireland monastery 38/3
Cloncurry N Australia copper mining 113/1
Clonfert Ireland monastery 38/3
Clonmacnoise Ireland monastery 38/3
Clontibret N Ireland ⚔73/4
Clovis King of Franks 34T
Cloyne Ireland bishopric 26/2
Clusium (*mod.* Chiusi) N Italy Etruscan city 30/1
Clyde-Carlingford Cairns Scotland 15/4
Clysma Red Sea early port 25/1; Roman Empire 25/2
Cnossus (*Gr.* Knossos) Crete Roman Empire 24/2, 31/3
Coahuila province of N Mexico 97/1; US military action 111/4
Coahuiltec Indian tribe of N Mexico 63/1
Coalbrookdale C England Industrial Revolution 98/1
Coblenz (*n/s* Koblenz) W Germany WW1 119/3; administrative centre 137/5
Cochimi Indian tribe of W Mexico 63/1
Cochin region of S India early trade 59/3; Portuguese rule 66/2, 67/1; Dutch settlement 67/1; British rule 104/1
Cochin-China region of S Indo-China expansion into Cambodia 71/2; French control 101/1
Cocos Islands (*now* under Australian administration *called* Cocos-Keeling Islands) Indian Ocean British control 101/2
Coele Roman province of SE Anatolia 31/3
Coelho, Duarte Portuguese soldier 64/2
Colchester (Camulodunum)
Colchis ancient country of the Caucasus, Ionian colonisation 19/4; 22/3, 31/3
Coldizzi Slav tribe of SE Germany 54/2
Cold War 148-9
Colenso S Africa ⚔103/4
Colima province of C Mexico 97/1
Cologne (*anc.* Colonia Agrippina *Ger.* Köln) W Germany medieval city 54/1, 55/3; Hanseatic city 59/2; archbishopric 34/4; WW1 119/3; WW2 133/2
Colombia independence from Spain 97/1; exports and foreign investment 96/3; population 96/2; political development 143/1; economy 142/2, 3; 150/1
Colombo Ceylon early trade 59/3; Portuguese trade 67/1; Dutch trade 66/2; capital of British colony 105/3
Colón Panama Canal Zone 111/4

Colonia Agrippina (*a/c* Colonia Agrippinesis *mod.* Köln *Eng.* Cologne) NW Germany Mithraic site 26/1; Roman Empire 24/2, 30/3; bishopric 26/2
Colonial Theme Byzantine province of E Anatolia 42/2
Colorado state of W USA Depression 130/2; population 145/1
Colossae W Anatolia town of Achaemenid Empire 20/5
Columba, St. 38/3
Columban, St. 38/3
Columbia SE USA burned 93/5
Columbus, Christopher 64-65
Comacchio N Italy captured by Venice 36/2
Comanche plains Indian tribe of S USA 63/1
Combe-Capelle France site of early man 3/3
COMECON 137/3
Commagene region of SE Anatolia Roman province 31/3
Commenda W Africa early British settlement 60/2 (inset)
Comminges independent fief of SW France 72/2
Como N Italy Lombard League 55/3
Comoro Islands E Africa spread of Islam 61/2; French colonisation 101/2; independence 138/1
Compiègne NE France WW1 119/3
Comtat Venaissin S France Papal state 72/2
Conakry W Africa occupied by French 103/3
Concord NE USA ✕92/1
Condatomagus (*mod.* La Graufesenque) S France Roman Empire 24/2
Confederate States of America 93/4
Confederation of the Rhine 91/1
Confucius Chinese philosopher 26T
Congo (*form.* Middle Congo *or* French Congo) region of C Africa independence 138/1; economy 151/1
Congo Free State (*later* Belgian Congo *now* Zaire) 101/2, 103/3
Connaught (*a/s* Connacht) region of W Ireland Norman-Angevin overlordship 53/6; Presidency 73/4
Connecticut NE USA colony 67/3; Depression 131/2; population 145/1
Connell's Prairie NW USA ✕95/2
Consentia (*mod.* Cosenza) S Italy Roman Empire 30/1
Constance (*anc.* Constantia *Ger.* Konstanz) S Germany Frankish kingdom 55/3
Constanţa (Tomi)
Constanţa (*Turk.* Küstence) E Romania WW1 119/3
Constantia (Salamis)
Constantinople (*anc.* Byzantium *mod.* Istanbul) NW Turkey centre of early Christianity 26/1; Avar attack 32/1; patriarchate 38/2; Arab attacks 41/1; Byzantine Empire 42/4; trade 58/3; WW1 119/3
Conway Castle N Wales 53/7
Cook, Capt. James 64-65
Cook Islands S Pacific early Polynesian settlement 10/2; New Zealand possession 139/1 (inset)
Cook Strait New Zealand rail ferry 112/2
Cooktown E Australia early settlement 113/1
Copán E Mexico Mayan site 12/2
Copenhagen (*Dan.* København) Denmark ✕90/3; WW2 133/2
Coppa Nevigata S Italy site 14/1
Copts Christian people of Egypt 38/1
Coptus Lower Egypt Roman Empire 31/3; bishopric 27/2
Coquilhatville (*now* Mbandaka) NW Belgian Congo 38/4
Cora Indian tribe of C Mexico 63/1
Coracesium S Anatolia 19/4
Coral Sea S Pacific ✕135/1
Corbie N France monastery 34/4
Corcyra (*mod.* Corfu *Gr.* Kerkira) island of NW Greece Dorian colony 19/4
Córdoba (*anc.* Corduba) S Spain Muslim conquest 40/1; Umayyad Caliphate and Muslim city 36/2, 37/1; reconquered from Muslims 37/4; Mediterranean trade 58/3; Civil War 129/4
Corduba (*mod.* Córdoba) S Spain Roman Empire 24/2, 30/3; bishopric 26/2
Corfe Castle S England 36/3
Corfu (*anc.* Corcyra *mod. Gr.* Kerkira) island of W Greece Byzantine Empire 42/3; under Venetian rule 48/1; Ottoman siege 48/2
Corinium (Cirencester)
Corinth (*Lat.* Corinthus *Gr.* Korinthos) C Greece parent state 19/4; archbishopric 27/2; Byzantine Empire 43/1
Corinth SE USA 93/5
Corinthus (*Gr.* Korinthos *Eng.* Corinth) C Greece town of Roman Empire 24/2, 31/3
Cork S Ireland monastery 38/3
Cormantin W Africa early Dutch settlement 60/2 (inset)
Corneto (Tarquinia)
Cornwall county of SW England early tin source 14/3; rebellion 73/4
Corregidor C Philippines surrender to Japanese 135/1
Corsica island of W Mediterranean Muslim conquest 40/1; Saracen attack 37/1; Byzantine Empire 42/1; Pisan conquest 36/2; Genoese rule 73/5; annexed by France 114/3
Corte-Real, Gaspar and Miguel Portuguese explorers 64/2

Cortés, Hernando conqueror of Mexico 68T/1
Cortona N Italy Etruscan city 19/4, 30/1
Corunna (*Sp.* La Coruña) NW Spain ✕90/1
Cos island of E Aegean bishopric 27/2
Cosa N Italy Roman Empire 30/1
Cosenza (Cosentia)
Cossacks S Russia attacked by Ottomans 85/1; anti-Bolshevik activity 121/2
Cossaei tribe of W Persia 22/3
Costa Rica country of C America independence 97/1; political development 143/1; economy 142/2, 3; 150/1
Costoboci early tribe of SE Europe 31/3
Cotyora (*mod.* Ordu) N Anatolia Ionian colony 19/4
Courland (*Ger.* Kurland) region of W Russia occupied by Teutonic Knights 54/4; Reformation 75/1
Courtrai (*Dut.* Kortrijk) Belgium ✕52/2
Court St. Etienne N France early Hallstatt site 15/6
Coventry C England Industrial Revolution 98/1; WW2 132/1
Cracow (*Pol.* Kraków) SE Poland bishopric 38/2, 53/1; Hanseatic city 59/2
Craigavon N Ireland IRA 137/6
Crécy N France ✕56/5
Cree sub-arctic Indian tribe of N Canada 63/1
Creek Indian tribe of SE USA 95/2
Crema N Italy Lombard League 55/3
Cremona N Italy Latin colony 30/1; Lombard League 55/3; Signorial domination 56/3
Crete (*Lat.* Creta *mod. Gr.* Kriti) migrations to Greece and Aegean 18-19; Muslim conquest 41/1; Byzantine Empire 36/2, 43/1; Venetian territory 73/1; Ottoman province 124/1; cession to Greece 116/1; German capture 133/2
Criccieth N Wales castle 53/7
Crimea (*Russ.* Krym) S Russia conquered by Mongols 46/1; acquired by Russia 85/1; Ottoman vassal khanate 49/1
Crna Gora (Montenegro)
Croatia (*S. Cr.* Hrvatska) region of N Yugoslavia conversion to Christianity 38/2; Mongol invasion 46/2; under Hungarian Kingdom 56/2; forms part of Yugoslavia 128/2; WW2 133/2
Croats Slav people of SE Europe 32/2
Cro-Magnon France site of early man 3/3
Cromarty N Scotland WW1 118/3
Cromna N Anatolia Ionian colony 19/4
Crooked Creek C USA ✕95/2
Cross, Cape SW Africa Portuguese discovery 64/1
Crossmaglen N Ireland IRA 137/6
Croton (*mod.* Crotone) S Italy Achaean colony 19/4; Roman colony 31/2, 3
Crow plains Indian tribe of W Canada 63/1
Crown Point (*Fr.* Fort St. Frédéric) Quebec capture by British 86/1
Croydon NE Australia early settlement 113/1
Crumlin S Wales Industrial Revolution 98/1
Cruni Bulgaria Ionian colony 19/4
Crusades 36T, 38T, 40/3, 43/3
Ctesiphon (*a/c* Tayspun) Mesopotamia early trade 25/1; Roman Empire 31/3
Cuba discovered 64/2; Spanish colony 66/1, 4; 69/3, 86/1; independence 97/1; exports and investment 96/3; US Protectorate 143/1; Cold War crisis 149/5
Cuddapah S India ceded to Britain 87/3
Cultural Revolution China 140T
Cumae C Italy Ionian colony 19/4, 23/2; Roman Empire 30/1
Cumberland House C Canada fort 68/5
Cuna Indian tribe of C America 63/1
Cunaxa Mesopotamia ✕21/5
Curaçao island of S West Indies captured by Dutch from Spanish 69/3; Dutch settlement and colonisation 97/1, 139/1 (inset)
Curium Cyprus Greek colony 19/4
Curlew Mts NW Ireland ✕73/4
Cusae Lower Egypt 21/1
Custozza N Italy ✕114/3
Cutch (Kutch)
Cuttack E India ceded to Britain 87/3
Cuxhaven N Germany WW1 119/3
Cuzco Peru Inca Empire 68/2
Cydonia (Khania)
Cymru (Wales)
Cynoscephalae C Greece ✕22/4
Cynossema W Anatolia ✕23/2
Cyprus (*Gr.* Kypros *Turk.* Kıbrıs *anc.* Alashiya) Greek and Phoenician colonisation 19/4; Muslim expansion 41/1; Byzantine Empire 37/2, 40/3, 43/1; Venetian territory 49/1; acquired by Turks 48/2; annexed by Britain 125/2; independence 138/1; invaded by Turkey 140/1
Cyrenaica region of N Africa Greek settlement 11/1; Roman province 31/3; Muslim conquest 41/1; Ottoman rule 61/2; Italian conquest 103/3
Cyrene (*It.* Cirene) Dorian colony 19/4; spread of Christianity and Judaism 26/1; Achaemenid Empire 20/5; centre of Roman province 24/2, 31/3; early bishopric 27/2
Cyropolis (*a/c* Krukath) C Asia Alexander's route 23/3; Achaemenid Empire 21/5
Cyrus King of Persia 21/5

Cythera (*a/c* Cerigo *mod. Gr.* Kithira) *island* S Greece colonisation 19/1; captured by Athens 23/2
Cytorus N Anatolia Ionian colony 19/4
Cyzicus NW Anatolia ✕23/2; Ionian colony 19/4; early archbishopric 27/2
Czechoslovakia created 128/2; inter-war alliances 128/1; socio-political development 131/3; territory lost to Germany and Hungary 129/5, 132-3; Comecon and Warsaw Pact 137/3, 149/1
Czechs post-War migration to West 136/1
Czernowitz (*now Russ.* Chernovtsy *Rom.* Cernăuţi) E Austro-Hungarian Empire WW1 119/3

Dabarkot NW India Harappan site 9/5
Dąbromierz (Hohenfriedeberg)
Dacca Bangladesh industry 105/3
Dachau S Germany concentration camp 132/1
Dacia (*mod.* Romania) province of Roman Empire 31/3; Byzantine Empire 43/1
Dade Massacre SE USA ✕95/2
Daghestan region of Caucasus acquired by Russia 125/1
Dagobert I King of Franks 34T
Dagon (*mod.* Rangoon) S Burma Buddhism 70/1
Dahae early tribe of C Asia 23/3
Dahomey (*n/c* Benin) country of W Africa early state 61/2; French colony 100/2, 103/3; independence 138/1
Daima NW Africa Stone and Iron Age site 11/1
Daimabad S India site 9/1
Daimyo Japanese military class 50T, 51/3
Dairen (*Russ.* Dalny) Manchuria ceded to Russia and Japan 107/4; Russo-Japanese war 127/4
Dai Viet kingdom of N Indo-China 51/2
Dakar Senegal, W Africa French settlement 103/3
Daleminzi Slav tribe of C Germany 54/2, 55/1
Dalmatia region of E Adriatic Byzantine Empire 43/3; acquired by Habsburgs 78/3
Dalny (Dairen)
Daman (*Port.* Damão) NW India Portuguese settlement 105/3
Damascus (*Fr.* Damas *Ar.* Ash Sham *or* Dimashq) Syria Assyrian Empire 17/4; Roman Empire 25/2; early trade 25/1, 58/3; archbishopric 38/1; Muslim conquest 41/1; Byzantine Empire 43/1; Ottoman Empire 49/1; WW1 125/2
Damb Buthi N India early site 9/5
Damietta (*Ar.* Dumyat) N Egypt Byzantine Empire 43/1
Danakil tribe of NE Africa 60/1
Da Nang (*Fr.* Tourane) C Indo-China Vietnamese war 148/3
Danebury S England Iron Age site 15/6
Danelaw England under Scandinavian control 36T
Danes people of N Europe 37/1, 3; 115/1
Danzig (*Pol.* Gdańsk) N Poland to Prussia 78/4; Hanseatic city 59/2; Baltic trade 58/3; 18C financial centre 82/4; Free City 128/2
Dardanelles (*Turk.* Çanakkale Boğazı *anc.* Hellespont) straits, NW Turkey demilitarised and remilitarised 128/2
Dardani early people of the Balkans 22/3
Dar es Salaam E Africa occupied by Germans 103/3
Darfur region of W Sudan stone age culture 11/1; early state 60/1, 61/2
Darius I, of Persia 22/1
Dartford SE England Industrial Revolution 98/1
Darwin N Australia early settlement 113/1; Allied base in WW2 135/1
Dascylium NW Anatolia Greek colony 19/4
Daugavpils (Dünaburg)
Dauphiné region of SE France French Royal domain 52/2, 56/5; province of France 80/1
David King of Israelites 21/4
Davis, John English explorer 64-65
Dead Buffalo Lake E USA ✕95/2
Debre Birhan Ethiopia monastery 38/1
Debre Markos Ethiopian monastery 38/1
Decapolis Judaea 26/3
Deccan region of C India Sultanate 48/2
Dego N Italy ✕90/1
Deheubarth dist. of Wales 36/3
Deira ancient kingdom of N England 33/3, 35/3
Delagoa Bay SE Africa early trade 61/2; Portuguese settlement 87/2
Delaware state of E USA settled by Swedes 67/3; British colony 92/1; Depression 131/2; population 145/1
Delaware Indian tribe of NE USA 63/1
Delhi city and region of N India Mongol invasion 47/1; Mughal Empire 48/2, 47/1, 3; Indian Mutiny 104/1
Delian League Greece 23/2
Delium E Greece ✕23/2
Delphi C Greece early settlement 15/6
Demetrias E Greece Byzantine Empire 43/1
Denain N France ✕81/5
Denbigh N Wales ✕53/7
Denizli (Laodicea)
Denmark conversion to Christianity 38/2; rise of 52/3; union with Norway and Sweden 72/1, 114/4; Reformation 75/1; emancipation of peasantry 82/1; loss

Loyang N China Chou site 9/6; early trade 25/1; sacked by Hsiung-nu 33/1
Lozi tribe of C Africa 60/1
Lu E China Chou domain 9/6; state 28/1
Lü C China Western Chou domain 9/6
Luanda Angola early trade 67/1; Portuguese settlement 61/2
Luango early state of W Africa 61/2
Luang Prabang SE Asia early political centre 51/2
Luba early kingdom of C Africa 60/1, 61/2
Lübeck N Germany urban revolt 57/1; Hanseatic city 59/2; Reformation 75/1; bishopric 79/1; WW1 119/3; WW2 133/2
Lublin Poland medieval fair 59/2; WW1 119/3
Lubumbashi (Elisabethville)
Lubusi S Africa Iron Age site 11/1
Lucania region of S Italy part of Kingdom of Naples 56/3
Lucca N Italy Republican commune 56/3; independent republic 73/5, 88/3
Lucerne (Ger. Luzern) early Swiss canton 54/5
Łuck (Lutsk)
Lucknow N India Indian Mutiny 104/1; industry 105/3
Ludendorff offensive 118-9
Lüderitz SW Africa German settlement 103/5
Lugansk (between 1935-58 and since 1970 called Voroshilovgrad) Ukraine 1905 Revolution 120/1
Lugdunensis Roman province of N France 30/1
Lugdunum (mod. Lyon Eng. Lyons) C France Roman Empire 24/2, 30/3; archbishopric 26/2
Luluabourg (now Kananga) C Belgian Congo 138/4
Lumbini Tibet Buddhist site 27/1
Luna (mod. Luni) N Italy Roman colony 30/1
Lund S Sweden bishopric 38/2; Danish archbishopric 53/3
Lunda early kingdom of C Africa 60/1, 61/2
Lüneburg N Germany Hanseatic city 59/2
Lungchow SW China treaty port 107/4
Lunghsi NW China Han commanderie 29/3
Lungyu NW China T'ang province 50/1
Luni (Luna)
Lusatia (Ger. Lausitz) region of E Germany under medieval German Empire 55/1, 3; acquired by Habsburgs 56/2; modern German Empire 79/1
Lusitania (mod. Portugal) province of Roman Empire 30/1
Lusizzi Slav tribe of Germany 55/1
Lutetia (mod. Paris) N France Roman Empire 30/3
Lutsk (Pol. Łuck) W Russia WW1 119/3
Lutter W Germany ⚔74/4
Lutynia (Leuthen)
Lützen C Germany ⚔74/4, 91/1
Luvians (a/c Luwians) ancient people of Anatolia 6/3, 16/2
Luxembourg (Ger. Luxemburg) Burgundian possession 73/3; German customs union 98/3; German Confederation 114/5; WW1 118/1; EEC and NATO 137/3
Luxeuil E France monastery 38/3
Luxor Upper Egypt 21/1
Luzern (Lucerne)
Luzon island of N Philippines American occupation 110/4; Japanese occupation 135/1
Luzzara N Italy ⚔81/5
Lvov (Pol. Łwów) W Ukraine industry 147/1
Lycia country of SW Anatolia 19/4; Roman Empire 31/3
Lycians early people of W Anatolia 18/2
Lydia country of W Anatolia 22/1; Byzantine Empire 43/1
Lyon (Lyons)
Lyonnais region of C France Royal domain 52/2
Lyons (anc. Lugdunum Fr. Lyon) C France medieval fair 59/2; 18C financial centre 82/4; St Bartholomew Massacre 74/3; centre of French Revolution 89/2
Lys river NE France WW1 119/3 (inset)
Lystra S Anatolia early bishopric 27/2

Maastricht town of Spanish Netherlands 77/1
Mabueni S Africa Iron Age site 11/1
Macao (Port. Macau) S China early Portuguese trade 67/1; Portuguese settlement 66/2; Portuguese colony 101/2, 107/4, 139/1
Macassar (Indon. Makasar) East Indies Dutch settlement 66/2, 71/2
Macau (Macao)
Macclesfield C England Industrial Revolution 98/1
Macedonia region of SE Europe 19/4; conquered by Persians 22/1; Antigonid Kingdom 22/4; Roman province 31/3; Byzantine Empire 43/1; Ottoman province 124/1; divided between Serbia, Greece and Bulgaria 116/1; Greek-Bulgarian conflict 128/2
Macedonians Slav people of SE Europe 115/1
Machaerus Judaea area of revolt 26/3
Machili S Africa Iron Age site 11/1
Macias Nguema Biyogo (Fernando Po)
Mackay E Australia early settlement 113/1
Macon USA early site 12/3
Macquarie Harbour Tasmania penal settlement 113/1
Macú Indian tribe of S America 63/1
Mada (a/c Media) country of NW Persia satrapy of Achaemenid Empire 21/5

Madagascar (form. Malagasy Republic) Indonesian settlement 11/1, 60/1, 3; settlement from Africa 61/2; French penetration 103/3; French colony 100/2, 103/3; independence 138/1; political development 140/1; economy 150/1
Madeira island of E Atlantic Portuguese exploration 64/1; Portuguese territory 100/2, 138/1
Madhya Bharat state of C India 105/5
Madhya Pradesh (form. Central Provinces) state of C India 105/5
Madras (now Tamil Nadu) state and city, S India British settlement 66/2; captured by French 87/2 (inset); under British rule 104/1; trade and industry 105/3
Madrid C Spain 18C financial centre 82/4; captured by French 90/1; Civil War 129/4
Madura island of E Indies Dutch control 71/4; joins Indonesia 139/2
Madura S India industry 105/3
Maes Howe Scotland site 15/4
Mafeking S Africa Boer War 103/4
Magadha early kingdom of NE India 29/4
Magdeburg E Germany bishopric 38/2; archbishopric 52/1, 79/1; Reformation 74/4, 75/1; Hanseatic city 59/2; industrial development 99/2; WW1 119/3
Magellan Strait S America first sailed 64/2
Magenta N Italy ⚔114/3
Magersfontein S Africa ⚔103/4
Maghreb (collective name for Algeria, Morocco and Tunisia)
Maginot Line E France defence system 132/1
Magna Graecia the Greek colonies of S Italy 19/4, 23/2
Magnesia (a/c Magnesia ad Maeandrum) W Anatolia ⚔22/1
Magnitogorsk C Russia industry 147/1; urban growth 146/2
Magnus the Good King of Norway 52T
Magyars invade W Europe 37/1
Maha-Kosala early country of C India 29/4
Maharashtra state of W India 29/4
Mahayana Buddhism 26T, 70/1
Mahdia (a/s Mehdia) Tunisia Pisan raids 36/2
Mahé SW India French settlement 87/2 (inset), 105/3
Mahón Minorca, Spain Civil War 129/4
Mähren (Moravia)
Maidstone SE England rebellion 73/4; Industrial Revolution 98/1
Mainake S Spain Ionian colony 18/4
Maine state of NE USA British settlement 67/3; Depression 131/2; population 111/5, 145/1
Maine region of N France 52/2, 72/2, 80/1
Mainpuri N India centre of Mutiny 104/1
Mainz (anc. Mogontiacum) C Germany archbishopric 34/4, 38/3, 79/1; medieval trade 58/1
Majapahit Java early Empire 51/2; trade 59/3
Majdanek E Poland concentration camp 132/1
Majorca (Sp. Mallorca) Civil War 129/4
Majuba Hill S Africa ⚔103/2
Majuro island of Marshalls, C Pacific occupied by US 135/1
Makakam SE Borneo Hindu-Buddhist remains 51/2
Makapan S Africa site of early man 3/3
Makasar (Macassar)
Makran region of SE Persia Muslim conquest 41/1
Makurra state of NE Africa 60/1
Malabar district of S India ceded to Britain 87/3
Malaca (mod. Málaga) S Spain Roman Empire 24/2, 30/3
Malacca (Mal. Melaka) district of S Malaya early sultanate 51/2; early trade 59/3, 67/1; captured by Portuguese 66/2, 70/3; European discovery 65/2; captured by Dutch 66/2, 70/3; under Portuguese rule 71/2; British possession 71/5, 101/1
Málaga (anc. Malaca) S Spain 18C urban development 83/4; ⚔81/5; Civil War 129/4
Malaga Cove W USA site 62/4
Malagasy Republic (Madagascar)
Malapati S Africa Iron Age site 11/1
Malatya (anc. Melitene) E Turkey revolt against Ottoman rule 48/2
Malavas people of NW India 29/5
Malawi (form. Nyasaland) country of C Africa independence 138/1; political development 140/1; economy 150/1
Malaya Iron and Bronze Age sites 8/3; spread of Islam 40/5, 70/1; British control 101/2; occupied by Japanese 134/1. See also Malaysia
Malaysia (state formed by amalgamation of Malaya, Sarawak and Sabah) independence 139/1; economy 150/1; confrontation with Indonesia 139/2
Malay States SE Asia British protectorate 71/5. See also Malaya, Malaysia
Malbork (Marienburg)
Maldives islands of N Indian Ocean acquired by British 87/2; protectorate 101/2; independence 139/1
Mali (form. French Sudan) country of West Africa independence 138/1; political development 140/1; economy 150/1

Mali Empire early state of W Africa 60/1
Malinalco Mexico Aztec temple 62/2
Malindi Kenya Muslim colony 60/1; early Portuguese trade 61/2
Mallia Crete palace site 19/1
Mallorca (Majorca)
Mallus W Anatolia Ionian colony 19/4
Malmédy E Belgium ceded by Germany 128/2
Maloyaroslavets W Russia ⚔91/1
Malplaquet N France ⚔81/5
Malta island of C Mediterranean Norman conquest 36/; British colony 101/2; WW2 133/4; independence 138/
Małujowice (Mollwitz)
Maluku (Moluccas)
Malvinas, Islas (Falkland Islands)
Mameluke Empire Egypt/Palestine Mongol invasion 46/1
Mamelukes (a/s Mamluk) 40/2
Manassas (a/c Bull Run) E USA ⚔93/5
Manchanagara district of Java Dutch control 71/4
Manchester N England industrial development 98/1
Manchouli N China treaty town 107/4
Manchukuo (name given to Manchuria as Japanese puppet state)
Manchuria (called 1932-45 Manchukuo) region of NE China Manchu homeland 106/1; occupied by Russia 107/4; Russo-Japanese war 127/4; Russian and Japanese spheres of influence 127/3; warlord control 122/2; Japanese puppet state 123/3, 4; 127/5; reoccupied by Russia 135/1
Manchus people of NE China, under the Ming 51/4; homeland expansion 106/1
Mandalay C Burma trade 71/2; terminus of Burma Road 127/5; occupied by Japanese 134/1; 134/2
Mandan plains Indian tribe of C Canada 63/1
Mangalore S India industry 105/3
Mang-vu Siam early trade 59/3
Manhao SW China treaty town 107/4
Manila C Philippines early trade 67/1; Spanish settlement 66/2; captured by Japanese 135/1
Manipur state of E India 71/2, 104/2, 105/5
Manisa W Anatolia Ottoman Empire 49/1
Manitoba province of C Canada economic development 111/1; joins Confederation 101/1
Mannheim W Germany industrial development 99/2; WW2 133/2
Mantinea C Greece ⚔23/2
Mantua (It. Mantova) N Italy Lombard League 55/3; Signorial domination 56/3; 73/5
Manuel I Byzantine Emperor 42T
Manuel's Fort N USA fur station 94/1
Manunggul Cave W Philippines Iron Age site 8/3
Manus Island W Pacific US base 135/1
Manzikert E Anatolia ⚔42/4, 43/1
Mao-Mao Kenyan guerrilla movement 138/1
Maoris New Zealand tribe 112/2, 3
Mao Tse-tung 122T
Mapungubwe early state of SE Africa 60/1
Maracanda (mod. Samarkand) Alexander's route 23/3 Achaemenid Empire 21/5; early trade 25/1
Maranga C Andes early site 12/4
Maranhão province of Brazil 97/1
Mărăşeşti Romania WW1 119/3
Marash (Turk. Maraş) N Anatolia Byzantine Empire 43/3
Maratha Confederacy N India 87/3; in alliance with British 87/2
Marathon C Greece ⚔20/5, 22/1
Maravi early state of E Africa 61/2
Marche region of C France 52/2; annexed by France 72/2
Marches (It. Le Marche) province of Italy unification 114/3
Marches, of Wales 73/4
Marcianopolis Bulgaria early archbishopric 27/2; Byzantine Empire 43/1
Marcomanni early tribe of C Europe 30/3, 31/4
Marco Polo route 59/3
Mardi early tribe of N Persia 22/3
Marengo N Italy ⚔90/1
Mari Mesopotamia early urban settlement 16/1
Mari people of C Russia 44/3, 45/2, 85/1
Marianas (form. Ladrones) islands of W Pacific German colony 101/4; US occupation 135/1
Marie Galante island of W Indies French settlement 66/4 (inset)
Marienburg (Pol. Malbork) N Poland seat of Teutonic Order 54/4
Marienwerder (Pol. Kwidzyn) N Poland founded by Teutonic Knights 54/4; 1920 plebiscite 128/2
Maritime Provinces (Russ. Primorskiy Kray) Russ. Far East acquired from China 107/4
Mariupol (now Zhdanov) S Russia industry 85/4
Marj Dabik SE Anatolia ⚔49/1
Mark W Germany Reformation 74/4
Market Harborough C England Industrial Revolution 98/1
Marksville USA Hopewell site 12/3

Marlborough province of S Island, New Zealand 112/2
Marne *river* NE France WW1 119/2; ⚔118/3 (inset)
Maroc (Morocco)
Marqab Syria 40/3
Marquesas Islands S Pacific Polynesian dispersal centre 11/2; French colony 139/1 (inset)
Marrakesh (*Fr.* Marrakech) Morocco early trade 58/3, 61/2
Marruecos (Morocco)
Marsala (Lilybaeum)
Marseilles (*Fr.* Marseille *anc.* Massilia) S France Mediterranean trade 58/3; galley port 80/1; centre of French Revolution 89/2
Marshall Islands C Pacific German colony 101/2; occupied by US 135/1
Marshall Plan 136T
Marston Moor N England ⚔76/4
Martinique island of W Indies French settlement 66/4, 69/3; attacked by British 86/1; French territory 97/1, 100/2, 139/1 (inset)
Martyropolis E Anatolia early bishopric 27/2
Mary (Merv)
Maryland state of E USA colony 67/3, 92/1; Civil War 93/5; Depression 131/2; population 111/5, 145/1
Masada Judaea Roman siege 26/3
Masai tribe of E Africa 60/1
Masampo S Korea Russo-Japanese war 127/4
Mashhad (Meshed)
Masovia (*a/s* Mazovia *Pol.* Mazowsze) region of Poland 53/1, 54/4
Masqat (Muscat)
Massachuset Indian tribe of NE USA 63/1
Massachusetts state of NE USA British colony 92/1; Depression 131/2; population 111/5, 145/1
Massachusetts Bay NE USA British colony 67/3
Massagetae tribe of C Asia 23/3
Massawa N Ethiopia Ottoman settlement 48/2, 61/2; Italian attack 103/3
Massilia (*mod.* Marseille *Eng.* Marseilles) S France Roman Empire 24/2, 30/2, 3; bishopric 26/2
Masulipatam S India early trade 25/1
Mataco Indian tribe of S America 63/1
Matadi W Belgian Congo 138/4
Mataram Sultanate of Java Dutch control 71/2
Matjiesrivier S Africa site of early man 3/3
Mato Grosso province of Brazil 97/1
Matsu *island* SE China Nationalist outpost 149/1
Matsue W Japan 126/2
Matsuyama W Japan 126/2
Matthias Corvinus king of Hungary 72/1, T
Maubeuge NE France WW1 119/2
Mauer Germany site of early man 3/3
Mauretania region of NW Africa conversion to Christianity 26/1
Maurice (Mauritius)
Mauritania country of NW Africa independence from France 138/1; political development 140/1; economy 150/1
Mauritius (*Fr.* Maurice) *island* Indian Ocean early trade 66/2; British colony 101/1, 2
Mauthausen Austria concentration camp 132/1
Maya people and civilisation of C America 12/2, 13/1, 62/2
Mayapán Mayan city of E Mexico destroyed 62/2
Maykop Caucasus early urban centre 16/1
Maysville Road C USA settlers' route 94/1
Mazaca (*mod.* Kayseri) C Anatolia Achaemenid Empire 21/5
Mazovia (Masovia)
Mazowsze (Masovia)
Mbandaka (Coquilhatville)
Meadows, The W USA⚔94/2
Meath early kingdom of C Ireland 53/6
Meaux N France unrest 57/1; St. Bartholomew Massacre 74/3
Mecca (*Ar.* Al Makkah) W Arabia birth of Islam 41/1; early trade 58/3; Ottoman Empire 48/2; WW1 125/2
Mechta Tunisia site of early man 3/3
Mecklenburg N Germany duchy 79/1; Reformation 74/4, 75/1; unification of Germany 98/3, 115/2
Medes ancient people of NW Persia 20T
Media (*a/c* Mada) ancient country of NW Persia in Alexander's Empire 22/3
Media Atropatene Hellenised kingdom of NW Persia 22/4
Medina (*Ar.* Al Madinah) W Arabia centre of Islam 41/1; early trade 58/3; Ottoman Empire 48/2; WW1 125/2
Medina del Campo N Spain medieval fair 59/2
Medina de Rioseco N Spain medieval fair 59/2
Mediolanum (*mod.* Milano *Eng.* Milan) N Italy Roman Empire 24/2, 30/3; bishopric 26/2
Mediterranean Sea Greek colonisation 18/4; Phoenicians 18/4; Roman routes 24/2; Saracen invasions 37/1; Norman and Venetian expansion and Byzantine reconquest 36/2; early trade routes 24/2, 58/3; WW2 132-3
Meersen, Partition of 35/6
Meerut N India Indian Mutiny 104/1
Megara C Greece Greek parent state 19/4

Megara-Hyblaea Sicily Greek colony 19/4
Megiddo Palestine ⚔WW1 125/2
Mehdia (Mahdia)
Mehemmed I Ottoman ruler 48T, 49/1
Mehemmed II Ottoman ruler 48T, 49/1
Mehi N India Harappan site 9/5
Meiji Restoration Japan 126T
Meissen district of E Germany 52/1, 55/1, 3
Melaka (Malacca)
Melanesia region of W Pacific early settlement 10/2
Melbourne SE Australia founded 113/1
Melilla (*anc.* Rusaddir) N Morocco Mediterranean trade 58/3; acquired by Habsburgs 72/1
Melitene (*mod.* Malatya) E Anatolia spread of Mithraism 26/1; Roman Empire 24/2, 31/3; early archbishopric 27/2; Byzantine Empire 42/2
Mello N France civil unrest 57/1
Melolo S East Indies Iron Age site 8/3
Melville Island N Australia 113/1
Memel (*Lith.* Klaipeda) NW Russia founded by Teutonic Knights 54/4; WW1 119/3
Memel Territory (*Ger.* Memelgebiet *or* Memelland) region of SW Lithuania annexed by Germany 129/3
Memphis Lower Egypt city of Ancient Egypt 21/1; Alexander's route 22/3; Achaemenid Empire 20/5; Roman Empire 24/2, 31/3; Byzantine Empire 43/1
Memphis SE USA⚔92/5; civil unrest 144/3
Mende N Greece early bishopric 19/4
Menes king of Egypt 16T
Mengtze (*Fr.* Mong-tseu) SW China treaty port 107/4
Mennonites sect 74/2
Menominee Indian tribe of C USA 63/1
Menorca (Minorca)
Mentese early emirate of SW Anatolia 49/1
Mercia early kingdom of C England 35/3, 38/3
Meremere N Island, New Zealand ⚔112/3
Mérida (*anc.* Emerita Augusta) SW Spain Civil War 129/4
Mérida SE Mexico early Spanish city 66/1
Merimbe Egypt Stone Age site 11/1
Merina early state in Madagascar 103/3
Merkits Mongolian tribe 47/1
Meroë Sudan Iron Age site 11/1; city of Alwa 60/1
Merovingian kingdom 35/2
Mersa Matruh (Paraetonium)
Merse (of Berwick) SE Scotland acquired by Edward III 56/4
Mersin E Anatolia early trade 17/4; destroyed 18/2
Merthyr Tydfil S Wales Industrial Revolution 98/1
Merv (*since 1937* Mary *anc.* Alexandria) Russ. C Asia early trade 59/3; spread of Christianity 26/1; early archbishopric 39/1; Muslim conquest 41/1; Safavid Empire 48/2
Mesaverde SW USA site 62/4
Mesembria Bulgaria Greek colony 19/4
Mesen (Messines)
Meshchera E Slav tribe of C Russia 85/1
Meshed (*Pers.* Mashhad) Alexander's Empire 23/3
Mesoamerica classic period 12/3
Mesopotamia (*mod.* Iraq) earliest settlement 7/2; early empires 16-17; spread of Mithraism 26/1; Alexander's Empire 23/2; Roman Empire 31/3; Muslim conquest 41/1; WW1 125/2
Messana (*mod.* Messina) Sicily Roman Empire 24/2, 30/3, 23/2
Messapii early people of S Italy 30/1
Messenia ancient region of SW Greece 18/3
Messina (*anc.* Zancle *later* Messana) Sicily early bishopric 26/2; Norman conquest 36/2; 18C urban development 82/4; WW2 133/2
Messines (*Dut.* Mesen) Belgium medieval fair 58/1; WW1 118/3 (inset)
Metaurus N Italy ⚔30/2
Methven C Scotland ⚔56/4
Metz NE France annexed to France 151/4; centre of French Revolution 89/2; WW1 119/3; WW2 133/2
Meuse (*Dut.* Maas) *river* NE France WW1 119/3 (inset)
Mexico Aztec Empire 62/2; Spanish colonisation 68/1; imperial trade 66/1; independence 101/1; exports and foreign investment 96/3; population 96/2; US intervention 143/1; political development 97/1; economy 109/1, 142-3
Mi C China Western Chou site 9/6
Miami Indian tribe of C USA 63/1
Michigan state of N USA Depression 131/2; population 111/5, 145/1
Michoacán province of C Mexico 97/1
Micmac Indian tribe of NE Canada 63/1
Middle East (*a/c* Near East) WW1 125/2; Cold War 148/4
Midhurst S England Industrial Revolution 98/1
Midland S USA site of early man 3/3
Midnapore district of NE India ceded to Britain 87/3, 105/4
Midway island of C Pacific US occupation 110/4; WW2 ⚔135/1; US base 149/1 (inset)
Mie prefecture of C Japan 126/2
Milan (*It.* Milano *anc.* Mediolanum) N Italy Lombard League 55/3; medieval trade 58/1; Signorial domination 56/3; Duchy 73/5; industrial development 99/2

Milas (Mylasa)
Milazzo (Mylae)
Miletus W Anatolia Cretan settlement 19/1, 4; Greek parent state 22/1; Roman Empire 31/3; bishopric 27/2; Byzantine Empire 43/1
Milev Algeria early bishopric 26/2
Milford Haven S Wales port 98/1
Military Frontier 78/3
Milizi Slav tribe of E Germany 55/1
Milk Creek C USA ⚔95/2
Milne Bay E New Guinea ⚔135/1
Milwaukee N USA civil unrest 144/3
Minas Gerais province of C Brazil 97/1
Mindanao island of S Philippines Muslim expansion 40/5; Spanish control 70/3; US occupation 104/3; Japanese occupation 135/1; political unrest 139/2
Minden NW Germany bishopric 79/1
Ming Empire China 51/4
Mingrelia Caucasus princedom under Ottoman Empire 124/1
Ming Voyages 59/3
Minneapolis-St. Paul N USA industry 111/2
Minnesota state of N USA site of early man 3/3; Depression 130/2; industry 110/3; population 111/5, 145/1
Minoan civilisation 18T
Minorca (*Sp.* Menorca) British naval base and⚔87/1; Civil War 129/4
Minsk W Russia early town of Polotsk 45/2; WW1 119/3; Bolshevik seizure 121/2; WW2 133/2; urban growth 147/1; industry 147/1
Minturnae (*mod.* Minturno) C Italy Roman colony 30/1
Minusinsk SC Siberia founded 84/2
Minyueh region of S China 28/1, 2; Han commanderie 29/3
Mirzoyan (Dzhambul)
Misenum C Italy Roman Empire 30/3
Miskito Indian tribe of C America 63/1
Mison C Indo-China Hindu-Buddhist temple 51/2
Mississippi state of S USA Civil War 92/5; Depression 131/2; population 111/5, 145/1
Missouri state of C USA Civil War 92/5; Depression 131/2; population 111/5, 145/1
Mitanni ancient kingdom of Middle East 7/3, 20/2
Mithraism 26T, 26/1
Mitla Mexico Mixtec site 62/2
Mito C Japan 126/2
Mitylene (Mytilene)
Mixtec early people of C Mexico 12/2
Miyagi prefecture of N Japan 126/2
Miyazaki city and prefecture of W Japan 126/2
Mlu Prei Cambodia early site 8/3
Mobile S USA fur station 94/1; ⚔93/5
Moçambique (Mozambique)
Moçâmedes Angola Portuguese settlement 103/3
Moche C Andes site 12/4
Modena (*anc.* Mutina) N Italy Mithraic site 26/1; Lombard League 55/3; Republican commune 56/3; Renaissance Italy 73/5; unification of Italy 114/3
Modjokerto Java site of early man 3/3
Modoc plateau Indian tribe of NW USA 63/1
Moesia region of Balkans district of Byzantine Empire 43/1
Moesiae late Roman province of Greece 31/4
Moesia Inferior Roman province of the Balkans 31/3
Moesia Superior Roman province of the Balkans 31/3
Mogadishu (*n/s* Muqdisho *It.* Mogadiscio) Somalia Muslim colony 60/1; early trade 58/3; Italian occupation 103/3
Mogador (*now* Essaouira) Morocco Stone Age site 11/1
Mogilev W Russia Hanseatic trade 59/2; WW1 119/2; WW2 133/2; industry 147/1
Mogontiacum (*mod.* Mainz) W Germany Roman Empire 24/2, 30/3
Mohács Hungary ⚔48/2
Mohammed founder of Islam 40T, 41/1
Mohave Indian tribe of SW USA 63/1
Mohenjo-Daro N India early urban settlement 9/1, 16/1; Harappan site 9/5
Mohi Hungary ⚔46/2
Moira Baths C England Industrial Revolution 98/1
Mojos forest Indian tribe of S America 63/1
Mokpo S Korea Russo-Japanese war 127/4; 1950-53 War 148/2
Moldavia (*Turk.* Boğdan *Rom.* Moldova) region of Romania/Russia Hungarian 56/2; under Ottoman control 49/1; occupied by Russia 91/1; part of Romania 116/1
Mollwitz (*Pol.* Małujowice) SW Poland ⚔78/2
Molotov (Perm)
Moluccas (*Indon.* Maluku *Dut.* Malukken *form.* Spice Islands) islands of E Indies Muslim expansion 70/1; European discovery 70/3; early Portuguese trade 67/1; Dutch control 71/2; independent republic 139/2
Molukken (Moluccas)
Mombasa Kenya Muslim colony 60-61; early trade 61/2, 66/2; British occupation 100/3

eipus, Lake (*Russ.* Chudskoye Ozero *Est.* Peipsi Järv) / Russia ✕45/2
eking (*form. Mong.* Khanbalik) N China site of early an 3/3; early trade 59/3; Ming capital 51/4; warlord tacks 22/2; Japanese occupation 127/5; industry 08/1
elew (Palau)
ella Palestine early bishopric 27/2
ella Macedonia 20/5, 22/3
eloponnesian War 23/2
eloponnesus (*Eng.* Peloponnese *a/c* Morea) region of Greece 18-19
elusium n Egypt Alexander's Empire 22/3; Roman mpire 26/2, 31/3
elym W Siberia founded 84/2
emaquid NE USA ✕95/2
emba *island* Tanzania Muslim colony 60/1
embina N USA fur station 94/1
embroke S Wales Scandinavian settlement 37/1; WW1 18/3
enang state of Malaya British possession 71/5; WW2 34/1
eninj E Africa site of early man 3/3
eninsular War 90/1
ennsylvania state of E USA colony 67/3, 92/1; Civil Var 93/5; Depression 131/2; population 111/5, 145/1
ennsylvania Road NE USA settlers' route 94/1
enobscot NE USA founded 67/3
ensacola SE USA Spanish post 67/3; fur station 94/1
enydarran S Wales Industrial Revolution 98/1
enza C Russia founded 85/1; 1905 Revolution 120/1; Bolshevik seizure 121/2
epin King of Franks 34T
equot Fort NE USA ✕95/2
erak state of Malaya 71/5
erath Mesopotamia early archbishopric 27/2
erche N France fief 72/2
ereslavets SW Russia 45/2
ereyaslavl Ukraine bishopric 38/2; early principality 45/2
ereyaslavl N Russia town of Vladimir-Suzdal 45/2
ergamum (*Gr.* Pergamon *Turk.* Bergama) W Anatolia Roman Empire 24/2, 31/3; early bishopric 27/2
erge S Anatolia early archbishopric 27/2
érigord region of C France English possession 52/2; annexed to France 72/2
erinthus SE Europe Greek colony 19/4
erlis state of Malaya tributary to Siam 71/5
erm (*1940-57 called* Molotov) C Russia founded 85/1; ndustry 147/1; urban growth 146/2; Bolshevik seizure 121/2
ermians people of N Russia 38/2, 45/2
ernambuco (*now* Recife) Brazil early Portuguese territory 66/1; Confederation of the Equator 96/1
erovsk (Kzyl-Orda)
erpignan S France fort 80/1
erryville SE USA ✕93/5
ersepolis Persia early trade 25/1; Alexander's Empire 23/3; Achaemenid Empire 21/5; Muslim conquest 41/1
ersia (*now* Iran) war with Greece 22/1; Achaemenid empire 21/5; attacked by White Huns 32/1; expansion of Christianity 39/1; Muslim conquest 41/4; under Abbasid sovereignty 41/2; Mongol conquest 46-7; Safavid Empire 49/1; independent kingdom 125/1; British and Russian spheres of influence 125/1
ersian Gulf (*a/c* Arabian Gulf *or* The Gulf) WW1 125/2; oil 151/1
ersis (*a/c* Fars, Parsa) S Persia Alexander's Empire 23/3
erth W Australia early settlement 113/1
eru Spanish colonisation 66/1, 69/2; independence 97/1; war with Chile 97/4; political developments 142-3; economy 150/1
erusia (*mod.* Perugia) N Italy Roman Empire 30/1, 31/3
eshawar Pakistan industry under British rule 105/3; capital of NW Frontier Agency 105/5
esto (Posidonia)
eterborough E England Industrial Revolution 98/1
etra Jordan early trade 25/1; Roman Empire 31/3; early archbishopric 27/2
etralona Greece site of early man 3/3
etrograd (*before 1914* St. Petersburg *since 1924* Leningrad) WW1 119/3; Russian Revolution 121/2
etropavlovsk (*now* Petropavlovsk-Kamchatskiy) Russ. Far East founded 84/2; industry 147/1
etsamo (*Russ.* Pechenga) NW Russia Russian conquest from Finland 133/2
ettau (Poetovio)
falz (Palatinate)
falz-Sulzbach W Germany principality 79/1
haistos Crete palace site 19/1
halaborwa SE Africa 60/1
hanagoria S Russia Greek colony 19/4
han Rang S Indo-China Hindu-Buddhist temple 51/2
haselis SW Anatolia Greek colony 19/4
hasis Caucasus Greek colony 19/4; Roman Empire 33/1
hazania (*mod.* Fezzan) region of S Libya 31/3

Philadelphia (*mod.* Alaşehir) W Anatolia early church 27/2
Philadelphia E USA founded 67/3; industry 109/1
Philadelphia (Amman)
Philiphaugh S Scotland ✕76/4
Philippi N Greece Roman Empire 27/2
Philippines early sites 8/3; spread of Islam 40/5; early trade 67/1; Spanish conquest 71/2; acquired by US 102/2, 110/4; occupied by Japanese 127/5, 135/1; independence 139/1; political development 141/1; US bases 149/1; industry and economy 150/1
Philippopolis (*mod.* Plovdiv *Turk.* Filibe) Bulgaria Roman Empire 31/3; Byzantine Empire 43/1; Ottoman Empire 48/1
Philistines displaced 18/2
Philomelium (*mod.* Akşehir) C Anatolia Byzantine Empire 43/3
Phnom Laang Cambodia early site 8/3
Phnom Penh Cambodia 70/1, 71/2; Vietnam war 148/3
Phocaea W Anatolia Greek colony 19/4
Phocis ancient territory of C Greece 18/3
Phoenicia at time of Greeks 19/4; Roman province 31/3
Phoenicians move into Africa 11/1
Phopo Hill E Africa Iron Age site 11/1
Phrygia ancient country of W Anatolia 19/4, 22/3; Byzantine Empire 43/1
Phrygians early people of Anatolia 18/2
Phylakopi Aegean Mycenaean palace site 19/1
Piacenza (*anc.* Placentia) N Italy Lombard League 55/3; Signorial domination 56/3; medieval fair 59/2
Piauí state of NE Brazil 97/1
Picardy (*Fr.* Picardie) region of N France annexed from Burgundy 72/2, 80/1; WW1 118/3 (inset)
Picentes early tribe of N Italy 25/1
Pictavi W France early bishopric 26/2
Picton S Island, New Zealand railway 112/1
Picts early tribe of Scotland 32/1, 38/3
Piedmont (*It.* Piemonte) region of N Italy 88/3, 114/3
Pigs, Bay of Cuba CIA invasion 149/5
Pilos (Navarino, Pylos)
Pilsen (*Cz.* Plzeň) Czechoslovakia industrial development 99/2
Pima Indian tribe of N Mexico 63/1
Pinega N Russia town of Novgorod Empire 45/2
Pinkie Scotland ✕73/4
Pinsk W Russia town of Turov-Pinsk 45/2
Piombino N Italy Duchy 73/5; French rule 91/1
Piqillacta C Andes early site 12/5
Piro forest Indian tribe of S America 63/1
Pisa (*anc.* Pisae) N Italy medieval city 55/3; Mediterranean trade 36/2, 58/1; raids and conquests 36/2; Republican commune 56/3
Pisae (*mod.* Pisa) N Italy Roman Empire 30/1, 31/3; bishopric 27/2
Piscataway Fort NE USA ✕95/2
Pishpek (Frunze)
Pisidia ancient country of C Anatolia 22/3, 43/1
Pistoia (*anc.* Pistoriae) N Italy medieval city 55/3
Pitcairn Island C Pacific British colony 139/1 (inset)
Pithecusa S Italy Greek colony 19/4
Pit River W USA ✕94/2
Pittsburgh E USA industry 109/1, 110/2
Pityus Caucasus Greek colony 19/4; early bishopric 27/2
Pizarro, Francisco Spanish explorer 68/2
Placentia (*mod.* Piacenza) N Italy Latin colony 30/1
Plassey E India ✕87/2 (inset)
Plataea C Greece ✕ 20/5, 22/1
Plate River (*Sp.* Río de la Plata) Argentina explored 64/2
Plevna (*now* Pleven) Bulgaria WW1 119/3
PLO Palestinian nationalist movement 140T
Ploeşti Romania WW2 133/2
Plovdiv (Philippopolis)
Plymouth SW England naval base 87/1; Industrial Revolution 98/1; WW1 118/3; WW2 132/1
Plymouth NE USA founded 67/3
Plzeň (Pilsen)
Podolia region of S Ukraine acquired by Lithuania 56/2
Poduca S India early port 25/1
Poetovio (*mod.* Ptuj *Ger.* Pettau) N Yugoslavia Mithraic site 27/1; Roman Empire 31/3
Pohai (*Kor.* Parhae *mod.* Manchuria) NE China early state 51/1
Pohang S Korea 1950-53 war 148/2
Point of Rocks C USA ✕94/2
Poitiers (*anc.* Limonum) C France ✕34/4, 40/1, 56/5; 17C revolts 77/2; seat of intendant 80/1; centre of French Revolution 89/2
Poitou region of W France French Royal domain 52/2; province of France 80/1
Pola (*mod.* Pula) N Yugoslavia Roman Empire 31/3; WW1 119/3
Polabii Slavic tribe of N Germany 54/1, 2
Poland conversion to Christianity 38/2; under Boleslav Chrobry 52/1; Mongol invasion 46/2; union with Lithuania 56/2; Black Death 57/1; Empire of Casimir IV 72/1; acquired by Russia 85/1; agriculture and peasant emancipation 82/1; Reformation 75/1; Partitions 79/4; revolt against Russia 88/1; WW1 119/3; independence

after WW1 120/3; socio-political development 128/1, 131/3; WW2 132/1; territorial changes 136/1, 137/5; Warsaw Pact and Comecon 137/3, 149/1; economy 150/1
Poles post-WW1 migration to Poland 128/3; post-WW2 migration to West 136/1
POLISARIO W Sahara guerrilla movement 138/1, 140/1
Polish Corridor 128/2
Polotsk W Russia early city and principality 45/2; Hanseatic trading post 59/2
Polovtsy tribe of C Russia 44-5
Poltava Ukraine town of Pereyaslavl 45/2; industry and urban growth 84/4; 1905 Revolution 120/1; Bolshevik seizure 121/2
Poltoratsk (Ashkhabad)
Polyanye Slav tribe of the Ukraine 44/1
Polynesia islands of C Pacific early settlement 10/2
Pomerania (*Ger.* Pommern *Pol.* Pomorze) region of N Europe acquired by Poland 52/1; medieval German Empire 55/3; acquired by Prussia 78/2; Reformation 75/1; unification of Germany 79/1, 115/2
Pomerania, East part of Germany 79/1
Pomerania, Swedish ceded to Prussia 114/4
Pomerania, West to Sweden 77/3
Pomeranians Slav tribe of N Europe 54/2
Pomerelia (*Ger.* Pommerellen) region of N Europe occupied by Teutonic Knights 54/4, 56/2
Pomo Indian tribe of NW USA 63/1
Pompeiopolis S Anatolia Roman Empire 31/3
Ponce de León Spanish explorer 64/3
Pondicherry (*Fr.* Pondichéry) SE India French settlement 66/2; captured by British 87/2 (inset); French enclave 105/3
Pondo region of SE Africa British administration 102/2
Pons Saravi E France Mithraic site 26/1
Ponthieu region of NE France under English rule 52/2; Burgundian possession 73/3
Pontia (Ponza)
Pontianak W Borneo Dutch settlement 71/2
Pontus district of N Anatolia 19/4; Roman province 31/4; Byzantine Empire 43/1
Ponza (Pontia) *island* C Italy Mithraic site 26/1
Poona W India industry 108/1
Populonia N Italy Etruscan city 19/4, 30/1
Porolissensis Roman province of E Europe 31/3
Porolissum Romania Roman Empire 31/3
Portage la Prairie (Fort La Reine)
Port Arthur (*Chin.* Lushun *Jap.* Ryojun) Manchuria ceded to Russia and Japan 84/3, 107/4; Russo-Japanese war 127/4
Port Arthur (*now* Thunder Bay) C Canada growth 111/5
Port Arthur Tasmania penal settlement 113/1
Port Augusta S Australia settlement 113/1
Port Chalmers S Island, New Zealand 112/2
Port Elizabeth SE Africa British settlement 102/2, 103/3
Port Essington N Australia founded 113/1
Port-Francqui (*now* Ilebo) C Belgian Congo 138/1
Port Hedland W Australia early settlement 112/1
Port Hudson S USA ✕92/5
Portland S England WW1 118/3
Portland SE Australia founded 113/1
Port Lincoln S Australia settlement 113/1
Port Macquarie SE Australia penal settlement 113/1
Port Moresby SE New Guinea Allied base WW2 135/1
Porto Novo SE India ✕87/2
Port Pirie S Australia settlement 113/1
Port Royal Jamaica British naval base 86/1
Port Said N Egypt Egyptian-Israeli war 141/3
Portsmouth S England naval base 87/1; Industrial Revolution 98/1; WW1 118/3
Portsmouth NE USA settlement 67/3
Portugal (*anc.* Lusitania) Jewish migration 39/4; Muslim conquest 41/1; reconquest 37/4; voyages of discovery 64-65; expansion overseas 66-7, 69/2; colonial empire 101/2; WW1 118-9; NATO and EFTA 137/3, 149/1; US bases 149/1; economy 150/1
Portuguese East Africa (*now* Mozambique) 87/2, 101/2
Portuguese Guinea (*now* Guinea-Bissau) W Africa Portuguese colony 100/2; independence 138/1
Portuguese Timor E Indies annexed by Indonesia 139/1, 2
Porus early kingdom of NW India 23/3
Posidonia (*later* Paestum *mod.* Pesto) S Italy Greek colony 19/4
Posen (*Pol.* Poznań) W Poland unification of Germany 115/2; ceded by Germany 128/2
Potaissa Romania Roman Empire 24/2
Potawatomi Indian tribe of C USA 63/1
Potidaea N Greece Dorian colony 19/4
Potosí Peru Spanish silver mine 66/1
Powhatan Indian tribe of E USA 63/1
Powys district of Wales 33/3, 53/7
Poynings Law English rule in Ireland 72T
Poznań (Posen)
Pozzuoli (Puteoli)

Slovakia - Swaziland

lovakia short-lived Soviet republic 120/3; forms part of zechoslovakia 128/2; occupied by Hungary in WW2 32/1
lovenes Slav tribe of S Europe 32/2
lovenia constituent republic of Yugoslavia 128/2
luys (*n/s* Sluis *Fr.* Ecluse) Netherlands ⚔56/5
maldings Slav tribe of E Europe 54/2
mederevo (Semendre)
molensk W Russia bishopric 38/2; Hanseatic trade 9/2; captured by Napoleon 91/1; Bolshevik seizure 21/2; (principality) 45/2; acquired by Lithuania 56/2; dustry 147/1
myrna (*mod.* Izmir) W Anatolia Roman Empire 31/3; ne of seven churches of Asia 27/2; Byzantine Empire 9/1; Ottoman Empire 49/1; Greek occupation 129/2
naketown USA early site 12/3
oba Sudan monastery 38/1; early town 60/1
obibor Poland concentration camp 132/1
ociety Islands (*Fr.* Iles de la Société) S Pacific olynesian settlement 10/2; European discovery 65/4; ench colony 139/1 (inset)
oča (Isonzo)
ocotra *island* Arabian Sea early bishopric 38/1; cquired by Britain 101/2
oerabaja (Surabaya)
oest W Germany Hanseatic city 59/2
ofala Mozambique early trade 66/2; Portuguese ettlement 61/2
ofia (*anc.* Serdica *a/s* Sardica *med.* Sredets) Bulgaria ttoman control 49/1; 18C urban development 82/4; ommunist uprising 120/3; WW2 133/2
ogabe clan territory of W Japan 51/3
ogdiana (*a/c* Sogdia, Suguda) ancient region of C Asia mit of Alexander's Empire 23/3; Chinese protectorate 0/1
ogdian Rock C Asia besieged by Alexander 23/3
öğüt NW Anatolia Ottoman centre 49/1
oissons N France monastery 34/4; WW1 119/2
okoto N Nigeria city and sultanate 60-61; occupied by ritish 103/3
ole Bank E England Dutch naval victory 81/3
olferino N Italy ⚔114/3
oli SE Anatolia Greek colony 19/4
olms former county of C Germany 79/1
olomon Islands SW Pacific early Melanesian ettlement 10/2; British protectorate 101/1 (inset); ccupied by Japanese 135/1; independence 139/1 inset)
olovetskiy N Russia monastery 38/2
olutré France site of early man 3/3
omali people of NE Africa 60-61
omalia (*form.* British and Italian Somaliland) ndependence 138/1; political development 140/1; conomy 150/1
omme *river* NE France WW1 offensive 119/3 (inset)
omme Bionne France La Tène site 15/6
onghay early empire of W Africa 60/2
onora Pass W USA 94/1
oochow E China in Ch'ing economy 107/2; treaty port 07/4; industry 123/4
opatma S India trading port 25/1
opron (*Ger.* Odenburg) Hungary Hallstatt site 15/6; to Hungary after plebiscite 129/2
ora C Italy Latin colony 30/1
orbs Slavic tribe of C Europe 33/5, 34/4, 54/2
oshangane tribe of SE Africa 102/2
otho tribe of S Africa 102/2
otka-Koh NW India Harappan site 9/5
ousse (*anc.* Hadrumetum) Tunisia Ottoman Empire 24/1
South Africa Union 101/2; immigration from Europe and India 109/2; Republic 138/1; political development 40/1
Southampton S England Industrial Revolution 98/1; WW2 132/1
South Arabia (South Yemen)
South Australia settlement and development 101/1, 13/1
South Carolina state of SE USA colony 67/3, 92/1; Civil War 93/5; Depression 131/2; population 111/5, 45/1
South Dakota state of N USA Depression 131/2; population 111/5, 145/1
South-East Asia early civilisations 8/3; Mongol attacks 51/2; 1511-1825 70-71; post 1945 conflicts 141/1, 148/1, 3
Southern Rhodesia (*now* Zimbabwe *f/c* Rhodesia) British colony 101/2, 103/3
South Island (*Maori* Te Waipounamu) New Zealand settlement and development 112/2
Southland province of S Island, New Zealand 112/2
South Moluccas E Indonesia republic suppressed 139/2
South Tyrol (*Ger.* Südtirol *It.* Alto Adige) region of Austro-Hungarian Empire acquired by Italy 128/2
South Vietnam independence 139/1; war 148/3. See also Vietnam, Indo-China
South West Africa (*a/c* Namibia *form.* German South West Africa) German colony 101/2, 103/3; S African control 138/1, 140/1; economy 150/1
South Yemen (*now called* People's Democratic Republic of Yemen *form.* Federation of South Arabia *earlier* Protectorate of South Arabia *earlier* Aden Protectorate) independence 138/1; political development 140/1; economy 150/1
Soviet Union (USSR)
Sowerby Bridge N England Industrial Revolution 98/1
Sozopol (Apollonia)
Spa Belgium 1920 Conference 128/2
Spain (*anc.* Hispania) Celtic penetration 15/6; early invasions 32/1; conversion to Christianity 38/2; Jewish migrations 39/4; Muslim conquest 41/1;Umayyad caliphate 40/2; Reconquista 37/4; Union of Castile and Aragon 72/1; Habsburg possession 72/1; voyages of discovery 64-5; overseas expansion 66-69; overseas settlements 66/4; colonisation of America 86/1; Reformation 75/1; War of the Spanish Succession 81/5; opposition to Napoleon 90/1; colonial empire 88/1; 19C alliances 117/2; 20C socio-political change 131/3; Civil War 129/4; US bases 149/1; economy 98/2, 150/1
Spalato (*anc.* Spalatum *mod.* Split) Yugoslavia Byzantine Empire 43/1
Spalding E England Industrial Revolution 98/1
Spalding's Mission NW USA 94/1
Spanish-American War 111T
Spanish Guinea (*now* Equatorial Guinea) W Africa colony 101/1
Spanish March 34/4
Spanish Sahara (*a/c* Western Sahara *includes* Rio de Oro) NW Africa Spanish colony 103/3; partition between Morocco and Mauritania 138/1, 140/1; economy 150/1
Spanish Succession, War of the 80T, 81/5
Sparda (*Lat.* Lydia) region of W Anatolia satrapy of Achaemenid Empire 20/5
Sparta (*a/c* Lacedaemon) S Greece Mycenaean palace site 19/1; Peloponnesian War 23/2; Roman Empire 24/2, 31/3
Spartalos N Greece ⚔23/2
Spasinou Charax Mesopotamia town of Achaemenid Empire 21/5
Sphacteria S Greece ⚔23/2
Spice Islands (Moluccas)
Spion Kop S Africa ⚔103/4
Spirit Cave N Siam early site 8/3
Split (Spalato)
Spokane House NW USA fur station 94/1
Spoletium (*mod.* Spoleto) N Italy Latin colony 30/1; Dukedom 42/1
Spotsylvania E USA ⚔93/5
Springbok Flats S Africa site of early man 3/3
Spy Belgium site of early man 3/3
Sredets (Sofia, Serdica)
Sredne-Kolymsk NE Siberia founded 84/2
Srem (Syrmia)
Sri Ksetra S Burma Hindu-Buddhist remains 51/2
Sri Lanka (Ceylon)
Srinagar N India capital of Kashmir 105/3
Srivijaya E Indies early empire 51/2
Stabroek (*now* Georgetown) Guyana Dutch settlement 66/4
Staffarda N Italy ⚔81/4
Stafford C England Industrial Revolution 98/1
Stalin (Varna)
Stalin, Joseph 146T
Stalinabad (Dushanbe)
Stalingrad (*until 1925* Tsaritsyn *since 1961* Volgograd) S Russia WW2 132-3
Stalino (Donetsk)
Stalinogorsk (Novomoskovskiy)
Stalinsk (Novokuznetsk)
Stamford C England Industrial Revolution 98/1
Stanley, Sir Henry Morton African exploration 102/1
Stanleyville (*now* Kisangani) S Belgian Congo Congo crisis 138/4
Starčevo Yugoslavia early site 14/1
Stargard E Germany Hanseatic trade 59/2
Stavanger S Norway WW2 132/1
Stavropol (*1940-44* Voroshilovsk) S Russia industry 147/1
Stavropol (Tolyatti)
Stębark (Tannenberg)
Steiermark (Styria)
Steinheim Germany site of early man 3/3
Steptoe Butte NW USA ⚔94/2
Sterkfontein S Africa site of early man 3/3
Stettin (*now* Szczecin) N Poland Hanseatic city 59/2; Swedish Empire 77/3; WW2 133/2
Stillman's Defeat N USA ⚔95/2
Stirling Bridge C Scotland ⚔56/4
Stobi S Yugoslavia Roman Empire 31/3; early archbishopric 27/2
Stockholm Sweden Hanseatic city 59/2; 18C urban development 82/4; in Swedish Empire 77/3
Stockport N England Industrial Revolution 98/1
Stockstadt W Germany Mithraic site 26/2
Stoke-on-Trent C England Industrial Revolution 98/1
Stony Lake N USA ⚔95/2
Stormberg S Africa ⚔103/4
Stourbridge W England medieval fair 59/2; Industrial Revolution 98/1
Stowmarket England Industrial Revolution 98/1
Stralsund N Germany Hanseatic city 59/2
Strasbourg (*Ger.* Strassburg *anc.* Argentoratum) E France centre of French Revolution 79/2; industrial development 98/2
Strassburg (*Fr.* Strasbourg) SW Germany royal mint 54/1; medieval fair 59/2; 18C urban development 82/4; Reformation 75/1; gained by France 81/2; bishopric 79/1; WW1 119/3
Stratford-on-Avon C England Industrial Revolution 98/1
Strathclyde N Britain medieval kingdom 33/3, 38/3
Stratonicea W Anatolia Roman Empire 31/3
Stresa N Italy 1935 Conference 128/2
Stuttgart S Germany industrial development 98/1; WW2 132/1
Stutthof (*now Pol.* Sztutowo) NE Germany concentration camp 132/1
Styria (*Ger.* Steiermark) province of SE Austria medieval German Empire 55/1, 3; acquired by Habsburgs 56/2; Duchy 79/1
Suakin E Sudan Ottoman settlement 61/2
Suceava (Suczawa)
Suczawa (*n/s* Suceava) Romania under Ottoman control 49/1
Sudan region of N Africa 60-61
Sudan (*form.* Anglo-Egyptian Sudan) Mahdist state 103/3; British control 124/1; Anglo-Egyptian condominium 103/3; independence 138/1, 140/1; economy 150/1
Sudbury E England Industrial Revolution 98/1
Sudbury NE USA ⚔95/4
Sudetenland C Europe German annexation 129/5
Suebi (Sueves)
Suessa Aurunca (*mod.* Sessa Aurunca) C Italy Latin colony 30/1
Sueves (*Lat.* Suebi) early tribe of SW Europe 32/2, 34/1
Suez (*Ar.* As Suways) N Egypt Ottoman port 48/2; Egyptian-Israeli war 140/3
Suez Canal N Egypt opening 109/4; Egyptian-Israeli war 141/3; Anglo-French attack 140/1
Sugambri early tribe of NW Europe 30/3
Suguda (*a/c* Sogdia *or* Sogdiana) C Asia satrapy of Achaemenid Empire 21/5
Suhar E Arabia Muslim conquest 41/1
Sui C China Western Chou domain 9/6
Suifen NE China treaty port 107/4
Suiyuan former province of N China 123/3
Sukhothai C Thailand Buddhist site 27/1; major political centre 51/2
Sukhum-Kale (*mod.* Sukhumi *anc.* Dioscurias) Caucasus conquered by Russia 85/1
Sulawesi (Celebes)
Suleiman Ottoman ruler 48T
Sumatra (*Indon.* Sumatera) E Indies spread of Buddhism 27/1; Muslim expansion 40/5; early sites 8/3; early trade 59/3; Dutch possession 101/2; occupied by Japanese 135/1
Sumer Mesopotamia 17/3
Sumerians ancient people of Mesopotamia 16/2, 17/3
Sunda Kalapa (*mod.* Jakarta) Java Islamic town 70/1
Sunderland NE England Industrial Revolution 98/1
Sung N China Chou domain 9/6; warring state 28/1
Sungchou C China T'ang prefecture 50/1
Sung Empire China conquered by Mongols 47/1, 3
Sungkiang E China British attack 107/3
Süntel N Germany ⚔34/4
Sun Yat-sen Chinese president 122T
Suomussalmi C Finland WW2 132/1
Surabaya (*Dut.* Soerabaja) Java trading centre 71/2
Surakarta district of Java Dutch control 71/2
Surashtra early state of W India, 29/4
Surat NW India Mughal port 59/3; Ottoman siege 48/2; industry 105/3
Surgut W Siberia founded 84/2
Surinam (*Dut.* Suriname *form.* Dutch Guiana) country of S America 142-3
Susa SW Persia early urban settlement 16/1, 17/4; Assyrian Empire 20/2, 3; early trade 24/1; Alexander's route 22/3; Persian Royal Road 21/5
Susiana (*a/c* Elam *mod.* Khuzistan) region of SW Persia province of Alexander's Empire 22/3
Susquehanna Indian tribe of NE USA 63/1
Sussex early kingdom of S England 35/3, 38/3
Sutkagen-Dor NW India Harappan site 9/5
Sutrium N Italy Latin colony 30/1
Suvar E Russia early town 45/2
Suzdal C Russia town of Vladimir-Suzdal 45/2
Sverdlovsk (*until 1924* Yekaterinburg) C Russia urban growth 146/2; industry 147/1
Swabia (*Ger.* Schwaben) region of S Germany province of medieval German Empire 55/1, 3
Swakopmund SW Africa German settlement 103/3
Swanscombe England site of early man 3/3
Swansea S Wales Industrial Revolution 98/1
Swartkrans S Africa site of early man 3/3
Swatow S China treaty port 107/4; Japanese occupation 127/5
Swaziland country of SE Africa British protectorate 101/1, 103/4; independence 138/1; economy 150/1

hyatira (*mod.* Akhisar) W Anatolia one of seven
urches of Asia 27/2
ahuanaco Empire C Andes site 12/5, 13/1
berias (*Heb.* Teverya) Israel town of Judaea 26/3
bet (*anc.* Bhota) C Asia spread of Buddhism 27/1;
rly expansion 33/1; unified kingdom 50/1; part of
ongol Empire 46/1, 3; Chinese protectorate 106/1;
itish sphere of influence 107/4; absorbed by China
89/1
bur (*mod.* Tivoli) C Italy Roman Empire 30/1
chitt W Africa Stone Age site 11/1
cinum (Pavia)
conderoga (*Fr.* Fort Carillon) NE USA British capture
French fort 86/1
dore *island* Moluccas, E Indies Islamic town 70/1;
rtuguese settlement 70/3; Dutch settlement 71/2
en early state of W China 28/1
enshui NW China Han commanderie 29/3
entai Shan *mountain* E China Buddhist site 27/1
entsin NE China treaty port 107/4; Boxer uprising
07/3; Japanese occupation 127/5
eum N Anatolia Greek colony 19/4
flis (*n/c* Tbilisi) Caucasus Muslim conquest 41/1;
ongol conquest 47/4; Ottoman conquest 48/2; urban
owth 146/2
ighina (Bender)
glath-Pileser I King of Assyria 20/3
glath-Pileser III King of Assyria 20/3
granocerta (*mod* Siirt) E Anatolia Roman Empire
/3
ikal E Mexico Mayan site 12/2, 13/1
imbira forest Indian tribe of N Brazil 63/1
imbuktu (*Fr.* Tombouctou) W Africa trans-Saharan
ade 60-61; occupied by French 103/3
imgad (Thamugadi)
imor *island* of E Indies early Portuguese colony 67/2;
utch/Portuguese control 101/2; occupied by Japanese
WW2 135/1; joined Indonesia 139/2
imucua Indian tribe of SE USA 63/1
imur's Empire Persia 47/4
ingis (*mod.* Tangier) Morocco Roman Empire 24/2,
0/3; early bishopric 26/2
ingitana NW Africa region of Roman Empire 30/3
inian *island* Marianas, C Pacific occupied by US in
W2 135/1
innevelly district of S India ceded to Britain 87/2
ipasa Algeria early bishopric 26/2
iphsah (Thapsacus)
ippecanoe N E USA ✕94/2
ippermuir C Scotland ✕76/4
ippu Tib's Domain E Africa 103/3
ipton C England Industrial Revolution 98/1
irana Albania Ottoman Empire 124/1
irguşor Romania Mithraic site 26/1
irol, Tirolo (Tyrol)
iryns S Greece Mycenaean palace 19/1
iverton SW England Industrial Revolution 98/1
ivertsy Slav tribe of W Russia 44/1
ivoli (Tibur)
jeribon (Cheribon)
laxcala region of C Mexico early kingdom 62/2;
efence against Cortés 68/1; modern state 97/1
lemcen NW Africa early trade 58/3
lingit coast Indian tribe of NW Canada 63/1
mutarakan S Russia 44/1
obago island of W Indies French rule 66/4; dependency
Trinidad 139/1 (inset)
obolsk W Siberia founded 84/2; on railway to east
4/3
obruk (*Ar.* Tubruq) N Libya WW2 132/1
ochigi prefecture of C Japan 126/2
odmorden N England Industrial Revolution 98/1
ogo (*form.* Togoland) country of W Africa
dependence 138/1; economy 150/1
ogoland W Africa German colony 100/2, 103/3. *For*
ench mandate see Togo
okushima city and prefecture of W Japan 126/1, 2
okyo (*form.* Edo) C Japan industrialisation 126/2;
W2 135/1
oledo (*anc.* Toletum) C Spain Muslim conquest 41/1;
ivil War 129/4
oletum (*mod.* Toledo) C Spain Roman Empire 24/2,
0/3; archbishopric 26/2
olmeta (Ptolemais)
olosa (*mod.* Toulouse) S France Roman Empire 24/2,
0/2; archbishopric 26/2
oltecs early people of Mexico 62T
olyatti (*until 1964* Stavropol) C Russia foundation and
dustry 146/2, 147/1
omassee SE USA ✕95/1
ombouctou (Timbuktu)
omi (*now* Constanţa) Romania early trade 24/1; Greek
olony 19/4; Roman Empire 24/2, 30/3
omsk C Siberia founded 84/2; on railway to east 84/3;
dustry 147/1
onbridge SE England Industrial Revolution 98/1
Tonga island kingdom of S Pacific early settlement 10/2;
British protectorate 101/2; independence 139/1 (inset)
Tongking (*Fr.* Tonkin) region of N Indo-China Hindu-
Buddhist state 71/2; tributary state of China 106/1

Tongking, Gulf of Vietnamese war 148/3
Tønsberg Norway Hanseatic trade 59/2
Toowoomba E Australia early settlement 113/1
Topa Inca emperor 62T, 63/3
Torhout Belgium medieval fair 58/1
Torino (Turin)
Torki people of S Russia 45/2
Torone N Greece Ionian colony 19/4
Toronto E Canada growth 111/1
Toropets W Russia early town of Smolensk 45/2
Torres Strait Australia/New Guinea European discovery
65/4
Tortona N Italy Lombard League 55/3
Toruń (Thorn)
Torzhok W Russia early town of Novgorod Empire 45/2
Toscana (Tuscany)
Totonac Indian tribe of C Mexico 63/1
Tottori city and prefecture of W Japan 126/1, 2
Touat (Tuat)
Toul NE France annexed 72/2
Toulon (*anc.* Telo Martius) S France naval base 87/1;
executions during French Revolution 89/2
Toulouse (*anc.* Tolosa) S France Muslim conquest
41/1; St. Bartholomew Massacre 74/3; *parlement* 80/1
Toungoo C Burma 51/2
Touraine region of C France French Royal domain 52/2
Tourane (*mod.* Da Nang) C Vietnam early trade 71/2
Tournai region of Belgium Burgundian possession 73/3
Tours (*anc.* Caesarodunum *later* Turones) C France
archbishopric 34/4; 17C revolts 77/2; seat of intendant
80/1
Townsville E Australia early settlement 113/1
Toyama city and prefecture of C Japan 126/2
Trabzon (*Eng.* Trebizond *anc.* Trapezus) NE Anatolia
49/1
Trachonitis ancient district of N Palestine 26/3
Trafalgar S Spain ✕90/1, 3
Trajectum (*mod.* Utrecht) Netherlands bishopric 26/2
Tra Kieu C Indo-China Hindu-Buddhist temple 51/2
Transjordan country of N Arabia Ottoman province
124/1; British mandate 132/1
Transkei region of SE Africa annexed by Cape Province
103/2; independent Bantustan 140/1
Transnistria SW Russia WW2 133/2
Transoxiana ancient region of C Asia, Muslim conquest
41/1, 2
Trans-Siberian Railway 127/5
Transvaal S Africa Boer republic 103/2, 4
Transylvania region of Hungary/Romania Empire of
Mathias Corvinus 72/1; part of Austro-Hungarian Empire
128/2
Trapezus (*mod.* Trabzon *Eng.* Trebizond) NE Anatolia
early trade 24/1; Greek colony 19/4; Roman Empire
25/2, 31/3; early bishopric 27/2
Traprain Law Scotland Iron Age site 15/6
Trasimenus C Italy ✕30/2
Travancore former state of S India 87/2, 3; 104/1
Traverse des Sioux N USA fur station 94/1
Trebia N Italy ✕30/2
Trebizond (*Turk.* Trabzon *anc.* Trapezus) NE Anatolia
Byzantine Empire 43/1; early trade 58/3; Ottoman Empire
49/1
Trebizond, Empire of NE Anatolia 42/4, 49/1
Treblinka Poland concentration camp 132/1
Trelleborg Denmark circular fortification 52/3
Trengganu state of Malaya tributary to Siam 71/5
Trent (Trient)
Trent, Council of 75T
Trentino (Trient)
Trento (Trient)
Tres Zapotes C Mexico early site 12/2
Treves (Trier, Augusta Treverorum)
Treviso (*anc.* Tarvisium) N Italy Signorial domination
56/3
Trévoux E France seat of intendant 80/1
Trichinopoly S India ceded to Britain 87/3; ✕87/2
Trient (*It.* Trento *or (district)* Trentino *Eng.* Trent *anc.*
Tridentum) S Germany bishopric 79/1
Trier (*Eng.* Treves *Fr.* Trèves *anc.* Augusta Treverorum)
W Germany archbishopric 34/4, 79/1
Trieste (*anc.* Tergeste *S. Cr.* Trst) WW1 119/3; WW2
133/2
Trincomalee Ceylon captured by British 87/2
Trinidad island of W Indies discovery 65/3; Spanish
settlement 66/4; British colony 97/1; independence
139/1 (inset)
Trinil Java site of early man 3/3
Trío Indian tribe of S America 63/1
Triple Alliance 81/4, 117/2
Triple Entente 116T
Tripoli (*Ar.* Tarabulus al Gharb *anc.* Oea) N Libya
Muslim conquest 48/2; trans-Saharan trade 61/2;
Mediterranean trade 58/3; Italian occupation 103/3
Tripoli (*Ar.* Tarabulus ash Sham *anc.* Tripolis) Syria
Roman Empire 31/3; early bishopric 27/2; Byzantine
Empire 43/1; Venetian trade 37/2; Crusaders 40/3
Tripolitania N Africa district of Byzantine Empire 43/1;
under Almohads 60/1; Italian occupation 103/3
Tripura district of NE India Partition 105/5
Tristan da Cunha S Atlantic British colony 100/2

Troas (*Eng.* Troy) W Anatolia early archbishopric 27/2
Troesmis Romania Roman Empire 31/3
Trois Rivières Quebec French post 67/3
Troitskaya Lavra N Russia monastery 38/2
Troitsko-Pechorsk N Russia monastery 38/2
Trondheim (*f/c* Nidaros) C Norway bishopric 38/2;
Hanseatic trade 59/2; WW2 132/1
Tropaeum Traiani Romania Roman Empire 31/3
Troy (*Lat.* Ilium *Gr.* Troas) NW Anatolia early city 16/1,
2; 18/3
Troyes NE France medieval fair 58/1; St. Bartholomew
Massacre 74/3
Trst (Trieste)
Trucial Coast (*later* Trucial Oman, Trucial States *now*
United Arab Emirates) E Arabia British control 125/1;
WW1 125/2
Truckee W USA ✕94/2
Truk Caroline Islands, C Pacific Japanese base in WW2
135/1
Ts'ai N China Chou domain 9/6
Tsangko SW China Han commanderie 29/3
Tsangwu S China Han commanderie 29/3
Tsaritsyn (*1925-61* Stalingrad *now* Volgograd) S
Russia founded 85/1; urban growth 146/2; industry
147/1; Bolshevik seizure 121/2
Tselinograd (*until 1961* Akmolinsk) Kazakh SSR Russ.
C Asia industry 147/1
Tsimshian Indian tribe of NW Canada 63/1
Tsinan N China railway 107/4
Tsinghai province of NW China incorporated into
Manchu (Ch'ing) Empire 106/1
Tsingtao E China German treaty port 107/4; Japanese
occupation 135/1
Tsitsihar Manchuria 122/4
Tsou N China Chou site 9/6
Tsu C Japan 134/3
Tsunyi C China on Long March 122/4
Tsurugaoka (Shonai)
Tswana tribe of S Africa 102/2
Tuat (*Fr.* Touat) Sahara early trade 58/3; 60-61
Tubrug (Tobruk)
Tucano Indian tribe of S America 63/1
Tuchi N China T'ang prefecture 50/1
Tucson SE USA on trail West 94/1
Tugursk Russ. Far East founded 84/2
Tukharistan region of C Asia Chinese protectorate 50/1
Tukulti-Ninurta I King of Assyria 20/3
Tula Mexico Toltec centre 62/2
Tula C Russia industrial development and urban growth
146-47
Tulmaythah (Ptolemais)
Tulúm Mexico fortified site 62/2
Tumasik (*now* Singapore) Malaya 51/2
Tumbes Peru Pizarro's landing 68/2
Tumbes Andean Indian tribe 63/1
Tunes (Tunis)
T'ung SE China Western Chou domain 9/6
Tungirsk SE Siberia founded 84/2
Tungusy people of Siberia 84/2
Tunhsi Western Chou site 9/6
Tunhwang W China early trade and silk route 25/1;
Buddhist site 27/1; conquered by Han 28/2
Tunis (*anc.* Tunes) N Africa early trade 58/3; acquired by
Habsburgs 72/1; Ottoman conquest 48/2, 61/2; French
occupation 103/3
Tunisia under the Almohads 60/1; autonomy under
Ottoman Empire 124/1; French protectorate 103/3; under
Vichy control 132/1; WW2 132/2; independence 138/1;
economy 150/1
Tupinambá forest Indian tribe of E Brazil 63/1
Turckheim W France ✕81/4
Turfan NW China silk route 25/1; administrative centre
of Later Han 28/2
Turin (*It.* Torino *anc.* Taurasia *later* Augusta Taurinorum)
N Italy Lombard League 55/3; 18C urban development
82/4; ✕81/5
Turinsk W Siberia founded 84/2
Turkestan region of C Asia spread of Buddhism 27/1;
during T'ang Empire 50/1; Chinese protectorate 106/1
Turkey on break-up of Ottoman Empire 124/1; war with
Greece 125/4; Greek occupation of west 129/2;
European alliances WW1 128/1; neutral in WW2 132/1;
Baghdad Pact and NATO 148/4, 149/1. See also
Anatolia, Asia Minor, Ottoman Empire
Turkmen tribe of C Asia, conquered by Russia 84/3
Turks tribes on China's northern borders 50/1; invasion
of Anatolia 41/2; movements after WW1 129/3. See also
Ottoman Empire
Turks and Caicos Islands W Indies British colony
100/2
Turnhout Belgium medieval fair 58/1, 59/2
Turnu-Severin (Drobetae)
Turones (*mod.* Tours) C France archbishopric 26/2
Turov-Pinsk early principality of W Russia 45/2
Turukhansk C Siberia founded 84/2
Tuscany (*It.* Toscana) region of N Italy medieval German
Empire 55/3; unification of Italy 114/3
Tuscararas SE USA ✕94/2
Tutchone sub-arctic tribe of NW Canada 63/1
Tutub Mesopotamia 17/3

Tuvalu (*form.* Ellice Islands) C Pacific British colony 139/1 (inset)

Tver (*since 1931* Kalinin) W Russia early town of Vladimir-Suzdal 45/2

Two Sicilies kingdom 114/3

Tyana C Anatolia early bishopric 27/2; Byzantine Empire 43/3

Tynedale N England Franchise of 56/4

Tyras (*mod.* Akkerman *since 1944* Belgorod-Dnestrovskiy *Rom.* Cetatea-Alba) S Russia Roman Empire 31/3

Tyre (*anc.* Tyrus *Ar.* Sur) Lebanon early trade 17/4, 24/1; Phoenician city 19/4; besieged by Alexander 22/3; early archbishopric 27/2; Crusades 40/3

Tyrol (*Ger.* Tirol *It.* Tirolo) region of W Austria medieval German Empire 55/3; acquired by Habsburgs 78/3; County 79/1; peasant revolt 88/1; South Tyrol to Italy 128/2

Tyrus (*Eng.* Tyre *Ar.* Sur) Lebanon Roman Empire 25/2, 31/3

Tyumen C Russia founded 84/2; on railway to east 84/3; industry 147/1

Tzintzuntzán Mexico Tarascan site 62/2

Ubangi-Shari (Oubangui-Chari,Central African Republic)

Udaipur former state of C India 104/1

Udinsk S Siberia founded 84/2

Udmurty people of C Russia 85/1

Udon Thani N Thailand Vietnamese war 148/3

Udyana region of NW India 29/4

Uesugi E Japan clan territory 51/3

Ufa C Russia founded 85/1; industry 147/1

Uganda British protectorate 101/2, 103/3; independence 138/1; political development 140/1; economy 150/1

Ugarit (*mod.* Ras Shamra) ancient city of Syria Hittite Empire 20/2

Uighurs Turkic tribe of C Asia 47/1, 50/1

Ujiji C Africa meeting of Livingstone and Stanley 102/1

Ukraine region of SW USSR post-WW1 independence 129/2; WW2 132-3; industrial development 84/4

Ukrainians people of S Russia, emigration to West 129/3

Ulan Bator (*Mong.* Ulaanbaatar *form.* Urga) Mongolia 120/4

Ulan-Ude (*until 1934* Verkhneudinsk) E Siberia industry 147/1

Ulm S Germany ✕90/1

Ulster province of N Ireland early kingdom 73/4; IRA 137/6

Ulyanovsk (Simbirsk)

Umatilla NW USA ✕94/2

Umayyads Muslim dynasty, Caliphate 34/4, 40/1

Umbrians Italic tribe of C Italy 30/1

Umma Mesopotamia Sumerian city 17/3

Unao N India Indian Mutiny 104/1

U.S.S.R. formation 120-1; alliances in 1930's 128/1; fighting against Japan 135/1; WW2 132-3; territorial gains after WW2 137/4; Warsaw Pact and Comecon 149/1; development 147/1; Cold War 149/1

UNITA Angolan guerrilla movement 138T, 140/1

United Arab Emirates (*form.* Trucial States *earlier* Trucial Oman, Trucial Coast) federation of sheikhdoms, Persian Gulf creation 138/1; economy 150/1

United Arab Republic name given to union of Egypt and Syria 1958-61, retained by Egypt after dissolution until 1972

United Kingdom socio-political development 131/3; NATO and EEC 137/3, 149/1; economy 150/1. See also England, Scotland, Wales, Great Britain, Ulster

United Netherlands 79/1

United Provinces (*now* Uttar Pradesh) state of N India 105/3

United Provinces (*a/c* Dutch Republic) occupied by France 81/4

United States Thirteen Colonies and revolutionary war 86/1; War of Independence 92/1; industrialisation 110/2, 109/1; westward expansion 94/1; Indian wars 95/1; railway development 95/3; Civil War 92-3; population 111/5; Great Depression 130/3; 20C economic and industrial development 144-5; WW2 in Asia and Pacific 135/1; WW2 against Axis in West 132-3; involvement in Latin America 111/4, 143/1; in Cold War 148-9; NATO 148/1

Unsan N Korea 1950-53 war 148/2

Unterwalden original Swiss canton 54/5

Upper Burma annexed by British 104/2

Upper Emigrant Trail S USA settlers' route 94/1

Upper Palatinate S Germany Reformation 75/1

Upper Volta (*Fr.* Haute-Volta) country of W Africa independence 138/1; economy 150/1

Uppland E Sweden early kingdom 53/5

Uppsala E Sweden bishopric 38/2

Ur (of the Chaldees) Mesopotamia 17/3, 4

Urals *mountains* industrial region of USSR 147/1

Urartu (*mod.* Armenia) state of ancient Near East 20/3

Urbs Vetus (Volsinii)

Urewe E Africa Iron Age site 11/1

Urfa (Edessa)

Urga (*mod.* Ulan-Bator *Mong.* Ulaanbaatar) Mongolia seat of Lamaistic patriarch 106/1

Urgench C Asia Muslim trade 59/3

Uri original Swiss canton 54/5

Uruguay part of Brazil 97/1; independence 97/1; political development 143/1; industry and economy 142/2, 3; 150/1

Uruk (*a/c* Erech) Mesopotamia ancient city 16/1, 17/3, 4

Urumchi NW China silk route 25/1

Üsküb (*S. Cr.* Skoplje, *Maced.* Skopje) Yugoslavia Ottoman Empire 49/1

Ust-Kutsk C Siberia founded 84/2

Ust-Sysolsk (Syktyvkar)

Ust-Vilyuysk E Siberia founded 84/2

Ust-Vym N Russia bishopric 38/2

Utah state of W USA ceded by Mexico 97/1; Depression 130/3; population 111/5, 145/1

Ute Indian tribe of SW USA 63/1

Utica Tunisia Stone Age site 11/1; Punic city 19/4; Roman Empire 30/2

U Tong S Thailand Hindu-Buddhist remains 51/2

Utrecht (*anc.* Trajectum) Holland bishopric 38/3; Burgundian possession 73/3; province of Dutch Republic 77/1

Uttar Pradesh (*from* United Province) state of N India 105/5

Uttoxeter C England Industrial Revolution 98/1

Uvinza E Africa Iron Age site 11/1

Uvja (*a/c* Elam) W Persia province of Achaemenid Empire 21/5

Uxii ancient tribe of W Persia 22/3

Vače Yugoslavia Hallstatt site 15/6

Vadhapura Indo-China early trade 25/1

Vagarshapat (*since 1945* Echmiadzin) Armenia early archbishopric 27/2

Vaisali W Burma Hindu-Buddhist remains 51/2

Valencia (*anc.* Valentia) E Spain bishopric 38/2; reconquered by Aragon 37/4; 18C urban development 82/4; Muslim minority 75/1; ✕90/1; Civil War 129/4

Valentia (*mod.* Valence) S France bishopric 26/1

Valentia (Valencia)

Valladolid N Spain Lutheran minority 75/1; Civil War 129/4

Valley Road NE USA settlers' route 94/1

Valmy NE France ✕89/2

Valois region of NE France 72/2

Valona (*anc.* Avlona *Turk.* Avlonya *now Alb.* Vlorë) S Adriatic Ottoman town 48/2

Vancouver W Canada growth 111/1

Vandals Germanic tribe, invasion of Europe and N Africa 32/1, 2; 34/1

Van Diemen's Land (*mod.* Tasmania) early trade 113/4

Vanga ancient country of E India 29/4

Varangians Russia Viking raiders 44/1/T

Varna (*anc.* Odessus *1949-57* Stalin) E Bulgaria ✕49/1

Vasio S France bishopric 27/2

Vassily III king of Muscovy 72/1

Vatsa early kingdom of N India 29/4

Vaud Switzerland Reformation 75/1

Veletians Slav tribe of NW Europe 55/1

Velia (Elea)

Velikiye Luki W Russia WW2 133/2

Velitrae C Italy Latin colony 30/1

Velsuna (Volsinii)

Vendée region of W France 80/1; uprising 89/2

Vendôme region of NW France 72/2

Venetia (*It.* Venezia) region of N Italy exchanged for Austrian Netherlands 78/3, 88/3; unification of Italy 114/3

Venetian Empire (Venice)

Venetian Republic NE Italy 79/1. See also Venice

Venezia (Venetia, Venice)

Venezuela European discovery 65/3; independence 97/1; US influence 111/4; political development 143/1; economy 142/2, 3, 150/1

Venice (*It.* Venezia *anc.* Venetia) expansion into Adriatic and Aegean 37/4; Reformation 75/1; republican commune 56/3; early trade 58/3; Black Death 57/1; 18C financial centre 82/4; WW1 119/3

Ventspils (Windau)

Venusia (*mod.* Venosa) C Italy Latin colony 30/1

Vera Cruz E Mexico modern province 97/1

Vercelli N Italy Lombard League 55/3; Signorial domination 56/3

Verden N Germany bishopric 79/1

Verdun E France annexed to France 72/2; WW1 119/2 (inset)

Verdun, Treaty of 35/5

Vereeniging, Peace of Boer War 102T/4

Verkhne-Angarsk S Siberia founded 84/2

Verkhne-Kolymsk E Siberia founded 84/2

Verkhne-Udinsk (Ulan-Ude)

Verkholensk S Siberia founded 84/2

Verkhoturye W Siberia founded 84/2

Vermandois,region of NE France Royal domain 52/2; Burgundian possession 73/3

Vermont state of NE USA Depression 131/2; population 111/5, 145/1

Vernyy (*since 1921* Alma-Ata) Russ. C Asia industry 147/1

Veroia (Beroea)

Verona N Italy Roman Empire 24/2; Lombard League 55/3; Signorial domination 56/3; 18C financial centre 82/4

Verrazzano Italian navigator 65/2

Versailles N France 80/1

Vértesszöllős Hungary site of early man 3/3

Verulamium (*mod.* St. Albans) S England Roman Empire 30/3; bishopric 26/2

Vesontio (*mod.* Besançon) E France Roman Empire 30/3; archbishopric 26/2

Vetulonia C Italy Etruscan city 19/4

Via Appia (*Eng.* Appian Way) C Italy Roman road from Rome to Brindisi 30/1

Via Flaminia (*Eng.* Flaminian Way) C Italy Roman road from Rome to Rimini 30/1

Via Valeria C Italy Roman road 30/1

Viborg (Viipuri, Vyborg)

Vicenza N Italy Lombard League 55/3

Vichy France satellite state of Germany in WW2 132/1

Vicksburg S USA ✕92/5

Victoria state of SE Australia settlement and development 113/4

Victoria W Canada growth 111/1

Videha ancient kingdom of E India 29/4

Vidin W Bulgaria Ottoman Empire 49/1

Vienna (*anc.* Vindobona *Ger.* Wien *form. Turk.* Beç) Austria siege of 48/2

Vienna (*mod.* Vienne) S France Roman Empire 30/3; archbishopric 26/1

Vientiane Laos trading centre 71/2

Vietnam 1945-75 war 148/3; unification of north and south 141/1; economy 150/1. See also North Vietnam, South Vietnam, Indo-China

Viipuri (*Sw.* Viborg *Russ.* Vyborg) SE Finland captured by Russia 132/1

Vijaya (*mod.* Binh Dinh) S Indo-China capital of Champa Kingdom 51/2

Vilcaconga Peru ✕Pizarro/Inca 68/2

Vilcashuamán Peru ✕Pizarro/Inca 68/2

Villalón N Spain medieval fair 59/2

Villaviciosa Spain ✕81/5

Vilna (*Pol.* Wilno *Russ.* Vilno *Lith.* Vilnius) Lithuania/Poland WW1 119/3; Polish seizure 129/2

Vimeiro Portugal ✕90/1

Viminacium Yugoslavia early trade 24/1; Roman Empire 24/2

Vincennes C USA fur station 94/1

Vindobona (*Eng.* Vienna *Ger.* Wien) Austria Roman Empire 24/2

Viracocha Inca emperor 62T

Virginia state of E USA colony 67/3; Civil War 93/5; Depression 131/2; population 111/5, 145/1

Virginia City W USA mining site 94/1

Virgin Islands W Indies British and Danish settlement 66/4; British colony 79/1; Danish islands acquired by US 111/4 (inset); 139/1 (inset)

Viroconium (*mod.* Wroxeter) England Roman Empire 30/3

Visby Gotland, E Sweden Hanseatic city 59/2

Visé Belgium medieval fair 58/1

Visigoths Germanic invaders of Europe 32/1, 2; 34/1,

Vitebsk W Russia Hanseatic trade 59/2; industry 147/1

Vitoria N Spain ✕90/1

Vittorio Veneto N Italy WW1 ✕119/3

Vivarium S Italy bishopric 27/2

Vix France Hallstatt site 15/1

Vizagapatam district of E India ceded to Britain 87/3

Vlaanderen (Flanders)

Vladikavkaz (*since 1931* Ordzhonikidze *except 1944-54* Dzaudzhikau) Caucasus acquired by Russia 85/1; 1905 Revolution 120/1

Vladimir C Russia early city of Vladimir-Suzdal 45/2; bishopric 38/2; 1905 Revolution 120/1

Vladimir (*now* Vladimir-Volynsky *Pol.* Włozimierz *Lat.* Lodomeria) W Russia early city of Vladimir-Volynsk 45/2

Vladimir-Suzdal early principality of C Russia 45/2

Vladimir-Volynsk early principality of W Russia 45/2

Vladivostok *Russ.* Far East on Trans-Siberian railway 127/4, 5; urban growth 146/2; industry 147/1

Vlorë (Valona, Avlona, Avlonya)

Volaterrae (*mod.* Volterra) C Italy Etruscan city 19/4

Volci C Italy Etruscan city 19/4

Volga Bulgars early people of C Russia 44/1, 3; 45/2

Volga-Ural Oilfield Siberia 147/1

Volgograd (*between 1925-61* Stalingrad *early Tsaritsyn*) C Russia industry and urban growth 146-7

Volhynia region of W Ukraine acquired by Lithuania 56/2

Vologda C Russia city of Muscovy 85/1

Volsci Italic tribe of C Italy 30/1